The Modern Historiography Reader:

Western Sources

Historiography—the history of historical writing—is one of the most important and basic areas of study for all historians. Yet in such a broad and expanding field, how should students find their way through it?

In *The Modern Historiography Reader: Western Sources*, Adam Budd guides readers through European and North American developments in history-writing since the eighteenth century. Starting with Enlightenment history and moving through subjects such as moral history, national history, the emergence of history as a profession, and the impact of scientific principles on history, he then looks at some of the most important developments in twentieth-century historiography such as social history, traumatic memory, postcolonialism, gender history, postmodernism, and the history of material objects.

This is the only book that brings together historiographical writing from anthropology, literary theory, philosophy, psychology, and sociology—as well as history. Each of the thirteen thematic sections begins with a clear introduction that familiarizes readers with the topics and articles, setting them in their wider contexts. They explain what historiography is, how historians' perspectives and sources determine the kinds of questions they ask, and discuss how social and ideological developments have shaped historical writing over the past three centuries.

With a glossary of critical terms and reading lists for each section, *The Modern Historiography Reader: Western Sources* is the perfect introduction to modern historiography.

Adam Budd directs the historical methods courses in the Graduate School of History and Classics at the University of Edinburgh. He also teaches historiography, bibliography, and eighteenth-century literary history, and has published on related topics. His study of medicine and literary culture in the Scottish Enlightenment is forthcoming.

Routledge Readers in History

The Decolonization Reader
Edited by James Le Sueur

The Enlightenment: A Sourcebook and
Reader
Edited by Olga Gomez, Francesca
Greensides and Paul Hyland

The European Women's History
Reader
Edited by Christine Collette and Fiona
Montgomery

The Fascism Reader
Edited by Aristotle A. Kallis

The Feminist History Reader
Edited by Sue Morgan

The Global History Reader
Edited by Bruce Mazlish and Akira
Iriye

The History and Narrative Reader
Edited by Geoffrey Roberts

The Irish Women's History Reader
Edited by Alan Hayes and Diane
Urquhart

The Modern Historiography Reader:
Western Sources
Edited by Adam Budd

The Nature of History Reader
Edited by Keith Jenkins and Alun
Munslow

The Oral History Reader
Edited by Robert Perks and Alistair
Thomson

The Postmodern History Reader
Edited by Keith Jenkins

The Postmodernism Reader:
Foundational Texts
Edited by Michael Drolet

Renaissance Thought: A Reader
Edited by Robert Black

The Slavery Reader
Edited by Gad Heuman and James Walvin

The Terrorism Reader
Edited by David J. Whittaker

The Victorian Studies Reader
Edited by Kelly Boyd and Rohan
McWilliam

The Witchcraft Reader
Edited by Darren Oldridge

The World War Two Reader
Edited by Gordon Martel

The

Modern Historiography

Reader

Western Sources

Edited by

Adam Budd

Routledge
Taylor & Francis Group

LONDON AND NEW YORK

First published 2009 by Routledge
2 Park Square, Milton Park, Abingdon, Oxon OX14 4RN

Simultaneously published in the USA and Canada
by Routledge
711 Third Avenue, New York, NY 10017

Reprinted 2010

Routledge is an imprint of the Taylor & Francis Group, an informa business

Typeset in Perpetua and Bell Gothic by
RefineCatch Limited, Bungay, Suffolk

British Library Cataloguing in Publication Data
A catalogue record for this book is available from the British Library

Library of Congress Cataloging in Publication Data
Budd, Adam.
The modern historiography reader : Western sources / [edited by] Adam Budd.
    p. cm. — (Routledge readers in history)
  1. Historiography. I. Title.
  D13.B765 2008
  907.2—dc22
  2008015243

ISBN 10: 0–415–45886–2 (hbk)
ISBN 10: 0–415–45887–0 (pbk)

ISBN 13: 978–0–415–45886–3 (hbk)
ISBN 13: 978–0–415–45887–0 (pbk)

History is . . . a science in movement. Like all those which have the human spirit for its object, this newcomer in the field of rational knowledge is also a science in its infancy. . . . Now at last, it struggles to penetrate beneath the mere surface of actions, rejecting not only the temptations of legend and rhetoric, but the still more dangerous modern poisons of routine learning and empiricism parading as common sense.

Marc Bloch, *The Historian's Craft* (1941) 13.

Contents

Preface

THE PAST WILL NEVER CHANGE, but the ways we think about it have never stopped changing. Readers of history, including historians themselves, ask why we have chosen to examine and describe the past in particular ways. Why have we sometimes focused on the lives and accomplishments of Great Men using government papers, and at other times studied the private thoughts of obscure people using their dusty diaries? Do historians express the concerns of their time, or do their creative insights or even their childhoods lead them to certain subjects? Over the past three centuries we have considered the documents that record history, the books that describe it, the memories that inform it, the emotions that deny it, the objects that have marked it, the people who have seen it, the scholars who write it, and the readers who consume it. *The modern period* has been usefully defined by referring to the distinctive questions that have been asked about history from the Enlightenment to the present. This *Reader* offers an introduction to those last three centuries of critical discussion about what history is, what historians should do, and why history is important.

Just as our questions about history have changed, our critical vocabulary has changed too. Back in the mid-eighteenth century, the word *Historiography* simply referred to the writing of history—a *historiographer* was someone who wrote about the past. These days, *Historiography* refers to the history of historical writing, not only focusing on what historians have written but also examining how and why historians have thought about the past. Many students choose to become historians not just because they are fascinated by specific events but also because they are intrigued by the concerns historians have raised—or have refused to raise. They might adopt new methods of research, address different problems, or perhaps analyze "major" events from a "minority" viewpoint. For the most part, historians have embraced historiography because it leads them to think in new ways about what they do, to consider their literary styles, their positions in society, and the changing nature of their tasks as researchers, authors, and teachers. Together with their students, historians in universities are composing new courses devoted to the critical history of historical writing.

History is to the humanities and social sciences what mathematics is to the natural sciences—we all draw on its insights, even when we don't call ourselves historians. That is why this *Reader* includes writing by anthropologists, literary theorists, philosophers, psychologists, and sociologists, whose fields have always drawn on insights from history. Since these authors comment from outside History departments, their perspectives invigorate historiography in refreshing ways and encourage discussion beyond its specialist terms. As the earlier sections in this book will show, readers and writers have wondered about the nature of historical writing well before the first graduate-level seminar in History was offered in Europe (at Berlin in 1826) and in North America (at Johns Hopkins University in 1876)—and these questions have persisted within and beyond universities.

Visitors and curators at museums and art galleries have always been concerned with historiography. Let's focus on the painting that appears on the cover of this book. For most of the time since February 2000, this imposing group portrait appeared at the end of a long corridor in The National Portrait Gallery in London.[i] It depicts seven historians who have served on the editorial board of *Past and Present*, a journal that emerged from a shoestring enterprise to become one of the world's most distinguished forums for historical scholarship. The artist, Stephen Farthing, used imaginative techniques to encourage critical thinking about these historians and their work. These seven never posed together—Farthing sketched and interviewed them separately in 1999; he then assembled them on his canvas. Those on the left were members of the Communist Party of Great Britain and had been involved in the journal from its founding in 1952. The colourful setting, with its torn book covers, half-filled shelves, and shifting proportions, invites us to analyze it closely. Christopher Hill, who is seated, has three hands. Rodney Hilton, standing in the blue jacket, has sunken into (or is emerging from) an empty bookcase. At the centre, beyond the group, the only visible door leads to darkness. Everyone stands atop a rug that reprints the journal's cover-page, recalling the famous Ditchley portrait of Elizabeth I, who marked her ownership of England by standing on a map of it.[ii] Surely this is an ironic analogy, for even those historians who are not Marxists might have mixed feelings about their association with royal power. Do the historians' positions in the portrait suggest their sense of self or a greater recognition of their ownership of history?

This portrait is intriguing in part because it raises questions rather than provides answers. Surely many of the fifty-six authors in this *Reader* try to do both, but by assembling their writings together in one place, I hope to evoke a sense of dialogue about historiography. I have included the writings of historians and theorists that will be familiar to many readers, and set them among essays that are less known but still influential—even when their influence extends to suggesting useful contexts for our interpretations. One consequence of historiography is that editors realize that our books create historical knowledge by suggesting that our choices represent intrinsic authority about the past. Similarly, the *The* in this book's title implies comprehensiveness—when of course it simply is not possible (or even desirable) to present the range and depth of questions that have informed historical writing from 1700 to the present. But hopefully, by arranging these documents according to suggestive themes rather than strict chronology, and by including both familiar and unfamiliar voices, this *Reader* introduces and orients new readers in this expanding field. The lists of Further Reading at the close of each

i   The painting was commissioned by the Gallery in 1999 and unveiled in February 2000; it was exhibited in the late-twentieth-century gallery until February 2006. From left to right, the subjects are: Eric Hobsbawm, Christopher Hill, Rodney Hilton, Lawrence Stone, John Elliott, Joan Thirsk, and Keith Thomas. See David Saywell and Jacob Simon, eds, *The Complete Illustrated Catalogue: National Portrait Gallery, London* (London: Unicorn Press, 2004), 731. Its catalogue number is NPG 6518; further details and a larger image can be consulted at http://www.npg.org.uk.
ii This is NPG 2561, by Marcus Gheeraerts the Younger (1592). It can be consulted at http://www.npg.org.uk.

thematic section are an important part of this book, because they suggest pathways it hasn't followed, to inspire ideas for further research.

Finally, a few words about my guiding editorial principles. This book provides interpretive introductions to the questions and contexts that are raised in each of its thirteen sections. I have restricted the scope of this book to historiography in Western Europe and North America, from the early Enlightenment to the present—and I am relieved to see that new studies in global historiography, which reach beyond the West and stretch further than the modern period, are entering into print.[iii] The number of endnotes and length of Further Reading lists in each editorial introduction reflect the complexity of current debates on the topics at issue. I have tried to highlight the recurrence of particular ideas across time and place during the past three hundred years, which is why, as the book develops, the number of editorial cross-references increases. I have avoided anticipating developments in historiography, for few things can be more discouraging (not to say annoying) than a zealous narrator who likes to leap forward. The Index lists the critical terms, historical figures, and theorists who appear in the introductions; the Glossary clarifies those terms and lists related books and articles.

Although each introduction attempts to familiarize readers with the material that follows it, I have deliberately included the key terms and formulations used by the authors themselves. Too much paraphrasing risks implying that an editor can say it better than the author, or that readers need to hear the same concept repeated in different ways. Since new concepts generate new terms, it is important to become familiar with the words, tone, and formulations that these writers offer, which is why interpretive context rather than repetition is best for clarifying the authors' meaning. Having learned to swim in the frigid lakes of central Ontario, I am the last person to say that difficulty enhances learning. However, I do think that our sense of unfamiliarity is a useful response to encountering new ideas, and that it should lead us to ask why some concepts challenge more than others, and why certain points that seem obvious now were radical earlier (and vice versa). If the study of historiography sharpens our curiosity, then it fulfils its promise.

Throughout this book, I have capitalized *History* when referring to history as a formal academic field; similarly *Anthropology* and *Sociology*. Terms that appear in **bold** can be consulted in both the Glossary and Index—but in the interests of style, these appear in bold only on their first appearance in each editorial introduction. The Index lists all authors and important critical terms where they appear throughout the book.

One final note about the format of this book. I have sought to include each reading in its original length whenever it was feasible, indicating my excisions with ellipses [. . .]. I have occasionally provided explanatory notes to the texts, marking them with [-Ed.]. These appear as footnotes in Roman numerals. Authorial notes from the original sources appear as numbered endnotes. My internal clarifications are marked in square brackets. At the head of each reading, a bibliographical reference cites the most recent or accessible edition of the original source, indicating which pages I have excised. I eagerly invite readers to consult the originals so they can study these readings in full.

---

iii See, for example, Georg G. Iggers and Q. Edward Wang. *A Global History of Modern Historiography* (London: Longmans, 2008); Daniel Woolf, *A Short History of History* (Cambridge: Cambridge University Press), forthcoming. The global *Oxford History of Historical Writing*, in five volumes under the general editorship of Daniel Woolf, is scheduled for release in 2009 and 2010.

Further reading in Modern Historiography

Bentley, Michael (ed.) *Companion to Historiography* (London: Routledge, 1997).

——— . *Modernizing England's Past: English Historiography in the Age of Modernism, 1870–1970* (Cambridge: Cambridge University Press, 2006).

——— . *Modern Historiography: An Introduction* (London: Routledge, 1999).

Berger, Stefan, et al. (eds) *Writing History: Theory and Practice* (London: Hodder Arnold, 2003).

Black, Jeremy. *Maps and History: Constructing Images of the Past* (New Haven: Yale University Press, 1997).

Breisach, Ernst. *Historiography: Ancient, Medieval, and Modern.* Third edition. (Chicago: University of Chicago Press, 2007).

Brown, Donald E. *Hierarchy, History, and Human Nature: The Social Origins of Historical Consciousness* (Tucson: University of Arizona Press, 1988).

Burke, Peter. *History and Social Theory* (Cambridge: Polity Press, 1993).

——— (ed.) *New Perspectives on Historical Writing.* Second edition. (Cambridge: Polity Press, 1991).

Burns, Robert M. (ed.) *Historiography: Critical Concepts in Historical Studies.* 5 vols. (London: Routledge, 2005).

——— and Hugh Rayment-Pickard (eds) *Philosophies of History: From Enlightenment to Postmodernity* (Oxford: Blackwell, 2000).

Burrow, John. *A History of Histories* (London: Allen Lane, 2007).

Carr, David, et al. (eds) *The Ethics of History* (Evanston, IL: Northwestern University Press, 2004).

Fay, Brian, et al. (eds) *History and Theory: Contemporary Readings* (Oxford: Blackwell, 1998).

Haskell, Francis. *History and Its Images: Art and the Interpretation of the Past* (New Haven: Yale University Press, 1993).

Hughes-Warrington, Marnie. *Fifty Key Thinkers on History* (London: Routledge, 2000).

Iggers, Georg G. *Historiography in the Twentieth Century, with a New Epilogue* (Middletown, CT: Wesleyan University Press, 2005).

—— . and Q. Edward Wang. *A Global History of Modern Historiography* (London: Longmans, 2008).

Jenkins, Keith et al. (eds) *Manifestoes for History* (London: Routledge, 2007).

Jordanova, Ludmilla. *History as Practice*. Second edition. (London: Hodder Arnold, 2006).

Kelley, Donald R. *Faces of History: Historical Inquiry from Herodotus to Herder.* (New Haven: Yale University Press, 1998).

—— . *Fortunes of History: Historical Inquiry from Herder to Huizinga* (New Haven: Yale University Press, 2003).

—— . *Frontiers of History: Historical Inquiry in the Twentieth Century* (New Haven: Yale University Press, 2006).

Kramer, Lloyd and Sarah Maza (eds) *A Companion to Western Historical Thought* (Oxford: Blackwell, 2002).

Lorenz, Chris. "Comparative Historiography: Problems and Perspectives", *History and Theory* 38 (1999), 25–39.

Manning, Patrick. *Navigating World History: Past, Present, and Future of a Global Field* (Basingstoke: Palgrave, 2003).

Lowenthal, David. *The Heritage Crusade and the Spoils of History* (Cambridge: Cambridge University Press, 1998).

Momigliano, Arnaldo. *Classical Foundations of Modern Historiography*. New edition. (Berkeley: University of California Press, 1992).

Monkkonnen, Eric H. (ed.) *Engaging the Past: The Uses of History across the Social Sciences* (Durham, NC: Duke University Press, 1994).

Munslow, Alun. *The Routledge Companion to History* (London: Routledge, 2000).

Orr, Linda. "The Revenge of Literature: A History of History," *New Literary History* 18 (1986–1987), 1–21.

Patterson, Annabel. *Nobody's Perfect: A New Whig Interpretation of History* (New Haven: Yale University Press, 2002).

Sato, Masayuki. "Comparative Ideas of Chronology," *History and Theory* 30 (1991), 275–301.

Steig, Margaret F. *The Origin and Development of Scholarly Historical Journals* (Tuscaloosa, AL: University of Alabama Press, 1986).

Stuchtey, Benedict and Eckhardt Fuchs (eds) *Writing World History: 1800–2000* (Oxford: Oxford University Press, 2003).

Woolf, D. R. (ed.) *A Global Encyclopedia of Historical Writing* (New York: Garland, 1998). 2 vols.

—— . *A Short History of History* (Cambridge: Cambridge University Press), forthcoming.

Acknowledgements

This *Reader* grew out of my courses in modern historiography, for which I couldn't find a bound collection of primary texts that ranged from the start of the eighteenth century. In many respects, Fritz Stern's *The Varieties of History: From Voltaire to the Present* is excellent, but since Stern interpreted "the present" in 1956 (adding just two documents in 1970), his selections and introductions require revision. Over the past fifty years more has been published on the critical history of historical writing than during the previous three centuries. Since this *Reader* collects major texts with less familiar but still influential material, from the start I have looked to colleagues as well as my students for advice.

First I wish to thank the authors and their executors for kindly allowing me to include their work between, and on, these covers. Some read parts of the manuscript and provided helpful suggestions; others sent informative emails and responded quickly to my questions. Although I accepted most but not all of their comments, I remain grateful for their support of a project that could include neither the true range nor depth of modern historiography. These contributors include: Karen Blu, Stephen Farthing, Anthony Giddens, David Halperin, Natsu Hattori, Gertrude Himmelfarb, Cornelius Holtorf, Georg Iggers, Michael Ignatieff, Neil McKendrick, Daniel Miller, Adam Phillips, Mark Phillips, H. P. Rickman, Joan Scott, Bonnie Smith, Chris Tilley, and Hayden White. From the start, Daniel Woolf has commented wisely on my interpretations, for which I am grateful. Among my students, Julia Boll, Daniel Fritsch, Tyler Griffith, Helen O'Shea, and Beryl Pong made valuable suggestions.

I have been fortunate to have benefited from the amazing expertise of Rachel Bower, research assistant *extraordinaire*. My stepfather, Graham Berman, generously read the entire manuscript and gave detailed comments, late at night and during his well-deserved holidays. Likewise, I wish to thank my friends and colleagues, including Thomas Ahnert, Thomas Baker, Crispin Bates, Robert Budd, Peter Burke, John Burrow, Frank Cogliano, Bill Dorman, Dennis Dworkin, Bashabi Fraser, Elspeth Jajdelska, Stephen Kemp, Sue Morgan, Stana Nenadic, Nancy Partner, Silvia Sebastiani, Richard Sher, Jill Stephenson, and Hope Thompson.

At Routledge, I have thoroughly enjoyed working with the great editorial triumvirate of Annamarie Kino, Julene Knox, and Eve Setch.

Much of this book was written with one or both of my wee'uns attempting to climb up onto my lap, with Nadine patiently persuading them to let me write a grown-up book with only grown-ups in mind. But overhearing Yael explaining to Sadie that she should always ask us "why also?" after receiving our answers to "why?" inspired me throughout. I lovingly dedicate this book to the three of them.

The publishers would like to thank the following for permission to reprint their material:

John Emerich Edward, Lord Acton, "Inaugural Lecture: 'On the Study of History' ", *Lectures on Modern History* (London, 1952), 1–28. Reproduced by kind permission.

Carl Becker, "Everyman His Own Historian", Presidential Address. *American Historical Review* 37 (January 1932), 221–36. Reproduced by permission of the American Historical Association.

Marc Bloch, "Introduction", *The Historian's Craft*. 1941. Trans. Peter Putnam. Copyright 1953 and renewed 1981 by Alfred A. Knopf, a division of Random House Inc. Used by permission of Alfred A. Knopf, a division of Random House Inc.

Bonnie G. Smith, "What is a Historian?" reprinted by permission of the publisher from *The Gender of History: Men, Women, and Historical Practice* by Bonnie G. Smith, pp. 70–102 (Cambridge MA: Harvard University Press). Copyright © 1998 by the President and Fellows of Harvard College.

Giambattista Vico, "Principles of the New Science Concerning the Common Nature of Nations", from *New Science* by Giambattista Vico, translated by David Marsh, introduction by David Grafton (Penguin Classics, 1999). Copyright © David Marsh, 1999. Introduction © Anthony Grafton, 1999. Reproduced by permission of Penguin Books.

Erich Auerbach, "Vico and Aesthetic Historism", 1959. *Scenes from the Drama of European Literature* (Minneapolis: University of Minnesota Press, 1984).

William Godwin, "Of History and Romance", in *Caleb Williams*, Maurice Hindle (ed.) (Harmondsworth: Penguin, 1988), 359–73.

Mark Salber Phillips, "Relocating Inwardness: Historical Distance and the Transition from Enlightenment to Romantic Historiography". Reproduced by permission from the Modern Language Association from *PMLA* 118 (2003) 436–49, 442–9. © 2003 by the Modern Language Association of America.

Wilhelm von Humbolt, from "On the Historian's Task". 1822. Trans. Louis O. Mink, *History and Theory* 6 (1967), 57–71. Reproduced with permission of Wiley-Blackwell Publishing Ltd.

Leopold von Ranke. Two Prefaces. (1) "Preface to the First Edition of Histories of the Latin and German Nations", 1825. *Theory and Practice in History*, Georg Iggers (ed.). Trans. W. Iggers (Indianapolis: Bobbs-Merrill, 1973). (2) "Preface to *History of the Popes, Their Church and State*", 1834. Trans. E. Fowler. Revised by Konrad von Moltke (New York: Colonial Press, 1901), v–xi. Reproduced by kind permission of Georg Iggers.

Anthony Grafton, "How the Historian Found His Muse: Ranke's Path to the Footnote". Reprinted by permission of the publisher from *The Footnote: A Curious History* by Anthony Grafton, pp. 62–72; 92–3, (Cambridge, MA: Harvard University Press). Copyright © 1997 by Les Editions du Seuil. All rights reserved.

Anthony Grafton, "How the Historian Found His Muse: Ranke's Path to the Footnote". *The Footnote: A Curious History*. (Cambridge: Harvard University Press, 1997), 62–72; 92–3. Originally published as *Les Origines Tragiques de L'Erudition*, Editions du Seuil. Reproduced with permission.

Herbert Butterfield, "The Underlying Assumption", from *The Whig Interpretation of History* by Herbert Butterfield. Copyright 1931 by Herbert Butterfield. Used by permission of W. W. Norton & Company.

Émile Durkheim, "History, Function, and Cause". 1902. *Selected Writings*. Trans. Anthony Giddens. Copyright © 1972 Cambridge University Press, reprinted with permission.

Wilhelm Dilthey, from "Human Life: Lived and Rethought", *Introduction to the Human Sciences*. 1923. Trans. W. Kluback and M. Weinbaum. Westport, CT: Greenwood Press, 1957. 22–3.

Wilhelm Dilthey, "Construction of the Historical World", *Dilthey's Epistemology and Methodology*, 1910 [*Gesammelte Schriften* vol. 7]. Trans. H. P. Rickman. Copyright © 1976 Cambridge University Press, reprinted with permission.

Max Weber, from "On the Concept of Sociology and the 'Meaning' of Social Conduct", *Basic Concepts in Sociology*, 1922. Trans. H. P. Secher (London: Peter Owen, 1962), 29–33. Reproduced with permission.

R. G. Collingwood, "Oswald Spengler and the Theory of Historical Cycles", *Antiquity* (1927), 311–25. Reproduced by permission of Antiquity Publications Ltd.

Fernand Braudel, "History and the Social Sciences", 1958. Trans. Keith Folca. Peter Burke (ed.), *Economy and Society in Early Modern Europe*, 11–21. Copyright © 1972. Routledge. Reproduced by permission of Taylor and Francis Books UK.

Thomas Kuhn, "Introduction: A Role for History", *The Structure of Scientific Revolutions* (Chicago: University of Chicago Press, 1963), 1–9. Reproduced with permission.

The Editors, "Introduction" *Past and Present* 1 (1952): i–iii. By permission of Oxford University Press.

E. P. Thompson, "Preface" from *The Making of the English Working Class*, by E.P. Thompson copyright © 1963 by E.P. Thompson. Used by permission of Pantheon Books, a division of Random House, Inc.

E. P. Thompson, "Preface", *The Making of the English Working Class*. 1963 (London, Penguin, 1980), 9–13. Reprinted by permission of the publisher, Victor Gollancz, an imprint of The Orion Publishing Group.

Gertrude Himmelfarb, "The 'Group': British Marxist Historians", *New History and the Old: Critical Essays and Reappraisals*. 1986 (Cambridge, MA: Harvard University Press, 1987 (revd edn 2004)), 70–94. Reproduced by kind permission of the author.

[Editorial Collective.] "Editorials." *History Workshop Journal* 1 (1976): 1–3. Reproduced by permission of Oxford University Press.

Roy Porter, "The Patient's View: Doing Medical History from Below." *Theory and Society* 14 (1985): 175–98. Wellcome Institute for the History of Medicine, London. With kind permission from Springer Science and Business Media.

Michael Ignatieff, "The Nightmare from Which We Are Trying to Awake", from *Warrior's Honor: Ethnic War and the Modern Conscience*, by Michael Ignatieff (London: Chatto and Windus, 1998). Reprinted by permission of The Random House Group Ltd.

Hannah Arendt, "Judgment, Appeal, and Execution", from *Eichmann in Jerusalem: A Report on the Banality of Evil* by Hannah Arendt. Copyright renewed © 1991, 1992 by Lotte Kohler. Used by permission of Viking Penguin, a division of Penguin Group (USA) Inc.

Adam Phillips, "Close-Ups", *History Workshop Journal* 57 (2004), 142–9. Copyright © 2004 by Oxford University Press Reprinted by permission of Oxford University Press.

Hayden White, "The Historical Text as Literary Artifact", from Hayden White, *Tropics of Discourse: Essays in Cultural Criticism*, 81–100. Copyright © 1978 The Johns Hopkins University Press.

Paul Ricoeur, "*The Reality of the Historical Past*". Copyright © 1984 by Marquette University Press. Used by permission of the publisher. All rights reserved, www.marquette.edu/mupress/

Joan Wallach Scott, "Gender: A Useful Category of Historical Analysis", in *Gender and the Politics of History* (New York: Columbia University Press, 1988), 41–50. Reproduced with permission.

Michel Foucault, "Objective," from *The History of Sexuality: Volume 1, An Introduction* by Michel Foucault, translated by Robert Hurley (Allen Lane 1979, first published as "La Volonté du savoir" 1976). Copyright © Editions Gallimard, 1976. Translation copyright © Random House, Inc. 1978. Reproduced by permission of Penguin Books Ltd.

Michel Foucault, *The History of Sexuality*. Copyright © Random House 1978, Inc., New York. Originally published in French as *La Volonté du Savoir*. Copyright © Editions Gallimard 1976. Reprinted by permission of Georges Borchardt, Inc., for the Editions Gallimard.

David Halperin, "Forgetting Foucault: Acts, Identities, and the History of Sexuality", *How To Do the History of Homosexuality* (Chicago: Chicago University Press, 2002), 26–44. Reproduced with permission.

Clifford Geertz, "Thick Description: Toward an Interpretive Theory of Culture," *The Interpretation of Cultures: Selected Essays* (New York; London: Hutchison, 1973), 3–30. Reprinted by permission of Basic Books, a member of Perseus Books Group.

Edward Said, "Introduction", from *Orientalism* by Edward Said. Copyright © 1978 by Edward W. Said. Used by permission of Pantheon Books, a division of Random House, Inc.

David Cannadine, "Beginnings", *Ornamentalism: How the British Saw Their Empire* (Oxford: Oxford University Press, 2001), 3–10. By permission of Oxford University Press, Inc.

David Cannadine, "Beginnings", *Ornamentalism: How the British Saw Their Empire* (Allen Lane 2001, Penguin Books 2002). Copyright © David Cannadine, 2001. Reproduced by Penguin Books Ltd.

George Fredrickson, "The Concept of Racism in Historical Discourse", from Fredrickson, George M.: *Racism*. © 2002 Princeton University Press, 2003 paperback edition. Reprinted by permission of Princeton University Press.

Daniel Miller and Chris Tilney, "Editorial", *Journal of Material Culture* 1 (1986), 5–14. Reproduced with permission from Daniel Miller and Chris Tilney. Copyright © 1986 Sage Publications, by permission of Sage Publications Ltd.

Marcel Mauss, "Introduction", from *The Gift: Forms and Functions of Exchange in Archaic Societies*. 1923–4. Trans. W. D. Halls, 1–9. Copyright © 1990 Routledge, reproduced by permission of Taylor and Francis Books UK.

Neil McKendrick, "Introduction", *The Birth of a Consumer Society: The Commercialization of Eighteenth-Century England* (London: Europa, 1982), 1–6. Reproduced by kind permission of the author.

Georges Vigarello, "Introduction", *Concepts of Cleanliness: Changing Attitudes in France since the Middle Ages*. Copyright © 1988 Cambridge University Press, reprinted with permission.

Cornelius Holtorf, "Notes on the Life History of a Potshard". Unpublished MS. Reproduced by
    kind permission of the author.

While every effort has been made to trace and acknowledge ownership of copyright material
used in this volume, the Publishers will be glad to make suitable arrangements with any
copyright holders whom it has not been possible to contact.

PART 1

The historian's task

INTRODUCTION

THIS FIRST SECTION INTRODUCES key questions that modern historians have brought to their research—and, in turn, continue to ask historians and their readers. None of these four historians knew one another, they read and wrote in different circumstances, and they chose to focus on distinct areas of European and North American history. Yet each considered history-writing to be an urgent moral task that demands new questions not only of past events, but also of past values. Each of these authors seized on their present moment because it seemed to offer a unique intellectual opportunity. The unique clarity of their moment was offered by new ethical standards, an eagerness to uncover and explain the dynamics of intimate relationships, a surge of impatient optimism, and the terrifying insights of writing during wartime. Taken together, the length of the sources in this section makes it by far the longest in this volume. Now this does not just attest to the particular enthusiasm of these historians—after all, two of these documents were originally delivered as lectures; the manuscript of another amounts to a doomed prisoner's final testament; and the last is from a chapter in an energetically-argued monograph. More than any other section in this book, these readings propose a wide range of questions on a less settled group of shared concerns.

Lord Acton was an unusually cosmopolitan Victorian aristocrat, whose ultimate failure to realize his scholarly ambitions illustrates concerns that will resurface throughout this book. He was born in Italy, travelled in Europe and America throughout his life, and assumed an English peerage through his mother's remarriage into an ancient anglo-Catholic family. Acton was fluent in all the major European languages, and through his studies in Germany developed a lifelong conviction that it is the intellectual's moral responsibility to defend liberty of thought from the stifling authority of hierarchical institutions. He contributed articles to a number of periodicals over many decades, arguing for the importance of liberal thinking among Catholics, which entailed questioning the "immoral" belief that papal hierarchy can allow anyone to speak infallible truth. Through his political and social connections in London, Acton was offered the prestigious Regius Professorship in Modern History at Cambridge in 1895, but this turned out to be a mixed blessing. It brought Acton the supportive colleagues, admiring students, and splendid libraries he required to prepare the massive *Cambridge Modern History* that he was asked to organize the following year. Ironically, however, the stimulating intellectual world of Cambridge forced him to face the fact that his uncompromising moralism could not be reconciled with his impartial approach to historical research.

In his famous inaugural lecture, Lord Acton trumpeted his moral view of history through his dramatic and confident declaration of his and his students' special place in the tide of world history. Speaking to a largely receptive male audience of professors, politicians, and students, he declared that,

> Unlike the dreaming prehistoric world, ours knows the need and the duty to make itself master of the earlier times, and to forfeit nothing of their wisdom or their warnings, [ours] has devoted its best energy and treasure to the sovereign purpose of detecting error and vindicating entrusted truth.

Acton's confidence in the belief that *previous* ages were dreaming but that *ours* is awake and aware of its duties is characteristic of the literary genre to which an inaugural lecture belongs. For his audience would have expected that their newly-appointed Professor of History would offer rousing declarations on the purpose and meaning of their shared pursuits. And yet there are ambiguities in Acton's words that complicate his argument and reveal a deeper meaning to those points he wished to stress. Exploring them, even briefly, offers a useful entry point into what the four writers in this section proposed when they considered what historians should do.

Acton provided two observations about the practice of history and he aimed to secure two fundamental points about his duty as a historian—and indeed about his students' duties as aspiring historians. First, Acton argued that the current historical moment—the one that belongs to him and to these students—was unique because it was only at this time that humankind had shrugged off its old willingness to remain ignorant of the past, of those circumstances that created the present. He easily could have found examples of this from the literature, social theories, and political attitudes of the time, but Acton would probably have focused on religion first: in his view, the turn of the twentieth century marked the triumphant moment when one could respectfully embrace the religion of one's choice even when disagreeing with the dogmatic teachings that the same religion had once commanded. Armed with a new refusal to dream their way through life, only now would we take up the "Need and duty" to learn about the past—and therefore to grasp the power to master history's significance. The second point is that, for Acton, the present had all the tools and resources it needed to succeed in this new mission; indeed, he and his students seemed to have been so well-endowed with historical resources that they could have made the best even of those aspects of the past that their predecessors couldn't understand.

The first point made a claim about where the historian stands; the second referred to the methods he or she uses. While Acton had his own views on the importance of perspective and on **methodology**, all historians share his view that both of these are important. Perhaps more meaningful and more unique are two deeper points that Acton's lecture emphasizes: The history of humanity is the history of steady progress from ignorance to knowledge and from enslavement to liberty, and as the special inheritors of this knowledge historians have the solemn duty to teach the world the difference between right and wrong. For Acton, we are not mere researchers of the past but, rather, we are the moral teachers of the present: with all the special advantages that the present and privileged moment provides, the historian and his students are obliged to point out humanity's past errors and to explain the rightness of God's plan—that, as he memorably declared, "History is the true demonstration of Religion".

Acton's moral imperative, confident as it sounds in his powerful rhetoric of universal values, caused him severe problems when it came to his own work as a historian. On the one hand, Acton believed that "there is virtue in the saying that a historian is seen at his best when he does not appear"; in other words, the ideal historian communicates, "do not imagine you are listening to me; it is history itself that speaks". But on the other hand, how can a historian let the documents do the talking when he has the moral obligation to point out "the converging and combined conditions of advancing civilization"? Such balancing of **objective** presentation with **subjective** framing was, tragically, beyond Acton's abilities. At the time of his death in 1902, Acton had written nothing of the projected *Universal History of Liberty* to which he had devoted his entire working life; his ambitious plans for the *Cambridge Modern History* had to be scrapped and the volumes revised. Today, his vast library, filled with thousands of index cards and scribbled notes, remains a warning to those who visit it in the Cambridge University Library: moral justification of the past can only sit uneasily with the ideal of reaching historical objectivity, and it led, in Acton's case, to scholarly paralysis.

Precisely forty years after Acton gave his inaugural lecture, Oxford University nominated Carl Becker, a famous American professor of History at Cornell, for the prestigious Harmsworth Professorship of American History. But Becker modestly refused it, saying that he didn't know enough about American History to accept such a position (strictly speaking this was correct—he was not an Americanist by training). By the time of his death in 1945, Becker had written 15 books, roughly 75 articles, and nearly 200 reviews—and one of his own works was a major textbook on American History. In contrast to Acton's confidence in the **positive** nature of historical progress and in the historian's moral duty to vindicate religious truths, Becker was a sceptic whose argument in "Everyman His Own Historian", which he read to loud applause at the annual conference of the American Historical Association in 1931, still reverberates. This lecture was received enthusiastically because its articulate attack on the "scientific" school of history seemed to rest on principles of common-sense, and its rhetoric appealed to a democratic spirit that seemed to have been lost among the previous generation of "aristocratic" historians. The scientific ideal among historians had enjoyed considerable popularity and prestige in America at the turn of the twentieth century, ever since its principles were imported to American colleges from German universities in the late nineteenth century. "Facts properly arranged interpret themselves", declared Albert Beveridge, a popular politician and historian at the time. Becker's powerful reply, that "History is the memory of things said and done", shifted the focus away from facts toward human memory, with all the personal beliefs, opinions, feelings that "memory" implies. Historians do more than just arrange facts, according to Becker: they use their imaginations to create visions of history that serve their present needs. At times Becker sounds like the dreaming prehistoric mentioned by Acton. When we read Becker's paper some 75 years later, as we debate the possibility of a truly objective history, we still use many of the arguments that Becker displayed in "Everyman His Own Historian". Despite the sinister uses that historical **relativism** has served at various times in the twentieth century, Becker asked us to examine rather than dismiss the role of imagination and memory in the creation of historical truth.

Few historians of the twentieth century inspire as much respect and admiration as the French historian Marc Bloch—not only for his influential approach to historical research but also for the fact that he was murdered by the Nazis while working for the French Resistance. Bloch's historical approach stresses the social and historical meaning of human beliefs, and his own life (and death) illustrate the brutal consequences that conflicting beliefs entail—even for a scholar whose life seemed more devoted to historical research than to politics. Whereas Acton believed that historians have a moral duty to emphasize the progress of human history and Becker focused on the imaginative nature of historical writing, Bloch advocated a **comparative method** of historical research. Since, for Bloch, historical research should try to recuperate the "collective consciousness" of the people whose ideas, feelings, and actions created the world we now inhabit, historians should use a wide range of scholarly approaches (from economics, sociology, geography, linguistics, and religious studies) to compare human beliefs across nations and across time periods. Indeed, for Bloch, history itself was time in movement, orchestrated by the relationship between our perspectives and those elements of the past which are visible to us. Since recent history is more accessible to us than the distant past, historians should adopt a regressive method, working backward through time, aiming to examine the past but not to judge it using current moral values. An energetic scholar who devoted his career to fulfilling the intellectual aims of the journal *Annales d'Histoire Sociale* that he co-founded in 1929 (see its founding statement in Part 5), Bloch objected to the traditional boundaries that separated "historians" from "sociologists" and other social scientists whose perspectives could, collectively, provide a deeper vision of history. This selection from Bloch's writing, in which he seeks to answer his young son's question "What is the use of History?" was written while Bloch was in hiding in Nazi-occupied France, without access to his books or other research materials. It was written shortly before his capture and death, and remains a key document in twentieth-century **historiography**.

Historians have long recognized that their subjective judgements influence the historical narratives they create. We must therefore read history critically in our effort to understand the past. Acton's history was influenced by his belief that he had a moral and indeed religious duty to justify the achievement of certain historical figures. It was refreshing but not quite revolutionary for Becker and for Bloch to point out that historians needed to reconsider the academic traditions from which they wrote and taught history. Yet it was not until the later decades of the twentieth century, when historians began to examine the questions about personal bias, which had been raised largely through feminist scholars, that the subjective aspects of professional judgement began to command serious attention.

The evolution of social and political rights and the associated expansion of possible personal choices have been intertwined with changes in our private beliefs about the right places of women and men in society. It is therefore crucial that historians focus on those experiences that shape our notions of gender. In turn, as Bonnie Smith points out, we will find that there is a history of the "Historian as Professional", a history filled with personal drama, sometimes painful, sometimes inspiring, which created a psychological and social identity for historians. To assume this identity, historians have assigned specific roles to women in historical writing. Male historians have done this despite the significant and emotionally meaningful place that women have held in their personal and professional lives. But as educational, social, and political conventions have insisted, these historians have enjoyed their "authorial presence" at the expense of the women whose stories and experiences they have suppressed, ignored, or otherwise silenced. It is the task of current historians, then, not merely to recover the neglected history of "forgotten" people, but also to cultivate a critical self-consciousness of the ways in which our own practice as historians can shape a meaningful sense of the human past.

Chapter 1

John Emerich Edward, Lord Acton

INAUGURAL LECTURE ON THE STUDY OF HISTORY

John Emerich Edward, Lord Acton (1834–1902), "Inaugural Lecture: 'On the Study of History' ", 1895, *Lectures on Modern History* (London: Macmillan, 1930), 1–6, 8–12, 15–18, 27–8.

FELLOW STUDENTS—
[. . .]

You have often heard it said that Modern History is a subject to which neither beginning nor end can be assigned. No beginning, because the dense web of the fortunes of man is woven without a void; because, in society as in nature, the structure is continuous, and we can trace things back uninterruptedly, until we dimly descry the Declaration of Independence in the forests of Germany. No end, because, on the same principle, history made and history making are scientifically inseparable and separately unmeaning.

"Politics," said Sir John Seeley, "are vulgar when they are not liberalised by history, and history fades into mere literature when it loses sight of its relation to practical politics." Everybody perceives the sense in which this is true. For the science of politics is the one science that is deposited by the stream of history, like grains of gold in the sand of a river; and the knowledge of the past, the record of truths revealed by experience, is eminently practical, as an instrument of action and a power that goes to the making of the future.[1] In France, such is the weight attached to the study of our own time, that there is an appointed course of contemporary history, with appropriate text-books.[2] That is a chair which, in the progressive division of labour by which both science and government prosper,[3] may some day be founded in this country. Meantime, we do well to acknowledge the points at which the two epochs diverge. For the contemporary differs from the modern in this, that many of its facts cannot by us be definitely ascertained. The living do not give up their secrets with the candour of the dead; one key is always excepted, and a generation passes before we can ensure accuracy. Common report and outward seeming are bad copies of the reality, as the initiated know it. Even of a thing so memorable as the war of 1870, the true cause is still obscure; much that we believed has been scattered to the winds in the last six months, and further revelations by important witnesses are about to appear. The use of history turns far more on certainty than on abundance of acquired information.

Beyond the question of certainty is the question of detachment. The process by which principles are discovered and appropriated is other than that by which, in practice, they are applied; and our most sacred and disinterested convictions ought to take shape in the tranquil regions of the air, above the tumult and the tempest of active life. For a man is justly despised who has one opinion in history and another in politics, one for abroad and another at home, one for opposition and another for office. History compels us to fasten on abiding issues, and rescues us from the temporary and transient. Politics and history are interwoven, but are not commensurate. Ours is a domain that reaches farther than affairs of state, and is not subject to the jurisdiction of governments. It is our function to keep in view and to command the movement of ideas, which are not the effect but the cause of public events; and even to allow some priority to ecclesiastical history over civil, since, by reason of the graver issues concerned, and the vital consequences of error, it opened the way in research, and was the first to be treated by close reasoners and scholars of the higher rank.

In the same manner, there is wisdom and depth in the philosophy which always considers the origin and the germ, and glories in history as one consistent epic.[4] Yet every student ought to know that mastery is acquired by resolved limitation. And confusion ensues from the theory of Montesquieu and of his school, who, adapting the same term to things unlike, insist that freedom is the primitive condition of the race from which we are sprung. If we are to account mind not matter, ideas not force, the spiritual property that gives dignity and grace and intellectual value to history, and its action on the ascending life of man, then we shall not be prone to explain the universal by the national, and civilisation by custom.[5] A speech of Antigone, a single sentence of Socrates, a few lines that were inscribed on an Indian rock before the Second Punic War, the footsteps of a silent yet prophetic people who dwelt by the Dead Sea, and perished in the fall of Jerusalem, come nearer to our lives than the ancestral wisdom of barbarians who fed their swine on the Hercynian acorns.

For our present purpose, then, I describe as Modern History that which begins four hundred years ago, which is marked off by an evident and intelligible line from the time immediately preceding, and displays in its course specific and distinctive characteristics of its own. The modern age did not proceed from the medieval by normal succession, with outward tokens of legitimate descent. Unheralded, it founded a new order of things, under a law of innovation, sapping the ancient reign of continuity. In those days Columbus subverted the notions of the world, and reversed the conditions of production, wealth, and power; in those days Machiavelli released government from the restraint of law; Erasmus diverted the current of ancient learning from profane into Christian channels; Luther broke the chain of authority and tradition at the strongest link; and Copernicus erected an invincible power that set for ever the mark of progress upon the time that was to come. There is the same unbound originality and disregard for inherited sanctions in the rare philosophers as in the discovery of Divine Right, and the intruding Imperialism of Rome. The like effects are visible everywhere, and one generation beheld them all. It was an awakening of new life; the world revolved in a different orbit, determined by influences unknown before. After many ages persuaded of the headlong decline and impending dissolution of society,[6] and governed by usage and the will of masters who were in their graves, the sixteenth century went forth armed for untried experience, and ready to watch with hopefulness a prospect of incalculable change.

That forward movement divides it broadly from the older world; and the unity of the new is manifest in the universal spirit of investigation and discovery which did not cease to operate, and withstood the recurring efforts of reaction, until, by the advent of the reign of general ideas which we call the Revolution, it at length prevailed.[7] This successive deliverance and gradual passage, for good and evil, from subordination to independence is a phenomenon of primary import to us, because historical science has been one of its instruments.[8] If the Past has been an obstacle and a burden, knowledge of the Past is the safest and the surest emancipation. And the earnest search for it is one of the signs that distinguish the four centuries of which I speak from those that went before. The Middle Ages, which possessed good writers of contemporary narrative, were careless and impatient of older fact. They became content to be deceived, to live in a twilight of fiction, under clouds of false witness, inventing according to convenience, and glad to welcome the forger and the cheat. As time went on, the atmosphere of accredited mendacity thickened, until, in the Renaissance, the art of exposing falsehood dawned upon keen Italian minds. It was then that History as we understand it began to be understood, and the illustrious dynasty of scholars arose to whom we still look both for method and material. Unlike the dreaming prehistoric world, ours knows the need and the duty to make itself master of the earlier times, and to forfeit nothing of their wisdom or their warnings,[9] and has devoted its best energy and treasure to the sovereign purpose of detecting error and vindicating entrusted truth.

In this epoch of full-grown history men have not acquiesced in the given conditions of their lives. Taking little for granted they have sought to know the ground they stand on, and the road they travel, and the reason why. Over them, therefore, the historian has obtained an increasing ascendency.[10] The law of stability was overcome by the power of ideas, constantly varied and rapidly renewed;[11] ideas that give life and motion, that take wing and traverse seas and frontiers, making it futile to pursue the consecutive order of events in the seclusion of a separate nationality. They compel us to share the existence of societies wider than our own, to be familiar with distant and exotic types, to hold our march upon the loftier summits, along the central range, to live in the company of heroes, and saints, and men of genius, that no single country could produce. We cannot afford wantonly to lose sight of great men and memorable lives, and are bound to store up objects for admiration as far as may be;[12] for the effect of implacable research is constantly to reduce their number. No intellectual exercise, for instance, can be more invigorating than to watch the working of the mind of Napoleon, the most entirely known as well as the ablest of historic men. In another sphere, it is the vision of a higher world to be intimate with the character of Fénelon, the cherished model of politicians, ecclesiastics, and men of letters, the witness against one century and precursor of another, the advocate of the poor against oppression, of liberty in an age of arbitrary power, of tolerance in an age of persecution, of the humane virtues among men accustomed to sacrifice them to authority, the man of whom one enemy says that his cleverness was enough to strike terror, and another, that genius poured in torrents from his eyes. For the minds that are greatest and best alone furnish the instructive examples. A man of ordinary proportion or inferior metal knows not how to think out the rounded circle of his thought, how to divest his will of its surroundings and to rise above the pressure of time and race and circumstance, to choose the star that guides his course, to correct, and test, and assay his convictions by the light within, and, with a resolute conscience and ideal courage, to remodel and reconstitute the character which birth and education gave him.[13]

[. . .]

The first of human concerns is religion, and it is the salient feature of the modern centuries. They are signalised as the scene of Protestant developments. Starting from a time of extreme indifference, ignorance, and decline, they were at once occupied with that conflict which was to rage so long, and of which no man could imagine the infinite consequences. Dogmatic conviction—for I shun to speak of faith in connection with many characters of those days—dogmatic conviction rose to be the centre of universal interest, and remained down to Cromwell the supreme influence and motive of public policy. A time

came when the intensity of prolonged conflict, when even the energy of antagonistic assurance abated somewhat, and the controversial spirit began to make room for the scientific;
and as the storm subsided, and the area of settled questions emerged, much of the dispute
was abandoned to the serene and soothing touch of historians, invested as they are with the
prerogative of redeeming the cause of religion from many unjust reproaches, and from the
graver evil of reproaches that are just. Ranke used to say that Church interests prevailed in
politics until the Seven Years' War, and marked a phase of society that ended when the hosts
of Brandenburg went into action at Leuthen, chaunting their Lutheran hymns. That bold
proposition would be disputed even if applied to the present age. After Sir Robert Peel had
broken up his party, the leaders who followed him declared that no popery was the only
basis on which it could be reconstructed.[14] On the other side may be urged that, in July
1870, at the outbreak of the French war, the only government that insisted on the abolition
of the temporal power was Austria; and since then we have witnessed the fall of Castelar,
because he attempted to reconcile Spain with Rome.

Soon after 1850 several of the most intelligent men in France, struck by the arrested
increase of their own population and by the telling statistics from Further Britain, foretold
the coming preponderance of the English race. They did not foretell, what none could then
foresee, the still more sudden growth of Prussia, or that the three most important countries
of the globe would, by the end of the century, be those that chiefly belonged to the
conquests of the Reformation. So that in Religion, as in so many things, the product of
these centuries has favoured the new elements; and the centre of gravity, moving from the
Mediterranean nations to the Oceanic, from the Latin to the Teuton, has also passed from
the Catholic to the Protestant.[15]

Out of these controversies proceeded political as well as historical science. It was in the
Puritan phase, before the restoration of the Stuarts, that theology, blending with politics,
effected a fundamental change. The essentially English reformation of the seventeenth
century was less a struggle between churches than between sects, often subdivided by
questions of discipline and self-regulation rather than by dogma. The sectaries cherished no
purpose or prospect of prevailing over the nations; and they were concerned with the
individual more than with the congregation, with conventicles, not with State churches.
Their view was narrowed, but their sight was sharpened. It appeared to them that governments and institutions are made to pass away, like things of earth, whilst souls are immortal;
that there is no more proportion between liberty and power than between eternity and
time; that, therefore, the sphere of enforced command ought to be restricted within fixed
limits, and that which had been done by authority, and outward discipline, and organised
violence, should be attempted by division of power, and committed to the intellect and the
conscience of free men.[16] Thus was exchanged the dominion of will over will for the
dominion of reason over reason. The true apostles of toleration are not those who sought
protection for their own beliefs, or who had none to protect; but men to whom, irrespective
of their cause, it was a political, a moral, and a theological dogma, a question of conscience
involving both religion and policy. Such a man was Socinus; and others arose in the smaller
sects,—the Independent founder of the colony of Rhode Island, and the Quaker patriarch of
Pennsylvania. Much of the energy and zeal which had laboured for authority of doctrine was
employed for liberty of prophesying. The air was filled with the enthusiasm of a new cry;
but the cause was still the same. It became a boast that religion was the mother of freedom,
that freedom was the lawful offspring of religion; and this transmutation, this subversion of
established forms of political life by the development of religious thought, brings us to the
heart of my subject; to the significant and central feature of the historic cycles before us.
Beginning with the strongest religious movement and the most refined despotism ever
known, it has led to the superiority of politics over divinity in the life of nations, and

terminates in the equal claim of every man to be unhindered by man in the fulfilment of duty to God—a doctrine laden with storm and havoc, which is the secret essence of the Rights of Man, and the indestructible soul of Revolution.

When we consider what the adverse forces were, their sustained resistance, their frequent recovery, the critical moments when the struggle seemed for ever desperate, in 1685, in 1772, in 1808, it is no hyperbole to say that the progress of the world towards self-government would have been arrested but for the strength afforde, by the religious motive in the seventeenth century. And this constancy of progress, of progress in the direction of organised and assured freedom, is the characteristic fact of Modern History, and its tribute to the theory of Providence.[17] Many persons, I am well assured, would detect that this is a very old story, and a trivial common-place, and would challenge proof that the world is making progress in aught but intellect, that it is gaining in freedom, or that increase in freedom is either a progress or a gain. Ranke, who was my own master, rejected the view that I have stated; Comte, the master of better men, believed that we drag a lengthening chain under the gathered weight of the dead hand and many of our recent classics—Carlyle, Newman, Froude—were persuaded that there is no progress justifying the ways of God to man, and that the mere consolidation of liberty is like the motion of creatures whose advance is in the direction of their tails. They deem that anxious precaution against bad government is an obstruction to good, and degrades morality and mind by placing the capable at the mercy of the incapable, dethroning enlightened virtue for the benefit of the average man. They hold that great and salutary things are done for mankind by power concentrated, not by power balanced and cancelled and dispersed, and that the whig theory, sprung from decomposing sects, the theory that authority is legitimate only by virtue of its checks, and that the sovereign is dependent on the subject, is rebellion against the divine will manifested all down the stream of time.

I state the objection not that we may plunge into the crucial controversy of a science that is not identical with ours. but in order to make my drift clear by the defining. No political dogma is as serviceable to my purpose here as the historian's maxim to do the best he can for the other side, and to avoid pertinacity or emphasis on his own. Like the economic precept *laissez faire*, which the eighteenth century derived from Colbert, it has been an important, if not a final step in the making of method. The strongest and most impressive personalities, it is true, like Macaulay, Thiers, and the two greatest of living writers, Mommsen and Treitschke, project their own broad shadow upon their pages. This is a practice proper to great men, and a great man may be worth several immaculate historians. Otherwise there is virtue in the saying that a historian is seen at his best when he does not appear. Better for us is the example of the Bishop of Oxford, who never lets us know what he thinks of anything but the matter before him; and of his illustrious French rival, Fustel de Coulanges, who said to an excited audience: "Do not imagine you are listening to me; it is history itself that speaks." We can found no philosophy on the observation of four hundred years, excluding three thousand. It would be an imperfect and a fallacious induction. But I hope that even this narrow and disedifying section of history will aid you to see that the action of Christ who is risen on mankind whom he redeemed fails not, but increases; that the wisdom of divine rule appears not in the perfection but in the improvement of the world; and that achieved liberty is the one ethical result that rests on the converging and combined conditions of advancing civilisation.[18] Then you will understand what a famous philosopher said, that History is the true demonstration of Religion.[19]

[. . .]

For our purpose, the main thing to learn is not the art of accumulating material, but the sublimer art of investigating it, of discerning truth from falsehood and certainty from doubt.

It is by solidity of criticism more than by the plenitude of erudition, that the study of history strengthens, and straightens, and extends the mind.[20] And the accession of the critic in the place of the indefatigable compiler, of the artist in coloured narrative, the skilled limner of character, the persuasive advocate of good, or other, causes, amounts to a transfer of government, to a change of dynasty, in the historic realm. For the critic is one who, when he lights on an interesting statement, begins by suspecting it. He remains in suspense until he has subjected his authority to three operations. First, he asks whether he has read the passage as the author wrote it. For the transcriber, and the editor, and the official or officious censor on the top of the editor, have played strange tricks, and have much to answer for. And if they are not to blame, it may turn out that the author wrote his book twice over, that you can discover the first jet, the progressive variations, things added, and things struck out. Next is the question where the writer got his information. If from a previous writer, it can be ascertained, and the inquiry has to be repeated. If from unpublished papers, they must be traced, and when the fountain-head is reached, or the track disappears, the question of veracity arises. The responsible writer's character, his position, antecedents, and probable motives have to be examined into; and this is what, in a different and adapted sense of the word, may be called the higher criticism, in comparison with the servile and often mechanical work of pursuing statements to their root. For a historian has to be treated as a witness, and not believed unless his sincerity is established.[21] The maxim that a man must be presumed to be innocent until his guilt is proved, was not made for him.

For us, then, the estimate of authorities, the weighing of testimony, is more meritorious than the potential discovery of new matter.[22] And modern history, which is the widest field of application, is not the best to learn our business in; for it is too wide, and the harvest has not been winnowed as in antiquity, and further on to the Crusades. It is better to examine what has been done for questions that are compact and circumscribed, such as the sources of Plutarch's *Pericles*, the two tracts on Athenian government, the origin of the epistle to Diognetus, the date of the life of St. Antony; and to learn from Schwegler how this analytical work began. More satisfying because more decisive has been the critical treatment of the medieval writers, parallel with the new editions, on which incredible labour has been lavished, and of which we have no better examples than the prefaces of Bishop Stubbs. An important event in this series was the attack on Dino Compagni, which, for the sake of Dante, roused the best Italian scholars to a not unequal contest. When we are told that England is behind the Continent in critical faculty, we must admit that this is true as to quantity, not as to quality of work. As they are no longer living, I will say of two Cambridge professors, Lightfoot and Hort, that they were critical scholars whom neither Frenchman nor German has surpassed.

The third distinctive note of the generation of writers who dug so deep a trench between history as known to our grandfathers and as it appears to us, is their dogma of impartiality. To an ordinary man the word means no more than justice. He considers that he may proclaim the merits of his own religion, of his prosperous and enlightened country, of his political persuasion, whether democracy, or liberal monarchy, or historic conservatism, without transgression or offence, so long as he is fair to the relative, though inferior, merits of others, and never treats men as saints or as rogues for the side they take. There is no impartiality, he would say, like that of a hanging judge. The men who, with the compass of criticism in their hands, sailed the uncharted sea of original research proposed a different view. History, to be above evasion or dispute, must stand on documents, not on opinions. They had their own notion of truthfulness, based on the exceeding difficulty of finding truth, and the still greater difficulty of impressing it when found. They thought it possible to write, with so much scruple, and simplicity, and insight, as to carry along with them every man of good will, and, whatever his feelings, to compel his assent. Ideas which, in religion and in politics, are truths, in history are forces. They must be respected; they must not be affirmed. By dint of a supreme reserve, by much self-control, by a timely and discreet indifference, by secrecy in the matter of the black cap, history might be lifted above contention, and made an accepted tribunal, and the same for all.[23] If men were truly sincere, and delivered judgment by no canons but those of evident morality, then Julian would be described in the same terms by Christian and pagan, Luther by Catholic and Protestant, Washington by Whig and Tory, Napoleon by patriotic Frenchman and patriotic German.[24]

I speak of this school with reverence, for the good it has done, by the assertion of historic truth and of its legitimate authority over the minds of men. It provides a discipline which every one of us does well to undergo, and perhaps also well to relinquish. For it is not the whole truth. Lanfrey's essay on Carnot, Chuquet's wars of the Revolution, Ropes's military histories, Roget's Geneva in the time of Calvin, will supply you with examples of a more robust impartiality than I have described. Renan calls it the luxury of an opulent and aristocratic society, doomed to vanish in an age of fierce and sordid striving. In our universities it has a magnificent and appointed refuge; and to serve its cause, which is sacred, because it is the cause of truth and honour, we may import a profitable lesson from the highly unscientific region of public life. There a man does not take long to find out that he is opposed by some who are abler and better than himself. And, in order to understand the cosmic force and the true connection of ideas, it is a source of power, and an excellent school of principle, not to rest until, by excluding the fallacies, the prejudices, the exaggerations which perpetual contention and the consequent precautions breed, we have made out for our opponents a stronger and more impressive case than they present themselves. Excepting one to which we are coming before I release you, there is no precept less faithfully observed by historians.

Ranke is the representative of the age which instituted the modern study of History. He taught it to be critical, to be colourless, and to be new. We meet him at every step, and he has done more for us than any other man. There are stronger books than any one of his, and some may have surpassed him in political, religious, philosophic insight, in vividness of the creative imagination, in originality, elevation, and depth of thought; but by the extent of important work well executed, by his influence on able men, and by the amount of knowledge which mankind receives and employs with the stamp of his mind upon it, he stands without a rival. I saw him last in 1877, when he was feeble, sunken, and almost blind, and scarcely able to read or write. He uttered his farewell with kindly emotion, and I feared that the next I should hear of him would be the news of his death. Two years later he began a Universal History, which is not without traces of weakness, but which, composed after the age of eighty-three, and carried, in seventeen volumes, far into the Middle Ages, brings to a close the most astonishing career in literature.

His course had been determined, in early life, by *Quentin Durward*. The shock of the discovery that Scott's Lewis the Eleventh was inconsistent with the original in Commynes made him resolve that his object thenceforth should be above all things to follow, without swerving, and in stern subordination and surrender, the lead of his authorities. He decided effectually to repress the poet, the patriot, the religious or political partisan, to sustain no cause, to banish himself from his books, and to write nothing that would gratify his own feelings or disclose his private convictions. When a strenuous divine, who, like him, had written on the Reformation, hailed him as a comrade, Ranke repelled his advances. "You," he said, "are in the first place a Christian: I am in the first place a historian. There is a gulf between us." He was the first eminent writer who exhibited what Michelet calls *le désintéressement des morts*. It was a moral triumph for him when he could refrain from judging, show that much might be said on both sides, and leave the rest to Providence. He would have felt sympathy with the two famous London physicians of our day, of whom it is told that they could not make up their minds on a case and reported dubiously. The head of the family insisted on a positive opinion. They answered that they were unable to give one, but he might easily find fifty doctors who could.

Niebuhr had pointed out that chroniclers who wrote before the invention of printing generally copied one predecessor at a time, and knew little about sifting or combining authorities. The suggestion became luminous in Ranke's hands, and with his light and dexterous touch he scrutinised and dissected the principal historians, from Machiavelli to the *Mémoires d'un Homme d'État*, with a rigour never before applied to moderns. But whilst Niebuhr dismissed the traditional story, replacing it with a construction of his own, it was Ranke's mission to preserve, not to undermine, and to set up masters whom, in their proper sphere, he could obey. The many excellent dissertations in which he displayed this art, though his successors in the next generation matched his skill and did still more thorough work, are the best introduction from which we can learn the technical process by which within living memory the study of modern history has been renewed. Ranke's contemporaries, weary of his neutrality and suspense, and of the useful but subordinate work that was done by beginners who borrowed his wand, thought that too much was made of these obscure preliminaries which a man may accomplish for himself, in the silence of his chamber, with less demand on the attention of the public. That may be reasonable in men who are practised in these fundamental technicalities. We who have to learn them, must immerse ourselves in the study of the great examples.

Apart from what is technical, method is only the reduplication of common sense, and is best acquired by observing its use by the ablest men in every variety of intellectual employment. Bentham acknowledged that he learned less from his own profession than from writers like Linnæus and Cullen; and Brougham advised the student of Law to begin with Dante. Liebig described his *Organic Chemistry* as an application of ideas found in Mill's *Logic*, and a distinguished physician, not to be named lest he should overhear me, read three books to enlarge his medical mind; and they were Gibbon; Grote, and Mill. He goes on to say, "An educated man cannot become so on one study alone, but must be brought under the influence of natural, civil, and moral modes of thought." I quote my colleague's golden words in order to reciprocate them. If men of science owe anything to us, we may learn much from them that is essential. For they can show how to test proof, how to secure fulness and soundness in induction, how to restrain and to employ with safety hypothesis and analogy. It is they who hold the secret of the mysterious property of the mind by which error ministers to truth, and truth slowly but irrevocably prevails. Theirs is the logic of discovery, the demonstration of the advance of knowledge and the development of ideas, which as the earthly wants and passions of men remain almost unchanged, are the charter of progress and the vital spark in history. And they often give us invaluable counsel when they attend to their own subjects and address their own people. Remember Darwin taking note only of those passages that raised difficulties in his way; the French philosopher complaining that his work stood still, because he found no more contradicting facts; Baer, who thinks error treated thoroughly nearly as remunerative as truth, by the discovery of new objections; for, as Sir Robert Ball warns us, it is by considering objections that we often learn. Faraday declares that "in knowledge, that man only is to be condemned and despised who is not in a state of transition." And John Hunter spoke for all of us when he said: "Never ask me what I have said or what I have written; but if you will ask me what my present opinions are, I will tell you."

From the first years of the century we have been quickened and enriched by contributors from every quarter. The jurists brought us that law of continuous growth which has transformed history from a chronicle of casual occurrences into the likeness of something organic. Towards 1820 divines began to recast their doctrines on the lines of development, of which Newman said, long after, that evolution had come to confirm it. Even the

Economists, who were practical men, dissolved their science into liquid history, affirming that it is not an auxiliary, but the actual subject-matter of their inquiry. Philosophers claim that, as early as 1804, they began to bow the metaphysical neck beneath the historical yoke. They taught that philosophy is only the amended sum of all philosophies, that systems pass with the age whose impress they bear, that the problem is to focus the rays of wandering but extant truth, and that history is the source of philosophy, if not quite a substitute for it. Comte begins a volume with the words that the preponderance of history over philosophy was the characteristic of the time he lived in. Since Cuvier first recognised the conjunction between the course of inductive discovery and the course of civilisation, science had its share in saturating the age with historic ways of thought, and subjecting all things to that influence for which the depressing names historicism and historical-mindedness have been devised.

There are certain faults which are corrigible mental defects on which I ought to say a few denouncing words, because they are common to us all. First: the want of an energetic understanding of the sequence and real significance of events, which would be fatal to a practical politician, is ruin to a student of history, who is the politician with his face turned backwards. It is playing at study, to see nothing but the unmeaning and unsuggestive surface, as we generally do. Then we have a curious proclivity to neglect, and by degrees to forget, what has been certainly known. An instance or two will explain my idea. The most popular English writer relates how it happened in his presence that the title of Tory was conferred upon the Conservative party. For it was an opprobrious name at the time, applied to men for whom the Irish Government offered head-money; so that if I have made too sure of progress, I may at least complacently point to this instance of our mended manners. One day, Titus Oates lost his temper with the men who refused to believe him, and, after looking about for a scorching imprecation, he began to call them Tories. The name remained; but its origin, attested by Defoe dropped out of common memory, as if one party were ashamed of their godfather, and the other did not care to be identified with his cause and character. You all know, I am sure, the story of the news of Trafalgar, and how, two days after it had arrived, Mr. Pitt, drawn by an enthusiastic crowd, went to dine in the city. When they drank the health of the minister who had saved his country, he declined the praise. "England," he said, "has saved herself by her own energy; and I hope that after having saved herself by her energy, she will save Europe by her example." In 1814, when this hope had been realised, the last speech of the great orator was remembered, and a medal was struck upon which the whole sentence was engraved, in four words of compressed Latin: *Seipsam virtute, Europam exemplo*. Now it was just at the time of his last appearance in public that Mr. Pitt heard of the overwhelming success of the French in Germany, and of the Austrian surrender at Ulm. His friends concluded that the contest on land was hopeless, and that it was time to abandon the Continent to the conqueror, and to fall back upon our new empire of the sea. Pitt did not agree with them. He said that Napoleon would meet with a check whenever he encountered a national resistance; and he declared that Spain was the place for it, and that then England would intervene. General Wellesley, fresh from India, was present. Ten years later, when he had accomplished that which Pitt had seen in the lucid prescience of his last days, he related at Paris what I scarcely hesitate to call the most astounding and profound prediction in all political history, where such things have not been rare.

I shall never again enjoy the opportunity of speaking my thoughts to such an audience as this, and on so privileged an occasion a lecturer may well be tempted to bethink himself whether he knows of any neglected truth, any cardinal proposition, that might serve as his selected epigraph, as a last signal, perhaps even as a target. I am not thinking of those shining precepts which are the registered property of every school; that is to say—Learn as much by writing as by reading; be not content with the best book; seek sidelights from the others; have no favourites; keep men and things apart; guard against the prestige of great names, see that your judgments are your own, and do not shrink from disagreement; no trusting without testing; be more severe to ideas than to actions; do not overlook the strength of the bad cause or the weakness of the good; never be surprised by the crumbling of an idol or the disclosure of a skeleton; judge talent at its best and character at its worst; suspect power more than vice, and study problems in preference to periods; for instance: the derivation of Luther, the scientific influence of Bacon, the predecessors of Adam Smith, the medieval masters of Rousseau, the consistency of Burke, the identity of the first Whig. Most of this, I suppose, is undisputed, and calls for no enlargement. But the weight of opinion is against me when I exhort you never to debase the moral currency or to lower the standard of rectitude, but to try others by the final maxim that governs your own lives, and to suffer no man and no cause to escape the undying penalty which history has the power to inflict on wrong. The plea in extenuation of guilt and mitigation of punishment is perpetual. At every step we are met by arguments which go to excuse, to palliate, to confound right and wrong, and reduce the just man to the level of the reprobate. The men who plot to baffle and resist us are, first of all, those who made history what it has become. They set up the principle that only a foolish Conservative judges the present time with the ideas of the past; that only a foolish Liberal judges the past with the ideas of the present.

The mission of that school was to make distant times, and especially the Middle Ages, then most distant of all, intelligible and acceptable to a society issuing from the eighteenth century. There were difficulties in the way; and among others this, that, in the first fervour of the Crusades, the men who took the Cross, after receiving communion, heartily devoted the day to the extermination of Jews. To judge them by a fixed standard, to call them sacrilegious fanatics or furious hypocrites, was to yield a gratuitous victory to Voltaire. It became a rule of policy to praise the spirit when you could not defend the deed. So that we have no common code; our moral notions are always fluid; and you must consider the times, the class from which men sprang, the surrounding influences, the masters in their schools, the preachers in their pulpits, the movement they obscurely obeyed, and so on, until responsibility is merged in numbers, and not a culprit is left for execution. A murderer was no criminal if he followed local custom, if neighbours approved, if he was encouraged by official advisers or prompted by just authority, if he acted for the reason of state or the pure love of religion, or if he sheltered himself behind the complicity of the Law. The depression of morality was flagrant; but the motives were those which have enabled us to contemplate with distressing complacency the secret of unhallowed lives. The code that is greatly modified by time and place, will vary according to the cause. The amnesty is an artifice that enables us to make exceptions, to tamper with weights and measures, to deal unequal justice to friends and enemies.

It is associated with that philosophy which Cato attributes to the gods. For we have a theory which justifies Providence by the event, and holds nothing so deserving as success, to which there can be no victory in a bad cause; prescription and duration legitimate; and whatever exists is right and reasonable; and as God manifests His will by that which He tolerates, we must conform to the divine decree by living to shape the future after the ratified image of the past. Another theory, less confidently urged, regards History as our guide, as much by showing errors to evade as examples to pursue. It is suspicious of illusions in success, and, though there may be hope of ultimate triumph for what is true, if not by its own attraction, by the gradual exhaustion of error, it admits no corresponding promise for what is ethically right. It deems the canonisation of the historic past more perilous than ignorance or denial, because it would perpetuate the reign of sin and acknowledge the sovereignty of wrong, and conceives it the part of real greatness of know how to stand and fall alone, stemming, for a lifetime, the contemporary flood.

[. . .]

If, in our uncertainty, we must often err, it may be sometimes better to risk excess in rigour than in indulgence, for then at least we do no injury by loss of principle. As Bayle has said, it is more probable that the secret motives of an indifferent action are bad than good; and this discouraging conclusion does not depend upon theology, for James Mozley supports the sceptic from the other flank, with all the artillery of Tractarian Oxford. "A Christian," he says, "is bound by his very creed to suspect evil, and cannot release himself. . . . He sees it where others do not; his instinct is divinely strengthened; his eye is supernaturally keen; he has a spiritual insight, and senses exercised to discern. . . . He owns the doctrine of original sin; that doctrine puts him necessarily on his guard against appearances, sustains his apprehension under perplexity, and prepares him for recognising anywhere what he knows to be everywhere."[25] There is a popular saying of Madame de Staël, that we forgive whatever we really understand. The paradox has been judiciously pruned by her descendant, the Duke de Broglie, in the words: "Beware of too much explaining, lest we end by too much excusing." History, says Froude, does teach that right and wrong are real distinctions. Opinions alter, manners change, creeds rise and fall, but the moral law is written on the tablets of eternity.[26] And if there are moments when we may resist the teaching of Froude, we have seldom the chance of resisting when he is supported by Mr. Goldwin Smith: "A sound historical morality will sanction strong measures in evil times; selfish ambition, treachery, murder, perjury, it will never sanction in the worst of times, for these are the things that make times evil—Justice has been justice, mercy has been mercy, honour has been honour, good faith has been good faith, truthfulness has been truthfulness from the beginning." The doctrine that, as Sir Thomas Browne says, morality is not ambulatory,[27] is expressed as follows by Burke, who, when true to himself, is the most intelligent of our instructors: "My principles enable me to form my judgment upon men and actions in history, just as they do in common life; and are not formed out of events and characters, either present or past. History is a preceptor of prudence, not of principles. The principles of true politics are those of morality enlarged; and I neither now do, nor ever will admit of any other."

Whatever a man's notions of these later centuries are, such, in the main, the man himself will be. Under the name of History, they cover the articles of his philosophic, his religious, and his political creed.[28] They give his measure; they denote his character: and, as praise is the shipwreck of historians, his preferences betray him more than his aversions. Modern History touches us so nearly, it is so deep a question of life and death, that we are bound to find our own way through it, and to owe our insight to ourselves. The historians of former ages, unapproachable for us in knowledge and in talent, cannot be our limit. We have the power to be more rigidly impersonal, disinterested and just than they; and to learn from undisguised and genuine records to look with remorse upon the past, and to the future with assured hope of better things; bearing this in mind, that if we lower our standard in History, we cannot uphold it in Church or State.

Notes

1   No political conclusions of any value for practice can be arrived at by direct experience. All true political science is, in one sense of the phrase, *a priori*, being deduced from the tendencies of things, tendencies known either through our general experience of human nature, or as the result of an analysis of the course of history, considered as a progressive evolution.—MILL, *Inaugural Address*, 51.

2   Contemporary history is, in Dr. Arnold's opinion, more important than either ancient or modern; and in fact superior to it by all the superiority of the end to the means.—SEELEY, *Lectures and Essays*, 306.

3   The law of all progress is one and the same, the evolution of the simple into the complex by successive differentiations.—*Edinburgh Review*, clvii. 428.

4   In our own history, above all, every step in advance has been at the same time a step backwards. It has often been shown how our latest constitution is, amidst all external differences, essentially the same as our earliest, how every struggle for right and freedom, from the thirteenth century onwards, has simply been a struggle for recovering something old.—FREEMAN, *Historical Essays*, iv. 253. Nothing but a thorough knowledge of the social system, based upon a regular study of its growth, can give us the power we require to affect it.—HARRISON, *Meaning of History*, 19.

5   The question which is at the bottom of all constitutional struggles, the question between the national will and the national law.—GARDINER, *Documents*, xviii. Religion, considered simply as the principle which balances the power of human opinion, which takes man out of the grasp of custom and fashion, and teaches him to refer himself to a higher tribunal, is an infinite aid to moral strength and elevation.—CHANNING, *Works*, iv. 83.

6   The older idea of a law of degeneracy, of a "fatal drift towards the worse," is as obsolete as astrology or the belief in witchcraft. The human race has become hopeful, sanguine.—SEELEY, *Rede Lecture*, 1887. *Fortnightly Review*, July 1887, 124.

7   That great statesman (Mr. Pitt) distinctly avowed that the application of philosophy to politics was at that time an innovation, and that it was an innovation worthy to be adopted. He was ready to make the same avowal in the present day which Mr. Pitt had made in 1792.—CANNING, 1st June 1827. *Parliamentary Review*, 1828, 71. American history knows but one avenue of success in American legislation, freedom from ancient prejudice. The best lawgivers in our colonies first became as little children.—BANCROFT, *History of the United States*, i. 494. Every American, from Jefferson and Gallatin down to the poorest squatter, seemed to nourish an idea that he was doing what he could to overthrow the tyranny which the past had fastened on the human mind.—ADAMS, *History of the United States*, i. 175.

8   The greatest changes of which we have had experience as yet are due to our increasing knowledge of history and nature. They have been produced by a few minds appearing in three or four favoured nations, in comparatively a short period of time. May we be allowed to imagine the minds of men everywhere working together during many ages for the completion of our knowledge? May not the increase of knowledge transfigure the world?—JOWETT, *Plato*, i. 414. Nothing, I believe, is so likely to beget in us a spirit of enlightened liberality, of Christian forbearance, of large-hearted moderation, as the careful study of the history of doctrine and the history of interpretation.—PEROWNE, *Psalms*, i. p. xxxi.

9   A man who does not know what has been thought by those who have gone before him is sure to set an undue value upon his own ideas.—M. PATTISON, *Memoirs*, 78.

10   All our hopes of the future depend on a sound understanding of the past.—HARRISON, *The Meaning of History*, 6.

11   The real history of mankind is that of the slow advance of resolved deed following laboriously just thought; and all the greatest men live in their purpose and effort more than it is possible for them to live in reality.—The things that actually happened were of small consequence—the thoughts that were developed are of infinite consequence.—RUSKIN. Facts are the mere dross of history. It is from the abstract truth which interpenetrates them, and lies latent among them like gold in the ore, that the mass derives its value.—MACAULAY, *Works*, v. 131.

12   [. . .] Instead of saying that the history of mankind is the history of the masses, it would be much more true to say that the history of mankind is the history of its great men.—KINGSLEY, *Lectures*, 329.

13   When you are in young years the whole mind is, as it were, fluid, and is capable of forming itself into any shape that the owner of the mind pleases to order it to form itself into.—CARLYLE, *On the Choice of Books*, 131.

14   The only real cry in the country is the proper and just old No Popery cry.—*Major Beresford*, July 1847. Unfortunately the strongest bond of union amongst them is an apprehension of Popery.—*Stanley*, 12th September 1847. The great Protectionist party having degenerated into a No Popery, No Jew Party, I am still more unfit now than I was in 1846 to lead it.—G. Bentinck, 26th December 1847; *Croker's Memoirs*, iii. 116, 132, 157.

15   In the case of Protestantism, this constitutional instability is now a simple matter of fact, which has become too plain to be denied. The system is not fixed, but in motion; and the motion is for the time in the direction of complete self-dissolution.—We take it for a transitory scheme, whose breaking up is to make room in due time for another and far more perfect state of the Church.—

The new order in which Protestantism is to become thus complete cannot be reached without the co-operation and help of Romanism.—NEVIN, *Mercersburg Review*, iv. 48.

16   The rights of individuals and the justice due to them are as dear and precious as those of states; indeed the latter are founded on the former, and the great end and object of them must be to secure and support the rights of individuals, or else vain is government.—CUSHING, in CONWAY, *Life of Paine*, i. 217. As it is owned the whole scheme of Scripture is not yet understood; so, if it ever comes to be understood, before the restitution of all things, and without miraculous interpositions, it must be in the same way as natural knowledge is come at—by the continuance and progress of learning and liberty.—BUTLER, *Analogy*, ii. 3.

17   All the world is, by the very law of its creation, in eternal progress; and the cause of all the evils of the world may be traced to that natural, but most deadly error of human indolence and corruption, that our business is to preserve and not to improve.—ARNOLD, *Life*, i. 259. In whatever state of knowledge we may conceive man to be placed, his progress towards a yet higher state need never fear a check, but must continue till the last existence of society.—HERSCHEL, *Prel. Dis.* 360. It is in the development of thought as in every other development; the present suffers from the past, and the future struggles hard in escaping from the present.—MAX MÜLLER, *Science of Thought*, 617. Most of the great positive evils of the world are in themselves removable, and will, if human affairs continue to improve, be in the end reduced within narrow limits. Poverty in any sense implying suffering may be completely extinguished by the wisdom of society combined with the good sense and providence of individuals.—All the grand sources, in short, of human suffering are in a great degree, many of them almost entirely, conquerable by human care and effort.—J. S. MILL, *Utilitarianism*, 21, 22. The ultimate standard of worth is personal worth, and the only progress that is worth striving after, the only acquisition that is truly good and enduring, is the growth of the soul.—BIXBY, *Crisis of Morals*, 210.

18   The experiment of free government is not one which can be tried once for all. Every generation must try it for itself. As each new generation starts up to the responsibilities of manhood, there is, as it were, a new launch of Liberty, and its voyage of experiment begins afresh.—WINTHROP, *Addresses*, 163. You are not to inquire how your trade may be increased, nor how you are to become a great and powerful people, but how your liberties can be secured. For liberty ought to be the direct end of your government.—PATRICK HENRY, 1788; WIRT, *Life of Henry*, 272.

19   The study of Modern History is, next to Theology itself, and only next in so far as Theology rests on a divine revelation, the most thoroughly religious training that the mind can receive. It is no paradox to say that Modern History, including Medieval History in the term, is co-extensive in its field of view, in its habits of criticism, in the persons of its most famous students, with Ecclesiastical History.—STUBBS, *Lectures*, 9. The belief that the course of events and the agency of man are subject to the laws of a divine order, which it is alike impossible for any one either fully to comprehend or effectually to resist—this belief is the ground of all our hope for the future destinies of mankind.—THIRLWALL, *Remains*, iii. 282. A true religion must consist of ideas and facts both; not of ideas alone without facts, for then it would be mere philosophy; nor of facts alone without ideas, of which those facts are the symbols, or out of which they are grounded; for then it would be mere history.—COLERIDGE, *Table Talk*, 144. It certainly appears strange that the men most conversant with the order of the visible universe should soonest suspect it empty of directing mind; and, on the other hand, that humanistic, moral and historical studies—which first open the terrible problems of suffering and grief, and contain all the reputed provocatives of denial and despair—should confirm, and enlarge rather than disturb, the prepossessions of natural piety.—MARTINEAU, *Essays*, i. 122.

20   This process consists in determining with documentary proofs, and by minute investigations duly set forth, the literal, precise, and positive inferences to be drawn at the present day from every authentic statement, without regard to commonly received notions, to sweeping generalities, or to possible consequences.—HARRISSE, *Discovery of America*, 1892, p. vi. Perhaps the time has not yet come for synthetic labours in the sphere of History. It may be that the student of the Past must still content himself with critical inquiries.—*Ib.* p. v. Few scholars are critics, few critics are philosophers, and few philosophers look with equal care on both sides of a question.—W. S. LANDOR in HOLYOAKE's *Agitator's Life*, ii. 15.

21   The only case in which such extraneous matters can be fairly called in is when facts are stated resting on testimony; then it is not only just, but it is necessary for the sake of truth, to inquire into the habits of mind of him by whom they are adduced.—BABBAGE, *Bridgewater Treatise*, p. xiv.

22   There is no part of our knowledge which it is more useful to obtain at first hand—to go to the fountain-head for—than our knowledge of History.—J. S. MILL, *Inaugural Address*, 34. The only

sound intellects are those which, in the first instance, set their standard of proof high.—J. S. MILL, *Examination of Hamilton's Philosophy*, 525.

23   There are so few men mentally capable of seeing both sides of a question; so few with consciences sensitively alive to the obligation of seeing both sides; so few placed under conditions either of circumstance or temper, which admit of their seeing both sides.—GREG, *Political Problems*, 1870, 173.

24   I was fond of Fleury for a reason which I express in the advertisement; because it presented a sort of photograph of ecclesiastical history without any comment upon it. In the event, that simple representation of the early centuries had a good deal to do with unsettling me.—NEWMAN, *Apologia*, 152. Church history falsely written is a school of vainglory, hatred, and uncharitableness; truly written, it is a discipline of humility, of charity, of mutual love.—SIR W. HAMILTON, *Discussions*, 506. The more trophies and crowns of honour the Church of former ages can be shown to have won in the service of her adorable head, the more tokens her history can be brought to furnish of his powerful presence in her midst, the more will we be pleased and rejoice, Protestant though we be.—NEVIN, *Mercersburg Review*, 1851, 168. To love truth for truth's sake is the principal part of human perfection in this world, and the seed-plot of all other virtues.—LOCKE, *Letter to Collins*.

25   A Christian is bound by his very creed to suspect evil, and cannot release himself.—His religion has brought evil to light in a way in which it never was before; it has shown its depth, subtlety, ubiquity; and a revelation, full of mercy on the one hand, is terrible in its exposure of the world's real state on the other. The Gospel fastens the sense of evil upon the mind; a Christian is enlightened, hardened, sharpened, as to evil; he sees it where others do not.—MOZLEY, *Essays*, i. 308. All satirists, of course, work in the direction of Christian doctrine, by the support they give to the doctrine of original sin, making a sort of meanness and badness a law of society.—MOZLEY, *Letters*, 333.

26   The eternal truths and rights of things exist, fortunately, independent of our thoughts or wishes, fixed as mathematics, inherent in the nature of man and the world. They are no more to be trifled with than gravitation.—FROUDE, *Inaugural Lecture at St. Andrews*, 1869, 41. What have men to do with interests? There is a right way and a wrong way. That is all we need think about.—CARLYLE to FROUDE, *Longman's Magazine*, December 1892, 151. As to History, it is full of indirect but very effective moral teaching. It is not only, as Bolingbroke called it, "Philosophy teaching by examples," but it is morality teaching by examples.—It is essentially the study which best helps the student to conceive large thoughts.—It is impossible to overvalue the moral teaching of History.—FITCH, *Lectures on Teaching*, 432. Judging from the past history of our race, in ninety-nine cases out of a hundred, war is a folly and a crime.—Where it is so, it is the saddest and the wildest of all follies, and the most heinous of all crimes.—GREG, *Essays on Political and Social Science*, 1853, i. 562.

27   Think not that morality is ambulatory; that vices in one age are not vices in another, or that virtues, which are under the everlasting seal of right reason, may be stamped by opinion.—SIR THOMAS BROWNE, *Works*, iv. 64.

28   The subject of modern History is of all others, to my mind, the most interesting, inasmuch as it includes all questions of the deepest interest relating not to human things only, but to divine.—ARNOLD, *Modern History*, 311.

Chapter 2

Carl Becker

EVERYMAN HIS OWN HISTORIAN

Carl Becker (1873–1945), "Everyman His Own Historian", 1931, Presidential Address, *American Historical Review* 37 (January 1932), 221–36.

I.

ONCE UPON A TIME, long long ago, I learned how to reduce a fraction to its lowest terms. Whether I could still perform that operation is uncertain; but the discipline involved in early training had its uses, since it taught me that in order to understand the essential nature of anything it is well to strip it of all superficial and irrelevant accretions—in short, to reduce it to its lowest terms. That operation I now venture, with some apprehension and all due apologies, to perform on the subject of history.

I ought first of all to explain that when I use the term history I mean knowledge of history. No doubt throughout all past time there actually occurred a series of events which, whether we know what it was or not, constitutes history in some ultimate sense. Nevertheless, much the greater part of these events we can know nothing about, not even that they occurred; many of them we can know only imperfectly; and even the few events that we think we know for sure we can never be absolutely certain of, since we can never revive them, never observe or test them directly. The event itself once occurred, but as an actual event it has disappeared; so that in dealing with it the only objective reality we can observe or test is some material trace which the event has left—usually a written document. With these traces of vanished events, these documents, we must be content since they are all we have; from them we infer what the event was, we affirm that it is a fact that the event was so and so. We do not say "Lincoln is assassinated"; we say "it is a fact that Lincoln was assassinated". The event *was*, but is no longer; it is only the affirmed fact about the event that *is*, that persists, and will persist until we discover that our affirmation is wrong or inadequate. Let us then admit that there are two histories: the actual series of events that once occurred; and the ideal series that we affirm and hold in memory. The first is absolute and unchanged—it was what it was whatever we do or say about it; the second is relative, always changing in response to the increase or refinement of knowledge. The two series correspond more or less, it is our aim to make the correspondence as exact as possible; but the actual series of events exists for us only in terms of the ideal series which we affirm and hold in memory. This is why I am forced to identify history with knowledge of history. For all practical purposes history is, for us and for the time being, what we know it to be.

It is history in this sense that I wish to reduce to its lowest terms. In order to do that I need a very simple definition. I once read that "History is the knowledge of events that have occurred in the past". That is a simple definition, but not simple enough. It contains three words that require examination. The first is knowledge. Knowledge is a formidable word. I always think of knowledge as something that is stored up in the *Encyclopædia Britannica* or the *Summa Theologica*; something difficult to acquire, something at all events that I have not. Resenting a definition that denies me the title of historian, I therefore ask what is most essential to knowledge. Well, memory, I should think (and I mean memory in the broad sense, the memory of events inferred as well as the memory of events observed); other things are necessary too, but memory is fundamental: without memory no knowledge. So our definition becomes, "History is the memory of events that have occurred in the past". But events—the word carries an implication of something grand, like the taking of the Bastille or the Spanish–American War. An occurrence need not be spectacular to be an event. If I drive a motor car down the crooked streets of Ithaca, that is an event—something done; if the traffic cop bawls me out, that is an event—something said; if I have evil thoughts of him for so doing, that is an event—something thought. In truth anything done, said, or thought is an event, important or not as may turn out. But since we do not ordinarily speak without thinking, at least in some rudimentary way, and since the psychologists tell us that we can not think without speaking, or at least not without having anticipatory vibrations in the larynx, we may well combine thought events and speech events under one term; and so our definition becomes, "History is the memory of things said and done in the past". But the past—the word is both misleading and unnecessary: misleading, because the past, used in connection with history, seems to imply the distant past, as if history ceased before we were born; unnecessary, because after all everything said or done is already in the past as soon as it is said or done. Therefore I will omit that word, and our definition becomes, "*History is the memory of things said and done*". This is a definition that reduces history to its lowest terms, and yet includes everything that is essential to understanding what it really is.

If the essence of history is the memory of things said and done, then it is obvious that every normal person, Mr. Everyman, knows some history. Of course we do what we can to conceal this invidious truth. Assuming a professional manner, we say that so and so knows no history, when we mean no more than that he failed to pass the examinations set for a higher degree; and simple-minded persons, undergraduates and others, taken in by academic classifications of knowledge, think they know no history because they have never taken a course in history in college, or have never read Gibbon's *Decline and Fall of the Roman Empire*. No doubt the academic convention has its uses, but it is one of the superficial accretions that must be stripped off if we would understand history reduced to its lowest terms. Mr. Everyman, as well as you and I, remembers things said and done, and must do so at every waking moment. Suppose Mr. Everyman to have awakened this morning unable to remember anything said or done. He would be a lost soul indeed. This has happened, this sudden loss of all historical knowledge. But normally it does not happen. Normally the memory of Mr. Everyman, when he awakens in the morning, reaches out into the country of the past and of distant places and instantaneously recreates his little world of endeavor, pulls together as it were things said and done in his yesterdays, and coördinates them with his present perceptions and with things to be said and done in his to-morrows. Without this historical knowledge, this memory of things said and done, his to-day would be aimless and his to-morrow without significance.

Since we are concerned with history in its lowest terms, we will suppose that Mr. Everyman is not a professor of history, but just an ordinary citizen without excess knowledge. Not having a lecture to prepare, his memory of things said and done, when he awakened this morning, presumably did not drag into consciousness any events connected with the Liman von Sanders mission or the Pseudo-Isidorian Decretals; it presumably dragged into consciousness an image of things said and done yesterday in the office, the highly significant fact that General Motors had dropped three points, a conference arranged for ten o'clock in the morning, a promise to play nine holes at four-thirty in the afternoon, and other historical events of similar import. Mr. Everyman knows more history than this, but at the moment of awakening this is sufficient: memory of things said and done, history functioning, at seven-thirty in the morning, in its very lowest terms, has effectively oriented Mr. Everyman in his little world of endeavor.

Yet not quite effectively after all perhaps; for unaided memory is notoriously fickle; and it may happen that Mr. Everyman, as he drinks his coffee, is uneasily aware of something said or done that he fails now to recall. A common enough occurrence, as we all know to our sorrow—this remembering, not the historical event, but only that there was an event which we ought to remember but can not. This is Mr. Everyman's difficulty, a bit of history lies dead and inert in the sources, unable to do any work for Mr. Everyman because his memory refuses to bring it alive in consciousness. What then does Mr. Everyman do? He does what any historian would do: he does a bit of historical research in the sources. From his little Private Record Office (I mean his vest pocket) he takes a book in MS., volume XXXV. it may be, and turns to page 23, and there he reads: "December 29, pay Smith's coal bill, 20 tons, $1017.20." Instantaneously a series of historical events comes to life in Mr. Everyman's mind. He has an image of himself ordering twenty tons of coal from Smith last summer, of Smith's wagons driving up to his house, and of the precious coal sliding dustily through the cellar window. Historical events, these are, not so important as the forging of the Isidorian Decretals, but still important to Mr. Everyman: historical events which he was not present to observe, but which, by an artificial extension of memory, he can form a clear picture of, because he has done a little original research in the manuscripts preserved in his Private Record Office.

The picture Mr. Everyman forms of Smith's wagons delivering the coal at his house is a picture of things said and done in the past. But it does not stand alone, it is not a pure antiquarian image to be enjoyed for its own sake; on the contrary, it is associated with a picture of things to be said and done in the future; so that throughout the day Mr. Everyman intermittently holds in mind, together with a picture of Smith's coal wagons, a picture of himself going at four o'clock in the afternoon to Smith's office in order to pay his bill. At four o'clock Mr. Everyman is accordingly at Smith's office. "I wish to pay that coal bill", he says. Smith looks dubious and disappointed, takes down a ledger (or a filing case), does a bit of original research in his Private Record Office, and announces: "You don't owe me any money, Mr. Everyman. You ordered the coal here all right, but I didn't have the kind you wanted, and so turned the order over to Brown. It was Brown delivered your coal: he's the man you owe." Whereupon Mr. Everyman goes to Brown's office; and Brown takes down a ledger, does a bit of original research in his Private Record Office, which happily confirms the researches of Smith; and Mr. Everyman pays his bill, and in the evening, after returning from the Country Club, makes a further search in another collection of documents, where, sure enough, he finds a bill from Brown, properly drawn, for twenty tons of stove coal, $1017.20. The research is now completed. Since his mind rests satisfied, Mr. Everyman has found the explanation of the series of events that concerned him.

Mr. Everyman would be astonished to learn that he is an historian, yet it is obvious, isn't it, that he has performed all the essential operations involved in historical research. Needing or wanting to do something (which happened to be, not to deliver a lecture or write a book, but to pay a bill; and this is what misleads him and us as to what he is really doing), the first step was to recall things said and done. Unaided memory proving inadequate, a further step was essential—the examination of certain documents in order to discover the necessary but as yet unknown facts. Unhappily the documents were found to give conflicting reports, so that a critical comparison of the texts had to be instituted in order to eliminate error. All this having been satisfactorily accomplished, Mr. Everyman is ready for the final operation— the formation in his mind, by an artificial extension of memory, of a picture, a definitive picture let us hope, of a selected series of historical events—of himself ordering coal from Smith, of Smith turning the order over to Brown, and of Brown delivering the coal at his house. In the light of this picture Mr. Everyman could, and did, pay his bill. If Mr. Everyman had undertaken these researches in order to write a book instead of to pay a bill, no one would think of denying that he was an historian.

II.

I have tried to reduce history to its lowest terms, first by defining it as the memory of things said and done, second by showing concretely how the memory of things said and done is essential to the performance of the simplest acts of daily life. I wish now to note the more general implications of Mr. Everyman's activities. In the realm of affairs Mr. Everyman has been paying his coal bill; in the realm of consciousness he has been doing that fundamental thing which enables man alone to have, properly speaking, a history: he has been reënforcing and enriching his immediate perceptions to the end that he may live in a world of semblance more spacious and satisfying than is to be found within the narrow confines of the fleeting present moment.

We are apt to think of the past as dead, the future as nonexistent, the present alone as real; and prematurely wise or disillusioned counselors have urged us to burn always with "a hard, gemlike flame" in order to give "the highest quality to the moments as they pass, and simply for those moments' sake". This no doubt is what the glowworm does; but I think that man, who alone is properly aware that the present moment passes, can for that very reason make no good use of the present moment simply for its own sake. Strictly speaking, the present doesn't exist for us, or is at best no more than an infinitesimal point in time, gone before we can note it as present. Nevertheless, we must have a present; and so we create one by robbing the past, by holding on to the most recent events and pretending that they all belong to our immediate perceptions. If, for example, I raise my arm, the total event is a series of occurrences of which the first are past before the last have taken place; and yet you perceive it as a single movement executed in one present instant. This telescoping of succes- sive events into a single instant philosophers call the 'specious present'. Doubtless they would assign rather narrow limits to the specious present; but I will willfully make a free use of it, and say that we can extend the specious present as much as we like. In common speech we do so: we speak of the 'present hour', the 'present year', the 'present generation'. Perhaps all living creatures have a specious present; but man has this superiority, as Pascal says, that he is aware of himself and the universe, can as it were hold himself at arm's length and with some measure of objectivity watch himself and his fellows functioning in the world during a brief span of alloted years. Of all the creatures, man alone has a specious present that may be deliberately and purposefully enlarged and diversified and enriched.

The extent to which the specious present may thus be enlarged and enriched will depend upon knowledge, the artificial extension of memory, the memory of things said and done in the past and distant places. But not upon knowledge alone; rather upon knowledge directed by purpose. The specious present is an unstable pattern of thought, incessantly changing in response to our immediate perceptions and the purposes that arise therefrom. At any given moment each one of us (professional historian no less than Mr. Everyman) weaves into this unstable pattern such actual or artificial memories as may be necessary to orient us in our little world of endeavor. But to be oriented in our little world of endeavor we must be prepared for what is coming to us (the payment of a coal bill, the delivery of a presidential address, the establishment of a League of Nations, or whatever); and to be prepared for what is coming to us it is necessary, not only to recall certain past events, but to anticipate (note I do not say predict) the future. Thus from the specious present, which always includes more or less of the past, the future refuses to be excluded; and the more of the past we drag into the specious present, the more an hypothetical, patterned future is likely to crowd into it also. Which comes first, which is cause and which effect, whether our memories construct a pattern of past events at the behest of our desires and hopes, or whether our desires and hopes spring from a pattern of past events imposed upon us by experience and knowledge, I shall not attempt to say. What I suspect is that memory of past and anticipation of future events work together, go hand in hand as it were in a friendly way, without disputing over priority and leadership.

At all events they go together, so that in a very real sense it is impossible to divorce history from life: Mr. Everyman can not do what he needs or desires to do without recalling past events; he can not recall past events without in some subtle fashion relating them to what he needs or desires to do. This is the natural function of history, of history reduced to its lowest terms, of history conceived as the memory of things said and done: memory of things said and done (whether in our immediate yesterdays or in the long past of mankind), running hand in hand with the anticipation of things to be said and done, enables us, each to the extent of his knowledge and imagination, to be intelligent, to push back the narrow confines of the fleeting present moment so that what we are doing may be judged in the light of what we have done and what we hope to do. In this sense all *living* history, as Croce says, is contemporaneous: in so far as we think the past (and otherwise the past, however fully related in documents, is nothing to us) it becomes an integral and living part of our present world of semblance.

It must then be obvious that living history, the ideal series of events that we affirm and hold in memory, since it is so intimately associated with what we are doing and with what we hope to do, can not be precisely the same for all at any given time, or the same for one generation as for another. History in this sense can not be reduced to a verifiable set of statistics or formulated in terms of universally valid mathematical formulas. It is rather an imaginative creation, a personal possession which each one of us, Mr. Everyman, fashions out of his individual experience, adapts to his practical or emotional needs, and adorns as well as may be to suit his æsthetic tastes. In thus creating his own history, there are, nevertheless, limits which Mr. Everyman may not overstep without incurring penalties. The limits are set by his fellows. If Mr. Everyman lived quite alone in an unconditioned world he would be free to affirm and hold in memory any ideal series of events that struck his fancy, and thus create a world of semblance quite in accord with the heart's desire. Unfortunately, Mr. Everyman has to live in a world of Browns and Smiths; a sad experience, which has taught him the expediency of recalling certain events with much exactness. In all the immediately practical affairs of life Mr. Everyman is a good historian, as expert, in conducting the researches necessary for paying his coal bill, as need be. His expertness comes partly from long practice, but chiefly from the circumstance that his researches are prescribed and guided by very definite and practical objects which concern him intimately. The problem of what documents to consult, what facts to select, troubles Mr. Everyman not at all. Since he is not writing a book on "Some Aspects of the Coal Industry Objectively Considered", it does not occur to him to collect all the facts and let them speak for themselves. Wishing merely to pay his coal bill, he selects only such facts as may be relevant; and not wishing to pay it twice, he is sufficiently aware, without ever having read Bernheim's *Lehrbuch*, that the relevant facts must be clearly established by the testimony of independent witnesses not self-deceived. He does not know, or need to know, that his personal interest in the performance is a disturbing bias which will prevent him from learning the whole truth or arriving at ultimate causes. Mr. Everyman does not wish to learn the whole truth or to arrive at ultimate causes. He wishes to pay his coal bill. That is to say, he wishes to adjust himself to a practical situation, and on that low pragmatic level he is a good historian precisely because he is not disinterested: he will solve his problems, if he does solve them, by virtue of his intelligence and not by virtue of his indifference.

Nevertheless, Mr. Everyman does not live by bread alone; and on all proper occasions his memory of things said and done, easily enlarging his specious present beyond the narrow circle of daily affairs, will, must inevitably, in mere compensation for the intolerable dullness and vexation of the fleeting present moment, fashion for him a more spacious world than that of the immediately practical. He can readily recall the days of his youth, the places he has lived in, the ventures he has made, the adventures he has had—all the crowded events of a lifetime; and beyond and around this central pattern of personally experienced events, there will be embroidered a more dimly seen pattern of artificial memories, memories of things reputed to have been said and done in past times which he has not known, in distant places which he has not seen. This outer pattern of remembered events that encloses and completes the central pattern of his personal experience, Mr. Everyman has woven, he could not tell you how, out of the most diverse threads of information, picked up in the most casual way, from the most unrelated sources—from things learned at home and in school, from knowledge gained in business or profession, from newspapers glanced at, from books (yes, even history books) read or heard of, from remembered scraps of newsreels or educational films or *ex cathedra* utterances of presidents and kings, from fifteen-minute discourses on the history of civilization broadcast by the courtesy (it may be) of Pepsodent, the Bulova Watch Company, or the Shepard Stores in Boston. Daily and hourly, from a thousand unnoted sources, there is lodged in Mr. Everyman's mind a mass of unrelated and related information and misinformation, of impressions and images, out of which he somehow manages, undeliberately for the most part, to fashion a history, a patterned picture of remembered things said and done in past times and distant places. It is not possible, it is not essential, that this picture should be complete or completely true: it is essential that it should be useful to Mr. Everyman; and that it may be useful to him he will hold in memory, of all the things he might hold in memory, those things only which can be related with some reasonable degree of relevance and harmony to his idea of himself and of what he is doing in the world and what he hopes to do.

In constructing this more remote and far-flung pattern of remembered things, Mr. Everyman works with something of the freedom of a creative artist; the history which he imaginatively recreates as an artificial extension of his personal experience will inevitably be an engaging blend of fact and fancy, a mythical adaptation of that which actually happened. In part it will be true, in part false; as a whole perhaps neither true nor false, but only the most convenient form of error. Not that Mr. Everyman wishes or intends to deceive himself or others. Mr. Everyman has a wholesome respect for cold, hard facts, never suspecting how malleable they are, how easy it is to coax and cajole them; but he necessarily takes the facts as they come to him, and is enamored of those that seem best suited to his interests or promise most in the way of emotional satisfaction. The exact truth of remembered events he has in any case no time, and no need, to curiously question or meticulously verify. No doubt he can, if he be an American, call up an image of the signing of the Declaration of Independence in 1776 as readily as he can call up an image of Smith's coal wagons creaking up the hill last summer. He suspects the one image no more than the other; but the signing of the Declaration, touching not his practical interests, calls for no careful historical research on his part. He may perhaps, without knowing why, affirm and hold in memory that the Declaration was signed by the members of the Continental Congress on the fourth of July. It is a vivid and sufficient image which Mr. Everyman may hold to the end of his days without incurring penalties. Neither Brown nor Smith has any interest in setting him right; nor will any court ever send him a summons for failing to recall that the Declaration, "being engrossed and compared at the table, was signed by the members" on the second of August. As an actual event, the signing of the Declaration was what it was; as a remembered event it will be, for Mr. Everyman, what Mr. Everyman contrives to make it: will have for him significance and magic, much or little or none at all, as it fits well or ill into his little world of interests and aspirations and emotional comforts.

III.

What then of us, historians by profession? What have we to do with Mr. Everyman, or he with us? More, I venture to believe, than we are apt to think. For each of us is Mr. Everyman too. Each of us is subject to the limitations of time and place; and for each of us, no less than for the Browns and Smiths of the world, the pattern of remembered things said and done will be woven, safeguard the process how we may, at the behest of circumstance and purpose.

True it is that although each of us is Mr. Everyman, each is something more than his own historian. Mr. Everyman, being but an informal historian, is under no bond to remember what is irrelevant to his personal affairs. But we are historians by profession. Our profession, less intimately bound up with the practical activities, is to be directly concerned with the ideal series of events that is only of casual or occasional import to others; it is our business in life to be ever preoccupied with that far-flung pattern of artificial memories that encloses and completes the central pattern of individual experience. We are Mr. Everybody's historian as well as our own, since our histories serve the double purpose, which written histories have always served, of keeping alive the recollection of memorable men and events. We are thus of that ancient and honorable company of wise men of the tribe, of bards and story-tellers and minstrels, of soothsayers and priests, to whom in successive ages has been entrusted the keeping of the useful myths. Let not the harmless, necessary word 'myth' put us out of countenance. In the history of history a myth is a once valid but now discarded version of the human story, as our now valid versions will in due course be relegated to the category of discarded myths. With our predecessors, the bards and story-tellers and priests, we have therefore this in common: that it is our function, as it was theirs, not to create, but to preserve and perpetuate the social tradition; to harmonize, as well as ignorance and prejudice permit, the actual and the remembered series of events; to enlarge and enrich the specious present common to us all to the end that 'society' (the tribe, the nation, or all mankind) may judge of what it is doing in the light of what it has done and what it hopes to do.

History as the artificial extension of the social memory (and I willingly concede that there are other appropriate ways of apprehending human experience) is an art of long standing, necessarily so since it springs instinctively from the impulse to enlarge the range of immediate experience; and however camouflaged by the disfiguring jargon of science, it is still in essence what it has always been. History in this sense is story, in aim always a true story; a story that employs all the devices of literary art (statement and generalization, narration and description, comparison and comment and analogy) to present the succession of events in the life of man, and from the succession of events thus presented to derive a satisfactory meaning. The history written by historians, like the history informally fashioned by Mr. Everyman, is thus a convenient blend of truth and fancy, of what we commonly distinguish as 'fact' and 'interpretation'. In primitive times, when tradition is orally transmitted, bards and story-tellers frankly embroider or improvise the facts to heighten the dramatic import of the story. With the use of written records, history, gradually differentiated from fiction, is understood as the story of events that actually occurred; and with the increase and refinement of knowledge the historian recognizes that his first duty is to be sure of his facts, let their meaning be what it may. Nevertheless, in every age history is taken to be a story of actual events from which a significant meaning may be derived; and in every age the illusion is that the present version is valid because the related facts are true, whereas former versions are invalid because based upon inaccurate or inadequate facts.

Never was this conviction more impressively displayed than in our own time—that age of erudition in which we live, or from which we are perhaps just emerging. Finding the course of history littered with the *débris* of exploded philosophies, the historians of the last century, unwilling to be forever duped, turned away (as they fondly hoped) from 'interpretation' to the rigorous examination of the factual event, just as it occurred. Perfecting the technique of investigation, they laboriously collected and edited the sources of information, and with incredible persistence and ingenuity ran illusive error to earth, letting the significance of the Middle Ages wait until it was certainly known "whether Charles the Fat was at Ingelheim or Lustnau on July 1, 887", shedding their "life-blood", in many a hard fought battle, "for the sublime truths of Sac and Soc". I have no quarrel with this so great concern with hoti's business. One of the first duties of man is not to be duped, to be aware of his world; and to derive the significance of human experience from events that never occurred is surely an enterprise of doubtful value. To establish the facts is always in order, and is indeed the first duty of the historian; but to suppose that the facts, once established in all their fullness, will 'speak for themselves' is an illusion. It was perhaps peculiarly the illusion of those historians of the last century who found some special magic in the word 'scientific'. The scientific historian, it seems, was one who set forth the facts without injecting any extraneous meaning into them. He was the objective man whom Nietzsche described—"a mirror: accustomed to prostration before something that wants to be known, . . . he waits until something comes, and then expands himself sensitively, so that even the light footsteps and gliding past of spiritual things may not be lost in his surface and film".[1] "It is not I who speak, but history which speaks through me", was Fustel's reproof to applauding students. "If a certain philosophy emerges from this scientific history, it must be permitted to emerge naturally, of its own accord, all but independently of the will of the historian."[2] Thus the scientific historian deliberately renounced philosophy only to submit to it without being aware. His philosophy was just this, that by not taking thought a cubit would be added to his stature. With no other preconception than the will to know, the historian would reflect in his surface and film the "order of events throughout past times in all places"; so that, in the fullness of time, when innumerable patient expert scholars, by "exhausting the sources", should have reflected without refracting the truth of all the facts, the definitive and impregnable meaning of human experience would emerge of its own accord to enlighten and emancipate mankind. Hoping to find something without looking for it, expecting to obtain final answers to life's riddle by resolutely refusing to ask questions—it was surely the most romantic species of realism yet invented, the oddest attempt ever made to get something for nothing!

That mood is passing. The fullness of time is not yet, overmuch learning proves a weariness to the flesh, and a younger generation that knows not Von Ranke is eager to believe that Fustel's counsel, if one of perfection, is equally one of futility. Even the most disinterested historian has at least one preconception, which is the fixed idea that he has none. The facts of history are already set forth, implicitly, in the sources; and the historian who could restate without reshaping them would, by submerging and suffocating the mind in diffuse existence, accomplish the superfluous task of depriving human experience of all significance. Left to themselves, the facts do not speak; left to themselves they do not exist, not really, since for all practical purposes there is no fact until some one affirms it. The least the historian can do with any historical fact is to select and affirm it. To select and affirm even the simplest complex of facts is to give them a certain place in a certain pattern of ideas, and this alone is sufficient to give them a special meaning. However 'hard' or 'cold' they may be, historical facts are after all not material substances which, like bricks or scantlings, possess definite shape and clear, persistent outline. To set forth historical facts is not comparable to dumping a barrow of bricks. A brick retains its form and pressure wherever placed; but the form and substance of historical facts, having a negotiable existence only in literary discourse, vary with the words employed to convey them. Since history is not part of the external material world, but an imaginative reconstruction of vanished events, its form and substance are inseparable: in the realm of literary discourse substance, being an idea, *is* form; and form, conveying the idea, *is* substance. It is thus not the undiscriminated fact, but the perceiving mind of the historian that speaks: the special meaning which the facts are made to convey emerges from the substance-form which the historian employs to recreate imaginatively a series of events not present to perception.

In constructing this substance-form of vanished events, the historian, like Mr. Every-man, like the bards and story-tellers of an earlier time, will be conditioned by the specious present in which alone he can be aware of his world. Being neither omniscient nor omnipresent, the historian is not the same person always and everywhere; and for him, as for Mr. Everyman, the form and significance of remembered events, like the extension and velocity of physical objects, will vary with the time and place of the observer. After fifty years we can clearly see that it was not history which spoke through Fustel, but Fustel who spoke through history. We see less clearly perhaps that the voice of Fustel was the voice, amplified and freed from static as one may say, of Mr. Everyman; what the admiring students applauded on that famous occasion was neither history nor Fustel, but a deftly colored pattern of selected events which Fustel fashioned, all the more skillfully for not being aware of doing so, in the service of Mr. Everyman's emotional needs—the emotional satisfaction, so essential to Frenchmen at that time, of perceiving that French institutions were not of German origin. And so it must always be. Played upon by all the diverse, unnoted influences of his own time, the historian will elicit history out of documents by the same principle, however more consciously and expertly applied, that Mr. Everyman employs to breed legends out of remembered episodes and oral tradition.

Berate him as we will for not reading our books, Mr. Everyman is stronger than we are, and sooner or later we must adapt our knowledge to his necessities. Otherwise he will leave us to our own devices, leave us it may be to cultivate a species of dry professional arrogance growing out of the thin soil of antiquarian research. Such research, valuable not in itself but for some ulterior purpose, will be of little import except in so far as it is transmuted into common knowledge. The history that lies inert in unread books does no work in the world. The history that does work in the world, the history that influences the course of history, is living history, that pattern of remembered events, whether true or false, that enlarges and enriches the collective specious present, the specious present of Mr. Everyman. It is for this reason that the history of history is a record of the "new history" that in every age rises to confound and supplant the old. It should be a relief to us to renounce omniscience, to recognize that every generation, our own included, will, must inevitably, understand the past and anticipate the future in the light of its own restricted experience, must inevitably play on the dead whatever tricks it finds necessary for its own peace of mind. The appropriate trick for any age is not a malicious invention designed to take anyone in, but an unconscious and necessary effort on the part of 'society' to understand what it is doing in the light of what it has done and what it hopes to do. We, historians by profession, share in this necessary effort. But we do not impose our version of the human story on Mr. Everyman; in the end it is rather Mr. Everyman who imposes his version on us—compelling us, in an age of political revolution, to see that history is past politics, in an age of social stress and conflict to search for the economic interpretation. If we remain too long recalcitrant Mr. Everyman will ignore us, shelving our recondite works behind glass doors rarely opened. Our proper function is not to repeat the past but to make use of it, to correct and rationalize for common use Mr. Everyman's mythological adaptation of what actually happened. We are surely under bond to be as honest and as intelligent as human frailty permits; but the secret of our success in the long run is in conforming to the temper of Mr. Everyman, which we seem to guide only because we are so sure, eventually, to follow it.

Neither the value nor the dignity of history need suffer by regarding it as a foreshortened and incomplete representation of the reality that once was, an unstable pattern of remembered things redesigned and newly colored to suit the convenience of those who make use of it. Nor need our labors be the less highly prized because our task is limited, our contributions of incidental and temporary significance. History is an indispensable even though not the highest form of intellectual endeavor, since it makes, as Santayana says, a gift of "great interests . . . to the heart. A barbarian is no less subject to the past than is the civic man who knows what the past is and means to be loyal to it; but the barbarian, for want of a transpersonal memory, crawls among superstitions which he cannot understand or revoke and among people whom he may hate or love, but whom he can never think of raising to a higher plane, to the level of a purer happiness. The whole dignity of human endeavor is thus bound up with historic issues, and as conscience needs to be controlled by experience if it is to become rational, so personal experience itself needs to be enlarged ideally if the failures and successes it reports are to touch impersonal interests."[3]

I do not present this view of history as one that is stable and must prevail. Whatever validity it may claim, it is certain, on its own premises, to be supplanted; for its premises, imposed upon us by the climate of opinion in which we live and think, predispose us to regard all things, and all principles of things, as no more than "inconstant modes or fashions", as but the "concurrence, renewed from moment to moment, of forces parting sooner or later on their way". It is the limitation of the genetic approach to human experience that it must be content to transform problems since it can never solve them. However accurately we may determine the 'facts' of history, the facts themselves and our interpretations of them, and our interpretation of our own interpretations, will be seen in a different perspective or a less vivid light as mankind moves into the unknown future. Regarded historically, as a process of becoming, man and his world can obviously be understood only tentatively, since it is by definition something still in the making, something as yet unfinished. Unfortunately for the 'permanent contribution' and the universally valid philosophy, time passes; time, the enemy of man as the Greeks thought; to-morrow and to-morrow and to-morrow creeps in this petty pace, and all our yesterdays diminish and grow dim: so that, in the lengthening perspective of the centuries, even the most striking events (the Declaration of Independence, the French Revolution, the Great War itself; like the Diet of Worms before them, like the signing of the Magna Carta and the coronation of Charlemagne and the crossing of the Rubicon and the battle of Marathon) must inevitably, for posterity, fade away into pale replicas of the original picture, for each succeeding generation losing, as they recede into a more distant past, some significance that once was noted in them, some quality of enchantment that once was theirs.

Notes

1   *Beyond Good and Evil*, p. 140.
2   Quoted in *English Historical Review*, V. 1.
3   *The Life of Reason*, V. 68.

Chapter 3

Marc Bloch

INTRODUCTION TO *THE* HISTORIAN'S CRAFT

Marc Bloch (1886–1944), "Introduction", *The Historian's Craft,* 1941. Trans. Peter Putnam (New York: Knopf, 1953), 3–7, 9–19.

"TELL ME, DADDY. What is the use of history?"

[. . .]

The question far transcends the minor scruples of a professional conscience. Indeed, our entire Western civilization is concerned in it.

For, unlike others, our civilization has always been extremely attentive to its past. Everything has inclined it in this direction: both the Christian and the classical heritage. Our first masters, the Greeks and the Romans, were history-writing peoples. Christianity is a religion of historians. Other religious systems have been able to found their beliefs and their rites on a mythology nearly outside human time. For sacred books, the Christians have books of history, and their liturgies commemorate, together with episodes from the terrestrial life of a God, the annals of the church and the lives of the saints. Christianity is historical in another and, perhaps, even deeper sense. The destiny of humankind, placed between the Fall and the Judgment, appears to its eyes as a long adventure, of which each life, each individual pilgrimage, is in its turn a reflection. It is in time and, therefore, in history that the great drama of Sin and Redemption, the central axis of all Christian thought, is unfolded. Our art, our literary monuments, resound with echoes of the past. Our men of action have its real or pretended lessons incessantly on their lips. Of course, differences of group psychology can be noted. Cournot long ago observed that the French people in the mass, everlastingly inclined to reconstruct the world on lines of reason, live their collective memories much less intensely than the Germans, for example.[1] Without doubt, too, civilizations may change. It is not in itself inconceivable that ours may, one day, turn away from history, and historians would do well to reflect upon this possibility. If they do not take care, there is danger that badly understood history could involve good history in its disrepute. But should we come to this, it would be at the cost of a serious rupture with our most unvarying intellectual traditions.

For the present, our discussion has reached only the stage of probing the conscience. And, indeed, whenever our exacting Western society, in the continuing crisis of growth, begins to doubt itself, it asks itself whether it has done well in trying to learn from the past, and whether it has learned rightly. Read what was written before the war, or, for that matter, what might be written today. Among the confused murmurings of the present, you will almost certainly hear this complaint mingling its voice with the others. I myself chanced to overhear its echo in the very heart of the great drama. It was in June 1940—the very day, if I remember aright, of the German entry into Paris. In a Norman garden, stripped of our troops, we of the general staff consumed our idle hours in ruminating over the causes of the disaster. "Are we to believe that history has betrayed us?" one of us cried. So it was that the anguish of a mature man united its bitter accents with the simple curiosity of the boy. Both demand an answer.

"What is the use of history?"

What is here meant by "use"? But, before proceeding to this question, let me insert one word of apology. The circumstances of my present life, the impossibility of reaching any large library, and the loss of my own books have made me dependent upon my notes and upon memory. Both the supplementary reading and the research demanded by the very laws of the craft I here propose to describe have been denied me. Will it, one day, be granted to me to fill in the gaps? Never entirely, I fear. I can therefore only ask indulgence. I should say: "I plead guilty," were it not that, by so doing, I might seem overly presumptuous in assuming responsibility for the evils of destiny.

[. . .]

But here a new question arises. What is it, exactly, that constitutes the legitimacy of an intellectual endeavor?

No one today, I believe, would dare to say, with the orthodox positivists, that the value of a line of research is to be measured by its ability to promote action. Experience has surely taught us that it is impossible to decide in advance whether even the most abstract speculations may not eventually prove extraordinarily helpful in practice. It would inflict a strange mutilation upon humanity to deny it a right to appease its intellectual appetites apart from all consideration of its material welfare. Even were history obliged to be eternally indifferent to *homo faber* or to *homo politicus*, it would be sufficiently justified by its necessity for the full flowering of *homo sapiens*. Yet, even with this limitation, the question is not immediately resolved.

The nature of our intelligence is such that it is stimulated far less by the will to know than by the will to understand, and, from this, it results that the only sciences which it admits to be authentic are those which succeed in establishing explanatory relationships between phenomena. The rest is, as Malebranche put it, mere "polymathy." Now, polymathy can well assume the form either of recreation or of mania, but it cannot today, any more than in the time of Malebranche, pass for one of the proper tasks of the intellect. Even apart from any application to conduct, history will rightfully claim its place among those sciences truly worthy of endeavor only in proportion as it promises us, not simply a disjointed and, you might say, a nearly infinite enumeration, but a rational classification and progressive intelligibility.

However, it is undeniable that a science will always seem to us somehow incomplete if it cannot, sooner or later, in one way or another, aid us to live better. Moreover, should we not feel this sentiment with particular force as regards history, so much the more clearly destined to work for the profit of man, in that it has man himself and his actions for its theme? In fact, a long-standing penchant prompts us, almost by instinct, to demand of it the means to direct our actions and, therefore, as in the case of the conquered soldier mentioned above, we become indignant if, perchance, it seems incapable of giving us guidance. The question of the use of history, in the strict and "pragmatic" sense of the word "use," is not to be confounded with that of its strictly intellectual legitimacy. Moreover, this question of use must always come second in the order of things, for, to act reasonably, it is first necessary to understand. Common sense dictates that we no longer avoid this problem.

Certain among our would-be counselors have already given answers to these questions. They have sought to chide our optimism. The most indulgent have said that history is both unprofitable and unsound; others, with a severity which admits of no compromise, that it is pernicious. One of them, and not the least celebrated, has declared it "the most dangerous compound yet contrived by the chemistry of the intellect." These condemnations offer a terrible temptation, in that they justify ignorance in advance. Fortunately for those of us who still retain our intellectual curiosity, there is, perhaps, an appeal from their verdict. His view curiosity, there is, perhaps, an appeal from their verdict.

But if the debate is to be revived, it is important that it be based upon more trust-worthy data.

For there is one precaution which the ordinary detractors of history seem not to have heeded. Their words lack neither eloquence nor wit, but they have, for the most part, neglected to ask themselves exactly what it is they are discussing. The picture which they have formed for themselves of our studies has not been drawn in the workshop. It savors rather of the debating-platform than of the study. Above all, it is out of date. Therefore, when all is said and done, it may well be that all their energy has been expended only to conjure away a phantom. Our effort here must be very different. The methods whose value and certainty we shall attempt to assess are those actually used in research, right down to the lowly and delicate technical details. Our problems will be the same as those which the historian's material imposes upon him every day. In a word, our primary objective is to explain how and why a historian practices his trade. It will then be the business of the reader to decide whether this trade is worth practicing.

Let us take care, however. Even thus defined and limited, the task is not so simple as it seems. It might be, were we dealing with one of the practical arts which are sufficiently explained when time-tested manual operations are enumerated one after another. But history is neither watchmaking nor cabinet construction. It is an endeavor toward better understanding and, consequently, a thing in movement. To limit oneself to describing a science just as it is will always be to betray it a little. It is still more important to tell how it expects to improve itself in the course of time. Now, such an undertaking inevitably involves a rather large dose of personal opinion. Indeed, every science is continually beset at each stage of its development by diverging tendencies, and it is scarcely possible to decide which is now dominant without prophesying the future. We shall not shirk this obligation. The dread of responsibility is as discreditable in intellectual matters as in any others. But it is only honest to give the reader fair warning.

The more so, as the difficulties which every study of methodology encounters vary greatly according to the point which the particular discipline has reached upon the always irregular curve of its development. For example, fifty years ago, when Newton still reigned supreme, it was far easier than today to frame, with all the precision of a blueprint, a thesis on mechanics. But history is still in that stage which is very indulgent of statements of positive certainties.

For history is not only a science in movement. Like all those which have the human spirit for their object, this newcomer in the field of rational knowledge is also a science in its infancy. Or to explain more fully, having grown old in embryo as mere narrative, for long encumbered with legend, and for still longer pre-occupied with only the most obvious events, it is still very young as a rational attempt at analysis. Now, at last, it struggles to penetrate beneath the mere surface of actions, rejecting not only the temptations of legend and rhetoric, but the still more dangerous modern poisons of routine learning and empiricism parading as common sense. In several of the most essential problems of method, it has not passed beyond the first tentative gropings, and that is why Fustel de Coulanges and, even before him, Bayle came very near the truth when they called it "the most difficult of all the sciences."

But is this merely an illusion? However uncertain our road at many points, we are, it seems to me, at the present hour better placed than our predecessors to see a little light on the path ahead.

The generations just prior to our own, in the last decades of the nineteenth century and even in the first years of the twentieth, were as if mesmerized by the Comtian conception of physical science. This hypnotic *schema*, extending to every province of the intellect, seemed to them to prove that no authentic discipline could exist which did not lead, by immediate and irrefutable demonstrations, to the formulation of absolute certainties in the form of sovereign and universal laws. Such was the nearly unanimous opinion at the time, but when applied to historical studies it gave birth, depending upon the temperament of the individual historian, to two opposing schools.

The first believed it really possible and tried their best to establish a science of human evolution which would conform to a sort of pan-scientific ideal. They were willing to abandon, as outside a true science of man, a great many eminently human realities which appeared to them stubbornly insusceptible to rational comprehension. This residue they scornfully called mere events or happenstance. It was also a good part of the most intimate and individual side of life. Such was, in sum, the position of the sociological school founded by Durkheim. (Of course the early rigidity of principle was gradually softened in practice, though reluctantly, by men too intelligent not to yield before the force of things as they are.) To this great scientific effort our studies are vastly indebted. It has taught us to analyze more profoundly, to grasp our problems more firmly, and even, I dare say, to think less shoddily. It will be spoken of here only with infinite gratitude and respect. If it seems sterile now, that is only the price that all intellectual movements must pay, sooner or later, for their moment of fertility.

The other school of inquirers took a quite different point of view. Unsuccessful in cramming the stuff of history into the legalistic framework of physical science, and particularly disturbed, because of their early training, by the difficulties, doubts, and many fresh beginnings required by documentary criticism, they drew from their inquiries the moral lesson of a disillusioned humility. In the final reckoning, they felt that they were devoting their talents to a discipline which promised neither very positive conclusions in the present, nor the hope of progress in the future. They tended to view history less as truly scientific knowledge than as a sort of æsthetic play, a hygienic exercise favorable to health of mind. They have sometimes been called *historiens historisants*, possessing the truly "historical" point of view; but such a judgment does injury to our profession, for it seems to find the essence of history in the very denial of its possibilities. For my part, I should prefer to find a more expressive symbol for them in the moment of French thought with which they are associated.

[. . .]

Our mental climate has changed. The kinetic theory of gases, Einstein's mechanics, and the quantum theory have profoundly altered that concept of science which, only yesterday, was unanimously accepted. They have not weakened it; they have only made it more flexible. For certainty, they have often substituted the infinitely probable; for the strictly measurable, the notion of the eternal relativity of measurement. Their influence has even affected the countless minds (and, alas, I must number mine among them) which, thanks to defects in intelligence or early training, have been able to follow the great metamorphosis only at a distance and as if by a reflected light. Hence, we are much better prepared to admit that a scholarly discipline may pretend to the dignity of a science without insisting upon Euclidian demonstrations or immutable laws of repetition. We find it far easier to regard certainty and universality as questions of degree. We no longer feel obliged to impose upon every subject of knowledge a uniform intellectual pattern, borrowed from natural science, since, even there, that pattern has ceased to be entirely applicable. We do not yet know what the sciences of man will some day be. We do know that in order to exist—and, it goes without saying, to exist in accordance with the fundamental laws of reason—they need neither disclaim nor feel ashamed of their own distinctive character.

I should like professional historians and, above all, the younger ones to reflect upon these hesitancies, these incessant soul-searchings, of our craft. It will be the surest way they can prepare themselves, by a deliberate choice, to direct their efforts reasonably. I should desire above all to see ever-increasing numbers of them arrive at that broadened and deepened history which some of us—more every day—have begun to conceive. If my book can help them, I shall feel that it was not in vain. I confess that that is, in part, its aim.

But I do not write exclusively, or even chiefly, for the private use of the guild. The uncertainties of our science must not, I think, be hidden from the curiosity of the world. They are our excuse for being. They bring freshness to our studies. Surely we have the right to claim for history the indulgence due to all new ventures. The incomplete, if it is perpetually straining to realize itself, is quite as enticing as the most perfect success. To paraphrase Péguy, the good husbandman takes as much pleasure in plowing and sowing as in the harvest.

It is fitting that these few words of introduction be concluded with a confession. Each science, taken by itself, represents but a fragment of the universal march toward knowledge. I have given an example above; in order to understand and appreciate one's own methods of investigation, however specialized, it is indispensable to see their connection with all simultaneous tendencies in other fields. Now this study of methods for their own sake is, in its turn, a specialized trade, whose technicians are called philosophers. That is a title to which I cannot pretend. Through this gap in my education this essay will doubtless lose much in both precision of language and breadth of horizon. I submit it for what it is and no more: the memorandum of a craftsman who has always liked to reflect over his daily task, the notebook of a journeyman who has long handled the ruler and the level, without imagining himself to be a mathematician.

Note

1   The antihistorical Frenchman: Cournot, *Souvenirs*, p. 43, on the subject of the absence of any royalist sentiment at the end of the Empire, remarks: ". . . for the explanation of the singular fact before us, I believe we must also take into account the scant popularity of our history and the underdeveloped consciousness of historical tradition among our lower classes, for reasons too lengthy for analysis."

Chapter 4

Bonnie G. Smith

WHAT IS A HISTORIAN?

Bonnie G. Smith, "What is a Historian?", *The Gender of History: Men, Women and Historical Practice* (Cambridge, MA: Harvard University Press, 1998), 70–79, 81–7, 89–91.

"**WHAT IS AN AUTHOR?**" the philosopher Michel Foucault asked some two decades ago, and although this question has fascinated literary theorists, it has barely interested historians, who are more absorbed by wrestling with issues of "truth" and "objectivity."[1] The accomplishments of scientific history are unquestioningly attributed to great historians, technically expert and visionary practitioners who soar beyond the passions and interests of ordinary people in ways that allow them to produce compelling if not always perfect history. Studies of one or two great historians per generation often serve to make up historiography, but while we examine the fortunes of modern history we rarely consider the shape of historiography itself and what it has meant to the profession to have its achievements contained in the biographies of a handful of great authors. What is the use to which these biographies are put, and how have these lives of great historians fortified the founding claims of objectivity? Why has the story of the scholar who wrestles to free his talent from the bias and banality of the quotidian been so central an ingredient of professionalization, yet so little explored? In this connection, "What is an author?" would indeed be a useful question for historians to ask, especially regarding their various nineteenth-century heroes.

The question of the "historian" becomes more pressing when considered in light of the way in which certain figures and the topic of the nation-state are seen as central to all accounts of nineteenth-century historical work. Female amateurs, with their ardent readership, disappear from historiography; far from informing history, they seem to clot it. Social and cultural history, especially when addressing women's concerns and issues of everyday life, come to have little value. No matter how much cachet social history may have from time to time, politics and the men who write about it are the "meat and potatoes" of great history. However, when seen as produced by intellectual and cultural forces that laced historiography with gender, the biographies of the great male historians—those who wrote about politics—help explain how we have come to exalt the male historian and devalue or even erase women's historical work.

The towering figures of modern historiography, by many accounts, have childhood experiences only incidentally, attend schools where they may study alongside other fledgling practitioners, often take a wife and have children (known but dimly to future generations), and then proceed to write important histories, usually from university positions or while holding important posts as public figures. Each of these institutions, however—including family, school, friendship, and marriage—was a locus of historical writing, a place where the historian was in fact "produced" as an exemplar for historiography and where politics acquired its gloss. Seen as separate from history—a separate sphere, in fact—the household was often a place where historians wrote their first serious works, using tools and gazing at artifacts that are more frequently associated with leisure rather than toil. Sex (rarely associated with the founding practices of modern historical writing) and children (the result of sex) were also in the orbit of historical work. Yet most historiography sees the narrative of everyday life, the narrative of family, childhood, sex, and marriage, as irrelevant to great historical writing and to the recasting of the discipline in the nineteenth century. To the contrary, this chapter argues that household, sex, and marriage have contributed key crucial material for gendering historiography by providing standards for the important and the unimportant, the brilliant and the derivative.

The adolescent road to historical science

Historical narrative and its values took shape in the conditions of nineteenth-century boyhood. John Lothrop Motley, age ten in 1824, wrote to his parents from boarding school outside Boston: "I want to see you very much. I suppose you remember that it is my turn to come home on Saturday next? This is Thursday, the day on which we speak. I was third best . . . My nose has bled very often lately, but I believe it will not bleed much more. I have had a pain in my side once or twice."[2] Motley's schooltime preparation for becoming a historian involved intensive training in languages, accompanied by his own growing thirst for reading, a thirst unwittingly fostered by a school where linguistic drill, math, and some science filled the curriculum. "In the morning, from half-past five to seven, I study French," he wrote his mother a year later. "After breakfast I study Spanish, from nine to half past ten, when we go out and stay about ten or fifteen minutes; and when we come in, I study Greek until twelve, when we are dismissed; and in the afternoon I study Cicero and recite to Dr. Beck, a German."[3] Motley asked his father for books, complaining about the lack of reading material; when a reading room finally did materialize at the school, it still failed to satisfy his cravings. No one contributed books, and the few newspapers were "a hundred years old" and all mutilated within an hour of being deposited. "Reading is not to be thought of, as there are no books in school."[4]

Motley went on to become a major U.S. historian of Europe, as well as an ambassador, but his education, one that was common for most important male historians of the nineteenth century, raises questions about its pertinence to the momentous changes occurring in historical writing and training. The first experience for many boys was despair at being wrenched from home, and their letters expressed a pathetic longing for family members and family rituals. "My dear Mamma," thirteen-year-old Thomas Macaulay wrote from school in 1813, "I do not remember being ever more gloomy in my life than when I first left Clapham."[5] In his letters, Macaulay counted the days till vacation, begged his parents to let him return for his birthday, and bombarded his mother with his memories of their happy walks and talks together. Sharing accommodations with forty other boys, the shy and quiet William Lecky, at school in the 1850s, disliked the size of his school—its very unhomelike atmosphere.[6] Young students not only wrote to their parents but sent off touching notes to brothers, sisters, aunts, uncles, and grandparents. Leopold von Ranke, Frederic Maitland, Henry Adams—innumerable historical authors sent heartfelt letters back to the domestic sphere, recounting their deprivation and loneliness. "Each evening, in the notebook where I entered my expenditures," remembered Ernest Lavisse, minister of public instruction and editor of a twelve-volume history of the world, "I counted, 'Only so many days left 'til vacation'—and the last days seemed very long."[7]

School stood in marked contrast to the domestic sphere. "When the door of the *collège* shut, I was stupefied, and time did nothing but augment my sense of being a prisoner," Edgar Quinet wrote about entering boarding school at the age of twelve.[8] For him, the sense of imprisonment stemmed from the difference between the school's rhythms and values and those of the home. He loved keeping a little garden, harvesting wheat and baking the flour into pastries, and roaming wild. But the most striking aspect of his confinement in boarding school was "the coldness toward one's own family that one was supposed to show in front of other students. One would incur merciless ridicule by embracing one's relatives effusively before witnesses."[9] There were respites from school's antidomestic values. Macaulay's greatest vacation delight was making plum and apple pies; his father, however, feared the boy's irrepressible "love of domesticity."[10] Carsten Niebuhr, whose son Barthold spent less of his youth learning at school than most historians, also worried that his son's "attachment to home was excessive."[11]

School rituals for the most part emphasized differences between the boy's world of study and the domestic world of family. Quinet, who made his first Communion later than usual, after he had entered boarding school, was keenly aware that the Catholic religion he was adopting diverged profoundly from the tolerant spirituality of his mother. Although raised a Lutheran, she had taken him to Mass regularly and exposed him to a wide variety of religious practices, but Quinet's religious instruction in boarding school made him fear that the priest would force a choice between the Holy Mother Church and his biological mother, and he knew that the Church considered her damned. Happy at being confirmed, "my only anguish was the absence of my mother."[12] Impersonal religious practices replaced domestic and village ones, and the "mother tongue" was swallowed up in the classical curriculum based mostly on Latin and Greek.

[. . .]

Thus, the training of these soon-to-be historians was not in history but in languages—so much so, that drills in language and in a different kind of formal system (math) absorbed almost all his school program. Lavisse's six years preparing for university were spent "writing Greek and Latin prose, Greek and Latin translations, Latin and French speeches, Latin and French essays, [and] Latin poetry."[13] Leopold von Ranke attended Schulpforta in Saxony, a school known for perpetuating the kind of classical and other linguistic training first made important during the Renaissance. "I believe," he later remembered of his five years there (1809–1814), "that I read both the *Iliad* and the *Odyssey* through three times."[14] He even sent letters home to his parents in Latin.[15] Ranke, like other young German scholars, was required to do extensive language drill, but he also came to profit from philological studies as they were then revolutionizing the study of the classics. Inspired by Johann Winckelmann, Friedrich August Wolf, and scholars of antiquity in general, these drills aimed for textual translations that—through relentless pursuit of philological details —would be precise, accurate, and free of anachronisms.[16] In most cases, however, both newer and older methods of teaching languages gave low priority to the study of history, if it was considered at all. "History came into the school work only so far as necessary for understanding the classical texts, and then for the most part in a bare and dry fashion," reported Frederick Pollock.[17] In fact, students had no idea whether Julius Caesar preceded Virgil; or Homer, Plato; they only knew which was taught first in the curriculum. Lavisse wrote Latin speeches "for the most diverse characters. I gave Marsilio Ficino's funeral oration for Cosimo de' Medici, . . . and I let one of Seneca's slaves profit from the Saturnalia season to tell his master (a minister and courtier under Nero) some naked truths . . . [But] these were people I hardly knew, speaking on subjects about which I knew even less, for our teachers said little about these people or about Rome at the time of Scipio, or imperial Rome, or . . ."[18]

For the moment, then, history was an aside, a by-product or diversion in the study of the languages, It might enter the curriculum or the life of a boy because of the succession of wars and revolutions. The French Revolution, for example, moved the seventeen-year-old Barthold Niebuhr to start listing its major events. At Paulsen's school, one teacher of Greek and theology had a "great predilection for political harangues,"[19] and in the days of Bismarck's rising star students could easily induce him to speak more about current events. In the course of the school year, students everywhere debated pertinent topics and noted forth-coming debates on extracurricular political issues. "To day is a whole holiday," the thirteen-year-old Macaulay wrote home, "and I have employed it principally in taking notes for a speech [on] 'whether the Crusades were or were not beneficial to Europe.' "[20] When the debates were over, he commented: "I do not much like political subjects, for they make the boys rather too warm in defence of this or that Party." For Macaulay, such debates gave priority back to the home: "When some of the boys have their fathers in the house of commons, they fight for their father's party, right or wrong."[21] Other topics that the boys debated were the fall of Rome, the Peloponnesian Wars, and other major incidents found in Greek and Latin texts. In this case Macaulay was already constructing a hierarchy of right and wrong (objectivity and bias), with the family falling on the side of inferiority and error. Extraphilological debates evoked heated passions in the boys: "In the evening study hall, those who were 'strong in disputation' would go over their material, getting emotional, enfevered, the blood rushing to their cheeks, gesticulating, . . . their arms outstretched or raised."[22] But there was little historical knowledge informing this drive; most were animated by the competition for class ranking, or by the boyish experience of what their own disputes were like.

The main focus remained the "word"—the fervor with which it was pronounced, its intricate usages, and its grammatical constructions. Students wrote compositions of their own with the aim of duplicating the most sought-after *color latinus*. Paulsen remembered that the greatest excitement occurred when the teacher returned the corrected compositions. "To each of us he read out a list of mistakes, pointing out the worst blunders and also any mistakes of special interest, which gave him the opportunity to make instructive comments or witty remarks. If we had committed any grammatical blunders, we felt genuinely and deeply ashamed . . . [for having] offended against the logic and spirit of the language of the Romans."[23]

Accomplishments in classical languages were crucial because education involved being distinguished from other students through recitation and disputation, which were constantly ranked. Familial identity having been lost or discredited, a new persona took shape around what now mattered: "the grades in the record books, the weekly ranking of our composi-tions, our appearance on the honors list on prize day, when the general, the prefect, and the attorney-general sat on the platform in formal dress."[24] Ranking was often done on a daily basis: Motley, as we see in one of the letters he wrote as a ten-year-old, ranked third for that day's recitation. The English historian William Lecky, who hated the Cheltenham School he attended early in the 1850s, generally resisted the intense competition for prizes but none-theless ranked tenth out of forty students tested to enter the University of Dublin; he also went on to become a magnificent orator. Despite Lecky's continual protests that he was "indifferent to college ambitions and competitions," he wrote to a friend after a debate in

1858: "This evening the Committee have made up the Oratory marks and I have got the Gold Medal, which is, I confess, very gratifying to me . . . My marking, they seem to think, is the highest which has been in the Society for some years. It is a fraction above what Plunket got last year."[25] Macaulay, like most other boys, wrote home at the onset of each examination period, informing his parents of his anxieties about competition from a particular student in the rankings, and then reporting on everyone's standing in every subject after the new class rankings had appeared. As Lavisse wrote, schoolmasters incited this psychically demanding competition: "I entered in my notebook my victories over Genaudet, Paul Grizot, and Sage; or, by the same token, my defeats."[26]

Many had initial difficulties not only with the constant quest for prizes and place, but also with the physical discipline and the mandated rough-housing. The latter constituted another side to the struggle for self-redefinition once the family had been left behind. Teachers struck or beat students as part of making them learn: "The discipline consisted in, first, a strong hand on the boys' heads, and a sharp cane on their hands," Stubbs recalled of primary school.[27] Paulsen, as a schoolboy, was struck sharply on the head with a pencil when his answers in Latin were slow in coming. Initially John Richard Green concentrated all his effort on avoiding beatings, but then one day he gave a wrong answer in class and received a thrashing. "I was simply stupefied,—for my father had never struck me." The ice once broken, he went to his regular punishments willingly, like all the rest.[28]

Frequent as pedagogical physicality was, the students' abuse of one other was equally common and usually more brutal. Macaulay silently endured beatings from a young bully, and told his parents only when the student had left the school for good. "I was generally beaten or taunted by him ten times a day. Though I was much too wise and perhaps a little too proud to let him perceive that I felt or heeded what he chose to do, yet I assure you my silence did not give consent. He is gone at last."[29] Lecky, although "horrified at the faces streaming with blood and men half insensible," was fascinated enough by the physical brutality of schools in his youth to produce accounts in his letters of student attacks on the police, one of which he dubbed "the Massacre of College Green."[30] In Germany, exactly at the moment when the conventions of scientific history were being established, this fighting continued on into university years in the form of dueling—a practice that was common and that seemed to absorb much student energy. "I have been here now about three weeks," the eighteen-year-old Motley wrote to his parents from Göttingen in 1832, "and during that time as many as forty [duels] have been fought *to my knowledge*, and I know of as many as one hundred and fifty more that are to take place directly." Motley characterized the duels as serious, though not usually deadly. "But the face is often most barbarously mangled, and indeed it is almost an impossibility to meet a student who has not at least one or two large scars in his visage."[31] A most important ritual of German student life was that of *Brüderschaft*, in which students adopted the familiar form of address *(Du)*, drank a glass of wine together, linked arms, and kissed. This ceremony meant that the two would never fight a duel with each other.

The rituals of school life constituted an important indicator of values that differentiated high from low. Words in texts ranked above matters dealing with home and family. How one dealt with texts provided an important new identity to replace the domestic one. These textual moments were punctuated by physical pain and struggle, which also enacted not only a hierarchy between the word and the body but also between those who gave pain and those who received it. In examining schoolboy violence and its connection with abstract knowledge, Walter Ong has interpreted this phenomenon as unambiguously male, while Elaine Scarry has discussed bodily pain mostly in terms of an unproblematically male body. Yet histories of World War I, in describing the feminization of wounded soldiers, suggest that warfare and inflicting pain have highly gendered effects. Pain in violence and torture, Scarry maintains, makes one all body, nothing but an object of a superior's power. In so marking out the pained body as an inferior body—in coming to an understanding of the "weaker sex," we might say—the entire process of life in elite schools further delineated the masculine study of the word from the inferior feminine body.

A band of "brothers" whose adolescent combat and mastery of the classics united them and organized a worldview, educated young men, by the time they reached eighteen, had received a formation in the gendering of knowledge that distanced them from most young women. Carrying a Latin book in his pocket as a youth, Lavisse noted that foolish young women in church often asked to share his "missal." "One of them, a smiling, lisping girl from Touraine, said to me, 'I have a Lathin name—Hermione Vidi. Vidi meanzth I saw.' "[32] Niebuhr, barely eighteen, had utter contempt for a certain Madame de R.—"a miserable twaddler, shallow and insipid," who dared discuss with him whether the hand of God was more visible in nature or in the course of history. Upholding the latter position, Niebuhr claimed to get the best of her, and this he deduced from her gracious treatment of him over the next weeks. "[But] the honor that is my due can only be conferred on me by men, . . . for they have it in rich abundance to bestow . . . I will receive roses and myrtle from female hands, but no laurels; I only wish to plant them, and then be crowned by three or five men."[33] Twenty-one-year-old J. R. Green wanted a wife "who will never invade my study."[34]

These young men resented women who attempted to engage them on an intellectual terrain that, through their adolescent years, had been limited to a gendered competition and combat which valorized their own sex. By now they associated the keepers and subjects of knowledge with masculinity. Niebuhr had such a strict standard of gender order in intellectual matters that a visit to Westminster Abbey in 1798 both satisfied and appalled him. He "looked with gratitude" at "the busts of so many great men," but their ignoble company—"so many nameless and insignificant persons" whose tombs were graced by such "a quantity of nonsense"—sickened him. "One man writes a Hebrew inscription on the tomb of his daughter; on another, I think also belonging to a woman, there is an Abyssinian inscription."[35] Great men beside insignificant women, foreign languages (that he had mastered) assigned to commoners and the weaker sex, upset the ordering of knowledge constructed during adolescence. Young men's linguistic competition for academic honors had set standards for a common masculinity.

[. . .]

By the time these historians were nearing manhood, their lives had shifted from household matters and family routines to linguistic study in the classics and to the issues of war and politics. They pursued these topics in competition with one another, but also imbibed them as the subject matter of classical texts. Thus, it seems no accident that the premier historical writing of the nineteenth century would come to focus on finding objective truths in the words of state documents sequestered in closely guarded places like archives. Authentication, classification, dating, and other procedures had less to do with the feel of some universal past (as Lavisse complained) than with a kind of linguistic ritual that took place behind closed doors, among like-minded and similarly trained men. The thick walls of the boarding schools, so insistently invoked by Ranke a half-century later, prepared the temperament for cloistered archival study of the word, the sentence, the text—for objectification of political documents and the creation of a modern discipline of history. Though history employed already existing conventions, it performed a simulation of highly problematic, even troubled youthful workings of gender.

Young historians had rescripted the world during their school years, finding the most significant components to be knowledge of words, texts, struggles or wars, and the construction of powerful personalities.[36] Concomitantly they had identified characteristics, emotions, and subject positions associated with the inferiority of women, social life, and the home and that they would denounce as somehow contaminating the field of study. "I constantly become more and more estranged from the world in the ordinary sense of the word," the eighteen-year-old Niebuhr wrote his alarmed parents.[37] At age nineteen Hippolyte Taine claimed that, several years earlier, he had already become "master of myself; I had accustomed my body and soul to do my will. And thus I saved myself from those brutal passions that blind and stupefy man, and prevent his studying human destiny."[38] With personal passions and familial attachments pushed aside at the *lycée*, Taine had prepared himself for "la science," where he could "think a lot, discover many new things, contemplate and produce beautiful works." Besides this dispassionate study, Taine at age twenty had only one other goal: the companionship of like-minded, accomplished men, or what he called "love." In the world of disinterested contemplation, the perfect companion "is not a woman, but a man," he wrote to one of his high school competitors, whom he hoped to include in "the brotherly pursuit of truth."[39] The band of scholars that had become so hardened in the struggle for adolescent truth would remain intact to pursue "la science."

Objective scholarship had also been coded male through study of classical texts that imprinted an image of the hero-scholar on the adolescent mind. Boys who beat and bruised each other while they competed for prizes in their studies followed a junior version of the model found in Caesar or Cicero—a model of men who waged war and politics but who also wrote. Among the ancients, Niebuhr maintained, war, public office, and scholarship were gloriously combined in the life of a single man.[40] "From the particular direction of my mind and talents," he informed his parents, "I believe that nature has intended me for a literary man, an historian of ancient and modern times, a statesman, and perhaps a man of the world."[41] The experience of youth made up the professional credo, allowing Niebuhr to maintain the same comrades, pursue the same struggles, and keep up the scholarly study of texts that had showed him this route in the first place. At the same time men who chose this course or who later studied history could maintain the "objectivity" of such appraisals, for study was the higher, complex mental scrutiny that stood in opposition to the objectification in beatings, boyhood fights, and the brutal repression of a boy's domestic identity. Successfully producing the *color latinus* and the facts ended beatings and stabilized the adolescent's status, permitting him a new subjectivity. Objective study of the "word," repression of everything outside study in classical texts, brought both distinction and personal heroism. In the adolescent *agon* of boy versus master, boy versus boy, and boy versus the text—through the perpetual struggle against inferiority, the body, femininity—the adult historian painfully and passionately emerged. These tales of youth would be successfully reworked into historical science as distinguishing the winners from the beaten, the higher from the lower, and would become its foundational political narrative.[42]

Households and great historians

The twenty-one-year-old J. R. Green, who wanted a wife who would stay out of his study, nonetheless sought one "who can decipher my horrible scrawl and copy my manuscripts for the printer."[43] Green, who married Alice Stopford in 1877, was typical of those historians who needed household help to accomplish their numerous works.[44] Many wives of historians assiduously worked on their husband's projects, or even wrote books themselves. During the course of nineteenth-century professionalization and even into the late twentieth century, much historical writing and research was familial. Family members were researchers, copyists, collaborators, editors, proofreaders, and ghostwriters, and a great deal of writing took place at home.

François Guizot, who would serve as prime minister under the July Monarchy, earned his living in the 1820s and 1830s by teaching university courses and by writing, with full-time help from his first and second wives. At first, because Guizot's courses were irregular and even (in the 1820s) suspended as too liberal, the family survived only because of money brought in from their joint writing. Guizot and his first wife, Pauline Meulun Guizot, envisioned gathering large collections of documents, one on French history and another on England, so that she could do much of the compilation and copying. Although they eventually completed both collections, and published them along with histories of the two topics, Pauline Guizot worried about the initial difficulties in getting a publishing commit-ment. "As you know, I wanted to find something which would give us a settled employment, and prove the foundation of a different sort of life than ours is now . . . It was to get over this difficulty that we thought of undertaking those two great works. They have both fallen through, and we soon shall have lost a year from the time when we had hoped to lay the first stone of the little fortune which we must build in one way or another."[45] Pauline Guizot wrote novels and pedagogical works, read books and took notes for François's articles, conducted the correspondence for his editorship of the *Revue Française*, helped her hus-band prepare his lectures, and finally edited the collection of documents on the English Revolution. The Guizot household was a literary workshop, and this continued after Pauline's death. Second wife Eliza Dillon Guizot also wrote. In the early 1830s, she sent to her husband the following outline of "their" work: "I am rewriting my chapter on the state of Gaul, and I shall have to write it a third time . . . I think that I shall be obliged to retouch the chapter on the Gallic wars." She was also preparing a review essay, which, when done, "we will put in your portfolio to use when the opportunity presents itself."[46]

Sister combinations such as the Stricklands were almost as common as female dynas-ties—for example, Sarah Taylor Austin, her daughter, and her granddaughter (Janet Ross), or Julia Cartwright and Cecilia Ady. François Guizot and his daughters, Pauline Guizot de Witt and Henriette Guizot de Witt, were another authorial team of history. Guizot pre-pared his daughters by writing them long letters not on everyday life but on such topics as their use of the comma. Equally pervasive were husband-wife collaborations, such as those of Alice Stopford Green and J. R. Green, Barbara Hammond and J. H. Hammond, Mary Ritter Beard and Charles Beard.[47] Despite the modern ethos of separate spheres for men and women, historical writing was implicated in domesticity, the family, and sexuality—all of which were rich in possibilities for authorial confusion and unprofessional influences.

As the demands for high-level scholarship and extensive research intensified, historians organized their households into efficient, complex systems. Max Müller noted, on a visit to the home of Eugène Burnouf, that the famed scholar had "four little daughters who were evidently helping him in collecting and alphabetically arranging a number of slips on which he had jotted down whatever had struck him as important in his reading during the day."[48] The historian Thomas Frederick Tout had his wife, sister-in-law, and other female relatives working for him. This joint authorship ensured that female relatives were the ones most familiar with the historian's work; consequently, they were the natural editors of his post-humous publications and his most knowledgeable biographers. Such publications were an essential stage in creating the persona of the autonomous historian: the stage in which the wife dismissed her own contribution.

Thus, in the periods of both nascent and mature professionalization, history had author-teams that worked in household workshops. Around this complexity arose conventions that formulated authorship as singular and male, as a public and extrafamilial undertaking. For instance, when a scholarly reviewer was assessing a work by a husband and wife, custom dictated attributing authorship to the man alone. The reviewer could do this, say, by talking about "Charles Beard's" *Rise of American Civilization* series and by noting "the assistance of his wife," and then proceeding as if Charles Beard were the sole author. The Beards' jointly written book *The American Spirit*, it was said, resembled "an encyclopedia of Charles Beard's reading for the past decade."[49] A compliment to the muse who had inspired the brilliant man indicated to a knowing readership that the wife's contribution had been negligible. These conventions veiled the complex authorship of many works.[50] An equally common convention comprised more explicit sneers at the pretensions of intellectual wives to any kind of accomplishment: Harriet Grote, who wrote several books—including the biography of her husband, George Grote, a historian of Greece—"seldom under-rated her husband, and never herself," quipped Arnaldo Momigliano.[51]

Such work continued the process of distancing a higher, intellectual life from a domestic, affective one. Originating in the assiduous research of well-trained and self-abnegating historians, the best professional accounts contained their own positive truth because each author had put aside politics, class, gender, and other passions and interests, as well as concerns for literary drama, in order to achieve an autonomous, universally valid text. As history became professionalized, however, these claims to scientific impersonality were made into a discipline composed of such diverse ingredients as offices at home and work, research assistants, copyrights and royalties, translations, editions, editors, readers, and an academic hierarchy of flesh-and-blood human beings that reinforced professorial authority. While professional standards invoked impersonality, professionalism developed as an arena charged with human affect and fantasy. The scientifically minded French scholar Gabriel Monod confessed that a review of Ferdinand Gregorovius' biography of Lucrezia Borgia had "made my mouth water" for a "more intimate acquaintance with this 'loose, amiable'" woman[52] and he praised the rapturous Jules Michelet because he could "not escape the contagion of his enthusiasm, his hopes, and his youthful heart."[53] Reformers often had trouble avoiding not just sexual but familial terms, since they saw their new science as based on "principles," in the words of one, "that are transmitted from the fathers to the sons."[54] Initially envisioning their environment as a "workshop," they found the most important quality was "deference toward their masters."[55] Even into the mid-twentieth century, historical science could incite romantic expressions of masculine identity: "I study history," R. G. Collingwood wrote, "to learn what it is to be a man."[56]

Articulations of sexual excitement and emotional enthusiasm were rewritten into a complex historiographic script that depicted the great historian as someone struggling with the pettiness of everyday life and ultimately soaring beyond it to reach the realms of universal truth. Few historians have presented such a challenge to the task of rescripting as the passionate Jules Michelet, a perennial and exciting focus of historiographic attention. Yet Michelet's sexual and intellectual relationships with women, especially his second wife, have, ironically, for the past century facilitated depictions of him as a great author. They have shown the ways in which a driven man overcame a wide array of familial, marital, and other difficulties to pursue his obsession with history. In the process, for almost a century the portrait of Michelet's personal life—theoretically irrelevant to historiography—has served various intellectual schools, partisan politics, personal advancement, and a number of other causes. For all its specificity and intimate detail, the story may have a familiar ring.
[. . .]

Jules's second marriage, to Athénaïs Mialaret, was a complicated, literary experience.
[. . .]

According to both their accounts, Athénaïs Michelet did research and reported on it, wrote sections of Jules's books, discussed projects and recorded details of their daily conversations on topics for books, and offered her judgments on the work that was published under his name. She wrote books of her own, one of them a story of her childhood. He drafted an unpublished manuscript, "Mémoires d'une jeune fille honnête" ("Memoirs of an

Upright Young Woman"), about her young adulthood, After his death, she continued publishing: selections from his journal, a story of his youth, a posthumous edition of their love
letters. During their years together, Jules kept a journal in which he recorded her personal
feelings and many incidents in their work life.

[. . .]

The collaboration of Jules and Athénaïs Michelet on such works of "natural" history as
L'Oiseau (The Bird; 1856), *L'Insecte (The Insect*; 1857), *La Mer (The Sea*; 1861), *and La Montagne*
(The Mountain; 1867) and on other writings was fraught with the ambiguities of domestic
literary production.[57] Although *The Bird* was published under Jules's name, he himself
broached the question of authorship, first by dedicating *The Bird* to Athénaïs as the product
of "home and hearth, of our sweet nightly conversations."[58] That work, Jules explained,
issued from domestic "hours of leisure, afternoon conversations, winter reading, summer-
time chats," and other joint efforts.[59] A reviewer in the *Moniteur*—not the only one to
acknowledge the hint of collaboration—cited the work as having "the style of a superior man
softened by the grace and delicate sensitivity of a woman."[60] Jules himself wrote to journalists suggesting its familial origins and asking them "to take this into account" in their reviews.
The next year, he reported the authorship of *The Insect* somewhat differently to an Italian
journalist; it was, he said, "in reality the work of my wife, but composed and edited by
me."[61] Victor Hugo offered praise after receiving a complimentary copy of *The Insect:* "Your
wife is in it, and I've sensed her passing in these subterranean corridors like a fairy, like
a *luciole* guiding your genius with her ardent light."[62] In the wills he wrote in 1865 and
1872, Jules bequeathed Athénaïs the literary rights to his books and papers, not only
because she had served as secretary, researcher, and proofreader, but because she had
"written considerable sections of these books."[63]

When Jules died in 1874, his widow put aside some of the projects on which she had
been working with special interest. She sorted out the papers that he himself had not
destroyed, and used them as the basis for several books, including a summary of his youth, an
abridged version of his journal, a history, a travel book, and a biography. Jules's son-in-law
(a literary figure of some influence but slight reputation) and grandchildren contested his
legacy in court. Athénaïs won, however, taking as her patron in these publishing endeavors
Gabriel Monod—a friend of the family, a founder of the *Revue Historique*, and a pioneer in
the development of scientific historical writing in France. Monod introduced selections from
Michelet's work, wrote an appreciation of him in his book *Renan, Taine, Michelet* (which also
paid tribute to Athénaïs' devotion to her husband's memory and to her continuation of his
work), wrote a biography, and gave a course at the Collège de France on Jules's historical
writing. Just before her death, Athénaïs gave Monod control over the disposition of many of
her husband's papers. With that, her real troubles began.

From Monod to Lucien Febvre and beyond, attention to Jules Michelet swelled among
prominent French intellectuals, but it was invariably accompanied by extraordinary invective
toward Athénaïs—invective that has become ever more pronounced over the course of the
twentieth century. Monod, who during Athénaïs' lifetime acknowledged her contribution to
Jules's work ("faithful trustee of his ideas"),[64] and credited her with the publication of many
posthumous papers, deftly changed course. Practitioner of a different, more scientific history, Monod attributed his choice of career to Jules, but "the feelings I have for him are not
those of a disciple for a master whose doctrine one adopts."[65] Jules Michelet embodied a
French historical spirit, "a sympathy for the untolled dead who were our ancestors,"[66] and as
such served as the model historian of French nationalism, so deeply important to Monod's
generation of scientific historians.[67]

[. . .]

Monod never definitively separated Jules from his wife. He neither ruptured the bond celebrated in Michelet's journal nor completely discredited the sense of fusion Athénaïs had promoted in handling posthumous publications. Other authors were bolder. In 1902 Daniel Halévy published a widely read article in the *Revue de Paris* on Michelet's second marriage—an article that asserted the utter worthlessness of Michelet's work after his dismissal from all his positions by Napoleon III (and by implication after his marriage).[68] But Halévy also explicitly attributed this failure to Athénaïs, who, he maintained, "suffered from spiritual frigidity" that contrasted sharply with Jules's "feverish mysticism and enthusiasm."[69] Distinct but also disturbed, she aimed for total and unnatural domination of her husband—"from the bedroom, because that was an essential step, to the worktable. It was the worktable she aspired to, and Michelet at first defended it, while she controlled the bed. For several months, the marriage was chaste. Finally Michelet gained control in bed, and, soon after, Athénaïs gained access to the worktable."[70]

[. . .]

The trope has remained powerful. For example, Roland Barthes's *Michelet lui-même* (published in English simply as *Michelet*) maintains that the widow "falsified Michelet's manuscripts, stupidly falsifying the themes—i.e., Michelet himself."[71] An exception to the prevailing view is Arthur Mitzman's recent study of Michelet, which has generously tried to absolve Athénaïs from many of these charges by explaining that she had no training as a scholar.[72] Moreover, as Mitzman points out and as his own work shows, this "abusive widow," even though she may have suppressed some sexually explicit material, still allowed so much to be published that Michelet's obsessions are more than amply documented. Mitzman also notes that the modern editors' version of Jules's love letters (a "sacred relic," the editors claim, canonizing Jules) omits Athénaïs', which she had included in the original edition. The omission often makes Jules's letters unintelligible. Mitzman continues to refer to the "false Michelet" created by his widow, but he acknowledges the interactive nature of the writings, at least the posthumous ones.

One might assume that feminist scholarship would support Mitzman's sympathetic treatment of a woman author, endorse appreciation of her work, and strive to establish at least a historically accurate contextualization of her accomplishments. However, this scholarship also runs the risk of replicating the historiographic problem of authorship—as would happen if, for instance, one argued that Athénaïs was a genius equal to her husband, or if one tried to carve her out as a distinct author. Devising some way of treating Athénaïs as a historian or author is not my intent. I broach the subject of her authorship only to suggest (along with Mitzman) its dialogic and collaborative qualities, to indicate the way in which she edited passages in the travel journals to describe women instead of men, and to note that a major part of the much-condemned editing of Jules's love letters involved omitting those letters in which he discussed her sexual and physiological state and the doctors' opinions of it.

The attacks on Athénaïs' authorship are interesting in themselves because, by using gender to create a historical author, they help define the historical field. To take another example: Michelet's editors wondered whether Athénaïs "reconciled her literary pretensions and her wifely love without asking herself if literary genius wasn't profoundly individual, if the most faithful writer doesn't find himself alone with his conscience and his talent when he writes, and if the first duty of fidelity toward his memory isn't to respect to the letter the work he has left behind."[73] Such statements remind us that the language of scholarship combines passages listing archival citations and professions of "respect to the letter" with emotionally or sexually loaded phrases. Hayden White has described the rhetorical style of scientific history as "genial" and "middle-brow," yet this history has simultaneously been highly charged, contentious, and loaded with gendered fantasy, passion, and outrage. The case of Michelet's widow shows all of these being deployed to establish the scientific confines of history, whose boundaries she so clearly challenged.[74]

The great author, created in so gendered a way, has served the authorial dilemmas of other historians. For example, Lucien Febvre's editorship of the new edition of Jules's work and his postwar devotion to and creation of the cult of Michelet covered ambiguities in his own authorship of the *Annales* and other works during the 1930s and World War II. Febvre cofounded the *Annales* with Marc Bloch, and their collaboration was never easy, as many historians point out. From the mid-1930s, funding for the *Encyclopédie française* enabled Febvre to employ an assistant, Lucie Varga, a young Austrian historian and regular contributor to the *Annales* with whom he became romantically involved. Febvre—whose wife, Suzanne Dognon Febvre, was also a scholar—relied on Varga for research, and her detailed commentaries on newly published works allowed him to produce book reviews quickly. By the late 1930s, his romantic relationship posed a threat to his marriage and career; Varga lost her job, and never found another in the field of history.[75] Another dilemma emerged under the Occupation, when, as Natalie Davis has pointed out, Febvre and Bloch were at odds over whether the cover of the journal should carry Bloch's name (which was Jewish). To Bloch's insistence that they resist the Nazis' anti-Semitic policies, Febvre responded, "So what if there's only one name on the cover? It's the enterprise that counts."[76] Davis illuminates the difficulties of authorship during the Occupation, citing the many alternatives, compromises, and resistances that were possible. Febvre chose neither to collaborate openly nor to resist openly, but rather took a middle way that would allow him to continue to appear an important historical author. Michelet's authorship having been firmly established in the gendered historiographic discourse of the preceding decades, Febvre consolidated his own by incanting the ritualized attacks on the abusive widow and by overseeing a project that, among other things, would strive to destroy her claims to authorship.

[. . .]

If, as Hayden White suggests, factual storytelling or narrativity "moralizes reality," then Michelet scholarship (and this account has merely touched on a few highlights) had a direct relationship to the political reality of French history. Michelet's biography as a historian recapitulated the story of postrevolutionary France, using gender as its trope. Before 1848, Michelet engaged in heroic struggles for greatness as a historian, muting other attachments; but that revolutionary year was a watershed for him, just as it was for France—entrancing him, even enslaving him to an "illegitimate" ruler. Michelet continued to be productive, even opening new avenues of research, but his "enslavement" was continually wearing. Michelet died in 1874, and with the advent of a republicanism born of military defeat came French decline, as well as the abuse of his writings, an erosion of his genius. But the interwar period launched his rebirth, as well as that of history and of France, culminating in the triumph of scientism, planning, technocracy, and the professions that would rehabilitate France as they rehabilitated Michelet's reputation. Narrating Michelet—an enormous project of the postwar French Academy—moralized the story of France, using gender to mark out where science ended and error began. Though France was destitute economically and defeated militarily, its tradition of individual genius would help it survive.

These conclusions about Michelet and the history of modern France are speculative, and secondary to my real concern: the relationship between gender and historiography, between authorship and objectivity, between the state and the household as important historical topics. Recently, Lionel Gossman has proposed a "middle ground" between claims that history corresponds to reality (or objectivity) and claims that history may be relative or arbitrary ("decisionism").[77] Instead of saying that history is commensurable with reality, Gossman suggests that good historical accounts have some degree of commensurability among themselves, while in place of arbitrariness, decisionism, or relativity, he invokes "the ability to change one's mind for good reason."[78] In trying to apply these hypotheses to the case of Michelet's widow, I find myself in agreement with the objective conclusions about her scholarly inadequacy; that is, in all good faith I could also write a commensurable account about her inadequacy as a historical writer. In addition, the changing evaluations of Michelet as author make perfectly good sense, allowing both commensurability and relativity their day. But Gossman's criteria still fail to account for the repetitious attention to someone so insignificant as Athénaïs Michelet. Only exploring the ways in which gender is constitutive of history can do that.

Michelet, like most central figures in historiography, has been useful to individual careers not so much for the way he provides a nationalist refuge to those, like Febvre, who may have unconsciously worried about their own decisions during the tortured time of war and holocaust, but for the way he has helped construct the individual fantasy life of the scientific historian entranced by achievements of great historians. Wrapped in the mantle of science and impartiality, the saga in which Michelet was mutilated by his widow and rescued by heroic researchers is a melodrama whose psychological dimensions we should begin attending to, if only to achieve a better understanding of the world of history. Like most professionals, Febvre, the surviving cofounder of the *Annales*—so deeply indebted to Michelet's work on mountains and seas, to the sense of the local in Michelet's travel journals, and to the complicated relationship between historical actors and their environments on which Michelet pondered—fantasized unique and singular authors as the forefathers of and contributors to his new school of history, and he worked to script it that way, as had many before him. The category "author," as Foucault proposed, has helped organize the discipline around the classification of historical writing and the development of other critical procedures that the invocation of a single author facilitates, allowing for such genealogies of influence and parentage to arise.

"What is a historian?" we ask, altering Foucault's query. Until now, a historian has been the embodiment of universal truth, who, constructed from bits of psychological detail and out of the purifying trials dealt by the contingencies of daily life, human passion, and devouring women, emerges as a genderless genius with a name that radiates extraordinary power. It is time to begin thinking about the ways in which this authorial presence has in fact been gendered as masculine, and how it comes into being through repetitious pairings of a male "original" with a female "copy(ist)" or "falsifier" or "fake." In the nineteenth century, the process of creating the high and the low was part of educational practice, as well as of adult work. Although beatings have stopped in school, the agon of the winner and loser figures in our visual and historical culture. In historiography itself the great historian, coupled with his absent, inferior, unoriginal partner, remains the ever-present touchstone for misogynistic, scientific standards.[79]

Notes

1   Michel Foucault, "Qu'est-ce que c'est l'auteur?" *Bulletin de la Société Française de Philosophie*, 64 (1969), 73–104. Among the recent works on truth in history, see Joyce Appleby, Lynn Hunt, and Margaret Jacob, *Telling the Truth about History* (New York: Norton, 1994); Robert F. Berkhofer, *Beyond the Great Story: History as Text and Discourse* (Cambridge, Mass.: Harvard University Press, 1995); F. A. Ankersmith and Hans Kellner, eds., *A New Philosophy of History* (Chicago: University of Chicago Press, 1995).

2   John Motley to his father, May 13, 1824, in *The Correspondence of John Lothrop Motley*, ed. George William Curtis, 2 vols. (New York: Harper and Brothers, 1889), I, 1.

3   John Motley to his mother, May 31, 1825, ibid., I, 5.

4   John Motley to his brother, July 26, 1829, ibid., I, 8.

5   Thomas Macaulay to Selina Mills Macaulay, February 3, 1813, in *The Letters of Thomas Babington Macaulay*, ed. Thomas Pinney (Cambridge: Cambridge University Press, 1974), I, 14.

6   *A Memoir of the Right Hon. William Edward Hartpole Lecky* (London: Longmans, Green, 1909), 8–9.

7   Ernest Lavisse, *Souvenirs* (Paris: Calmann-Lévy, 1988; orig. pub. 1912), 130.

8   Edgar Quinet, *Historie de mes idées: Autobiographie*, ed. Simone Bernard-Griffiths (Paris: Flammarion, 1972; orig. pub. 1858), 121.

9   Ibid., 125.

10   John Clive, *Macaulay: The Shaping of the Historian* (New York: Knopf, 1973), 23–39.

11   *Life and Letters of Barthold George Niebuhr*, ed. Dora Hensler, 3 vols. (New York: Harper's, 1854), I, 24.

12   Quinet, *Histoire de mes idées*, 130.

13   Lavisse, *Souvenirs*, 212.

14   Leopold von Ranke, *Sur einigen Lebensgeschichte*, in Ranke, *Sämmtliche Werke*, ed. Alfred Dove (Leipzig: Duncker & Humblot, 1890), LIII–LIV, 21.

15   Eugen Guglia, *Lepold von Rankes Leben und Werke* (Leipzig: Grunow, 1893), 18.

16   Important studies of the changes in philology are Suzanne Marchand, *Down from Olympus: Archeology and Philhellenism in Germany, 1750–1970* (Princeton: Princeton University Press, 1996); Anthony Grafton, "Prolegomena to Friedrich August Wolf," in Grafton, *Defenders of the Text: The Traditions of Scholarship in an Age of Science, 1450–1800* (Cambridge, Mass.: Harvard University Press, 1991), 214–243.

17   Frederick Pollock, *For My Grandson* (London: John Murray, 1933), 20–25, quoted in C. H. S. Fifoot, *Frederic William Maitland: A Life* (Cambridge, Mass.: Harvard University Press, 1971), 21.

18   Lavisse, *Souvenirs*, 216.

19   Paulsen, *Autobiography*, 148.

20   Thomas Macaulay to Selina Mills Macaulay, March 17, 1813, in Macaulay, *Letters*, I, 22.

21   Thomas Macaulay to Zachary Macaulay, March 23, 1813, in Macaulay, *Letters*, I, 23.

22   Lavisse, *Souvenirs*, 216.

23   Paulsen, *Autobiography*, 152–153.

24   Lavisse, *Souvenirs*, 166.

25   William Lecky to Knightley Chetwode, June 16, 1859, in Lecky, *A Memoir*, 17.

26   Lavisse, *Souvenirs*, 166.

27   Stubbs, *Letters*, 10.

28   *Letters of John Richard Green*, ed. Leslie Stephen (London: Macmillan, 1901), 7.

29   Thomas Macaulay to Selina Mills Macaulay, January 31, 1815, in Macaulay, *Letters*, I, 57.

30   William Lecky to Knightley Chetwode, March 1858, in Lecky, *A Memoir*, 13.

31   John Motley to his mother, July 1, 1832, in Motley, *Letters*, I, 20–21.

32   Lavisse, *Souvenirs*, 213.

33   Barthold Niebuhr to his parents, September 7, 1794, in Niebuhr, *Life and Letters*, I, 44.

34   John Green to W. B. Dawkins, July 25, 1859, in *Letters of John Richard Green*, 31.

35   Barthold Niebuhr to Amelia Behrens (his fiancée), August 10, 1798, in Niebuhr, *Life and Letters*, 114–115.

36   Allan Megill has recently outlined the concept of objectivity as having cognitive, procedural, dialectical, and other discrete meanings that may even operate at odds with one another. Here I employ several of those meanings, rather than treating objectivity as a unitary concept. See Megill, *Rethinking Objectivity* (Durham, N.C.: Duke University Press, 1994), 1–20.

37   Barthold Niebuhr to his parents, November 15, 1794, in Niebuhr, *Life and Letters*, I, 47.

38   *Hippolyte Taine: Sa vie et sa correspondance*, 4 vols. (Paris: Hachette, 1902–1907), I, 24. This quotation is in the introduction to an unfinished manuscript entitled "La destinée humaine," which Taine wrote as a youth.

39   Hippolyte Taine to Prévost-Paradol, March 2, 1849, ibid., I, 51.

40   Barthold Niebuhr to Dora Hensler, September 6, 1797, in Niebuhr, *Life and Letters*, I, 84.

41   Barthold Niebuhr to his parents, November 7, 1794, ibid., I, 115.

42   The conclusions of this section are based on Walter Ong, *Fighting for Life: Contest, Sexuality, and Consciousness* (Ithaca: Cornell University Press, 1981); Walter Ong, *Literacy and Orality* (New York: Methuen, 1982); Megill, "Introduction," in Megill, ed., *Rethinking Objectivity*, 1–20; Johannes Fabian, "Language, History, and Anthropology," *Philosophy of the Social Sciences*, 1 (1971), 19–47; Martin Heidegger, *Being and Time*, trans. John Macquarrie and Edward Robinson (New York: Harper and Row, 1962); and such studies in the history of science as Mario Biagioli, "Scientific Revolution, Social Bricolage, and Etiquette," in Roy Porter and Mikulás Teich, eds., *The Scientific Revolution in National Context* (Cambridge: Cambridge University Press, 1992), 11–54.

43   John Green to W. B. Dawkins, July 25, 1859, in *Letters of John Richard Green*, 31.

44   R. B. McDowell, *Alice Stopford Green: A Passionate Historian* (Dublin: Allen Figgis, 1967); *Letters of John Richard Green*, passim.

45   Henriette Guizot de Witt, *Monsieur Guizot in Private Life, 1787–1874*, trans. M. C. M. Simpson (Boston: Estes and Lauriat, 1881), 76.

46   Ibid., 117–118.

47   On the comma, see François Guizot to Henriette Guizot, June 3, 1839, ibid., 187–190. On the Hammonds, see Stewart Weaver, *A Marriage in History: The Lives and Work of Barbara and J. H. Hammond* (Stanford: Stanford University Press, 1997). Primary material on Barbara Hammond is in the archives of Lady Margaret Hall, Oxford University. See also Anne Ridler, *A Victorian Postbag* (Oxford: Perpetua, 1988).

48   F. Max Müller, *My Autobiography: A Fragment* (London: Longmans, Green, 1901), 163.

49   For example, Bernard C. Borning. *The Political and Social Thought of Charles A. Beard* (Seattle: University of Washington Press, 1962); Richard Hofstadter, *The Progressive Historians* (New York: Knopf, 1968); Cushing Strout, *The Pragmatic Revolt in America: Carl Becker and Charles Beard* (New Haven: Yale University Press, 1958); Forrest McDonald, "Charles A. Beard," in Marcus Cunliffe and Robin W. Winks, eds., *Pastmasters* (New York: Harper and Row, 1969), 110–141; Howard K. Beale, ed., *Charles A. Beard* (Louisville: University of Kentucky Press, 1954); Marvin C. Swanson, ed., *Charles A. Beard* (Greencastle, Ind.: DePauw University, 1976).

50   Jack Stillinger, *Multiple Authorship and the Myth of Solitary Genius* (New York: Oxford, 1991), calls for a more complex view of authorship that would acknowledge the work of editors, but his book tends to reinforce the view that men were geniuses whose editors and wives made no "substantive" contributions. For instance, although John Stuart Mill calls the "whole mode of thinking" in *On Liberty* his wife's, Stillinger says that scholars should really focus on Harriet's editorial role (ibid., 66) and stop worrying about whether she had ideas—she didn't, he implies. Ultimately, he describes her roles as "the middle-aged Mill being spruced up by his wife for attractive autobiographical presentation" (ibid., 182).

      Another fascinating recognition of authorial complexity comes in Lionel Gossman, *Towards a Rational Historiography* (Philadelphia: American Philosophical Society, 1989), which sympathetically describes the community of criticism absorbed into scholarly publications. Yet when speaking of a work by Stephen Toulmin and two other authors, Gossman (except for the first mention) cites it exclusively as Toulmin's, even referring to "his" thought, argument, thesis, and so on.

51   Arnaldo Momigliano, *George Grote and the Study of Greek History* (London: H. K. Lewis, 1952), 7.

52   Gabriel Monod to Gaston de Paris, August 6, 1874, in Bibliothèque Nationale, Manuscrit nouvelle acquisition française 24450, Fonds Gaston de Paris, fols. 131–132.

53   Gabriel Monod, *Renan, Taine, Michelet*, 5th ed. (Paris: Calmann-Lévy, n.d.), 178.

54   Victor Duruy, quoted in William R. Keylor, *Academy and Community: The Foundation of the French Historical Profession* (Cambridge, Mass.: Harvard University Press, 1975), 70.

55   Ernest Lavisse, quoted ibid., 70–71.

56   See Bonnie G. Smith, "Gender, Objectivity, and the Rise of Scientific History," in Wolfgang Natter, Theodore Schatzki, and John Paul Jones, eds. *Objectivity and Its Other* (New York: Guilford, 1995).

57   On these works and their very important connection to Michelet's evolving conceptualization of historical issues, see Linda Orr, *Jules Michelet: Nature, History, and Language* (Ithaca: Cornell University Press, 1976).

58   Jules Michelet, *Oeuvres complètes*, ed. Paul Viallaneix (Paris: Flammarion, 1986), XVII, 45.

59   Ibid.

60   Ibid., 41.

61   Ibid., 279.

62   Ibid., 280.

63   Will composed in 1872, quoted ibid., 188.

64   Monod, *Renan, Taine, Michelet*, 289.

65   Ibid., 179.

66   Ibid., 178.

67   Keylor, *Academy and Community*, 43–44 and passim.

68   Daniel Halévy, "Le mariage de Michelet," *Revue de Paris*, 15, no. 9 (August 1902), 557–579.

69   Ibid., 577.

70   Daniel Halévy, *Jules Michelet* (Paris: Hachette, 1928), 133.

71   Roland Barthes, *Michelet*, trans. Richard Howard (New York: Hill and Wang, 1987; orig. pub. 1954), 206.

72   Arthur Mitzman, *Michelet, Historian: Rebirth and Romanticism in Nineteenth-Century France* (New Haven: Yale University Press, 1990). Mitzman's two appendixes excusing Athénaïs provided the inspiration for this chapter.

73   Michelet, *Journal*, I, 25.

74   In this regard, readers can consult the way in which Peter Novick uses such words as "sexy," "hot," and "fashionable" to discredit certain groups of historians. See also Hayden White, *The Content of the Form: Narrative Discourse and Historical Representation* (Baltimore: Johns Hopkins University Press, 1987), 71.

75   See Peter Schöttler, *Lucie Varga: Les autorités invisible* (Paris: Cerf, 1991). Schöttler has done an extraordinary job discovering the details of Varga's obscure life and reprinting her essays and articles. He suggests Bloch's misogynistic attitude toward women intellectuals, but, more important, Bloch's distress at finding his collaboration with Febvre still further complicated by Varga's work. Schöttler was loath to reveal the extent of Varga and Febvre's relationship: "La vie scientifique et l'amour . . . are not considered pertinent in accounts of the life of a scholar." Nonetheless, Schöttler considered it necessary to reveal the romance because "its consequences were sufficiently determining that one could not keep it quiet without falsifying history" (57, n. 142). This ambiguous statement may refer to Varga's subsequent employment selling vacuum cleaners, then working in an advertising agency, after which, under Vichy, her utter destitution kept her from getting the necessary medicine to treat her diabetes. She died in 1942 at the age of thirty-four.

    Natalie Zemon Davis, "Women and the World of the *Annales*," *History Workshop Journal*, 33 (1992), 121–137, describes the contributions of Suzanne Dognon Febvre to Lucien Febvre's work, and considers the important part played by Paule Braudel in Fernand Braudel's work.

76   Lucien Febvre to Marc Bloch, 1941, quoted in Natalie Davis, "Rabelais among the Censors," *Representations*, 32 (Fall 1990), 5.

77   Lionel Gossman, *Towards a Rational Historiography* (Philadelphia: American Philosophical Society, 1989), 61–62.

78   Ibid., 62 and passim.

79   On this point, see R. Howard Bloch, "Medieval Misogyny," *Representations*, 20 (Fall 1987), 1–24.

Further Reading: Chapters 1 to 4

For a list of surveys and introductions to modern historiography, see the Further Reading section that follows the Preface, p. xvi.

JOHN EMERICH EDWARD DALBERG, LORD ACTON (1834–1902)

Altholz, Josef L. *The Liberal Catholic Movement in England: The "Rambler" and its Contributors, 1848–1864* (London: Burns & Oates, 1962).

——, Damian McElrath and J. C. Holland (eds) *The Correspondence of Lord Acton and Richard Simpson.* 3 vols (Cambridge: Cambridge University Press, 1971–5).

Butterfield, Herbert. *Lord Acton* (London: Historical Association, 1948).

——. *Man on His Past. The Study of the History of Historical Scholarship* (Cambridge: Cambridge University Press, 1955).

Chadwick, Owen. *Acton and Gladstone* (London: Athlone Press, 1978).

——. *Acton and History* (Cambridge: Cambridge University Press, 1998).

Fasnacht, George Eugène. *Acton's Political Philosophy: An Analysis* (London: Hollis and Carter, 1952).

Hill, Roland. *Lord Acton* (New Haven: Yale University Press, 2000).

Himmelfarb, Gertrude. *Lord Acton: A Study in Conscience and Politics* (London: Routledge & Kegan Paul, 1952).

Kochan, Lionel. *Acton on History* (London: Andre Deutsch, 1954).

Matthew, David. *Lord Acton and His Times* (London: Eyre & Spottiswoode, 1968).

MacElrath, Damian. *Lord Acton: The Decisive Decade, 1864–1874* (Louvain: Bureaux de la R.H.E., Bibliothèque de l'Université; Publications universitaires de Louvain, 1970).

Paul, H. *Letters of Lord Acton to Mary Gladstone* (London: George Allen, 1904).

Schuettinger, Robert L. "Bibliography of the Works of Lord Acton". *Lord Acton: Historian of Liberty* (La Salle, IL: Open Court, 1976). 191–35.

——. *Lord Acton, Historian of Liberty* (La Salle, IL: Open Court, 1976).

Tulloch, Hugh. *Acton* (New York: St Martin's Press, 1988).

Watson, G. *Lord Acton's History of Liberty: A Study of His Library, with an Edited Text of His History of Liberty Notes* (Aldershot: Scolar Press, 1994).

CARL LOTUS BECKER (1873–1945)

Alpern, Mildred. "Carl Becker's Modern History: New Roads Barely Trodden". *The History Teacher* 19(1) (1985): 111–121.

Appleby, Joyce. "The Power of History". *The American Historical Review* 103(1) (1998): 1–14.

Braeman, John and John C. Rule. "Carl Becker: Twentieth-Century Philosophe". *American Quarterly* 13(4) (1961): 534–539.

Cairns, John C. "Carl Becker: An American Liberal". *The Journal of Politics* 16(4) (1954): 623–44.

Gershoy, Leo. "Introduction". *Progress and Power. Carl Becker* (New York: A. A. Knopf, 1949).

——. "Zagorin's Interpretation of Becker: Some Observations". *The American Historical Review* 62(1) (1956): 12–17.

Gottschalk, Louis. "Carl Becker: Skeptic or Humanist?" *Journal of Modern History* 18(2) (1946): 160–62.

Klein, Milton M. "Everyman His Own Historian: Carl Becker as Historiographer". *The History Teacher* 19(1) (1985): 101–109.

McNeill, William H. "Carl Becker, Historian". *The History Teacher* 19(1) (1985): 89–100.

New York State Association of European Historians. "Carl Becker's Heavenly City Revisited: Studies Resulting from a Symposium held at Colgate University October 13, 1956" (Ithaca, NY: Cornell University Press, 1958).

Novick, Peter. *That Noble Dream: The "Objectivity Question" and the American Historical Profession* (Cambridge: Cambridge University Press, 1988).

Rockwood, Raymond O. (ed.) *Carl Becker's Heavenly City Revisited* (Ithaca, NY: Cornell University Pres, 1958).

Smith, Charlotte Watkins. *Carl Becker* (Ithaca, NY: Cornell University Press, 1956).

Snyder, Phil L. "Carl L. Becker and the Great War: A Crisis for a Humane Intelligence". *Western Political Quarterly* 9(1) (1956): 1–10.

—— . (ed.) *Detachment and the Writing of History: Essays and Letters of Carl L. Becker* (Ithaca, NY: Cornell University Press, 1958).

Strout, Cushing. *The Pragmatic Revolt in American History: Carl Becker and Charles Beard* (New Haven: Yale University Press, 1958).

Wilkins, Burleigh Taylor. *Carl Becker: a Biographical Study in American Intellectual History* (Cambridge MA: MIT Press; Harvard University Press, 1961).

Zagorin, Perez. "Carl Becker on History, Professor Becker's Two Histories: A Skeptical Fallacy". *The American Historical Review* 62(1) (1956): 1–11.

MARC BLOCH (1886–1944)

Brewer, W. M. "Review: The Historian's Craft". *The Journal of Negro History* 39(1) (1954): 69–71.

Brown, Elizabeth A. R. "The Tyranny of a Construct: Feudalism and Historians of Medieval Europe". *The American Historical Review* 79(4) (1974): 1063–88.

Burke, Peter. "Strengths and Weaknesses of the History of Mentalities". *History of European Ideas* 7(5) (1986): 439–51.

—— . *The French Historical Revolution: The Annales School, 1929–89* (Stanford, CA: Stanford University Press, 1990).

Fink, Carole. *Marc Bloch: A Life in History* (Cambridge; New York: Cambridge University Press, 1989).

—— . "Marc Bloch (1886–1944)." *Medieval Scholarship: Biographical Studies on the Formation of a Discipline*, Helen Damico and Joseph B. Zavadil (eds) (New York: Garland, 1995): 205–17.

Friedman, Susan W. *Marc Bloch, Sociology and Geography: Encountering Changing Disciplines* (Cambridge: Cambridge University Press, 1996).

Gildea, Robert. "Historians in Harness". *Times Online* <www.timesonline.co.uk>. 30 July 2004.

Hill, Alette Olin, Boyd H. Hill Jr., William H. Sewell and Sylvia L. Thrupp. "AHR Forum: Marc Bloch and Comparative History". *The American Historical Review* 85(4) (1980): 828–57.

Huppert, George. "Lucien Febvre and Marc Bloch: The Creation of the *Annales*". *The French Review* 55(4) (1982): 510–13.

Keylor, William R. *Academy and Community: The Foundation of the French Historical Profession* (Cambridge, MA: Harvard University Press, 1975).

Kraus, Michael. "Review: The Historian's Craft". *The Mississippi Valley Historical Review* 40(4) (1954): 721–22.

Lyon, Bryce. "Marc Bloch: Did He Repudiate *Annales* History?" *Journal of Medical History* 11 (1987): 181–91.

Lyon, Bryce and Mary Lyon (eds) *The Birth of Annales History: The Letters of Lucien Febvre and Marc to Henri Pirenne, 1921–1935* (Brussels: Académie Royale de Belgique, 1991).

Noiriel, Gérard. "Marc Bloch (1886–1944)". *The Columbia History of Twentieth-Century French Thought*, Lawrence D. Kritzman and Brian Reilly (eds). Trans. Malcolm DeBevoise (New York: Columbia University Press, 2006: 439–41).

Revel, Jacques and Lynn Hunt (eds) *Histories: French Constructions of the Past* (New York: New Press, 1995).

Rhodes, Robert Colbert. "Emile Durkheim and the Historical Thought of Marc Bloch". *Theory and Society* 5(1) (1978): 45–73.

Sewell, William H., Jr. "Marc Bloch and the Logic of Comparative History". *History and Theory* 6(2) (1967): 208–218.

Spang, Rebecca. "Marc Bloch: His Life and Legacy". *History Workshop Journal* 59 (2005): 284–6.

Stirling, Katherine. "Rereading Marc Bloch". *History Compass* 5(2) (2007): 525–38.

PART 2

Vico and the meaning of historical origins

INTRODUCTION

IN THE EARLY EIGHTEENTH CENTURY, the Italian historian and philosopher Giambattista Vico said that his book "has cost me nearly an entire scholarly career spent in tireless researches"—and he was not merely complaining. He was also revealing a central element of his lengthy study, *Scienza Nuova*. Echoing the titles of Bacon's and Galileo's world-changing treatises,[i] Vico's *Principles of the New Science concerning the Common Nature of Nations* was an ambitious attempt to "trace the *ideal eternal history* through which the history of every nation passes". Vico asserted that discovering the origins and development of human history requires that we make a strenuous imaginative and intellectual effort to think like those who lived in the past. Important examples of the expressions of distant human cultures, such as Homer's poems or the statues in medieval churches, contain traces of their creators' ideas about their world. So in Vico's view, we must devote ourselves to studying those relevant even if "dead" languages, laws, religions, myths, and symbols. Underlying this theory is Vico's important and possibly quite original insight, that the study of history requires moving beyond an accumulated knowledge of old facts or the collector's enjoyment of pretty antiques: studying history requires that we enter imaginatively and sympathetically into remote human experiences through an intensive education. This view of a historical sensibility defines a distinctly modern approach to history, which is one reason why this second Part explores the meaning and enduring relevance of Vico's insights.

When Vico applied this theory to the question of whether Homer really was the rational philosopher or "most agreeable historian of the early ages of Greece" that admirers such as Plato and, later, the noted eighteenth-century essayist Hester Chapone claimed him to be, Vico

---

i   Galileo's *Two New Sciences* (originally published as *Discorsi e Dimostrazioni Matematiche, intorno a due nuove scienze*) was published in 1638; Bacon's *Novum Organon* was printed in 1620.

used his erudite reading of *The Illiad* to conclude that Homer was part of the violent pre-philosophical culture that his poem celebrated. And yet, one must be quick to add, by recognizing Homer as culturally primitive, Vico was not demeaning the value of his poetry. On the contrary, a central point for Vico is that appreciation of historical material requires recognition of its own internal perspective, and this means assuming past and not current values. Indeed, in Vico's view, those who lived in Homer's time were in some ways superior to us, since they were "poetic" (that is, not abstract thinkers) by their very nature. If some of these notions are common sense now, none of these ideas were common sense in Vico's time, when Homer had been envisioned as a cultured sage rather than a primitive poet who relished the barbaric behaviour that he depicted. As the great twentieth-century literary historian Erich Auerbach points out, it was Vico's notion of the primitive poet that Johann Gottfried Herder and other German romantic writers of the late eighteenth century called "the folk genius". Like Vico, the romantics prized such "natural" genius as the original sources of human inspiration that would later evolve into current cultural and national sensibilities.

Why is this notion of genius important for exploring the meaning of historical origins? Anyone who reads Vico for the first time might be puzzled or amused by his extravagant characterizations of early humans as instinctive poets or by his seemingly arbitrary view that human civilization should be understood through a three-part structure. So it is important to stress that Vico's originality—and his enormous influence on historiography—lies in his notion of historical understanding: he was the first to argue that history must account for the history of human *ideas* rather than the causes of political *events*. For Vico, all human knowledge (*scientia*) contains traces of the ancient ideas that were held by our distant predecessors, which leads to another of his powerful insights: it is not only possible for us to appreciate the historical meaning of those ancient ideas, but also that we will achieve such understanding only by making the interpretive effort to adopt the perspectives held back then. Reading Vico today itself requires something of that effort, since those elements of his theory of history that are original and essential are those which seem to us most familiar—which student of history today would minimize the importance (and difficulty) of considering historical sources in their own contexts? And who would doubt the need for historical researchers to be attuned to and curious about those elements of the past that seem familiar and yet are truly quite distant from our own experience? While we may disapprove of the practices of previous generations (such as slavery), perhaps we wonder whether our disapproval arises from our recognition that, had we been born into that culture, we too might have been blameworthy. All of these views, which now seem so current, Vico described in his *Scienza Nuova* of 1745. But unlike Bacon and Galileo, Vico was hardly read in his own lifetime—and indeed his innovative theory about Homer was not published until after his death.

Since Vico lived and wrote in Naples, which was not a major centre for sympathetic philosophers of history, he could not participate in the lively social and intellectual networks that came to be known as the Enlightenment.[ii] Since he couldn't speak or read German or

ii   On Vico's disaffection with the intellectual environment in his native city, see his *Autobiography of Giambattista Vico*. Trans. M. H. Fisch and T. G. Bergin (Ithaca: Cornell University Press, 1944), 128–35. In his study of parallels between Naples and Edinburgh in the mid-eighteenth century, John Robertson points to Vico's awareness of local academic discourse without doubting Vico's relative isolation from wider European trends. See *The Case for the Enlightenment: Scotland and Naples, 1680–1760* (Cambridge: Cambridge University Press, 2005), 209–10. See also Elvira Chiosi, "Academicians and academies in eighteenth-century Naples". Trans. Mark Weir, *Journal of the History of Collections* 19 (2007): 177–90.

English, his ability to communicate with fellow European intellectuals in "The Republic of Letters" also was curtailed significantly—as was his knowledge of sources published in those languages.[iii] Moreover, Vico's relative intellectual isolation meant that his thought and his writing did not go through the valuable processes of collective discussion and opportunity for popularization that Scottish Enlightenment authors such as Adam Ferguson and his student Dugald Stewart enjoyed. Perhaps the most famous interpreter of Vico was Isaiah Berlin, who remarked that Vico did not have enough literary talent for his considerable intellect: "he cannot keep a cool head in the storm of inspiration; he is at times carried away by the flood of disorganised ideas."[iv] But as Auerbach puts it, Vico was the first to articulate our modern notion of historical understanding. As we will find in subsequent Parts of this Reader, Vico's innovative two-part argument—that we can enter in the minds of previous ages, and that the ideas which characterize those periods ought to be judged according to their own values— anticipated an enduringly influential notion, later termed historicism (sometimes called "historism"). Unlike Vico's academic treatise, the article on "History" from the *Encyclopaedia Britannica* (possibly written by Ferguson), and Stewart's introductory discussion of conjectural history from his edition of Adam Smith's *Essays*, reflect the polished style of their time and place and to some extent the shared vision of friends and colleagues.[v] Still, the methodology and historiography that they espoused provide a compelling contrast to Vico's historicism, inviting us to consider the nature and importance of historical origins among readers and writers of this intellectually fertile period.

For Ferguson and the other economists, philosophers, and historians who constituted the Scottish Enlightenment, social life is a necessary and essential expression of human nature. Therefore there are "naturally" just two types of historical enquiry: "civil" and "ecclesiastical"—the first charts the rise and decline of nations or countries in order to understand the motivations and circumstances that caused their successes and failures. The second reveals how citizens acted according to their religious beliefs. Together, these two types of history can take the form of biography, particular history, and general history; biography is limited to focusing on the motivations and consequences of "those who act any considerable part in history". Since the only writings that merit the name of history as a genre of scholarship are either on military or civil topics, historians should focus on political figures and political events. So it comes as no surprise that Ferguson's two remaining forms of history focus on the history of nations. Some fifty years earlier, Lord Bolingbroke famously remarked that "History is philosophy [that is, morality] teaching by examples"—so all one needs to do is focus on what has taken place to distinguish right from wrong. Although Ferguson was wide-ranging in

iii   A. Grafton, "Introduction," *New Science* by G. Vico. Trans. D. Marsh (Harmondsworth: Penguin, 2001), xxii–xxiii.
iv   "Vico's Concept of Knowledge", *Against the Current: Essays in the History of Ideas*, H. Hardy (ed.) (Princeton: Princeton University Press, 2001), 114.
v   Since Adam Ferguson signed the "Historical Chart" that appeared with this article in the *Britannica*, and since there are passages in "History" that correspond directly to passages in Ferguson's *Essay on Civil Society* (1767) it is likely that Ferguson was the author or a contributing author to this article. However, Silvia Sebastiani has argued persuasively that there are elements of the article that contradict Ferguson's views on religion, casting doubt on his authorship. See S. Sebastiani, "Conjectural History vs. The Bible: Eighteenth-Century Scottish Historians and the Idea of History in the *Encyclopedia Britannica*", *Cromohs* 6 (2001): 1–6.

his approach to national histories, like Acton one century later, he values those historical writings that will have a moral effect on the reader's conduct as a citizen.[vi]

The final reading in this Part describes **conjectural history**, a method of addressing periods in human history for which no documentation exists, by offering speculations based on what we believe is universal in human nature. By the late eighteenth century, confidence in the ability of moral philosophers to speculate accurately about history was at its height: as an example, the moralist and politician Edmund Burke wrote to the historian William Robertson, assuring him that

> I have always thought with you, that we possess at this time very great advan-
> tages towards the knowledge of human Nature. We need no longer go to History
> to trace it in all its stages and periods.[vii]

Coming from one of the most important and respected political writers of the time, written to the most famous historian of the time, such agreement between Burke and Robertson might seem hugely unscholarly today—but it was philosophically sound and even morally correct back then.[viii] Stewart included this short but influential essay on conjectural history in his edition of the philosophical works of Adam Smith. Smith was only one among many figures associated with the Scottish Enlightenment, whose general project was to articulate a "Science of Man"—a complete rational understanding of human motivation, conduct, and society based on a universal theory of civilization.[ix] This argument for **stadial history**, which organized the past in distinct "ages" or "stages" in order to define the present and to predict the future, anticipates the popularity of historical stage-theories in the nineteenth century (which we will survey in Part 6). As a method of using a psychological stage-theory of human nature as well as a belief in social progress (which was not always optimistic), conjectural history provided an innovative departure from historical models that depended on arbitrarily-chosen elements, such as "a vague reference of laws to the wisdom of particular legislators" or "accidental circumstances, which it is now impossible to ascertain". The result, according to one of Smith's students, was "new and important views . . . much less artificial" than those of conventional histories—for they depended not on the historian's clever artifice but on the natural qualities of history's human subjects. While Stewart allowed that conjectural history will draw more on knowledge of nature than on actual events, this method is still superior, since events can be "particular accidents which are not likely again to occur", whereas the human mind is the dominant force of nature in history. Conjectural history, then, tried to define

vi   For Bolingbroke's quotation, see his *Letters on the Study and Use of History* (London: Millar, 1752), 16, 58.

vii See Burke's letter to Robertson, 9 June 1777, in *The Correspondence of Edmund Burke*, George H. Guttridge (ed.) (Cambridge: Cambridge University Press, 1961), vol. 3, 351.

viii It is important to point out that while there are conjectural elements to Robertson's historical works, he did engage in research to an intense degree by eighteenth-century standards, even though it was limited to examining printed documents and corresponding with scholars in various parts of Europe.

ix   For a valuable discussion of conjectural histories, see Mark Salber Phillips, *Society and Senti-ment: Genres of Historical Writing in Britain, 1740–1820* (Princeton: Princeton University Press, 2000), 171–90. For Smith's four-stage theory of human development, see his *Lectures in Jurisprudence*, R. L. Meek, D. D. Raphael, and P. G. Stein (eds) (Oxford: Oxford University Press, 1978), 201–10, 459–60.

a general history of national development based on a general theory of human nature, rather than by listing the specific facts of a nation's history.

Stewart observed that conjectural history can be also found in moral, political, and literary writing. This is because each of those genres ultimately corresponds to human experience, which always refers to the psychological basis of all knowledge and of all action. For these historians, then, the origin of historical understanding was their theory of the mind. Stewart suggested that only conjectural history can provide insight into obscure periods in our past; it also satisfies our curiosity and corrects false assumptions—both of which, for the philosophical historians of the Scottish Enlightenment, enable us to lead more tranquil and productive lives.

Chapter 5

Giambattista Vico

PRINCIPLES OF THE NEW SCIENCE CONCERNING THE COMMON NATURE OF NATIONS

Giambattista Vico (1668–1744), "Principles of the New Science Concerning the Common Nature of Nations", 1725. *New Science.* Trans. David Marsh (Harmondsworth: Penguin, 1999), 24–5, 128–9, 152–3, 355–7, 367. Paragraph numbers that appear in square brackets refer to a numbering system that scholars have used to identify and compare passages across the various editions and translations of Vico's book. The original text appears in Andrea Battistini (ed.) *Vico: Opere* (Milan: Mondadori, 1990), 2 vols.

[34] In seeking the basic principle of the common origins of languages and letters, we find that the first peoples of pagan antiquity were, by a demonstrable necessity of their nature, *poets* who spoke by means of *poetic symbols*. This discovery provides the master key of my New Science, but making it has cost me nearly an entire scholarly career spent in tireless researches. For to our more civilized natures, the poetic nature of the first people is utterly impossible to imagine, and can be understood only with the greatest effort. Their symbols were certain *imaginative general categories*, or archetypes. These were largely images of animate beings, such as gods and heroes, which they formed in their imagination, and to which they assigned all the specifics and particulars comprised by each generic category. (In precisely this way, the myths of civilized ages, such as the plots of the New Comedy, are rational archetypes derived from moral philosophy; and from these myths, our comic poets create in their characters these imaginative archetypes, which are simply the most complete ideas of human types in each genre.) We find, then, that the divine and heroic symbols were true myths, or true mythical speech. And we discover that, in describing the early age of the Greek peoples, the meaning of their allegories is based on identity rather than analogy, and is thus historical rather than philosophical.

These archetypes – which is what myths are in essence – were created by people endowed with vigorous imaginations but feeble powers of reasoning. So they prove to be true poetic statements, which are feelings clothed in powerful passions, and thus filled with sublimity and arousing wonder. We further find that poetic expression springs from two sources: the poverty of language, and the need to explain and be understood. This engendered the vividness of heroic speech, which was the direct successor of the mute language of the divine age, which had conveyed ideas through gestures and objects naturally related to them. Eventually, following the inevitable natural course of human institutions, the Assyrians, Syrians, Phoenicians, Egyptians, Greeks, and Romans developed languages, which began with heroic verse, then passed to iambics, and finally ended in prose. This progression is confirmed by the history of ancient poetry. And it explains why we find so many natural versifiers are born in German-speaking lands, particularly in the peasant region of Silesia; and why the first authors in Spanish, French, and Italian wrote in verse.

[35] From these three languages, we may derive a conceptual dictionary, which properly defines words in all the different articulate languages. [. . .] I studied the timeless attributes of the fathers who lived in the age when languages were formed, both in the state of families and in the first heroic cities. Then, in fifteen different languages, both living and dead, I derived proper definitions of the words for father, which varied according to their different attributes. (Of the three sections in that edition which satisfy me, this is the third.) This lexicon proves necessary if we are to learn the language of the ideal eternal history through which the histories of all nations in time pass. And it is necessary if we are to be scientific in citing authorities that confirm our observations about the natural law of nations, and about particular kinds of jurisprudence.

[36] There were, then, *three* languages, proper to *three* ages in which *three* kinds of government ruled, conforming to *three* kinds of civil natures, which change as nations follow their course. And we find that these languages were accompanied by an appropriate kind of jurisprudence, which in each age followed the same order.
[. . .]

[346] We shall find that these sublime proofs of natural theology are confirmed by the three kinds of logical proofs. First, by reasoning about the origins of divine and human institutions in the pagan world, we arrive at their first beginnings, beyond which only foolish curiosity would attempt to go – which is the hallmark of first principles. Second, we shall explain the particular manner in which they arose, or what I call their nascence or nature – which is the hallmark of a science. Finally, we shall find confirmation of these proofs in the eternal properties which are preserved by human institutions and determined by their 'nature', meaning the time, place, and manner of their origins [. . .]

[347] In exploring the origins of human institutions, my Science rigorously analyses our human notions about what is necessary or useful, which are the two perennial sources of the natural law of nations, as Axiom 11 states. Hence, in another principal aspect, my New Science is a *history of human ideas*, which forms the basis for constructing a metaphysics of the human mind. Axiom 106 states that sciences must begin at the point when their subject matter begins. Hence, the queen of the sciences, metaphysics, began when the first men began to think in human fashion, and not when philosophers began to reflect on human ideas. (The latter notion is found in Johann Jakob Brucker's recent *Philosophical History of the Theory of Ideas*, an erudite and scholarly little book which includes the latest controversies between the foremost geniuses of our age, Leibniz and Newton.)

[348] We must, then, determine the earliest times and places of this history: that is, when and where human thought arose. And we must gain certainty for these times and places by applying the appropriate chronology and geography, which might be called *metaphysical*. To this end, my Science applies a new critical art, similarly metaphysical, to the founders of the nations: for they must have lived more than a thousand years before those

writers with whom previous criticism has dealt. And as a criterion, I have adopted the common sense of the human race, which (as Axiom 11 states) is taught by divine providence and is common to all nations. This common sense is determined by the necessary harmony of human institutions, which is the source of all the beauty of the civil world. Hence, the predominant proofs of my Science follow this form: given the orders established by divine providence, human institutions *had to, have to, and will have to* develop in the way described by my Science. (Nor would this change even if infinite worlds were to arise from time to time throughout eternity, which is certainly false in fact.)

[349] Thus, my New Science also traces the *ideal eternal history* through which the history of every nation passes in time; and it follows each nation in its birth, growth, maturity, decline, and fall. Now, according to the first irrefutable principle stated above, the world of nations is clearly a human creation, and its nature reflected in the human mind. Hence, I would venture to say that anyone who studies my Science will retrace this ideal eternal history for himself, recreating it by the criterion that it *had to, has to, and will have to* be so. For there can be no more certain history than that which is recounted by its creator. In this way, my Science proceeds like geometry which, by constructing and contemplating its basic elements, creates its own world of measurable quantities. So does my Science, but with greater reality, just as the orders of human affairs are more real than points, lines, surfaces, and figures. This is an indication that my proofs are divine and should afford my reader something like divine pleasure. For in God knowledge and creation are the same thing.

[. . .]

[391] The third principal aspect of my New Science is the *history of human ideas*. As we have seen, human ideas sprang from the divine ideas formed by early people when they contemplated the heavens with the 'eyes of the body', as we say, rather than the eyes of the mind. In their science of augury, the Romans used the verb *contemplari* for observing the parts of the heavens whence auguries came or the auspices were taken. This verb referred to the precincts of the heavens, *templa coeli*, which was the Latin name for the regions marked out by augurs with their divining wands. Similar rites must have given the Greeks their early *theārēmata* and *mathēmata*, things divine and sublime to contemplate, which ultimately became metaphysical and mathematical abstractions.

This is the civil and historical meaning of the poetic tag 'From Jupiter the Muse began', *A Iove principium Musae*. For, as we have just seen, Jupiter's lightning bolts were the origin of the first Muse, which Homer calls the knowledge of good and evil. Later, philosophers found it all too easy to impose their interpretation of the phrase as the biblical maxim, 'The beginning of wisdom is piety.' The first Muse must have been Urania, who contemplates the heavens for the taking of auguries, and who later came to symbolize astronomy, as we shall see. Earlier, we divided poetic metaphysics into subordinate sciences, which all share the poetic nature of their mother. Just so, my history of ideas will trace the crude origins which gave rise both to the practical sciences, which are customarily used by various nations, and to the speculative sciences, which are perfected and pursued by scholars.

[. . .]

[780] [. . .] Plato's belief in Homer's sublime and esoteric wisdom became so firmly embedded that all the other philosophers eagerly followed his view, especially Plutarch, who dedicated an entire book to the subject. In response to them, I propose to examine *whether Homer was in fact a philosopher*. [. . .]

The esoteric wisdom attributed to Homer

[781] If we are to judge this question, we must concede that Homer shared the popular feelings and customs of the barbarous Greeks of his time: for such feelings and customs constitute the proper materials of all poets. And we must concede that Homer means what he says when he asserts that the gods are ranked by their physical strength. Homer illustrates this in his myth of the great chain, in which Jupiter cites his supreme strength to prove that he alone is the king of gods and men. Only such a belief makes it credible that Minerva first helps the mortal Diomedes wound Venus and Mars, and then in the battle of the gods disarms Venus and strikes Mars with a rock. [. . .] And let us concede that Homer describes the fearful customs current among the barbarous people of Greece. (Even though many think that the Greeks spread civilization throughout the world, these customs run contrary to what theorists have called the 'eternal' practices of the natural law of nations.) First, the Greeks poisoned their arrows, which is why Ulysses goes to Ephyra in search of poisonous herbs. And second, they denied burial to enemies killed in battle, whose bodies were left as carrion for crows and dogs. This is why Priam paid so much to ransom his son Hector, even after Achilles had bound his corpse to a chariot and dragged it around the walls of Troy for three days.

[782] Poets are the teachers of the masses, and the aim of poetry is to tame their savagery. So it was unworthy of a wise man, versed in savage feelings and customs, to arouse such admiration of them that the masses found pleasure and hence encouragement from his myths. And it was unworthy of a wise man to arouse the pleasure of the knavish masses by describing the knaveries of the gods, to say nothing of the heroes. In the battle of the gods, we find Mars insulting Minerva as a 'dog-fly', and Minerva striking Diana in the chest. Even the two kings, Agamemnon, commander of the Greek allies, and Achilles, the greatest of the Greek heroes, call each other dogs – an insult which the servants in our comedies would scarcely utter today.

[783] As for Agamemnon's supposed wisdom, good heavens, what can we call it but folly? When Apollo sends a deadly plague and decimates the Greek army for the seizing of Chryseis, this commander of the Greeks has to be compelled by Achilles to do his duty and restore Chryseis to her father Chryses, who is the priest of Apollo. Then, considering his dignity slighted, Agamemnon decides to regain his honour by observing a justice commensurate with his great wisdom: he wrongfully seizes Briseis from Achilles. In response, the hero who carries Troy's fate in his heel withdraws in disgust, taking with him his men and ships, and allows Hector to kill any Greeks who have survived the plague.

This is the Homer who was previously regarded as the founder of Greek polity or civilization! From this incident, he weaves the whole fabric of the entire *Iliad*, whose principal characters are two Greek leaders: the commander Agamemnon, and the hero Achilles, whose character we discussed in the Heroism of Early Peoples. This is Homer, the incomparable creator of poetic archetypes, whose greatest characters are completely unsuited to our present civilized and social nature, but are perfectly suited to the heroic nature of punctilious nobles!

[784] What shall we say, then, when Homer relates that his heroes take so much pleasure in wine, and that in their greatest afflictions they take comfort in drunkenness, especially the wise Ulysses? Such precepts of consolation are truly worthy of a philosopher!

[785] [. . .] even if we concede that Homer thought them necessary to making himself understood by the wild and savage masses, it is clear that no mind civilized and refined by philosophy could have succeeded in inventing such similes, which are truly incomparable. And no mind rendered humane and compassionate by philosophy could have created the truculent and ferocious style which Homer uses in describing the great variety of bloody

battles, and the great variety of extravagantly cruel kinds of slaughter, which constitute the particular sublimity of the *Iliad*.

[. . .]

Philosophical proofs for the discovery of the true Homer

[. . .]

[816] Poetic archetypes, which are the essence of myths, were created by primitive people because their nature was incapable of abstracting forms and properties. As a result, they represent the *manner of thinking of entire peoples* as expressed within the natural limits of their barbarism. It is an invariable property of such poetic myths that they magnify the ideas of particular things. In a golden passage in his *Rhetoric*, Aristotle observes that people with limited ideas generalize particulars into maxims. The reason for this must be that, when the human mind, with its infinite powers, is constricted by the vigour of the senses, it can only express its nearly divine nature by enlarging particulars in the imagination. This may explain why the gods and heroes are imagined as superhumanly large in both Greek and Latin poetry. And in the medieval return of barbarism, the paintings of God the Father, Jesus Christ, and the Virgin Mary portray them as extraordinarily large.

Chapter 6

Erich Auerbach

VICO AND AESTHETIC HISTORISM

Erich Auerbach (1892–1957), "Vico and Aesthetic Historism", 1949. *Scenes from the Drama of European Listerature* (Minneapolis: University of Minnesota Press, 1984), 183–98.

MODERN CRITICS OF ART or of literature consider and admire, with the same preparedness for understanding, Giotto and Michelangelo, Michelangelo and Rembrandt, Rembrandt and Picasso, Picasso and a Persian miniature; or Racine and Shakespeare, Chaucer and Alexander Pope, the Chinese lyrics and T. S. Eliot. The preference they may give to one or the other of the various periods or artists is no longer imposed upon them by certain aesthetic rules or judgments dominating the feelings of all our contemporaries, but such preferences are merely personal predilections originating from individual taste or individual experiences. A critic who would condemn the art of Shakespeare or of Rembrandt or even the drawings of the ice age primitives as being of bad taste because they do not conform to the aesthetic standards established by classical Greek or Roman theory would not be taken seriously by anybody.

This largeness of our aesthetic horizon is a consequence of our historical perspective; it is based on historism, i.e., on the conviction that every civilization and every period has its own possibilities of aesthetic perfection; that the works of art of the different peoples and periods, as well as their general forms of life, must be understood as products of variable individual conditions, and have to be judged each by its own development, not by absolute rules of beauty and ugliness. General and aesthetic historism is a precious (and also a very dangerous) acquisition of the human mind; it is a comparatively recent one. Before the sixteenth century, the historical and geographical horizon of the Europeans was not large enough for such conceptions; and even in the Renaissance, the seventeenth, and the beginning of the eighteenth century, the first moves toward historism were overbalanced by currents which worked against it; especially by the admiration of Greek and Roman civilization, which focused the attention on classical art and poetry; these became models to be imitated, and nothing is more contrary to aesthetic historism than imitation of models. It promotes absolute standards and rules of beauty, and creates an aesthetic dogmatism such as was admirably achieved by the French civilization of the time of Louis XIV. Besides this there was another current in the sixteenth and seventeenth centuries acting against historical perspective: the revival of the ancient concept of absolute human nature. The sudden enlargement of the horizon, the discovery of the variety and relativity of human religions, laws, customs, and tastes which occurred in the Renaissance, did not lead, in most cases, to historical perspective, that is to say, to an attempt to understand them all and to acknowledge their relative merits; it led, on the contrary, to the rejection of all of them, to a struggle against the variety of historical forms, to a struggle against history, and to a powerful revival of the concept of true or original or uncorrupted absolute human nature as opposed to history. History seemed to be nothing but "the actions and institutions of men," arbitrary, erroneous, pernicious, and even fraudulent. The worthlessness of such institutions seemed to be proved sufficiently by their variety; and the task of mankind seemed to be to replace them all by absolute standards according to the law of nature. There were indeed very different opinions about the nature of this nature; between those who identified human nature with the primitive uncivilized origins of mankind, and those who, on the contrary, identified nature with enlightened reason, there were all kinds of shades and gradations. But the static and absolute character of this human nature, as opposed to the changes of history, is common to all these theories of human nature and natural law. Montesquieu introduced a certain amount of historical perspective by his explanation of the variety of human forms of government, by climate and other material conditions; with the ideas of Diderot and Rousseau the concept of general and of human nature became strongly dynamic; but it was still a nature opposed to history.

Aesthetic historism, followed by general historism, practically originated in the second half of the eighteenth century, as a reaction against the European predominance of French classicism; the preromantic and romantic currents created it and spread it all over Europe. The most vigorous impulse came from Germany, from the so-called Storm and Stress group of the 1770's, from the first works of Herder and Goethe and their friends; later from the Schlegel brothers and the other German romantics. Herder and his followers started from the conception of the original folk genius as the creator of true poetry; in strong opposition to all theories which based poetry and art on highly developed civilization, good taste, imitation of models, and well-defined rules, they believed that poetry is the work of free instinct and imagination, and that it is most spontaneous and genuine in the early periods of civilization, in the youth of mankind, when instinct, imagination, and oral tradition were stronger than reason and reflection, when "poetry was the natural language of men"; hence their predilection for folk songs and folk tales, their theory that ancient epic poetry (parts of the Bible, Homer, the epic poetry of the Middle Ages) were not consciously composed by individuals, but had grown up and were synthetized unconsciously from many anonymous contributions—songs or tales—originating from the depth of the folk genius; hence finally their conviction that even in modern times true poetry can be reborn only from a return to its eternal source, the folk genius, with its unconscious and instinctive development of traditions. These men conceived history, not as a series of exterior facts and conscious actions of men, not as a series of mistakes and frauds, but as a subconscious, slow, and organic evolution of "forces," which were considered as manifestations of the Divinity. They admired the variety of historical forms as the realization of the infinite variety of the divine spirit, manifesting itself through the genius of the various peoples and periods. The divinization of history led to an enthusiastic research into the individual historical and aesthetic forms, to the attempt to understand them all by their own individual conditions of growth and development, to a contemptuous rejection of all aesthetic systems based on absolute and rationalistic standards. [. . .] Although this interest was extended to foreign national forms in the literary and scientific activities of the romantics, it led many of them, especially in Germany, to an extremely nationalistic attitude toward their own fatherland, which they considered as the synthesis and supreme realization of folk genius. Contemporary circumstances and events—the political disaggregation of Germany, the French Revolution, Napoleon's domination—contributed to the development of such feelings.

Now, it is one of the most astonishing facts in the history of ideas that very similar principles had been conceived and published half a century before their first preromantic appearance by an elderly Neapolitan scholar, Giambattista Vico (1668–1744), in his *Scienza Nuova*, which appeared first in 1725—by a man totally ignorant of all the conditions which, fifty years later, fostered and promoted such ideas. [. . .] He did not even know Shakespeare; his education had been classical and rationalistic, and he had no opportunity to become interested in Nordic folklore. The Storm and Stress movement was specifically Nordic in its aspect: it originated in a milieu of youthful liberty, it was promoted by a whole group of young men bound together by the same enthusiastic feelings. Vico was a solitary old professor at the University of Naples who had taught Latin figures of speech all his life and had written hyperbolical eulogies for the various Neapolitan viceroys and other important personalities. Nor had he any appreciable influence upon the preromantic and romantic movements. The difficulties of his style and the baroque atmosphere of his book, an atmosphere totally different from romanticism, covered it with a cloud of impenetrability. [. . .]

Vico arrived very late at the maturity of his ideas. [. . .] He was in his fifties when he finally succeeded in finding a form for his theory of cognition which satisfied him, and even filled him with enthusiasm. In this ultimate form, the theory says that there is no knowledge without creation; only the creator has knowledge of what he has created himself; the physical world—*il mondo della natura*—has been created by God; therefore only God can understand it; but the historical or political world, the world of mankind—*il mondo delle nazioni*—can be understood by men, because men have made it. I have no time now to discuss the theological implications of this much debated theory, considered in its relations with Vico's conception of Divine Providence. For our purpose, it is sufficient to stress the fact that Vico had achieved by this theory the predominance of the historical sciences, based on the certitude that men can understand men, that all possible forms of human life and thinking, as created and experienced by men, must be found in the potentialities of the human mind (*dentro le modificazioni della nostra medesima mente umana*); that therefore we are capable of re-evoking human history from the depth of our own consciousness.

The impulse to this theory of cognition was given to Vico undoubtedly by his own historical discoveries. He had no scientific knowledge of primitive civilizations, and a very incomplete and vague knowledge of the Middle Ages; he was supported only by his scholar-ship in classical philology and Roman law. It is almost a miracle that a man, at the beginning of the eighteenth century in Naples, with such material for his research, could create a vision of world history based on the discovery of the magic character of primitive civilization. Certainly, he was inspired by the theories of natural law, by Spinoza, Hobbes, and especially by Grotius; or better, he was inspired by his opposition to their theories. Still, there are few similar examples in the history of human thought of isolated creation due to such an extent to the particular quality of the author's mind. He combined an almost mystical faith in the eternal order of human history with a tremendous power of productive imagination in the interpretation of myth, ancient poetry, and law.

In his view, the first men were neither innocent and happy beings living in accordance with an idyllic law of nature, nor terrible beasts moved only by the purely material instinct of self-preservation. He also rejected the concept of primitive society as founded by reason and common sense in the form of mutual agreement by contract. For him, primitive men were orginally solitary nomads living in orderless promiscuity within the chaos of a mysteri-ous and for this very reason horrible nature. They had no faculties of reasoning; they only had very strong sensations and a strength of imagination such as civilized men can hardly understand. When, after the deluge, the first thunderstorm broke out, a minority of them, terror-struck by thunder and lightning, conceived a first form of religion, which modern scholars would call animistic: they personified nature, their imagination created a world of magic personifications, a world of living deities expressing their might and their will by the natural phenomena; and this minority of primitive men, in order to understand the will of the deities, to appease their wrath and to win their support, created a system of fantastic and magic ceremonies, formulas and sacrifices which governed all their life. They established sanctuaries at certain fixed places and became settled; hiding their sexual relations as a religious taboo, they became monogamous, thus founding the first families: primitive magic religion is the base of social institutions. It is also the origin of agriculture; the settlers were the first who cultivated the soil. The primitive society of isolated families is strongly patriarchal; the father is priest and judge; by his exclusive knowledge of the magic ceremonies, he has absolute power over all the members of his family; and the sacred formulas according to which he rules them are of extreme severity; these laws are strictly bound to the ritual wording, ignoring flexibility and consideration of special circumstances. Vico called the life of these primitive fathers a severe poem; they had huge bodies, and called themselves giants, *gigantes*, sons of the Earth, because they were the first to bury their dead and to worship their memory: the first nobility. Their conceptions and expressions were inspired by personifications and images; the mental order in which they conceived the surrounding world and created their institutions was not rational, but magic and fantastic. Vico calls it poetic; they were poets by their very nature; their wisdom, their metaphysics, their laws, all their life was "poetic." This is the first age of mankind, the golden age (golden because of the harvests), the age of the gods.

The development from the first to the second, the heroic age, is mainly political and economic. Stationary life and family constitution had given to the minority of settlers a superiority of wealth, material power, and religious prestige over the remnant of nomads, who finally were obliged to have recourse to the families of the fathers for protection and better living conditions; they were accepted as labor-slaves, as dependent members of the family of the first fathers or "heroes"; they were not admitted to the ritual ceremonies, and consequently had no human rights, no legal matrimony, no legitimate children, no property. But after a certain time the slaves or *famuli* began to rebel; a revolutionary movement developed, religious as well as social, for participation in the ceremonies, in legal rights and property. This movement obliged the isolated fathers to unite for defense, and to constitute the first communities, the heroic republics. They were oligarchical states, where religious, political, and economic power was entirely in the hands of the heroes; by maintaining the secrecy and inviolability of the divine mysteries they opposed all innovations in religion, law, and political structure. They preserved during this second period (which still was mentally "poetic" in the sense Vico uses this word) their narrow-minded virtue, their cruel discipline, and their magic formalism, still unable and unwilling to act by rationalistic considerations, symbolizing their life and their institutions in mythical concepts and strongly believing themselves to be of a higher nature than the rest of men. But rationalistic forms of mind, promoted by the revolutionary leaders of the plebeians (the former *famuli*), developed more and more. Step by step the plebeians tore away from the heroes their rights and prerogatives. With the final victory of the plebeians begins the third period of history, the age of men, a rationalistic and democratic period, where imagination and poetry have lost their creative power, where poetry is only an embellishment of life and an elegant pastime, where all men are considered as equals and are governed by elastic and liberal religions and laws. There is no doubt about the striking similarity between Vico's ideas and those of Herder and his followers. The poetical irrationalism and the creative imagination of primitive men are concepts common to both; both say that primitive men were poets by their very nature, that their language, their conception of nature and history, their entire life was poetry; both considered enlightened rationalism as unpoetical. But the concept of poetry, the basic concept, is entirely different. Vico admired his primitive giants and heroes as much as, perhaps even more than, Herder loved and cultivated the folk genius. Their power of imagination and expression, the concrete realism of their sublime metaphoric language, the unity of concept pervading all their life became for this poor old professor the model of creative greatness. He even admired—with an admiration so overwhelming that it proved to be stronger than his horror—the terrible cruelty of their magic formalism. These last words—the terrible cruelty of their magic formalism—well illustrate the immense discrepancy between his concepts and those of Herder. Herder's conception of the youth of mankind had grown on the ground of Rousseau's theory of original nature; it had been nourished and inspired by folk songs and folk tales; it is not political. The motive of magic animism is not entirely absent from his concepts, but it does not dominate, and it is not developed to its concrete implications and consequences. He saw the original state of mankind as a state of nature, and nature, for him, was liberty: liberty of feeling, of instinct, of inspiration, absence of laws and institutions, in striking contrast to the laws, conventions, and rules of rationalized society. He would never have conceived the idea that primitive imagination created institutions more severe and ferocious, boundaries more narrow and insurmountable than any civilized society can possibly do. But that is Vico's idea; it is the very essence of his system. The aim of primitive imagination, in his view, is not liberty, but, on the contrary, establishment of fixed limits, as a psychological and material protection against the chaos of the surrounding world. And later on, mythical imagination serves as the base of a political system and as a weapon in the struggle for political and economic power. The ages of the gods and the heroes, with their all pervading "poetry," are not at all poetical in the romantic sense, although, in both cases, poetry means imagination opposed to reason. The imagination of the folk genius produces folklore and traditions; the imagination of the giants and heroes produces myths which symbolize institutions according to the eternal law of Divine Providence. [. . .]

[. . .]

Vico did not show any special interest in the folk genius of the different individual peoples. His aim was to establish eternal laws—the laws of Divine Providence which govern history: an evolution of human civilization through distinct stages, an evolution which would develop again and again, in eternal cycles, wherever men should live. His suggestive analysis of the different periods stresses their individual aspect only in order to prove that they are typical stages of this evolution; [. . .]

In this movement of early European historism, Vico's ideas did not play an important part; his work was not sufficiently known. It seems to me that this is due not only to a casual combination of unfavorable circumstances, but primarily to the fact that his vision of human history lacked some of the most important elements of romantic historism, and possessed others which could hardly be understood and appreciated in the preromantic and early romantic period. The slow process of his gradual discovery in Europe began in the 1820's; later in the nineteenth century his influence still remained sporadic, and many leading textbooks of history of philosophy did not even mention his name. But in the last forty years this has changed; his name and his ideas have become important and familiar to an ever increasing number of European and American scholars and authors; the admirable activity Croce and Nicolini devoted to the publication and interpretation of his work met with considerable and steadily growing success. Some of his basic ideas seem to have acquired their full weight only for our time and our generation; as far as I know, no great author has been as much impressed by his work as James Joyce. There are, as it seems to me, three main ideas which are and may prove to be in future of great significance for our conceptions of aesthetics and history.

First, his discovery of the magic formalism of primitive men, with its power to create and to maintain institutions symbolized by myth; it includes a conception of poetry which has, undoubtedly, some relationship to modern forms of artistic expression. The complete unit of magic "poetry" or myth with political structure in primitive society, the interpretation of myths as symbols of political and economic struggles and developments, the concept of concrete realism in primitive language and myth are extremely suggestive of certain modern tendencies. By the word "tendencies," I do not allude to certain parties or countries, but to trends of thought and feeling spread all over our world.

The second point is Vico's theory of cognition. The entire development of human history, as made by men, is potentially contained in the human mind, and may therefore, by a process of research and re-evocation, be understood by men. The re-evocation is not only analytic; it has to be synthetic, as an understanding of every historical stage as an integral whole, of its genius (its *Geist*, as the German romantics would have said), a genius pervading all human activities and expressions of the period concerned. By this theory, Vico created the principle of historical understanding, entirely unknown to his contemporaries; the romantics knew and practiced this principle, but they never found such a powerful and suggestive epistemological base for it.

Finally, I want to stress his particular conception of historical perspective; it can best be explained by his interpretation of human nature. Against all contemporary theorists, who believed in an absolute and unchanging human nature as opposed to the variety and changes of history, Vico created and passionately maintained the concept of the historical nature of men. He identified human history and human nature, he conceived human nature as a function of history. There are many passages in the *Scienza Nuova* where the word *natura* should best be translated by "historical development" or "stage of historical development." Divine Providence makes human nature change from period to period, and in each period the institutions are in full accordance with the human nature of the period; the distinction between human nature and human history disappears; as Vico puts it, human history is a permanent Platonic state. This sounds rather ironical in a man who did not believe in progress, but in a cyclical movement of history. However, Vico was not ironical; he meant it in earnest.

Chapter 7

Anonymous

HISTORY

[Anon: Adam Ferguson? (1723–1816)], "History", *Encyclopaedia Britannica* (2nd edn) (Edinburgh: Balfour et al., 1780), Vol. 5, 3649, 3678–84.

HISTORY, IN GENERAL, SIGNIFIES an account of some remarkable facts which have happened in the world, arranged in the true order in which they actually took place, together with the causes to which they were owing, and the different effects they have produced, as far as can be discovered.—The word is Greek, Ιϛορια; and literally denotes a search of curious things, or a desire of knowing, or even a rehearsal of things we have seen; [it] properly signifies to know a thing by having seen it. But the idea is now much more extensive, and is applied to the knowledge of things taken from the report of others. The origin is from the verb Ιϛορια "I know;" and hence it is, that among the ancients several of their great men were called *polyhistores*, i.e. persons of various and general knowledge.

Sometimes, however, the word history is used to signify a description of things, as well as an account of facts. Thus Theophrastus calls his work, in which he has treated of the nature and properties of plants, an *history of plants*; and we have a treatise of Aristotle, intitled an *history of animals*; and to this day the descriptions of plants, animals, and minerals, are called by the general name of *natural history*.

But what chiefly merits the name of history, and what is here considered as such, is an account of the principal transactions of mankind since the beginning of the world; and which naturally divides itself into two parts, namely, *civil* and *ecclesiastical*. The first contains the history of mankind in their various relations to one another, and their behaviour, for their own emolument, or that of others, in common life; the second considers them as acting, or pretending to act, in obedience to what they believe to be the will of the Supreme Being.— Civil history, therefore, includes an account of all the different states that have existed in the world, and likewise of those men who in different ages of the world have most eminently distinguished themselves either for their good or evil actions. This last part of civil history is usually termed BIOGRAPHY.

History is now considered as a very considerable branch of polite literature: few accomplishments are more valued than an accurate knowledge of the histories of different nations; and scarce any literary production is more regarded than a well-written history of any nation.

With regard to the study of history, we must consider, that all the revolutions which have happened in the world, have been owing to two causes. 1. The connections between the different states existing together in the world at the same time, or their different situations with regard to one another; and, 2. The different characters of the people who in all ages constituted these states, their different geniuses and dispositions, &c. by which they were either prompted to undertake such and such actions of themselves, or were easily induced to it by others. The person who would study history, therefore, ought in the first place to make himself acquainted with the state of the world in general in all different ages; what nations inhabited the different parts of it; what their extent of territory was; at what particular time they arose, and when they declined. He is then to inform himself of the various events which have happened to each particular nation; and, in so doing, he will discover many of the causes of those revolutions, which before he only knew as facts. Thus, for instance, a person may know the Roman history from the time of Romulus, without knowing in the least why the city of Rome happened to be built at that time. This cannot be understood without a particular knowledge of the former state of Italy, and even of Greece and Asia; seeing the origin of the Romans is commonly traced as high as Æneas, one of the heroes of Troy. But when all this is done, which indeed requires no small labour, the historian hath yet to study the genius and dispositions of the different nations, the characters of those who were the principal directors of their actions, whether kings, ministers, generals, or priests; and when this is accomplished, he will discover the causes of those transactions in the different nations which have given rise to the great revolutions above mentioned: after which, he may assume the character of one who is perfectly versed in history.

[. . .]

Art. I. Of truth in history

TRUTH is, as it were, the very life and soul of history, by which it is distinguished from fable or romance. An historian therefore ought not only to be a man of probity, but void of all passion or bias. He must have the steadiness of a philosopher, joined with the vivacity of a poet or orator. Without the former, he will be insensibly swayed by some passion, to give a false colouring to the actions or characters he describes, as favour or dislike to parties or persons affect his mind. Whereas he ought to be of no party, nor to have either friend or foe while writing; but to preserve himself in a state of the greatest indifferency to all, that he may judge of things as they really are in their own nature, and not as connected with this or that person or party. And with this firm and sedate temper, a lively imagination is requisite; without which his descriptions will be flat and cold, nor will he be able to convey to his readers a just and adequate idea of great and generous actions. Nor is the assistance of a good judgment less necessary than any of the former qualities, to direct him what is proper to be said and what to be omitted, and to treat every thing in a manner suitable to its importance. And since these are the qualifications necessary for an historian, it may perhaps seem the less strange, that we have so few good histories.

But historical truth consists of two parts; one is, Not not to say any thing we know to be false: Tho' it is not sufficient to excuse an historian in relating a falsehood, that he did not know it was so when he wrote it; unless he first used all the means in his power to inform himself of the truth. For then undoubtedly, an invincible error is as pardonable in history as in morality. But the generality of writers in this kind content themselves with taking their accounts from hearsays, or transcribing them from others; without duly weighing the evidence on which they are founded, or giving themselves the trouble of a strict inquiry. Few will use the dilligence necessary to inform themselves of the certainty of what they undertake to relate. And as the want of this greatly abates the pleasure of reading such writers, while persons read with diffidence; so nothing more recommends an historian, than such industry. [. . .] But as an historian ought not to assert what he knows to be false; so he should likewise be cautious in relating things which are doubtful, and acquaint his readers with the evidence he goes upon in such facts, from whence they may be able to judge how far it is proper to credit them. So Herodotus tells us what things he saw himself in his travels, and what he heard from the information of the Egyptian priests and others with whom he conversed. And Curtius, in the life of Alexander, speaking of the affairs of India, ingenuously confesses, that he wrote more than he fully believed. "For (says he) I neither dare to affirm positively, what I doubt of; nor can I think it proper to omit what I have been told." By such a conduct the author secures his credit, whether the things prove really true or false; and gives room for further inquiry, without imposing on his readers.

The other branch of historical truth is, Not to omit any thing that is true, and necessary to set the matter treated of in a clear and full light. In the actions of past ages, or distant countries, wherein the writer has no personal concern, he can have no great inducement to break in upon this rule. But where interest or party is engaged, it requires no small candour, as well as firmness of mind, constantly to adhere to it. Affection to some, aversion to others, fear of disobliging friends or those in power, will often interpose, and try his integrity. Besides, an omission is less obvious to censure, than a false assertion: for the one may be easily ascribed to ignorance or forgetfulness; whereas the other will, if discovered, be commonly looked upon as design. He therefore, who in such circumstances, from a generous love to truth, is superior to all motives to betray or stifle it, justly deserves the character of a brave, as well as honest man. What Polybius says upon this head is very well worth remarking: "A good man ought to love his friends and his country, and to have a like disposition with them, both towards their friends and enemies. But when he takes upon him the character of an historian, they must all be forgot. He must often speak well of his enemies, and commend them when their actions deserve it; and sometimes blame, and even upbraid his greatest friends, when their conduct makes it necessary. Nor must he forbear sometimes to reprove, and at other times to commend, the same persons; since all are liable to mistake in their management, and there are scarce any persons who are always in the wrong. Therefore, in history, all personal considerations should be laid aside, and regard had only to their actions."

What a different view of mankind and their actions should we have, were these rules observed by all historians? Integrity is undoubtedly the principal qualification of an historian; when we can depend upon this, other imperfections are more easily passed over. Suetonius is said to have written the lives of the first twelve Roman emperors with the same freedom where-with they themselves lived. What better character can be given of a writer? The same ingenuous temper appears in the two Grecian historians above mentioned, Thucydides and Polybius: The former of whom, though banished by his countrymen the Athenians, yet expresses no marks of resentment in his history, either against them in general, or even against the chief authors of it, when he has occasion to mention them; and the latter does not forbear censuring, what he thought blameable in his nearest relations and friends. [. . .]

Art. II. The *subject* or *argument* of history

THE *subject* in general is facts, together with such things as are either connected with them, or may at least be requisite to set them in a just and proper light. But although the principal design of history be to acquaint us with facts, yet all facts do not merit the regard of an historian; but such only as may be thought of use and service for the conduct of human life. Nor is it allowable for him, like the poet, to form the plan and scheme of his work as he pleases. His business is to report things as he finds them, without any colouring or disguise to make them more pleasing and palatable to his reader, which would be to convert his history into a novel. Indeed, some histories afford more pleasure and entertainment than others, from the nature of the things of which they consist; and it may be esteemed the happiness of an historian to meet with such a subject, but it is not his fault if it be otherwise. Thus Herodotus begins his history with shewing, that the barbarians gave the first occasion to the wars between them and the Greeks, and ends it with an account of the punishment which, after some ages, they suffered from the Greeks on that account. Such a relation must not only be very agreeable to his countrymen the Grecians, for whose sakes it was written; but likewise very instructive, by informing them of the justice of Providence in punishing public injuries in this world, wherein societies, as such, are only capable of punishment. And therefore those examples might be of use to caution them against the like practices. On the contrary, Thucydides begins his history with the unhappy state of his countrymen the Athenians; and in the course of it plainly intimates, that they were the cause of the calamitous war between them and the Lacedemonians. Whereas, had he been more inclined to please and gratify his countrymen, than to write the truth, he might have set things in such a light as to have made their enemies appear the aggressors. But he scorned to court applause at the expence of truth and justice, and has set a noble example of integrity to all future historians. But as all actions do not merit a place in history, it requires no small judgment in an historian to select such only as are proper. Cicero observes very justly, that history "is conversant in great and memorable actions." For this reason, an historian should always keep posterity in view, and relate nothing which may not, upon some account or other, be worth the notice of after ages. To descend to trivial and minute matters, such as frequently occur in the common affairs of life, is below the dignity of history. Such writers ought rather to be deemed journalists than historians, who have no view or expectation that their works should survive them. But the skilful historian is fired with a more noble ambition. His design is to acquaint succeeding ages with what remarkable occurrences happened in the world before them; to do justice to the memory of great and virtuous men; and at the same time to perpetuate his own.

[. . .]

[. . .] [A]lthough facts in general are the proper subject of history, yet they may be differently considered with regard to the extent of them, as they relate either to particular persons, or communities of men. And from this consideration, history has been distinguished into three sorts, viz. *biography, particular*, and *general history*. The lives of single persons is called *biography*. By *particular history* is meant that of particular states, whether for a shorter or longer space of time. And *general history* contains an account of several states existing together in the same period of time.

1. The subjects of *biography* are the lives either of public or private persons; for many useful observations in the conduct of human life may be made from just accounts of those who have been eminent and beneficial to the world in either station. Nay, the lives of vitious persons are not without their use, as warnings to others, by observing the fatal consequences which sooner or later generally follow such practices. But, for those who exposed their lives, or otherwise employed their time and labour for the service of their fellow creatures, it seems but a just debt that their memories should be perpetuated after them, and posterity acquainted with their benefactors. The expectation of this was no small incentive to virtue in the Pagan world. And perhaps every one, upon due reflection, will be convinced how natural this passion is to mankind in general. And it was for this reason, probably, that Virgil places

not only his heroes, but also the inventors of useful arts and sciences, and other persons of distinguished merit, in the Elysian fields, where he thus describes them:

> Here patriots live, who, for their country's good,
> In fighting fields were prodigal of blood:
> Priests of unblemish'd lives here make abode,
> And poets worthy their inspiring god;
> And searching wits of more mechanic parts,
> Who grac'd their age with new-invented arts;
> Those who to worth their bounty did extend,
> And those who knew that bounty to commend:
> The heads of these with holy fillets bound,
> And all their temples were with garlands crown'd.
> ÆNEID, I. vi. v. 66.

In the lives of public persons, their public characters are principally, but not solely, to be regarded. The world is inquisitive to know the conduct of princes and other great men, as well in private as public. And both, as has been said, may be of service, considering the influence of their examples. But to be over-inquisitive in searching into the weaknesses and infirmities of the greatest or best of men, is, to say no more of it, but a needless curiosity. In the writers of this kind, Plutarch is justly allowed to excel.
[. . .]
Now, in such histories as these, to go farther back than is requisite to set the subject in a just light, seems as improper as it is unnecessary.
The general subject or argument of history, in its several branches, may be reduced to these four heads; *narration, reflections, speeches,* and *digressions.*
I. By *narration* is meant a description of facts or actions, with such things as are necessarily connected with them, namely, persons, time, place, design, and event.
As to *actions* themselves, it is the business of the historian to acquaint his readers with the manner in which they were performed; what measures were concerted on all sides, and how they were conducted, whether with vigilance, courage, prudence, and caution, or the contrary, according to the nature of the action; as likewise, if any unforeseen accidents fell out, by which the designed measures were either promoted or broken. All actions may be referred to two sorts, military and civil. And as war arises from injustice, and injuries received, on one side or the other, it is fit the reader should be informed who were the aggressors. For though war is never to be desired, yet it is sometimes necessary. In the description of battles, regard should be had equally to both parties, the number of forces, conduct of the generals, in what manner they engaged, what turns and changes happened in the engagement, either from accidents, courage, or stratagem, and how it issued. The like circumstances should all be observed in sieges and other actions. But the most agreeable scene of history arises from a state of peace. Here the writer acquaints us with the constitution of states, the nature of their laws, the manners and customs of the inhabitants, the advantages of concord and unanimity, with the disadvantages of contention and discord; the invention of arts and sciences, in what manner they were improved and cultivated, and by whom; with many other things, both pleasant and profitable in the conduct of life.
As to *persons*, the characters of all those should be described who act any considerable part in an history. This excites the curiosity of the reader, and makes him more attentive to what is said of them; as every one is more inquisitive to hear what relates to others, in proportion to his knowledge of them. And it will likewise be of use to observe, how their

actions agree with their characters, and what were the effects of their different qualifications and abilities.

[. . .]

But an accurate historian goes yet further, and considers the *causes* of actions, and what were the *designs* and views of those persons who were principally concerned in them. Some, as Polybius has well observed, are apt to confound the beginnings of actions with their springs and causes, which ought to be carefully separated. For the causes are often very remote, and to be looked for at a considerable distance from the actions themselves. [. . .] Again, the true springs and causes of action are to be distinguished from such as are only feigned and pretended. For generally the worse designs men have in view, the more solicitous they are to cover them with specious pretences. It is the historian's business, therefore, to lay open, and expose to view, these arts of politicians.

[. . .] But in order to our being well assured of a person's real designs, and to make the accounts of them more credible, it is proper we should be acquainted with his disposition, manners, way of life, virtues, or vices; that by comparing his actions with these, we may see how far they agree and suit each other. For this reason Sallust is so particular in his description of Catiline, and Livy of Hannibal; by which it appears credible, that the one was capable of entering into such a conspiracy against his country, and the other of performing such great things as are related concerning him. But if the causes of actions lie in the dark and unknown, a prudent historian will not trouble himself, or his readers, with vain and trifling conjectures, unless something very probable offers itself.

Lastly, an historian should relate the *issue* and *event* of the actions he describes. This is undoubtedly the most useful part of history; since the greatest advantage arising from it is to teach us experience, from what has happened in the world before us. When we learn from the examples of others the happy effects of wisdom, prudence, integrity, and other virtues, it naturally excites us to an imitation of them, and to pursue the same measures in our own conduct. And, on the contrary, by perceiving the unhappy consequences which have followed from violence, deceit, rashness, or the like vices, we are deterred from such practices. But since the wisest and most prudent measures do not always meet with the desired success, and many cross accidents may happen to frustrate the best concerted designs; when we meet with instances of this nature, it prepares us for the like events, and keeps us from too great a confidence in our own schemes. However, as this is not commonly the case, but in the ordinary course of human affairs like causes usually produce like effects; the numerous examples of the happy consequences of virtue and wisdom, recorded in history, are sufficient to determine us in the choice of our measures, and to encourage us to hope for an answerable success, though we cannot be certain we shall in no instance meet with a disappointment. And therefore Polybius very justly observes, that "he who takes from history the causes, manner, and end of actions, and omits to take notice whether the event was answerable to the means made use of, leaves nothing in it but a bare amusement, without any benefit or instruction." These then are the several things necessary to be attended to in historical narrations, but the proper disposition of them must be left to the skill and prudence of the writer.

Chapter 8

Dugald Stewart

ON CONJECTURAL HISTORY

Dugald Stewart (1753–1828), "On Conjectural History", *Essays on Philosophical Subjects,* by Adam Smith (London: T. Cadell, 1795), xl–xlvi.

THE DISSERTATION on the Origin of Languages, which now forms a part of the same volume with the Theory of Moral Sentiments, was, I believe, first annexed to the second edition of that work. It is an essay of great ingenuity, and on which the author himself set a high value; but, in a general review of his publications, it deserves our attention less, on account of the opinions it contains, than as a specimen of a particular sort of enquiry, which, so far as I know, is entirely of modern origin, and which seems, in a peculiar degree, to have interested Mr. SMITH's curiosity. Something very similar to it may be traced in all his different works, whether moral, political, or literary; and on all these subjects he has exemplified it with the happiest success.

When, in such a period of society as that in which we live, we compare our intellectual acquirements, our opinions, manners, and institutions, with those which prevail among rude tribes, it cannot fail to occur to us as an interesting question, by what gradual steps the transition has been made from the first simple efforts of uncultivated nature, to a state of things so wonderfully artificial [i.e. as a product of artistic accomplishment or craftsmanship] and complicated. Whence has arisen that systematical beauty which we admire in the structure of a cultivated language; that analogy which runs through the mixture of languages spoken by the most remote and unconnected nations; and those peculiarities by which they are all distinguished from each other? Whence the origin of the different sciences and of the different arts; and by what chain has the mind been led from their first rudiments to their last and most refined improvements? Whence the astonishing fabric of the political union; the fundamental principles which are common to all governments; and the different forms which civilized society has assumed in different ages of the world? On most of these subjects very little information is to be expected from history; for long before that stage of society when men begin to think of recording their transactions, many of the most important steps of their progress have been made. A few insulated facts may perhaps be collected from the casual observations of travellers, who have viewed the arrangements of rude nations;

but nothing, it is evident, can be obtained in this way, which approaches to a regular and connected detail of human improvement.

In this want of direct evidence, we are under a necessity of supplying the place of fact by conjecture; and when we are unable to ascertain how men have actually conducted themselves upon particular occasions, of considering in what manner they are likely to have proceeded, from the principles of their nature, and the circumstances of their external situation. In such enquiries, the detached facts which travels and voyages afford us, may frequently serve as land-marks to our speculations; and sometimes our conclusions *a priori*, may tend to confirm the credibility of facts, which, on a superficial view, appeared to be doubtful or incredible.

Nor are such theoretical views of human affairs subservient merely to the gratification of curiosity. In examining the history of mankind, as well as in examining the phenomena of the material world, when we cannot trace the process by which an event *has been* produced, it is often of importance to be able to shew how it *may have been* produced by natural causes. Thus, in the instance which has suggested these remarks, although it is impossible to determine with certainty what the steps were by which any particular language was formed, yet if we can shew, from the known principles of human nature, how all its various parts might gradually have arisen, the mind is not only to a certain degree satisfied, but a check is given to that indolent philosophy, which refers to a miracle, whatever appearances, both in the natural and moral worlds, it is unable to explain.

To this species of philosophical investigation, which has no appropriated name in our language, I shall take the liberty of giving the title of *Theoretical* or *Conjectural History*; an expression which coincides pretty nearly in its meaning with that of *Natural History*, as employed by Mr. HUME[1], and with what some French writers have called *Histoire Raisonnée*.

The mathematical sciences, both pure and mixed, afford, in many of their branches, very favourable subjects for theoretical history; and a very competent judge, the late M. d'ALEMBERT, has recommended this arrangement of their elementary principles, which is founded on the natural succession of inventions and discoveries, as the best adapted for interesting the curiosity and exercising the genius of students. The same author points out as a model a passage in MONTUCLA's History of Mathematics, where an attempt is made to exhibit the gradual progress of philosophical speculation, from the first conclusions suggested by a general survey of the heavens, to the doctrines of COPERNICUS. It is somewhat remarkable, that a theoretical history of this very science (in which we have, perhaps, a better opportunity than in any other instance whatever, of comparing the natural advances of the mind with the actual succession of hypothetical systems) was one of Mr. SMITH's earliest compositions, and is one of the very small number of his manuscripts which he did not destroy before his death.

I already hinted, that enquiries perfectly analagous to these may be applied to the modes of government, and to the municipal institutions which have obtained among different nations. It is but lately, however, that these important subjects have been considered in this point of view; the greater part of politicians before the time of MONTESQUIEU, having contented themselves with an historical statement of facts, and with a vague reference of laws to the wisdom of particular legislators, or to accidental circumstances, which it is now impossible to ascertain. MONTESQUIEU, on the contrary, considered laws as originating chiefly from the circumstances of society; and attempted to account, from the changes in the condition of mankind, which take place in the different stages of their progress, for the corresponding alterations which their institutions undergo. It is thus, that in his occasional elucidations of the Roman jurisprudence, instead of bewildering himself among the erudition of scholiasts and of antiquaries, we frequently find him borrowing his lights from the most remote and unconnected quarters of the globe, and combining the casual observations of illiterate travellers and navigators, into a philosophical commentary on the history of law and of manners.

The advances made in this line of enquiry since MONTESQUIEU's time have been great. Lord KAMES, in his Historical Law Tracts, has given some excellent specimens of it, particularly in his Essays on the History of Property and of Criminal Law, and many ingenious speculations of the same kind occur in the works of Mr. MILLAR.

In Mr. SMITH's writings, whatever be the nature of his subject, he seldom misses an opportunity of indulging his curiosity, in tracing from the principles of human nature, or from the circumstances of society, the origin of the opinions and the institutions which he describes. I formerly mentioned a fragment concerning the History of Astronomy which he has left for publication; and I have heard him say more than once, that he had projected, in the earlier part of his life, a history of the other sciences on the same plan. In his Wealth of Nations, various disquisitions are introduced which have a like object in view, particularly the theoretical delineation he has given of the natural progress of opulence in a country; and his investigation of the causes which have inverted this order in the different countries of modern Europe. His lectures on jurisprudence seem, from the account of them formerly given, to have abounded in such enquiries.

I am informed by the same gentleman who favoured me with the account of Mr. SMITH's lectures at Glasgow, that he had heard him sometimes hint an intention of writing a treatise upon the Greek and Roman republics. "And after all that has been published on that subject, I am convinced (says he), that the observations of Mr. SMITH would have suggested many new and important views concerning the internal and domestic circumstances of those nations, which would have displayed their several systems of policy, in a light much less artificial than that in which they have hitherto appeared."

The same turn of thinking was frequently, in his social hours, applied to more familiar subjects; and the fanciful theories which, without the least affectation of ingenuity, he was continually starting upon all the common topics of discourse, gave to his conversation a novelty and variety that were quite inexhaustible. Hence too the minuteness and accuracy of his knowledge on many trifling articles which, in the course of his speculations, he had been led to consider from some new and interesting point of view; and of which his lively and circumstantial descriptions amused his friends the more, that he seemed to be habitually inattentive, in so remarkable a degree, to what was passing around him.

I have been led into these remarks by the Dissertation on the Formation of Languages, which exhibits a very beautiful specimen of theoretical history, applied to a subject equally curious and difficult. The analogy between the train of thinking from which it has taken its rise, and that which has suggested a variety of his other disquisitions, will, I hope, be a sufficient apology for the length of this digression; more particularly, as it will enable me to simplify the account which I am to give afterwards, of his enquiries concerning political economy.

I shall only observe farther on this head, that when different theoretical histories are proposed by different writers, of the progress of the human mind in any one line of exertion, these theories are not always to be understood as standing in opposition to each other. If the progress delineated in all of them be plausible, it is possible at least, that they may all have been realized; for human affairs never exhibit, in any two instances, a perfect uniformity. But whether they have been realized or no, is often a question of little consequence. In most cases, it is of more importance to ascertain the progress that is most simple, than the progress that is most agreeable to fact; for, paradoxical as the proposition may appear, it is certainly true, that the real progress is not always the most natural. It may have been determined by particular accidents, which are not likely again to occur, and which cannot be considered as forming any part of that general provision which nature has made for the improvement of the race.

Note

1   See his Natural History of Religion.

Further Reading: Chapters 5 to 8

Adams, H. P. *The Life and Writings of Giambattista Vico* (London: Allen & Unwin, 1935).

Auerbach, Erich. "The New Science of Giambattista Vico", *Modern Language Notes* 64(3) (1949), 196–7.

Bayer, Thora Ilin. "The Future of Vico Studies: Vico at the Millennium", *New Vico Studies* 18 (2000), 71–76.

Bedani, Gino. *Vico Revisited* (Oxford: Berg, 1989).

Berlin, Isaiah. "On Vico", *Philosophical Quarterly* 35 (1985), 281–9.

——. *Three Critics of the Enlightenment: Vico, Hammann, Herder*, Henry Hardy (ed.) (Princeton, NJ: Princeton University Press, 2000).

——. *Vico and Herder: Two Studies in the History of Ideas* (London: Hogarth Press, 1976).

Black, David W. *Vico and Moral Perception* (New York: Peter Lang, 1996).

Breslin, Charles. "Philosophy or Philology: Auerbach and Aesthetic Historicism", *Journal of the History of Ideas* 22(3) (1961): 369–81.

Burke, Peter. *Vico* (Oxford: Oxford University Press, 1985).

Caponigri, A. Robert. *Time and Idea: The Theory of History in Giambattista Vico* (London: Routledge & Kegan Paul, 1953).

Collingwood, R. G. *The Idea of History*. 1946. Introduction Jan van der Dussen (Oxford: Oxford University Press, 1994).

Croce, B. *The Philosophy of Giambattista Vico*. Trans. R. G. Collingwood. 1913. Introduction Alan Sica (New Brunswick NJ; London: Transaction, 2002).

Damrosch, David. "Auerbach in Exile". *Comparative Literature* 47(2) (1995), 97–117.

Haddock, B. A. "Vico and Anachronism", *Political Studies* 24(4) (1976), 483–7.

Herder, J. G. *Another Philosophy of History and Selected Writings*. Trans. and ed. I. D. Evrigenis and D. Pellerin (Indianapolis: Hackett, 2004).

Iggers, Georg. "Historicism: The History and Meaning of the Term", *Journal of the History of Ideas* 56 (1995), 129–52.

Levine, Joseph M. "Giambattista Vico and the Quarrel between the Ancients and the Moderns", *Journal of the History of Ideas* 52(1) (1991), 55–79.

Lilla, Mark. *G. B. Vico: The Making of an Anti-Modern* (Cambridge, MA: Harvard University Press, 1993).

Mali, Joseph. "On Giambattista Vico", *History of European Ideas* 21(2) (1995), 287–90.

——. *The Rehabilitation of Myth: Vico's "New Science"* (Cambridge: Cambridge University Press, 1992).

Megill, Allan. "Aesthetic Theory and Historical Consciousness in the Eighteenth Century", *History and Theory* 17(1) (1978), 29–62.

Miller, Cecilia. *Giambattista Vico: Imagination and Historical Knowledge* (Basingstoke: Macmillan, 1993).

Morrison, James C. "Review: Three Interpretations of Vico", *Journal of the History of Ideas* 39(3) (1978), 511–18.

Pompa, Leon. *Vico: A Study of the "New Science"*. 1975. (2nd edn) (Cambridge: Cambridge University Press, 1990).

Preece, W. E. "The Organization of Knowledge and the Planning of Encyclopaedias: The Case of the *Encyclopaedia Britannica*", *Cahiers d'histoire mondiale* 9 (1966), 799–819.

Robertson, John. *The Case for the Enlightenment: Scotland and Naples, 1680–1760* (Cambridge: Cambridge University Press, 2005).

Said, Edward. "Eric Auerbach: Critic of the Earthly World", *Boundary 2* 31(2) (2004), 11–34.

Stone, H. *Vico's Cultural History: The Production and Transmission of Ideas in Naples, 1685–1750* (Leiden, New York and Cologne: E. J. Brill, 1997).

Tagliacozzo, Giorgio. "Vico: A Philosopher of the Eighteenth- and Twentieth-Century", *Italica* 59(2) (1982), 93–108.

——— . (ed.). *Vico: Past and Present* (Atlantic Highlands, NJ.: Humanities Press, 1981).

——— . and Donald Phillip Verene. *Giambattista Vico's Science of Humanity* (Baltimore, MD: Johns Hopkins University Press, 1976).

——— . *New Vico Studies* (Atlantic Highlands, NJ: Humanities Press (1983–)).

——— . and Michael Mooney (eds). *Vico and Contemporary Thought* (Atlantic Highlands, NJ: Humanities Press, 1979).

——— . and Vanessa Rumble (eds). *A Bibliography of Vico in English (1884–1984)* (Bowling Green, OH: Philosophy Documentation Center, Bowling Green State University, 1986).

Tagliacozzo, Giorgio and Hayden V. White (eds). *Giambattista Vico: An International Symposium* (Baltimore, MD: The Johns Hopkins University Press, 1969).

Verene, Donald Phillip. *The New Art of Autobiography: an Essay on the Life of Giambatista Vico Written by Himself* (Oxford: Oxford University Press, 1991).

Vico, Giambattista. *The Autobiography of Giambattista Vico.* Trans. M. H. Fisch and T. G. Bergin (Ithaca, NY: Cornell University Press, 1944).

Wilson, Edmund. *To the Finland Station: A Study in the Writing and Acting of History* (New York: Harcourt Brace, and London: Secker and Warburg, 1940).

Zagorin, Perez. "Berlin on Vico". *The Philosophical Quarterly* 35 (1985), 290–96.

PART 3

Historical writing and moral psychology

INTRODUCTION

PERHAPS MORE VIVIDLY THAN in any other section, these readings seem to feature contradictory approaches to the study of history, and yet their basic criteria for defining the purpose and meaning of historical writing have resonated through the centuries. Since their influence will be found in most of the Parts that follow, the conflicting views of these Enlightenment writers, Hester Chapone and William Godwin—along with the psychological observations of Lord Kames—should therefore be seen as complementary elements in modern historiography.

On both sides of the Atlantic and across the British Isles, the moral essayist Hester Chapone was so widely admired for her essays that publishers released more than thirty printings of them between 1771 and 1800. Chapone defined historical writing as the record of "heroic actions and exalted characters", a phrase which would become familiar to readers of that grand reference text of the Scottish Enlightenment, the *Encyclopaedia Britannica* (see Part 2). Adopting the style of letter-writing, which was familiar both to readers of sentimental novels and of moral essays, Chapone advised her young niece that heroic narratives will persuade her to act morally. This is because studying the historical narrative of true heroism "cultivates a taste for intellectual improvement," after which "[you] will embrace, with a clearer choice, those principles of Virtue and Religion, which the judgement must ever approve, in proportion as it becomes enlightened". Some twenty years later, the radical political writer and novelist William Godwin questioned the very content and means of composing this kind of history, in ways that also challenged fundamental notions of how historical writing can or should affect our behaviour. Godwin's ideas were shared by a growing number of Romantic philosophers, poets, and critics, who celebrated the mind's dynamic nature and emphasized the imaginative ("romantic") power of art (see Part 4). Comparing Chapone with Godwin provides a useful view of the principles that mark the transition from Enlightenment to Romantic historiography at the end of the eighteenth century.

To be sure, Chapone and Godwin agreed that the study of history should encourage a positive moral outcome, and indeed they shared the belief that historical writing ought to focus on the lives of individuals rather than on the abstract conjectures of philosophers. In this important respect, Godwin and Chapone wanted history to be grounded in actual thoughts and actions rather than merely concepts and theories. But their ideas of what constitutes history and its reader's state of mind were strikingly different. Godwin opened by dismissing historians who aim to provide "tranquillity of the soul" simply by producing historical abstractions that are organised around themes rather than actual human lives. He then offered a taste of his **subjective** and psychological rather than **objective** and public concerns by attacking Enlightenment historians: "[they] are ready from the slightest glance to decipher the whole character. Not so genuine scholars". Like Vico earlier in the century, Godwin proposed that historians and their readers should cultivate a passionate curiosity about the world, and that truly meaningful historical writing should create powerful emotional experiences through the description of feelings and insight into private motivation. Chapone also rejected **conjectural history** (see Part 2), but she retained an Enlightenment emphasis on mental tranquillity: in her view, any exchange of sentiments would take the form of readers engaging in polite conversations that remind each other of forgotten historical details, with the general aim to "restore [the mind] to an exulting sense of dignity". Similarly, she assumed that her reader's wish for tranquillity would lead her to turn immediately from intolerable depictions of vice to consoling depictions of virtue. But for Godwin, history ought to pack an emotional punch in order to inspire moral feelings: "there must be friction and heat, before the virtue will operate". His innovative notion of historical writing provides an *exchange of ideas* or *investigation of details* that takes place in the passionate but subjective privacy of the reader's mind, and is therefore technically and conceptually distinct from the mere *depiction* of heroic men that Chapone required for her thus enlightened readers to act morally. Indeed, Chapone's Enlightenment ideal of historical reading is one which takes place in a public context, whereas Godwin's Romantic ideal stems from a deeply emotional mental state: it is only through an imaginative sympathy with what history enables us to envision that we can drink a historian's meaning without even noticing that we are doing so—he says we can "insensibly imbibe [its] same spirit". By proposing that virtue is the natural result of choices informed by reading the right kinds of history, Chapone required a textual transparency for heroic historical writing and a exclusively public sphere for morality. It also suggests that, in Chapone's view, reading history widens women's social spheres by extending the possible topics of meaningful female discourse. At one point in her essay she suggested that men tend to read history for narrowly political rather than expansively social reasons, which leads to disputes and partisanship.[i]

Despite their similar writing styles—Godwin also adopts a personal tone by adopting the first-person viewpoint—there are so many differences between these writers that it might seem that they are speaking different languages. The shift from objective to subjective morality that defines the differences between Chapone and Godwin can be explained by the innovative aesthetic theory published by the Scottish legal historian Henry Home, Lord Kames (which appeared 10 years before Chapone's book and 35 years before Godwin's essay). Kames was

---

i   Chapone explained to her female reader that, "as *you* will not read with a critical [that is, disputatious] view, nor enter deeply into politics, I think you may be allow'd to choose that which is most entertaining". See "On the Manner and Course of Reading History", *Letters on the Improvement of the Mind*, 212. For a more extensive discussion of gender and the functions of historical reading during the late eighteenth century, see M. Phillips, *Society and Sentiment* (Princeton: Princeton University Press, 2000), 103–28. Phillips quotes this passage on 113.

one of the first to focus on our state of mind when we are so immersed in a book, painting, or theatrical performance, that "we perceive every object as in our sight; and the mind, totally occupied with an interesting event, finds no leisure for reflection of any sort". Kames provided a descriptive term for this experience, **ideal presence**, and he suggested that this mental state is strongest when we are envisioning another person's suffering. Therefore ideal presence, evoked even through writing that depicts fictions, serves a strongly moral purpose: "language, by means of fiction, has the command of our sympathy for the good of others". Remember that when Chapone recommended how to study history, she mentioned social events at which friends discussed their reading, to remind each other of forgotten details. But the moral value of reading for Kames, however, requires an intensely private experience that vanishes the moment we are made aware of it. While Chapone remained focused on the content of the history that we ought to read, Kames and Godwin were concerned primarily with the feelings and beliefs that such writing evokes.

The psychology that informed Godwin gestures back to Kames's interest in the emotional state of history's sympathetic readers. But Chapone believed that good choices will follow, quite naturally and automatically, from reading the right historical narratives. Surely Chapone would have agreed with Kames that the moral value of historical writing originates in the reader's mind. But Godwin went much further by dwelling on the special ability of certain kinds of historical writing to cultivate sympathetic feelings. Those historical texts that are morally affecting would enable us actually to see a subject of history in his or her public and private life—they would allow readers "to follow him into his closet [i.e. private room]". Since generating an emotional response to historical writing is most important, Godwin went so far as to declare that "I should be better employed in studying this one man, than in perusing the abridgement of Universal History in sixty volumes". This is because the most valuable reading involves the solemn act of self-investigation in which we view in ourselves those intimate details that we have seen in others. Chapone's choice of historical works resided in a literary tradition that had established its reliability and respectability among generations of readers in polite society. But Godwin questioned whether history based on its popularity or even its factual basis can provide his moral and psychological ideal. He pointed to writers of "romances" (by which he means novels) who use their "enthusiastic and sublime licence of imagination" to affect readers in ways that recorders of facts cannot do; moreover, since novelists create the characters they depict, they are more authoritative than historians, who assemble materials they have merely collected from other sources. Controversially, Godwin remarked that "romance [is] a bolder species of composition than history"—because novelists alone aim to achieve the moral goal of arousing powerful sympathetic feelings.

Now on the one hand, it is this observation that led Godwin to invite energetic readers to "proceed at once to the naked and scattered materials, out of which the historian has constructed his work [so that] they may investigate the story for themselves", whereas Chapone's concern for social propriety and moral guidance led her to say that if one "should wish to know more of any particular people or period than you find in Rollin ... there are, I believe, French or English translations of all the original historians from whom he extracted his materials". On the other hand, by referring readers to the scattered materials that the historian uses to build and to verify his narrative, Godwin revealed his own mixed feelings about the kinds of knowledge that readers can acquire from novels and histories. While novels may have offered a more emotionally resonant view of the world that emerged from the mind of a creative writer, only history can offer verifiable information about the world before its writing took place. Within each section in this book, we will see this internal tension about the relative force and meaning of historical knowledge playing itself out.

In his discussion of the transition from Enlightenment to Romantic historiography, the historian Mark Salber Phillips pointed out that sympathy was an important moral issue for authors in both periods. After all, those leading authors who defined Enlightenment history by adopting a rational approach to the Science of Man (such as David Hume and Adam Smith) also participated in what came to be known as "the age of sensibility" by emphasizing the physical senses as our primary source of knowledge. They affirmed the importance of feeling rather than rational judgement as the key to our process of making ethical decisions. To show just how innovative that view was, it might be useful to mention that only two generations earlier, John Locke had claimed that morality could be defined as objectively as a mathematical equation.[ii] So it is ironic, Phillips suggests, that when these Enlightenment authors wrote history, they strove to create a certain **historical distance** between themselves and the materials they described, at times evoking a sense of distance or of closeness between their readers and the history they read. This was partly because these discussions of historical understanding took place in literary essays and were not put into scholarly practice—they were descriptive rather than **methodological**. As we will see in the next Part, it was Romantics such as Godwin who brought together notions of emotional sensibility, the cultivation of ideal presence, and the moral dimensions of each, in historical writing. Historians may suggest that they are intellectually distant or at odds with the topics they are describing, and yet they may still use language to create a sympathetic or sentimental relationship between the reader and their historical text. It is important, Phillips argues, to notice how revealing such literary craftsmanship—whether conscious or not—can be for understanding the historian's imagined proximity to his or her materials, to language, and to his or her future readers.

Phillips shows that studying the ways historians orchestrate distance is also useful because when historians position their readers they reveal their ideological, stylistic, and cognitive values. They also present an implicit theory of how history should be understood. For instance, when museums define nationally-important events by organizing artefacts in a particular way and then encasing them in glass for our passive view, the resulting expansion of historical distance communicates certain political values. E. P. Thompson introduced his study of the English working class (see Part 9) by employing a style that is powerfully specific, leading us to focus on "the poor stockinger, the Luddite cropper, the 'obsolete' hand-loom weaver"—he reduced historical distance to evoke our emotional concern for poor people. It was not merely his literary style that achieved that evocation of distance, but also his concerns with **ideology**, psychology, and emotion. We have seen that Chapone assumed that her reader would turn away quickly from depressing depictions because they would delay her wish for an uplifting view of history. This reveals an aesthetic approach to cognition that is quite different from Godwin's view that historical writing is most impressive when it moves us imaginatively and emotionally. But, paradoxically, Chapone seems to share Godwin's view that historical writing can affect us in those ways—otherwise, why would her readers need to turn away? The psychology of readers and the morals that historical writing should impart are concerns shared by each of the readings that follow.

ii   See *Essay concerning Human Understanding*, ed. Peter H. Nidditch (Oxford: Oxford University Press, 1975), 547 [4.3.18].

Chapter 9

Hester Chapone

ON THE MANNER AND COURSE OF READING HISTORY

Hester Chapone (1727–1801), "On the Manner and Course of Reading History", 1773, *Letters on the Improvement of the Mind* (H. Hughes for J. Walter, 1773), 185–92, 205–7, 209.

MY DEAR NIECE,

WHEN I recommend to you to gain some in sight into the general history of the world, perhaps you will think I propose a formidable task; but, your apprehensions will vanish, when you consider that of near half the globe we have no histories at all;—that, of other parts of it, a few facts only are known to us—and that, even of those nations, which make the greatest figure in history, the early ages are involved in obscurity and fable. It is not indeed allowable to be totally ignorant even of those fables, because they are the frequent subjects of poetry and painting, and are often referred to in more authentic histories.

The first recorders of actions are generally poets: in the historical songs of the bards are found the only accounts of the first ages of every state; but in these we must naturally expect to find truth mixed with fiction, and often disguised in allegory. In such early times, before science has enlightened the minds of men, the people are ready to believe every thing—and the historian, having no restraints from the fear of contradiction or criticism, delivers the most improbable and absurd tales as an account of the lives and actions of their forefathers: thus the first heroes of every nation are gods, or the sons of gods; and every great event is accompanied with some supernatural agency. Homer, whom I have already mentioned as a poet, you will find the most agreeable historian of the early ages of Greece—and Virgil will show you the supposed origin of the Carthaginians and Romans.

It will be necessary for you to observe some regular plan in your historical studies, which can never be pursued with advantage otherwise than in a continued series. I do not mean to confine you solely to that kind of reading—on the contrary, I wish you frequently to relax with poetry or some other amusement, whilst you are pursuing your course of history; I only mean to warn you against mixing *ancient* history with *modern*, or *general* histories of one place with *particular reigns* in another—by which desultory manner of reading, many people distract and confound their memories, and retain nothing to any purpose from such a confused mass of materials.

[. . .]

The want of memory is a great discouragement in historical pursuits, and is what every body complains of. Many artificial helps have been invented, of which, those who have tried them can best tell you the effects: but the most natural and pleasant expedient is that of conversation with a friend, who is acquainted with the history which you are reading. By such conversations, you will find out how much is usually retained of what is read, and you will learn to select those characters and facts which are best worth preserving; for, it is by trying to remember every thing without distinction, that young people are so apt to lose every trace of what they read. By repeating to your friend what you can recollect, you will fix it in your memory; and, if you should omit any striking particular, which ought to be retained, that friend will remind you of it, and will direct your attention to it on a second perusal. It is a good rule, to cast your eye each day over what you read the day before, and to look over the contents of every book when you have finished it.

Rollin's work takes in a large compass—but, of all the ancient nations it treats of, perhaps there are only the Grecians and Romans, whose stories ought to be read with any anxious desire of retaining them perfectly: for the rest—such as the Assyrians, Egyptians, &c.—I believe, you would find, on examination, that most of those, who are supposed tolerably well read in history, remember no more than a few of the most remarkable facts and characters. I tell you this, to prevent your being discouraged on finding so little remain in your mind after reading these less interesting parts of ancient history.

But, when you come to the Grecian and Roman stories, I expect to find you deeply interested and highly entertained; and, of consequence, eager to treasure up in your memory, those heroic actions and exalted characters, by which a young mind is naturally so much animated and impressed. As Greece and Rome were distinguished as much for genius as valour, and were the theatres, not only of the greatest military actions—the noblest efforts of liberty and patriotism—but of the highest perfection of arts and sciences, their immortal fame is a subject of wonder and emulation, even to these distant ages; and, it is thought a shameful degree of ignorance, even in our sex, to be unacquainted with the nature and revolutions of their governments, and with the characters and stories of their most illustrious heroes—Perhaps when you are told that the government and the national character of your own countrymen have been compared with those of the Romans, it may not be an useless amusement, in reading the Roman history, to carry this observation in your mind, and to examine how far the parallel holds good. The French have been thought to resemble the Athenians in their genius, though not in their love of liberty. These little hints sometimes serve to awaken reflection and attention in young readers—I leave you to make what use of them you please.

When you have got through Rollin, if you add *Vertot's Revolutions Romaines*—a short, and very entertaining work—you may be said to have read as much as is *absolutely necessary* of ancient history. Plutarch's Lives of famous Greeks and Romans—a book deservedly of the highest reputation—can never be read to so much advantage as immediately after the histories of Greece and Rome: I should even prefer reading each life in Plutarch, immediately after the history of each particular Hero, as you meet with them in Rollin or in Vertot.

If hereafter you should choose to enlarge your plan, and should wish to know more of any particular people or period than you find in Rollin, the sources from which he drew may be open to you—for there are, I believe, French or English translations of all the original historians, from whom he extracted his materials.

Crevier's continuation of Rollin, I believe, gives the best account of the Roman

emperors down to Constantine. What shocking instances, will you there meet with, of the terrible effects of lawless power on the human mind!—How will you be amazed to see the most promising characters changed by flattery and self-indulgence into monsters that disgrace humanity!—To read a series of such lives as those of Tiberius, Nero, or Domitian would be intolerable, were we not consoled by the view of those excellent emperors, who remained uncorrupted through all temptations. When the mind—disgusted, depressed, and terrified—turns from the contemplation of those depths of vice, to which the human nature may be sunk, a Titus, the delight of mankind—a Trajan—an Antoninus—restore it to an exulting sense of the dignity, to which that nature may be exalted by virtue. Nothing is more awful than this consideration: a human creature given up to vice is infinitely below the most abject brute; the same creature, trained by virtue to the utmost perfection of his nature, "is but a little lower than the angels, and is crowned with glory and immortality".
[. . .]

Thus much may suffice for that moderate scheme, which I think is best suited to your sex and age. There are several excellent histories, and memoirs of particular reigns and periods, which I have taken no notice of in this circumscribed plan—but with which, if you should happen to have a taste for the study, you will hereafter choose to be acquainted: these will be read with most advantage, after you have gained some general view of history—and they will then serve to refresh your memory, and settle your ideas distinctly, as well as enable you to compare different accounts of the persons and facts which they treat of, and to form your opinions of them on just grounds.

As I cannot, with certainty, foresee what degree of application or genius for such pursuits you will be mistress of, I shall leave the deficiencies of this collection to be supplied by the suggestions of your more informed friends—who, if you explain to them how far you wish to extend your knowledge, will direct you to the proper books.

But if, instead of an eager desire for this kind of knowledge, you should happen to feel that distaste for it, which is too common in young ladies, who have been indulged in reading only works of mere amusement, you will perhaps rather think that I want mercy in offering you so large a plan, than that there needs an apology for the deficiencies of it; but, comfort yourself with the assurance that a taste for history will grow and improve by reading: that as you get acquainted with one period or nation, your curiosity cannot fail to be awakened for what concerns those immediately connected with it; and thus, you will insensibly be led on, from one degree of knowledge to another.

If you waste in trivial amusement the next three of four years of your life, which are the prime season of improvement, believe me, you will hereafter bitterly regret their loss: when you come to feel yourself inferior in knowledge to almost every one you converse with—and, above all, if you should ever be a mother, when you feel your own inability to direct and assist the pursuits of your children—you will then find ignorance a severe mortification and a real evil. Let this, my dear, animate your industry—and let not a modest opinion of your own capacity be a discouragement to your endeavours after knowledge; a moderate understanding, with diligent and well-directed application, will go much farther than a more lively genius, if attended with that impatience and inattention, which too often accompanies quick parts. It is not from want of capacity that so many women are such trifling insipid companions—so ill qualified for the friendship and conversation of a sensible man—or for the task of governing and instructing a family; it is much oftener from the neglect of exercising the talents, which they really have, and from omitting to cultivate a taste for intellectual improvement: by this neglect, they lose the sincerest of pleasures: a pleasure, which would remain when almost every other forsakes them—which neither fortune nor age can deprive them of—and which would be a comfort and resource in almost every possible situation of life.
[. . .]

The studies, which I have recommended to you, must be likewise subservient to the same views: the pursuit of knowledge, when it is guided and controlled by the principles I have established, will conduce to many valuable ends: the habit of industry, it will give you—the nobler kind of friendships, for which it will qualify you, and its tendency to promote a candid and liberal way of thinking, are obvious advantages. I might add, that a mind well informed in the various pursuits which interest mankind, and the influence of such pursuits on their happiness, will embrace, with a clearer choice, and will more steadily adhere to, those principles of Virtue and Religion, which the judgment must ever approve, in proportion as it becomes enlightened.

Your most
affectionate Aunt.

Chapter 10

Henry Home, Lord Kames

ON IDEAL PRESENCE

Henry Home, Lord Kames (1696–1782), "On Ideal Presence", 1762, *Elements of Criticism* (London: Miller, 1762), Vol. 1, 104–18, 121–7.

Emotions caused by fiction

THE ATTENTIVE READER will observe, that in accounting for passions and emotions, no cause hitherto has been assigned but what hath a real existence. Whether it be a being, action, or quality, that moveth us, it is supposed to be an object of our knowledge, or at least of our belief. This observation discovers to us that the subject [of this study] is not yet exhausted; because our passions, as all the world know, are moved by fiction as well as by truth. In judging beforehand of man, so remarkably addicted to truth and reality, one should little dream that fiction could have any effect upon him. But man's intellectual faculties are too imperfect to dive far even into his own nature. [. . .]

That the objects of our senses really exist in the way and manner we perceive, is a branch of intuitive knowledge. When I see a man walking, a tree growing, or cattle grazing, I have a conviction that these things are precisely as they appear. If I be a spectator of any transaction or event, I have a conviction of the real existence of the persons engaged, of their words, and of their actions. Nature determines us to rely on the veracity of our senses. And indeed, if our senses did not convince us of the reality of their objects, they could not in any degree answer their end.

By the power of memory, a thing formerly seen may be recalled to the mind with different degrees of accuracy. We commonly are satisfied with a slight recollection of the chief circumstances; and, in such recollection, the 'thing is not figured as present nor any image formed. I retain the consciousness of my present situation, and barely remember that formerly I was a spectator. But with respect to an interesting object or event which made a strong impression, the mind sometimes, not satisfied with a cursory review, chuses to revolve every circumstance. In this case, I conceive myself to be a spectator as I was originally; and I perceive every particular passing in my presence, in the same manner as when I was in reality a spectator. For example, I saw yesterday a beautiful woman in tears for the loss of an only child, and was greatly moved with her distress. Not satisfied with a slight recollection or bare remembrance, I insist on the melancholy scene. Conceiving myself to be in the place where I was an eye-witness, every circumstance appears to me as at first. I think I see the woman in tears and hear her moans. Hence it may be justly said, that in a complete idea of memory there is no past nor future. A thing recalled to the mind with the accuracy I have been describing, is perceived as in our view, and consequently as presently existing. [. . .]

Lamentable is the imperfection of language, almost in every particular that falls not under external sense. I am talking of a matter exceeding clear in itself, and of which every person must be conscious; and yet I find no small difficulty to express it clearly in words; for it is not accurate to talk of incidents long past as passing in our sight, nor of hearing at present what we really heard yesterday or perhaps a year ago. To this necessity I am reduced, by want of proper words to describe ideal presence and to distinguish it from real presence. And thus in the description, a plain subject becomes obscure and intricate. When I recall any thing in the distinctest manner, so as to form an idea or image of it as present; I have not words to describe this act, other than that I perceive the thing as a spectator, and as existing in my presence. This means not that I am really a spectator; but only that I conceive myself to be a spectator, and have a consciousness of presence similar to what a real spectator hath.

As many rules of criticism depend on ideal presence, the reader, it is expected, will take some pains to form an exact notion of it, as distinguished on the one hand from real presence, and on the other from a superficial or reflective remembrance. It is distinguished from the former by the following circumstance. Ideal presence arising from an act of memory, may properly be termed *a waking dream*; because, like a dream, it vanisheth upon the first reflection of our present situation. Real presence, on the contrary, vouched by eye-sight, commands our belief, not only during the direct perception, but in reflecting after-ward upon the object. And to distinguish ideal presence from the latter, I give the following illustration. Two internal acts, both of them exertions of memory, are clearly distinguish-able. When I think of an event as past, without forming any image, it is barely reflecting or remembering that I was an eye-witness. But when I recall the event so distinctly as to form a complete image of it, I perceive it ideally as passing in my presence; and this ideal perception is an act of intuition, into which reflection enters not more than into an act of sight.

Though ideal presence be distinguished from real presence on the one side and from reflective remembrance on the other, it is however variable without any precise limits; rising sometimes toward the former, and often sinking toward the latter. In a vigorous exertion of memory, ideal presence is extremely distinct. When a man, as in a reverie, drops himself out of his thoughts, he perceives every thing as passing before him, and hath a consciousness of presence similar to that of a spectator. There is no other difference, but that in the former the consciousness of presence is less firm and clear than in the latter. But this is seldom the case. Ideal presence is often faint, and the image so obscure as not to differ widely from reflective remembrance.

Hitherto of an idea of memory. I proceed to consider the idea of a thing I never saw, raised in me by speech, by writing, or by painting. This idea, with respect to the present matter, is of the same nature with an idea of memory, being either complete or incomplete. An important event, by a lively and accurate description, rouses my attention and insensibly transforms me into a spectator: I perceive ideally every incident as passing in my presence. On the other hand, a slight or superficial narrative produceth only a faint and incomplete idea, precisely similar to a reflective recollection of memory. Of such idea, ideal presence makes no part. Past time is a circumstance that enters into this idea, as it doth into a reflective idea of memory. I believe that Scipio existed about 2000 years ago, and that he overcame Hannibal in the famous battle of Zama. When I revolve in so cursory a manner that memorable event, I consider it as long past. But supposing me to be warmed with the story, perhaps by a beautiful description, I am insensibly transformed to a spectator. I perceive these two heroes in act to engage; I perceive them brandishing their swords, and exhorting their troops; and in this manner I attend them through every circumstance of the battle. This event being present to my mind during the whole progress of my thoughts, admits not any time but the present.

I have had occasion to observe, that ideas both of memory and of speech, produce emotions of the same kind with what are produced by an immediate view of the object; only fainter, in proportion as an idea is fainter than an original perception. The insight we have now got, unfolds the means by which this effect is produced. Ideal presence supplies the want of real presence; and in idea we perceive persons acting and suffering, precisely as in an original survey. If our sympathy be engaged by the latter, it must also in some measure be engaged by the former. The distinctness of ideal presence, as above mentioned, approacheth sometimes to the distinctness of real presence; and the consciousness of presence is the same in both. This is the cause of the pleasure that is felt in a reverie, where a man, losing sight of himself, is totally occupied with the objects passing in his mind, which he conceives to be really existing in his presence. The power of speech to raise emotions, depends entirely on the artifice of raising such lively and distinct images as are here described. The reader's passions are never sensibly moved, till he be thrown into a kind of reverie; in which state, losing the consciousness of self, and of reading, his present occupation, he conceives every incident as passing in his presence, precisely as if he were an eye-witness. A general or reflective remembrance hath not this effect. It may be agreeable in some slight degree; but the ideas suggested by it, are too faint and obscure to raise any thing like a sympathetic emotion. And were they ever so lively, they pass with too much precipitation to have this effect. Our emotions are never instantaneous: even those that come the soonest to perfection, have different periods of birth, growth, and maturity; and to give opportunity for these different periods, it is necessary that the cause of every emotion be present to the mind a due time. The emotion is completed by reiterated impressions. We know this to be the case of objects of sight: we are scarce sensible of any emotion in a quick succession even of the most beautiful objects. And if this hold in the succession of original perceptions, how much more in the succession of ideas?

Though all this while, I have been only describing what passeth in the mind of every one and what every one must be conscious of, it was necessary to enlarge upon it; because, however clear in the internal conception, it is far from being so when described in words. Ideal presence, though of general importance, hath scarce ever been touched by any writer; and at any rate it could not be overlooked in accounting for the effects produced by fiction. Upon this point, the reader I guess has prevented me. It already must have occurred to him, that if, in reading, ideal presence be the means by which our passions are moved, it makes no difference whether the subject be a fable or a reality. When ideal presence is complete, we perceive every object as in our sight; and the mind, totally occupied with an interesting event, finds no leisure for reflection of any sort. [. . .]

In support of the foregoing theory, I add what I reckon a decisive argument. Upon examination it will be found, that genuine history commands our passions by means of ideal presence solely; and therefore that with respect to this effect, genuine history stands upon the same footing with fable. To me it appears clear, that our sympathy must vanish so soon as we begin to reflect upon the incidents related in either. The reflection that a story is a pure fiction, will indeed prevent our sympathy; but so will equally the reflection that the persons described are no longer existing. It is present distress only that moves my pity. My concern vanishes with the distress; for I cannot pity any person who at present is happy. According to this theory, founded clearly on human nature, a man long dead and insensible now of past misfortunes, cannot move our pity more than if he had never existed. The misfortunes described in a genuine history command our belief: but then we believe also, that these misfortunes are at an end, and that the persons described are at present under no distress. What effect, for example, can the belief of the rape of Lucretia have to raise our sympathy, when she died above 2000 years ago, and hath at present no painful feeling of the injury done her? The effect of history in point of instruction, depends in some measure upon its veracity. But history cannot reach the heart, while we indulge any reflection upon the facts. Such reflection, if it engage our belief, never fails at the same time to poison our pleasure, by convincing us that our sympathy for those who are dead and gone is absurd. And if reflection be laid aside, history stands upon the same footing with fable. What effect either of them may have to raise our sympathy, depends on the vivacity of the ideas they raise; and with respect to that circumstance, fable is generally more successful than history.

Of all the means for making an impression of ideal presence, theatrical representation is the most powerful. That words independent of action have the same power in a less degree, every one of sensibility must have felt: A good tragedy will extort tears in private, though not so forcibly as upon the stage. This power belongs also to painting. A good historical picture makes a deeper impression than can be made by words, though not equal to what is made by theatrical action. And as ideal presence depends on a lively impression, painting seems to possess a middle place betwixt reading and acting. In making an impression of ideal presence, it is not less superior to the former than inferior to the latter.

It must not however be thought, that our passions can be raised by painting to such a height as can be done by words. Of all the successive incidents that concur to produce a great event, a picture has the choice but of one, because it is confined to a single instant of time. And though the impression it makes, is the deepest that can be made instantaneously; yet seldom can a passion be raised to any height in an instant, or by a single impression. It was observed above, that our passions, those especially of the sympathetic kind, require a succession of impressions; and for that reason, reading and still more acting have greatly the advantage, by the opportunity of reiterating impressions without end.

Upon the whole, it is by means of ideal presence that our passions are excited; and till words produce that charm they avail nothing. Even real events intitled to our belief, must be conceived present and passing in our sight before they can move us.
[. . .]
       [. . .] Matters of fact, it is true, and truth in general, may be inculcated without taking advantage of ideal presence. But without it, the finest speaker or writer would in vain attempt to move any of our passion: our sympathy would be confined to objects that are really present: and language would lose entirely that signal power it possesseth, of making us sympathize with beings removed at the greatest distance of time as well as of place. Nor is the influence of language, by means of this ideal presence, confined to the heart. It reaches also in some measure the understanding, and contributes to belief. When events are related in a lively manner and every circumstance appears as passing before us, it is with difficulty that we suffer the truth of the facts to be questioned. A historian accordingly who hath a genius for narration, seldom fails to engage our belief. The same facts related in a manner cold and indistinct, are not suffered to pass without examination. A thing ill described, is like an object seen at a distance or through a mist: we doubt whether it be a reality or a fiction.
[. . .]
       For accomplishing the task undertaken in the beginning of the present section, what only remains is, to show the final cause of the power that fiction hath over the mind of man. I have already mentioned, that language, by means of fiction, has the command of our sympathy for the good of others. By the same means, our sympathy may be also raised for our own good. In the third section it [was] observed, that examples both of virtue and of vice

raise virtuous emotions; which becoming stronger by exercise, tend to make us virtuous by habit as well as by principle. I now further observe, that examples drawn from real events, are not so frequent as to contribute much to a habit of virtue. If they be, they are not recorded by historians. It therefore shows great wisdom, to form us in such a manner, as to be susceptible of the same improvement from fable that we receive from genuine history. By this admirable contrivance, examples to improve us in virtue may be multiplied without end. No other sort of discipline contributes more to make virtue habitual; and no other sort is so agreeable in the application. I add another final cause with thorough satisfaction; because it shows, that the author of our nature is not less kindly provident for the happiness of his creatures, than for the regularity of their conduct. The power that fiction hath over the mind of man, is the source of an endless variety of refined amusement, always ready to employ a vacant hour. Such amusement is a fine resource in solitude; and by sweetening the temper, improves society.

Chapter 11

William Godwin

OF HISTORY AND ROMANCE

William Godwin (1756–1836), "Of History and Romance", 1797, *Caleb Williams,* Maurice Hindle (ed.) (Harmondsworth: Penguin, 1988), 359–73.

THE STUDY OF HISTORY may well be ranked among those pursuits which are most worthy to be chosen by a rational being.

The study of history divides itself into two principal branches; the study of mankind in a mass, of the progress, the fluctuations, the interests and the vices of society; and the study of the individual.

The history of a nation might be written in the first of these senses, entirely in terms of abstraction, and without descending so much as to name one of those individuals of which the nation is composed.

It is curious, and it is important, to trace the progress of mankind from the savage to the civilised state; to observe the points of similitude between the savages of America and the savages of ancient Italy or Greece; to investigate the rise of property moveable to immoveable; and thus to ascertain the causes that operate universally upon masses of men under given circumstances, without being turned aside in their operation by the varying character of individuals.

The fundamental article in this branch of historical investigation, is the progress and varieties of civilisation. But there are many subordinate channels into which it has formed itself. We may study the history of eloquence or the history of philosophy. We may apply ourselves to the consideration of the arts of life, and the arts of refinement and pleasure. There lie before us the history of wealth and the history of commerce. We may study the progress of revenue and the arts of taxation. We may follow the varieties of climates, and trace their effect on the human body and the human mind. Nay, we may descend still lower; we may [. . .] apply ourselves entirely to the examination of medals and coins.

There are those who conceive that history, in one or all the kinds here enumerated, is the only species of history deserving a serious attention. They disdain the records of individuals. To interest our passions, or employ our thoughts about personal events, be they of patriots, of authors, of heroes or kings, they regard as a symptom of effeminacy. Their mighty minds cannot descend to be busied about anything less than the condition of nations, and the collation and comparison of successive ages. Whatever would disturb by exciting our feelings the torpid tranquillity of the soul, they [hold] in unspeakable abhorrence.

It is to be feared that one of the causes that have dictated the panegyric which has so often been pronounced upon this species of history, is its dry and repulsive nature. Men who by persevering exertions have conquered a subject in defiance of innumerable obstacles, will almost always be able to ascribe to it a disproportionate value. Men who have not done this, often imagine they shall acquire at a cheap rate among the ignorant the reputation of profound, by praising, in the style of an adept, that which few men venture so much as to approach. Difficulty has a tendency to magnify to almost all eyes the excellence of that which only through difficulty can be attained.

The mind of man does not love abstractions. Its genuine and native taste, as it discovers itself in children and uneducated persons, rests entirely in individualities. It is only by perseverance and custom that we are brought to have a relish for philosophy, mathematical, natural or moral. There was a time when the man, now most eagerly attached to them, shrunk with terror from their thorny path.

But the abstractions of philosophy, when we are grown familiar with them, often present to our minds a simplicity and precision, that may well supply the place of entire individuality. The abstractions of history are more cumbrous and unwieldy. In their own nature perhaps they are capable of simplicity. But this species of science is yet in its infancy. He who would study the history of nations abstracted from individuals whose passions and peculiarities are interesting to our minds, will find it a dry and frigid science. It will supply him with no clear ideas. The mass, as fast as he endeavours to cement and unite it, crumbles from his grasp, like a lump of sand. Those who study revenue or almost any other of the complex subjects above enumerated are ordinarily found, with immense pains to have compiled a species of knowledge which is no sooner accumulated than it perishes, and rather to have confounded themselves with a labyrinth of particulars, than to have risen to the dignity of principles.

Let us proceed to the consideration of the second great branch of the study of society. In doing so we shall be insensibly led to assign to the first branch its proper rank.

The study of individual men can never fail to be an object of the highest importance. It is only by comparison that we come to know any thing of mind or ourselves. We go forth into the world; we see what man is; we enquire what he was; and when we return home to engage in the solemn act of self-investigation, our most useful employment is to produce the materials we have collected abroad, and, by a sort of magnetism, cause those particulars to start out to view in ourselves, which might otherwise have lain for ever undetected.

But the study of individual history has a higher use than merely as it conduces to the elucidation of science. It is the most fruitful source of activity and motive. If a man were condemned to perfect solitude, he would probably sink into the deepest and most invariable lethargy of soul. If he only associate, as most individuals are destined to do, with ordinary men, he will be in danger of becoming such as they are. It is the contemplation of illustrious men, such as we find scattered through the long succession of ages, that kindles into a flame the hidden fire within us. The excellence indeed of sages, of patriots and poets, as we find it exhibited at the end of their maturity, is too apt to overwhelm and discourage us with its lustre. But history takes away the cause of our depression. It enables us to view minutely and in detail what to the uninstructed eye was too powerful to be gazed at; and, by tracing the progress of the virtuous and the wise from its first dawn to its meridian lustre, shows us that they were composed of materials merely human. [. . .] While we admire the poet and the hero, and sympathise with his generous ambition or his ardent exertions, we insensibly imbibe the same spirit, and burn with kindred fires.

But let us suppose that the genuine purpose of history, was to enable us to understand

how history can be repeated

the machine of society, and to direct it to its best purposes. Even here individual history will perhaps be found in point of importance to take the lead of general. General history will furnish us precedents in abundance, will show us how that which happened in one country has been repeated in another, and may perhaps even instruct us how that which has occurred in the annals of mankind, may under similar circumstances be produced again. But, if the energy of our minds should lead us to aspire to something more animated and noble than dull repetition, if we love the happiness of mankind enough to feel ourselves impelled to explore new and untrodden paths, we must then not rest contented with considering society in a mass, but must analyse the materials of which it is composed. It will be necessary for us to scrutinise the nature of man, before we can pronounce what it is of which social man is capable. Laying aside the generalities of historical abstraction, we must mark the operation of human passions; must observe the empire of motives whether grovelling or elevated; and must note the influence that one human being exercises over another, and the ascendancy of the daring and the wise over the vulgar multitude. It is thus, and thus only, that we shall be enabled to add, to the knowledge of the past, a sagacity that can penetrate into the depths of futurity. We shall not only understand those events as they arise which are no better than old incidents under new names, but shall judge truly of such conjunctures and combinations, their sources and effects, as, though they have never yet occurred, are within the capacities of our nature. He that would prove the liberal and spirited benefactor of his species, must connect the two branches of history together, and regard the knowledge of the individual, as that which can alone give energy and utility to the records of our social existence.

From these considerations one inference may be deduced, which constitutes perhaps the most important rule that can be laid down respecting the study of history. This is, the wisdom of studying the detail, and not in abridgement. The prolixity of dullness is indeed contemptible. But the copiousness of wisdom and genius is treasure inestimable. To read a history which, expanding itself through several volumes, treats only of a short period, is true economy. To read historical abridgements, in which each point of the subject is touched upon only, and immediately dismissed, is a wanton prodigality of time worthy only of folly or of madness.

The figures which present themselves in such a history, are like the groups that we sometimes see placed in the distance of a landscape, that are just sufficiently marked to distinguish the man from the brute, or the male from the female, but are totally unsusceptible of discrimination of form or expression of sentiment. The men I would study upon the canvas of history, are men worth the becoming intimately acquainted with.

It is in history, as it is in life. Superficial acquaintance is nothing. A scene incessantly floating, cannot instruct us; it can scarcely become a source of amusement to a cultivated mind. I would stop the flying figures, that I may mark them more clearly. There must be an exchange of real sentiments, or an investigation of subtle peculiarities, before improvement can be the result. There is a magnetical virtue in man, but there must be friction and heat, before the virtue will operate.

Pretenders indeed to universal science, who examine nothing, but imagine they understand everything, are ready from the slightest glance to decipher the whole character. Not so the genuine scholar. His curiosity is never satiated. He is ever upon the watch for further and still further particulars. Trembling for his own fallibility and frailty, he employs every precaution to guard himself against them.

There are characters in history that may almost be said to be worth an eternal study. They are epitomes of the best and most exalted features, purified from their grossness. I am not contented to observe such a man upon the public stage, I would follow him into his closet. I would see the friend and the father of a family, as well as the patriot. I would read his works and his letters, if any remain to us. I would observe the turn of his thoughts and the character of his phraseology. I would study his public orations. I would collate his behaviour in prosperity with his behaviour in adversity. I should be glad to know the course of his studies, and the arrangement of his time. I should rejoice to have, or to be enabled to make, if that were possible, a journal of his ordinary and minutest actions. I believe I should be better employed in this studying one man, than in perusing the abridgement of Universal History in sixty volumes. I would rather be acquainted with a few trivial particulars of the actions and dispositions of Virgil and Horace, than with the lives of many men, and the history of many nations.

This leads us to a second rule respecting the study of history. Those historians alone are worthy of attention and persevering study that treat of the development of great genius, or the exhibition of bold and masculine virtues. Modern history indeed we ought to peruse, because all that we wish must be connected with all that we are, and because it is incumbent upon us to explore the means by which the latter may be made, as it were, to slide into the former. But modern history, for the most part, is not to be perused for its own sake.

The ancients were giants, but we, their degenerate successors, are pygmies. There was something in the nature of the Greek and Roman republics that expanded and fired the soul. He that sees not this, if he have had an adequate opportunity to see it, must be destitute of some of the first principles of discrimination. He that feels not the comparative magnitude of their views, must be himself the partaker of a slow-working and unelevated soul.

To convince us of this, we need do no more than look into the biographical collection of Plutarch [AD 46–120]. Plutarch is neither lucid in his arrangement, eloquent in his manner, nor powerful in his conceptions. The effect he produces upon us, is the effect of his subject, and is scarcely in any respect aided by the skill of the writer.

[. . .]

The ancients on the other hand are men of a free and undaunted spirit. There is a conscious dignity in their mien that impresses us with awe. Whatever they undertake they undertake with a full and undivided soul. They proceed to their object with an unerring aim, and do not lose themselves in dark, inexplicable windings. He that shall study their history with an unbiassed spirit, will almost imagine that he is reading of a different species. He will not be blind to their mistakes, their abuses and their crimes, but he will confess that their minds are of a more decisive character, and their virtues more attractive and sublime.

We are sometimes told that the remoteness of the object in this case misleads us, and that we admire the ancients for this reason merely, because they are ancients. But this solution will not account for the phenomenon. Read on the one hand Thucydides and Livy, and on the other Hume and Voltaire and Robertson. When we admire the personages of the former, we simply enter into the feelings with which these authors recorded them. The latter neither experience such emotions nor excite them. The ancients were not ancients to their contemporaries,

> Les anciens étaient contemporains de leurs historiens, et nous ont pourtant appris à les admires. Assurément si la postérité jamais admire les nôtres, elle ne l'ausa pas appris de nous. [The ancients were their historians' contemporaries, and we have learned to admire them. Assuredly, if posterity ever admires our historians, it will not have learned to do so from us.]
>
> Rousseau: *Nouvelle Héloise*, Lettre XII

No: the difference is intrinsic, and the emotions will be generated as long as history endures.

[. . .]

Some persons, endowed with too much discernment and taste not to perceive the extreme disparity that subsists between the character of ancient and of modern times, have observed that ancient history carries no other impression to their minds than that of exaggeration and fable.

It is not necessary here to enter into a detail of the evidence upon which our belief of ancient history is founded. Let us take it for granted that it is a fable. Are all fables unworthy of regard? Ancient history, says Rousseau, is a tissue of such fables, as have a moral perfectly adapted to the human heart. I ask not, as a principal point, whether it be true or false? My first enquiry is, 'Can I derive instruction from it? Is it a genuine praxis upon the nature of man? Is it pregnant with the most generous motives and the most fascinating examples? If so, I had rather be profoundly versed in this fable, than in all the genuine histories that ever existed.'

It must be admitted indeed that all history bears too near a resemblance to fable. Nothing is more uncertain, more contradictory, more unsatisfactory than the evidence of facts. If this be the case in courts of justice, where truth is sometimes sifted with tenacious perseverance, how much more will it hold true of the historian? He can administer no oath, he cannot issue his precept, and summon his witnesses from distant provinces, he cannot arraign his personages and compel them to put in their answer. He must take what they choose to tell, the broken fragments, and the scattered ruins of evidence.

That history which comes nearest to truth, is the mere chronicle of facts, places and dates. But this is in reality no history. He that knows only on what day the Bastille was taken and on what spot Louis XVI perished, knows nothing. He professes the mere skeleton of history. The muscles, the articulations, every thing in which the life emphatically resides, is absent.

Read Sallust [86–34 BC]. To every action he assigns a motive. Rarely an uncertainty diversifies his page. He describes his characters with preciseness and decision. He seems to enter into the hearts of his personages, and unfolds their secret thoughts. Considered as fable, nothing can be more perfect. But neither is this history.

There is but one further mode of writing history, and this is the mode principally prevalent in modern times. In this mode, the narrator is sunk in the critic. The main body of the composition consists of a logical deduction and calculation of probabilities. This species of writing may be of use as a whetstone upon which to sharpen our faculty of discrimination, but it answers none of the legitimate purposes of history.

From these considerations it follows that the noblest and most excellent species of history, may be decided to be a composition in which, with a scanty substratum of facts and dates, the writer interweaves a number of happy, ingenious and instructive inventions, blending them into one continuous and indiscernible mass. It sufficiently corresponds with the denomination, under which Abbé Prévost [novelist, 1697–1763] acquired considerable applause, of historical romance. Abbé Prévost differs from Sallust, inasmuch as he made freer use of what may be styled, the *licentia historica*.

If then history be little better than romance under a graver name, it may not be foreign to the subject here treated, to enquire into the credit due to that species of literature, which bears the express stamp of invention, and calls itself romance or novel.

This sort of writing has been exposed to more obloquy and censure than any other.

The principal cause of this obloquy is sufficiently humorous and singular.

Novels, as an object of trade among booksellers, are of a peculiar cast. There are few by which immense sums of money can be expected to be gained. There is scarcely one by which some money is not gained. A class of readers, consisting of women and boys, and which is considerably numerous, requires a continual supply of books of this sort. The circulating libraries therefore must be furnished; while, in consequence of the discredit which has fallen upon romance, such works are rarely found to obtain a place in the collection of the gentleman or the scholar. An ingenious bookseller of the metropolis, speculating upon this circumstance, was accustomed to paste an advertisement in his window, to attract the eye of the curious passenger, and to fire his ambition, by informing him of a 'want of novels for the ensuing season'.

The critic and the moralist, in their estimate of romances, have borrowed the principle that regulates the speculations of trade. They have weighed novels [as a genre] and taken into their view the whole scum and surcharge of the press. But surely this is not the way in which literature would teach us to consider the subject.

When we speak of poetry, we do not fear to commend this species of composition, regardless of the miserable trash that from month to month finds its way from the press under the appellation of poetry. The like may be said of history, or of books of philosophy, natural and intellectual. There is no species of literature that would stand this ordeal.

If I would estimate truly any head of composition, nothing can be more unreasonable, than for me to take into account every pretender to literature that has started in it. In poetry I do not consider those persons who merely know how to count their syllables and tag a rhyme; still less those who print their effusion in the form of verse without being adequate to either of these. I recollect those authors only who are endowed with some of the essentials of poetry, with its imagery, its enthusiasm, or its empire over the soul of man. Just so in the cause before us, I should consider only those persons who had really written romance, not those who had vainly attempted it.

Romance then, strictly considered, may be pronounced to be one of the species of history. The difference between romance and what ordinarily bears the denomination history, is this. The historian is confined to individual incident and individual man, and must hang upon that his invention or conjecture as he can. The writer collects his materials from all sources, experience, report, and the records of human affairs; then generalises them; and finally selects, from their elements and the various combinations they afford, those instances which he is best qualified to portray, and which he judges most calculated to impress the heart and improve the faculties of his reader. In this point of view we should be apt to pronounce that romance was a bolder species of composition than history.

It has been affirmed by the critics that the species of composition which Abbé Prévost and others have attempted, and according to which, upon a slight substratum of fact, all the license of romantic invention is to be engrafted, is contrary to the principles of a just taste. History is by this means debauched and corrupted. Real characters are wantonly misrepresented. The reader, who has been interested by a romance of this sort, scarcely knows how to dismiss it from his mind when he comes to consider the genuine annals of the period to which it relates. The reality and the fiction, like two substances of disagreeing natures, will never adequately blend with each other. The invention of the writer is much too wanton not to discolour and confound the facts with which he is concerned; while on the other hand, his imagination is fettered and checked at every turn by facts that will not wholly accommodate themselves to the colour of his piece, or the moral he would adduce from it.

These observations, which have been directed against the production of historical romance, will be found not wholly inapplicable to those which assume the graver and more authentic name of history. The reader will be miserably deluded if, while he reads history, he suffers himself to imagine that he is reading facts. Profound scholars are so well aware of this, that, when they would study the history of any country, they pass over the historians that have adorned and decorated the facts, and proceed at once to the naked and scattered materials, out of which the historian constructed his work. This they do, that they may investigate the story for themselves; or, more accurately speaking, that each man, instead of resting in the inventions of another, may invent his history for himself, and possess his creed as he possesses his property, single and incommunicable.

Philosophers, we are told, have been accustomed by old prescription to blunder in the dark; but there is perhaps no darkness, if we consider the case maturely, so complete as that of the historian. It is a trite observation, to say that the true history of a public transaction is never known till many years after the event. The places, the dates, those things which immediately meet the eye of the spectator, are indeed as well known as they are ever likely to be. But the comments of the actors come out afterwards; to what are we the wiser? Whitlock and Clarendon,[i] who lived upon the spot, differ as much in their view of the transactions, as Hume and the whig historians have since done. Yet all are probably honest. If you be a superficial thinker, you will take up with one or other of their representations, as best suits your prejudices. But, if you are a profound one, you will see so many incongruities and absurdities in all, as deeply to impress you with the scepticism of history.

The man of taste and discrimination, who has properly weighed these causes, will be apt to exclaim, 'Dismiss me from the falsehood and impossibility of history, and deliver me over to the reality of romance.'

The conjectures of the historian must be built upon a knowledge of the characters of his personages. But we never know any man's character. My most intimate and sagacious friend continually misapprehends my motives. He is in most cases a little worse judge of them than myself and I am perpetually mistaken. The materials are abundant for the history of Alexander, Caesar, Cicero and Queen Elizabeth. Yet how widely do the best informed persons differ respecting them? Perhaps by all their character is misrepresented. The conjectures therefore respecting their motives in each particular transaction must be eternally fallacious. The writer of romance stands in this respect upon higher ground. He must be permitted, we should naturally suppose, to understand the character which is the creature of his own fancy.

The writer of romance then is to be considered as the writer of real history; while he who was formerly called the historian, must be contented to step down into the place of his rival, with this disadvantage, that he is a romance writer, without the arduous, the enthusiastic and the sublime licence of imagination, that belong to that species of composition. True history consists in a delineation of consistent, human character, in a display of the manner in which such a character acts under successive circumstances, in showing how character increases and assimilates new substances to its own, and how it decays, together with the catastrophe into which by its own gravity it naturally declines.

There is however, after all, a deduction to be made from this eulogium of the romance writer. To write romance is a task too great for the powers of man, and under which he must be expected to totter. No man can hold the rod so even, but that it will tremble and vary from its course. To sketch a few bold outlines of character is no desperate undertaking; but to tell precisely how such a person would act in a given situation, requires a sagacity scarcely less than divine. We never conceive a situation, or those minute shades in a character that would modify its conduct. Naturalists tell us that a single grain of sand more or less on the surface of the earth, would have altered its motion, and, in process of ages, have diversified its events. We have no reason to suppose in this respect, that what is true in matter, is false in morals.

Here then the historian in some degree, though imperfectly, seems to recover his advantage upon the writer of romance. He indeed does not understand the character he

---

i   Bulstrode Whitelocke (1605–75), politician and friend of Robert Hyde, first earl of Clarendon (1609–1679), politician and defender of popular causes [-Ed.].

exhibits, but the events are taken out of his hands and determined by the system of the universe, and therefore, as far as his information extends, must be true. The romance writer, on the other hand, is continually straining at a foresight to which his faculties are incompetent, and continually fails. This is ludicrously illustrated in those few romances which attempt to exhibit the fictitious history of nations. That principle only which holds the planets in their course, is competent to produce that majestic series of events which characterises flux, and successive multitudes.

The result of the whole, is that the sciences and the arts of man are alike imperfect, and almost infantine. He that will not examine the collections and the efforts of man, till absurdity and folly are extirpated from among them, must be contented to remain in ignorance, and wait for the state, where he expects that faith will give place to sight, and conjecture be swallowed up in knowledge.

Chapter 12

Mark Salber Phillips

RELOCATING INWARDNESS: HISTORICAL DISTANCE AND THE TRANSITION FROM ENLIGHTENMENT TO ROMANTIC HISTORIOGRAPHY

Mark Salber Phillips, "Relocating Inwardness: Historical Distance and the Transition from Enlightenment to Romantic Historiography." *PMLA* 118 (2003): 436–9; 442–9.

> The perusal of a history seems a calm entertainment; but would be no entertainment at all, did not our hearts beat with correspondent movements to those which are described by the historian.
> —David Hume, *An Enquiry concerning the Principles of Morals* (1751 [112])

> [D]id any one ever gain from Hume's history anything like a picture of what may actually have been passing, in the minds, say, of Cavaliers or of Round-heads during the civil wars? Does any one feel that Hume has made him figure to himself with any precision what manner of men these were; how far they were like ourselves, how far different; what things they loved and hated, and what sort of conception they had formed of the things they loved and hated? And what kind of a notion can be framed of a period of history, unless we begin with that as a preliminary?
> —John Stuart Mill, "Carlyle's *French Revolution*" (1837 [135–36])

SOME OF THE MOST intriguing problems in intellectual history arise out of juxtapositions like the one presented in my two epigraphs. Both the eighteenth-century historian and his nineteenth-century critic appear to have an equal commitment to the importance of emotional engagement in the writing of history. Nevertheless, since Mill's remarks are part of an extended diatribe against the unsympathizing qualities of the histor-ians of the previous age, these two apparently similar declarations evidently conceal a deep disagreement about the nature and purposes of historical narrative. Clearly, if despite Hume's protestations about the importance of the emotions, Mill and his contemporaries found eighteenth-century writing bloodless and abstract, it was because they sought a different kind of engagement in the writing of history.

Hostility to the work of the previous age served an obvious purpose for the Enlightenment's immediate successors (for ease of reference I will simply call them Romantics), but the accusation Mill brought against Hume and his contemporaries has continued to be raised by more recent critics. From R. G. Collingwood to Hayden White,[1] philosophers and historians have repeated Mill's complaint, and even those more sympathetic to the historical thought of the Enlightenment have generally interested themselves primarily in its speculative and abstract qualities, neglecting the sympathetic element evident in my quotation from Hume. The result, inevitably, has been to accentuate the sense of a sharp divide between the two periods, reinscribing in modern accounts the antagonism between Romantic inwardness and Enlightenment abstraction that is such an important part of the Romantics' reaction against their predecessors.

The nineteenth century's rejection of an allegedly ahistorical Enlightenment has often been taken as a founding moment of a modern historical understanding—indeed of modernity itself. A more careful reading of eighteenth-century historical writing, however, suggests some lines of continuity that the Romantic generation was less likely to appreciate. In fact, *pace* Mill and later critics, the historiography of the eighteenth century was deeply interested in engaging the reader's emotions to promote sympathy with the events and experiences of other times. This was, after all, an age of sensibility as well as of enlightenment. Nor was the sentimentalism a superficial feature of historical writing, a matter merely of style or passing literary fashion. On the contrary, the Enlightenment's preoccupation with sympathy and inwardness, no less than its often discussed conjectural method, expressed the central preoccupation of eighteenth-century historical thought, which was the desire to frame a new kind of history that would encompass a much wider view of social life.

In this essay, I explore the continuities and discontinuities between these two periods. A short discussion of a theoretical character will take us away from the eighteenth century for a while, but it permits a more precise analysis of what changed and what remained essentially the same in the shift from the inwardness of sensibility to that of Romanticism.

Historical distance

Questions of distance have been debated in a number of disciplines, including aesthetics, narratology, theater, political sociology, and anthropology. Among a long list of notable discussions of social, conceptual, or aesthetic distance, one might pick out Edward Bullough's idea of "the aesthetic attitude," Victor Shklovsky's "estrangement," Bertolt Brecht's "alienation effects," Karl Mannheim's "social distance," Norbert Elias's "civilizing process," Georg Simmel's "stranger," Mieke Bal's "focalization," or Johannes Fabian's "refusal of coevalness." History, however, has largely escaped this kind of discussion—though Friedrich Nietzsche's *On the Advantage and Disadvantage of History for Life* stands as a brilliant exception.[2] Even so, the construction of relations of engagement and detachment, proximity and distance would seem to be a central issue for all kinds of historical description—including historical representation in biography, museums, and film, as well as in traditional genres of historical writing. The reason for this silence, I suggest, is that a prescriptive idea of historical distance has become so incorporated in our common understandings of history that the idea has been lost to view. Like our way of constructing pictorial space since the Renaissance, historical distance now seems something given, not constructed—a natural way of marking the procession of time, not the outcome of a specific tradition of historical thought. Indeed, our commitment to a certain kind of detachment has become so incorporated into the discipline that the idea of historical distance seems hardly distinguishable from the idea of history itself.

Though practice, in fact, has been far more flexible than prescription, historians generally greet the idea of distance in strongly positive terms. Often called objectivity, distance is assumed to be a function of temporality, a clarity of vision that comes with the passage of time. This view of historical distance, however, is only a starting point, since it must be evident that every history faces the task of positioning its audience in relation to a past. Thus distance is not simply given but also constructed, and the range of distance constructions is broad. It comprehends all points along a gradient of distance, including immediacy as well as detachment. (We have no trouble recognizing that both a bungalow and a skyscraper have height; equally, we can say that every representation of the past manipulates distance, however foreshortened or extended.) Distance refers not only to matters of form or rhetoric but also to other significant dimensions of engagement or disengagement. As a result, questions about distance can be directed to a history's ideological implication as well as to its affective coloration, to its cognitive assumptions as well as to its formal traits.

If every history must position its readers in some relation of proximity or detachment to the past it describes, the issue of distance is as relevant to the long history of historical writing as it is to recent practice. Thus, if a strong attachment to both the methods and the rhetoric of analytic distance informs the work of Fernand Braudel or Eric Hobsbawm, what comparisons might we make to the writings of Adam Ferguson or Henry Thomas Buckle? If contemporary readers are drawn to the intriguing microhistories of Carlo Ginzburg or to the literary vivacity of Simon Schama, surely other audiences were drawn to similar qualities in the histories of their own day. Romantic narratives will quickly come to mind—Thomas Carlyle's *Past and Present*, for instance, or Jules Michelet's *Le peuple*—but we might also think of works in the chronicling tradition, like Dino Compagni's powerful eyewitness account of Florentine politics in the time of Dante or perhaps that most influential work of English historiography, John Foxe's *Acts and Monuments*.

These last examples indicate that the questions of presence and distance I am raising are not confined to genres we now regard as canonically historiographical. Not only chronicle and martyrology but also biography and memoir often carry with them a particular sense of immediacy, and the same is true for local history, family history, and much literary history. By the same token, antiquarianism, universal history, and encyclopedic writing are generally presented in the impersonal tones of disinterested inquiry. Indeed, if we press the question, it is soon apparent that tacit assumptions about distantiation and proximity are a key element in the way in which we distinguish the various historiographical genres. The distinctions we draw among history, memoir, and journalism or between microhistory and general history surely depend on the ability of audiences to recognize and accept assumptions of this kind. And what is the currently fashionable contrast between history and memory if not a problem of distance?

Nor is there any reason to limit the discussion to textual representations. Though they employ different vocabularies, history painting, photography, and documentary film all raise similar questions. Museums, too, with their combination of concrete materials and a public setting, present some of the issues in their most tangible and accessible form. Few readers of Emmanuel LeRoy Ladurie's *Montaillou* or Laurel Thatcher Ulrich's *The Midwife's Tale*, for example, are likely to reflect on the sentimental attractions of microhistory, but it takes no special museological awareness to spot parallel changes that have been taking place in historical and anthropological museums over the past generation. When faced with the varied displays of London's Imperial War Museum, for example, visitors can easily distinguish the traditional mahogany-and-glass cases filled with swords and military uniforms from newer displays like *The Trench Experience* or *The Blitz Experience*, where (as the titles indicate) we are invited to relive a specific moment or milieu from the past.

The parallel between written microhistory and recent museum practice suggests some characteristic features of recent historical sensibilities, especially our pervasive interest in everyday experience and affective proximity. Nevertheless, at any given moment of historical thought, we should not expect to find a consistent stance either of engagement or detachment. Even in the scope of a single work, distance is not a simple matter; rather, it is a variable and complex effect, shaped by balances or tensions among a variety of separable aspects of narrative construction and social or intellectual commitment. In the case of the War Museum, for example, an analysis of the Blitz exhibition would need to raise separate questions about formal vocabulary, affective coloration, and ideological implication. And beyond these aspects of distance there remains another dimension of our relation to the past that is concerned with what, at any given time, we judge to be most capable of explanation or understanding. This matter of cognitive distance surely plays an important part in establishing historical perspective, and, like the other dimensions of distance I have outlined, it is part of the complex interplay of engagements that marks the historical outlook of a given period.

These different kinds of distances do not stand in fixed or predetermined relations; on the contrary, it is worth the effort to separate the affective from the ideological or the ideological from the cognitive, because each of these dimensions makes its own contribution to the reader's experience. Nor are the formal devices of narrative always used for the same purposes. Close-up description, for example, is often pursued as a way of enlisting the reader's sympathies in a political cause, as Edward Thompson explicitly does in "seeking to rescue the poor stockinger, the Luddite cropper, the 'obsolete' hand-loom weaver . . . from the enormous condescension of posterity" (12). Yet detailed narration is not always a strategy for creating sympathy, nor is immediacy in description always paired with ideological identification. The grisly description of the dismemberment of Damien the regicide that opens Michel Foucault's *Discipline and Punish* is not calculated to make us identify with the criminal or to spur us to sympathy with efforts of penal reform; on the contrary, this horrific description is intended to shock us into abandoning our comfort with other, much more familiar regimes of punishment. In these terms, the graphic description of Damien's death spectacle serves as a kind of Brechtian alienation effect. It is intended to force on us the detachment necessary to recognize what is at stake in other forms of punishment, specifically what Foucault saw as a new regime of surveillance instituted by the reforms of the Enlightenment.

[. . .]

Hume on tragedy and historical distance

In a striking passage in the essay "Of Tragedy," [1757] Hume wrote that when Clarendon, the great historian of the English Revolution, approaches the execution of the king, he "hurries over the king's death, without giving one circumstance of it." Clarendon evidently

> considers it as too horrid a scene to be contemplasted with any satisfaction, or even without the utmost pain and aversion. He himself, as well as the readers of that age, were too deeply concerned in the events, and felt a pain from subjects, which an historian and a reader of another age would regard as the most pathetic and most interesting, and, by consequence, the most agreeable.
>
> (*Essays* 223–24)

Hume's subject in this essay is an old question in literary criticism: why tragedy pleases.[3] In this context, his reference to history, though surely indicative of a wider interest, is brief and tantalizing. Even so, his sympathetic understanding of Clarendon's reticence, combined with his clear sense that the event that was most painful to an earlier generation has become most "interesting" to his own, points to an intriguing awareness of the ductility of historical distance. Despite the brevity of his remarks, Hume gives more than a hint of the many-sidedness of the subject.

First, there is the important issue of variability, which Hume put at the center of his discussion. He clearly accepts that both Clarendon and his audience found themselves in a kind of proximity to the regicide that ruled out some possible representations of the event, especially (we surmise) the kind of detailed, pathetic treatment that Hume would offer his readers in the *History of England*. The implication is that variation in distance should not be considered a fault; rather, change in historical perspective is not only legitimate but also inevitable. This sense is reinforced by the suggestion that the alteration has little to do with the historian's individual preferences, being as much a property of the audience as of the writer.

Second, Hume recognized that distance must be considered both as a reflection of something occurring outside the text and as a construction that operates within the text to shape the emotional responses of the reader. Clearly, we can understand the change in distance that separates Clarendon's sense of history from Hume's only if we consider the difference in experience between their two generations. But if the passage of time has led to new political perceptions, the result will be registered as much in the form and rhetoric of the narrative as in its content. Clarendon's account was appropriate for its age, but no one now, Hume seems to say, could rest content with its hurried, uncircumstantial narrative; the contemporary reader, attracted by the pathos of the story, would be eager to hear the tragedy unfold in all its evocative detail.

Third, the literary context of Hume's discussion is important. Unlike those essays that deal with issues of history, politics, or political economy, "Of Tragedy" specifically addresses a tradition of belles lettres. The question of tragedy's power to move the emotions goes back, of course, to Aristotle's discussion of catharsis in the *Poetics*, but Hume's real interlocutors in this essay are Jean-Baptiste Dubos and Bernard Fontenelle, two key figures in French beletrist tradition. Hume does not initially come to Clarendon's writing from a historiographical concern; instead, he approaches the issue of historical distance from within a tradition of letters that has long been interested in literature's power to engage the emotions. The discussion of tragedy seems to have helped him see an analogy in history, and to a large extent he has simply extended an established question to a new genre[4]—though in doing so he has also expanded the issue in important ways that are appropriate to his preoccupation with historical writing.[5]

The complexities of distance in eighteenth-century narratives

Hume emphasized the emotional impact of historical narrative, but at bottom the stakes were as much ideological as affective. If Clarendon's avoidance of this "infinitely disagreeable" subject had an evident political meaning (223), so must the fact that a later reader could regard the same events as "pathetic" and "agreeable." This layering of one kind of distance over another—formal, affective, ideological, and (ultimately) cognitive—reminds us not to think of distance as a single, unitary dimension. Instead, as we explore the theory and practice of historical writing in the eighteenth century, we need to be alert to the variety of distances in play and the different ways in which they may combine.

Looked at in this way, the problem of understanding eighteenth-century historiography becomes a matter of reconciling different postures in relation to the past—postures that often appear in the same author and even in the same text. On the one hand, there was a strong impulse in the Enlightenment to approach history as a kind of laboratory for establishing a naturalistic science of humankind. The result was a generalizing spirit that later critics came to deride but that had inestimable importance at the time, since it underpinned the confidence of eighteenth-century historians that they held in their grasp principles of explanation that elevated their understanding beyond anything available to earlier writers. This was the spirit expressed by the Edinburgh clergyman and minor literary figure John Logan in a brief work entitled *Elements of the Philosophy of History*: "To common minds every thing appears particular. A Philosopher sees in the great, and observes a whole. The curious collect and describe. The scientific arrange and generalize" (10).

This side of Enlightenment historiography is well known;[6] less so its other, more sentimental face. There is plenty of evidence that historians, much like the novelists and poets of the day, were keenly interested in engaging the reader's sympathies, especially by presenting scenes of virtue in distress. This dimension of Enlightenment historiography may be lost if we choose to focus exclusively on the more philosophical texts, but—following Hume's lead in the essay "Of Tragedy"—we will find it strongly articulated in works on belles lettres.

Raising the issue of distance leads us to recognize a split between two important features of the historical outlook of the eighteenth century. To simplify considerably, much of the most interesting historical work of the Enlightenment drew its strength from a theory of knowledge that assumed the importance of cognitive distance. Only the comprehensive philosophical eye, it was thought, could discern the underlying patterns that give order to the development of society. At the same time, if we turn our attention to matters of form and of morals, we see that the discussion of narrative in this period was strongly concerned with cultivating a sense of immediacy. History no less than fiction, it was argued, should exercise the moral imagination of its readers by presenting them with scenes that are as vivid and affecting as possible. This tension between cognitive distantiation and affective proximity becomes still more interesting when we recognize that many of the same voices speak prominently on both sides of this divide, most notably Kames, Smith, and Hume.

For those of us who read eighteenth-century histories with sympathy, the strain between these two impulses provides a tension that adds life and interest to this literature. At the same time, recognizing the division makes it easier to understand how the work of this period fell out of favor with a subsequent generation of readers, who came to focus their attention on only one side of the Enlightenment's historiographical legacy. The sentimentalism of Hume and his contemporaries contributed a great deal to the growing taste for immediacy in historical writing, but in encouraging this tendency, these writers unintentionally fostered a new climate of taste by which their own works would come to be judged as excessively cold and detached. The result was a second shift in distance, much like the one that Hume recognized as separating his generation from that of Clarendon.

Eighteenth-century inwardness: Kames's *Elements of Criticism*

The most remarkable instance of this double distance is Smith,[7] but Henry Home, Lord Kames, provides a more manageable example for a brief discussion. When we think of Kames as a historical thinker, we generally have in mind the conjecturalist program of his *Sketches of the History of Man*. When we turn to his *Elements of Criticism* (1762), however, we find a different emphasis. Here the central issue is not the progress of humankind but the moral psychology of the reader. Kames's argument, in essence, is that literary representation has the same power to stir the passions as actual experience, but only if the scene represented carries with it a high degree of vividness. This vivacity results in a loss of critical distance, turning the reader's experience into a kind of "waking dream." Kames called this crucial effect "ideal presence," and he claimed for it a profoundly important role in the moral education of humankind. Though literary representation will always have an impact that is weaker than the force of experience itself, "ideal presence" allows the lessons of experience to be prepared for or repeated in ways that account for "that extensive influence which language hath over the heart" (1: 95–96).

Ideal presence, as the name implies, is an aesthetic principle whose specific concern is the abbreviation of distance. In practice, much of Kames's critical writing amounts to reiterated injunctions to make description as actual and vivid as possible. "Writers of genius," he wrote, "sensible that the eye is the best avenue to the heart, represent every thing as passing in our sight; and from readers or hearers, transform us, as it were, into spectators: . . . in a word every thing becomes dramatic as much as possible." Plutarch, he added, observes that Thucydides "makes his reader a spectator, and inspires him with the same passions as if he were an eyewitness" (2: 347–48). Similarly, in another place he wrote, "The force of language consists in raising complete images; which have the effect to transport the reader as by magic into the very place and time of the important action, and to convert him as it were into a spectator, beholding every thing that passes" (2: 326).[8]

The notion of transporting the reader into "the very place and time" of the event would become significant not only for historical narrative itself but also for a whole family of associated genres, including the historical novel, biography, and literary history. The phrase carries with it a strong sense of the transformation of historical distance that would become pervasive in the early part of the next century. But Kames was not singling out historical evocation as such—though as the reference to Plutarch's judgment on Thucydides shows, history is one among many literatures that demonstrate the truth of his central principle. "Upon examination," he writes, "it will be found, that genuine history commands our passions by means of ideal presence solely; and therefore that with respect to this effect, genuine history stands upon the same footing with fable. To me it appears clear, that our sympathy must vanish so soon as we begin to reflect upon the incidents related in either." If we think that a story is nothing but fiction, he continues, the effect will be dissipated, but the same is true if we reflect that the persons described are no longer alive: "a man long dead, and insensible now of past misfortunes, cannot move our pity more than if he had never existed" (1: 87–88).[9]

Romantic reactions: the reception of Hume's *history*

There is no room here to describe the complex balance of irony and sentiment, speculativeness and spectatorship that shapes Hume's practice as a historian (see Phillips, *Society*, chs. 1–2). Instead, I want only to show that the reception of his great narrative is a way of tracing the changes of sensibility that affected historical writing as much as they did any other literature in the early part of the nineteenth century. In "My Own Life," Hume recalled the first appearance of his work and claims that Britons of every religious and political stripe were united "in their rage against the man, who had presumed to shed a generous tear for the fate of Charles I and the Earl of Strafford" (xxx). The picture he paints is, of course, exaggeratedly negative. Nonetheless, it serves as a useful reminder of the political and religious partisanship that played a central role in the response to Hume's work in this early phase. This ideological critique did not disappear in the nineteenth century; in fact, it reached a culmination in George Brodie's *History of the British Empire*, published in 1822, and it remained an element in the reception of T. B. Macaulay's history. Gradually, however, a different sort of discontent comes into view, one that paints Hume's history as intellectually abstract and emotionally thin. This second phase of criticism held the work up to new criteria of judgment, and it embraced all of Enlightenment historiography in its condemnation.

The first articulation of this criticism that I know of comes from James Mackintosh, the Whig historian and politician. In his journals for 1811, Mackintosh sketched a brief but admiring portrait of Hume: "No other narrative seems to unite, in the same degree, the two qualities of being instructive and affecting. No historian approached him in the union of the talent of painting pathetic scenes with that of exhibiting comprehensive views of human affairs" (2: 168).[10] It is hard to imagine a better summary of the tension between proximity and detachment that this essay explores, but Mackintosh attached to this praise a criticism that would be prophetic for the growing reaction against the historical outlook of the Enlightenment. In Mackintosh's view, Hume's skeptical and rationalist temper seemed a limitation on his capacity for historical sympathy. Too often, Mackintosh thought, Hume used his intelligence in the place of evidence. He "was too habitually a speculator and too little of an antiquary, to have a great power of throwing back his mind into former ages, and of clothing his persons and events in their moral dress; his personages are too modern and argumentative—if we must not say too rational" (2: 169).

Despite Hume's failures of sympathy, Mackintosh still judged Hume the greatest of historians, but two decades later the balance had shifted decisively. In the review of Carlyle with which I began, Mill permitted himself to wonder whether Hume, William Robertson, and Edward Gibbon, for all their talents, should be considered historians at all. Their histories, he charged, were populated by "mere shadows and dim abstractions" whom no reader would recognize as "beings of his own flesh and blood." Mill asked, "Does Hume throw his own mind into the mind of an Anglo-Saxon, or an Anglo-Norman? . .. Would not the sight, if it could be had, of a single table or pair of shoes made by an Anglo-Saxon, tell us, directly and by inference, more of his whole way of life, more of how men thought and acted among the Anglo-Saxons, than Hume, with all his narrative skill, has contrived to tell us from all his materials?" (135).

Carlyle, Macaulay, and others made much the same point, urging on historians the task of retrieving a quality of immediacy that, depending on the occasion, these critics identified with the freshness of primary documents, the vividness of Herodotus, or the fictional imagination of Walter Scott.[11] None of them, it is clear, thought that, in repudiating the qualities of aloofness and abstraction they identified with their Enlightenment predecessors, they might actually be following in the footsteps of Hume and Smith themselves.

Locations of inwardness from Enlightenment to Romanticism

Our image of the historical sensibility of the Enlightenment as wholly abstract and detached is in many ways a myth created by the Romantics as a foil for their own critique. For this reason, I have tried to show that alongside its "philosophical" detachment, Enlightenment historiography also responded to a strong sentimentalist influence that focused on the aesthetic attractions and moral training that result from soliciting the reader's sympathy. In the larger picture, then, we need to balance these two aspects of eighteenth-century historiography, keeping in mind that this period combined a view of historical knowledge that emphasizes generality with a view of narrative that stresses the aesthetic and ethical value of immediacy.

When the problem of continuity is stated in this way, some elements of discontinuity stand out more clearly. The Romantics deepened the desire for immediacy in some areas where sentimentalism had prepared the way, but they also brought a new demand for engagement in other areas where eighteenth-century historical thought valued a greater degree of distantiation. The stylistic changes that we normally identify with Romantic historiography can be seen as a further stage in a long-standing movement toward actuality and immediacy; but the shift to a new sense of proximity or engagement on both ideological and cognitive grounds has fewer precedents in the eighteenth century and therefore contributes more fundamentally to the sense we have of encountering a new historical sensibility.

Both groups of writers were interested in finding ways to make history more vivid or dramatic, but for the eighteenth-century writers the search for immediacy centered on the psychology of reading, not on the quality of knowing. Their program called for strategies to involve readers as closely as possible in the narrative, so that they would respond more like witnesses than detached observers. Consequently, in belletrist discussion attention to formal distance was tied to the desire to abridge affective distance, and affective distance in turn was regarded as key to the ethical value of historical writing. The historian's own relation to the past, however, was not explicitly at issue, and we miss the characteristically historicist view that an equivalent abridgment of distance cognitively would provide a clearer or deeper understanding of realities remote from the present.

In Smith and Kames, in other words, the abridging effects of sympathy belong to the setting of criticism and moral psychology, not that of historical method or explanation. When they wrote about historical narrative, after all, both men were writing in a tradition of belles lettres. From within this sphere they reworked the traditional view that history teaches by presenting ideal examples of character and action, replacing it with a new sense that history might contribute to virtue by providing vicarious exercises for the moral imagination. But it has to be recognized that these sentimentalist doctrines did not immediately move beyond the issue of ethical instruction or change how Smith and Kames thought about historical understanding.

This is what changed in the new century, in ways that begin to be seen in Mill's criticism of Hume's failure to "throw his mind" into the situation of another time. Mill's attack on the Enlightenment expressed a view of historical knowledge that was central to important strands of nineteenth-century thought and has continued to have enormous influence in shaping the views of the historical profession. The key feature of this way of thinking about history is the opposition it established between distance and insight. Historical understanding was not construed as a matter of simple identification with the past. (Such naïveté was the hallmark of the chroniclers and romancers that so attracted the Romantic imagination.) Rather, genuine historical understanding begins from a recognition of difference but strives to overcome the opacity of the past by an act of the imagination. More superficial minds, it was thought, might content themselves with the simplicities of factual knowledge or the abstractions of empty generalization. But when one wanted to understand the real experience of past times, neither abstract theorizing nor external observation would do. Instead, historians would need to cultivate special qualities of historical insight in order to see more directly into past experience.

This view of historical understanding—given ideological impetus by the sense of engagement common to both liberal and nationalist ideologies and codified as a historical epistemology by Wilhelm Dilthey, Benedetto Croce, Friedrich Meinecke, and R. G. Collingwood—has done a great deal to shape subsequent thinking about the proper forms of historical writing. For the historians of the Enlightenment, who began with quite different ideas about historical distance, the continuing influence of this now canonical view has created a persistently hostile climate of reception, from whose presuppositions only now are we beginning to liberate both Hume and ourselves.

Notes

1   According to White, "Hume viewed the historical record as little more than the record of human folly, which led him finally to become as bored with history as he had become with philosophy" (55). For Collingwood's hostility to Enlightenment historiography, see 71–85.

2   Alexis de Tocqueville's *Democracy* also has some suggestive passages on historical distance (chs. 1–4, 20). Among recent work by historians, see the rich essays by Carlo Ginzburg in *Wooden Eyes*.

3   Earl Wasserman's "The Pleasures of Tragedy" remains an excellent review of this theme.

4   Fontenelle's solution to the problem—a solution that Hume largely accepts—involves a kind of distantiation: "We weep for the misfortune of a hero, to whom we are attached. In the same instant we comfort ourselves, by reflecting, that it is nothing but a fiction" (*Réflexions sur la poétique*, as quoted by Hume [*Essays* 218n]).

5   "Of Tragedy" first appeared in *Four Dissertations*, published by Millar in 1757, a time when Hume was also engaged on his *History of England*.

6   See, for example, John Pocock's important recent study on Gibbon, *Barbarism and Civilization*.

7   Smith was the greatest political economist of the age, but his *Lectures on Rhetoric* was also its most searching examination of historical narrative. See my *Society and Sentiment*, chs. 1 and 3.

8   Similarly, Smith writes, "When we read in history concerning actions of proper and beneficent greatness of mind, how eagerly do we enter into such designs? . .. In imagination we become the very person whose actions are represented to us: we transport ourselves in fancy to the scenes of those distant and forgotten adventures, and imagine ourselves acting the part of a Scipio or a Camillus, a Timoleon or an Aristides" (*Moral Sentiments* 75).

9   Note the parallel between Kames's views and those of Fontenelle. But where Kames wished to discourage any kind of reflection that might interrupt the sense of immediacy, Fontenelle saw the consciousness of fiction as a necessary and useful attenuation of the impact of tragedy.

10   The *Memoirs* culls passages from Mackintosh's extensive manuscript journals, held in the British Library, which are a rich source of comment on his literary and historical reading, as well as on private and official life.

11   The Romantic period is rife with statements that indicate the desire for a new sense of proximity in historical writing. Macaulay, for example, makes reiterated use of images of abbreviated distance to describe his ambition for a new, more imaginatively constructed historical understanding: "To make the past present, to bring the distant near, to place us in the society of a great man or on the eminence which overlooks the field of a mighty battle, to invest with the reality of human flesh and blood beings whom we are too much inclined to consider as personified qualities in an allegory, to call up our ancestors before us with all their peculiarities of language, manner, and garb, to show us over their houses, to seat us at their tables, to rummage their old fashioned wardrobes . . ." (1).

Works cited

Bal, Mieke. *Narratology: Introduction to the Theory of Narrative*. Toronto: U of Toronto P, 1997.

Barrell, John. *The Political Theory of Painting from Reynolds to Hazlitt*. New Haven: Yale UP, 1986.

Blair, Hugh. *Lectures on Rhetoric*. 2 vols. Ed. Harold F. Harding. Carbondale: Southern Illinois UP, 1965.

Brecht, Bertolt. *Brecht on Theatre; The Development of an Aesthetic*. Ed. and trans. John Willett. New York: Hill, 1964.

Bullough, Edward. "Psychical Distance as a Factor in Art and an Esthetic Principle." *A Modern Book of Esthetics*. Ed. Melvin Rader. New York: Henry Holt, 1952. 315–42.

Campbell, Thomas. *Complete Poetical Works*. Ed. J. Logie Robertson. London: Oxford UP, 1907.

Collingwood, R. G. *Idea of History*. Ed. Jan van der Dussen. Oxford: Clarendon, 1993.

Elias, Norbert. *The Civilizing Process*. Trans. Edmund Jephcott. New York: Pantheon, 1982.

Fabian, Johannes. *Time and the Other: How Anthropology Makes Its Object*. New York: Columbia UP, 1983.

Foucault, Michel. *Discipline and Punish; The Birth of the Prison*. Trans. Alan Sheridan. New York: Vintage, 1995.

Ginzburg, Carlo. *Wooden Eyes: Nine Reflections on Distance*. Trans. Martin Ryle and Kate Soper. New York: Columbia UP, 2001

Hume, David. *An Enquiry concerning the Principles of Morals*. Ed. Tom L. Beauchamp. Oxford: Oxford UP, 1998.

———. *Essays, Moral, Political, and Literary*. Ed. Eugene Millar. Indianapolis: Liberty, 1987.

———. *History of England*. 6 vols. Indianapolis: Liberty, 1983.

———. "My Own Life." Hume, *History* 1: xxvii–xxxiv.

———. *Treatise of Human Nature*. Ed. David Norton and Mary Norton. Oxford: Oxford UP, 2000.

Kames, Henry Home, Lord. *Elements of Criticism*. 2 vols. Edinburgh, 1765.

Logan, John. *Elements of the Philosophy of History*. Edinburgh, 1781.

Lonsdale, Roger, ed. *The Poems of Thomas Gray, William Collins, Oliver Goldsmith*. London: Longmans, 1969.

Macaulay, Thomas Babington. "Hallam." *Critical and Historical Essays*. Ed. Alexander James Grieve. Vol. 1. London: Dent, 1961. 1–76.

Mackintosh, James. *Memoirs of the Life and Writings of Sir James Mackintosh*. Ed. R. Mackintosh. 2 vols. Boston, 1853.

Mannheim, Karl. "Social Contract and Social Distance." *Systematic Sociology: An Introduction to the Study of Society*. Ed. J. S. Eroes and W. A. C. Stewart. Vol. 8. London: Routledge, 1957. 43–55.

Mill, John Stuart. "Carlyle's *French Revolution*." Rev. of *The French Revolution: A History*, by Thomas Carlyle. *Essays on French History and Historians*. Ed. John M. Robson and John C. Cairns. Toronto: U of Toronto P, 1985. 133–66.

Millar, John. *Historical View of the English Government*. 4 vols. London, 1803.

Nietzsche, Friedrich. *On the Advantage and Disadvantage of History for Life*. Trans. P. Preuss. Indianapolis: Hackett, 1980.

Phillips, Mark Salber. "Historical Distance and the Historiography of Eighteenth-Century Britain." *History, Religion, and Culture: British Intellectual History, 1750–1950*. Ed. Stefan Collini, Richard Whatmore, and Brian Young. Cambridge: Cambridge UP, 2000. 31–47.

———. "Hume and Historical Distance." *Lumen* 21 (2002): 1–20.

———. *Society and Sentiment: Genres of Historical Writing in Britain, 1740–1820*. Princeton: Princeton UP, 2000.

Pocock, John. *Barbarism and Religion*. Cambridge: Cambridge UP, 1999.

Reynolds, Joshua. *Discourses on Art*. Ed. Robert Wark. New Haven: Yale UP, 1999.

Rousseau, Jean-Jacques. *The Social Contract*. The Social Contract *and Other Later Political Writings*. Ed. and trans. Victor Gourevitch. Cambridge: Cambridge UP, 1997. 39–152.

Shklovsky, Victor. *Theory of Prose*. Trans. Benjamin Sher. Normal: Dalkey Archive, 1991.

Simmel, Georg. "The Stranger." *The Sociology of Georg Simmel*. Ed. Kurt Wolff. London: Free, 1950. 402–08.

Smith, Adam. "History of Astronomy." *Essays on Philosophical Subjects*. Ed. W. P. D. Wightman and J. C. Bryce. Indianapolis: Liberty, 1982. 33–105.

———. *Inquiry into the Nature and Causes of the Wealth of Nations*. 2 vols. Ed. R. H. Campbell and A. S. Skinner. Indianapolis: Liberty, 1981.

———. *Lectures on Rhetoric and Belles Lettres*. Ed. J. C. Bryce. Indianapolis: Liberty, 1983.

———. *Theory of Moral Sentiments*. Ed. D. D. Raphael and A. L. Macfie. Indianapolis: Liberty, 1982.

Thompson, Edward. *The Making of the English Working Class*. Harmondsworth: Penguin, 1968.

Tocqueville, Alexis de. *Democracy in America*. Trans. Harvey Mansfield and Delba Winthrop. Vol. 2. Chicago: U of Chicago P, 2000.

Wasserman, Earl. "The Pleasures of Tragedy." *English Literary History* 14 (1947): 283–307.

White, Hayden. *Metahistory*. Baltimore: Johns Hopkins UP, 1973.

Further Reading: Chapters 9 to 12

Allan, David. *Virtue, Learning, and the Scottish Enlightenment: Ideas of Scholarship in Early Modern History* (Edinburgh: Edinburgh University Press, 1993).

Berry, Christopher J. *Social Theory of the Scottish Enlightenment* (Edinburgh: Edinburgh University Press, 1997).

Bryson, Gladys. *Man and Society: The Scottish Inquiry of the Eighteenth Century* (Princeton, NJ: Princeton University Press, 1945).

Colley, Linda. *Britons: Forging the Nation, 1707–1837* (New Haven, CT: Yale University Press, 1992).

Dwyer, John. "Enlightened Spectators and Classical Moralists: Sympathetic Relations in Eighteenth-Century Scotland", *Sociability and Society in Eighteenth-Century Scotland*, Dwyer and Richard Sher (eds). (Edinburgh: Mercat, 1993).

Hargreaves, Neil, "Revelation of Character in Eighteenth-Century Historiography and William Robertson's, *History of the Reign of Charles V*", *Eighteenth-Century Life* 27 (2003), 23–48.

Hicks, Philip. *Neoclassical History and English Culture: From Clarendon to Hume* (New York: St Martin's, 1996).

Hilson, J. C. "Hume: The Historian as Man of Feeling", *Augustan Worlds: Essays in Honour of A. R. Humphreys*, J.C. Hilson, M. Jones, and J. Watson (eds) (Leicester: Leicester University Press, 1978).

Hont, I. and M. Ignatieff, (eds). *Wealth and Virtue: The Shaping of Political Economy in the Scottish Enlightenment* (Cambridge: Cambridge University Press, 1983).

Jones, Chris. *Radical Sensibility: Literature and Ideas in the 1790s* (London: Routledge, 1993).

Kaufman, Robert. "The Sublime as Super-Genre of the Modern, or Hamlet in Revolution: Caleb Williams and His Problems", *Studies in Romanticism* 36 (Winter 1997), 541–74.

Kelly, Gary. *Women, Writing, and Revolution, 1790–1827* (Oxford: Clarendon, 1993).

Kidd, Colin. *Subverting Scotland's Past: Scottish Whig Historians and the Creation of an Anglo-British Identity, 1689–c.1830* (Cambridge: Cambridge University Press, 1993).

Klancher, Jon. "Godwin and the Genre Reformers: Necessity and Contingency in Romantic Narrative Theory", *Romanticism, History, and the Possibilities of Genre*, Tilottama Rajan and Julia M. Wright (eds) (Cambridge: Cambridge University Press, 1998), 21–38.

Klein, Lawrence. *Shaftesbury and the Culture of Politeness: Moral Discourse and Cultural Politics in Early Eighteenth-Century England* (Cambridge: Cambridge University Press, 1993).

Kramnick, I. *Bolingbroke and his Circle: The Politics of Nostalgia in the Age of Walpole* (Cambridge, MA: Harvard University Press, 1968).

Levine, Joseph. *The Battle of the Books: History and Literature in the Augustan Age* (Ithaca: Cornell University Press, 1991).

Locke, Don. *A Fantasy of Reason: The Life and Thought of William Godwin* (London: Routledge and Kegan Paul, 1980).

Meek, Ronald. *Social Science and the Ignoble Savage* (Cambridge: Cambridge University Press, 1976).

Mayer, Robert. *History and the Early English Novel: Matters of Fact from Bacon to Defoe* (Cambridge: Cambridge University Press, 1997).

Nadel, George. "The Philosophy of History before Historicism", *History and Theory* 3 (1963), 291–315.

O'Brien, Karen. *Narratives of Enlightenment: Cosmopolitan History from Voltaire to Gibbon* (Cambridge: Cambridge University Press, 1997).

Okie, Laird. *Augustan Historical Writing: Histories of England in the English Enlightenment* (Lanham, MD and London: University Press of America, 1991).

Peardon, Thomas Preston. *The Transition in English Historical Writing, 1760–1830* (New York: AMS, 1966).

Phillips, Mark. "Adam Smith and the History of Private Life: Social and Sentimental Narratives in Eighteenth-Century Historiography", *The Historical Imagination in Early Modern Britain*, D. R. Kelley and David Harris Sacks (eds) (Cambridge: Cambridge University Press, 1997).

Phillipson, Nicholas. *Hume* (London: Weidenfeld and Nicholson, 1989).

Pocock, J. G. A. *Barbarism and Religion*. 4 vols to date (Cambridge: Cambridge University Press, 1999–).

Pohl, Nicole and Betty Schellenberg. "A Bluestocking Historiography", *Huntington Library Quarterly* 65 (2002), 1–19.

Samuel, Raphael. *Theatres of Memory* (London: Verso, 1994).

Sher, Richard B. *The Enlightenment and the Book: Scottish Authors and Their Books in Eighteenth-Century Britain, Ireland, and America* (Chicago: University of Chicago Press, 2006).

Stewart, John. *The Moral and Political Philosophy of David Hume* (New York: Columbia University Press, 1963).

Taylor, Charles. *Sources of the Self: The Making of the Modern Identity* (Cambridge, MA: Harvard University Press, 1989).

Turner, Cheryl. *Living by the Pen: Women Writers in the Eighteenth Century* (London: Routledge, 1992).

Vance, John. *Samuel Johnson and the Sense of History* (Athens: University of Georgia Press, 1984).

Wood, Paul. "Hume, Reid, and the Science of the Mind", *Hume and Hume's Connexions*, M.A. Stewart and J. P. Wright (eds) (University Park: Pennsylvania State University Press, 1994).

—— . "The Natural History of Man in the Scottish Enlightenment", *History of Science* 27 (1989), 89–123.

Woolf, Daniel. "A Feminine Past? Gender, Genre, and Historical Knowledge in England, 1500–1800", *American Historical Review* 102 (1997), 645–79.

PART 4

The tasks of romantic history

INTRODUCTION

MOST HISTORIANS AGREE THAT the terms we use to divide the past into periods—such as medieval, Renaissance, and modern—are adjectives of convenience, chosen with hindsight to emphasize our own political, religious, or intellectual concerns. For example, those who lived during the medieval period probably considered themselves to be living in a present age rather than a middle age (for **modernity** had not yet arrived): so it is important that we use *medieval* merely for convenience and not for definition. But when we consider the artistic values, scholarly standards, and moral priorities that combine to create a romantic approach to history, romanticism seems more than a term of convenience. This is because specific ideas concerning historical writing, which date roughly from the time of the French Revolution to the mid-nineteenth century, were shared by authors and readers across Europe and North America. Even though these authors did not form a cohesive group or literary movement, romantic was a term that these authors used at the time to emphasize the role of imagination for creating and understanding their work.[i]

The romantics believed that historical writing, like novels (romances), must appeal to the reader's imagination by adopting an evocative literary style—so that the reader's imaginative experience would bring elements of the past to life. By appealing to a sense of national **mythology**, each of these romantic historians celebrated what they saw as their respectively unique national characteristics, therefore moving away from the Enlightenment emphasis on

---

i   Samuel Taylor Coleridge described the imaginative theory that informs his own *Lyrical Ballads* (1798): "my ideas should be directed to persons and characters supernatural, or at least romantic ... to transfer from our inward nature a human interest and a semblance of truth sufficient to procure for these shadows of imagination that willing suspension of disbelief for the moment, which constitutes poetic faith". See *Biographia Literaria,* J. Engell and W. J. Bate (eds) (Princeton: Princeton University Press, 1983) vol. 2, 5–6. This book was published in 1817, but Coleridge had voiced these views in public lectures from 1812 onward.

universality defined by human nature. The artistic freedom that this theory provided is one reason why romantic historians have also been called "literary" historians. Romantic notions were voiced even by authors who were separated by language, geography, and politics. For example, in 1828, Thomas Babington Macaulay wrote that "our historians . . . miserably neglect the art of narration, the art of interesting the affections and presenting pictures to the imagination". He contrasted history-writing with biographies that "[create] these effects without violating truth". This sounds very much like the views of the radical William Godwin, expressed in an unpublished essay that celebrated the imaginative vividness evoked by reading about private lives (see Part 3).[ii] Similarly, Macaulay's primary concern for imaginative effects rather than factual composition echoes the romantic poet Johann Wolfgang von Goethe who, in a private letter to a fellow poet, issued a passionate plea for instruction that enlivens the mind by inspiring our creative abilities.[iii] When Macaulay argued that "the effect of historical reading" should enable us to be "transported into a new state of society", he seemed to be invoking Lord Kames's notion of ideal presence, which contributed crucially to romantic theories of history (see Part 3). Macaulay's reference to the romantic reader's mental imagery as "new" reveals that the romantic historian is an inspired creator of powerful historical scenery rather than a cloistered writer calmly dedicated to recovering facts.[iv]

The sources in this section show that romantic approaches to history are charged with immediacy. Stylistically, many of these narratives sound more like impassioned speeches than carefully-argued scholarship; conceptually, authors in this section such as Jules Michelet, Mercy Otis Warren, and Francis Parkman were among the first in the modern period to consider their own experiences (or those of their friends and family) as historically significant. This new consciousness of the present-as-historical may be one reason why it is difficult to disentangle romantic writings about history from actual historical accounts. During the previous century, romances were fictional novels that masqueraded as true history—now, historians are employing the imagination to treat recent events as historical. These are basic reasons why the word romantic is useful to describe as well as define these historians of the early nineteenth century.

Perhaps their primary appeal to the imagination has caused romantic historians' works to

ii   See Godwin in Part 3. Among the many comments that the historian William Robertson received from readers, it is important to note Dugald Stewart's observation that his narrative talents provided "that unceasing interest which constitutes one of the principal charms in tales of fiction; an interest easy to support in relating a series of imaginary adventures, but which in historical composition, evinces, more than anything else, the hand of a master": see D. Stewart, *Account of the Life and Writings of William Robertson* (2nd edn) (London: 1802), 139. See also M. Phillips, *Society and Sentiment: Genres of Historical Writing in Britain: 1740–1820*, 89–90.

iii   Goethe's correspondent was Friedrich Schiller. See Friedrich Nietzsche's Foreword to "The Use and Abuse of History for Life" (1873); it opens by condemning all attempts at instruction that do not energise the reader by evoking imaginative vitality. He quoted a strongly-worded letter from Goethe: "I despise everything that merely instructs me without enriching or directly inspiring me". Like both Godwin and Macaulay, Goethe was responding to the confident historical conjectures of an eighteenth-century philosopher—in this case, Immanuel Kant. See Nietzsche, *Untimely Meditations*, ed. D. Breazeale, trans. R. J. Hollingdate (Cambridge: Cambridge University Press, 1997), 59; J. W. von Goethe, *Goethes Werke*, vol. 13 (Weimar: Hermann Böhlau, 1893), 346. The quote is my own translation.

iv   Similarly, when Macaulay turned to writing poetry, he proposed that his *Lays of Ancient Rome* (1842) "transform some portions of early Roman history back into the poetry out of which they were made"—despite his recognition that records of the original oral poems did not survive. See "Introduction", *Lays of Ancient Rome* (London: Longmans, 1842), 36.

[Marginal annotation, top left: "- almost a literary device to transport the reader to the event and to feel a connection to the people and past"]

[Marginal annotation, bottom left: "feel in order to create action"]

seem so dated: Thomas Carlyle's description of the Versailles court on the eve of the French Revolution, narrated with the urgency of the present tense, now reads like a novel in which the omniscient narrator describes and then dooms his characters. Warren's strongly patriotic narrative takes the form of an impassioned speech to her "countrymen" that shares her painful experience of living through and then writing about the American Revolution. Ironically, by basing her account on her first-hand experience of "the sudden convulsions, crowded scenes, and rapid changes, that flowed in quick succession", and by suggesting her own role in God's plan for spreading democratic government, her account seems personally authentic but therefore not quite credible as an objective history of American politics. Michelet's passion for his subject expresses itself through a sentimental vision of neglected ghosts haunting his country's archives—"as I breathed upon their dust I saw them rise"—illustrating his wish to get a poetic sense rather than a factual account of the times. Looking back from an academic perspective some two centuries later, few historical works have been discredited by succeeding generations as energetically as those represented in this section. These authors have been called "amateur historians" who illustrate what R. G. Collingwood (in Part 7) has called the scissors-and-paste method of historical composition. They used sources to evoke the times rather than to uncover and explain the facts.[v] At the same time, these historians did not see themselves as academic researchers, they did not teach students or cultivate disciples, and they tended not to enter into scholarly debate with their peers. These factors in the decline of their reputation among academics of subsequent generations should not distract us from appreciating their remarkable and unprecedented achievements.

Their task when composing history was to inform readers of their own national pasts by appealing to their imaginations, and to some extent their goals continue to shape the ethics and style of historical writing. As the eminent historian John Burrow has remarked in his discussion of Carlyle and Michelet, both giants of romantic history, "both conceived of the task of the historian as being to re-create and re-enact, and both threw their authorial personalities into the action, apostrophizing and extorting, in moods often of exultation, almost of frenzy."[vi] What are the critical values that each of these authors use to render the historical past into the imaginative present? Once we consider this question, we will be better prepared to discuss whether the eventual shift away from romanticism reflected changing political values, scholarly methods, or simply a new taste for how historians should represent themselves in their writing.

Macaulay's essay, cogently titled "History", was one of the first to use this compact and relatively accessible genre as a means to advance historical ideas. "History" first appeared anonymously in the *Edinburgh Review*, which meant that it was designed for educated but not academic readers.[vii] Accordingly, Macaulay's essay promoted popular consumption of historical writing—and his success was impressive, for he became one of the most widely-published historians of the nineteenth century. His essay was an articulate argument for history whose truth is conveyed by its imaginative effects on readers, rather than on factual content alone. Proclaiming that facts are the mere dross of history, Macaulay focused on the difficult task that historians face: like Godwin, he observed that "writers of history seem to entertain an aristocratic contempt for the writers of memoirs", and yet it was these highly popular writings on the personal experience of history that illustrated its value and disseminated its meaning.

v   See R. G. Collingwood, *The Idea of History* (Oxford: Oxford University Press, 1946), 257–61.

vi J. Burrow, *A History of History* (London: Allen Lane, 2007), 393.

vii See D. A. Spurgeon, "The *Edinburgh Review*", British Literary Magazines: The Romantic Age, *1789–1836*, A. Sullivan (ed.) (Westport CT: Greenwood Press, 1983), 139–44.

History should make use of the attractions characteristic of novels, since by doing so "men will not merely be described, but will be made intimately known to us". This was a dramatic argument, since in the early nineteenth century, history was seen as the most dignified of literary genres, whereas novels were only one short step above gossip—and indeed it was the novel's salacious attractions that made it morally suspect. Now Macaulay went on to declare that, using this new narrative method, "society would be shown from the highest to the lowest". But Macaulay was not anticipating the kind of people's history written in France by Jules Michelet or the history from below that we will examine in Part 8; he did not express a particularly democratic aim or wish to write people's history. He had very specific political and moral lessons in mind. As we will see (in Part 5), Macaulay was one of the earliest and most energetic promoters of what Herbert Butterfield has called the Whig interpretation of history, for which the history of Britain is the story of human progress. Macaulay needed to narrow his social vision considerably in order to write that story.

Readers have long described Carlyle as a prophet, although by the time he turned to writing history he held no religious beliefs. He has been seen as prophetic because his writings propose that it is the historian's task to interpret and communicate the spiritual meaning of the otherwise chaotic vastness of historical detail. Carlyle also tended to adopt a tortured grammatical style (which annoyed even his closest friends), lending him an oracular tone. Like Macaulay, Carlyle believed that historical writing should affect its readers in the same ways as fiction, and his powerful stylistic abilities helped to make historical narrative enormously popular throughout the nineteenth century. Using novelistic conventions including characterization and intensely atmospheric description, Carlyle focused on history's human and domestic elements, therefore posing a direct and insightful challenge to the Enlightenment view that history's moral lessons are self-evident for readers who can simply discern the consequences of human errors. We saw that the conjectural historians of the previous century tried to elaborate Lord Bolingbroke's claim that "History is philosophy [i.e. morality] teaching by examples", but Carlyle illustrated (and even celebrated) history's violent and unpredictable elements.[viii] This meant that, for Carlyle, the historian must make imaginatively demanding efforts to spell out history's moral lessons through a sense of history's ultimately mysterious unfolding. As one recent reader has suggested, Carlyle strove to "make vivid what was once indeed alive", just as novelists breathe life into fiction by giving a voice and a history to products of their own imagination.[ix]

Carlyle used his formidable literary talents to let his readers envision the past with a vividness unprecedented in the British historical tradition. He easily opposed those who challenged him to offer a contextual analysis of his subjects. In his essay on "Great Men", Carlyle suggested that taking a critical approach to defining heroic men of the past, by suggesting that they were "creatures of their Time", merely revealed "general blindness to spiritual lightning". For Carlyle, recognizing human greatness required the spiritual vision that only a romantic historian can provide. Taking up Macaulay's recent valuation of historical memoir, Carlyle's French Revolution relied on the memoirs recorded by those who survived the events that he described. This meant, however, that his book popularized numerous faulty recollections—none of the reading that Carlyle undertook when preparing his volumes included archival research or primary sources printed during the Revolution. Carlyle's narrative voice guides us through

viii H. St. John, Lord Bolingbroke, *Letters on the Study and Use of History*, 16, 58; see also J. D. Rosenberg, *Carlyle and the Burden of History* (Oxford: Clarendon Press, 1985), 176.
ix Rosenberg, 34.

the domestic atmosphere that orchestrated the ornate but fragile *ancien régime* (the pre-Revolutionary aristocracy), by using its own evocative power to excuse its lack of critical explanation. Indeed, the imaginative rather than documentary substance of Carlyle's *French Revolution* can be illustrated by the fact that, when the first draft of its first volume was accidentally destroyed in a fire, Carlyle swiftly rewrote it from memory. This also testifies to the palpable intensity of Carlyle's prophetic social vision, for his imaginative dedication to the brutally poor peasants of eighteenth-century France suggested their parallel in the squalid smoky tenements of nineteenth-century British cities. Through his feverish composition and skilled publication of *The French Revolution*, the violent overthrow of the weak French aristocracy and subsequent Terror served as Carlyle's romantic warning.

Across the English Channel, Michelet studied archival materials, but was devoted to celebrating the social ideals of the French Revolution rather than documenting its factual record. As a ground-breaking translator of Vico and a student of German philosophy, Michelet was steeped in social theories of civilization. But as he remarked, "his book is his life", and fittingly his *The History of France*, which filled 23 volumes, is energized by emotional experiences (see Bonnie Smith in Part 1). As a child Michelet's close relatives (including his father, to whom he was deeply attached) shared their first-hand recollections of the Revolution, and as an adult he was persecuted by the counter-revolutionary July Monarchy.[x] Michelet's *History* is a labour of love for his social ideals, and a celebration of the national spirit of the French people. His novelistic depiction of French history evokes our own sympathy for the people who struggled to realize their dream of *fraternité*. For this reason, Michelet's romantic style matches Carlyle's for vividness, but it argued for a communal rather than individual heroism. In the section that follows, Michelet began describing his research in French archives by adopting an impersonal tone, but this quickly gave way to first-person exclamations and resuscitations of the dead, illustrating his belief that "these papers are not papers, but lives of men". With the Revolution still reverberating through the social and ruling politics of France, Michelet's romanticism allowed him to express his allegiances and ideals in vivid language. Michelet's interest in history's human elements enabled him to write a powerful story, even if it ignored violent and contrary elements. In his *History of the French Revolution*, "the people" is synonymous with all that is good; the Parisian mob is never mentioned.

Although Warren published her *History* late in life (when she was nearly 80 years old), she knew the American Revolution first-hand—and had been writing about it from at least as early as 1775. Since she had become personally acquainted with friends and enemies of those Revolutionary ideas that she and her family had supported, her *History* is among the most personal and also the most partisan documents of the period. Like Parkman, whose first book was an autobiographical adventure story, Warren derived both her historical authority and her political bias from the fact that her historical account was based on personal experience and ideological commitments. Decades before she turned to history, Warren enjoyed popular success as a poet and playwright who used her pen to celebrate her pro-Revolutionary views. Indeed most of her plays, which were staged during the height of the American crisis, focused so narrowly on contemporary political conflicts that it is difficult to appreciate them today without a specialist knowledge of late-eighteenth-century New England history.[xi] The collection and publication of her poetry in book form in 1790 (dedicated to her "private friend" George

---

x   For the important role of Michelet's wife Athenaïs (1828–99) in the composition of his historical works, see Bonnie Smith in Part 1.

xi   For a useful survey, see M. Macdonald Hutcheson, "Mercy Warren, 1728–1814", *William and Mary Quarterly* 10 (July 1953), 378–402.

Washington) is evidence of the ideological success of her versified propaganda, which had originally appeared in Boston's political newspapers.

The writings of the major American historians George Bancroft and Francis Parkman retained dramatic elements reminiscent of staged performances. These historians used their considerable narrative skills to popularize their visions of American history by providing historical literature. Like Michelet, but unlike their predecessors in this section, these two historians researched in archives and also travelled widely to ground their historical projects in the reality of their times. Bancroft may have been the first American to receive a PhD in History from a German university (whose seminar training in ancient languages and source-criticism was unique in the West—see Part 5). Boston-born Parkman travelled to the western American frontier and throughout Quebec and Ontario, despite chronic illness, to experience first-hand the land and people he wanted to describe. They filled their volumes with extensive footnotes and bibliographical citations—they wanted readers to know that their books were learned, even if their references were not always precise. Bancroft and Parkman can be credited with widening the scope of American history by looking beyond individual "heroes" to depict the social groups, geography, political structures, and the history of exploration that defined America as a physical place as well as a new republic. Yet their ideological purpose, and heavy reliance on other sources (which were not always documented in the footnotes), together with their selective interpretation of unpublished materials, resulted in books that dramatized history and catered to the literary tastes of the time, while promoting the political views of the authors.

The first volume of Francis Parkman's massive seven-volume history of the French and British colonies in North America began with a peculiar mixture of confidence and apology. Echoing Carlyle, Parkman declared that "the clear light of History", ignited by the author-historian, will clarify America's origins. Writing at the height of the Civil War, when "half a million bayonets" were fighting to define American values, Parkman suggested that his work was of immediate national importance. His stark distinction between New England as the "offspring of a triumphant government" and New France as the creation "of an oppressed and fugitive people" revealed a conceptual simplicity which lent narrative force as well as conceptual clarity. Yet when Parkman revealed that "the amount of reading applied to [this] composition is far greater than the citations represent", he was asking readers to allow him certain creative and artistic freedoms, justifying this request by remarking that his aim is "to animate . . . the life of the past, and, so far as might be, clothe the skeleton with flesh". The belief that historical writing could bring the past to life in the mind of the reader was central to romantic history, and in this passage we see that one of its most confident practitioners understood that some explanation was required. Adopting literary rather than historical terms, Parkman proceeded to point out that "the narrator must seek to imbue himself with the life and spirit of the time"; by gesturing to his weak health, he identified himself as sympathetic enough to feel and therefore to stand in as "a sharer or a spectator of the action he describes". For Parkman, history can be written only once it has been imaginatively experienced by the especially sensitive historian.[xii]

By the late 1870s, in the midst of high unemployment and obvious social division during Reconstruction, Bancroft tried to provide historical justification for what he saw as the

xii   For Parkman's view that romance should be a guiding narrative principle that defines all American historical writing of this period, see his manuscript of August 1844, published in Wilbur R. Jacobs, "Francis Parkman's Oration 'Romance in America' ", *American Historical Review* 68 (April 1963), 692–97.

American government's constitutional obligation not to interfere in economic matters. His earlier expansiveness was declining into more conservative formulations that began to resemble Parkman's cranky conservative politics. As a recent biographer has pointed out, his interpretation of the Constitution entailed "selective quotation, judicious juggling of the evidence, and, in rare instances, plain distortion". But Bancroft, who had served as an American diplomat, Secretary of the Navy, and Presidential advisor, was writing to advocate a national mythology. Since this meant inspiring American readers to celebrate historically unique and divinely-granted freedoms guaranteed by their Constitution, his "selectivity and biased documentation . . . were legitimate scholarly methods, not falsifications of the record".[xiii] In other words, since Bancroft believed in the historic place of America as a divinely-created force of progress and liberty, these difficult times required his creative reconstruction rather than objective presentation. As shown by the stylistic techniques featured here, in the first chapter of The History of the Formation of the Constitution of the United States of America, Bancroft, like Warren, Carlyle, and Michelet, also idealized his own role as an imaginatively-engaged and thus trustworthy author. References to himself, to "the dawn of civilization", to his search for "moral truth", to an intellectual inheritance from ancient times, and foremost to America's realization of God's plan, had the cumulative effect of stirring up a romantic wave of dramatic images at the expense of providing a fair record of historical facts. None of this seems to have made Bancroft's histories less readable or less popular at the time, nor should they cloud our sense of the achievements of romantic history.

xiii See L. Handlin, George Bancroft: The Intellectual as Democrat (New York: Harper and Row, 1984), 331.

Chapter 13

Thomas Babington Macaulay

HISTORY[1]

Thomas Babington Macaulay (1800–1859), "History", 1828, *Critical, Historical, and Miscellaneous Essays, Edinburgh Review* (May 1828), 270–72, 277–80, 300–309.

TO WRITE HISTORY RESPECTABLY—that is, to abbreviate dispatches, and make extracts from speeches, to intersperse in due proportion epithets of praise and abhorrence, to draw up antithetical characters of great men, setting forth how many contradictory virtues and vices they united, and abounding in *withs* and *withouts*—all this is very easy. But to be a really great historian is perhaps the rarest of intellectual distinctions. Many scientific works are, in their kind, absolutely perfect. There are poems which we should be inclined to designate as faultless, or as disfigured only by blemishes which pass unnoticed in the general blaze of excellence. There are speeches, some speeches of Demosthenes particularly, in which it would be impossible to alter a word without altering it for the worse. But we are acquainted with no history which approaches to our notion of what a history ought to be—with no history which does not widely depart, either on the right hand or on the left, from the exact line.

The cause may easily be assigned. This province of literature is a debatable land. It lies on the confines of two distinct territories. It is under the jurisdiction of two hostile powers; and, like other districts similarly situated, it is ill-defined, ill-cultivated, and ill-regulated. Instead of being equally shared between its two rulers, the Reason and the Imagination, it falls alternately under the sole and absolute dominion of each. It is sometimes fiction. It is sometimes theory.

History, it has been said, is philosophy teaching by examples. Unhappily, what the philosophy gains in soundness and depth the examples generally lose in vividness. A perfect historian must possess an imagination sufficiently powerful to make his narrative affecting and picturesque. Yet he must control it so absolutely as to content himself with the materials which he finds, and to refrain from supplying deficiencies by additions of his own. He must be a profound and ingenious reasoner. Yet he must possess sufficient self-command to abstain from casting his facts in the mould of his hypothesis. Those who can justly estimate these almost insuperable difficulties will not think it strange that every writer should have failed, either in the narrative or in the speculative department of history.

It may be laid down as a general rule, though subject to considerable qualifications and exceptions, that history begins in novel and ends in essay. Of the romantic historians Herodotus is the earliest and the best. His animation, his simple-hearted tenderness, his wonderful talent for description and dialogue, and the pure sweet flow of his language, place him at the head of narrators. [. . .] He has written something better perhaps than the best history; but he has not written a good history; he is, from the first to the last chapter, an inventor. We do not here refer merely to those gross fictions with which he has been reproached by the critics of later times. We speak of that coloring which is equally diffused over his whole narrative, and which perpetually leaves the most sagacious reader in doubt what to reject and what to receive. The most authentic parts of his work bear the same relation to his wildest legends which Henry the Fifth bears to the Tempest. [. . .] Shakespeare gives us enumerations of armies, and returns of killed and wounded, which are not, we suspect, much less accurate than those of Herodotus There are passages in Herodotus nearly as long as acts of Shakespeare, in which everything is told dramatically, and in which the narrative serves only the purpose of stage-directions. It is possible, no doubt, that the substance of some real conversations may have been reported to the historian. But events, which, if they ever happened, happened in ages and nations so remote that the particulars could never have been known to him, are related with the greatest minuteness of detail. We have all that Candaules said to Gyges, and all that passed between Astyages and Harpagus. We are, therefore, unable to judge whether, in the account which he gives of transactions respecting which he might possibly have been well informed, we can trust to anything beyond the naked outline; whether, for example, the answer of Gelon to the ambassadors of the Grecian confederacy, or the expressions which passed between Aristides and Themisto-cles at their famous interview, have been correctly transmitted to us. The great events, are, no doubt, faithfully related. So, probably, are many of the slighter circumstances; but which of them it is impossible to ascertain. The fictions are so much like the facts, and the facts so much like the fictions, that, with respect to many most interesting particulars, our belief is neither given nor withheld, but remains in an uneasy and interminable state of abeyance. We know that there is truth; but we cannot exactly decide where it lies.
[. . .]

Some capricious and discontented artists have affected to consider portrait-painting as unworthy of a man of genius. Some critics have spoken in the same contemptuous manner of history. Johnson puts the case thus: The historian tells either what is false or what is true: in the former case he is no historian: in the latter he has no opportunity for displaying his abilities: for truth is one: and all who tell the truth must tell it alike.
[. . .]

Diversity, it is said, implies error: truth is one, and admits of no degrees. We answer, that this principle holds good only in abstract reasonings. When we talk of the truth of imitation in the fine arts, we mean an imperfect and a graduated truth. No picture is exactly like the original; nor is a picture good in proportion as it is like the original. When Sir Thomas Lawrence paints a handsome peeress, he does not contemplate her through a powerful microscope, and transfer to the canvas the pores of the skin, the bloodvessels of the eye, and all the other beauties which Gulliver discovered in the Brobdignaggian maids of honor. If he were to do this, the effect would not merely be unpleasant, but, unless the scale of the picture were proportionably enlarged, would be absolutely *false*. And, after all, a microscope of greater power than that which he had employed would convict him of innumerable omissions. The same may be said of history. Perfectly and absolutely true it cannot be: for, to be perfectly and absolutely true, it ought to record *all* the slightest particulars of the slightest transactions—all the things done and all the words uttered during the time of which it treats. The omission of any circumstance, however insignificant, would be a defect. If history were written thus, the Bodleian library would not contain the occurrences of a week. What is told in the fullest and most accurate annals bears an infinitely small proportion to what is suppressed. The difference between the copious work of Clarendon and the account of the civil wars in the abridgment of Goldsmith vanishes when compared with the immense mass of facts respecting which both are equally silent.

No picture, then, and no history, can present us with the whole truth: but those are the best pictures and the best histories which exhibit such parts of the truth as most nearly produce the effect of the whole. He who is deficient in the art of selection may, by showing nothing but the truth, produce all the effect of the grossest falsehood. It perpetually happens that one writer tells less truth than another, merely because he tells more truths. [. . .]

History has its foreground and its background: and it is principally in the management of its perspective that one artist differs from another. Some events must be represented on a large scale, others diminished; the great majority will be lost in the dimness of the horizon; and a general idea of their joint effect will be given by a few slight touches.

In this respect no writer has ever equalled Thucydides. He was a perfect master of the art of gradual diminution. His history is sometimes as concise as a chronological chart; yet it is always perspicuous. It is sometimes as minute as one of Lovelace's letters[i]; yet it is never prolix. He never fails to contract and to expand it in the right place. [. . .]

[I]t must be allowed that Thucydides has surpassed all his rivals in the art of historical narration, in the art of producing an effect on the imagination, by skilful selection and disposition, without indulging in the license of invention. But narration, though an important part of the business of a historian, is not the whole. To append a moral to a work of fiction is either useless or superfluous. A fiction may give a more impressive effect to what is already known; but it can teach nothing new. If it presents to us characters and trains of events to which our experience furnishes us with nothing similar, instead of deriving instruction from it, we pronounce it unnatural. We do not form our opinions from it; but we try it by our preconceived opinions. Fiction, therefore, is essentially imitative. Its merit consists in its resemblance to a model with which we are already familiar, or to which at least we can instantly refer. Hence it is that the anecdotes which interest us most strongly in authentic narrative are offensive when introduced into novels; that what is called the romantic part of history is in fact the least romantic. It is delightful as history, because it contradicts our previous notions of human nature, and of the connection of causes and effects. It is, on that very account, shocking and incongruous in fiction. In fiction, the principles are given, [i.e. assumed] to find the facts; In history, the facts are given, to find the principles; and the writer who does not explain the phenomena as well as state them performs only one half of his office. Facts are the mere dross of history. It is from the abstract truth which interpenetrates them, and lies latent among them like gold in the ore, that the mass derives its whole value: and the precious particles are generally combined with the baser in such a manner that the separation is a task of the utmost difficulty. [. . .]

[. . .] [I]n generalization, the writers of modern times have far surpassed those of antiquity. The historians of our own country are unequalled in depth and precision of reason; and, even in the works of our mere compilers, we often meet with speculations beyond the reach of Thucydides or Tacitus.

But it must, at the same time, be admitted that they have characteristic faults, so closely connected with their characteristic merits, and of such magnitude, that it may well be

---

i   Robert Lovelace: The articulate villain of Samuel Richardson's epistolary novel, *Clarissa* (1747–8). [-Ed.]

doubted whether, on the whole, this department of literature has gained or lost during the last two-and-twenty centuries.

The best historians of later times have been seduced from truth, not by their imagination, but by their reason. They far excel their predecessors in the art of deducing general principles from facts. But unhappily they have fallen into the error of distorting facts to suit general principles. They arrive at a theory from looking at some of the phenomena; and the remaining phenomena they strain or curtail to suit the theory. For this purpose it is not necessary that they should assert what is absolutely false; for all questions in morals and politics are questions of comparison and degree. Any proposition which does not involve a contradiction in terms may by possibility be true; and, if all the circumstances which raise a probability in its favor be stated and enforced, and those which lead to an opposite conclusion be omitted or lightly passed over, it may appear to be demonstrated. In every human character and transaction there is a mixture of good and evil: a little exaggeration, a little suppression, a judicious use of epithets, a watchful and searching skepticism with respect to the evidence on one side, a convenient credulity with respect to every report or tradition on the other, may easily make a saint of Laud, or a tyrant of Henry the Fourth.

This species of misrepresentation abounds in the most valuable works of modern historians. Herodotus tells his story like a slovenly witness, who, heated by partialities and prejudices, unacquainted with the established rules of evidence, and uninstructed as to the obligations of his oath, confounds what he imagines with what he has seen and heard, and brings out facts, reports, conjectures, and fancies, in one mass. Hume is an accomplished advocate. Without positively asserting much more than he can prove, he gives prominence to all the circumstances which support his case; he glides lightly over those which are unfavorable to it; his own witnesses are applauded and encouraged; the statements which seem to throw discredit on them are controverted; the contradictions into which they fall are explained away; a clear and connected abstract of their evidence is given. Everything that is offered on the other side is scrutinized with the utmost severity; every suspicious circumstance is a ground for comment and invective; what cannot be denied is extenuated, or passed by without notice; concessions even are sometimes made: but this insidious candor only increases the effect of the vast mass of sophistry.

[. . .]

The practice of distorting narrative into a conformity with theory is a vice not so unfavorable as at first sight it may appear to the interests of political science. We have compared the writers who indulge in it to advocates; and we may add, that their conflicting fallacies, like those of advocates, correct each other. It has always been held, in the most enlightened nations, that a tribunal will decide a judicial question most fairly when it has heard two able men argue, as unfairly as possible, on the two opposite sides of it; and we are inclined to think that this opinion is just. Sometimes, it is true, superior eloquence and dexterity will make the worse appear the better reason; but it is at least certain that the judge will be compelled to contemplate the case under two different aspects. It is certain that no important consideration will altogether escape notice.

This is at present the state of history. The poet laureate appears for the Church of England, Lingard for the Church of Rome. Brodie has moved to set aside the verdicts obtained by Hume; and the cause in which Mitford succeeded is, we understand, about to be reheard. In the midst of these disputes, however, history proper, if we may use the term, is disappearing. The high, grave, impartial summing up of Thucydides is nowhere to be found.

While our historians are practising all the arts of controversy, they miserably neglect the art of narration, the art of interesting the affections and presenting pictures to the imagination. That a writer may produce these effects without violating truth is sufficiently proved by many excellent biographical works. The immense popularity which well-written books of this kind have acquired deserves the serious consideration of historians. Voltaire's Charles the Twelfth, Marmontel's Memoirs, Boswell's Life of Johnson, Southey's account of Nelson, are perused with delight by the most frivolous and indolent. Whenever any tolerable book of the same description makes it appearance, the circulating libraries are mobbed; the book societies are in commotion; the new novel lies uncut; the magazines and newspapers fill their columns with extracts. In the mean time histories of great empires, written by men of eminent ability, lie unread on the shelves of ostentatious libraries.

The writers of history seem to entertain an aristocratical contempt for the writers of memoirs. They think it beneath the dignity of men who describe the revolutions of nations to dwell on the details which constitute the charm of biography. They have imposed on themselves a code of conventional decencies as absurd as that which has been the bane of the French drama. The most characteristic and interesting circumstances are omitted or softened down, because, as we are told, they are too trivial for the majesty of history. The majesty of history seems to resemble the majesty of the poor King of Spain, who died a martyr to ceremony because the proper dignitaries were not at hand to render him assistance.

That history would be more amusing if this etiquette were relaxed will, we suppose, be acknowledged. But would it be less dignified or less useful? What do we mean when we say that one past event is important and another insignificant? No past event has any intrinsic importance. The knowledge of it is valuable only as it leads us to form just calculations with respect to the future. A history which does not serve this purpose, though it may be filled with battles, treaties, and commotions, is as useless as the series of turnpike tickets collected by Sir Matthew Mite.

Let us suppose that Lord Clarendon, instead of filling hundreds of folio pages with copies of state papers, in which the same assertions and contradictions are repeated till the reader is overpowered with weariness, had condescended to be the Boswell of the Long Parliament. Let us suppose that he had exhibited to us the wise and lofty self-government of Hampden, leading while he seemed to follow, and propounding unanswerable arguments in the strongest forms with the modest air of an inquirer anxious for information: the delusions which misled the noble spirit of Vane; the course fanaticism which concealed the yet loftier genius of Cromwell, destined to control a mutinous army and a factious people, to abase the flag of Holland, to arrest the victorious arms of Sweden, and to hold the balance firm between the rival monarchies of France and Spain. Let us suppose that he had made his Cavaliers and Roundheads talk in their own style; that he had reported some of the ribaldry of Rupert's pages, and some of the cant of Harrison and Fleetwood. Would not his work in that case have been more interesting? Would it not have been more accurate?

A history in which every particular incident may be true may on the whole be false. The circumstances which have most influence on the happiness of mankind, the changes of manners and morals, the transition of communities from poverty to wealth, from knowledge to ignorance, from ferocity to humanity—these are, for the most part, noiseless revolutions. Their progress is rarely indicated by what historians are pleased to call important events. They are not achieved by armies, or enacted by senates. They are sanctioned by no treaties and recorded in no archives. They are carried on in every school, in every church, behind ten thousand counters, at ten thousand firesides. The upper current of society presents no certain criterion by which we can judge of the direction in which the under current flows. We read of defeats and victories. But we know that nations may be miserable amidst victories and prosperous amidst defeats. We read of the fall of wise ministers and of the rise of profligate favorites. But we must remember how small a proportion the good or evil effected by a single statesman can bear to the good or evil of a great social system.

Bishop Watson compares a geologist to a gnat mounted on an elephant, and laying down theories as to the whole internal structure of the vast animal, from the phenomena of the hide. The comparison is unjust to the geologists; but it is very applicable to those historians who write as if the body politic were homogeneous, who look only on the surface of affairs, and never think of the mighty and various organization which lies deep below.

[. . .]

The effect of historical reading is analogous, in many respects, to that produced by foreign travel. The student, like the tourist, is transported into a new state of society. He sees new fashions. He hears new modes of expression. His mind is enlarged by contemplating the wide diversities of laws, of morals, and of manners. But men may travel far, and return with minds contracted as if they had never stirred from their own market-town. In the same manner men may know the dates of many battles and the genealogies of many royal houses, and yet be no wiser. Most people look at past times as princes look at foreign countries. More than one illustrious stranger has landed on our island amidst the shouts of a mob, has dined with the king, has hunted with the master of the stag-hounds, has seen the guards reviewed, and a knight of the garter installed, has cantered along Regent street, has visited St. Paul's, and noted down its dimensions; and has then departed, thinking that he has seen England. He has, in fact, seen a few public buildings, public men, and public ceremonies. But of the vast and complex system of society, of the fine shades of national character, of the practical operation of government and laws, he knows nothing. He who would understand these things rightly must not confine his observations to palaces and solemn days. He must see ordinary men as they appear in their ordinary business and in their ordinary pleasures. He must mingle in the crowds of the exchange and the coffee-house. He must obtain admittance to the convivial table and the domestic hearth. He must bear with vulgar expressions. He must not shrink from exploring even the retreats of misery. He who wishes to understand the condition of mankind in former ages must proceed on the same principle. If he attends only to public transactions, to wars, congresses, and debates, his studies will be as unprofitable as the travels of those imperial, royal, and serene sovereigns who form their judgment of our island from having gone in state to a few fine sights, and from having held formal conferences with a few great officers.

The perfect historian is he in whose work the character and spirit of an age is exhibited in miniature. He relates no fact, he attributes no expression to his characters, which is not authenticated by sufficient testimony. But, by judicious selection, rejection, and arrangement, he gives to truth those attractions which have been usurped by fiction. In his narrative a due subordination is observed: some transactions are prominent; others retire. But the scale on which he represents them is increased or diminished, not according to the dignity of the persons concerned in them, but according to the degree in which they elucidate the condition of society and the nature of man. He shows us the court, the camp, and the senate. But he shows us also the nation. He considers no anecdote, no peculiarity of manner, no familiar saying, as too insignificant for his notice which is not too insignificant to illustrate the operation of laws, of religion, and of education, and to mark the progress of the human mind. Men will not merely be described, but will be made intimately known to us. The changes of manners will be indicated, not merely by a few general phrases or a few extracts from statistical documents, but by appropriate images presented in every line.

[. . .]

The early part of our imaginary history would be rich with coloring from romance, ballad, and chronicle. We should find ourselves in the company of knights such as those of Froissart, and of pilgrims such as those who rode with Chaucer from the Tabard. Society would be shown from the highest to the lowest,—from the royal cloth of state to the den of the outlaw; from the throne of the legate, to the chimney-corner where the begging friar regaled himself. Palmers, minstrels, crusaders,—the stately monastery, with the good cheer in its refectory and the high-mass in its chapel,—the manor-house, with its hunting and hawking,—the tournament, with the heralds and ladies, the trumpets and the cloth of gold,—would give truth and life to the representation. We should perceive, in a thousand slight touches, the importance of the privileged burgher, and the fierce and haughty spirit which swelled under the collar of the degraded villain. The revival of letters would not merely be described in a few magnificent periods. We should discern, in innumerable particulars, the fermentation of mind, the eager appetite for knowledge, which distinguished the sixteenth from the fifteenth century. In the Reformation we should see, not merely a schism which changed the ecclesiastical constitution of England and the mutual relations of the European powers, but a moral war which raged in every family, which set the father against the son, and the son against the father, the mother against the daughter, and the daughter against the mother. Henry would be painted with the skill of Tacitus. We should have the change of his character from his profuse and joyous youth to his savage and imperious old age. We should perceive the gradual progress of selfish and tyrannical passions in a mind not naturally insensible or ungenerous; and to the last we should detect some remains of that open and noble temper which endeared him to a people whom he oppressed, struggling with the hardness of despotism and the irritability of disease. We should see Elizabeth in all her weakness and in all her strength, surrounded by the handsome favorites whom she never trusted, and the wise old statesmen whom she never dismissed, uniting in herself the most contradictory qualities of both her parents,—the conquetry, the caprice, the petty malice of Anne,—the haughty and resolute spirit of Henry. We have no hesitation in saying that a great artist might produce a portrait of this remarkable woman at least as striking as that in the novel of Kenilworth, without employing a single trait not authenticated by ample testimony. In the mean time, we should see arts cultivated, wealth accumulated, the conveniences of life improved. We should see the keeps, where nobles, insecure themselves, spread insecurity around them, gradually giving place to the halls of peaceful opulence, to the oriels of Longleat, and the stately pinnacles of Burleigh. We should see towns extended, deserts cultivated, the hamlets of fishermen turned into wealthy havens, the meal of the peasant improved, and his hut more commodiously furnished. We should see those opinions and feelings which produced the great struggle against the house of Stuart slowly growing up in the bosom of private families, before they manifested themselves in parliamentary debates. Then would come the civil war. Those skirmishes on which Clarendon dwells so minutely would be told, as Thucydides would have told them, with perspicuous conciseness. They are merely connecting links. But the great characteristics of the age, the loyal enthusiasm of the brave English gentry, the fierce licentiousness, the swearing, dicing, drunken reprobates, whose excesses disgrace the royal cause,—the austerity of the Presbyterian Sabbaths in the city, the extravagance of the independent preachers in the camp, the precise garb, the severe countenance, the petty scruples, the affected accent, the absurd names and phrases which marked the Puritans,—the valor, the policy, the public spirit, which lurked beneath these ungraceful disguises,—the dreams of the raving Fifth-monarchy-man, the dreams, scarcely less wild, of the philosophic republican,—all these would enter into the representation, and render it at once more exact and more striking.

The instruction derived from history thus written would be of a vivid and practical character. It would be received by the imagination as well as by the reason. It would be not merely traced on the mind, but branded into it. Many truths, too, would be learned, which can be learned in no other manner. As the history of States is generally written, the greatest and most momentous revolutions seem to come upon them like supernatural inflictions, without warning or cause. But the fact is, that such revolutions are almost always the consequences of moral changes, which have gradually passed on the mass of the community, and which ordinarily proceed far before their progress is indicated by any public measure. An intimate knowledge of the domestic history of nations is therefore absolutely necessary to the prognosis of political events. A narrative, defective in this respect, is as useless as a medical treatise which should pass by all the symptoms attendant on the early stage of a disease and mention only what occurs when the patient is beyond the reach of remedies.

A historian, such as we have been attempting to describe, would indeed be an intellectual prodigy. In his mind, powers scarcely compatible with each other must be tempered into an exquisite harmony. We shall sooner see another Shakspeare or another Homer. The highest excellence to which any single faculty can be brought would be less surprising than such a happy and delicate combination of qualities. Yet the contemplation of imaginary models is not an unpleasant or useless employment of the mind. It cannot indeed produce perfection; but it produces improvement, and nourishes that generous and liberal fastidiousness which is not inconsistent with the strongest sensibility to merit, and which, while it exalts our conceptions of the art, does not render us unjust to the artist.

Note

1   *The Romance of History. England.* By HENRY NEELE. London, 1828.

Chapter 14

Thomas Carlyle

(1) ASTRÆA REDUX[i]

Thomas Carlyle (1795–1881):

(1) "Astræa Redux", 1837, *The French Revolution: A History* (London: James Fraser, 1837), 39–46.

(2) "The Hero as Divinity", 1840, *On Heroes, Hero-Worship, and the Hero in History* (London: Chapman and Hall, 1844), 3–4, 15–17.

A **PARADOXICAL PHILOSOPHER**, carrying to the uttermost length that aphorism of Montesquieu's, 'Happy the people whose annals are tiresome,' has said, 'Happy the people whose annals are vacant.' In which saying, mad as it looks, may there not still be found some grain of reason? For truly, as it has been written, 'Silence is divine,' and of Heaven; so in all earthly things too there is a silence which is better than any speech. Consider it well, the Event, the Thing which can be spoken of and recorded, is it not, in all cases, some disruption, some solution of continuity? Were it even a glad Event, it involves change, involves loss (of active Force); and so far, either in the past or in the present, is an irregularity, a disease. Stillest perseverance were our blessedness; not dislocation and alteration,—could they be avoided.

The oak grows silently, in the forest, a thousand years; only in the thousandth year, when the woodman arrives with his axe, is there heard an echoing through the solitudes; and the oak announces itself when, with far-sounding crash, it *falls*. How silent too was the planting of the acorn; scattered from the lap of some wandering wind! Nay, when our oak flowered, or put on its leaves (its glad Events), what shout of proclamation could there be? Hardly from the most observant a word of recognition. These things *befel* not, they were slowly *done*; not in an hour, but through the flight of days: what was to be said of it? This hour seemed altogether as the last was, as the next would be.

It is thus everywhere that foolish Rumour babbles not of what was done, but of what was misdone or undone; and foolish History (ever, more or less, the written epitomised synopsis of Rumour) knows so little that were not as well unknown. Attila Invasions, Walter-the-Penniless Crusades, Sicilian Vespers, Thirty-Years' Wars: mere sin and misery; not work, but hinderance of work! For the Earth, all this while, was yearly green and yellow with her kind harvests; the hand of the craftsman, the mind of the thinker rested not: and so, after all, and in spite of all, we have this so glorious high-domed blossoming World; concerning which, poor History may well ask, with wonder, Whence *it* came? She knows so little of it, knows so much of what obstructed it, what would have rendered it impossible. Such, nevertheless, by necessity or foolish choice is her rule and practice; whereby that paradox, 'Happy the people whose annals are vacant,' is not without its true side.

And yet, what seems more pertinent to note here, there is a stillness, not of unobstructed growth, but of passive inertness, the symptom of imminent downfal. As victory is silent, so is defeat. Of the opposing forces the weaker has resigned itself; the stronger marches on, noiseless now, but rapid, inevitable: the fall and overturn will not be noiseless. How all grows, and has its period, even as the herbs of the fields, be it annual, centennial, millennial! All grows and dies, each by its own wondrous laws, in wondrous fashion of its own; spiritual things most wondrously of all. Inscrutable, to the wisest, are these latter; not to be proph-esied of, or understood. If when the oak stands proudliest flourishing to the eye, you know that its heart is sound, it is not so with the man; how much less with the Society, with the Nation of men! Of such it may be affirmed even that the superficial aspect, that the inward feeling of full health, is generally ominous. For indeed it is of apoplexy, so to speak, and a plethoric lazy habit of body, that Churches, Kingships, Social Institutions, oftenest die. Sad, when such Institution plethorically says to itself, Take thy ease, thou hast goods laid up;— like the fool of the Gospel, to whom it was answered, Fool, *this night* thy life shall be required of thee!

Is it the healthy peace, or the ominous unhealthy, that rests on France, for these next ten years? Over which the Historian can pass lightly, without call to linger: for as yet events are not, much less performances. Time of sunniest stillness;—shall we call it, what all men thought it, the new Age of Gold? Call it, at least, of Paper; which, in many ways, is the succedaneum of Gold. Bank-paper, wherewith you can still buy when there is no gold left; Book-paper, splendent with Theories, Philosophies, Sensibilities,—beautiful art, not only of revealing Thought, but also of so beautifully hiding from us the want of Thought! Paper is made from the *rags* of things that did once exist; there are endless excellencies in Paper.— What wisest Philosophe, in this halcyon uneventful period, could prophesy that there was approaching, big with darkness and confusion, the event of events? Hope ushers in a Revolution,—as earthquakes are preceded by bright weather. On the Fifth of May, fifteen years hence, old Louis will not be sending for the Sacraments; but a new Louis, his grandson, with the whole pomp of astonished intoxicated France, will be opening the States General.

Dubarrydom and its d'Aiguillons are gone for ever. There is a young, still docile, well-intentioned King; a young, beautiful and bountiful, well-intentioned Queen; and with them all France as it were become young! Maupeou and his Parlement have to vanish into thick night; respectable Magistrates, not indifferent to the Nation, were it only for having been opponents of the Court, can descend unchained from their 'steep rocks at Croe in Combrailles' and elsewhere, and return singing praises: the old Parlement of Paris resumes its functions. Instead of a profligate bankrupt Abbé Terray, we have now, for Controller-General, a virtuous philosophic Turgot, with a whole Reformed France in his head. By whom whatsoever is wrong, in Finance or otherwise, will be righted,—as far as possible. Is it not as if Wisdom herself were henceforth to have seat and voice in the Council of Kings?

Turgot has taken office with the noblest plainness of speech to that effect; been listened to with the noblest royal trustfulness.[1] It is true, as King Louis objects, "they say he never goes to mass;" but liberal France likes him little worse for that; liberal France answers, "the Abbé Terray always went." Philosophism sees, for the first time, a Philosophe (or even a Philosopher) in office: she in all things will applausively second him; neither will light old Maurepas obstruct, if he can easily help it.

Then how 'sweet' are the manners; vice 'losing all its deformity;' becoming *decent* (as established things, making regulations for themselves, do); becoming almost a kind of 'sweet' virtue! Intelligence so abounds; irradiated by wit and the art of conversation. Philosophism sits joyful in her glittering saloons, the dinner-guest of Opulence grown ingenuous, the very Nobles proud to sit by her; and preaches, lifted up over all Bastilles, a coming millennium. From far Fernay, Patriarch Voltaire gives sign: veterans Diderot, d'Alembert have lived to see this day; these with their younger Marmontels, Morellets, Chamforts, Raynals, make glad the spicy board of rich ministering Dowager, of philosophic Farmer-General. O nights and suppers of the gods! Of a truth, the long-demonstrated will now be done; 'the Age of Revolutions approaches' (as Jean Jacques wrote), but then of happy blessed ones. Man awakens from his long somnambulism; chases the Fantasms that beleaguered and bewitched him. Behold the new morning glittering down the eastern steeps; fly, false Fantasms, from its shafts of light: let the Absurd fly utterly, forsaking this lower Earth for ever. It is Truth and *Astræa Redux* that (in the shape of Philosophism) henceforth reign. For what imaginable purpose was man made, if not to be 'happy?' By victorious Analysis, and Progress of the Species, happiness enough now awaits him. Kings can become philosophers; or else philosophers Kings. Let but Society be once rightly constituted,—by victorious Analysis! The stomach that is empty shall be filled; the throat that is dry shall be wetted with wine. Labour itself shall be all one as rest; not grievous, but joyous. Wheatfields, one would think, cannot come to grow untilled; no man made clayey, or made weary thereby;—unless indeed machinery will do it? Gratuitous Tailors and Restaurateurs may start up, at fit intervals, one as yet sees not how. But if each will, according to rule of Benevolence, have a care for all, then surely—no one will be un-cared for. Nay, who knows but, by sufficiently victorious Analysis, 'human life may be in-'definitely lengthened,' and men get rid of Death, as they have already done of the Devil? We shall then be happy in spite of Death and the Devil.—So preaches magniloquent Philosophism her *Redeunt Saturnia regna*.

The prophetic song of Paris and its Philosophes is audible enough in the Versailles Œil-de-Bœuf; and the Œil-de-Bœuf, intent chiefly on nearer blessedness, can answer, at worst, with a polite 'Why not?' Good old cheery Maurepas is too joyful a Prime Minister to dash the world's joy. Sufficient for the day be its own evil. Cheery old man, he cuts his jokes, and hovers careless along; his cloak well adjusted to the wind, if so be he may please all persons. The simple young King, whom a Maurepas cannot think of troubling with business, has retired into the interior apartments; taciturn, irresolute; though with a sharpness of temper at times: he, at length, determines on a little smith-work; and so, in apprenticeship with a Sieur Gamain (whom one day he shall have little cause to bless), is learning to make locks.[2] It appears further, he understood Geography; and could read English. Unhappy young King, his childlike trust in that foolish old Maurepas deserved another return. But friend and foe, destiny and himself have combined to do him hurt.

Meanwhile the fair young Queen, in her halls of state, walks like a goddess of Beauty, the cynosure of all eyes; as yet mingles not with affairs; heeds not the future; least of all, dreads it. Weber and Campan[3] have pictured her, there within the royal tapestries, in bright boudoirs, baths, peignoirs, and the Grand and Little Toilette; with a whole brilliant world waiting obsequious on her glance: fair young daughter of Time, what things has Time in store for thee! Like Earth's brightest Appearance, she moves gracefully, environed with the grandeur of Earth: a reality, and yet a magic vision; for, behold, shall not utter Darkness swallow it! The soft young heart adopts orphans, portions meritorious maids, delights to succour the poor,—such poor as come picturesquely in her way; and sets the fashion of doing it; for, as was said, Benevolence has now begun reigning. In her Duchess de Polignac, in her Princess de Lamballe, she enjoys something almost like friendship: now too, after seven long years, she has a child, and soon even a Dauphin, of her own; can reckon herself, as Queens go, happy in a husband.

Events? The grand events are but charitable Feats of Morals (*Fêtes des mœurs*), with their Prizes and Speeches; Poissarde Processions to the Dauphin's cradle; above all, Flirtations, their rise, progress, decline and fall. There are Snow-statues raised by the poor in hard winter, to a Queen who has given them fuel. There are masquerades, theatricals; beautify-ings of Little Trianon, purchase and repair of St. Cloud; journeyings from the summer Court-Elysium to the winter one. There are poutings and grudgings from the Sardinian Sisters-in-law (for the Princes too are wedded); little jealousies which Court-Etiquette can moderate. Wholly the lightest-hearted frivolous foam of Existence; yet an artfully refined foam; pleasant were it not so costly, like that which mantles on the wine of Champagne!

Monsieur, the King's elder Brother, has set up for a kind of wit; and leans towards the Philosophe side. Monseigneur d'Artois pulls the mask from a fair impertinent; fights a duel in consequence,—almost drawing blood.[4] He has breeches of a kind new in this world;—a fabulous kind: 'four tall lackeys,' says Mercier, as if he had seen it, 'hold him up in the air, that he may fall into the garment without vestige of wrinkle; from which rigorous encasement the same four, in the same way, and with more effort, must deliver him at night.'[5] This last is he who now, as a gray timeworn man, sits desolate at Grätz;[6] having winded up his destiny with the Three Days. In such sort are poor mortals swept and shovelled to and fro.

(2) THE HERO AS DIVINITY

WE HAVE UNDERTAKEN TO DISCOURSE HERE for a little on Great Men, their manner of appearance in our world's business, how they have shaped themselves in the world's history, what ideas men formed of them, what work they did;—on Heroes, namely, and on their reception and performance; what I call Hero-worship and the Heroic in human affairs. Too evidently this is a large topic; deserving quite other treatment than we can expect to give it at present. A large topic; indeed, an illimitable one; wide as Universal History itself. For, as I take it, Universal History, the history of what man has accomplished in this world, is at bottom the History of the Great Men who have worked here. They were the leaders of men, these great ones; the modellers, patterns, and in a wide sense creators, of whatsoever the general mass of men contrived to do or to attain; all things that we see standing accomplished in the world are properly the outer material result, the practical realisation and embodiment, of Thoughts that dwelt in the Great Men sent into the world: the soul of the whole world's history, it may justly be considered, were the history of these. Too clearly it is a topic we shall do no justice to in this place!

One comfort is, that Great Men, taken up in any way, are profitable company. We cannot look, however imperfectly, upon a great man, without gaining something by him. He is the living light-fountain, which it is good and pleasant to be near. The light which enlightens, which has enlightened the darkness of the world; and this not as a kindled lamp only, but rather as a natural luminary shining by the gift of Heaven; a flowing light-fountain, as I say, of native original insight, of manhood and heroic nobleness;—in whose radiance all souls feel that it is well with them. On any terms whatsoever, you will not grudge to wander in such neighbourhood for a while.

[. . .]

I am well aware that in these days Hero-worship, the thing I call Hero-worship, professes to have gone out, and finally ceased. This, for reasons which it will be worth while some time to inquire into, is an age that as it were denies the existence of great men; denies the desirableness of great men. Show our critics a great man, a Luther for example, they begin to what they call 'account' for him; not to worship him, but take the dimensions of him,—and bring him out to be a little kind of man! He was the 'creature of the Time,' they say; the Time called him forth, the Time did everything, he nothing—but what we the little critic could have done too! This seems to me but melancholy work. The Time call forth? Alas, we have known Times *call* loudly enough for their great man; but not find him when they called! He was not there; Providence had not sent him; the Time, *calling* its loudest, had to go down to confusion and wreck because he would not come when called.

For if we will think of it, no Time need have gone to ruin, could it have *found* a man great enough, a man wise and good enough: wisdom to discern truly what the Time wanted, valour to lead it on the right road thither; these are the salvation of any Time. But I liken common languid Times, with their unbelief, distress, perplexity, with their languid doubting characters and embarrassed circumstances, impotently crumbling-down into ever worse distress towards final ruin;—all this I liken to dry dead fuel, waiting for the lightning out of Heaven that shall kindle it. The great man, with his free force direct out of God's own hand, is the lightning. His word is the wise healing word which all can believe in. All blazes round him now, when he has once struck on it, into fire like his own. The dry mouldering sticks are thought to have called him forth. They did want him greatly; but as to calling him forth—!—Those are critics of small vision, I think, who cry: "See, is it not the sticks that made the fire?" No sadder proof can be given by a man of his own littleness than disbelief in great men. There is no sadder symptom of a generation than such general blindness to the spiritual lightning, with faith only in the heap of barren dead fuel. It is the last consummation of unbelief. In all epochs of the world's history, we shall find the Great Man to have been the indispensable saviour of his epoch;—the lightning, without which the fuel never would have burnt. The History of the World, I said already, was the Biography of Great Men.

Notes

1   Turgot's Letter: Condorcet, Vie de Turgot (Œuvres de Condorcet, t. v.) p. 67. The date is 24th August, 1774.
2   Campan, i. 125.
3   Campan, i. 100–151.—Weber, i. 11–50.
4   Besenval, ii. 282–330.
5   Mercier: Nouveau Paris, iii. 147.
6   AD 1834.

Chapter 15

Jules Michelet

ILLUSTRATIONS TO BOOK THE FOURTH

Jules Michelet (1798–1874), "Illustrations to Book the Fourth", 1844, *History of France.* Trans. Walter K. Kelly (London: Chapman and Hall, 1844), Vol. 1, 632, 634–6.

THE DOCUMENTS WHICH WERE to have followed this book are reserved for another place. They are derived, in a great measure, from the archives of the kingdom. One word only as to these archives, the functions which have made it the author's duty to search out the history of our antiquities to the bottom, the peaceful theatre of his labours, and the spot that has prompted them. His book is his life; it is the almost necessary result of the circumstances in which he has found himself placed. This consideration will perhaps entitle him to some indulgence on the part of the equitable reader.

Employed in the archives of the kingdom, and professor in the Ecole Normale, he has for many years concentrated his studies on the national history. The facts and ideas gathered in that rich depository of the official acts of the monarchy, were, thanks to this twofold position, taught to the young professors, who, in their turn, have been able to propagate them all over France.

[. . .]

Monarchical confiscation created the Trésor des Chartes; revolutionary confiscation made our archives such as we have them at this day. To the old Trésor des Chartes, thenceforth proscribed, were added its brethren the *Trésors* of St. Denis, St. Germain des Prés, and a host of other monasteries. The venerable and fragile papyri which still bear the names of Childebert and Clotaire, came forth from the ecclesiastical asylums to appear in this great review of the dead. In this violent and rapid concentration of so many monuments, many perished, many were destroyed: parchments had also their own revolutionary tribunal under the appellation of *Bureau du triage des titres*, a tribunal terrible and expeditious in its judgments; an immense number of muniments had a deadly designation applied to them: *titre féodal*; when that was said the matter was all over. Revolutionary confiscation not grounding its proceedings on texts and written titles, like monarchic confiscation, had no need of these parchments. Its one sole title was the social contract, as the Koran was his who burned the Alexandrian library.

If the Revolution did little service to knowledge in scrutinising and criticising the muniments, it served it greatly by the vast concentration it effected. It shook all this dust briskly: monasteries, châteaux, depositories of every kind, it emptied all, turned out every thing on the floor, and gathered all up together. The stores in the Louvre, for instance, were crammed full of papers, the very windows were blocked up, whilst the archivist hired out several rooms to the Académie. If one wanted to make researches he was obliged to have a candle in broad noon. The Revolution, once for all, let in daylight upon the dusty masses. [. . .]

At present the archives of France are no longer those of Europe. We still see on the doors of our halls the trace of inscriptions, reminding us of our losses; Bulles, Daterie, &c. Nevertheless, there still remain to us about a hundred and fifty *cartons*. Though the provinces refuse to let their archives be collected together, though even many ministerial offices continue to retain their own, want of space will at last induce them to get rid of them. We shall conquer, for we are death, we have its potent attraction; every revolution turns to our advantage. We have but to wait: "Patiens, quia æternus."

Soon or late the victors and the vanquished come to us. We have the whole monarchy from Alpha to Omega; Childebert's charter by the side of Louis XVI's will; we have the Republic in our iron chest, keys of the Bastile—minute of the rights of man—deputies' urns, and the great republican machine, the implement for stamping assignats. There is nothing, even to the pontificate, but has left us something; the pope has taken back his archives from us; but in reprisal we have kept the poles of the litter on which he was carried to the emperor's coronation. Beside these bloody toys of Providence is placed the immutable standard of measure, which is examined every year. The temperature is invariable in the archives.

As for me, when I first entered these manuscript catacombs, this admirable necropolis of the national muniments, I would gladly have said, like the German entering the monastery of St. Vannes, "Here is the habitation I have chosen, and my rest for ever and ever!"

I was not long, however, before I perceived, that in the apparent silence of these galleries there was a movement, a murmur, which pertained not to death. These papers and parchments long left unregarded, desired nothing better than to return to the light of day. These papers are not papers, but lives of men, provinces, and peoples. First of all the families and the fiefs, blazoned in their dust, cried out against oblivion. The provinces rose up, alleging that centralisation had wrongfully thought to annihilate them. The ordonnances of our kings asserted that they had not been effaced by the multitude of modern laws. Had one hearkened to them all, as the grave-digger said on the field of battle, there was not one dead individual among them. They were all alive and talking, and surrounded the author with an army of a hundred languages, that rudely silenced the grand voice of the Republic and the Empire.

Softly, dead sirs, let us proceed in order, if you please. You all have a rightful claim on history. The private is very well as a private, the general as a general. The Fief is right, the Monarchy more so, and more again the Empire. You shall have your say, Godefroy; and you, Richelieu; and you, Bonaparte. The province shall revive; the old diversity of France shall be marked out by a strongly defined geography. It shall reappear, but on condition that as the diversity gradually wears away, the identification of the country shall succeed in its turn. Let the monarchy revive, let France revive! Let a great effort of classification serve for once as a clue through this chaos. Such a systemisation will be serviceable, however imperfect. To live again is something after all, even though the head sit awry on the shoulders, and the leg be not fitted quite as it should be to the thigh.

And in proportion as I breathed upon their dust I saw them rise. They drew from the sepulchre, one a hand, another its head; as in Michael Angelo's Day of Judgment, or in the

Dance of Death. This galvanic dance of theirs around me, I have endeavoured to reproduce in this book. Some, perhaps, will consider this neither handsome nor true; they will be shocked especially at the harshness of the provincial contrasts I have pointed out. It is enough for me to observe to my critics, that it may very possibly be they do not recognise their own ancestors, that we French possess, above all other nations, that gift which one of the ancients longed for, the gift of forgetting. The songs of Roland and Renaud, &c., have certainly been popular; the fabliaux succeeded them; and all this was so obsolete in the sixteenth century, that Joachim du Bellay lays it down, "There is nothing in our old literature but the Romance of the Rose:" these are his very words. In the time of Du Bellay, France was Rabelais; afterwards it was Voltaire. Rabelais now belongs to the domain of the erudite, Voltaire is less read than formerly. Thus does this people go on transforming and forgetting itself.

France, at this day one and identified, may very well deny that old heterogeneous France I have described. The Gascon will not recognise Gascony, nor the Provençal Provençe. To this I reply, that there is no longer a Gascony or a Provençe, but a France. I now present that France in the original diversity of its old provinces. The last books of this history will exhibit it in its unity.

Chapter 16

Mercy Otis Warren

AN ADDRESS TO THE INHABITANTS
OF THE UNITED STATES

Mercy Otis Warren (1728–1814), "An Address to the Inhabitants of the United States", 1805, *History of the Rise, Progress and Termination of the American Revolution* (Boston: Manning & Loring, 1805), iii–viii.

AT A PERIOD WHEN every manly arm was occupied, and every trait of talent or activity engaged, either in the cabinet or the field, apprehensive, that amidst the sudden convulsions, crowded scenes, and rapid changes, that flowed in quick succession, many circumstances might escape the more busy and active members of society, I have been induced to improve the leisure Providence had lent, to record as they passed, in the following pages, the new and unexperienced events exhibited in a land previously blessed with peace, liberty, simplicity, and virtue.

As circumstances were collected, facts related, and characters drawn, many years antecedent to any history since published, relative to the dismemberment of the colonies, and to American independence, there are few allusions to any later writers.

Connected by nature, friendship, and every social tie, with many of the first patriots, and most influential characters on the continent; in the habits of confidential and epistolary intercourse with several gentlemen employed abroad in the most distinguished stations, and with others since elevated to the highest grades of rank and distinction, I had the best means of information, through a long period that the colonies were in suspense, waiting the operation of foreign courts, and the success of their own enterprising spirit.

The solemnity that covered every countenance, when contemplating the sword uplifted, and the horrors of civil war rushing to habitations not inured to scenes of rapine and misery; even to the quiet cottage, where only concord and affection had reigned; stimulated to observation a mind that had not yielded to the assertion, that all political attentions lay out of the road of female life.

It is true there are certain appropriate duties assigned to each sex; and doubtless it is the more peculiar province of masculine strength, not only to repel the bold invader of the rights of his country and of mankind, but in the nervous [i.e. physical, vigorous -Ed.]

style of manly eloquence, to describe the blood-stained field, and relate the story of slaughtered armies.

Sensible of this, the trembling heart has recoiled at the magnitude of the undertaking, and the hand often shrunk back from the task; yet, recollecting that every domestic enjoyment depends on the unimpaired possession of civil and religious liberty, that a concern for the welfare of society ought equally to glow in every human breast, the work was not relinquished. The most interesting circumstances were collected, active characters portrayed, the principles of the times developed, and the changes marked; nor need it cause a blush to acknowledge, a detail was preserved with a view of transmitting it to the rising youth of my country, some of them in infancy, others in the European world, while the most interesting events lowered over their native land.

Conscious that truth has been the guide of my pen, and candor, as well as justice, the accompaniment of my wishes through every page, I can say, with an ingenious writer, "I have used my pen with the liberty of one, who neither hopes nor fears, nor has any interest in the success or failure of any party, and who speaks to posterity—perhaps very far remote."

The sympathizing heart has looked abroad and wept [for] the many victims of affliction, inevitably such in consequence of civil feuds and the concomitant miseries of war, either foreign or domestic. The reverses of life, and the instability of the world, have been viewed on the point of both extremes. Their delusory nature and character, have been contemplated as becomes the philosopher and the christian: the one teaches us from the analogies of nature, the necessity of changes, decay, and death; the other strengthens the mind to meet them with the rational hope of revival and renovation.

Several years have elapsed since the historical tracts, now with diffidence submitted to the public, have been arranged in their present order. Local circumstances, the decline of health, temporary deprivations of sight, the death of the most amiable of children, "the shaft flew thrice, and thrice my peace was slain",[i] have sometimes prompted to throw by the pen in despair. I draw a veil over the woe-fraught scenes that have pierced my own heart. "While the soul was melting inwardly, it has endeavoured to support outwardly, with decency and dignity, those accidents which admit of no redress, and to exert that spirit that enables to get the better of those that do."

Not indifferent to the opinion of the world, nor servilely courting its smiles, no further apology is offered for the attempt, though many may be necessary, for the incomplete execution of a design, that had rectitude for its basis, and a beneficent regard for the civil and religious rights of mankind, for its motive.

The liberal-minded will peruse with candor, rather than criticise with severity; nor will they think it necessary, that any apology should be offered, for sometimes introducing characters nearly connected with the author of the following annals; as they were early and zealously attached to the public cause, uniform in their principles, and constantly active in the great scenes that produced the revolution, and obtained independence for their country, truth precludes that reserve which might have been proper on less important occasions, and forbids to pass over in silence the names of such as expired before the conflict was finished, or have since retired from public scenes. The historian has never laid aside the tenderness of the sex or the friend; at the same time, she has endeavoured, on all occasions, that the strictest veracity should govern her heart, and the most exact impartiality be the guide of her pen.

---

i   Edward Young. *Night Thoughts* 1, 212. [-Ed.]

If the work should be so far useful or entertaining, as to obtain the sanction of the generous and virtuous part of the community, I cannot but be highly gratified and amply rewarded for the effort, soothed at the same time with the idea, that the motives were justifiable in the eye of Omniscience. Then, if it should not escape the remarks of the critic, or the censure of party, I shall feel no wound to my sensibility, but repose on my pillow as quietly as ever,——

> *While all the distant din the world can keep,*
> *Rolls o'er my grotto, and but soothes my sleep.* [ii]

Before this address to my countrymen is closed, I beg leave to observe, that as a new century has dawned upon us, the mind is naturally led to contemplate the great events that have run parallel with, and have just closed the last. From the revolutionary spirit of the times, the vast improvements in science, arts, and agriculture, the boldness of genius that marks the age, the investigation of new theories, and the changes in the political, civil, and religious characters of men, succeeding generations have reason to expect still more astonishing exhibitions in the next. In the mean time, Providence has clearly pointed out the duties of the present generation, particularly the paths which Americans ought to tread. The United States form a young republic, a confederacy which ought ever to be cemented by a union of interest and affection, under the influence of those principles which obtained their independence. These have indeed, at certain periods, appeared to be in the wane; but let them never be eradicated, by the jarring interests of parties, jealousies of the sister states, or the ambition of individuals! It has been observed, by a writer of celebrity,[1] that "that people, government, and constitution is the freest, which makes the best provision for the enacting of expedient and salutary laws." May this truth be evinced to all ages, by the wise and salutary laws that shall be enacted in the federal legislature of America!

May the hands of the executive of their own choice, be strengthened more by the unanimity and affection of the people, than by the dread of penal inflictions, or any restraints that might repress free inquiry, relative to the principles of their own government, and the conduct of its administrators! The world is now viewing America, as experimenting a new system of government, a FEDERAL REPUBLIC, including a territory to which the Kingdoms of Great Britain and Ireland bear little proportion. The practicability of support-ing such a system, has been doubted by some; if she succeeds, it will refute the assertion, that none but small states are adapted to republican government; if she does not, and the union should be dissolved, some ambitious son of Columbia, or some foreign adventurer, allured by the prize, may wade to empire through seas of blood, or the friends of monarchy may see a number of petty despots, stretching their sceptres over the disjointed parts of the continent. Thus by the mandate of a single sovereign, the degraded subjects of one state, under the bannerets of royalty, may be dragged to sheathe their swords in the bosoms of the inhabitants of another.

The state of the public mind, appears at present to be prepared to weigh these reflec-tions with solemnity, and to receive with pleasure an effort to trace the origin of the American revolution, to review the characters that effected it, and to justify the principles of the defection and final separation from the parent state. With an expanded heart, beating with high hopes of the continued freedom and prosperity of America, the writer indulges a modest expectation, that the following pages will be perused with kindness and candor: this

---

ii   Alexander Pope, "The First Satire of the Second Book of Horace, Imitated." 125–6. [-Ed.]

she claims, both in consideration of her sex, the uprightness of her intentions, and the fervency of her wishes for the happiness of all the human race.

Plymouth, Mass., March, 1805

Mercy Warren

Note

1   Paley's Moral Philosophy. [William Paley, *The Principles of Moral and Political Philosophy* (London, 1785), p. 448 (Book vi, Ch. V).]

Chapter 17

Francis Parkman

INTRODUCTION TO *PIONEERS OF FRANCE IN THE NEW WORLD*

Francis Parkman (1823–1893), "Introduction", *Pioneers of France in the New World*, 1833 (London: Macmillan, 1865), ix–xvi.

THE SPRINGS OF AMERICAN CIVILIZATION, unlike those of the elder world, lie revealed in the clear light of History. In appearance they are feeble; in reality, copious and full of force. Acting at the sources of life, instruments otherwise weak become mighty for good and evil, and men, lost elsewhere in the crowd, stand forth as agents of Destiny. In their toils, their sufferings, their conflicts, momentous questions were at stake, and issues vital to the future world,—the prevalence of races, the triumph of principles, health or disease, a blessing or a curse. On the obscure strife where men died by tens or by scores hung questions of as deep import for posterity as on those mighty contests of national adolescence where carnage is reckoned by thousands.

The subject to which the proposed series will be devoted is that of "France in the New World,"—the attempt of Feudalism, Monarchy, and Rome to master a continent where, at this hour, half a million of bayonets are vindicating the ascendency of a regulated freedom;—Feudalism still strong in life, though enveloped and overborne by new-born Centralization; Monarchy in the flush of triumphant power; Rome, nerved by disaster, springing with renewed vitality from ashes and corruption, and ranging the earth to reconquer abroad what she had lost at home. These banded powers, pushing into the wilderness their indomitable soldiers and devoted priests, unveiled the secrets of the barbarous continent, pierced the forests, traced and mapped out the streams, planted their emblems, built their forts, and claimed all as their own. New France was all head. Under king, noble, and Jesuit, the lank, lean body would not thrive. Even commerce wore the sword, decked itself with badges of nobility, aspired to forest seigniories and hordes of savage retainers.

Along the borders of the sea an adverse power was strengthening and widening, with slow but steadfast growth, full of blood and muscle,—a body without a head. Each had its strength, each its weakness, each its own modes of vigorous life: but the one was fruitful, the other barren; the one instinct with hope, the other darkening with shadows of despair.

By name, local position, and character, one of these communities of freemen stands forth as the most conspicuous representative of this antagonism;—Liberty and Absolutism, New England and New France. The one was the offspring of a triumphant government; the other, of an oppressed and fugitive people: the one, an unflinching champion of the Roman Catholic reaction; the other, a vanguard of the Reform. Each followed its natural laws of growth, and each came to its natural result. Vitalized by the principles of its foundation, the Puritan commonwealth grew apace. New England was preeminently the land of material progress. Here the prize was within every man's reach: patient industry need never doubt its reward; nay, in defiance of the four Gospels, assiduity in pursuit of gain was promoted to the rank of a duty, and thrift and godliness were linked in equivocal wedlock. Politically she was free; socially she suffered from that subtle and searching oppression which the dominant opinion of a free community may exercise over the members who compose it. As a whole, she grew upon the gaze of the world, a signal example of expansive energy; but she has not been fruitful in those salient and striking forms of character which often give a dramatic life to the annals of nations far less prosperous.

We turn to New France, and all is reversed. Here was a bold attempt to crush under the exactions of a grasping hierarchy, to stifle under the curbs and trappings of a feudal monarchy, a people compassed by influences of the wildest freedom,—whose schools were the forest and the sea, whose trade was an armed barter with savages, and whose daily life a lesson of lawless independence. But this fierce spirit had its vent. The story of New France is from the first a story of war: of war—for so her founders believed—with the adversary of mankind himself; war with savage tribes and potent forest commonwealths; war with the encroaching powers of Heresy and of England. Her brave, unthinking people were stamped with the soldier's virtues and the soldier's faults; and in their leaders were displayed, on a grand and novel stage, the energies, aspirations, and passions which belong to hopes vast and vague, ill-restricted powers, and stations of command.

The growth of New England was a result of the aggregate efforts of a busy multitude, each in his narrow circle toiling for himself, to gather competence or wealth. The expansion of New France was the achievement of a gigantic ambition striving to grasp a continent. It was a vain attempt. Long and valiantly her chiefs upheld their cause, leading to battle a vassal population, warlike as themselves. Borne down by numbers from without, wasted by corruption from within, New France fell at last; and out of her fall grew revolutions whose influence to this hour is felt through every nation of the civilized world.

The French dominion is a memory of the past; and when we evoke its departed shades, they rise upon us from their graves in strange, romantic guise. Again their ghostly camp-fires seem to burn, and the fitful light is cast around on lord and vassal and black-robed priest, mingled with wild forms of savage warriors, knit in close fellowship on the same stern errand. A boundless vision grows upon us; an untamed continent; vast wastes of forest verdure; mountains silent in primeval sleep; river, lake, and glimmering pool; wilderness oceans mingling with the sky. Such was the domain which France conquered for Civilization. Plumed helmets gleamed in the shade of its forests, priestly vestments in its dens and fastnesses of ancient barbarism. Men steeped in antique learning, pale with the close breath of the cloister, here spent the noon and evening of their lives, ruled savage hordes with a mild, parental sway, and stood serene before the direst shapes of death. Men of courtly nurture, heirs to the polish of a far-reaching ancestry, here, with their dauntless hardihood, put to shame the boldest sons of toil.

This memorable but half-forgotten chapter in the book of human life can be rightly read only by lights numerous and widely scattered. The earlier period of New France was prolific in a class of publications which are often of much historic value, but of which many are exceedingly rare. The writer, however, has at length gained access to them all. Of the unpublished records of the colonies, the archives of France are of course the grand deposit; but many documents of important bearing on the subject are to be found scattered in public and private libraries, chiefly in France and Canada. The task of collection has proved abundantly irksome and laborious. It has, however, been greatly lightened by the action of the governments of New York, Massachusetts, and Canada, in collecting from Europe copies of documents having more or less relation to their own history. It has been greatly lightened, too, by a most kind co-operation, for which the writer owes obligations too many for recognition at present, but of which he trusts to make fitting acknowledgment hereafter. [. . .]

In this [volume], and still more must it be the case in succeeding volumes, [that] the amount of reading applied to their composition is far greater than the citations represent, much of it being of a collateral and illustrative nature. This was essential to a plan whose aim it was, while scrupulously and rigorously adhering to the truth of facts, to animate them with the life of the past, and, so far as might be, clothe the skeleton with flesh. If, at times, it may seem that range has been allowed to fancy, it is so in appearance only; since the minutest details of narrative or description rest on authentic documents or on personal observation.

Faithfulness to the truth of history involves far more than a research, however patient and scrupulous, into special facts. Such facts may be detailed with the most minute exactness, and yet the narrative, taken as a whole, may be unmeaning or untrue. The narrator must seek to imbue himself with the life and spirit of the time. He must study events in their bearings near and remote; in the character, habits, and manners of those who took part in them, he must himself be, as it were, a sharer or a spectator of the action he describes.

With respect to that special research which, if inadequate, is still in the most emphatic sense indispensable, it has been the writer's aim to exhaust the existing material of every subject treated. While it would be folly to claim success in such an attempt, he has reason to hope that, so far at least as relates to the present volume, nothing of much importance has escaped him. With respect to the general preparation just alluded to, he has long been too fond of his theme to neglect any means within his reach of making his conception of it distinct and true.

To those who have aided him with information and documents, the extreme slowness in the progress of the work will naturally have caused surprise. This slowness was unavoidable. During the past eighteen years, the state of his health has exacted throughout an extreme caution in regard to mental application, reducing it at best within narrow and precarious limits, and often precluding it. Indeed, for two periods, each of several years, any attempt at bookish occupation would have been merely suicidal. A condition of sight arising from kindred sources has also retarded the work, since it has never permitted reading or writing continuously for much more than five minutes, and often has not permitted them at all. A previous work, "The Conspiracy of Pontiac," was written in similar circumstances.

The writer means, if possible, to carry the present design to its completion. Such a completion, however, will by no means be essential as regards the individual volumes of the series, since each will form a separate and independent work. The present work, it will be seen, contains two distinct and completed narratives. Some progress has been made in others.

Boston. January 1, 1865.

Chapter 18

George Bancroft

A RETROSPECT. MOVEMENTS TOWARD UNION. 1643–1781

George Bancroft (1800–1891), "A Retrospect. Movements Toward Union. 1643–1781", *History of the Formation of the Constitution of the United States of America* (New York: Appleton, 1882), Vol. 1, 3–6.

THE ORDER OF TIME brings us to the most cheering act in the political history of mankind, when thirteen republics, of which at least three reached from the sea to the Mississippi, formed themselves into one federal commonwealth. There was no revolt against the past, but a persistent and healthy progress. The sublime achievement was the work of a people led by statesmen of earnestness, perseverance, and public spirit, instructed by the widest experience in the forms of representative government, and warmed by that mutual love which proceeds from ancient connection, harmonious effort in perils, and common aspirations.

Scarcely one who wished me good speed when I first essayed to trace the history of America remains to greet me with a welcome as I near the goal. Deeply grateful as I am for the friends who rise up to gladden my old age, their encouragement must renew my grief for those who have gone before me.

While so much is changed in the living objects of personal respect and affection, infinitely greater are the transformations in the condition of the world. Power has come to dwell with every people, from the Arctic sea to the Mediterranean, from Portugal to the borders of Russia. From end to end of the United States, the slave has become a freeman; and the various forms of bondage have disappeared from European Christendom. Abounding harvests of scientific discovery have been garnered by numberless inquisitive minds, and the wildest forces of nature have been taught to become the docile helpmates of man. The application of steam to the purposes of travel on land and on water, the employment of a spark of light as the carrier of thought across continents and beneath oceans, have made of all the inhabitants of the earth one society. A journey round the world has become the pastime of a holiday vacation. The morning newspaper gathers up and brings us the noteworthy events of the last four-and-twenty hours in every quarter of the globe. All states are beginning to form parts of one system. The "new nations," which Shakespeare's prophetic eye saw rising on our eastern shore, dwell securely along two oceans, midway between their kin in Great Britain on the one side and the oldest surviving empire on the other.

More than two thousand years ago it was truly said that the nature of justice can be more easily discerned in a state than in one man.[1] It may now be studied in the collective states. The ignorance and prejudices that come from isolation are worn away in the conflict of the forms of culture. We learn to think the thought, to hope the hope of mankind. Former times spoke of the dawn of civilization in some one land; we live in the morning of the world. Day by day the men who guide public affairs are arraigned before the judgment-seat of the race. A government which adopts a merely selfish policy is pronounced to be the foe of the human family. The statesman who founds and builds up the well-being of his country on justice has all the nations for a cloud of witnesses, and, as one of our own poets[2] has said, "The linkéd hemispheres attest his deed." He thrills the world with joy; and man becomes of a nobler spirit as he learns to gauge his opinions and his acts by a scale commensurate with his nature.

History carries forward the study of ethics by following the footsteps of states from the earliest times of which there is a record. The individual who undertakes to capture truth by solitary thought loses his way in the mazes of speculation, or involves himself in mystic visions, so that the arms which he extends to embrace what are but formless shadows return empty to his own breast. To find moral truth, he must study man in action. The laws of which reason is conscious can be tested best by experience; and inductions will be the more sure, the larger the experience from which they are drawn. However great may be the number of those who persuade themselves that there is in man nothing superior to himself, history interposes with evidence that tyranny and wrong lead inevitably to decay; that freedom and right, however hard may be the struggle, always prove resistless. Through this assurance ancient nations learn to renew their youth; the rising generation is incited to take a generous part in the grand drama of time; and old age, staying itself upon sweet Hope as its companion and cherisher,[3] not bating a jot of courage, nor seeing cause to argue against the hand or the will of a higher power, stands waiting in the tranquil conviction that the path of humanity is still fresh with the dews of morning, that the Redeemer of the nations liveth.

Notes

1   Plato in the Republic, Book ii. Bekker, III. i. 78.
2   Emerson: The Adirondacks, 248.
3   Plato. Republic. Book i, Bekker, Pindar in III. i. 10.

Further reading: Chapters 13 to 18

Bann, Stephen. *The Clothing of Clio: A Study of the Representation of History in Nineteenth Century Britain and France* (Cambridge: Cambridge University Press, 1984).

——. *Romanticism and the Rise of History* (New York: Maxwell Macmillan, 1995).

Canary, Robert H. *George Bancroft* (New York: Twayne, 1974).

Crossley, Ceri. *French Historians and Romanticism: Thierry, Guizot, the Saint-Simonians, Quinet, Michelet* (London and New York: Routledge, 1993).

Culler, A. Dwight. *The Victorian Mirror of History* (New Haven: Yale University Press, 1985).

Fontana, Bianca Maria. *Rethinking the Politics of Commercial Society: The Edinburgh Review, 1802–1832* (Cambridge: Cambridge University Press, 1985).

Gooch, G. P. *History and Historians in the Nineteenth Century* (Boston: Beacon Press, 1959).

Hamburger, Joseph. *Macaulay and the Whig Tradition* (Chicago: University of Chicago Press, 1976).

Heyck, T. W. *The Transformation of Intellectual Life in Britain* (London: Croom Helm, 1982).

Klancher, Jon. *The Making of English Reading Audiences, 1790–1832* (Madison: University of Wisconsin Press, 1987).

Levine, Philippa. *The Amateur and the Professional: Antiquarians, Historians, and Archaeologists in Victorian England, 1838–1886* (Cambridge: Cambridge University Press, 1986).

McGann, Jerome J. *The Romantic Ideology: A Critical Investigation* (Chicago: University of Chicago Press, 1983).

Morgan, Peter. *Literary Critics and Reviewers in Early Nineteenth-Century Britain* (Beckenham: Croom Helm, 1983).

Orr, Linda. *Headless History: Nineteenth-Century French Historiography of the Revolution* (Ithaca, NY: Cornell University Press, 1990).

Peer, Larry H. (ed.) *The Romantic Manifesto: An Anthology* (New York: Peter Lang, 1988).

Rigney, Ann. *Imperfect Histories: The Elusive Past and the Legacy of Romantic Historicism* (Ithaca: Cornell University Press, 2001). 13–58.

Trevor-Roper, Hugh. *The Romantic Movement and the Study of History* (London: Athlone Press, 1969).

Vitzthum, Richard C. *The American Compromise: Theme and Method in the Histories of Bancroft, Parkman, and Adams* (Norman: University of Oklahoma Press, 1974).

Williams, Raymond. *Culture and Society, 1780–1950* (London: Chatto & Windus, 1958).

MACAULAY, THOMAS BABINGTON (1800–1859)

Burrow, John W. *A Liberal Descent: Victorian Historians and the English Past* (Cambridge: Cambridge University Press, 1981).

Clive, John. *Macaulay: The Shaping of the Historian* (London: Secker & Warburg, 1973).

—— and Thomas Pinney (eds) *Thomas Babington Macaulay: Selected Writings* (Chicago: University of Chicago Press, 1972).

Cruikshank, Margaret. *Thomas Babington Macaulay* (Boston, MA: Twayne, 1978).

Edwards, Owen Dudley. *Macaulay* (London: Weidenfeld & Nicholson, 1988).

Firth, Charles Harding. *A Commentary on Macaulay's History of England* (London: Macmillan, 1938).

Gay, Peter. *Style in History* (New York: McGraw-Hill, 1974).

Geyl, Pieter. *Debates with Historians* (London: Batsford, 1955).

Gilley, Sheridan. "Macaulay as Historian", *The Australian Journal of Politics and History* 29 (1983), 328–43.

Hamburger, J. *Macaulay and the Whig Tradition* (Chicago: University of Chicago Press, 1976).

Jann, Rosemary. *The Art and Science of Victorian History* (Columbus, OH: Ohio State University Press, 1985).

Knowles, David. *Lord Macaulay, 1800–1859: A Lecture* (Cambridge: Cambridge University Press, 1960).

Levine, G. *The Boundaries of Fiction: Carlyle, Macaulay, Newman* (Princeton, NJ: Princeton University Press, 1968).

Millgate, Jane. *Macaulay* (London: Routledge & Kegan Paul, 1973).

Stunt, Timothy C. F. "Thomas Babington Macaulay and Frederick the Great", *Historical Journal* 23(4) (1980), 939–47.

Trevelyan, George Otto. *The Life and Letters of Lord Macaulay.* 2 vols (New York: Harper, 1875).

Young, Kenneth. *Macaulay*, Ian Scott-Kilvert (ed.) (Harlow: Longmans, 1976).

CARLYLE, THOMAS (1795–1881)

Ben-Israel, Hedva. *English Historians on the French Revolution* (Cambridge: Cambridge University Press, 1968).

Campbell, Ian. *Thomas Carlyle* (London: Hamish Hamilton, 1974).

Cobban, Alfred. "Carlyle's 'French' Revolution", *History* 48 (1963), 306–16.

Dale, Peter Allan. *The Victorian Critic and the Idea of History: Carlyle, Arnold, Pater* (Cambridge, MA: Harvard University Press, 1977).

Froude, James Anthony. *Thomas Carlyle: A History of His Life in London, 1834–1881* (London: Longman, 1884).

Gooch, G.P. *History and Historians in the Nineteenth Century.* 1913, 2nd edn (London: Longman, 1952).

Kenyon, John. *The History Men: The Historical in England since the Renaissance.* 1983, 2nd edn (London: Weidenfeld & Nicholson, 1993).

Le Quesne, A. Lawrence. *Carlyle* (Oxford: Oxford University Press, 1982).

Levine, G. *The Boundaries of Fiction: Carlyle, Macaulay, Newman* (Princeton, NJ: Princeton University Press, 1968).

Rosenberg, John D. *Carlyle and the Burden of History* (Oxford: Clarendon Press, 1985).

Sanders, Charles Richard et al. (eds) *The Collected Letters of Thomas and Jane Welsh Carlyle.* 24 vols (Edinburgh: Edinburgh University Press, 1970–99).

Seigel, Jules Paul. *Thomas Carlyle: The Critical Heritage* (London: Routledge; and New York: Barnes & Noble, 1971).

Tarr, Roger L. *Thomas Carlyle: A Descriptive Bibliography* (Oxford: Oxford University Press, 1989).

MICHELET, JULES (1798–1874)

Barnes, Harry Elmer. *A History of Historical Writing.* 1937 (2nd edn) (Norman: University of Oklahoma Press, 1962).

Barthes, Roland. *Michelet.* Trans. Richard Howard (Oxford: Basil Blackwell, 1987).

Burrows, T. "Their Patron Saint and Eponymous Hero: Jules Michelet and the *Annales* School", *Clio* 12(1) (1982), 67–81.

Crossley, Ceri. *French Historians and Romanticism: Thierry, Guizot, the Saint-Simonians, Quinet, Michelet* (London: Routledge, 1993).

Febvre, Lucien. *Michelet et la Renaissance* (Paris: Flammarion, 1992).

Gooch, G.P. *History and Historians in the Nineteenth Century* (London: Longman, 1952).

Gossman, Lionel. *Between History and Literature* (Cambridge, MA: Harvard University Press, 1990).

Haac, Oscar A. *Jules Michelet* (Boston, MA: Twayne Publishers, 1982).

Kaplan, Edward K. *Michelet's Poetic Vision: A Romantic Philosophy of Nature, Man, Woman* (Amherst, MA: University of Massachusetts Press, 1977).

Kippur, Stephen A. *Jules Michelet: A Study of Mind and Sensibility* (Albany, NY: State University of New York Press, 1981).

"Michelet Issue". *Clio* 6(2) (1977).

Mitzman, Arthur. *Michelet, Historian: Rebirth and Romanticism in Nineteenth Century France* (New Haven, CT: Yale University Press, 1990).

Orr, Linda. *Jules Michelet: Nature, History, and Language* (Ithaca, NY: Cornell University Press, 1976).

Thompson, James Westfall. *A History of Historical Writing*, Vol. 2 (New York: Macmillan, 1942). 2 vols.

Weber, Eugen. "Great Man at Work: Michelet Reconsidered", *American Scholar* 60 (1991), 53–72.

White, Hayden. *Metahistory* (Baltimore: Johns Hopkins University Press, 1973).

Wilson, Edmund. *To the Finland Station: A Study in the Writing and Action of History.* 1972 (Harmondsworth: Penguin, 1991).

WARREN, MERCY OTIS (1728–1814)

Anthony, Katharine. *First Lady of the Revolution: The Life of Mercy Otis Warren* (Garden City, NY: Doubleday, 1958).

Brown, Alice. *Mercy Warren* (London: John Murray, 1896).

Cohen, Lester H. "Explaining the Revolution: Ideology and Ethics in Mercy Otis Warren's Historical Theory", *The William and Mary Quarterly* 3rd Ser., 37(2) (1980), 200–218.

—— . "Mercy Otis Warren: The Politics of Language and the Aesthetics of Self", *American Quarterly* 35(5) (1983), 481–98.

Emerson, Everett (ed.) *American Literature, 1764–1789: The Revolutionary Years* (Madison: University of Winconsin Press, 1977).

Friedman, Lawrence J. and Arthur H. Shaffer. "Mercy Otis Warren and the Politics of Historical Nationalism", *The New England Quarterly* 48(2) (1975), 194–215.

Hayes, Edmund M. "Mercy Otis Warren: The Defeat", *The New England Quarterly* 49(3) (1976), 440–58.

Hutcheson, Maud Macdonald. "Mercy Warren, 1728–1814", *The William and Mary Quarterly* 3rd Ser., 10(3) (1953), 378–402.

Laska, Vera. *Remember the Ladies: Outstanding Women of the American Revolution* (Boston: Bicentennial Commission, 1976).

Richards, Jeffrey H. *Mercy Otis Warren* (New York: Twayne, 1995).

Shaffer, Arthur H. *The Politics of History: Writing the History of the American Revolution, 1783–1815* (Chicago: Precedent, 1975).

Zagarri, Rosemarie. *A Woman's Dilemma: Mercy Otis Warren and the American Revolution* (Wheeling, IL: Harlan Davidson, 1995).

PARKMAN, FRANCIS (1823–1893)

Doughty, Howard. *Francis Parkman* (New York: Macmillan, 1962).

Eccles, W. J. "The History of New France According to Francis Parkman", *The William and Mary Quarterly* 3rd Ser., 18(2) (1961), 163–75.

Farnham, Charles Haight. *A Life of Francis Parkman* (London: Macmillan, 1900).

Gale, Robert L. *Francis Parkman* (New York: Twayne Publishers, 1973).

Jacobs, Wilbur R. *Francis Parkman, Historian as Hero: The Formative Years* (Austin: University of Texas Press, 1991).

—— . "Highlights of Parkman's Formative Period", *The Pacific Historical Review* 27(2) (1958), 149–58.

—— . "Some of Parkman's Literary Devices", *The New England Quarterly* 31(2) (1958), 244–52.

Jennings, Francis. "Francis Parkman: A Brahmin among Untouchables", *The William and Mary Quarterly* 3rd Ser., 42(3) (1985), 305–28.

Levin, David. *History as Romantic Art: Bancroft, Prescott, Motley, and Parkman* (Stanford, CA: Stanford University Press, 1959).

Morison, Samuel Eliot. *The Parkman Reader* (Boston: Little Brown and Co., 1955).

Pease, O. A. *Parkman's History: The Historian As Literary Artist* (New Haven, CT: Yale University Press, 1953).

Schafer, Joseph. "Francis Parkman, 1823–1893", *The Mississippi Valley Historical Review* 10(4) (1924), 351–364.

Schröder, Ingo W. "From Parkman to Postcolonial Theory: What's New in the Ethnohistory of Missions?" *Ethnohistory* 46(4) (1999), 809–15.

Townsend, Kim. "Francis Parkman and the Male Tradition", *American Quarterly* 38(1) (1986), 97–113.

Tyler, Moses Coit. "Review: A Half Century of Conflict", *Political Science Quarterly* 7(4) (1982): 726–29.

Wade, Mason. *Francis Parkman: Heroic Historian* (New York: Viking, 1942).

BANCROFT, GEORGE (1800–1891)

Blumenthal, Henry. "George Bancroft in Berlin: 1867–1874", *The New England Quarterly* 37(2) (1964), 224–41.

Canary, Robert H. *George Bancroft* (New York: Twayne, 1974).

Dawes, N. H. and F. T. Nichols. "Revaluing George Bancroft", *The New England Quarterly* 6(2) (1933), 278–93.

Green, Samuel Swett. *George Bancroft. From Proceedings of the American Antiquarian Society . . .1891* (Worcester, MA, 1891).

Handlin, Lilian. *George Bancroft, the Intellectual as Democrat* (New York: Harper & Row, 1984).

Kraus, Michael. "George Bancroft 1834–1934", *The New England Quarterly* 7(4) (1934): 662–86.

Levin, David. *History as Romantic Art: Bancroft, Prescott, Motley, and Parkman* (Stanford, CA: Stanford University Press 1959).

Nye, Russell Blaine. *George Bancroft: Brahmin Rebel* (New York: Knopf, 1944).

—— . "George Bancroft, Early Critic of German Literature", *Modern Language Notes* 58(2) (1943), 128–30.

—— . "Introduction", *The History of the United States of America from the Discovery of the Continent*. George Bancroft. (Chicago: University of Chicago Press, 1966).

Stewart, Watt. "George Bancroft Historian of the American People", *The Mississippi Valley Historical Review* 19(1) (1932), 77–86.

Vitzhum, Richard C. "Theme and Method in Bancroft's History of the United States", *The New England Quarterly* 41(3) (1968), 362–80.

PART 5

Historicism, the historian's craft, and the new century

INTRODUCTION

UNLIKE THE ROMANTIC HISTORIANS, whose widespread popularity soared during the same period, the German philosopher Wilhelm von Humboldt and historian Leopold von Ranke responded to the conjectural historians of the eighteenth century in purely academic terms. In their lectures they rejected the Enlightenment view that human history followed a rational plan according to natural principles, which philosophy could supply when documentation did not exist. Rather than paint missing historical episodes using their literary imaginations, Humboldt and Ranke argued that philosophical conjecture should be replaced by an empirical examination of authentic historical documents. Moreover, Humboldt and Ranke proposed a new theory of historical consciousness, which was soon called historicism (see Vico in Part 2). For the philosophers of the previous century, the study of human nature can prove the existence of general principles, and of events that are the result of human instinct. The study of human history, on the other hand, can reveal actions of specific people or unique events resulting from their decisions and behaviour in particular circumstances. Therefore, Humboldt and Ranke argued, the objective details that we can unearth from archival documents provide evidence of human agency and of historical context, which themselves are the keys to recounting the past. Further, unlike the romantics, Humboldt and Ranke neither sought popularity among general readers nor tried to cultivate a powerful literary style. Instead, they wrote for their students and colleagues, and outlined the approaches and training that their historicist ideals would require. As a recent scholar has remarked, "professional zeal for exactitude, exhaustiveness, and causal explanation tended to tilt the balance from narrative to analysis".[i] Despite their turn away from catering to popular taste, the enduring prestige and influence of nineteenth-century German historicism continues to be felt in a wide range of disciplines.

---

i   J. Burrow, *A History of Histories* (London: Allen Lane, 2007), 470.

Since the rise and dominance of a scientific approach to history in the late nineteenth century was due largely to the intellectual inspiration and engaging educational techniques fostered by Ranke—which were encouraged under Humboldt's patronage—the documents that follow remain especially valuable to those interested in the history of modern historical scholarship.[ii] None of the romantic historians held long-term positions in universities, and their widely popular writings had little effect on the practice of history within the academy, but Humboldt and Ranke were true academic pioneers. Indeed, it would be fair to say that Ranke is the father of the critical techniques that defines the research, teaching, and writing of history today in universities from Paris to Tokyo and from Berlin to Chicago—and under his direct influence, the historian-as-professional was born. No section in this book will be referenced more frequently than this one.

In 1810, as a senior administrator in the Prussian government, Humboldt established the first German university to adopt *universitas litterarum* as its explicit guiding principle, and the University of Berlin became the global model for bringing research and teaching together. It was the first institution at which students in history would be taught by an active researcher, and where historians would instruct students in their own scholarly methods. Ranke was the first historian to train students in the exacting criticism of original sources by using the group-seminar format; the seminar would become a familiar teaching structure, particularly in America and in France, where it was soon imported by Ranke's enthusiastic American and French disciples.[iii] Ranke's seminar (from *seminarium*, "seeding ground"), where students would meet to discuss their research, made academic researchers into professional teachers of history. The clearest indication of Ranke's influence is that, nearly two centuries later, the seminar remains the preferred introduction to professional historical training in the West.[iv]

Apart from their institutional legacies, Humboldt and Ranke advocated a theory of history that would shape the views of generations of historians, philosophers, and their readers. Historicism, as Humboldt described it in 1821 and as Ranke practised it from 1824, remains a cornerstone for current historical practice—requiring consideration from historians who argue against it and those who want to move beyond it, as we will see in later sections. Anthony Grafton illustrates Ranke's continuing importance in current discussions on historical

---

ii   Iggers has suggested that, "in a basic way, the history of German and American historical thought not only is but must be organized around the issue of the acceptance or rejection of Ranke." See "The Image of Ranke in American and German Historical Thought", *History and Theory* 2 (1962), 17–40.

iii In 1895, possibly half of all professional historians in America had studied in Germany: see J. F. Jameson, "*The American Historical Review, 1895–1920*", *AHR* 26 (1920), 2. John Higham sees Ranke's influence at other stages of American education, suggesting that it was Ranke's American students who referred to his educational principles when they "imposed a complete four-year sequence from ancient to American history on the nation's high schools". See *History: Professional Scholarship in America* (Baltimore: Johns Hopkins University Press, 1963), 112. On Ranke's legacy in France, see W. Keylor, *Academy and Community: The Foundation of the French Historical Profession* (Cambridge, MA: Harvard University Press, 1975), 36–7.

iv   Ranke's teaching and methods also found their way to Asia during the nineteenth century: Ranke's student Ludwig Reiss founded *Shigaku Zasshi* ("Journal of Historical Science") in 1889, which remains the leading historical journal in Japan. See Teijirô Muramatsu, *Westerners in the Modernization of Japan*, trans. L. E. Riggs and M. Takechi (Tokyo: Hitachi, 1995). For the view that the "two practices of scientific history, the seminar and archival research, were as foundational to and influential in the profession as the ideals of truth and objectivity", see B. G. Smith, "Gender and the Practices of Scientific History: The Seminar and Archival Research in the Nineteenth Century", *American Historical Review* 100 (1995), 1150–176.

writing—even among the non-specialist readers for whom this essay was written. Grafton discussed Ranke's use of footnotes, both as a rhetorical device that demonstrates an historian's erudition and as a stylistic device that risks distracting the reader from the main body of the historian's text. Despite Ranke's reputation for creating the field of historical science (and reinventing the German word for it, *Geschichtswissenschaft*),[v] Grafton showed that Ranke was reluctant to display his depth of research (and debts to research) in this particular way—and Ranke's use of footnotes remains unreliable. It is paradoxical that the first "scientist" of history disliked this scientifically conventional means of referencing his sources. Although most of the other historians in this volume don't refer to Ranke or Humboldt directly, once we focus on the historical methods and theory that these two advocated, we will see why a new generation of scholars during the early twentieth century strove to emerge from the academic dominance of German historical science.

In his lecture, Humboldt was keenly aware that his view of historical inquiry faced a dual challenge, from the "philosophical" (conjectural) and "artistic" (that is, romantic) historians (see Parts 3 and 4). The first group, whose prestige lingered into the early nineteenth century, created fundamental problems both in its moral ambition and in its methodological approach. He refutes Lord Bolingbroke's axiom ("History is philosophy [morality] teaching by examples") that echoes through the writings of Enlightenment historians:

> History does not primarily serve us by showing us through specific examples, often misleading and rarely enlightening, what to do and what to avoid. History's true and immeasurable usefulness lies rather in its power to enliven and refine our sense of acting on reality ... by clearly recognizing the truth of the predominating trend of ideas at a given time and by adhering to this truth with determination.

We cannot rely on a rational or natural plan that gives shape to history, for which the historian merely needs to extract specific episodes that will teach us how to live. Rather, we need to approach history as a task that requires research into the causes and consequences of human creativity and human action: only by focusing on the role of specific ideas in the production of specific historical events can history be useful. Similarly, unlike the romantics, "the historian *subordinates his imagination* to experience and the investigation of reality" (my emphasis). Historians need to use their intuition to make connections among oceans of otherwise meaningless facts, and yet this ability must be the fruit of intensive study of such facts, "by making its own the structure of all occurrences". For Humboldt, moral vision was a consequence and not a cause of historical study: "everything depends on this fusion of the inquiring intellect and the object of inquiry"—which is why a primary focus on the materials of history without the application of one's own values will produce historical writing of truly enduring value.

Ranke was at work completing his *Histories of the Latin and Germanic Nations* when Humboldt delivered his lecture to the Royal Prussian Academy of Sciences in 1821. This was the first of what would become an astounding sixty volumes of historical books, and the one that led Humboldt to appoint Ranke as a professor at Berlin. Right from the start of his

v   This term had been coined by Johann Martin Chladenius in 1752, but was not widely used until its adoption by and attribution to Ranke in the mid-nineteenth century. See Rüdiger vom Bruch, "Geschichtswissenschaft", S. Jordan (ed.), *Lexikon Geschichtswissenschaft* (Stuttgart: Hundert Grundbegriffe, 2002), 124–30.

stick to the facts

Preface to the *Histories*, Ranke outlined his research principles and suggested their practical limitations. He declared that his ambition was to present the shared origins and evolution of France, Italy, and Spain as well as Germany, Britain, and Scandinavia. Ranke emphasized the methodology on which every aspect of his research and writing would be based: "strict presentation of facts, no matter how conditional and unattractive they might be, is undoubtedly the supreme law". So this meant that Ranke would focus only on original information, by examining records that were created at the time that the historical events took place. The ultimate goal, he famously stated, was not to judge the past or to interpret history through an ethical or moral lens, but "to show how, essentially, things happened" (*wie es eigentlich gewesen*).[vi]

Ranke was aware that there were important consequences for such a grand project that would dwell only on original documentary evidence, and his summary of his methods made that clear. Since only certain historical events were set in motion by or provided the occasion for written documents, the history that Ranke could write must be very limited in its scope. Ranke openly admitted that his work is imperfect because it dealt only with particulars. Yet, as later critics of scientific history pointed out, it was not merely Ranke's limited scope as a researcher which could cause misinterpretation, it was his narrow focus on politics and policy—since it was largely governments and aristocrats who generated and maintained a documentary history—that created a narrow definition of what *history*, *sources*, and *nation* might mean. If we take Italy as just one example from Ranke's Preface, we see that he has focused on the political events that led to its development as a modern state. Yet it is unlikely that the sense of national identity of those minority groups that lived in Italy at the time, but did not produce documents that Ranke could access, would be understood through a narrative of progress from division to unity. Moreover, as anthropologists and **cultural historians** have shown, nations also express their history through documents that are not found in archives or libraries: surely linguistic, artistic, religious, and architectural history merit a place in the history of nations— as Marc Bloch and Lucien Febvre, later in this section, proposed.

Further, as mid-twentieth-century historians pointed out, an historicist position that seeks merely to record documented events without engaging with ethical or moral concerns, risks neglecting the psychological realities of the people who lived them. In other words, the required selectivity of Ranke's method, and his enduring distaste for generalizations, brings us back to Grafton's point—that, in fact, Ranke tried to resist using documentary footnotes. This may be because footnotes suggest that it is the original sources, and not the historian's critical interpretation of them, which provide historical authority. So like the literary historians, even Ranke cultivated a narrative style and critical interpretation that suited his viewpoint.

Ironically, the scholarly rigour that developed independently of romanticism's popular appeal, and which brought closed archives into accessible print, returned to haunt its later practitioners. In America, scientific history would soon hold wide appeal among academic historians, for it lent academic prestige and a sense of intellectual freedom: "the scientific approach cut the fetters that had entangled history with older academic subjects and had

---

vi   Anticipating twentieth-century concerns with the historian's use of narrative to reveal the past (see Part 10), it might be useful to point out that in 1824 Ranke said he wanted to tell (*sagen*) rather than to show (*zeigen*) "how, essentially, things happened". So he might have been more self-conscious of his own narrative shaping of the evidence in the original version of his essay, which has been obscured by the fact that the verb *zeigen* replaced *sagen* in the German edition of Ranke's collected works (published in the 1870s), whose text has been cited ever since. I am grateful to Georg Iggers for this illuminating point.

subordinated it to literature and philosophy".[vii] Yet general readers and younger historians, who by 1910 could train in America rather than Germany, raised moral and aesthetic objections to scientific history. Theodore Roosevelt berated the 1912 annual meeting of the American Historical Association:

> Many hardworking students, alive to the deficiencies of romance-writing, have grown to distrust not only all historical writing that is romantic, but all historical writing that is vivid. . . . The immense importance of full knowledge of a mass of dry facts and gray details has so impressed them as to make them feel that the dryness and the grayness are in themselves meritorious.

The historians of the new century, he concluded, "must have the power to take the science of history and turn it into literature".[viii] By doing so, historical writing could once again engage the attention of non-specialists, address the causes and consequences of recent events that remain within living memory, and look beyond political history to focus on topics more relevant to current readers. James Harvey Robinson, who had been trained in Europe with one of Ranke's disciples, was one of the keenest advocates for The New History, which sought to reform scientific history by widening its scope and by shortening its perspective.[ix] By taking up the once-romantic project of exploring a wider social range of historical elements, and by focusing on the recent past, Robinson argued, historical writing could be practically relevant to current times.

By the time that Robinson wrote his polemic against the drier aspects of scientific history, the Rankean focus on archival sources, together with his emphasis on recounting details rather than evoking contexts, meant that the historical profession was focusing on political history from a narrowly quantitative point of view. Robinson's argument communicated an impatience with traditional means and goals that would seem to reach beyond the historical profession, and it closed with a climactic vision of the future:

> The "New History" is escaping from the limitations formerly imposed upon the study of the past. It will come in time consciously to meet our daily needs; it will avail itself of all those discoveries that are being made about mankind by anthropologists, economists, psychologists, and sociologists.

This utopian melody chimed in with other socially-oriented ambitions of the American Progressive Era of this period. Robinson's eagerness to make history relevant by focusing on topics that interested current readers opened the profession to researchers trained in the social sciences. Paradoxically, however, by expanding the historical field both academically and socially, Robinson also sought to improve the profession's prestige, in much the same way as Ranke tried to create history as a distinct field within the Humanities nearly a century earlier.

vii J. Higham, *History: Professional Scholarship in America*, 96–7.

viii T. Roosevelt, "History as Literature", *American Historical Review* 18 (1913), 475. As late as 1908, a previous President of the Association declared at their annual meeting that Ranke is "our first leader": see George Burton Adams, "History and the Philosophy of History", *American Historical Review* 14 (1909), 236.

ix For a summary of Robinson's intellectual background, see Peter Novick, *That Noble Dream: The "Objectivity Question" and the American Historical Profession* (Cambridge: Cambridge University Press, 1988), 104.

Moreover, powerful political interests were closely allied to the New Historians' turn away from political history, for Roosevelt was not only an intellectual ally; he was President from 1901 to 1909, an advocate of Progressive policies, and indeed was instrumental in the founding of the US Progressive Party during the same year that *The New History* was published— citing Robinson in his own address to members of the American Historical Association a few months later.[x]

Like nineteenth-century America, France also had sent many of its most gifted historians to Germany for training in Ranke's critical methods.[xi] But two related strains developed in contemporary French historical education that were distinct from the American context. They also led to dissatisfaction with scientific history, which was voiced clearly by Bloch and Febvre in their inaugural issue of *Annales d'histoire économique et sociale* (1929). On the one hand, since the German defeat of France some sixty years earlier (in 1871), the educational system in France taught a strongly patriotic version of history. On the other, French archivists and historians sought to emulate objective historical methods. Like the academic situation in America, historical publications had become increasingly specialized. French scientific historians had adopted "an obsessive empiricism and the indiscriminate accumulation of facts". As a result, "the vast bulk of historical scholarship produced by the French universities was of little interest to anyone but specialists".[xii] A general sense of civic and patriotic responsibility, shared by academics and the reading public, pressed historical writing to address current national interests and experiences.

The next Part in this book will include materials relating to Émile Durkheim and the rise of sociology, whose speedy rise to prominence in France was closely related to this public and professional dissatisfaction with historical science. In the meantime, this Part features the energetic approach declared by the editors of the *Annales* journal (an essay by Bloch appears in Part 1). Their innovative devotion to an international and interdisciplinary study of history successfully created social history as a prestigious alternative to the conflicting aims of historical science in France. Their journal, *Annales: Histoire, Sciences-sociales*, remains a globally-admired forum for cross-disciplinary historical scholarship.

Bloch and Febvre's open letter to their readers (who they hoped would include their peers as well as non-specialists) described a divorce among historians whose focus on different periods meant that they did not collaborate on research. Their new journal promised to offer a forum for a collaboration whose results will bring "many cultural benefits [and] innovations in intuition". This subtle reference to Ranke's concern with intuition suggested Bloch and Febvre's hope that historians working together on a range of historical topics, problems, and periods would develop a broader range of research methods and produce more learned interpretations of their findings. The *Annales* group of historians would soon begin to fashion an approach to what would be called **total history**, which studied long-term changes in social, cultural, economic, and linguistic structures in specific geographical areas (see Part 7). Geography was important for the *Annales* historians, since by defining an area objectively, by its physical location, they could study the transitional nature of politics, society, and culture over the long term. This approach required training in the numerous social sciences, and collaboration among historians working in fields that had once seemed distinct but now were

---

x   For an introduction to Progressivism, see A. A. Ekirch, Jr. *Progressivism in America: A Study of the Era from Theodore Roosevelt to Woodrow Wilson* (New York: New Viewpoints, 1974).
xi   Keylor, *Academy and Community*, 27, 36.
xii Keylor, 106–7.

unified by an innovative historical project. As we will see, historians continue to share these ambitions.

The situation among professional historians in England during the early twentieth century was in some respects parallel to those in Germany, France, and America. One important similarity with France was the English adoption of Ranke's critical methods, which did not challenge the romantic tendency to view the past as the obvious background for present-day successes. In England, historicist methods did not require adopting an historicist outlook. Even George Macaulay Trevelyan, a giant of academic and popular history during the early twentieth century (and a grand-nephew of Thomas Macaulay), in his widely-read and respected books celebrated a seemingly inherited belief that English history provides its own explanation for current English liberties. In his famous lecture on the historiography of this period, E. H. Carr observed that "between the middle of the last century and 1914 it was scarcely possible for a British historian to conceive of historical change except for the better".[xiii] Herbert Butterfield's glittering indictment of this **Whig interpretation of history** (named for the partisan political vision that triumphed in the event that they styled The Glorious Revolution of 1689) provided insight into two important elements of English historical writing during the inter-war years. First, it suggested the difficulty of departing from this seductive view of English historical progress, where the past contains seeds of the therefore inevitable present. Ironically, this view provided the kind of rousing utilitarianism that the "New Historians," on the other side of the Atlantic, also demanded — and which Butterfield now called "a failure of historical understanding". Second, it illustrated the ultimate fragility of Butterfield's call for an historical approach that emphasized "the complexity of human change and the unpredictable character of [its] ultimate consequences". For Butterfield's spirited attack on Whig historiography was published in 1931, early in his long career; after the devastating war that followed, his own outlook took a more celebratory approach to historical events. In 1949, for instance, Butterfield declared that the Scientific Revolution of Copernicus, Galileo, and Newton outshone "everything since the rise of Christianity and reduced the Renaissance and Reformation to the rank of mere episodes".[xiv] This Whiggish view was a long stretch from the interpretive neutrality that his earlier historicist treatise had demanded. No historian's historiography can resist historical forces for long.

xiii E. H. Carr, "Society and the Individual," in *What Is History?* (New York: Vintage, 1961), 45.
xiv H. Butterfield, *The Origins of Modern Science, 1300–1800* (London: G. Bell, 1949), vii.

Chapter 19

Wilhelm von Humboldt

ON THE HISTORIAN'S TASK

Wilhelm von Humboldt (1767–1835), "On the Historian's Task", 1822. Trans. Louis O. Mink, *History and Theory* 6 (1967), 57–61, 63–5, 69–71.

THE HISTORIAN'S TASK IS to present what actually happened. The more purely and completely he achieves this, the more perfectly has he solved his problem. A simple presentation is at the same time the primary, indispensable condition of his work and the highest achievement he will be able to attain. Regarded in this way, he seems to be merely receptive and reproductive, not himself active and creative.

An event, however, is only partially visible in the world of the senses; the rest has to be added by intuition, inference, and guesswork. The manifestations of an event are scattered, disjointed, isolated; what it is that gives unity to this patchwork, puts the isolated fragment into its proper perspective, and gives shape to the whole, remains removed from direct observation. For observation can perceive circumstances which either accompany or follow one another, but not their inner causal nexus, on which, after all, their inner truth is solely dependent. If one is trying to talk about the most significant fact, but at the same time attempting strictly to tell only what actually happened, one soon notices how, unless the greatest care is employed in the choice and evaluation of expressions, minute determinants will creep in beyond the actual happening, and will give rise to falsehood and uncertainty. Language itself contributes to this state of affairs since – growing out of the fullness of the soul as it does – it frequently lacks expressions which are free from all connotations. Nothing is rarer, therefore, than a narrative which is literally true; nothing is better proof of a sound, well-ordered, and critical intelligence and of a free, objective attitude. Thus historical truth is, as it were, rather like the clouds which take shape for the eye only at a distance. For this reason, the facts of history are in their several connecting circumstances little more than the results of tradition and scholarship which one has agreed to accept as true, because they – being most highly probable in themselves – also fit best into the context of the whole.

One has, however, scarcely arrived at the skeleton of an event by a crude sorting out of what actually happened. What is so achieved is the necessary basis of history, its raw material, but not history itself. To stop here would be to sacrifice the actual inner truth, well-founded within the causal nexus, for an outward, literal, and seeming truth; it would mean choosing actual error in order to escape the potential danger of error. The truth of any event is predicated on the addition – mentioned above – of that invisible part of every fact, and it is this part, therefore, which the historian has to add. Regarded in this way, he does become active, even creative – not by bringing forth what does not have existence, but in giving shape by his own powers to that which by mere intuition he could not have perceived as it really was. Differently from the poet, but in a way similar to him, he must work the collected fragments into a whole.

It may seem questionable to have the field of the historian touch that of the poet at even one point. However, their activities are undeniably related. For if the historian, as has been said, can only reveal the truth of an event by presentation, by filling in and connecting the disjointed fragments of direct observation, he can do so, like the poet, only through his imagination. The crucial difference, which removes all potential dangers, lies in the fact that the historian subordinates his imagination to experience and the investigation of reality. In this subordination, the imagination does not act as pure fantasy and is, therefore, more properly called the intuitive faculty or connective ability. But this by itself would still assign too low a place to history. The striving for the truth of events seems obvious enough. It is, however, the most difficult attainment conceivable. For if truth were ever conquered completely, all that which determines the reality of things, like a chain of necessity, would lie uncovered. The historian must therefore seek the necessity of events; he must not, like the poet, merely impose on his material the appearance of necessity; rather, he must keep constantly in mind the ideas which are the laws of necessity, because only by being steeped in them can he find evidence of them in any pure inquiry into the real in its reality.

The historian has all the strands of temporal activity and all the expressions of eternal ideas as his province. The whole of existence is, more or less directly, the object of his endeavors, and thus he must pursue all the manifestations of the mind. Speculation, experience, and fiction are, therefore, merely different manifestations of the mind, not distinct activities of it, opposed to and limiting one another.

Thus two methods have to be followed simultaneously in the approach to historical truth; the first is the exact, impartial, critical investigation of events; the second is the connecting of the events explored and the intuitive understanding of them which could not be reached by the first means. To follow only the first path is to miss the essence of truth itself; to neglect this path, however, by overemphasizing the second one is to risk falsification of truth in its details. Even a simple depiction of nature cannot be merely an enumeration and depiction of parts or the measuring of sides and angles; there is also the breath of life in the whole and an inner character which speaks through it which can be neither measured nor merely described. Description of nature, too, will be subjected to the second method, which for such description is the representation of the form of both the universal and the individual existence of natural objects. In history there is likewise no intention of finding something isolated by means of that second method, and even less are there to be any imaginative additions to the material. The historian's mind is merely supposed to understand better the genuinely intelligible material by making its own the structure of all occurrences; thus it must learn to perceive more in that material than could be achieved by the mere operation of the intellect. Everything depends on this fusion of the inquiring intellect and the object of the inquiry. The more profoundly the historian understands mankind and its actions through intuition and study, the more humane his disposition is by nature and circumstances, and the more freely he gives rein to his humanity, the more completely will he solve the problems of his profession. The chronicles prove this point. No one can deny that the better ones among them are based on the most genuine historical truth despite the fact that they contain many factual misrepresentations and many an obvious fairy tale. They are closely related to the older type of so-called memoirs, although in these the close attention paid to the individual already jeopardizes that more general concern with humanity which history requires even when it is dealing with an isolated phenomenon. [. . .]

It is the historian who is supposed to awaken and to stimulate a sensibility for reality, and his activity is defined subjectively by the elaboration of that concept as it is defined objectively by the historical narrative. Every intellectual activity which affects man as a whole possesses something which might be called its essential element, its activating power, the secret of its influence on the mind; and it is so different from the objects affected by it that they often serve merely to bring it to the attention of the mind in new and different ways. In mathematics this essential element consists in isolating number and line; in metaphysics it consists in abstracting from all experience; and in art it is the wonderful manipulation of nature, so that everything in the created work appears to be taken from nature although nothing exactly like it actually exists. The element in which history operates is the sense of reality, and it contains the awareness of the transience of existence in time, and of dependence upon past and present causes; at the same time, there is the consciousness of spiritual freedom and the recognition of reason, so that reality, despite its seeming contingency, is nevertheless bound by an inner necessity. If the mind surveys only one single human life, it will be struck by the different ways in which history stimulates and captivates. Hence the historian, in order to perform the task of his profession, has to compose the narrative of events in such a way that the reader's emotions will be stirred by it as if by reality itself.

It is in this way that history is related to active life. History does not primarily serve us by showing us through specific examples, often misleading and rarely enlightening, what to do and what to avoid. History's true and immeasurable usefulness lies rather in its power to enliven and refine our sense of acting on reality, and this occurs more through the form attached to events than through the events themselves. It prevents the sense of reality from slipping into the realm of pure ideas, and yet subjects it to ideas. And on this narrow middle path it constantly keeps alive in the mind the notion that there is no successful intervention in the flow of events except by clearly recognizing the truth of the predominating trend of ideas at a given time and by adhering to this truth with determination. It is this inner effect that history must always produce, irrespective of the subject matter, whether it be the narration of a continuous pattern of events or of a single event. The historian worthy of his title must show every event as part of a whole, or, what amounts to the same thing, must reveal the form of history *per se* in every event described. [. . .]

Here we have to proceed with great caution lest the mere mention of ideas already impair historical accuracy in its pure form. For although both artist and historian imitate and represent, their aims are quite different. The artist merely takes away from reality its ephemeral appearance, merely touches reality in order to fly away from it; the historian is searching for reality alone and has to plunge deeply into it. It is precisely for this reason, and because the historian cannot be satisfied merely with the loose external relationships of the individual events, that he has to proceed to the center of things from which their true nexus can be understood. He has to seek the truth of an event in a way similar to the artist's seeking the truth of form. Events in history are even less obviously perceptible than appearances in the world of the senses and cannot be simply read off. An understanding of them is the combined product of their constitution and the sensibility supplied by the beholder. Here, as in art, not everything can be derived logically, one thing from another, by mere operation of the intellect, and dissected into concepts. One can only grasp that which is right, subtle, and hidden, because the mind is properly attuned to grasping it. The historian, like the draftsman, will produce only caricatures if he merely depicts the specific

assuming causes falsifies the history

circumstances of an event by connecting them with each other as they seemingly present themselves. He must render strict account of their inner nexus, must establish for himself a picture of the active forces, must recognize their trends at a given moment, must inquire into the relationship of both forces and trends to the existing state of affairs and to the changes that have preceded it. To do this, however, the historian must be familiar in the first place with the conditions, the operation and interdependence of these forces, as a complete understanding of the specific always presupposes a knowledge of the general, under which it is comprehended. It is in this sense that the understanding of events must be guided by ideas. It is, of course, self-evident that these ideas emerge from the mass of events themselves, or, to be more precise, originate in the mind through contemplation of these events undertaken in a truly historical spirit: the ideas are not borrowed by history like an alien addition, a mistake so easily made by so-called philosophical history. Historical truth is, generally speaking, much more threatened by philosophical than by artistic handling, since the latter is at least accustomed to granting freedom to its subject matter. Philosophy dictates a goal to events. This search for final causes, even though it may be deduced from the essence of man and nature itself, distorts and falsifies every independent judgment of the characteristic working of forces.

[. . .]

All understanding presupposes in the person who understands, as a condition of its possibility, an analogue of that which will actually be understood later: an original antecedent congruity between subject and object. Understanding is not merely an extension of the subject, nor is it merely a borrowing from the object; it is, rather, both simultaneously. Understanding always is the application of a pre-existent general idea to something new and specific. When two beings are completely separated by a chasm, there is no bridge of communication between them; and in order to understand each other, they must, in some other sense, have already understood each other. In the case of history that antecedent of understanding is quite obvious, since everything which is active in world history is also moving within the human heart. The more deeply, therefore, the soul of a nation feels everything human, and the more tenderly, purely, and diversely it is moved by this, the greater will be its chances to produce historians in the true sense of the word. To this condition one must add the critical practice which tests and corrects preconceived ideas against the object until both clarity and certainly emerge through this repeated interaction.

In this way, through a study of the creative forces of world history, the historian conceives for himself a general picture of the form of the connection of all events, and it is within this realm that the ideas discussed above are contained. They are not being projected into history, but are the essence of history itself. For every force, living or dead, acts according to the laws of its nature, and all occurrences are inseparably linked in space and time.

[. . .]

Every human individuality is an idea rooted in actuality, and this idea shines forth so brilliantly from some individuals that it seems to have assumed the form of an individual merely to use it as a vehicle for expressing itself. When one traces human activity, after all its determining causes have been subtracted there remains something original which transforms these influences instead of being suffocated by them; in this very element there is an incessantly active drive to give outward shape to its inner, unique nature. It is the same with the individuality of nations, and in many areas of history the inner drive is more easily recognizable in them than in individuals, since man in certain periods and under certain circumstances develops, as it were, in groups. The spiritual principle of individuality therefore remains active in the midst of the history of nations guided by needs, passions, and apparent accidents, and it is more powerful than those elements. This principle seeks to express its innate idea, and it succeeds as the most fragile plant, by the organic expansion of its cells, will succeed in splitting walls which had otherwise withstood the wear of centuries. In addition to the directions which nations and individuals impart to mankind by their actions, they leave behind them forms of spiritual individuality which are more enduring and effective than deeds or events.

There are, however, also ideal forms which, although they do not constitute human individuality, are related to it, if only indirectly. Language is one of them. For although every language reflects the spirit of its people, it also has an earlier, more independent base, and its uniqueness and internal cohesion are so powerful and determining that its independence is more influential than influenced, so that every important language appears as a unique vehicle for the creation and communication of ideas.

[. . .]

Human judgment cannot perceive the plans of the governance of the world directly but can only divine them in the ideas through which they manifest themselves, and therefore all history is the realization of an idea. In the idea resides both its motivating force and its goal. And thus, merely by steeping oneself in the contemplation of the creative forces one travels along a more correct route to those final causes to which the intellect naturally aspires. The goal of history can only be the actualization of the idea which is to be realized by mankind in every way and in all shapes in which the finite form may enter into a union with the idea. The course of events can end only at the point where both are no longer capable of further mutual integration.

Thus we have arrived at the ideas which must guide the historian, and we can now return to the comparison undertaken above between the historian and the artist. What knowledge of nature and the study of organic structures are to the latter, research into the forces appearing in life as active and guiding is to the former; what to the latter are proportion, symmetry, and the concept of pure form, to the former are the ideas which unfold themselves serenely and majestically in the nexus of world events without, however, being part of them. In its final, yet simplest solution the historian's task is the presentation of the struggle of an idea to realize itself in actuality. For the idea will not always be successful in its first attempt; not infrequently will it become perverted because it is unable to master completely the actively resisting matter.

There are two things which the course of this inquiry has attempted to keep firmly in mind: that there is an idea, not itself directly perceptible, in everything that happens, but that this idea can be recognized only in the events themselves. The historian must, therefore, not exclude the power of the idea from his presentation by seeking everything exclusively in his material sources; he must at least leave room for the activity of the idea. Going beyond that, moreover, he must be spiritually receptive to the idea and actively open to perceiving and appropriating it. Above all, he must take great care not to attribute to reality arbitrarily created ideas of his own, and not to sacrifice any of the living richness of the parts in his search for the coherent pattern of the whole. This freedom and subtlety of approach must become so much a part of his nature that he will bring them to bear on the investigation of every event. For no event is separated completely from the general nexus of things, and part of every occurrence lies beyond the pale of direct perception, as we have shown above. If the historian lacks this freedom of approach, he cannot perceive events in their scope and depth; if he lacks subtlety and tact, he will destroy their simple and living truth.

Chapter 20

Leopold von Ranke

(1) PREFACE TO THE FIRST EDITION OF *HISTORIES OF THE LATIN AND GERMAN NATIONS*

Leopold von Ranke (1795–1886):

(1) "Preface to the First Edition of *Histories of the Latin and German Nations*", 1824, Georg Iggers (ed.), trans. Wilma Iggers (Indianapolis: Bobbs-Merrill, 1973), 135–8.

(2) "Preface to *History of the Popes, Their Church and State*", 1834. Trans. E. Fowler. Revised by Konrad von Moltke (New York: Colonial Press, 1901), v–xi.

THE **PRESENT BOOK**, I readily admit, seemed to me more perfect before it was printed than it does now that it is in print. However, I count on favorably inclined readers to pay less attention to its faults than to its possible virtues. Since I do not entirely trust it to make its own way, however, I shall preface it with a brief explanation about its purpose, subject, and form.

The intention of a historian depends on his viewpoint, about which two things must be said here. First of all, I regard the Latin and the Germanic nations as a unit. I reject three analogous concepts: one, the concept of a universal Christendom (which would embrace even the Armenians); two, the concept of the unity of Europe, for since the Turks are Asiatics and since the Russian Empire comprises the whole north of Asia, their situations could not be thoroughly understood without penetrating and drawing in the total Asian situation. Finally, my point of view also excludes the almost exactly analogous concept, that of a Latin Christendom. Slavic, Latvian, and Magyar tribes belonging to the latter have a peculiar and special nature which is not included here. The author remains close to home with the tribally related peoples of either purely Germanic or Germano-Latin origin, whose history is the nucleus of all recent history, and touches on what is foreign only in passing as something peripheral.

In the following introduction an attempt will be made to show, mainly by tracing the thread of foreign undertakings, to what extent these nations have evolved in unity and kindred movement. This is one aspect of the viewpoint on which this book is based. The other aspect is directly expressed by the content of the book, which embraces only a small part of the history of these nations, what might well be called the beginning of the modern history—only histories, not history. This book considers, on the one hand, the founding of the Spanish monarchy and the end of Italian freedom; on the other hand, the creation of a dual opposition, a political one by the French, an ecclesiastical one by the Reformation—in other words, the division of our nations into two hostile parts on which all our history rests. My account starts from the moment when Italy, united in herself, enjoyed at least external freedom and may perhaps be considered as a ruling force, since she supplied the Pope. It seeks to portray the division of Italy, the invasion of the French and the Spaniards, the end in some states of all freedom and in others of self-determination, and finally the victory of the Spaniards and the beginning of their domination. Furthermore, my book starts with the political insignificance of the Spanish kingdoms and continues to their unification—to the alignment of the united kingdom against the infidels and its influence on the internal development of Christianity. It seeks to make clear how the struggle against the infidels led to the discovery of America and the conquest of great kingdoms there, but above all how the attempt to strengthen Christianity led to Spanish domination over Italy, Germany, and the Netherlands. Thirdly, my chronicle continues from the time when Charles VIII sets out in the vanguard of Christendom in its struggle against the Turks through all the changing fortunes and misfortunes of the French up to the time, forty-one years later, when Francis calls these very Turks to aid against the Emperor. Finally, in tracing the beginnings of the opposition of a political party in Germany against the Emperor and of an ecclesiastical party in Europe against the Pope, this chronicle seeks to pave the way for a more complete insight into the history of the great schism brought about by the Reformation. This very schism is to be observed in its early course. This book tries to comprehend in their unity all these and the other related histories of the Latin and Germanic nations. To history has been given the function of judging the past, of instructing men for the profit of future years. The present attempt does not aspire to such a lofty undertaking. It merely wants to show how, essentially, things happened.

But from what sources could this be newly investigated? The foundations of the present writing, the origins of its subject matter, are memoirs, diaries, letters, reports from embassies, and original narratives of eyewitnesses. Other writings were considered only when they seemed either to have been immediately deduced from the former or to equal them through some kind of original information. Every page shows which these works were; a second book to be published simultaneously with the present one will present the method of research and the critical results.

Form results from intent and subject matter. One cannot demand of a historical work the same free development which at least in theory is sought in a poetic work, and I do not know if one is right in believing such free development to have been found in the works of the Greek and Roman masters. Strict presentation of facts, no matter how conditional and unattractive they might be, is undoubtedly the supreme law. The development of the unity and progress of the events came next in order of importance. Therefore instead of starting, as might have been expected, with a general description of public conditions in Europe— which would have diffused, if not confused, my point of view—I preferred to discuss every people, every power, every individual in greater detail only at the moment when they appeared in a pronouncedly active or leading role. I was unconcerned about the fact that occasionally I had already mentioned them previously. For how could I avoid mentioning their existence? In this way the general line of their development, the direction they took, the ideas which motivated them could be grasped all the better.

Finally, what will be said of the treatment of particulars, which constitutes such an important part of historical work? Will it not often seem hard, fragmentary, colorless, tiring? There are noble models for this procedure, ancient ones and—let us not fail to recognize this—also modern ones. But I did not dare imitate them. Their world was different from mine. A lofty ideal does exist: to grasp the event itself in its human comprehensibility, its unity, and its fullness. It should be possible to attain this goal. I know how far I am from having achieved it. One tries, one strives, but in the end one has not reached the goal. Only let no one become impatient about this failure! The main thing is always what we deal with: as Jakobi says, our subject is mankind as it is, explicable or inexplicable, the life of the individual, of the generations, of the peoples, and at times the hand of God over them.

(2) PREFACE TO *HISTORY OF THE POPES, THEIR CHURCH AND STATE*

The power of Rome in the early years and Middle Ages is universally known; in modern times, Rome has also experienced a great epoch of rejuvenated dominance over the world. After the decline of her importance in the first half of the sixteenth century, she once more succeeded in becoming the center of faith and opinion of the Romanic nations of southern Europe, making bold and at times successful attempts to recover her dominion over those of the North.

This period of a revived church-temporal power—its renovation and internal development, its progress and decline—I intend to describe, at least in outline; an undertaking which, however imperfectly it may be performed, could never have been attempted had I not found opportunity to avail myself of certain materials hitherto unknown. My first duty is to give a general indication of these materials and their sources.

In an earlier work I have already stated the contents of our Berlin manuscripts; but Vienna is incomparably richer than Berlin in treasures of this kind.

Besides its essentially German character, Vienna possesses also an element more extensively European: the most diversified manners and languages meet in all classes, from the highest to the lowest, and Italy in particular is fully and vividly represented. Even the collections in this city present a comprehensiveness of character, attributable to the policy of the state and its geographical position: its ancient connection with Spain, Belgium, and Lombardy and its proximity to, and ecclesiastical relations with, Rome. The Viennese have from the earliest times displayed a taste for collecting, possessing, and preserving, whence it arises that even the original and purely national collections of the imperial library are of great value; to these, various foreign collections have since been added. A number of volumes similar to the Berlin Informazioni were purchased at Modena from the house of Rangone; from Venice were acquired the invaluable manuscripts of the Doge Marco Foscarini, including his materials for a continuation of his literary undertaking, the "Italian Chronicles," of which no trace is elsewhere to be found; and the bequest of Prince Eugene added a rich collection of historical and political manuscripts that had been gathered together, with comprehensive judgment, by that distinguished statesman. The reader is animated by feelings of pleasure and hope on examining the catalogues and perceiving in them the unexplored knowledge that will enable him to supply the deficiencies manifest in almost all printed works of modern history. A whole futurity of study! And at the distance of a few steps only, Vienna presents literary support still more important. The Imperial Archives contain, as might be expected, the most authentic and valuable records for the elucidation of German history in general, but particularly also of Italian history. It is true that the greater part of the Venetian archives have been restored, after many wanderings, to Venice; but there still remains in Vienna a mass of Venetian manuscripts far from unimportant: dispatches, in the original or as copies, and abstracts thereof made for the use of the state, called "Rubricaries"; reports which, in many instances, are the only copies extant; official registers of public functionaries, chronicles, and diaries. The reports relating to Gregory XIII and Sixtus V to be found in the present volumes are for the most part derived from the archives of Vienna. I cannot sufficiently praise the unconditional liberality with which I was permitted to have access to these.

And perhaps I ought here to particularize the many and various aids afforded me in furtherance of my work, both at home and abroad; but I feel restrained by a scruple (whether well founded or not, I am unable to decide) that I should have to mention so many names, some of them of great eminence, as would give my gratitude the appearance of vainglory—and a work that has every reason to present itself modestly might assume an air of pretension ill suited to its purposes.

Next to Vienna, my attention was principally directed to Venice and Rome.

It was formerly the most invariable practice of great houses in Venice to form a cabinet of manuscripts as an adjunct to the library. It was in the nature of things that these would relate principally to the affairs of the republic. They represent the part taken by the respective families in public affairs and were preserved as records and memorials of the house for the instruction of its younger members. Some of these private collections still remain, and I had access to several; but much the larger number were destroyed in the general ruin of 1797 or since then. If more have been preserved than might have been expected, the gratitude of the world is due chiefly to the librarians of St. Mark, who labored to save from the universal wreck whatever the utmost resources of their institution would permit them to secure. Accordingly this library possesses a considerable store of manuscripts, indispensable to the history of the city and state, and which are even valuable aids toward that of Europe. But the inquirer must not expect too much from it: it is a somewhat recent acquisition gathered, almost at random, from private collections, incomplete and without unity of plan. It is not to be compared with the riches of the State archives especially as these are now arranged. I have already given a sketch of the Venetian archives in my inquiry into the conspiracy of 1618 and will not repeat what I there said. For my Roman investigations the reports of the ambassadors returning from Rome were above all desirable; but I had good reason to use other collections for this study, because gaps are always unavoidable, and these archives must necessarily have sustained losses in their many wanderings. In different places I gathered together forty-eight reports relating to Rome, the oldest dating from the year 1500. Nineteen were of the sixteenth century and twenty-one of the seventeenth century; these formed an almost complete series, having only a few breaks here and there. Of the eighteenth century there were, it is true, only eight, but these, too, were very instructive and welcome. In the majority of cases I saw and used the originals. They contained a great number of interesting observations derived from immediate experience that would otherwise have been lost with the passing of contemporaries. These first gave me hopes of a coherent narrative.

[It will be obvious that Rome alone could supply the means for verifying and extending these materials.]

But was it to be expected that a foreigner, and one professing a different faith, would there be permitted to have free access to the public collections for the purpose of revealing the secrets of the papacy? This would not perhaps have been so ill-advised as it may appear since no research can bring to light anything worse that what is already assumed by unfounded conjecture and received by the world as established truth. But I cannot boast of having had any such experience. I was enabled to take cognizance of the treasures contained in the Vatican and to use a number of volumes suited to my purpose; but the freedom of access which I could have wished was by no means accorded.

Fortunately, however, other collections were thrown open to me from which I could acquire information, which, if not complete, was nonetheless very extensive and authentic. In the times of flourishing aristocracy, more particularly in the seventeenth century, it was customary throughout Europe for the great families who had administered the affairs of state to retain possession of some of the public documents. This practice prevailed in Rome to a greater extent, perhaps, than in any other state. The reigning kinsmen of the pontiff, who in all ages exercised considerable power, usually bequeathed a large part of the state papers accumulated during their administration to the perpetual possession of the princely houses they founded. These constituted a part of the family endowments. In the palaces which they erected, a few rooms, usually in the upper part of the building, were always reserved for books and manuscripts, to which each succeeding generation contributed. Thus, to a certain extent the private collections of Rome may be regarded as the public ones, as the archives of state were dispersed among the descendants of reigning houses without any objection being made to the practice, much in the same manner as the redundancy of public wealth was suffered to flow into the coffers of the papal kindred; and certain private galleries, such as the Borghese or Doria, became greatly superior to the Vatican both in extent and historical importance, though the latter is distinguished by its selection of masterpieces. The manuscripts preserved in the Barberini, Chigi, Altieri, Albani, and Corsini palaces are accordingly of inestimable value for the aid they give toward a history of the popes, their State, and their Church. The State archives, recently established, are particularly important for their collection of registers illustrative of the Middle Ages; part of the history of this period still awaits a discoverer here; but, as far as my knowledge extends, I do not believe that much is to be gained from it for later centuries. Its value is small, unless I have been purposely deceived, when compared with the wealth and magnificence of private collections. Each of these comprises, as may be readily supposed, the papers of that epoch in which the pope of the family reigned; but as the kindred of each pontiff usually retained an eminent station; as men are in general desirous of extending and completing a collection once begun, and as opportunities were frequent in Rome, from the literary traffic in manuscripts established there; so the whole of these private collections possess many valuable documents illustrating other periods, both proximate and remote. The richest of all (in consequence of important bequests) is the Barberiniana; that of the Corsini Palace has been remarkable from its commencement for the care and judgment with which it has been formed.

I was fortunate enough to be permitted to use all these collections, as well as others of less importance, and in some instances with unrestricted freedom. An unexpected harvest of authentic and suitable materials thus lay before me as, for example: the correspondence of the nuncios with the instructions given to them and the reports which were brought back; detailed biographies of several popes, written with greater freedom because they were not intended for the public; accounts of the lives of distinguished cardinals; official and private journals; discussions of particular circumstances and transactions; memoranda and deliberations; reports on the administration of the provinces, their trade and manufactures; statistical tables and accounts of receipts and disbursements. These documents, for the most part entirely unknown, were prepared by men acquainted with their subject in practical terms and were of a credibility which, though it does not supersede the necessity for a searching and critical examination, is equal to that usually accorded to the testimony of well-informed contemporaries. The oldest of these manuscripts of which I made use related to the conspiracy of the Porcari against Nicholas V. Of other manuscripts on the fifteenth century I met with only a few, but on entering the sixteenth century, they became more numerous and more comprehensive at every step. Through the whole course of the seventeenth century, during which so little is known with certainty respecting Rome, they afford information all the more valuable because of its previous dearth. After the commencement of the eighteenth century, the documents decrease in number and intrinsic value; but at that time the Roman State and Court had already lost much of their influence and importance. I shall discuss these Roman manuscripts, as well as the Venetian, in detail at the end of the work, and will there note whatever I may find deserving attention, and which I could not well introduce in the course of the narrative. The large mass of materials, both manuscript and printed, lying before me renders a stringent condensation indispensable.

An Italian or Roman, a Catholic, would undertake the subject in a very different manner. Through expressions of personal veneration—or, perhaps, in the present state of opinion, of personal hatred—he would give to his work a peculiar, and, no doubt, more brilliant coloring; on many points he would be more elaborate, more ecclesiastical, more local. In these respects a Protestant, a North German, cannot be expected to compete with him. He regards the papal power with feelings of more indifference and must, from the first, renounce that warmth of expression which arises from partiality or hostility and which might, perhaps, produce a certain impression in Europe. In the last resort, we lack the true sympathy for such matters of ecclesiastical or canonical detail; on the other hand, our position affords us different—and, if I am not mistaken, more purely historical—perspectives. For what is there in the present day that can make the history of the papal power of importance to us? Not its particular relation to ourselves; for it no longer exercises any essential influence, nor does it create in us solicitude of any kind; the times are past in which we had anything to fear; we now feel ourselves perfectly secure. It must be its world historical development and influence. The papal power was, however, not so unchangeable as is commonly supposed. If we consider the question apart from those principles upon which its existence depends and which it cannot abandon without consigning itself to destruction, we shall find it affected, quite as deeply as any other government and to the very essence of its being, by the various destinies to which the nations of Europe have been subjected. As the history of the world has varied; as one nation or another has gained the ascendancy; as the fabric of social life has been disturbed; so also has the papal power been affected: its maxims, its objectives, and its pretensions have undergone essential changes; and its influence, above all, has been subjected to the greatest variations. If we consider the long list of names so frequently repeated through successive ages, from Pius I in the second century to our contemporaries, Pius VII and VIII, in the nineteenth, we receive an impression of uninterrupted stability; but we must not permit ourselves to be misled. The popes of different periods are, in fact, distinguished by differences as strongly marked as those existing between the various dynasties of a kingdom. To us who are outsiders precisely these mutations present the most interesting subject of contemplation. We see in them a portion of general history, of the overall development of the world; and this is true not only of periods when Rome held undisputed rule but also, and perhaps even more remarkably, of those periods shaken by the conflicting forces of action and counteraction, such as the times which the present work is intended to encompass—the sixteenth and seventeenth centuries—times when the papacy was menaced and endangered, yet maintained and fortified itself, nay, even reextended its influence, striding onward for a period but at last receding again and tottering to its fall; times in which the mind of the western nations was pre-eminently occupied by ecclesiastical questions and when the power, which, abandoned and assailed by one party, was upheld and defended with fresh zeal by the other, necessarily assumed a great universal importance. It is from this point of view that our natural position invites us to consider this history, and this I will now attempt.

Chapter 21

Anthony Grafton

HOW THE HISTORIAN FOUND HIS MUSE: RANKE'S PATH TO THE FOOTNOTE

Anthony Grafton, "How the Historian Found His Muse: Ranke's Path to the Footnote", *The Footnote: A Curious History* (Cambridge, MA: Harvard University Press, 1997), 62–72, 92–3.

THE ROAD THAT RANKE FOLLOWED as he learned to dramatize the central importance of documents to the historian's enterprise was in some ways more direct, in others much more crooked than he remembered as an old man. To follow Ranke back to the origins of his new German history, we must begin in the middle of the American Middle West. Around the turn of the century, many American universities began to make themselves over, following what they saw as the German model. Professors, many of whom had enjoyed the adventure of studying in scholarly Göttingen, romantic Heidelberg, or metropolitan Berlin, began to enroll graduate students and offer specialized seminars at home. They carved out new spaces for these advanced courses—often within the impressively crenelated university libraries of the time, in rooms equipped with reference books and primary sources. Students from Berkeley to Baltimore could learn dead languages, master bibliographies, and apply sophisticated research techniques, just as their teachers had. And they could do so without having to live in Germany, drink beer, and translate texts, extemporaneously, into as well as out of Gothic and Anglo-Saxon, as German professors required the members of seminars to do.

The discovery of the truth about the past—to be obtained by German forms of scholarship—took on the moral prestige of a crusade and the cultural allure of a fashion. It captured academic hearts in Middle America as well as on the coasts.[1] Before the First World War, the historians at the University of Illinois decided to create a historical seminar of the German kind. To adorn their meeting room they bought portraits of the greatest American and the greatest non-American historian they could think of: respectively Francis Parkman and Edward Gibbon. Though Ranke lost out in the competition to have his picture on the wall, he received a consolation prize. A letter of his, bought from a dealer in Frankfurt, was also framed and hung in the seminar whose patron saint he naturally was.

Years later, when the university found a new function for the room, the letter disappeared. Perhaps some historical aficionado of wide interests and low morals stole it.

Fortunately, a copy of this lost manuscript has survived. Ranke directed the letter—one of the few early ones that have been published—to his publisher, Georg Reimer, a great literary entrepreneur, who brought out such fundamental works of German literature and scholarship as the *Fairy Tales* of the brothers Grimm. In it Ranke addressed, with understandable anxiety, the delicate question of whether his first book could survive the state censorhip unharmed.[2] But he also raised, with even more anxiety, the question of the footnote. Surprisingly—especially to the late-twentieth-century reader, who expects learned authors to demand space for footnotes and hard-driving publishers to refuse it—Ranke insisted that he had felt it necessary to use notes only because a young author had to cite his sources. At all events, he had kept the distasteful things as short as possible: "I carefully avoided going in for real annotation. But I felt citation was indispensable in the work of a beginner who has to make his way and earn confidence." Ranke still hoped to find a way to avoid disfiguring his text with footnote cues and his pages with swelling feet of claylike annotation. Perhaps, he suggested, one could number the lines on each page or in each section, as was already normal practice in editions of classical authors, and put the notes at the end, keyed to the text. At best he saw the presence of annotation in his work as a necessary evil.[3]

Historians, young or old, are not on oath in letters to their publishers. But when the young and unknown Ranke professed his lack of interest in the formal aspects of documentation and his distaste for the appearance of pedantry, he was not striking a pose—even though he knew that his publisher cared as much about style as about science. The collection of Ranke's papers in Berlin includes not only his working notebooks, but part of the manuscript of his first book. Like the references in his finished book, those in the draft are the extremely short citations Ranke claimed to prefer: authors, titles, page numbers. Some pages have no footnotes at all; others have several footnote numbers, but not all of the references are filled in. And many footnotes give the author's name and the title, but no page number. All of the notes, finally, were added after Ranke had written out the entire text.[4] The document yields at least two obvious inferences. In the first place, Ranke, the founding father of the modern historian's craft, practiced it with no more discipline than his professional grandchildren and great-grandchildren. He composed his text as a whole. Only then did he search his books and notes, extracts and summaries, for the evidence to support it: he used a salt-shaker to add references to an already completed stew. This seems to have been Ranke's consistent practice. Even when, as an old man, he worked with and through secretaries, his methods underwent no fundamental change. The young men had to chase up references, for which Ranke supplied only hints, and which now and then did not exist at all, "a point on which Ranke was always very hard to convince."[5]

In fact, the scantiness of the notes in Ranke's *Geschichten* [Historian] led to the worst public embarrassment of his career. In 1828 he learned that he had offered powerful ammunition to his fiercest critic. Heinrich Leo, another young Berlin historian, responded to his rival's rapid ascent to the academic stratosphere with understandable jealousy—as well as a passionate desire to save the literary ideal of history that he cherished from Ranke's many stylistic and intellectual sins. He did his best to puncture what he saw as the hot air balloon of Ranke's purported scholarship. In a long and dismissive review, he criticized Ranke's style and his philosophy, predicting that his inchoate, sentimental book would find its warmest reception "among learned ladies"—"bey gelehrten Weibern." Worse still, Leo identified many passages where Ranke's text did not correspond precisely to the source quoted in the footnotes.[6] Ranke was appalled and infuriated by this "devilish review," which attacked him "on the most sensitive point of his research."[7] In a long reply he argued that support for every assertion Leo had contested could be found in one of the texts he had cited—though not necessarily in the passage referred to by any given footnote. The reader who wished to test Ranke's use of the originals must compare all of them systematically, as Leo had evidently failed to. "I cite," Ranke wrote in an indignant foonote, "for those who want to find, but not for those who look in order *not* to find. Incidentally, this book is not the sort that one can scrutinize over a cup of coffee, with just one of the editions I cited in one's hand."[8] Leo's rejoinder to this rebuttal was even more dismissive than his original review, and his judgment of the *Geschichten* even more absurdly negative. But he had no trouble using Ranke's own words to show that his victim's practices as a writer of footnotes were genuinely problematic. Leo advised Ranke to give up footnotes entirely in the future. A simple list of the sources used in each section would serve the reader better than annotations randomly attached to portions of the text "in which one finds things completely different from those in the citations."[9] Michael Bernays described the footnotes in Ranke's first book as exemplary: "No one who deserves to read Ranke would want to do without notes of this kind. But everyone realizes that the material they contain could not be moved into the text."[10] No praise would have pleased its recipient more. But not all his original readers would have agreed.

For all his modern erudition, Ranke evidently retained his allegiance to the classical notion of what a history should look like. Far from joyously accepting that a history should tell the double story of the historical past and the historian's research, Ranke shied away from disfiguring his powerful narrative and set-piece battle scenes with the ugly contrivances of scholarly mechanics. In this he was far from alone among Germany's historical revolutionaries. Barthold Georg Niebuhr, the revisionist who won fame by insisting that the traditional narrative of Rome's early history must be dissected by source-criticism and then reframed as a social analysis of the city's rise, loved the details of historical investigation and lectured about them to his students at Berlin.[11] He too, however, thought that the best historical narrative was a classical one, free of notes. He longed to write without a learned apparatus, if he could only solve all the technical problems and then push them out of the way: "Should the learned work, which reconstructs the material, ever be finished, I found it an appealing thought to write a straight narrative history of the Romans, without investigations, proofs, and erudition, as it would have been written 1800 years ago."[12] For Niebuhr as for Ranke, the hope proved impossible to fulfill: the historian who had eaten from the tree of source-criticism could not regain the innocence needed to write a simple narrative. But their aspirations remained rhetorical and literary, to an extent that would surprise many later professional historians. Some American scholars of an older generation, sure of their own right to claim professional descent from Ranke, regarded writing well as incompatible with the duties of a professional historian.[13] In doing so they hardly followed their master.

Ranke, after all, wished—as he said in an all-too-often quoted and all-too-rarely analyzed phrase—"only to say, how it really was"—"nur sagen, wie es eigentlich gewesen."[14] But what does that mean? As Hajo Holborn and others have shown, Ranke's famous dictum about his intentions as a historian was in fact a strategically placed citation of an even more famous passage from Thucydides (1.22).[15] One who cited the most profound of Greek political historians as his model for serious, accurate exposition could hardly be eager to obscure the literary relation between their texts by adding a commentary to the body of his own work.

More than one recent critic has pointed out that footnotes interrupt a narrative. References detract from the illusion of veracity and immediacy that Ranke and so many other nineteenth-century historians wished to create, since they continually interrupt the single story told by an omniscient narrator (Noel Coward made the same point more memorably when he remarked that having to read a footnote resembles having to go downstairs to answer the door while in the midst of making love).[16] Ranke's desire to imitate a classical historical model and his modern tastes both militated against the heavy use of notes. No wonder, then, that Ranke struggled to preserve the coherence of his narrative—and even tried, by placing the full texts of documents after his own text, to give the reader the experience of two kinds of authenticity, the literary and the documentary. No wonder, either, that modern scholars are not sure whether to treat him as the first scientific historian or the last Romantic.[17] Many distinguished later historians also rebelled against the need to provide rich documentation. Fustel de Coulanges, a passionate believer in the importance of full and accurate use of sources, only gradually and grudgingly accepted what he saw as the new fad of providing extensive formal documentation.[18] Ernst Kantorowicz, as we have seen, caused a scandal with his brilliant, best-selling *Kaiser Friedrich II*, which at first possessed no apparatus at all.[19] They and others were Ranke's heirs to an extent that they and their critics did not suspect.

Ranke, then, had footnotes forced upon him. But what of the second, and more important, component of his learned apparatus—the extended commentary on his sources, in the form of an essay on historians or a selection of primary documents with commentary? Appendices in fact formed the more distinguished and distinctive part of Ranke's commentary on his own text. They called forth his best efforts as researcher and as writer. They made clear to intelligent readers that his views about the possibility of obtaining absolute accuracy in describing the past were nowhere near so simple as modern versions of his thought, whether intended as praise o? as caricature, have suggested. And they gave the experience of reading Ranke something of the same symphonic density, the same continual interplay between chronological narrative and systematic reflection, that Gibbon offered his readers.

For all its originality and its impact, however, Ranke's textual apparatus also came into being in a different, and a more complex, way than he himself claimed. In his late dictations Ranke portrayed his turn to criticism as a conversion experience, with all the unpredictability and shock value that normally invests such moments. Like someone falling through a weak spot in an apparently solid floor, he recalled, he suddenly saw that history must rest on thick pillars and joists which only criticism could fashion and put in place. That insight became the foundation of the second volume of his *Geschichten*, in which he dealt with the sources and their problems. No one, he thought, had anticipated his moment of revelation—even the classical scholars, whose revolutionary work on Greek and Roman history and literature presented some apparent parallels to his own enterprise. Ranke expected Niebuhr's support, but recognized no fundamental debt to Niebuhr's method: "Here I had regard neither for Niebuhr, who really wanted more to provide the tradition with a meaning, nor, in particular, for Gottfried Hermann, who criticized authors on points of detail—though I promised myself that great men of this sort would applaud me."[20]

[. . .]

Ranke innovated in many ways. He combined narrative with analytical history, on the grand scale. He dramatized the process of criticism as powerfully as the events it enabled him to reconstruct. And he set the stage for new research projects and forms of exposition—many of which he himself devised and carried out. Nothing quite like his *Geschichten* had appeared before. But he and his first book did not represent the beginnings of documented, critical history. If not in 1824, when? If not Ranke, who? Like so many genealogies, that of the footnote turns out to have more branches and twists than one might have expected. The next one leads away from historicism and back into the Enlightenment, away from the hard-pressed teacher begging for books and travel grants and into the well-stocked libraries of several eighteenth-century gentlemen.

Notes

1   See e.g. B. Perry, *And Gladly Teach* (Boston and New York, 1935).

2   On Reimer see G. Lüdtke, *Der Verlag Walter de Gruyter & Co.* (Berlin, 1924; repr. Berlin, 1978), 51–62.

3   G. Stanton Ford, "A Ranke Letter," *Journal of Modern History*, 32 (1960), 143: "Sorgfältig habe ich mich vor der eigentlichen Adnotation gehütet: das Citat schien mir in dem Werk eines Anfängers, der sich erst Bahn machen und Glauben verdienen soll, unerläszlich."

4   Ranke Nachlass, Staatsbibliothek zu Berlin, Preussischer Kulturbesitz (Haus II), Fasz. 1, I.

5   T. Wiedemann, "Sechzehn Jahre in der Werkstatt Leopold von Ranke's," *Deutsche Revue*, December 1891, 333: "wovon Ranke immer nur sehr schwer überzeugt wurde."

6   "H. L. Manin" [H. Leo], review of Ranke, in *Ergänzungsblätter zur Jenaischen Allgemeinen Literatur-Zeitung*, 16 (1828), nos. 17–18, cols. 129–140, esp. 136: "Doch wozu noch mehr anführen?—Man schlage nach, auf jedem Blatte fast wird ein verdrehtes, ein nichtssagendes oder nachlässig benutztes Citat zu finden seyn. Heisst das nun nackte Wahrheit? Heisst das gründliche Erforschung des Einzelnen?" ("But why cite more evidence? One need simply look, and on every page one finds a distorted, a meaningless or a carelessly used quotation. Should this be called the naked truth? Should this be called thorough research into the details?"). On the philosophical dimension of the debate between Leo and Ranke see G. G. Iggers, *The German Conception of History* (Middletown, Conn., 1968), 66–69, and S. Baur, "Rankes Historik, Teil I: Der junge Ranke" (Diss., Freie Universität Berlin, 1996), 125–138.

7   L. von Ranke, *Das Briefwerk*, ed. W. P. Fuchs (Hamburg, 1949), 156–161, 165, 168, 240: "auf dem kitzlichsten Punkt der Forschung."

8   L. Ranke, "Replik," *Intelligenzblatt der Allgemeinen Literatur-Zeitung* (May 1828), no. 131, cols. 193–199, at 195–196 n.: "Ich citire für die, welche finden wollen, aber nicht für solche, die da suchen, um *nicht* zu finden. Bey einer Tasse Kaffee, mit einem einzigen der citirten Ausgaben in der Hand, lässt sich übrigens diess Buch nicht prüfen"; cf. *Das Briefwerk*, ed. Fuchs, 159.

9   H. Leo, "Replik," *Intelligenzblatt der Jenaischen Allgem. Literatur-Zeitung* (June 1828), no. 39, cols. 305–312 at 310: "in denen ganz andere Dinge zu finden sind, als in den Citaten."

10   M. Bernays, "Zur Lehre von den Citaten und Noten," *Schriften zur Kritik und Litteraturgeschichte*, IV (Berlin, 1899), 333: "Keiner, der Ranke zu lesen verdient, möchte Noten dieser Art entbehren; jeder aber sieht ein, dass ihr Inhalt sich in den Text nicht schicken würde."

11   See now the remarkable study by G. Walther, *Niebuhrs Forschung* (Stuttgart, 1993), with ample references to the older literature.

12   B. G. Niebuhr, *Briefe. Neue Folge, 1816–1830*, ed. E. Vischer, IV: *Briefe aus Bonn (Juli bis Dezember 1830)* (Bern and Munich, 1984), 117: "Es war für mich ein reizender Gedanke, wenn dies gelehrte Werk, wodurch der Stoff wieder geschaffen wird, vollendet seyn würde, eine ganz erzählende Geschichte der Römer zu schreiben, ohne Untersuchung, Erweis und Gelehrsamkeit; wie man sie vor 1800 Jahren geschrieben haben würde." Cf. W. Nippel, " 'Geschichte' und 'Altertümer': Zur Periodisierung in der Althistorie," *Geschichtsdiskurs*, ed. W. Küttler et al., I (Frankfurt, 1993), 310–311.

13   For Ranke's qualities as a writer see the fine account by P. Gay, *Style in History* (London, 1975), chap. 2. Two further acts of resistance against the necessity of providing footnotes, both carried out by distinguished historians who had minutely precise knowledge of the documents they used, are described in a characteristically elegant essay by J. H. Hexter, "Garrett Mattingly, Historian," *From the Renaissance to the Counter-Reformation*, ed. C. H. Carter (London, 1966), 13–28 at 15–17, and in the sharply contrasting treatments of G. H. Selement, "Perry Miller: A Note on His Sources in *The New England Mind: The Seventeenth Century*," *William and Mary Quarterly*, 31 (1974), 453–464, and P. Miller, *Sources for "The New England Mind: The Seventeenth Century,"* ed. J. Hoopes (Williamsburg, Va., 1981); on the second case cf. D. Levin, *Exemplary Elders* (Athens and London, 1990), 30–32.

14   For the wording of this text see W. P. Fuchs, "Was heisst das: 'bloss zeigen, wie es eigentlich gewesen'?" *Geschichte in Wissenschaft und Unterricht*, 11 (1979), 655–667, showing that in 1874 Ranke changed the original phrase quoted in the text, to make it read "bloss zeigen, wie es eigentlich gewesen."

15   H. Holborn, *History and the Humanities* (Garden City, N.Y., 1972), 90–91; K. Repgen, "Ueber Rankes Diktum von 1824: 'Bloss sagen, wie es eigentlich gewesen,' " *Historisches Jahrbuch*, 102 (1982), 439–449; R. S. Stroud, " 'Wie es eigentlich gewesen' and Thucydides 2.48.3," *Hermes*, 115 (1987) 379–382 (who refutes much of Repgen's analysis). Cf. F. Gilbert, *History, Politics, or Culture?* (Princeton, 1990).

16   L. Gossman, *Between History and Literature* (Cambridge, Mass. and London, 1990), 249–250;
      F. Hartog, *Le xixe siècle et l'historire* (Paris, 1988), esp. 112–115; G. Pomata, "Versions of Narrative:
      Overt and Covert Narrators in Nineteenth Century Historiography," *History Workshop*, 27 (1989),
      1–17. For Noel Coward I am indebted to B. Hilbert, "Elegy for Excursus: The Descent of the
      Footnote," *College English*, 51 (1989), 401.

17   He seems to play both roles in Pomata, 12 and 14.

18   See Fustel's declaration, published by Camille Jullian in 1891, in Hartog, 360: "J'appartiens à une
      génération qui n'est plus jeune, et dans laquelle les travailleurs s'imposaient deux règles: d'abord
      d'étudier un sujet d'après toutes les sources observées directement et de près, ensuite de ne
      présenter au lecteur que le résultat de leurs recherches; on lui épargnait l'appareil d'érudition,
      l'érudition étant pour l'auteur seul et non pour le lecteur; quelques indications au bas des pages
      suffisaient au lecteur, qu'on invitait à vérifier. Depuis une vingtaine d'années les procédés habituels
      ont changé: l'usage aujourd'hui est de présenter au lecteur l'appareil d'érudition plutôt que les
      résultats. On tient plus à l'échafaudage qu'à la construction. L'érudition a changé ses formes et ses
      procédés; elle n'est pas plus profonde, et l'exactitude n'est pas d'aujourd'hui; mais l'érudition veut
      se montrer davantage. On veut avant tout paraître érudit." ("I belong to a generation no longer
      young, in which researchers followed two rules. First of all, they approached each subject through
      direct and close study of all the sources. Then they offered the reader only the results of their
      researches, sparing him the paraphernalia of learning. Learning was reserved for the author alone,
      and not for the reader. Some references in footnotes sufficed for the reader, who was thus invited to
      make his own verification. Some twenty years ago, normal methods underwent a transformation.
      Today, the standard practice is to present the reader with the paraphernalia of learning rather than
      the results. The scaffolding matters more than the structure. Learning has changed its forms and
      methods. It is no longer deep, and precision is not a virtue of the present day. But learning wishes to
      make more of a display of itself. Scholars wish above all to appear learned.")

19   See e.g. Y. Malkiel, "Ernst H. Kantorowicz," in *On Four Modern Humanists*, ed. A. R. Evans, Jr.
      (Princeton, 1970), 150–151, 181–192. Malkiel points out that Kantorowicz's views changed con-
      siderably in later life, when he normally wrote in English, without artistic ambitions and with a
      sharp sense of the dangers that historical theses not derived from documents posed. He attacked a
      proposal to eliminate footnotes from *Speculum*, the main American journal of medieval studies, and
      supplied the work that he wrote in Berkeley and Princeton with a splendidly elaborate technical
      apparatus.

20   Ranke, *Sämmtliche Werke*, 53/54 (Leipzig, 1890), 62: "Ich habe hier weder auf Niebuhr, der
      eigentlich mehr der Tradition einen Sinn verschaffen will, noch vollends auf Gottfried Hermann,
      der die Autoren im einzelnen kritisirt, Rücksicht genommen, obwohl ich mir bei grossen Männern
      dieser Art Beifall versprach."

Chapter 22

James Harvey Robinson

THE NEW HISTORY

James Harvey Robinson (1863–1936), "The New History", 1911, *The New History: Essays Illustrating the Modern Historical Outlook* (New York: Macmillan, 1931), 1, 4–10, 13–16, 23–5.

IN ITS AMPLEST MEANING history includes every trace and vestige of everything that man has done or thought since first he appeared on the earth. It may aspire to follow the fate of nations or it may depict the habits and emotions of the most obscure individual. Its sources of information extend from the rude flint hatchets of Chelles to this morning's newspaper. [. . .]

[. . .]

I open a more recent volume which treats the whole of Europe in the eighteenth century, as it approached the momentous crisis of the French Revolution. Its author could hardly fail to realize the necessity of sifting his material most critically in order to make clear the regenerative workings of the new spirit of enlightenment amid conditions essentially difficult for us to understand. He does not hesitate, however, to insert such statements as these: "Zinzendorf died in 1742, Stahremberg in 1745, Kinsky in 1748. While Uhlfeld became on Zinzendorf's death nominally chancellor, Bartenstein remained from 1740 to 1753 Minister of Foreign Affairs, and had the greatest influence in the secret conference of Ministers." Very true; but were there not, perhaps, other things better worth telling about an ill-understood century than the dates of the deaths of the members of an Austrian cabinet?

[. . .]

The tendency to catalogue mere names of persons and places which have not the least importance for the reader, or which for want of space must be left as undetermined as x, y, and z in an unsolved equation, is too common to require further illustration. The question forces itself upon us, why do writers include such seemingly irrelevant and unedifying details? Sometimes, doubtless, from mere thoughtlessness; the names mean something to the writer, who mistakenly infers that they are eloquent in themselves. Or he may suppose that they give greater vivacity to his tale, or will form the nucleus about which future knowledge may crystallize. Names but once mentioned, however, rarely add vividness to a story, but rather obscure it; [. . .]

It is, however, often urged that even the hastiest and driest chronicle of the "chief events" in the world's history is a good thing, — that we get at least a chronological outline which we carry about with us as a guide, which enables us to put our future knowledge in its proper relations. We learn important dates so as to read intelligently later of events of which in school we learn only the names. We prepare ourselves to place our contingent knowledge of literature, philosophy, institutions, and art in what is called an "historic setting." Many of us have, however, come to suspect that such an outline amounts to very little. It recommends itself, it is true, as the easiest kind of history to teach, since it requires no thought, — only memory. I once had occasion to ask a college professor of great erudition and culture, who had resided several years in the Orient, the date of the Hegira, which, with that of Marathon, and the battle of Crécy, is generally regarded as part of the equipment of every educated gentleman. He did not know the date, however, any better than I did, so we looked it up in a dictionary. We might, indeed, have saved a minute or two if we had had the information at our tongue's end, but we had never missed it before.

A sensible carpenter or plumber does not constantly carry a saw in his hip pocket, or a coil of lead pipe over his shoulder, in order to be ready for a distant emergency. He very properly goes to his shop and his tool chest for his tools and materials. No more, in these days of cheap and convenient books of reference, need the student of history go heavy-armed for intellectual encounters. Of course all knowledge, even that which is well forgot-ten, may beget a certain habit of accuracy and sense of proportion, but formulas should follow knowledge, as they do in our best mathematical textbooks; in historical instruction we have ordinarily given our formulas first.

The really fundamental reason for hastening to introduce the reader as early as possible to the son of Peter of Aragon, to Zinzendorf, and that historic spot, Chateauneuf-en-Thimerais, has doubtless been the venerable predilection for merely political events and persons which has until recently dominated our writers of popular history. Carlyle's warn-ing has passed unheeded, that far away from senate houses, battle fields, and king's ante-chambers, "the mighty tide of thought and action was still rolling on its wondrous course." Elaborate attempts have indeed been made to justify this seemingly disproportionate fond-ness for political and military affairs. We are bluntly told by Mr. Freeman that "History is past politics." To Ranke the purpose of history was to clarify our notions of the origin and nature of the State, which forms the basis of the continuity that we believe we observe in human development. [. . .]

It is impossible to discuss here the intricate question of the rôle of the State in the past; nor is it necessary to do so, for no one denies its great importance or would advocate its neglect in our historical manuals. The real question is, has not our bias for political history led us to include a great many trifling details of dynasties and military history which merely confound the reader and take up precious space that should be devoted to certain great issues hitherto neglected? [. . .] Man is more than a warrior, a subject, or a princely ruler; the State is by no means his sole interest. [. . .] He has, through the ages, made voyages, extended commerce, founded cities, established great universities, written books, built glorious cathedrals, painted pictures, and sought out many inventions. The propriety of including these human interests in our historical manuals is being more and more widely recognized, but political history still retains its supreme position, and past political events are still looked upon by the public as history *par excellence*.

In contrast, and even in seeming contradiction, to the tradition which gives prominence to political events and personages, there is a curious element of the sensational in our popular histories. There is a kind of history which does not concern itself with the normal conduct and serious achievements of mankind in the past, but, like melodrama, purposely selects the picturesque and lurid as its theme. The annals of France, a modern writer assures us, will always command special attention, for "No other modern nation has undergone changes more frequent, more radical, more sudden, bloody, and dramatic." Then, too: "No land has given birth to men more great, more good, more brave; none has been cursed with men more vile. No people have climbed higher in the arduous pathway of victory; none have been so pitilessly stricken down in defeat." In short, "France has furnished the epic poem of modern history." The writer would therefore convince us that the more prodigious the occurrences narrated, the better the history. A distinguished chemist once considerately told me that it seemed to him that the certitude of history varied in inverse ratio to what we know about it. He might have added that sometimes, in common with the *Police Gazette*, its intrinsic interest appears to vary in direct ratio to its gruesomeness.

There would be less objection to perpetuating the conception of history as a chronicle of heroic persons and romantic occurrences, were it not that the craving for the dramatic can be better met by confessed fiction, and that those who see in history an epic poem give us very imperfect and erroneous notions of the past. [. . .]

[. . .]

We are, further, ordinarily taught to view mankind as in a periodic state of turmoil. Historical writers do all they can, by studied neglect, to disguise the importance of the lucid intervals during which the greater part of human progress has taken place. They skip lightly from one commotion to another. They have not time to explain what the French Revolution was by rationally describing the *Ancien régime*, which can alone give it any meaning, but after the quotation from La Bruyère, regarding certain fierce animals, "black, livid, and burnt by the sun," and a repetition of that careless phrase, "After us, the deluge," they hasten on to the Reign of Terror as the beall and end-all of the bloody affair. And in this way they make a second St. Bartholomew's of one of the grandest and, in its essential reforms, most peaceful of changes which ever overtook France or Europe. Obviously the real significance of a revolution is to be measured by the extent to which general conditions were changed and new things substituted for the old. The old must, therefore, be studied quite as carefully as the new—more carefully, indeed, since our sympathies are usually with the new, and our knowledge of the more recent is fuller than that of the more remote. Hence, we might far better busy ourselves with the reasons why arbitrary imprisonments, the guilds, the sale of offices, and so forth, were defended by many thoughtful, well-intentioned citizens than waste time in a gratuitous denunciation of them.

[. . .]

[. . .] Now I firmly believe that "institutions" (which are after all only national habits) can be made interesting. I use the word "institutions" in a very broad sense to include the ways in which people have thought and acted in the past, their tastes and their achievements in many fields besides the political. Events are the more or less clear expression of "institutions" in this sense, and the events properly selected will serve to make the "institutions" clear.

Hitherto writers have been prone to deal with events for their own sake; a deeper insight will surely lead us, as time goes on, to reject the anomalous and seemingly accidental occurrences and dwell rather upon those which illustrate some profound historical truth. And there is a very simple principle by which the relevant and useful may be determined and the irrelevant rejected. Is the fact or occurrence one which will aid the reader to grasp the meaning of any great period of human development or the true nature of any momentous institution? It should then be cherished as a precious means to an end, and the more engaging it is, the better; its inherent interest will only facilitate our work, not embarrass it. On the other hand, is an event seemingly fortuitous, isolated, and anomalous,—like the story of Rienzi, the September massacres, or the murder of Marat? We should then hesitate to include it on its own merits,—at least in a brief historical manual—for, interesting as it may be as an heroic or terrible incident, it may mislead the reader and divert his attention from the prevailing interests, preoccupations and permanent achievements of the past. [. . .]

Society is to-day engaged in a tremendous and unprecedented effort to better itself in manifold ways. Never has our knowledge of the world and of man been so great as it now is; never before has there been so much general good will and so much intelligent social activity as now prevails. The part that each of us can play in forwarding some phase of this reform will depend upon our understanding of existing conditions and opinion, and these can only be explained, as has been shown, by following more or less carefully the processes that produced them. We must develop historical-mindedness upon a far more generous scale than hitherto, for this will add a still deficient element in our intellectual equipment and will promote rational progress as nothing else can do. The present has hitherto been the willing victim of the past; the time has now come when it should turn on the past and exploit it in the interests of advance.

The "New History" is escaping from the limitations formerly imposed upon the study of the past. It will come in time consciously to meet our daily needs; it will avail itself of all those discoveries that are being made about mankind by anthropologists, economists, psychologists, and sociologists—discoveries which during the past fifty years have served to revolutionize our ideas of the origin, progress, and prospects of our race. There is no branch of organic or inorganic science which has not undergone the most remarkable changes during the last half century, and many new branches of social science, even the names of which would have been unknown to historians in the middle of the nineteenth century, have been added to the long list. It is inevitable that history should be involved in this revolutionary process, but since it must be confessed that this necessity has escaped many contemporaneous writers, it is no wonder that the intelligent public continues to accept somewhat archaic ideas of the scope and character of history.

The title of this little volume has been chosen with the view of emphasizing the fact that history should not be regarded as a stationary subject which can only progress by refining its methods and accumulating, criticizing, and assimilating new material, but that it is bound to alter its ideals and aims with the general progress of society and of the social sciences, and that it should ultimately play an infinitely more important rôle in our intellectual life than it has hitherto done.

We can only understand where we are if we understand how we got to this point

Chapter 23

Marc Bloch and Lucien Febvre

PREFACE: TO OUR READERS

Marc Bloch (1886–1944) and Lucien Febvre (1878–1956), "Preface: To Our Readers", Trans. Adeline Amar and Adam Budd, 2008, *Annales d'histoire économique et sociale* 1 (1929), 1–2.

THANKS TO THE BROAD VISION of a great editor, and thanks to the combined work of French and foreign contributors, whose eagerness has delighted and encouraged us, our *Annales*—a purpose that has long matured—can today be issued and can attempt to be useful. For this, we thank the real authors.

Yet another periodical, not to mention a periodical in economic and social history? We know that our journal is not the first of its kind in French, European, or worldwide production. Yet we believe that, next to its magnificent elder kin, it will take its own place under the sun. It is influenced by their examples yet brings its own spirit.

Both of us historians, we have had nearly similar experiences and have drawn the same conclusions from them; we have long been aware of the wrongs that can be caused by a divorce that has now become conventional. While historians apply their well-tried tricks to documents of the past, more and more men devote their activities—sometimes feverishly—to studying contemporary societies and economies: these are two different classes of researchers, made to understand each other and yet who usually come into regular contact without knowing each other. And there is more. Even among the historians, just like among researchers preoccupied with the present, there are many compartments: researchers working on antiquity, on the medieval and modern periods, who are devoted to describing societies considered "civilised"—to use an old term the meaning of which changes a bit more each day—or, on the contrary, researchers attracted to societies one has to call primitive, or exotic, by a lack of more appropriate words. Nothing would be better, of course, than if one could try and follow one's neighbour's work, while working on a legitimate specialisation, working hard to cultivate one's own garden. But the walls are so high that, very often, they block the view. Yet one can imagine how many excellent suggestions about methods and interpretations of facts, how many cultural benefits, innovations in intuition, would come to light, out of more frequent intellectual interactions between these various groups! This is the price of the future of economic history, and also the right intelligence of those facts that tomorrow will be history.

We aim to challenge these very devastating schisms. We will not use method articles here and theoretical dissertations there. We will use example and fact. Researchers of various origins and specialisations are put together here, but driven by the same spirit of precise impartiality they will offer the result of their research on those subjects of which they are specialists and that they themselves have chosen. It seems impossible for us that informed and intelligent readers will not quickly find the necessary lessons out of such contact. Our enterprise is an act of faith in the exemplary virtue that resides in sincere, meticulous, and securely equipped work.

The Directors

[Marc Bloch and Lucien Febvre]

Chapter 24

Herbert Butterfield

THE UNDERLYING ASSUMPTION

Herbert Butterfield (1900–1979), "The Underlying Assumption", *The Whig Interpretation of History* (London: G. Bell, 1931), 9–26.

THE PRIMARY ASSUMPTION of all attempts to understand the men of the past must be the belief that we can in some degree enter into minds that are unlike our own. If this belief were unfounded it would seem that men must be for ever locked away from one another, and all generations must be regarded as a world and a law unto themselves. If we were unable to enter in any way into the mind of a presentday Roman Catholic priest, for example, and similarly into the mind of an atheistical orator in Hyde Park, it is difficult to see how we could know anything of the still stranger men of the sixteenth century, or pretend to understand the process of history-making which has moulded us into the world of to-day. In reality the historian postulates that the world is in some sense always the same world and that even the men most dissimilar are never absolutely unlike. And though a sentence from Aquinas[i] may fall so strangely upon modern ears that it becomes plausible to dismiss the man as a fool or a mind utterly and absolutely alien, I take it that to dismiss a man in this way is a method of blocking up the mind against him, and against something important in both human nature and its history; it is really the refusal to a historical personage of the effort of historical understanding. Precisely because of his unlikeness to ourselves Aquinas is the more enticing subject for the historical imagination; for the chief aim of the historian is the elucidation of the unlikenesses between past and present and his chief function is to act in this way as the mediator between other generations and our own. It is not for him to stress and magnify the similarities between one age and another, and he is riding after a whole flock of misapprehensions if he goes to hunt for the present in the past. Rather it is his work to destroy those very analogies which we imagined to exist. When he shows us that Magna Carta is a feudal document in a feudal setting, with implications different from those we had taken for granted, he is disillusioning us concerning something in the past which we had assumed to be too like something in the present. That whole

---

i   Thomas Aquinas (c.1225–73), Italian theologian. [-Ed.]

process of specialised research which has in so many fields revised the previously accepted whig interpretation of history, has set our bearings afresh in one period after another, by referring matters in this way to their context, and so discovering their unlikeness to the world of the present-day.

It is part and parcel of the whig interpretation of history that it studies the past with reference to the present; and though there may be a sense in which this is unobjectionable if its implications are carefully considered, and there may be a sense in which it is inescapable, it has often been an obstruction to historical understanding because it has been taken to mean the study of the past with direct and perpetual reference to the present. Through this system of immediate reference to the present-day, historical personages can easily and irresistibly be classed into the men who furthered progress and the men who tried to hinder it; so that a handy rule of thumb exists by which the historian can select and reject, and can make his points of emphasis. On this system the historian is bound to construe his function as demanding him to be vigilant for likenesses between past and present, instead of being vigilant for unlikenesses; so that he will find it easy to say that he has seen the present in the past, he will imagine that he has discovered a 'root' or an 'anticipation' of the 20th century, when in reality he is in a world of different connotations altogether, and he has merely tumbled upon what could be shown to be a misleading analogy. Working upon the same system the whig historian can draw lines through certain events, some such line as that which leads through Martin Luther and a long succession of whigs to modern liberty; and if he is not careful he begins to forget that this line is merely a mental trick of his; he comes to imagine that it represents something like a line of causation. The total result of this method is to impose a certain form upon the whole historical story, and to produce a scheme of general history which is bound to converge beautifully upon the present – all demonstrating throughout the ages the workings of an obvious principle of progress, of which the Protestants and whigs have been the perennial allies while Catholics and tories have perpetually formed obstruction. A caricature of this result is to be seen in a popular view that is still not quite eradicated: the view that the Middle Ages represented a period of darkness when man was kept tongue-tied by authority – a period against which the Renaissance was the reaction and the Reformation the great rebellion. It is illustrated to perfection in the argument of a man denouncing Roman Catholicism at a street corner, who said: 'When the Pope ruled England them was called the Dark Ages.'

The whig historian stands on the summit of the 20th century, and organises his scheme of history from the point of view of his own day; and he is a subtle man to overturn from his mountain-top where he can fortify himself with plausible argument. He can say that events take on their due proportions when observed through the lapse of time. He can say that events must be judged by their ultimate issues, which, since we can trace them no farther, we must at least follow down to the present. He can say that it is only in relation to the 20th century that one happening or another in the past has relevance or significance for us. He can use all the arguments that are so handy to men when discussion is dragged into the market place and philosophy is dethroned by common sense; so that it is no simple matter to demonstrate how the whig historian, from his mountain-top, sees the course of history only inverted and aslant. The fallacy lies in the fact that if the historian working on the 16th century keeps the 20th century in his mind, he makes direct reference across all the intervening period between Luther or the Popes and the world of our own day. And this immediate juxtaposition of past and present, though it makes everything easy and makes some inferences perilously obvious, is bound to lead to an over-simplification of the relations between events and a complete misapprehension of the relations between past and present.

This attitude to history is not by any means the one which the historical specialist adopts at the precise moment when he is engaged upon his particular research; and indeed as we come closer to the past we find it impossible to follow these principles consistently even though we may have accepted them verbally. In spite of ourselves and in spite of our theories we forget that we had set out to study the past for the sake of the present, we cannot save ourselves from tumbling headlong into it and being immersed in it for its own sake; and very soon we may be concentrated upon the most useless things in the world – Marie Antoinette's ear-rings or the adventures of the Jacobites. But the attitude is one which we tend to adopt when we are visualising the general course of history or commenting on it, and it is one into which the specialist himself often slides when he comes to the point of relating his special piece of work to the larger historical story. In other words it represents a fallacy and an unexamined habit of mind into which we fall when we treat of history on the broad scale. It is something which intervenes between the work of the historical specialist and that work, partly of organisation and partly of abridgment, which the general historian carries out; it inserts itself at the change of focus that we make when we pass from the microscopic view of a particular period to our bird's-eye view of the whole; and when it comes it brings with it that whig interpretation of history which is so different from the story that the research student has to tell.

There is an alternative line of assumption upon which the historian can base himself when he comes to his study of the past; and it is the one upon which he does seem more or less consciously to act and to direct his mind when he is engaged upon a piece of research. On this view he comes to his labours conscious of the fact that he is trying to understand the past for the sake of the past, and though it is true that he can never entirely abstract himself from his own age, it is none the less certain that this consciousness of his purpose is a very different one from that of the whig historian, who tells himself that he is studying the past for the sake of the present. Real historical understanding is not achieved by the subordination of the past to the present, but rather by our making the past our present and attempting to see life with the eyes of another century than our own. It is not reached by assuming that our own age is the absolute to which Luther and Calvin and their generation are only relative; it is only reached by fully accepting the fact that their generation was as valid as our generation, their issues as momentous as our issues and their day as full and as vital to them as our day is to us. The twentieth century which has its own hairs to split may have little patience with Arius and Athanasius who burdened the world with a quarrel about a diphthong, but the historian has not achieved historical understanding, has not reached that kind of understanding in which the mind can find rest, until he has seen that that diphthong was bound to be the most urgent matter in the universe to those people. It is when the emphasis is laid in this way upon the historian's attempt to understand the past, that it becomes clear how much he is concerned to elucidate the unlikenesses between past and present. Instead of being moved to indignation by something in the past which at first seems alien and perhaps even wicked to our own day, instead of leaving it in the outer darkness, he makes the effort to bring this thing into the context where it is natural, and he elucidates the matter by showing its relation to other things which we do understand. Whereas the man who keeps his eye on the present tends to ask some such question as, How did religious liberty arise? while the whig historian by a subtle organisation of his sympathies tends to read it as the question, To whom must we be grateful for our religious liberty? the historian who is engaged upon studying the 16th century at close hand is more likely to find himself asking why men in those days were so given to persecution. This is in a special sense the historian's question for it is a question about the past rather than about the present, and in answering it the historian is on his own ground and is making the kind of contribution which he is most fitted to make. It is in this sense that he is always forgiving sins by the mere fact that he is finding out why they happened. The things which are most alien to ourselves are the very object of his exposition. And until he has shown why men persecuted in the

16th century one may doubt whether he is competent to discuss the further question of how religious liberty has come down to the 20th.

But after this attempt to understand the past the historian seeks to study change taking place in the past, to work out the manner in which transitions are made, and to examine the way in which things happen in this world. If we could put all the historians together and look at their total co-operative achievement they are studying all that process of mutation which has turned the past into our present. And from the work of any historian who has concentrated his researches upon any change or transition, there emerges a truth of history which seems to combine with a truth of philosophy. It is nothing less than the whole of the past, with its complexity of movement, its entanglement of issues, and its intricate interactions, which produced the whole of the complex present; and this, which is itself an assumption and not a conclusion of historical study, is the only safe piece of causation that a historian can put his hand upon, the only thing which he can positively assert about the relationship between past and present. When the need arises to sort and disentangle from the present one fact or feature that is required to be traced back into history, the historian is faced with more unravelling than a mind can do, and finds the network of interactions so intricate, that it is impossible to point to any one thing in the sixteenth century as the cause of any one thing in the twentieth. It is as much as the historian can do to trace with some probability the sequence of events from one generation to another, without seeking to draw the incalculably complex diagram of causes and effects for ever interlacing down to the third and fourth generations. Any action which any man has ever taken is part of that whole set of circumstances which at a given moment conditions the whole mass of things that are to happen next. To understand that action is to recover the thousand threads that connect it with other things, to establish it in a system of relations; in other words to place it in its historical context. But it is not easy to work out its consequences, for they are merged in the results of everything else that was conspiring to produce change at that moment. We do not know where Luther would have been if his movement had not chimed with the ambitions of princes. We do not know what would have happened to the princes if Luther had not come to their aid.

The volume and complexity of historical research are at the same time the result and the demonstration of the fact that the more we examine the way in which things happen, the more we are driven from the simple to the complex. It is only by undertaking an actual piece of research and looking at some point in history through the microscope that we can really visualise the complicated movements that lie behind any historical change. It is only by this method that we can discover the tricks that time plays with the purposes of men, as it turns those purposes to ends not realised; or learn the complex processes by which the world comes through a transition that seems a natural and easy step in progress to us when we look back upon it. It is only by this method that we can come to see the curious mediations that circumstances must provide before men can grow out of a complex or open their minds to a new thing. Perhaps the greatest of all the lessons of history is this demonstration of the complexity of human change and the unpredictable character of the ultimate consequences of any given act or decision of men; and on the face of it this is a lesson that can only be learned in detail. It is a lesson that is bound to be lost in abridgment, and that is why abridgments of history are sometimes calculated to propagate the very reverse of the truth of history. The historian seeks to explain how the past came to be turned into the present but there is a very real sense in which the only explanation he can give is to unfold the whole story and reveal the complexity by telling it in detail. In reality the process of mutation which produced the present is as long and complicated as all the most lengthy and complicated works of historical research placed end to end, and knit together and regarded as one whole.

The fallacy of the whig historian lies in the way in which he takes his short cut through this complexity. The difficulty of the general historian is that he has to abridge and that he must do it without altering the meaning and the peculiar message of history. The danger in any survey of the past is lest we argue in a circle and impute lessons to history which history has never taught and historical research has never discovered – lessons which are really inferences from the particular organisation that we have given to our knowledge. We may believe in some doctrine of evolution or some idea of progress and we may use this in our interpretation of the history of centuries; but what our history contributes is not evolution but rather the realisation of how crooked and perverse the ways of progress are, with what wilfulness and waste it twists and turns, and takes anything but the straight track to its goal, and how often it seems to go astray, and to be deflected by any conjuncture, to return to us – if it does return – by a backdoor. We may believe in some providence that guides the destiny of men and we may if we like read this into our history; but what our history brings to us is not proof of providence but rather the realisation of how mysterious are its ways, how strange its caprices – the knowledge that this providence uses any means to get to its end and works often at cross-purposes with itself and is curiously wayward. Our assumptions do not matter if we are conscious that they are assumptions, but the most fallacious thing in the world is to organise our historical knowledge upon an assumption without realising what we are doing, and then to make inferences from that organisation and claim that these are the voice of history. It is at this point that we tend to fall into what I have nicknamed the whig fallacy.

The whig method of approach is closely connected with the question of the abridgment of history; for both the method and the kind of history that results from it would be impossible if all the facts were told in all their fullness. The theory that is behind the whig interpretation – the theory that we study the past for the sake of the present – is one that is really introduced for the purpose of facilitating the abridgment of history; and its effect is to provide us with a handy rule of thumb by which we can easily discover what was important in the past, for the simple reason that, by definition, we mean what is important 'from our point of view.' No one could mistake the aptness of this theory for a school of writers who might show the least inclination to undervalue one side of the historical story; and indeed there would be no point in holding it if it were not for the fact that it serves to simplify the study of history by providing an excuse for leaving things out. The theory is important because it provides us in the long run with a path through the complexity of history; it really gives us a short cut through that maze of interactions by which the past was turned into our present; it helps us to circumvent the real problem of historical study. If we can exclude certain things on the ground that they have no direct bearing on the present, we have removed the most troublesome elements in the complexity and the crooked is made straight. There is no doubt that the application of this principle must produce in history a bias in favour of the whigs and must fall unfavourably on Catholics and tories. Whig history in other words is not a genuine abridgment, for it is really based upon what is an implicit principle of selection. The adoption of this principle and this method commits us to a certain organisation of the whole historical story. A very different case arises when the historian, examining the 16th century, sets out to discover the things which were important to that age itself or were influential at that time. And if we could imagine a general survey of the centuries which should be an abridgment of all the works of historical research, and if we were then to compare this with a survey of the whole period which was compiled on the whig principle, that is to say, 'from the point of view of the present,' we should not only find that the complications had been greatly over-simplified in the whig version, but we should find the story recast and the most important valuations amended; in other words we should find an abridged history which tells a different story altogether. According to the consistency with which we have applied the principle of direct reference to the present, we are driven to that version of history which is called the whig interpretation.

Further Reading: Chapters 19 to 24

Acton, Lord. "German Schools of History", *English Historical Review* 1 (1886), 7–42.

Bently, M. *Modernising England's Past: English Historiography in the Age of Modernism 1870–1970* (Cambridge: Cambridge University Press, 2005).

Burguière, André. "The Fate of the History of the *Mentalités* in the *Annales*". *Society for Comparative Study of Society and History* 24 (1982), 424–37.

Burke, Peter. *The French Historical Revolution: The Annales School, 1929–1989* (Stanford: Stanford University Press, 1990).

Galbraith, John S. "Some Reflections on the Profession of History", *Pacific Historical Review* 35 (February 1966), 1–14.

Herubel, J.-P. "The '*Annales* Movement' and Its Historiography: A Selective Bibliography", *French Historical Studies* 18 (Spring 1993), 346–55.

Hingham, John. *History: Professional Scholarship in America* (Baltimore: Johns Hopkins University Press, 1965).

Iggers, Georg. *The German Conception of History* (Middletown, CT: Wesleyan University Press, 1968).

—— . "Historicism: The History and Meaning of the Term", *Journal of the History of Ideas* 56 (1995), 129–52.

Kenyon, John. *The History Men: The Historical Profession in England since the Renaissance* (Pittsburgh: University of Pittsburgh Press, 1983).

Keylor, W. *Academy and Community: The Foundation of the French Historical Profession* (Cambridge, MA: Harvard University Press, 1975).

Krieger, L. *Ranke: The Meaning of History* (Chicago: University of Chicago Press, 1977).

Lamprecht, Karl Gotthard. "Historical Development and Present Character of the Science of History", *What Is History? Five Lectures on the Modern Science of History*. Trans. E. A. Andrews (London: Macmillan, 1905), 1–36.

Lodge, Richard. *The Study of History in a Scottish University: an Inaugural Lecture delivered on 22 October 1894* (Glasgow: Glasgow University Press, 1894).

Momigliano, Arnaldo. "The Introduction of History as an Academic Subject and Its Implications". *Ottavo, contributo alla storia degli studi classici e del mondo antico* (Rome, 1987), 161–78.

Novick, P. *That Noble Dream: The "Objectivity Question" and the American Historical Profession* (Cambridge: Cambridge University Press, 1988).

Reill, P. H. *The German Enlightenment and the Rise of Historicism* (Berkeley: University of California Press, 1975).

Revel, Jacques. "The *Annales*: Continuities and Discontinuities", *Review* 1(3/4) (1978), 9–18.

Ringer, Fritz. *The Decline of the German Mandarins: The German Academic Community, 1890–1933* (Cambridge, MA: Harvard University Press, 1969).

Trevelyan, George Macaulay. "Clio, A Muse" 1903 (revd edn). *Clio, A Muse, and Other Essays* (London: Longmans. 1913), 1–55.

Trevor-Roper, Hugh. "History: Professional and Lay", *History and Imagination*, H. R. Trevor-Roper et al. (eds) (London: Duckworth, 1982), 7–12.

White, Andrew D. "European Schools of History and Politics", *Johns Hopkins Studies in Historical and Political Science* 5 (1887), 471–546.

HUMBOLDT, WILHELM VON (1767–1835)

Iggers, Georg G. *The German Conception of History: The National Tradition of Historical Thought from Herder to the Present.* 1968 (Middletown, CT: Wesleyan University Press, 1983).

Sweet, P. R. *Wilhelm von Humboldt: A Biography.* 2 vols (Columbus: Ohio State University Press, 1978).

RANKE, LEOPOLD VON (1795–1886)

Dutcher, G. M., et al. *A Guide to Historical Literature* (Macmillan 1931). (New York: McGraw-Hill, 1974).

Fitzsimons, M. A. "Ranke: History as Worship", *The Review of Politics* 42(4) (1980), 533–55.

Geyl, Pieter. *Debates with Historians* (London: Batsford, 1955).

Gilbert, Felix. *History: Politics or Culture? Reflections on Ranke and Burckhardt* (Princeton, NJ: Princeton University Press, 1990).

Gooch, G. P. *History and Historians in the Nineteenth Century* (New York: Longmans, 1935).

Herkless, J. L. "Meinecke and the Ranke-Burckhardt Problem", *History and Theory* 9(3) (1970), 290–321.

Iggers, Georg G. *The German Conception of History: The National Tradition of Historical Thought from Herder to the Present.* 1968 (Middletown, CT: Wesleyan University Press, 1983).

—— . "The Image of Ranke in American and German Historical Thought", *History and Theory* 2(1) (1962), 17–40.

—— . and James M. Powell (eds). *Leopold von Ranke and the Shaping of the Historical Discipline* (Syracuse, NY: Syracuse University Press, 1990).

Krieger, Leonard. "Elements of Early Historicism: Experience, Theory, and History in Ranke", *History and Theory* 14(4) (1975), 1–14.

—— . *Ranke: The Meaning of History* (Chicago: University of Chicago Press, 1977).

Laue, Theodore von. *Leopold Ranke: The Formative Years* (Princeton, NJ: Princeton University Press, 1950).

Novick, P. *That Noble Dream: The "Objectivity Question" and the American Historical Profession* (Cambridge: Cambridge University Press, 1988).

Rüsen, Jörn. "Rhetoric and Aesthetics of History: Leopold von Ranke", *History and Theory* 29(2) (1990), 190–204.

Schevill, Ferdinand. "Ranke: Rise, Decline, and Persistence of a Reputation", *The Journal of Modern History* 24(3) (1952), 219–34.

Syracuse University. *The Leopold von Ranke Manuscript Collection of Syracuse University* (Syracuse, NY: Syracuse University Press, 1983).

White, Hayden. *Metahistory* (Baltimore, MD: Johns Hopkins University Press, 1973).

Wines, Roger (ed.) *The Secret of World History. Leopold von Ranke* (New York: Fordham University Press, 1981).

ROBINSON, JAMES HARVEY (1863–1936)

Barnes, Harry Elmer. "James Harvey Robinson". *American Masters of Social Science: An Approach to the Study of the Social Sciences Through the Neglected Field of Biography,* Howard W. Odum (ed.) (Port Washington, NY: Kennikat Press, 1926).

Braeman, John. "What is the Good of History? The Case of James Harvey Robinson", *Amerikastudien/ American Studies* 30 (1985), 75–89.

Breasted, James Henry. "Review: The New History", *The Journal of Philosophy, Psychology and Scientific Methods* 9(21) (1912), 585–7.

Crunden, Robert Morse. *Ministers of Reform: The Progressives' Achievement in American Civilization, 1889–1920* (New York: Basic Books, 1982).

Hendricks, Luther Virgil. *James Harvey Robinson: Teacher of History* (New York: King's Crown Press, 1946).

Novick, Peter. *That Noble Dream: The "Objectivity Question" and the American Historical Profession* (Cambridge: Cambridge University Press, 1988).

Ross, Dorothy. *The Origins of American Social Science* (Cambridge: Cambridge University Press, 1991).

Skotheim, Robert Allen. *American Intellectual Histories and Historians* (Princeton, NJ: Princeton University Press, 1966).

Strout, Cushing. *The Pragmatic Revolt in American History: Carl Becker and Charles Beard* (New Haven: Yale University Press, 1958).

Wells, H. G. "Introduction", *Mind in the Making. James Harvey Robinson* (London: Watts, 1940).

Whelan, Michael. "James Harvey Robinson: The New History and the 1916 Social Studies Report", *History Teacher* 24(2) (1991), 191–202.

White, Morton. *Social Thought in America: The Revolt Against Formalism* (Oxford: Oxford University Press, 1976).

FEBVRE, LUCIEN (1878–1956)

Berti, Silvia. "At the Roots of Unbelief", *Journal of the History of Ideas* 56(4) (1995), 555–75.

Braudel, F. "Lucien Febvre". *International Encyclopedia of the Social Sciences*, David L. Sills (ed.) (New York: Macmillan, The Free Press, 1968), Vol. 5, 348–50.

Burguière, A. "The Fate of the History of Mentalities in the *Annales*", *Comparative Studies in Society and History* 24(3) (1982), 424–37.

Burke, Peter. *The French Historical Revolution: The Annales School, 1929–89* (Stanford, CA: Stanford University Press, 1990).

Clark, Stuart. "French Historians and Early Modern Popular Culture", *Past and Present* 100 (1983), 62–99.

Davis, Natalie Zemon "Rabelais among the Censors (1940s, 1540s)", *Representations* 32(1) (1990), 1–32.

Fink, Carole. *Marc Bloch: A Life in History* (Cambridge: Cambridge University Press, 1989).

Hughes, H. Stuart. *The Obstructed Path: French Social Thought in the Years of Desperation 1930–1960* (New York: Harper & Row, 1969).

Hutton, Patrick H. "The History of Mentalities: The New Map of Cultural History", *History and Theory* 20(3) (1981), 237–59.

Lyon, Bryce and Mary Lyon (eds). *The Birth of Annales History: The Letters of Lucien Febvre and Marc Bloch to Henri Pirenne, 1921–1935* (Brussels: Académie Royale de Belgique, 1991).

Rhodes, Colbert. "Emile Durkheim and the Socio-Historical Thought of Lucien Febvre", *International Journal of Contemporary Sociology* 25 (1988), 65–82.

Schöttler, P. "Lucie Varge: A Central European Refugee in the Circle of the French 'Annales', 1934–1941", *History Workshop Journal* 33 (1992), 100–20.

—— . "The Rhine as an Object of Historical Controversy in the Inter-war Years: Towards a History of Frontier Mentalities", *History Workshop Journal* 39 (1995), 1–22.

Wootten, D. "Lucien Febvre and the Problem of Unbelief in the Early Modern Period", *Journal of Modern History* 60(4) (1988), 695–730.

BUTTERFIELD, SIR HERBERT (1900–1979)

Chadwick, Owen. "Acton and Butterfield", *Journal of Ecclesiastical History* 38 (1987), 386–405.

Coll, Alberto R. *The Wisdom of Statecraft: Sir Herbert Butterfield and the Philosophy of International Politics* (Durham, NC: Duke University Press, 1985).

Elliot, J. H. and H. G. Koenigsberger (eds). *The Diversity of History: Essays in Honour of Sir Herbert Butterfield* (London: Routledge and Kegan Paul, 1970).

Elton, G. R. "Herbert Butterfield and the Study of History", *Historical Journal* 27 (1984), 729–43.

Thompson, Kenneth W. (ed.). *Herbert Butterfield: The Ethics of History and Politics* (Washington, DC: University Press of America, 1980).

PART 6

The approach of
social science

INTRODUCTION

MANY OF THE AUTHORS featured in this section were considered sociologists in their own times, and are still considered so today, and their preoccupations with social structures have brought new perspectives to critical thinking about historical writing and research. Earlier in the nineteenth century, German historicism had advocated a scientific method of examining the past through its archival documents, and the result was a fairly narrow and elite focus on European political history and its great men. Social history requires a broader vision which, as the romantics showed, could not be fulfilled by examining documents alone (see Part 4). As the evocative style of social history became increasingly associated with amateurism and romanticism, it became prestigious among university-based professional historians. We will see that Ranke's **empiricism** (making intuitive generalizations based on factual research into the past) survives in the work of research sociologists such as Émile Durkheim and Max Weber, whose **comparative methods** used case studies (based on social research) to examine the institutions and values that structure societies. We will also see that contemporary concerns with the causes and consequences of violent revolution lent legitimacy if not urgency to the **deductive approaches** (which use a theoretical hypothesis to predict the outcome of future events) of J. S. Mill and Karl Marx, who studied the past through social philosophy. In all cases, current events shaped the development of social approaches to history. Just as the "hungry 1840s" energized Marx's **materialist approach** to inequality, the horrors of the First World War nearly eclipsed Durkheim's **progressive** social theory—because the belief that modern societies develop cooperatively seemed rather quaint considering the bloody industrial warfare that raged for years on European soil during the early decades of the twentieth century. So in many respects, these settle the ground that was laid by earlier historical theories, while posing the questions and introducing the critical vocabulary that now lends a recognizable shape to twentieth-century historiography.

Some of these sources presented ideas that have become familiar to those studying History (for example, Marx's notion that historical study should be guided by a recognition of inevitable economic pressures that divide societies), while others are more arcane (such as Mill's theory of progressive social design that transcends contemporary concerns). The theorists in this section have attracted considerable attention and fostered energetic debate since their first books were published—but some have fallen out of fashion, have long been misrepresented, or seem to have been made irrelevant because their ideas or methods have been disproved. Still, their emphasis on social organization as an inescapable fact of human existence, on understanding history in terms of social relationships, and their concern for studying the past apart from the study of specific events, have paved the way for historical discourse in the twentieth century. This is why several of these sources anticipate Bloch and Febvre's cross-disciplinary ambitions, Robinson's impatience with history's seeming social irrelevance, and Butterfield's attention to historians' own social values (see Part 5). Yet these sociologists took widely divergent approaches to the relations between their own emerging field and History. Durkheim insisted that with the advent of a morally meaningful and empirically scientific study of society, History provided merely the records of particular events. At the same time, Wilhelm Dilthey reflected on social traditions and historical methods to justify a new role for those who studied the human sciences—but, like Weber, he denied that **sociology** could ever provide truly *scientific* knowledge, since the individuals who comprise society define themselves through inner and intimate experiences that are too unique to be described in external or general terms. And yet, by focusing our attention on historians' own emotional abilities to truly understand the depth and meaning of the societies and individuals that they study, Dilthey anticipated twentieth-century psychological theorists (such as Adam Phillips in Part 9) and cultural anthropologists (like Clifford Geertz in Part 12), while he reminds us of Ranke's concern for the fundamental importance of the historian's intuition (in Part 5).

John Stuart Mill remains famous for his ethical philosophy, and yet his approach to **utilitarianism** was only one of the many contributions that he made to British intellectual history. Fairly early in his career as a public intellectual, Mill outlined a theory of human progress developed by Auguste Comte, a French philosopher whose "positive philosophy" encapsulated human history in a series of three evolutionary stages.[i] One consequence of Mill's essay "Of the Inverse Deductive, or Historical, Method" is that he used the term "social science" to describe this new field of study (it probably originated in Comte, along with "sociology"). Mill argued that the natural organization of individuals into social groups created social structures and institutions that would benefit subsequent generations. Therefore history should be understood in **stadial** terms, with distinct stages that lead towards a **positive** or progressive future. By adopting that basic viewpoint, Mill proposed that we can use history to provide the information that will construct the **empirical** basis of what would become the scientific principles of human society. In turn, understanding these principles could allow us to shape future events. Mill observed that European adherents to Comte's positive philosophy had made progress towards articulating empirical laws of social progress using historical evidence. Indeed, Comte tried to do this with the same degree of objective authority that characterized the natural sciences. But Mill believed that Comte's scientific rationalism failed to integrate the underlying characteristics of human nature. So Mill hoped to contribute to sociology's ultimate principles by observing that as societies develop, nature leads us to make better use of our speculative or intellectual abilities to make the most of limited resources. As a result, the quantity and quality of human knowledge improves as societies advance. By joining this observation with the

---

i   The best introduction to Comte in English translation is A. Comte, *Introduction to Positive Philosophy*, 1830, ed. and trans. Frederick Ferré (Indianapolis: Hackett, 1988).

sociological hypothesis provided by Comte, Mill triumphantly announced that "such practical instructions, founded on the highest branch of speculative sociology, will form the noblest and most beneficial portion of the Political Art".

Mill's attempt to define the social tendencies that would shape the future adopted both empirical and deductive elements. On the one hand, he clearly pointed out that "the ground of confidence in any concrete deductive science is not the *a priori* reasoning itself, but the accordance between its results and those of observation *a posteriori*." On the other hand he allowed that his enthusiasm for Comte's three-stage theory of human history (comprising theological, metaphysical, then positive stages) amounted to enthusiasm for a generalization: "this generalization appears to me to have that high degree of scientific evidence which is derived from the concurrence of the indications of human history with the probabilities derived from the constitution of the human mind". Mill's synthesis enjoyed considerable popularity throughout the mid- and late nineteenth century: his book commanded eight British editions in his lifetime, suggesting the willingness of Victorian readers to consider utopian alternatives to religion to envision the span of human history. Comte himself had hoped that positive philosophy would provide an alternative to religion, for he even published a *Positivist Calendar* that structured "the worship of humanity" by days and months named for famous men in Western science and literature.[ii]

Like Mill, his near-contemporary Marx spent the earlier part of his career attempting to address obvious inequalities. He also developed a social theory of history that was deductive, progressive, and socially engaged. Ironically, despite Marx's outrage at the evident human suffering caused by industrialization, his Comteian notion of history as a series of stages reflects a mid-nineteenth-century view of modernization as a one-way street from primitive society to cooperative utopia. While both Mill and Marx were committed to testing their theories against empirical evidence from history, and were impatient with historical theories that were not clearly relevant to the societies in which they lived, Marx had philosophical reasons for being more forceful in his articulation of those views: "social life is essentially practical", he wrote. "All mysteries which mislead theory into mysticism find their rational solution in human practice and in the comprehension of this practice."[iii] Within months of composing his "Premises of the Materialist Method of History", the young Marx declared his ultimate ambitions as a theorist: "philosophers have only *interpreted* the world in various ways; the point is to *change* it".[iv] Marx considered theory an essentially practical tool whose circulation will improve society. Now it is important to point out that the provocative material determinism for which Marx is now famous only represents an early stage in his considerably more sophisticated philosophy, and indeed while his name has become synonymous with communist political systems, his friend and co-author Friedrich Engels clearly insisted that "our conception of history is above all a guide to study, not a level for construction".[v] From a historiographic standpoint, then, we should appreciate Marx's early social theory of historical progress not just for its emphasis on the economic character of social relationships—although

ii   See A. Comte, *Calendrier Positiviste ou Système Générale de Commemoration Publique*, 1849 (Fontfroide le Haut: Éditions Fata Morgana, 1993).

iii "Theses on Feuerbach", 1845, *The German Ideology*. Trans. W. Lough (Amherst, NY: Prometheus, 1998), 571.

iv   "Theses on Feuerbach", 571.

v   See Walter L. Adamson, "Marxism and Historical Thought", *The Blackwell Companion to Western Historical Thought*, Lloyd Kramer and Sarah Maza (eds) (Oxford: Blackwell, 2006), 205–221.

this too has proved enormously influential for historians and sociologists—but also for the role his social theory was meant to play in the human drama of historical consciousness.

The powerful prose style and impressive self-confidence of Marx's early essay reflects his optimism for the success of the political revolutions that brewed across Europe during the "hungry 1840s" and finally ignited in France, Austria, Germany, and Italy.[vi] The eventual failures of the revolutions of 1848 led Marx to correct his view that historical theory was simply a picture of social reality whose readers will share his plan to change society for the better; his later writings assert that historical theory is needed to provoke society into revolutionary action. But why would revolution be a required element in a social theory of history? And what does it mean for a historical theorist to consider his own writing a social act that should directly affect the world he means to describe? Marx expressed his confidence in the social relevance of his theory: "the premises from which we begin are not arbitrary ones, not dogmas, but real premises from which abstraction can only be made in the imagination". When he proceeded to explain that social and political structures evolve naturally when individuals work to provide food and shelter, he expressed a self-evident fact—and its consequence, that people's thoughts are an immediate expression of this material labour, is plainly obvious to Marx. History, therefore, must begin with the natural and social fact either of the material work that we do to survive, or of the work we force others to do on our behalf. Marx then becomes more provocative, attacking the intellectual tradition in which he was taught: "in direct contrast to German philosophy which descends from heaven to earth, here it is a matter of ascending from earth to heaven"—in other words, his approach to the history of society claimed to reflect life as it is lived, rather than how it is imagined. The implication is that Marx's writing is an active and responsive element within that drama of social life, and that our reading of it is either alive to the material conditions that Marx describes, or decadently oblivious to them.

If this logic (and its **ideological** positioning of its readers) seems simplistic, Marx's rhetoric emphasizes the conceptual power of that simplicity. In cogent prose that sounds more like a slogan than a philosophy, Marx declared that "it is not consciousness that determines life, but life that determines consciousness", permitting only one interpretation: it is our material struggle to survive that creates our sense of ourselves and of society. Marx went so far as to demean as "trash" the notion that consciousness can be a productive force—and this partly distinguishes the "early" Marx from the "later" Marx. If we consider social life as an abstract idea rather than as a material fact, we would be negating the actual reality that all individuals either enjoy their leisure or are burdened with labour. Sociologists, in other words, are taught by real working people and not the other way round. Moreover, since historians are part of the social worlds in which they live, such negation by them extends the injustice that the division of labour has already set in motion. This is why, for Marx writing in the mid-1840s, those who cultivate historical consciousness are social agents included in a progressive movement towards a just revolution. It also explains why historical writing must use its linguistic tools to extend a political vision that is ultimately progressive and in a sense already understood by working people: the rousing *Communist Manifesto* had not yet been written, but we can already anticipate Marx's vision of a positive future realized in dynamic society rather than in abstract social theory. (We will focus more narrowly on the historical methods inspired by Marx in Part 8.)

---

vi   See Oscar J. Hammen, "The Spectre of Communism in the 1840s", *Journal of the History of Ideas* 14 (June 1953), 404–20; George R. Boyer, "The Historical Background of the Communist Manifesto [1848]", *Journal of Economic Perspectives* 12 (Fall 1998), 151–74.

Deeply read in Marx, but more concerned with the formation of social institutions than social conflict, Durkheim devoted his distinguished career to creating Sociology as a respected theoretical and research field: he held France's first academic position in social science (1896), founded the field's first academic journal *L'Année Sociologique* (1898), and was elected (1906) to the position that would become the first professorial chair in Sociology (1913). In his view, Sociology was not only independent from History but was also more deeply analytical, scientific, and morally meaningful than its stale and narrowly fact-gathering ancestor. Durkheim considered himself within Comte's progressive tradition, and yet his willingness to test his own social theories against historical evidence suggests a certain empirical aspect to his thinking. Adopting the objective language of the natural sciences (such as biology and physics), Durkheim followed Comte and to some extent Marx in his confidence that all human societies follow a series of stages—and for this reason he was responding to a deductive tradition, by expecting that the general theory of developmental stages allowed one to predict the future development of society. By defining and comparing the shared attitudes (their "collective representations" and "collective conscience") that give rise to social institutions, Durkheim hoped that his sociology would be in a superior position to discern the moral significance of its past and probable future.[vii] In other words, for Durkheim sociology could offer the confident insights to societies that psychology offers to individuals.

Although not as inflexibly as Marx, Durkheim proposed that social organization goes some way towards shaping human consciousness:

> It is society which informs our minds and wills, attuning them to the institutions which express that society. Consequently it is with society that the sociologist must begin ... sociology, so conceived, being a stranger to psychology, it arrives itself at a psychology, but one far more concrete and complex.[viii]

Despite Durkheim's famous denunciations of history as superficial for its narrow focus on what he called "particular events", his research methods used the gathering and comparing of social statistics as well as historical case studies to identify the social meanings generated by social institutions—and this was his important empirical contribution to historical study. His pioneering research into the quantitative incidence of suicide in France, for example, and his eagerness to explain its social meaning encouraged historians to research beyond the history of events to consider the changing meanings of social values over time. In the excerpt featured in this section, Durkheim belittled the field of history for its reluctance to compare its findings across periods, nations, and cultures; indeed, he would seem to be a clear anticipator of the *Annales* if only he did not go so far as to argue that once History begins to use its findings comparatively, it becomes Sociology (see Parts 1, 5 and 7). Nevertheless, Durkheim's attacks on history as a field are more ambivalent than confident, for his own logic suggests that without history's fact-based accomplishments, sociology's intellectual ground would be less secure, its claims less reliable.

Durkheim's exact contemporary Max Weber always considered himself a historian, so

vii On Durkheim's notion of the collective conscience, see M. J. Hawkins, "Continuity and Change in Durkheim's Theory of Social Solidarity", *Sociological Quarterly* 20 (1979), 155–64. Note Durkheim's influence on Bloch, who frequently used the term "collective consciousness" as an element of his comparative method of historical research (see Part 1).

viii See E. Durkheim, "The Contribution of Sociology to Psychology and Philosophy", *Rules of Sociological Method*, 1909. Trans. W. D. Halls (New York: Free Press, 1982), 237.

when he was hired to direct Germany's first Institute of Sociology as one of the country's first Professors of Sociology, he remarked that "I now happen to be a sociologist according to my appointment papers."[ix] Weber may have felt more at home in History than in Sociology since, in the early twentieth century the latter was still embracing **deductive** theories—while History was consciously attempting to approach research without preconceived hypotheses. Despite Weber's own sense that he was both inside and outside the field of sociology, his writing continues to exert a powerful influence over both Sociology and History. He provided the new field with a precise descriptive and critical vocabulary that distinguished between objective social facts (which Durkheim's students were trained to identify and explain) and subjective values that define societies themselves (which Durkheim had tended to overlook or misunderstand). Therefore, Weber is often understood to be a critic of Mill, Durkheim, and especially Marx, since their social theories depended on a general notion of human progress that either overlooked the unique values of specific societies or simply absorbed anomalous instances of social individualism into their general philosophical visions. Weber also asserted that while Sociology must try to avoid making value judgements, social meanings are so diverse, internally sophisticated, and therefore not quantifiable, that Sociology will never deliver knowledge that rests on a truly scientific basis—at least not in the same way this was taking place in the natural sciences. While these ideas may sound like an attempt to weaken Sociology as an academic discipline, in fact Weber contributed a more mature sense of both this new field's limitations and its unique abilities—and this invited greater collaboration between sociologists and historians, and helped to establish the comparative and interdisciplinary elements of the field now known as social history.

Another reason for Weber's influence on historians and sociologists stems from his interpretation of modern industrial societies: methodologically, his interpretation emphasized the role of culture in the production of social meanings and values; specifically, Weber's theory regarded "formal rationality"—intellectual, administrative, and political obsessions with achieving practical results as opposed to ethical ideals—as an essential condition of modern life in the industrialized world. In the excerpt included in this section, Weber set out to clarify the distinction between subjective and objective meaning in the social sciences, and we can see his attempt to avoid inserting his theory of rationality into that distinction: for if his theory provides the basis for his methodological vocabulary, then Weber runs the risk of contributing yet another deductive method that could exclude new insights based on new and unanticipated research. At the same time, Weber could not resist mentioning this theory—illustrating his assessment of those contributions he made to Sociology that will remain useful to historians.

It might seem peculiar to include Dilthey in a section devoted to history and the social sciences, since Dilthey thought sociologists unscientific because their methods were oriented around their causal theories, at the expense of seeking real insights or understanding of social phenomena. Like Weber, however, Dilthey's challenges to late-nineteenth-century social theory have enriched both Sociology and History—for example, his famous distinction between natural science that explains the external elements of things (*Erklären*) from the humanities that aspire to internal understanding (*Verstehen*) remains central to discussions in both fields. Incidentally, Weber remains tightly associated with the concept of *Verstehen* among historians of Sociology.[x] For Dilthey, in order to understand life (whether it be social or individual), we

ix   See H. H. Bruun, *Science, Values, and Politics in Max Weber's Methodology* (Copenhagen: Munksgaard, 1972), 38.
x   See M. Albrow, *Max Weber's Construction of Social Theory* (Basingstoke: Palgrave, 1990).

need to grasp a theory of knowledge that is attuned both to the emotional and intellectual nature of human experience as well as to the social values that our behaviour expresses. Since as researchers of the past we cannot experience our subject first-hand, we need to develop a sense of re-living that past by using our emotional, imaginative, and sympathetic abilities—and historians, like literary artists, in turn use narrative to communicate that internal understanding of history to future readers. Strongly anticipating late-twentieth-century **postmodernists** such as Hayden White (in Part 10), but also gesturing back to Kames's notion of ``**ideal presence**'' (in Part 3), Dilthey wrote (in 1910) that

> The narrative of the novelist or historian, which follows the historical course of events, makes us re-experience it. It is the triumph of re-experiencing that it supplements the fragments of a course of events in such a way that we believe ourselves to be confronted by continuity.

That quotation offers a rich range of concerns, but perhaps it is most useful to focus on Dilthey's moral view, that ``understanding [*Verstehen*] opens for [us] a wide realm of possibilities which do not exist within the limitations of real life''. Dilthey articulated a profound argument here, one which moved beyond empirical and deductive methods to challenge and extend the concerns of every social theorist featured in this section. The researcher or theorist now comprises the very source of the viewpoint that she or he provides: without empathic understanding of the historical subject in truly personal terms, reached through *our reflection on our own past*, we cannot appreciate either what past experience has ever meant for others, nor can we comprehend the social values that grew from and were expressed by that past experience. Moreover, for Dilthey, the historian's task widens our own imaginative and moral world, enabling us to offer the same kind of insights to our own readers.

Chapter 25

John Stuart Mill

THE HISTORICAL METHOD

John Stuart Mill (1806–1873), "The Historical Method", 1843, *A System of Logic ... A Connected View of the Principles of Evidence and the Methods of Scientific Investigation* (New York: Harper and Brothers, 1874), 631–4, 639–43.

STATES OF SOCIETY are like different constitutions or different ages in the physical frame [i.e. physical body], they are conditions not of one or a few organs or functions, but of the whole organism. Accordingly, the information which we possess respecting past ages, and respecting the various states of society now existing in different regions of the earth, does, when duly analyzed, exhibit uniformities. It is found that when one of the features of society is in a particular state, a state of many other features, more or less precisely determinate, always or usually co-exists with it.

But the uniformities of co-existence obtaining among phenomena which are effects of causes, must (as we have so often observed) be corollaries from the laws of causation by which these phenomena are really determined. The mutual correlation between the different elements of each state of society, is, therefore, a derivative law, resulting from the laws which regulate the succession between one state of society and another; for the proximate cause of every state of society is the state of society immediately preceding it. The fundamental problem, therefore, of the social science, is to find the laws according to which any state of society produces the state which succeeds it and takes its place. This opens the great and vexed question of the progressiveness of man and society; an idea involved in every just conception of social phenomena as the subject of a science.

§ 3. It is one of the characters, not absolutely peculiar to the sciences of human nature and society, but belonging to them in a peculiar degree, to be conversant with a subject-matter whose properties are changeable. I do not mean changeable from day to day, but from age to age; so that not only the qualities of individuals vary, but those of the majority are not the same in one age as in another.

The principal cause of this peculiarity is the extensive and constant reaction of the effects upon their causes. The circumstances in which mankind are placed, operating according to their own laws and to the laws of human nature, form the characters of the human beings;

but the human beings, in their turn, mould and shape the circumstances for themselves and for those who come after them. From this reciprocal action there must necessarily result either a cycle or a progress. In astronomy also, every fact is at once effect and cause; the successive positions of the various heavenly bodies produce changes both in the direction and in the intensity of the forces by which those positions are determined. But in the case of the solar system, these mutual actions bring around again, after a certain number of changes, the former state of circumstances; which, of course, leads to the perpetual recurrence of the same series in an unvarying order. Those bodies, in short, revolve in orbits: but there are (or, conformably to the laws of astronomy, there might be) others which, instead of an orbit, describe a trajectory—a course not returning into itself. One or other of these must be the type to which human affairs must conform.

One of the thinkers who earliest conceived the succession of historical events as subject to fixed laws, and endeavored to discover these laws by an analytical survey of history, Vico, the celebrated author of the *Scienza Nuova*, adopted the former of these opinions. He conceived the phenomena of human society as revolving in an orbit; as going through periodically the same series of changes. Though there were not wanting circumstances tending to give some plausibility to this view, it would not bear a close scrutiny: and those who have succeeded Vico in this kind of speculations have universally adopted the idea of a trajectory or progress, in lieu of an orbit or cycle.

The words Progress and Progressiveness are not here to be understood as synonymous with improvement and tendency to improvement. It is conceivable that the laws of human nature might determine, and even necessitate, a certain series of changes in man and society, which might not in every case, or which might not on the whole, be improvements. It is my belief, indeed, that the general tendency is, and will continue to be, saving occasional and temporary exceptions, one of improvement; a tendency toward a better and happier state. This, however, is not a question of the method of the social science, but a theorem of the science itself. For our purpose it is sufficient that there is a progressive change both in the character of the human race and in their outward circumstances, so far as moulded by themselves; that in each successive age the principal phenomena of society are different from what they were in the age preceding, and still more different from any previous age: the periods which most distinctly mark these successive changes being intervals of one gener-ation, during which a new set of human beings have been educated, have grown up from childhood, and taken possession of society.

The progressiveness of the human race is the foundation on which a method of philosophizing in the social science has been of late years erected, far superior to either of the two modes which had previously been prevalent, the chemical or experimental, and the geometrical modes. This method, which is now generally adopted by the most advanced thinkers on the Continent, consists in attempting, by a study and analysis of the general facts of history, to discover (what these philosophers term) the law of progress: which law, once ascertained, must according to them enable us to predict future events, just as after a few terms of an infinite series in algebra we are able to detect the principle of regularity in their formation, and to predict the rest of the series to any number of terms we please. The principal aim of historical speculation in France, of late years, has been to ascertain this law. But while I gladly acknowledge the great services which have been rendered to historical knowledge by this school, I can not but deem them to be mostly chargeable with a fundamental misconception of the true method of social philosophy. The misconception consists in supposing that the order of succession which we may be able to trace among the different states of society and civilization which history presents to us, even if that order were more rigidly uniform than it has yet been proved to be, could ever amount to a law of nature. It can only be an empirical law. The succession of states of the human mind and of human society can not have an independent law of its own; it must depend on the psychological and ethological laws which govern the action of circumstances on men and of men on circumstances. It is conceivable that those laws might be such, and the general circumstances of the human race such, as to determine the successive transformations of man and society to one given and unvarying order. But even if the case were so, it can not be the ultimate aim of science to discover an empirical law. Until that law could be connected with the psychological and ethological laws on which it must depend, and, by the consilience of deduction *a priori* with historical evidence, could be converted from an empirical law into a scientific one, it could not be relied on for the prediction of future events, beyond, at most, strictly adjacent cases. M. Comte alone, among the new historical school, has seen the necessity of thus connecting all our generalizations from history with the laws of human nature.

§ 4. But, while it is an imperative rule never to introduce any generalization from history into the social science unless sufficient grounds can be pointed out for it in human nature, I do not think any one will contend that it would have been possible, setting out from the principles of human nature and from the general circumstances of the position of our species, to determine *a priori* the order in which human development must take place, and to predict, consequently, the general facts of history up to the present time. After the first few terms of the series, the influence exercised over each generation by the generations which preceded it, becomes (as is well observed by the writer last referred to) more and more preponderant over all other influences; until at length what we now are and do, is in a very small degree the result of the universal circumstances of the human race, or even of our own circumstances acting through the original qualities of our species, but mainly of the qualities produced in us by the whole previous history of humanity. So long a series of actions and reactions between Circumstances and Man, each successive term being composed of an ever greater number and variety of parts, could not possibly be computed by human faculties from the elementary laws which produce it. The mere length of the series would be a sufficient obstacle, since a slight error in any one of the terms would augment in rapid progression at every subsequent step.

If, therefore, the series of the effects themselves did not, when examined as a whole, manifest any regularity, we should in vain attempt to construct a general science of society. We must in that case have contented ourselves with that subordinate order of sociological speculation formerly noticed, namely, with endeavoring to ascertain what would be the effect of the introduction of any new cause, in a state of society supposed to be fixed—a knowledge sufficient for the more common exigencies of daily political practice, but liable to fail in all cases in which the progressive movement of society is one of the influencing elements; and therefore more precarious in proportion as the case is more important. But since both the natural varieties of mankind, and the original diversities of local circumstances, are much less considerable than the points of agreement, there will naturally be a certain degree of uniformity in the progressive development of the species and of its works. And this uniformity tends to become greater, not less, as society advances; since the evolution of each people, which is at first determined exclusively by the nature and circumstances of that people, is gradually brought under the influence (which becomes stronger as civilization advances) of the other nations of the earth, and of the circumstances by which they have been influenced. History accordingly does, when judiciously examined, afford Empirical Laws of Society. And the problem of general sociology is to ascertain these, and connect them with the laws of human nature, by deductions showing that such were the derivative laws naturally to be expected as the consequences of those ultimate ones.

[. . .]

§ 6. While the derivative laws of social statics[i] are ascertained by analyzing different states of society, and comparing them with one another, without regard to the order of their succession, the consideration of the successive order is, on the contrary, predominant in the study of social dynamics,[ii] of which the aim is to observe and explain the sequences of social conditions. This branch of the social science would be as complete as it can be made, if every one of the leading general circumstances of each generation were traced to its causes in the generation immediately preceding. But the *consensus* is so complete (especially in modern history), that in the filiation of one generation and another, it is the whole which produces the whole, rather than any part a part. Little progress, therefore, can be made in establishing the filiation, directly from laws of human nature, without having first ascertained the immediate or derivative laws according to which social states generate one another as society advances; the *axiomata media* of General Sociology.

The empirical laws which are most readily obtained by generalization from history do not amount to this. They are not the "middle principles" themselves, but only evidence toward the establishment of such principles. They consist of certain general tendencies which may be perceived in society; a progressive increase of some social elements, and diminution of others, or a gradual change in the general character of certain elements. It is easily seen, for instance, that as society advances, mental tend more and more to prevail over bodily qualities, and masses over individuals; that the occupation of all that portion of mankind who are not under external restraint is at first chiefly military, but society becomes progressively more and more engrossed with productive pursuits, and the military spirit gradually gives way to the industrial; to which many similar truths might be added. And with generalizations of this description, ordinary inquirers, even of the historical school now predominant on the Continent, are satisfied. But these and all such results are still at too great a distance from the elementary laws of human nature on which they depend—too many links intervene, and the concurrence of causes at each link is far too complicated—to enable these propositions to be presented as direct corollaries from those elementary principles. They have, therefore, in the minds of most inquirers, remained in the state of empirical laws, applicable only within the bounds of actual observation; without any means of determining their real limits, and of judging whether the changes which have hitherto been in progress are destined to continue indefinitely, or to terminate, or even to be reversed.

[. . .]

In the difficult process of observation and comparison which is here required, it would evidently be a great assistance if it should happen to be the fact, that some one element in the complex existence of social man is pre-eminent over all others as the prime agent of the social movement. For we could then take the progress of that one element as the central chain, to each successive link of which, the corresponding links of all the other progressions being appended, the succession of the facts would by this alone be presented in a kind of spontaneous order, far more nearly approaching to the real order of their filiation than could be obtained by any other merely empirical process.

Now, the evidence of history and that of human nature combine, by a striking instance of consilience, to show that there really is one social element which is thus predominant, and almost paramount, among the agents of the social progression. This is, the

i   "The conditions of stability in the social union."
ii "The Theory of Society considered in a state of progressive movement."

state of the speculative faculties of mankind; including the nature of the beliefs which by any means they have arrived at, concerning themselves and the world by which they are surrounded.

It would be a great error, and one very little likely to be committed, to assert that speculation, intellectual activity, the pursuit of truth, is among the more powerful propensities of human nature, or holds a predominating place in the lives of any, save decidedly exceptional, individuals. But, notwithstanding the relative weakness of this principle among other sociological agents, its influence is the main determining cause of the social progress; all the other dispositions of our nature which contribute to that progress being dependent on it for the means of accomplishing their share of the work. Thus (to take the most obvious case first), the impelling force to most of the improvements effected in the arts of life, is the desire of increased material comfort; but as we can only act upon external objects in proportion to our knowledge of them, the state of knowledge at any time is the limit of the industrial improvements possible at that time; and the progress of industry must follow, and depend on, the progress of knowledge. The same thing may be shown to be true, though it is not quite so obvious, of the progress of the fine arts. Further, as the strongest propensities of uncultivated or half-cultivated human nature (being the purely selfish ones, and those of a sympathetic character which partake most of the nature of selfishness) evidently tend in themselves to disunite mankind, not to unite them—to make them rivals, not confederates, social existence is only possible by a disciplining of those more powerful propensities, which consists in subordinating them to a common system of opinions. The degree of this subordination is the measure of the completeness of the social union, and the nature of the common opinions determines its kind. But in order that mankind should conform their actions to any set of opinions, these opinions must exist, must be believed by them. And thus, the state of the speculative faculties, the character of the propositions assented to by the intellect, essentially determines the moral and political state of the community, as we have already seen that it determines the physical.

These conclusions, deduced from the laws of human nature, are in entire accordance with the general facts of history. Every considerable change historically known to us in the condition of any portion of mankind, when not brought about by external force, has been preceded by a change, of proportional extent, in the state of their knowledge, or in their prevalent beliefs. As between any given state of speculation, and the correlative state of every thing else, it was almost always the former which first showed itself; though the effects, no doubt, reacted potently upon the cause. Every considerable advance in material civilization has been preceded by an advance in knowledge: and when any great social change has come to pass, either in the way of gradual development or of sudden conflict, it has had for its precursor a great change in the opinions and modes of thinking of society. Polytheism, Judaism, Christianity, Protestantism, the critical philosophy of modern Europe, and its positive science—each of these has been a primary agent in making society what it was at each successive period, while society was but secondarily instrumental in making *them*, each of them (so far as causes can be assigned for its existence) being mainly an emanation not from the practical life of the period, but from the previous state of belief and thought. The weakness of the speculative propensity in mankind generally has not, therefore, prevented the progress of speculation from governing that of society at large; it has only, and too often, prevented progress altogether, where the intellectual progression has come to an early stand for want of sufficiently favorable circumstances.

From this accumulated evidence, we are justified in concluding, that the order of human progression in all respects will mainly depend on the order of progression in the intellectual convictions of mankind, that is, on the law of the successive transformations of human opinions. The question remains, whether this law can be determined; at first from history as an empirical law, then converted into a scientific theorem by deducing it *a priori* from the principles of human nature. As the progress of knowledge and the changes in the opinions of mankind are very slow, and manifest themselves in a well-defined manner only at long intervals, it can not be expected that the general order of sequence should be discoverable from the examination of less than a very considerable part of the duration of the social progress. It is necessary to take into consideration the whole of past time, from the first recorded condition of the human race, to the memorable phenomena of the last and present generations.

§ 8. The investigation which I have thus endeavored to characterize, has been systematically attempted, up to the present time, by M. Comte alone. His work is hitherto the only known example of the study of social phenomena according to this conception of the Historical Method. [. . .] Speculation he conceives to have, on every subject of human inquiry, three successive stages; in the first of which it tends to explain the phenomena by supernatural agencies, in the second by metaphysical abstractions, and in the third or final state confines itself to ascertaining their laws of succession and similitude. This generalization appears to me to have that high degree of scientific evidence which is derived from the concurrence of the indications of history with the probabilities derived from the constitution of the human mind. Nor could it be easily conceived, from the mere enunciation of such a proposition, what a flood of light it lets in upon the whole course of history, when its consequences are traced, by connecting with each of the three states of human intellect which it distinguishes, and with each successive modification of those three states, the correlative condition of other social phenomena.[iii]

But whatever decision competent judges may pronounce on the results arrived at by any individual inquirer, the method now characterized is that by which the derivative laws of social order and of social progress must be sought. By its aid we may hereafter succeed not only in looking far forward into the future history of the human race, but in determining what artificial means may be used, and to what extent, to accelerate the natural progress in so far as it is beneficial; to compensate for whatever may be its inherent inconveniences or disadvantages; and to guard against the dangers or accidents to which our species is exposed from the necessary incidents of its progression. Such practical instructions, founded on the highest branch of speculative sociology, will form the noblest and most beneficial portion of the Political Art.

That of this science and art even the foundations are but beginning to be laid, is sufficiently evident. But the superior minds are fairly turning themselves toward that object. It has become the aim of really scientific thinkers to connect by theories the facts of universal history: it is acknowledged to be one of the requisites of a general system of social doctrine, that it should explain, so far as the data exist, the main facts of history; and a Philosophy of History is generally admitted to be at once the verification, and the initial form, of the Philosophy of the Progress of Society.

If the endeavors now making in all the more cultivated nations, and beginning to be made even in England (usually the last to enter into the general movement of the European mind) for the construction of a Philosophy of History, shall be directed and controlled by those views of the nature of sociological evidence which I have (very briefly and imperfectly) attempted to characterize; they can not fail to give birth to a sociological system widely removed from the vague and conjectural character of all former attempts, and worthy to

---

iii   For Comte's text, see *Introduction to Positive Philosophy*, ed. and trans. Frederick Ferré (Indianapolis: Hackett, 1988). [-Ed.]

take its place, at last, among the sciences. When this time shall come, no important branch of human affairs will be any longer abandoned to empiricism and unscientific surmise: the circle of human knowledge will be complete, and it can only thereafter receive further enlargement by perpetual expansion from within.

Chapter 26

Karl Marx with Friedrich Engels

PREMISES OF THE MATERIALIST CONCEPTION OF HISTORY

Karl Marx (1818–1883) with Friedrich Engels (1820–1895), "Premises of the Materialist Conception of History", 1845, *The German Ideology*. Trans. and ed. S. Ryazanskaya (New York: Prometheus, 1998), 36–7, 41–3, 47–51.

THE PREMISES FROM WHICH WE BEGIN are not arbitrary ones, not dogmas, but real premises from which abstraction can only be made in the imagination. They are the real individuals, their activity and the material conditions of their life, both those which they find already existing and those produced by their activity. These premises can thus be verified in a purely empirical way.

The first premise of all human history is, of course, the existence of living human individuals. Thus the first fact to be established is the physical organisation of these individuals and their consequent relation to the rest of nature. Of course, we cannot here go either into the actual physical nature of man, or into the natural conditions in which man finds himself—geological, oro-hydrographical, climatic and so on.[2] All historical writing must set out from these natural bases and their modification in the course of history through the action of men.

Men can be distinguished from animals by consciousness, by religion or anything else you like. They themselves begin to distinguish themselves from animals as soon as they begin to *produce* their means of subsistence, a step which is conditioned by their physical organisation. By producing their means of subsistence men are indirectly producing their material life.

The way in which men produce their means of subsistence depends first of all on the nature of the means of subsistence they actually find in existence and have to reproduce.

This mode of production must not be considered simply as being the reproduction of the physical existence of the individuals. Rather it is a definite form of activity of these individuals, a definite form of expressing their life, a definite *mode of life* on their part. As individuals express their life, so they are. What they are, therefore, coincides with their production, both with *what* they produce and with *how* they produce. Hence what individuals are depends on the material conditions of their production.

This production only makes its appearance with the *increase of population*. In its turn this presupposes the *intercourse* [*Verkehr*] of individuals with one another. The form of this intercourse is again determined by production.

[. . .]

[4. The essence of the materialist conception of history. Social being and social consciousness]

The fact is, therefore, that definite individuals who are productively active in a definite way[3] enter into these definite social and political relations. Empirical observation must in each separate instance bring out empirically, and without any mystification and speculation, the connection of the social and political structure with production. The social structure and the state are continually evolving out of the life-process of definite individuals, however, of these individuals, not as they may appear in their own or other people's imagination, but as they *actually* are, i.e., as they act, produce materially, and hence as they work under definite material limits, presuppositions and conditions independent of their will.[4]

The production of ideas, of conceptions, of consciousness, is at first directly interwoven with the material activity and the material intercourse of men—the language of real life. Conceiving, thinking, the mental intercourse of men at this stage still appear as the direct efflux of their material behaviour. The same applies to mental production as expressed in the language of the politics, laws, morality, religion, metaphysics, etc., of a people. Men are the producers of their conceptions, ideas, etc., that is, real, active men, as they are conditioned by a definite development of their productive forces and of the intercourse corresponding to these, up to its furthest forms.[5] Consciousness [*das Bewusstsein*] can never be anything else than conscious being [*das bewusste Sein*], and the being of men is their actual life-process. If in all ideology men and their relations appear upside-down as in a *camera obscura*, this phenomenon arises just as much from their historical life-process as the inversion of objects on the retina does from their physical life-process.

In direct contrast to German philosophy which descends from heaven to earth, here it is a matter of ascending from earth to heaven. That is to say, not of setting out from what men say, imagine, conceive, nor from men as narrated, thought of, imagined, conceived, in order to arrive at men in the flesh; but setting out from real, active men, and on the basis of their real life-process demonstrating the development of the ideological reflexes and echoes of this life-process. The phantoms formed in the brains of men are also, necessarily, sublimates of their material life-process, which is empirically verifiable and bound to material premises. Morality, religion, metaphysics, and all the rest of ideology as well as the forms of consciousness corresponding to these, thus no longer retain the semblance of independence. They have no history, no development; but men, developing their material production and their material intercourse, alter, along with this their actual world, also their thinking and the products of their thinking. It is not consciousness that determines life, but life that determines consciousness. For the first manner of approach the starting-point is consciousness taken as the living individual; for the second manner of approach, which conforms to real life, it is the real living individuals themselves, and consciousness is considered solely as *their* consciousness.

This manner of approach is not devoid of premises. It starts out from the real premises and does not abandon them for a moment. Its premises are men, not in any fantastic isolation and fixity, but in their actual, empirically perceptible process of development under definite conditions. As soon as this active life-process is described, history ceases to be a collection of dead facts, as it is with the empiricists (themselves still abstract), or an imagined activity of imagined subjects, as with the idealists.

Where speculation ends, where real life starts, there consequently begins real, positive science, the expounding of the practical activity, of the practical process of development of men. Empty phrases about consciousness end, and real knowledge has to take their place. When the reality is described, a self-sufficient philosophy [*die selbständige Philosophie*] loses its medium of existence. At the best its place can only be taken by a summing-up of the most general results, abstractions which are derived from the observation of the historical development of men. These abstractions in themselves, divorced from real history, have no value whatsoever. They can only serve to facilitate the arrangement of historical material, to indicate the sequence of its separate strata. But they by no means afford a recipe or schema, as does philosophy, for neatly trimming the epochs of history. On the contrary, the difficulties begin only when one sets about the examination and arrangement of the material— whether of a past epoch or of the present—and its actual presentation. The removal of these difficulties is governed by premises which certainly cannot be stated here, but which only the study of the actual life-process and the activity of the individuals of each epoch will make evident. We shall select here some of these abstractions, which we use in contradistinction to ideology, and shall illustrate them by historical examples.[6]

[. . .]

[3. Primary historical relations, or the basic aspects of social activity: Production of the means of subsistence, production of new needs, reproduction of men (the family), social intercourse, consciousness][7]

Since we are dealing with the Germans, who are devoid of premises, we must begin by stating the first premise of all human existence and, therefore, of all history, the premise, namely, that men must be in a position to live in order to be able to "make history". But life involves before everything else eating and drinking, housing, clothing and various other things.[8] The first historical act is thus the production of the means to satisfy these needs, the production of material life itself. And indeed this is an historical act, a fundamental condition of all history, which today, as thousands of years ago, must daily and hourly be fulfilled merely in order to sustain human life. Even when the sensuous world is reduced to a minimum, to a stick as with Saint Bruno, it presupposes the action of prosocial product, and remains so as long as men exist at all. Consciousness is at first, of course, merely consciousness concerning the *immediate* sensuous environment and consciousness of the limited connection with other persons and things outside the individual who is growing self-conscious. At the same time it is consciousness of nature, which first confronts men as a completely alien, all-powerful and unassailable force, with which men's relations are purely animal and by which they are overawed like beasts; it is thus a purely animal consciousness of nature (natural religion) precisely because nature is as yet hardly altered by history—on the other hand, it is man's consciousness of the necessity of associating with the individuals around him, the beginning of the consciousness that he is living in society at all. This beginning is as animal as social life itself at this stage. It is mere herd-consciousness, and at this point man is distinguished from sheep only by the fact that with him consciousness takes the place of instinct or that his instinct is a conscious one.[9] This sheep-like or tribal consciousness receives its further development and extension through increased productivity, the increase of needs, and, what is fundamental to both of these, the increase of population. With these there develops the division of labour, which was originally nothing but the division of labour in the sexual act, then the division of labour which develops spontaneously or "naturally" by virtue of natural predisposition (e.g., physical strength), needs, accidents, etc., etc.[10] Division of labour only becomes truly such from the moment when a division of material and mental labour appears.[11] From this moment onwards consciousness *can* really flatter itself that it is something other than consciousness of existing practice, that it *really* represents something without representing something real; from now on consciousness is in a position to emancipate itself from the world and to proceed to the formation of "pure" theory, theology, philosophy, morality, etc. But even if this theory, theology, philosophy, morality, etc., come into contradiction with the existing relations, this can only occur because existing social relations have come into contradiction with existing productive forces; moreover, in a particular national sphere of relations this can also occur through the contradiction, arising not within the national orbit, but between this national consciousness and the practice of other nations, i.e., between the national and the general consciousness of a nation (as is happening now in Germany); but since this contradiction appears to exist only as a contradiction within the national consciousness, it seems to this nation that the struggle too is confined to this national muck, precisely because this nation represents this muck as such.

Incidentally, it is quite immaterial what consciousness starts to do on its own: out of all this trash we get only the one inference that these three moments, the productive forces, the state of society and consciousness, can and must come into contradiction with one another, because the *division of labour* implies the possibility, nay the fact, that intellectual and material activity, that enjoyment and labour, production and consumption, devolve on different individuals, and that the only possibility of their not coming into contradiction lies in negating in its turn the division of labour. It is self-evident, moreover, that "spectres", "bonds", "the higher being", "concept", "scruple", are merely idealist, speculative, mental expressions, the concepts apparently of the isolated individual, the mere images of very empirical fetters and limitations, within which move the mode of production of life, and the form of intercourse coupled with it.

Notes

1   [The following passage is crossed out in the manuscript:] The first *historical* act of these individuals distinguishing them from animals is not that they think, but that they begin *to produce their means of subsistence.*

2   [The following passage is crossed out in the manuscript:] These conditions determine not only the original, spontaneous organisation of men, especially racial differences, but also the entire further development, or lack of development, of men up to the present time.

3   [The manuscript originally had:] definite individuals under definite conditions of production.

4   [The following passage is crossed out in the manuscript:] The ideas which these individuals form are ideas either about their relation to nature or about their mutual relations or about their own nature. It is evident that in all these cases their ideas are the conscious expression—real or illusory—of their real relations and activities, of their production, of their intercourse, of their social and political conduct. The opposite assumption is only possible if in addition to the spirit of the real, materially evolved individuals a separate spirit is presupposed. If the conscious expression of the real relations of these individuals is illusory, if in their imagination they turn reality upside-down, then this in its turn is the result of their limited material mode of activity and their limited social relations arising from it.

5   [The manuscript originally had:] Men are the producers of their conceptions, ideas, etc., and precisely men conditioned by the mode of production of their material life, by their material intercourse and its further development in the social and political structure.

6   The clean copy ends here. The text that follows in this edition are the three parts of the rough copy of the manuscript.

7   [Marginal note by Marx:] *History.*

8   [Marginal note by Marx:] *Hegel.* Geological, hydrographical, etc., conditions. Human bodies. Needs, labour.

9   [Marginal note by Marx:] We see here immediately: this natural religion or this particular attitude to nature is determined by the form of society and vice versa. Here, as everywhere, the identity of nature and man also appears in such a way that the restricted attitude of men to nature determines their restricted relation to one another, and their restricted attitude to one another determines men's restricted relation to nature.

10   [Marginal note by Marx, which is crossed out in the manuscript:] Men's consciousness develops in the course of actual historical development.

11   [Marginal note by Marx:] The first form of ideologists, *priests*, is coincident.

Chapter 27

Émile Durkheim

HISTORY, FUNCTION AND CAUSE

Émile Durkheim (1858–1917), "History, Function and Cause", 1902, *Selected Writings*. Trans. Anthony Giddens (Cambridge: Cambridge University Press, 1972), 78–9.

(1) *Année Sociologique*, 1902(b) Review of works by Salvemini, Croce and Sorel on the nature of history, in *Année sociologique*, vol. 6, 1901–2.
(2) *Année Sociologique*, 1897(b) Review of Köhler: *Zur Urgeschichte der Ehe*, in *Année sociologique*, vol. 1, 1896–7.

(1)

HISTORY CAN ONLY BE a science on condition that it raises itself above the particular; but then it is the case that it ceases to be itself, and becomes a branch of sociology. It merges with dynamic sociology. History can remain a distinct discipline only if it confines itself to the study of each individual nation, taken by itself, and considered at the different moments of its development. But it is then no more than a narrative, which is mainly practical in objective. Its function is to put societies in a position to remind themselves of their past; it is the most distinctive form of collective memory. Having distinguished these two conceptions of history, it should be added that, more and more, they are destined to become inseparable. There is no longer any conflict between them but only a difference in degree. Scientific history, or sociology, must be founded upon the direct observation of concrete facts and, on the other hand, national history, history as art, can only gain through being penetrated by the general principles arrived at by the sociologist. For in order for a people to know its past well, it is still necessary to select from the multitude of phenomena in order to retain only those which are particularly vital; and in order to do that, we must have criteria, thus presupposing comparison. In the same way, in order to be able to discover with greater certainty the way in which the concrete events in a definite period of history are linked together, it is useful to know the general relationships of which specific relationships are instances and as if so many applications. There is not in reality, therefore, two separate disciplines, but two different points of view which, far from excluding each other, mutually presuppose each other. But this is no reason to confuse them, and to attribute to one what is a characteristic of the other.

(2)

AS SOON AS HISTORY BECOMES a comparative discipline, it is indistinguishable from sociology. Sociology, in turn, not only cannot do without history but needs historians who are, at the same time, sociologists. As long as sociology has to sneak like a stranger into the historical domain in order in some way to steal from it the facts in which it is interested, it cannot derive much profit from it. Finding itself in an unfamiliar context, one in which it has no roots, it is almost inevitable that sociology should be unable to perceive, or should see only vaguely, that which it actually has the greatest stake in observing with particular clarity. The historian, on the other hand, is accustomed to dealing with historical fact and handles it with ease. Thus, however antagonistic they may be, these two disciplines naturally tend to move toward one another, and everything suggests that they will be called upon to fuse into one common study, which recombines and unifies elements of both. For it appears equally impossible that the historian – the student whose role it is to discover facts – should neglect the comparisons which make use of this material, as that the sociologist, who compares them, should neglect how they have been discovered. To produce historians who know how to see historical facts as sociologists do, or – which amounts to the same thing – to produce sociologists who have mastered all of the techniques of history, is the objective which must be striven for from both sides. In this manner, the explanatory formulas of sociology will progressively extend to the whole universe of social facts, instead of reproducing only their most general outlines; and, at the same time, historical scholarship will become meaningful because it will be employed to resolve the most important problems which face mankind.

Chapter 28

Wilhelm Dilthey

(1) HUMAN LIFE: LIVED AND RETHOUGHT

Wilhelm Dilthey (1833–1911):

(1) "Human Life: Lived and Rethought", 1923, *Introduction to the Human Sciences*. Trans. W. Kluback and M. Weinbaum (Westport, CT: Greeenwood Press, 1957), 22–23.

(2) "Construction of the Historical World", 1910, *Dilthey's Epistemology and Methodology*. Trans. H. P. Rickman (Cambridge: Cambridge University Press, 1976), 226–8.

R EFLECTION ON LIFE shapes our life experience. It consolidates into an objective and generalized knowledge many detailed happenings (evoked in us by the bundle of urges and feelings) which occurred when our self met with the surrounding world and with fate. As human nature is always the same, so are the fundamental features of life's experience common to all men. Such features are the transitoriness and final futility of all things human, and yet our ability to enjoy the present hour; in strong men, or even in less strong characters, a tendency to overcome this transitoriness by building a solid framework of their existence, and in gentler or more meditative characters an emptiness and hence a longing for true stability in an invisible world; also the onrushing power of passions which, as in a dream, create phantasmagorias until their inherent illusions dissolve. Thus life's experience takes different forms in all individuals. But its common ground in all men covers the views of the power of destiny, of the corruptibility of all that we own, cherish or even hate and fear, and of ever present death which, all powerful for everyone of us, determines the significance and meaning of life.

From the chain of individuals arises a more generalized life experience. As men live with fellow men and with others before and after them, the regular repetition of particular experiences forms a tradition of terms describing them, which after a while becomes more and more accurate and certain. Their certainty rests on the ever increasing number of cases from which we draw our conclusions, also on a habit of subsuming cases under existing generalizations, and on constant re-examination. Even in an individual case where the tenets of our life's experience are not expressly and consciously remembered, such tenets influence us. All that dominates us as habit, usage or tradition, is founded on such generalized life's experience. But in all these experiences, the individualized as much as the generalized ones, the kind of certainty and the character of its formulation differ fundamentally from scientifically acquired universal truths. Scientific thinking can examine the method on which its certainty rests, and it can formulate and prove its principles with precision. But the origin of our knowledge of life cannot be similarly examined, and definite formulae cannot be devised for it.

In this group of life experiences belongs the fixed system of relations in which our self stands to other persons and to objects outside us. The reality of this our self, and of persons and things around us, and the normal relations between them constitute the framework of life experiences and of its gradually unfolding consciousness. The self, and persons and objects around us may be described as factors of empirical consciousness, and such consciousness exists only in the relations of these factors with each other. By whatever methods philosophical thinking may try to proceed and thereby abstract from individualized factors and their relations, the factors themselves remain the determinants and requisites of life itself, indestructible like life, and unchangeable through thinking, because such factors are founded in the life experiences of countless generations. Among such experiences which establish the reality of the world around us and our relations to it, the following are the most important: the world and our relations to it hem us in, oppress us in a manner which we cannot overcome, and they restrict our intentions unexpectedly and beyond our control. The essence of our inductions, the very sum of our knowledge rest on these presuppositions which, in turn, are founded on our empirical consciousness.

(2) CONSTRUCTION OF THE HISTORICAL WORLD

Empathy, re-creating and reliving

The approach of higher understanding to its object is determined by its task of discovering a vital connection in what is given. This is only possible if the context which exists in one's own experience and has been encountered in innumerable cases is always – and with all the potentialities contained in it – present and ready. This state of mind involved in the task of understanding we call empathy, be it with a man or a work. Thus every line of a poem is re-transformed into life through the inner context of experience from which the poem arose. Potentialities of the soul are evoked by the comprehension – by means of elementary understanding – of physically presented words. The soul follows the accustomed paths in which it enjoyed and suffered, desired and acted in similar situations. Innumerable roads are open, leading to the past and dreams of the future; innumerable lines of thought emerge from reading. Even by indicating the external situation the poem makes it easier for the poet's words to evoke the appropriate mood. Relevant here is what I have mentioned before, namely that expressions may contain more than the poet or artist is conscious of and, therefore, may recall more. If, therefore, understanding requires the presence of one's own mental experience this can be described as a projection of the self into some given expression.

On the basis of this empathy or transposition there arises the highest form of understanding in which the totality of mental life is active – re-creating or re-living. Understanding as such moves in the reverse order to the sequence of events. But full empathy depends on understanding moving with the order of events so that it keeps step with the course of life. It is in this way that empathy or transposition expands. Re-experiencing follows the line of events. We progress with the history of a period, with an event abroad or with the mental processes of a person close to us. Re-experiencing is perfected when the event has been filtered through the consciousness of a poet, artist or historian and lies before us in a fixed and permanent work.

[. . .] The narrative of the novelist or historian, which follows the historical course of events, makes us re-experience it. It is the triumph of re-experiencing that it supplements the fragments of a course of events in such a way that we believe ourselves to be confronted by continuity.

But what does this re-experiencing consist of? We are only interested in what the process accomplishes; there is no question of giving a psychological explanation. So we shall not discuss the relation of this concept to those of sympathy and empathy, though their relevance is clear from the fact that sympathy strengthens the energy of re-living. We must focus on the significance of re-living for grasping the world of mind. It rests on two factors; envisaging an environment or situation vividly always stimulates re-experiencing; imagination can strengthen or diminish the emphasis on attitudes, powers, feelings, aspirations and ideas contained in our own lives and this enables us to re-produce the mental life of another person. The curtain goes up and Richard appears. A flexible mind, following his words, facial expressions and movements, can now experience something which lies outside any possibility in its real life. [. . .]

This re-living plays a significant part in the acquisition of mental facts, which we owe to the historian and the poet. Life progressively limits a man's inherent potentialities. The shaping of each man's nature determines his further development. In short, he always discovers, whether he considers what determines his situation or the acquired characteristics of his personality, that the range of new perspectives on life and inner turns of personal existence is limited. But understanding opens for him a wide realm of possibilities which do not exist within the limitations of his real life. The possibility of experiencing religious states in one's own life is narrowly limited for me as for most of my contemporaries. But, when I read through the letters and writings of Luther, the reports of his contemporaries, the records of religious disputes and councils, and those of his dealings with officials, I experience a religious process, in which life and death are at issue, of such eruptive power and energy as is beyond the possibility of direct experience for a man of our time. But I can re-live it. I transpose myself into the circumstances; everything in them makes for an extraordinary development of religious feelings. I observe in the monasteries a technique of dealing with the invisible world which directs the monk's soul constantly towards transcendental matters; theological controversies become matters of inner life. I observe how what is thus formed in the monasteries *is spread* through innumerable channels – sermons, confessions, teaching and writings – to the laiety: and then *I notice* how councils and religious movements *have spread* the doctrine of the invisible church and universal priesthood everywhere and how it comes to be related to the liberation of personality in the secular sphere. Finally I see that what has been achieved by such struggles in lonely cells can survive, in spite of the church's opposition. [. . .] As Luther leads this movement we can understand his development through the links between common human features, the religious sphere, this historical setting and his personality. Thus this process reveals a religious world in him and his companions of the first period of the Reformation which widens our horizon of the possibilities of human existence. Only in this way do they become accessible to us. Thus the inner-directed man can experience many other existences in his imagination. Limited by circumstances he can yet glimpse alien beauty in the world and areas of life beyond his reach. Put generally: man, tied and limited by the reality of life is liberated not only by art – as has often been explained – but also by historical understanding. This effect of history, which its modern detractors have not noticed, is widened and deepened in the further stages of historical consciousness.

Chapter 29

Max Weber

ON THE CONCEPT OF SOCIOLOGY AND THE "MEANING" OF SOCIAL CONDUCT

Max Weber (1864–1920), "On the Concept of Sociology and the 'Meaning' of Social Conduct", 1922, *Basic Concepts in Sociology*. Trans. H. P. Secher (London: Peter Owen, 1962), 29–33.

THE TERM "SOCIOLOGY" is open to many different interpretations. In the context used here it shall mean that science which aims at the interpretative understanding of social behavior in order to gain an explanation of its causes, its course, and its effects. It will be called human "behavior" only in so far as the person or persons involved engage in some subjectively meaningful action. Such behavior may be mental or external; it may consist in action or omission to act. The term "social behavior" will be reserved for activities whose intent is related by the individuals involved to the conduct of others and is oriented accordingly.

A. Methodological foundations

1. "Meaning" is used here in two different senses. First, there is actual conduct by a specific actor in a given historical situation or the rough approximation based on a given quantity of cases involving many actors; and, second, there is the conceptually "ideal type" of subjective meaning attributed to a hypothetical actor in a given type of conduct. In neither sense can it be used as an objectively "valid" or as a metaphysically fathomable "true" meaning. Herein lies the distinction between the behavioral sciences, such as Sociology and History and the orthodox disciplines, such as Jurisprudence, Logic, Ethics, or Esthetics, whose purpose it is to determine the "true" and "valid" meaning of the objects of their analysis.

2. The line between meaningful and merely responsive behavior (i.e., subjectively not meaningful) is extremely fluid. [. . .] Meaningful, i.e. subjectively understandable conduct does not figure at all in many cases of psychophysical processes, or, if it does, is

recognizable only by the expert; mystical experiences which cannot be adequately communicated in words are never fully understandable for anyone who is not susceptible to such experiences. On the other hand, the ability to perform a similar action is not a precondition to understanding; it is not necessary "to be Caesar in order to understand Caesar." To be able to put one's self in the place of the actor is important for clearness of understanding but not an absolute precondition for meaningful interpretation. Understandable and non-understandable parts of a process are often inextricably intertwined.

3. All interpretation, as does science generally, strives for clarity and verifiable proof. Such proof of understanding will be either of a rational, i.e., logical or mathematical, or of an emotionally emphatic, artistically appreciative, character. Rational proof can be supplied in the sphere of behavior by a clear intellectual grasp of everything within its intended context of meaning. Emphatic proof in the sphere of behavior will be supplied by complete sympathetic emotional participation. Direct and unambiguous intelligibility is rational understanding of the highest order, especially in mathematically and logically related propositions. We understand plainly what it means when anyone uses the proposition $2 + 2 = 4$, or the Pythagorean theorem in reasoning or argument, or when a chain of reasoning is logically executed in accordance with accepted ways of thought. In the same way we understand the actions of a person who tries to achieve a certain goal by choosing appropriate means, if the facts of the situation on the basis of which he makes his choice are familiar to us. Any interpretation of such rationally purposeful action possesses—for an understanding of the means employed—the highest degree of proof. Not with the same accuracy, but still accurate enough for most purposes of explanation, it is possible to understand errors (including problem entanglements) to which we ourselves are susceptible or whose origin can be detected by sympathetic self-analysis. On the other hand, many ultimate *goals* or *values* toward which experience shows that human behavior may be oriented often cannot be understood as such, though it is possible to grasp them intellectually. The more radically they vary from our own ultimate values, the more difficult it is for us to understand them through sympathetic participation. Depending upon the circumstances of a particular case, it must then suffice to achieve only a purely intellectual understanding of such values or, failing that, a simple acceptance of them as given data. As far as is possible, the conduct motivated by these values can then be understood on the basis of whatever opportunities appear to be available for a sympathetic emotional and/or intellectual interpretation at different stages of its development. Here belong many zealous acts of religion or piety which are quite incomprehensible to those not susceptible to such values; as well as the extreme rationalistic fanaticism typical of the exponents of the "rights of man" theories which are abhorrent to those who, for their part, emphatically repudiate them.

As our susceptibility grows, the more readily are we able to experience such true passions as fear, anger, ambition, envy, jealousy, love, enthusiasm, pride, vengeance, pity, devotion and other desires of every kind, as well as the irrational behavior issuing from them. Even when the degree of intensity in which these emotions are found far surpasses our own potentialities for experiential understanding, we can still interpret intellectually their impact on the direction taken by our behavior as well as the choice of means used to implement it. For purposes of systematic scientific analysis it will be convenient to represent all irrational, emotionally conditioned elements of conduct as deviations from a conceptually pure type of goal-oriented behavior. For example, an analysis of a crisis on the stock exchange would be most conveniently attempted in the following manner: First, a determination of how it would have run its course in the absence of irrational factors; second, using the foregoing as a hypothetical premise, the irrational components are then singled out as "deviation" from the norm. In the same way, the determination of the rational course of a political or military campaign needs first to be made in the light of all known circumstances and known goals of the participants. Only then will it be possible to account for the casual significance of irrational factors as deviations from the ideal type.

The construction of a purely rational "goal-oriented" course of conduct, because of its clear understandability and rational unambiguity, serves sociology as an "ideal type". Thus we are aided in our understanding of the way in which actual goal-oriented conduct is influenced by irrational factors of every kind (such as emotion, errors) and which then can be classified as deviations from the original hypothesized behavior.

Only in this respect and because of methodological efficiency can the method of sociology be considered "rationalistic." Naturally, this procedure may not be interpreted as a rationalistic bias on the part of sociology, but simply as a methodological device. Neither can it be considered as evidence of the predominance of rationalism in human existence. To what extent the reality of rationalism does determine conduct is not to be considered here. That there is a danger of rationalistic interpretations in the wrong place will not be denied. Unfortunately, all experience confirms the existence of such a danger.

Further Reading: Chapters 25 to 29

Benedict, Ruth. *Patterns of Culture* (Boston: Houghton & Mifflin, 1934), 251–78.

Berlin, Isaiah. *Karl Marx: His Life and Environment* (3rd edn) (Oxford: Oxford University Press, 1963).

Burke, Peter. *History and Social Theory* (Cambridge: Polity, 1992).

Cabrera, Miguel. "In Search of an Alternative Social History". Trans. Marie McMahon, *Social History* 24(1) (1999), 74–89.

Conze, Werner. "Social History", *Journal of Social History* 1(1) (1967), 7–16.

Dorfman, Robert. "Economic Development from the Beginning to Rostow", *Journal of Economic Literature* 29 (1991), 573–91.

Elias, Norbert. *The Civilizing Process.* 1939. Trans. E. Jephcott. E. Dunning et al. (eds) (Oxford: Blackwell, 2000).

Hofstadter, Richard and Seymour Martin Lipset. *Sociology and History: Methods* (New York: Basic Books, 1968).

Keat, R. and J. Urry. *Social Theory as Science* (London: Routledge, 1975).

McLellan, David. *Karl Marx: His Life and Thought* (London: Macmillan, 1973).

—— . *The Young Hegelians and Karl Marx* (London: Macmillan, 1969).

Rosaldo, Renato. *Culture and Truth: The Remaking of Social Analysis* (Boston: Beacon, 1989).

Rigby, Stephen Henry. *Marxism and History: A Critical Introduction* (Manchester: Manchester University Press, 1987).

MILL, JOHN STUART (1806–1873)

August, Eugene R. *John Stuart Mill: A Mind at Large* (London: Vision Press, 1976).

Burns, J. H. "J. S. Mill and the Term 'Social Science' ", *Journal of the History of Ideas* 20(3) (1959), 431–2.

Carlisle, Janice. *John Stuart Mill and the Writing of Character* (Athens, GA: University of Georgia Press, 1991).

Cranston, Maurice. *John Stuart Mill* (London: Longmans, Green, 1958).

Halliday, Richard John. *John Stuart Mill* (London: Allen and Unwin, 1976).

Heans, S. J. "Was Mill a Moral Scientist?" *Philosophy* 67(259) (1992), 81–101.

Heydt, Colin. "Narrative, Imagination, and the Religion of Humanity in Mill's Ethics", *Journal of the History of Philosophy* 44(1) (2006), 99–115.

Hoag, Robert W. "Happiness and Freedom: Recent Work on John Stuart Mill", *Philosophy and Public Affairs* 15(2) (1986), 188–99.

Jong, Willem Remmelt de. *The Semantics of John Stuart Mill.* Trans. Herbert Donald Morton (Boston: Reidel, 1982).

McCloskey, Henry John. *John Stuart Mill: A Critical Study* (London: Macmillan, 1971).

Mill, John Stuart. *Collected Works.* John M. Robson (ed.) (Toronto: University of Toronto Press, 1963–91). 33 vols.

Skorupski, John. *John Stuart Mill* (London: Routledge, 1989).

Stafford, William. *John Stuart Mill* (Basingstoke: Macmillan, 1998).

Walsh, W. H. "The Limits of Scientific History", *Philosophical Analysis and History*, William H. Dray (ed.) (New York: Harper and Row, 1966), 54–74.

Wood, John Cunningham (ed.). *John Stuart Mill: Critical Assessments* (London: Croom Helm, 1987).

MARX, KARL (1818–1883) (*ALSO SEE FURTHER READING LIST FOLLOWING PART 8*).

Aguirre Rojas, Carlos Antonio. "Between Marx and Braudel: Making History, Knowing History", Fernand Braudel Center. *Review* 15 (1992), 175–219.

Ball, Terence. "History: Critique and Irony", *The Cambridge Companion to Marx*, Terrell Carver (ed.). (Cambridge: Cambridge University Press, 1991), 124–42.

Berlin, Sir Isaiah. *Karl Marx: His Life and Environment*. 1919 (4th edn) (New York: Oxford University Press, 2002).

Best, Steven. *The Politics of Historical Vision: Marx, Foucault, Habermas* (New York: Guildford, 1995).

Carver, Terrell. *Marx and Engels: The Intellectual Relationship* (Brighton: Wheatsheaf, 1983).

Cohen, Gerald A. *Karl Marx's Theory of History: A Defence* (Oxford: Oxford University Press, 1978).

Cohen, Marshall, Thomas Nagel and Thomas Scanlon (eds). *Marx, Justice, and History* (Princeton, NJ: Princeton University Press, 1980).

Fischer, Ernst. *Marx in His Own Words* (London: Allen Lane, 1970). Trans. Anna Bostock. Revised as *How to Read Karl Marx*. Introduction John Bellamy Foster (New York: Monthly Review Press, 1996).

Hobsbawm, Eric. "Marx and History", *New Left Review* 143 (1984), 39–50.

Kaye, Harvey J. *The British Marxist Historians: An Introductory Analysis* (Cambridge: Polity Press, 1984).

Lowith, Karl. *Max Weber and Karl Marx* (London: Routledge, 1993).

Mahon, Joseph. "Marx as a Social Historian", *History of European Ideas* 12 (1990), 749–66.

McLellan, David. *Karl Marx: His Life and Thought* (London: MacMillan, 1974).

——— . *Marxism after Marx: An Introduction* (Boston, MA: Houghton Mifflin, 1979).

Murray, Patrick. "Karl Marx as a Historical Materialist Historian of Political Economy", *History of Political Thought* 20 (1988), 90–105.

Oakley, Allen. *The Making of Marx's Critical Theory: A Bibliographical Analysis* (London: Routledge, 1983).

Rader, Melvin. *Marx's Interpretation of History* (Oxford: Oxford University Press, 1979).

Shaw, William H. *Marx's Theory of History* (Stanford: Stanford University Press, 1978).

Tagliacozzo, Giorgio (ed.). *Vico and Marx: Affinities and Contrasts* (Princeton, NJ and Atlantic Highlands, NJ: Humanities Press, 1983).

Wetherley, Paul (ed.). *Marx's Theory of History: Contemporary Debate* (Avebury: Brookfield, 1992).

Wood, Allen W. *Karl Marx*. (2nd edn) (London: Routledge & Kegan Paul, 2004).

ENGELS, FRIEDRICH (1820–1895)

Henderson, W. O. *The Life of Friedrich Engels*. 2 vols (London: Cass, 1976).

Hunt, Richard N. *The Political Ideas of Marx and Engels*. 2 vols (London: Macmillan, 1974–84).

Jones, Gareth Stedman. "Engels and the Genesis of Marxism", *New Left Review* 106 (1977), 79–104.

Lichtheim, George. *Marxism: An Historical and Critical Study* (London: Routledge, 1961).

McLellan, David. *Friedrich Engels* (New York: Viking Press, 1978).

Mayer, Gustav. *Friedrich Engels: A Biography*. Trans. Gilbert Highet and Helen Highet (London: Chapman & Hall, 1936).

Rigby, S. H. *Engels and the Formation of Marxism: History, Dialectics and Revolution* (Manchester: Manchester University Press, 1992).

Wolf, Eric R. "The Peasant War in Germany: Friedrich Engels as Social Historian", *Science and Society* 51 (1987), 82–92.

DURKHEIM, EMILE (1858–1917)

Bellah, Robert N. "Durkheim and History", *Emile Durkheim*. Robert A. Nisbet (ed.) (Englewood Cliffs, NJ: Spectrum, 1965), 153–76.

—— . "Durkheim and History", *American Sociological Review* 24(4) (1959), 447–61.

Burke, Peter. *History and Social Theory* (Cambridge: Polity Press, 1992).

Emirbayar, Mustafa. "Durkheim's Contribution to the Sociological Analysis of History", *Sociological Forum* 11(2) (1996), 263–84.

—— . "Useful Durkheim", *Sociological Theory* 14(2) (1996), 109–30.

Giddens, Anthony. *Capitalism and Modern Social Theory: An Analysis of the Writings of Marx, Durkheim and Max Weber* (Cambridge: Cambridge University Press, 1971).

Lukes, Steven. *Emile Durkheim: His Life and Work; a Historical and Critical Study*. 1973 (enlarged edn) (London: Penguin, 1992).

Rhodes, R. Colbert. "Emile Durkheim and the Historical Thought of Marc Bloch", *Theory and Society* 5(1) (1978), 45–73.

Walker, Lawrence D. "A Note on Historical Linguistics and Marc Bloch's Comparative Method", *History and Theory* 19(2) (1980), 154–64.

DILTHEY, WILHELM (1833–1911)

Bambach, C. R. *Heidegger, Dilthey and the Crisis of Historicism* (Ithaca, NY: Cornell University Press, 1995).

Bulhof, Ilse N. *Wilhelm Dilthey: A Hermeneutic Approach to the Study of History and Culture* (The Hague: Martinus Nijhoff, 1980).

—— . "Structure and Change in Wilhelm Dilthey's Philosophy of History", *History and Theory* 15(1) (1976), 21–32.

Collingwood, R. G. *The Idea of History*. 1946. Introduction Jan van der Dussen (Oxford: Oxford University Press, 1994).

Donoso, Anton. "Wilhelm Dilthey's Contribution to the Philosophy of History", *Philosophy Today* 12(3) (1968), 151–63.

Ermath, Michael. "Review: Historismus Redivivus, A New Dilthey?" *The Journal of Modern History* 48(1) (1976), 101–107.

—— . *Wilhelm Dilthey: The Critique of Historical Reason* (Chicago: University of Chicago Press, 1978).

Gallie, W. B. "Explanation in History and the Genetic Sciences", *Theories of History: Readings in Classical and Contemporary Sources*, Patrick Gardiner (ed.) (New York: Free Press, 1959), 213–25.

Hodges, Herbert A. *The Philosophy of Wilhelm Dilthey* (London: Routledge & Kegan Paul, 1952).

—— . *Wilhelm Dilthey: An Introduction*. 1944. (2nd edn) (London: Routledge & Kegan Paul, 1952).

Kluback, William. *Wilhelm Dilthey's Philosophy of History* (New York: Columbia University Press, 1956).

Makkreel, Rudolf A. *Dilthey: Philosopher of the Human Studies* 1972 (2nd edn) (Princeton, NJ: Princeton University Press, 1992).

—— . "Traditional Historicism, Contemporary Interpretations of Historicity, and the History of Philosophy", *New Literary History* 21(4) (1990), 977–91.

—— and Frithjof Rodi. "Introduction", *The Formation of the Historical World in the Human Sciences. Wilhelm Dilthey* (Princeton: Princeton University Press, 2002).

Masur, Gerhard. "Wilhelm Dilthey and the History of Ideas", *Journal of the History of Ideas* 13(1) (1952), 94–107.

Nelson, Eric Sean. "Review: The Formation of the Historical World in the Human Sciences", *Journal of the History of Philosophy* 42(2004), 113–115.

O'Hear, A. *Verstehen and Humane Understanding*. Royal Institute of Philosophy, Supplement 41 (Cambridge: Cambridge University Press, 1997).

Owensby, Jacob. *Dilthey and the Narrative of History* (Ithaca, NY: Cornell University Press, 1994).

Platinga, Theodore. "Commitment and Historical Understanding: A Critique of Dilthey", *Fides et Historia* 14 (1982), 29–36.

——. *Historical Understanding in the Thought of Wilhelm Dilthey* (Toronto: University of Toronto Press, 1980).

Rickman, H. P. *Dilthey Today: A Critical Appraisal of the Contemporary Relevance of his Work* (New York: Greenwood Press, 1988).

——. (ed.) *Meaning in History: W. Dilthey's Thoughts on History and Society* (London: Allen & Unwin, 1961).

——. *Wilhelm Dilthey: Pioneer of Human Studies* (Berkeley: University of California Press, 1980).

Tuttle, Howard Nelson. *Wilhelm Dilthey's Philosophy of Historical Understanding: A Critical Analysis* (Leiden: E. J. Brill, 1969).

Stein, Ludwig. "Historical Optimism: Wilhelm Dilthey", *The Philosophical Review* 33(4) (1924), 329–44.

MAX WEBER (1864–1920)

Antoni, Carlo. *From History to Sociology*. Foreword B. Croce. Trans. H. V. White (Detroit: Wayne State University Press, 1959).

Bendix, Reinhard. *Max Weber: An Intellectual Portrait* (Berkeley: University of California Press, 1960).

Burger, Thomas. *Max Weber's Theory of Concept Formation*. 1976. (expanded edn) (Durham, NC: Duke University Press, 1987).

Burke, Peter. *History and Social Theory* (Cambridge: Polity Press, 1992).

Eldridge, J. E. T. (ed.). *Max Weber: The Interpretation of Social Reality* (London: Nelson, 1972).

Freund, J. "German Sociology in the time of Max Weber", *A History of Sociological Analysis*, T Bottomore and R. Nisbet (eds) (London: Heinemann, 1979).

Giddens, Anthony. "Weber and Durkheim: Coincidence and Divergence", *Max Weber and his Contemporaries*, Wolfgang J. Mommsen and Jürgen Osterhammel (eds) (London: Allen & Unwin, 1987), 182–9.

——. *Politics and Sociology in the Thought of Max Weber* (London: Macmillan, 1972).

Helle, Horst J. "The Purpose of Max Weber's Sociology: Comments on Steven Seidman, 'The Main Aims of Max Weber's Sociology' ", *Canadian Journal of Sociology* 10(2) (1985), 195–201.

Hennis, Wilhelm. *Max Weber: Essays in Reconstruction*. Trans. Keith Tribe (London: Allen & Unwin, 1988).

Hughes, H. Stuart. *Consciousness and Society: The Reorientation of European Social Thought, 1890–1930* (London: MacGibbon & Key, 1959).

Kalberg, Stephen. *Max Weber's Comparative-Historical Sociology* (Chicago: University of Chicago Press, 1994).

Kronman, Anthony T. *Max Weber* (London: Edward Arnold, 1983).

Lash, Scott and Sam Whimster. *Max Weber, Rationality and Modernity* (London: Allen & Unwin, 1987).

Lehmann, Hartmut and Guenther Roth (eds). *Weber's "Protestant Ethic": Origins, Evidence, Contexts* (Cambridge: Cambridge University Press, 1982).

Lowith, Karl. *Max Weber and Karl Marx* (London: Routledge, 1993).

Mommsen, Wolfgang J. *The Age of Bureaucracy: Perspectives on the Political Sociology of Max Weber* (Oxford: Blackwell, 1984).

—— . *The Political and Social Theory of Max Weber: Collected Essays* (Chicago: University of Chicago Press, 1989).

—— and Osterhammel, Jürgen. *Max Weber and his Contemporaries* (London: Allen & Unwin, 1987).

Murvar, Vatro. *Max Weber Today, an Introduction to a Living Legacy: Selected Bibliography* (WI: Max Weber Colloquia & Symposia at University of Wisconsin-Milwaukee, 1983).

Parsons, Talcott. "Max Weber and the Contemporary Political Crisis", *The Review of Politics* 4 (1942), 61–76.

Roth, Guenther. "History and Sociology in the Work of Max Weber", *British Journal of Sociology* 27(3) (1976), 306–16.

—— and Wolfgang Schluchter. *Max Weber's Vision of History: Ethics and Methods* (Berkeley: University of California Press, 1979).

Scaff, Lawrence A. "Weber before Weberian Sociology", *British Journal of Sociology* 35(2) (1984), 190–215.

Seidman, Steven. "The Main Aims and Thematic Structures of Max Weber's Sociology", *Canadian Journal of Sociology/ Cahiers canadiens de sociologie* 9(4) (1984), 381–404.

—— . "Weber's Turn to Sociology: A Reply to Horst Helle", *Canadian Journal of Sociology/ Cahiers canadiens de sociologie* 10(2) (1985): 202–206.

Stammer, O. *Max Weber and Sociology Today*. Trans. Kathleen Morris (Oxford: Blackwell, 1971).

Weber, Marianne. *Max Weber*. 1926, ed. and trans. Harry Zohn (Oxford: Transaction Books, 1988).

Webster, Douglas. "Max Weber, Oswald Spengler and a Biographical Surmise", *Max Weber and his Contemporaries*, Wolfgang J. Mommsen and Jürgen Osterhammel (eds) (London: Allen & Unwin, 1987), 515–27.

PART 7

Historical time and historical structures

INTRODUCTION

HISTORICAL BOOKS HAD SPARKED controversy before the first volume of Oswald Spengler's *The Decline of the West* appeared in German bookstores during the final months of the First World War—but this was one of the first books to divide largely supportive responses of general readers from the overwhelmingly hostile reactions of professional historians.[i] Looking back, perhaps we should expect that Spengler's prophetic and apocalyptic vision of world history would be read sympathetically by demoralized German readers in 1918. Spengler's fellow scholars either ignored its popularity, ridiculed its seemingly unfounded generalizations, or they challenged Spengler on academic grounds. Still, the book remains in print some ninety years later, having been translated into every major Asian and European language, and so it offers a powerful suggestion of those concepts that appealed to readers at that time. Spengler argued for a global and timeless view of history, whereby the world's civilizations operated according to organic repetitions of birth, growth, and decline rather than according to a conventional and seemingly artificial positive framework that leads from beginnings to utopias—or, as Spengler impatiently describes it, "a scheme with its foolish linear progression and its meaningless proportions". Spengler's cyclical structure allowed him to write as both a historian and a prophet, for it allowed him to pinpoint the current moment in world history (decline) and predict the future (death and then rebirth) using familiar biological language. Read as one of many twentieth-century attempts to argue that a new structure for describing history will rejuvenate our understanding of the past, Spengler is immensely useful, even if his scholarly reputation itself has suffered steep decline. His *Decline of the West* was eagerly embraced by the Nazis (which Spengler always resented), he was ignored or ridiculed by his own colleagues, he was unable to complete his subsequent historical

---

i   For a useful survey of the popular and scholarly reception of Spengler's *Decline*, see H. Stuart Hughes, *Oswald Spengler: A Critical Estimate* (revd edn) (New York: Scribner's, 1962).

projects, and perhaps more than any other historical book of the period, this book has been described for nearly a century as unethical and even dangerous.[ii]

Despite the uses and abuses of Spengler's book, as well as its author's own attacks on historical frameworks, it too provided a fine example of the ways in which historians have "fabricated periods of history", as his eminent British contemporary R. G. Collingwood put it. As the sources in this section suggest, by dividing the past into distinct periods according to their preferred criteria, historians have distorted both their study and our vision of the past. European readers began to envision the past in terms of distinct periods at around the time of Napoleon's defeat in 1815—as one historian has explained, "new nation-states needed stories to justify their existence".[iii] Historians in the early and mid-twentieth century shared Spengler's concern with the consequences of historical periodization, particularly those who also used structural frameworks to reflect on a range of historical phenomena. These frameworks derive from fields as diverse as the archaeology of Roman Britain and the paradigm shifts that characterize the intellectual consequences of new scientific discoveries. Indeed we might have Spengler to thank for provoking Collingwood into publishing his early discussion of what he called historical sensibility in 1927, which would mature into his more famous pronouncements on related topics.[iv] For Collingwood, Spengler lacked a historical sense, the emotional and intellectual ability to envision the past through the eyes of those who lived it (a theory familiar to readers of Vico in Part 2). Collingwood considered that Spengler, lacking historical sensibility, was therefore blind to the similarities in human thought and experience in different times, places, cultures, and languages. Collingwood disputed Spengler's insistence that there are intrinsic differences between the eight historical civilizations that he described. He suggested that Spengler's progress or decline in the life-cycles of these civilizations implied not only some essentially mechanical aspect of human culture but also a complete intellectual and cultural separation between civilizations. Indeed, as another historian has carefully pointed out, neither of these views in Spengler is supported by historical fact.[v] Collingwood pointed out that despite Spengler's learned style, he did not cite his sources. Indeed, Spengler's high evaluation of Goethe and Nietzsche suggested his true concern was with fictional rather than truly historical materials. For example, Spengler ecstatically acclaimed Goethe's "godlike vision" when, upon the eve of a military battle, he declared that a new epoch of world history was about to begin. Now to say, before the event took place, that the men who were there could feel its monumental importance—Goethe says they could triumphantly claim "I was there"—reveals the degree to which Spengler was eager to trade a historical structure for a fictional

---

ii   For a powerful discussion of the ideological implications of such structural visions of history, see K. Popper, *The Poverty of Historicism*, 1957 (London: Routledge, 2002). Popper dedicated his book to "the memory of the countless men, women, and children . . . who fell victims to the fascist and communist belief in Inexorable Laws of Historical Destiny".

iii W. R. Reddy, "Anthropology and the History of Culture", *A Companion to Western Historical Thought*, L. Kramer and S. Maza (eds) (Oxford: Blackwell, 2002), 278.

iv   David Hollinger has paraphrased the general response of historians who, in the wake of Collingwood's *The Idea of History* (1946), would be asked to explain what they do: "we historians are on to something basic and complicated about human experience, and if you can't understand it you can read about it in Collingwood, and if you can't understand what he says, well, that's your problem". See "T. S. Kuhn's Theory of Science and Its Implications for History", *American Historical Review* 78 (April 1973), 370.

v   See William McNeill, *The Rise of the West: A History of the Human Community* (Chicago: University of Chicago Press, 1992). McNeill points to the connections between cultures or "civilizations" over the millennia; yet it is also important to point out that this book provides another, and much more recent, example of emplotment (see Part 10 and Glossary).

one. Like Goethe, who was defining an epoch before any part of it even took place, Spengler composes another kind of historical story. In that spirit of looking ahead: Hayden White will remark, in Part 10, that Spengler was committing the poetic fallacy. Spengler's prophetic vision, therefore, seems to reflect a notion of the spirit of his own age (*Zeitgeist*) rather than the wider historical topic he meant to address.

Underlying Collingwood's critical yet creative response to Spengler was their shared concern with aspects of human experience that previous approaches to history had either overlooked or undervalued. These include the cultural, intellectual, linguistic, and material elements of past lives. Fernand Braudel, a French historian and prominent member of the *Annales* group, was the most important figure to adopt this broadly lateral approach to history. He examined wider cultural aspects of history by using the methods and knowledge developed by related fields in the social sciences, including anthropology, economics, sociology, linguistics, and geography. For Braudel, history is structured in a non-linear way. He believed that only a non-linear and cross-disciplinary approach would allow us to consider all historical events and all evidence of human volition casting light on each other. This is what he called total history (*histoire globale*), to which he and his *Annales* colleagues aspired (see Part 5). It entailed adopting a historical viewpoint, right from the start, that envisions the past over the long term (*longue durée*). Braudel advocated a broad view of history that departed from studying the achievements or crises of nations, societies, and individuals, focusing more widely on the gradual changes that take place in a population defined according to its physical geography. For this reason, Braudel's famous study, *The Mediterranean and the Mediterranean World in the Age of Philip II* (1947) surveyed a vast range of historical changes, encompassing numerous cultural, national, and linguistic groups. Obviously, it is a very long book, running to more than 1200 pages in two volumes.

Braudel said that his ambition for total history was to illuminate the past rather than merely to shine light on bits of it—and in this particular respect, Braudel's criticism of nineteenth-century historical science was indebted to Durkheim (see Part 6).[vi] This would require a new conception of historical time, one which would depart from the short-term history of political events (*l'histoire evènementielle*) and of cyclical economic patterns over the medium term (*conjonctures*) that Braudel saw as artificial constructions invented by historians who preferred "a short time span, proportionate to individuals, to daily life, to our illusions, to our hasty sense of things—above all the time of the chronicle and the journalist".[vii] Short spans of time are attractive, Braudel pointed out, because they make it easier for historians to define causes and effects, even though doing so entails limiting their perspective to just those facts that seem relevant and to inserting their own knowledge of outcomes. For Braudel, the useful approximation between the historian's conception of time and the true nature of historical time could be found by envisioning a vast symphonic orchestra, in which each *conjoncture* (economic trend) and each *événement* (event) played the part of a single instrument. Now Spengler was also suspicious of the episodic nature of conventional histories, especially those spawned by the convenience of self-centred familiarity: "the ground of Western Europe forms a steady pole [chosen] for no better reason than that we are at home here—and around

vi   For a fine instance of Braudel's recurring metaphor, see "The Situation of History in 1950", in *On History*, trans. Sarah Matthews (Chicago: University of Chicago Press, 1980), 10–11.

vii My translation from the text on which the included excerpt is based. For a cogent discussion of Braudel's concept of time, with reference to his range of attempts to explain it, see U. Santamaria and A. M. Bailey, "A Note on Braudel's Structure as Duration", *History and Theory* 23 (1984), 78–83.

us thousands of years of global history . . . [of] great faraway cultures are made to revolve in all their modesty". Despite Spengler's attractiveness to nationalist currents in the Weimar Republic and later in the Third Reich, he advocated that historians shift away from the Euro-centric perspectives they typically assumed. Indeed, Spengler's might be the earliest and most evocative call for an approach to global history that moves beyond the narrowness of strictly Western concerns. However, unlike Spengler, Collingwood and Braudel described history as a truly dynamic process. They argued that historians must appreciate the unpredictable nature of historical development, something that a more structured theory of history, however organic in appearance, cannot accommodate. Where Spengler defined human cultures and their internal periods of development by key elements apparently distinctive to each, Collingwood and Braudel remained suspicious of historical theories that defined the field before they had examined the evidence. For this reason, Braudel's ridicule of "backward-looking pernicious humanism . . . preoccupied with [its] own place in the vast body of ancient and modern discovery" shares Spengler's enthusiasm for methodological challenges, but little else.

The American physicist-turned-historian Thomas Kuhn developed an approach to the history of science that famously used the world "revolution"—and his approach was itself revo-lutionary. Like these other twentieth-century historians, Kuhn wrote during a time when both historians and their readers were willing to question previously authoritative ways of approaching the past. When he was a graduate student in the 1950s, Kuhn was asked to teach a course on Aristotle's theory of dynamics, and he was puzzled to find that he could not do so without laughing at it. How was it possible to study the history of science when aspects of it seemed to be expressions of silly superstition rather than objective natural experiments? Like the other historians in this section, Kuhn found that he needed to furnish a new approach to the study of history and of our ordering of it. His approach questioned current notions of scientific progress, wondering about the unintended consequences of scientific education. He examined the revolutionary consequences of those scientific discoveries that had profound consequences not only on those who based their work on them but also on those of us who study the periods that are now defined by those discoveries. It would be fair to say that, although he was not the very first to do so, Kuhn challenged the reigning Whig interpretations of scientific history, providing a closer level of detail and more focused analysis than Butterfield had offered one generation earlier (see Part 5).

For Kuhn, it was important for historians to recognize that scientific discoveries revo-lutionize the way we think about the time when those discoveries had been made. For instance, we probably think of Newton as a hero of the Enlightenment because we identify him as the source of groundbreaking discoveries. But much else of Newton's influential work was not heroic nor "enlightened," and it merits historical study, too; such study would challenge our sense of who Newton was and what the Enlightenment, as a historical period or intellectual project, means. It follows for Kuhn, therefore, that careful historical insights into the history of science can only be drawn from the intellectual constellation of scientific ideas studied in historicist terms—the terms in which they were considered, disputed, and explored by their own historic scientific communities. Such studies eventually led Kuhn to observe that scientific progress was not simply a series of discoveries that led to increasingly accurate theories of nature, but rather progress is a word we use to describe the conceptual revolution that takes place when a scientific community accepts a new idea and then uses that idea to revolutionize how it defines—and how it sets about solving—new problems. Kuhn offered several technical terms to describe "the structure of scientific revolutions," the most famous (and perhaps most contentious) of which is paradigm shift. Since it is the scientist's colleagues who ultimately decide which scientific work is a true discovery, we need to study problems, theories, and tools—the *paradigm*—that those scientists use to make sense of what they examine. This is one reason why revolutions are so fruitful: "led by a new paradigm, scientists adopt new instruments and look in new places . . . what were ducks in the scientist's world before the revolution are rabbits afterward".[viii] For Kuhn, a true discovery shifts the very concepts, tools, and terms that scientists use. Scientific revolutions work by replacing one paradigm with the new one created by that discovery. This cyclical view of scientific revolutions is reminiscent of Spengler.

In the excerpt included here, Kuhn modestly asked whether "historical study can possibly effect the sort of conceptual transformation aimed at here". As a practising research scientist as well as a historian, Kuhn revealed his wish that his theory of scientific revolutions will inform the ways in which science is practised and taught. Rather than viewing its history as a logically positive process characterized by simple steps towards true knowledge, Kuhn asked us to consider the complex range of perspectives that science invites us to see. He seemed to have provoked his fellow scientists by claiming, in the final pages of his book, that "we may . . . have to relinquish the notion, explicit or implicit, that changes of paradigm carry scientists and those who learn from them closer to the truth".[ix] Like the other historians featured in this section, Kuhn looked at the history of the field in which he was trained, and focused on what he called the historical accidents, received beliefs, and elements of arbitrariness that shaped historical understanding. Without a critical examination of the ways in which we have used past events to define the structure of history, we deny ourselves the chance to engage with the past on its own terms.

viii Kuhn, *The Structure of Scientific Revolutions*, 3rd edn, 111.
ix   Kuhn, 170.

Chapter 30

Oswald Spengler

The Decline of the West:
FORM AND REALITY

Oswald Spengler (1880–1936), "Form and Reality", from Volume 1, 1918. Trans Julia Boll, 2008. *The Decline of the West. Outlines of a Morophology of World History (Der Untergang des Abendlandes. Umrisse einer Morphologie der Weltgeschichte)*, 1918 (Munich: Beck, 1923), 20–34[i]

Y ES—WHAT IS WORLD HISTORY? The tabulated idea of the past, an inner postulate, the expression of a sense of form, indeed. But even a very distinct *sense* is not an actual *form*. And as certain as we all feel and experience World History, with absolute certainty believe to perceive its form, it is also certain that even today we know its forms but we do not know its shape, which is the mirror of our inner life.

Certainly everybody, if asked, would state that he clearly and distinctly discerns the inner form of history. This illusion is based on nobody having ever seriously questioned it, on the fact that one does not doubt one's own knowledge, since nobody suspects just what could be questioned in this case. Indeed the *form* of World History is an untested intellectual property which, even among historians, is passed down from generation to generation. A small part of the scepticism that has been breaking down and deepening out the innate image of nature since Galileo, would be very necessary.

---

i   Editorial Note:

      For **morphology**, see the Glossary. Since Spengler adopts the tone and style of an impassioned speaker rather than a scholarly historian, his sentences are lengthy and filled with adjectives. Translation into written English requires breaking long sentences into shorter ones and, even more disconcertingly, translating the poet Goethe into English without reference to the original German text—since Spengler quotes from memory rather than from cited sources (an issue that Collingwood raises). At the same time, Spengler's German is highly allusive and therefore is more suggestive than any English translation can attempt to be. For instance, even in his title, *Abendland* refers not to the West specifically but to a more **mythological** notion of that part of the world that has been united by its cultural response to Greek antiquity and to the rise and spread of Christianity. In other words, while *West* is plainly geographical in English, Spengler intends a more suggestive reference to Europe's religious, artistic, linguistic, and intellectual heritage. This translation attempts to retain Spengler's vehemence and energy, despite making the required sacrifices to clarity and legibility.

Antiquity – The Middle Ages – Modern Times: this is an unbelievably poor and senseless scheme. Its absolute power over our historical thinking has prevented us, time and again, from properly conceiving the actual position of our little corner of the world, as it developed on the soil of Western Europe from the days of the German-Roman Empire. It has prevented us from understanding our relationship to the history of humanity in terms of its standing, form, and especially its life-span.

Future cultures will hardly believe that this scheme, with its foolish linear progression and its meaningless proportions, which becomes more impossible each century and which does not allow for the natural integration of new areas that emerge into our historical consciousness. Despite this, that scheme has never been seriously shaken from its indifference. It does not matter that it has become a habit among historians to raise objections to the scheme, because they have merely blurred the existing outline—without substituting it. There may be much talk about the Greek Middle Ages and Germanic antiquity, but a clear and internally necessary image, in which China, Mexico, the Axumian and Sassanid Empires can find an organic space has not been achieved. The relocation of the starting point of Modernity from the Crusades to the Renaissance and from there to the start of the nineteenth century only proves that the scheme itself continues to be held to be unshakeable.

This scheme restricts the *scope* of history. But worse, it also restricts our *vision* of history. Here, the ground of Western Europe[1] forms a steady pole for no better reason than that we, the creators of this historical perception, are at home here—around *us*, thousands of years of global history and great faraway cultures revolve in their modesty. This revolving planetary system is the result of a highly peculiar fabrication. One chooses a single landscape as the natural centre of a historical system. Here is the central sun. From here, all historical events receive their true light. From here, their significance is measured in perspective. But in reality, here speaks the scepticism-lacking vanity of us Western Europeans, in whose mind this phantom of "World History" unrolls. We have to thank this scheme for the dreadful optical illusion that has long become a habit, according to which the history of millennia such as that of China or Egypt shrinks to mere episodes in the distance, while within the proximity of our own position (since Luther and especially since Napoleon) the decades swell up uncannily. We know that a cloud seems to travel slower the higher it stands, and that a train only appears to crawl through distant landscapes, but we believe that the pace of the early Indian, Babylonian, and Egyptian histories really were slower than our recent past. And we perceive their substance as thinner, their forms as muffled and stretched, because we have not learned to give credit to their inner and outer distance.

That the existence of Athens, Florence, and Paris is more important for the culture of the West than the existence of Lo-yang and Pataliputra is self-evident. But should we make such esteem the basis of a pattern in World History? If so, then the Chinese historian would have the right to develop a World History in which the Crusades and the Renaissance, Caesar and Frederick the Great are regarded as trivial and passed over in silence. Seen morphologically, why should the eighteenth century be more important than one of the sixty centuries preceding it? Is it not ridiculous to juxtapose a "modern age," extending to a few centuries and mainly situated in Western Europe, with an "antiquity" extending to just as much millennia and to which the bulk of pre-Greek cultures is added as a mere attachment without us attempting a more profound structuring? To save the dated pattern, have not Egypt and Babylon, whose self-contained histories each by itself offset the alleged "World History" from Charlemagne to the World War and far beyond, been dismissed as mere prelude to antiquity? Have not the mighty complexities of Indian and Chinese culture, with an embarrassed face, been relegated to a footnote and the great American cultures, because they lack a cultural "relation," generally been ignored?

This scheme, familiar to the contemporary Western European, is what I call the

Ptolemaic system of history: in it, the high cultures describe their orbits around us as the alleged focal point of all world affairs. I regard this book as a Copernican discovery in the field of history: in it, a system takes its place in which antiquity and the West do not in any way occupy a privileged position next to India, Babylonia, China, Egypt, the Arabic and Mexican cultures. They are emerging single worlds that have just as much weight in the general picture of history, in greatness of spiritual conception, in their power of ascension, that they exceed Greek antiquity many times over.

[. . .]

It is a wholly untenable method to interpret World History while giving full vent to one's political, religious or social conviction. This is especially the case if one envisions the familiar three phases, not daring to shake it toward a direction leading away from one's own position. It is a mistake to apply concepts such as the *power of the mind* and *mankind*, the *happiness of the majority, economical evolution, enlightenment*, the *freedom of peoples, the submission of nature, world peace* and the like, as an absolute standard for millennia. By doing so, one just proves that others have not understood or achieved the right thing, when in reality they just wanted something else than we did. "Apparently what counts in life is life and not what results from it": this quote [probably from Goethe] should be set against every foolish attempt to solve the riddle of historical form with the help of a set programme.

The same picture is painted by historians of each individual art and science, national economy, and of course, philosophy. We see "the" art from the Egyptians (or the cave men) to the Impressionists, "the" music from the blind Homeric singer to the annual Wagner opera festival in Beirut, "the" social order from the prehistoric Swiss lake dwellers to Western socialism, all in the process of linear ascent which is based on some unchanging tendency, without considering the possibility that the arts have a measured lifespan, that they are linked to a landscape and a specific type of person as his means of expression, that these complete histories are the outer sum of a number of singular developments, of special arts which do not have anything in common but their name and parts of their technique.

Of each organism we know its speed, form, and life-span, and that each individual manifestation of life is determined by the species it belongs to. Nobody will assume from a thousand-year-old oak tree that it was just now on the point of starting its actual course of development. Nobody expects of a caterpillar, which he can see growing every day, will keep growing for a few more years. Here in the West, everybody has an unfailing sense of limits, which is identical with a sense of the inner form. In contrast to the history of the higher humanity, however, in the West there rules a wanton optimism which despises all historical and thus organic experiences in relation to the course of the future, so that in the coincidental present, everybody determines the "beginnings" of an extraordinarily outstanding linear "progress," not because it has been scientifically proven, but because it is what he wishes for. Here, unlimited possibilities are expected—never a natural end—and entirely naïve constructions of continuation are drawn up from the circumstances of each moment.

But mankind does not have an aim, an idea, a plan, just as any species of butterflies or orchids has an aim. *Mankind* is a zoological term or an empty word.[2] Were one to let this phantom disappear from the vicinity of historical problems of form, one would see appear a surprising richness of actual forms. There is an immense abundance, depth and liveliness, which up to now has been covered by a catchphrase, a plain pattern, personal "ideals." Instead of that dull image of a linear World History, which one can only maintain if one closes one's eyes to the outweighing number of facts, I see the spectacle of a plethora of powerful cultures, flourishing with primeval force from the womb of a maternal landscape to which each is strictly bound during the course of its existence, each impressing its own form onto its material: the human race, each culture having its own idea and passions, its own life, desires, feelings, its own death. There are colours, lights, and movements that no inner vision has yet discovered. There are cultures coming into bloom and aging, nations, languages, truths, gods, landscapes such as there are young and old oak and pine trees, blossoms, branches and leaves—but there is no aging "mankind." Each culture has its own new possibilities of expression, which appear, ripen, perish and do not return. There are many intrinsically different sculptures, arts, mathematics, physics, each with a determined lifespan, each self-contained, like each species of plant has its own blossoms and fruits, its own type of growth and decline. These cultures, organisms of the highest rank, grow up within a sublime futility, as the flowers in the field. They belong, like plants and animals, to Goethe's living nature, not to Newton's dead nature. I see the image of eternal creation and alteration in World History, a marvellous genesis and decline of organic forms. But the proper historian sees it in the shape of a tapeworm, which tirelessly "adds on" epochs.

Meanwhile, the succession *Antiquity – Middle Ages – Modern Times* has finally exhausted its expressive force. Full of nooks and crannies and shallow as it was as an academic basis, it also represented the not fully philosophical form which we had for the classification of our results, and under which we have filed *World History*. But the number of centuries which could be grouped under this pattern at the most has finally been reached. In the event of a quick increase in historical material, namely that which lies entirely outside of this order, the image begins to dissolve into indeterminable Chaos. Every historian that is not fully blind knows and feels this, and only in order to not sink completely, he holds on to the only pattern he knows for dear life. The term *Middle Ages*,[3] coined in 1667 by Professor Horn in Leyden, today has to cover a formless, continuously expanding mass which is only negatively restricted by what cannot be filed under any pretext under the other two passively ordered groups [*Antiquity* and *Modernity*]. The uneasy treatment and evaluation of the new Persian, Arabic and Russian history are obvious examples. It cannot be concealed any longer that this alleged history of the world actually did restrict itself to the region of the eastern Mediterranean and later, after the migration of the peoples, an event only important to us and thus highly overrated, which has a purely Occidental significance and does not regard the Arabic culture at all. Facing a sudden change of scene, "World History" restricts itself to West-Central Europe. Hegel had explained in all his naïveté that he would ignore those nations which did not fit into his system of history. But that was only an honest acknowledgement of methodological prerequisites, without which no [Western] historian would reach his aim. The disposition of all works of history can be examined at that. Today it is indeed a question of academic tact: which parts of historical developments shall be seriously acknowledged and which shall not? Ranke is a good example for that.

Today, we think in continents. Only our philosophers and historians have not learned that yet. What significance could terms and perspectives have, which come forth with a claim to universal validity and whose horizon does not exceed the spiritual atmosphere of the Western Europeans?

Now look at our best books. When Plato speaks of humanity, he thinks of the Greeks, in contrast to the Barbarians. This quite agrees with his ahistorical style of classical life and thought, and this premise leads to results that are right and meaningful for the Greeks. But if [the Englightenment philosopher] Kant reasons about ethical ideas, for example, then he claims the validity of his sentences for all men at all times. He does not voice that, since it is self-evident for him and for his reader. In his aesthetics, he does not formulate a principle of the art of Phidias or the art of Rembrandt, but straightaway one art for all in general. But what he determines as the necessary forms of thought are yet only the necessary forms of Occidental thought. One look at Aristotle and his intrinsically different results should have taught that here a mind is reflecting no less lucidly, but in a different way.

To Russian thought, the categories of the Occidental are as alien as to the latter those of the Chinese or the Greek. A real and full understanding of primeval worlds is as impossible to us as it is to the Russians and the Indians. For the modern Chinese and Arabs, with their very differently conditioned intellects, Philosophy from Kant to Bacon merely holds the value of a curiosity.

This is what the Occidental thinker lacks and just what he should not lack: insight into the historically-relative character of his results, which are expressions of an individual existence and only of this one. Knowledge of the necessary limits of these results, his conviction that his "irrefutable truths" and "eternal insights" are only true to him and only eternal within his part of the world, and that it is an obligation to look for those which men from other cultures have developed by themselves with the same conviction. This belongs to the completion of a philosophy of the future. Only this means to understand the formal language of history, of the living world, will work. Here nothing is permanent or general. No more talk of the forms of thought, the principle of the tragic, the duty of the state. Generalization means misjudging others by one's own standards.

The image becomes much more dubious if we turn to the thinkers of the Western European modernity of Schopenhauer, where the focal point of philosophy moves from the abstract-systematic to the practical-ethical and the problem of life (the will to live, to power, to deeds) takes the place of the problem of knowledge. Here, not only the ideal abstract of Kant's "human being" is being researched, but also the actual man as he had lived in historical times as a primitive or cultured man. It is senseless to maintain the structure of the highest conceptions with the help of the pattern *Antiquity – Middle Ages – Modern Times* and the ensuing geographical restriction. But it is the case here.

Let us consider Nietzsche's historical horizon. His conceptions of decadence, nihilism, the revaluation of all values, the will to power, which arise from the essence of Occidental civilisation and which are, purely and simply, crucial for its analysis. What was the basis of their creation? Romans and Greek, Renaissance and European present a fleeting side-long glance at misunderstood Indian philosophy, in short: *Antiquity – Middle Ages – Modern Times*. Strictly speaking, he did not get beyond these, nor did the other thinkers of his time.

Against all these arbitrary, narrow, external forms, dictated by individual wishes and forced onto history, I set the natural, the "Copernican" form of world affairs, which is to it and which only manifests itself to the unbiased visionary.

I remind you of Goethe. What he called *living nature* is exactly what is called *World History* in the broader sense, the world as history. Goethe, who as an artist time and again formed life, the development of its forms, becoming, not become, as he shows in *Wilhelm Meister* and *Wahrheit und Dichtung*, hated mathematics. Here, *world as a mechanism* was juxtaposed to *world as an organism, dead nature* juxtaposed to *living nature, law* juxtaposed to *form*. Each line he wrote as a natural scientist was supposed to call attention to the form of the nascent, "moulded form, which develops while living." Empathy, observation, comparison, the immediate inner certainty, the exact sensual fantasy – these were his means of coming close to the secret of moving things. And these are the means of historical research in general. There are no others at all. This godlike vision let him, at the campfire on the evening of the battle of Valmy, speak the words: "From here and now originates a new epoch of World History, and you can say you were part of it." No military leader, no diplomat, not to mention philosopher, has felt the rule of history with such immediacy. It is the most profound judgement ever to have ever been spoken over the great act of history in the moment of its completion.

And just as he followed the development of the form of a plant from a leaf, the emergence of the vertebrates, the growth of geological layers—the fate of nature and not its causality—here, the formal language of human history, its periodical structure, its organisational logic shall be developed from the abundance of all obvious details.

Man used to be numbered among the organisms of earth's surface, and with good reason. His bodily structure, his natural functions, his sensual appearance: all these belong to a more extensive unity. Only here, an exemption is made, despite a deeply felt relation of the fate of plants with the fate of man (an eternal subject of all poetry), despite the similarity of all human history with that of each other group of higher living beings (a subject of countless animal tales, myths, and fables). Here, one should compare by letting the world of human cultures take a pure and deep effect on the power of imagination, not by forcing it into a preconceived pattern. One should finally see objective denotations of organic states in the terms youth, rise, fullness, and decline, which until now have regularly been, and today more than ever are, expressions of subjective esteem and most personal interests of a social, moral or aesthetic nature. One should place antique culture as a self-contained event, as a body and expression of the antique soul, next to Egyptian, Indian, Babylonian, Chinese, Occidental culture and search for the typical in the changing fates of these great individuals, the necessary in the unrestrained abundance of coincidence. Only then will one see the unfolding of an image of World History which is natural to us, the people of the Occident, and to us alone.

Notes

1   Here, the historian is subjected to a fateful prejudice of geography (if not to say to a suggestion of a map's picture), which assumes a Continent of Europe, whereupon he feels obliged to conduct a corresponding differentiation to Asia. The term *Europe* should be deleted from history, but there is no *European* as a truly historical type. It is foolish, in the case of the Greeks, to speak of *European antiquity* (were Homer, Heraclitus, Pythagoras not *Asians* in geographically European terms?) and of their "mission" to culturally reconcile Asia and Europe. These are words stemming from a superficial interpretation of the map and which do not correspond to anything real. It was only the term *Europe* with the thought complex originating under its influence, which in our historical consciousness joined Russia with the Occident to a union not justified by anything meaningful. In a culture of readers only educated by books, a mere conceptualisation has led to dreadful consequences. In the person of Peter the Great, they have falsified the historical tendency of a primitive people by centuries, although the Russian instinct, rightly and utterly, separates *Europe* from "Mother Russia" with a hostility manifested in Tolstoy, Aksakow and Dostoevski. Orient and Occident are terms of real historical content. *Europe* is just hot air. Every great creation brought forth by antiquity originated under a negation evoked by the continental border between Rome and Cyprus, Byzantium and Alexandria. Everything which is called *European* culture originated between Weichsel [in Austria], Adria [in Slovenia] and Guadalquivir [in Spain]. And assuming that Greece lay in Europe in Pericles's times, today it does not lie there anymore.
2   "Humanity? That is an abstraction. There have always been just humans, and there will always be just humans" (Goethe to Luden).
3   The "Middle Ages" is the history of an area ruled by the Latin church and the Latin language of scholars. The enormous fates of Eastern Christianity, long before Boniface advanced through Turkmenistan to China and through Saba to Abyssinia, were not taken into consideration for this World History. [The earliest record of *Middle Ages* in English, according to the *Oxford English Dictionary*, is 1570.—Ed.]

Chapter 31

R. G. Collingwood

OSWALD SPENGLER AND THE THEORY

OF HISTORICAL CYCLES

R. G. Collingwood (1889–1943), "Oswald Spengler and the Theory of Historical Cycles",
Antiquity (1927), 311–14, 318–20, 322–25.

SINCE PLATO ANNOUNCED that the course of history returned upon itself in 72,000 years, since Polybius discerned a "circular movement" by which the history of states came back, over and over again, to the same point, the theory of historical cycles has been a commonplace of European thought. Familiar to the thinkers of the Renaissance, it was modified by Vico in the early eighteenth century and again by Hegel in the early nineteenth; and a complete history of the idea would show many curious transformations and cover a long period of time. Here no attempt will be made to summarize this story; the subject of the present paper is the latest and, to ourselves, most striking exposition of the general theory, contained in Dr Oswald Spengler's *Decline of the West*.[1]

Spengler's view of history presents it as a succession of cultures, each having a peculiar physiognomy of its own which it maintains and works out down to the smallest details, and each following a definite course of development through a sequence of phases that is identical for all. Every culture has its spring, its dawning phase, economically based on rural life and spiritually recognizable by a rich mythological imagination expressing in epic and legend the whole world-view which, later, is to be developed in philosophical and scientific form. Then follows its summer, at once a revolt against the mythology and scholasticism of the spring and their continuation; a period in which a young and vigorous urban intelligence pushes religion into the background and brings to the fore a strictly scientific form of consciousness. The autumn of the culture pushes this consciousness to its limit, while at the same time it sees the decay of religion and the impoverishment of inward life; rationalism, enlightenment, are its obvious marks. Last comes winter, the decay of culture and the reign of civilization, the materialistic life of the great cities, the cult of science only so far as science is useful, the withering of artistic and intellectual creativeness, the rise of academic and professional philosophy, the death of religion, and the drying-up of all the springs of spiritual life. The four-fold distinction of phases is not a necessity; at times it is convenient to distinguish more or fewer than four; but however many are distinguished in one culture the same number is necessarily distinguishable in all others. Thus, the revolt against Gothic which we call the Renaissance is a morphologically necessary phase of our culture; it is called the exhaustion of the early or primitive phase of a culture and the rise of the conscious or urban phase in which the individual working for himself takes the place of the anonymous corporate effort of the springtime. And therefore the same thing must happen in all cultures; in Egypt it is the revolt against the "pyramid style," in Greece the close of the archaic period, and so forth. Again, Napoleon in the western culture marks the exact point of transition from autumn to winter, from culture proper to civilization; the break-up of the state proper and the beginning of imperialism, the victory of the great city over the country, the triumph of money over politics. Hence Napoleon is exactly parallel (or, as Spengler calls it, "contemporary") with Alexander, who marks the transition from the Hellenic world to the Hellenistic; in no sense parallel with Caesar, who marks a phase *within* the "winter" period, and is "contemporary" with a phase in western history that still lies in the future. The point which we have now reached is the plutocracy disguised by demagogism, and called "democracy," which is represented by the second century B.C. in Rome.

Thus the cycle repeats itself in the smallest details, every phase reappearing in every cycle; yet what reappears is never the same phase—nothing can happen twice—but only something *homologous* with it, something which in the new cycle corresponds structurally with something in the old. Here comparative anatomy is the clue. A whale and an elephant lead radically different lives; everything about each is adapted to its own life; a whale is altogether whale and an elephant is elephantine through and through; but every organ and every bone in the one is homologous with an organ or a bone in the other. The task of morphology is to grasp at once the homology or correspondence of parts, and their differentiation by the fundamental difference between the two species. Merely to say "this bone in the elephant reminds me of that in the whale," is unscientific; and it is equally unscientific to say "a whale and an elephant are so different that nothing is gained by comparing them." Similarly it is unscientific merely to mention likenesses in history, a likeness between Alexander and Caesar, or between Buddha and Christ; and equally unscientific to say that the differences between cultures are so profound as to make likenesses impossible. The only scientific thing to do is to recognize at once the likeness and the difference, combining them into the notion of a homology or structural identity. We then see that Alexander and Caesar cannot be homologous, for they fall in the same culture; one closes its autumn, the other helps, though not crucially, to consolidate its winter; and that Buddha and Christ are still less to be compared, because the latter marks the creative spring of the Arabian culture, the former, the congealing winter of the Indian.

This conception is set forth at enormous length in a formless and chaotic volume, heavy with erudition and illuminated by a brilliant play of analogical insight, and a still more brilliant power of discrimination. The unforgettable things in the book are the passages in which the author characterizes such fundamental differences as those between classical things and their modern analogues: in which he illustrates the thesis that "Classical culture possessed no memory, no organ of history in the highest sense," or that the ancients thought of space as the non-existent—this he proves not simply by quoting philosophers but by analysing sculpture and architecture—whereas western man regards infinite space as his true home and proper environment; which again is proved not from Kant but from a study of Gothic and oil-painting. For the philosopher only makes explicit in his own peculiar way an idea which has necessarily been the common heritage of his entire culture; and nothing is more admirable than the way in which Spengler sees and expounds this important truth.

The strange thing is that he seems to think his ideas altogether new. Learned as he is, he is either very ignorant or very reticent concerning the history of his own science. He asserts over and over again that the morphology of historical cultures is a wholly new thing. He seems ready to admit, in a single cautious sentence, that with regard to political history the idea is old; but he denies that anyone has applied it to "*all* branches of a culture." That may be; all is a large word; but if he really knew of the cyclical doctrines of Plato, Polybius, Machiavelli, and above all Vico, which last both anticipates his own in all essentials and goes far beyond it in historical profundity; if he even knew of Professor Petrie's recent and fascinating exposition of the same doctrine, he cannot be acquitted of *suppressio veri*. [. . .]

[. . .]

The fact is that Spengler, with all his erudition and historical learning, lacks the true historical mind. Learning does not make the historian; there is a *sense* of history which is not acquired through erudition, and for this historical sense we look to Spengler in vain. History deals with the individual in all its individuality; the historian is concerned to discover the facts, the whole facts and nothing but the facts. Now comparative anatomy is not history but science; and Spengler's morphology is simply the comparative anatomy of historical periods. The historical morphologist is concerned not to discover what happened, but, assuming that he knows what happened, to generalize about its structure as compared with the structure of other happenings. His business is not to *work at* history, but to *talk about* it, on the assumption that someone else has already done the work—the work, that is, of finding out what the facts are, the historian's work. In this sense, Spengler nowhere shows the slightest desire to do a piece of historical work, or the slightest sign of having done one. His history consists of ready-made facts which he has found in books; and what he wants to do is to arrange these in patterns. When the man with historical sense reads a statement in a history book, he at once asks, is that really so? What evidence is there? How can I check the statement? and he sets to work doing over again, for himself, the work of determining the fact. This is because the historical sense means the feeling for historical thought as living thought, a that goes on within one's own mind, not a dead thought that can be treated as a finished product, cut adrift from its roots in the mind that thinks it, and played with like a pebble. Now the extraordinary thing about Spengler is that, after giving us a penetrating and vivid description of the difference between history and nature, and setting up the demand that we shall envisage "the world as history"—an admirable demand admirably stated—he goes on to consider the world not as history but precisely as nature, to study it, that is to say, through scientific and not historical spectacles, and to substitute for a truly genetic narrative, which would be history, a self-confessed morphology, which is science. And he is forced into doing this by his own philosophical errors, his errors, that is to say, concerning the structure of his own thought. He prepares us for all this, it is true, by his open scorn of logic and his statement that Goethe and Nietzsche are his only two masters; for neither Goethe nor Nietzsche, with all their poetic gifts and fine intelligence, had any grasp on the distinction between nature and history. And Spengler himself praises Goethe for confusing the two, for treating Nature as history and a culture as an organism.

The touchstone of the historical sense is the future. Science determines the future, foretells an eclipse or the like, just because the object of science is Nature and "Nature has no history." The laws of Nature are timeless truths. For history, time is the great reality; and the future is the infinite well-spring of those events which, when they happen, become present, and whose traces left upon the present enable us to reconstruct them when they are past. We cannot know the future, just because the future has not happened and therefore cannot leave its traces in the present. The historian who tries to forecast the future is like a tracker anxiously peering at a muddy road in order to descry the footsteps of the next person who is going to pass that way. All this, the historian knows instinctively. Ask him to forecast a single instant of the future, and he will laugh in your face. If anyone offers to foretell events, he speaks not as an historian but as a scientist or a clairvoyant. And if he offers to foretell events by means of historical thinking, he is either hoaxing his audience or saying historical when he means scientific. Spengler again and again claims that his morphology enables him to foretell the future. He even says that therein lies its chief merit and novelty; in which context, as usual, he refrains from mentioning his predecessors, the crowd of sociological writers, led by Marx, who have made just that claim.

[. . .]

If history is possible, if we can understand other cultures, we can do so only by re-thinking for ourselves their thoughts, cherishing within us the fundamental idea which framed their lives; and in that case their culture lives on within ours, as Euclidean geometry lives on within modern geometry and Herodotean history within the mind of the modern historian. But this is to destroy the idea of atomic cultures, and to assert not a mere plurality of cultures but a unity of that plurality, a unity which is the present culture, the heir of all its past. Against that conception Spengler struggles, because, having no historical sense, he does not *feel* it, and, being a bad philosopher, cannot understand it; yet that conception is presupposed on every page of his work. "The unities of place, time and action" I read, opening it at random, "are . . . an indication of what classical man felt about life" (p. 323). And how does Spengler know what classical man felt? Only by putting himself into the position of classical man and feeling it too. Unless he has done that, he is deliberately deceiving us; no man knows what another feels if he is incapable of feeling it himself.

Spengler's so-called philosophy of history is therefore, we may repeat, lacking in orientation, because it reduces history to a plurality of cultures between whose fundamental ideas there is no relation whatever; it is unsound on fundamentals, because its purpose—that of "predetermining the future"—is impossible in itself and in any case unrealizable by his methods; it is ill thought-out, because he shows no signs of having seen the fatal objections to it; and it is committed to the methodical falsification of facts because it distorts every fact falling—or alleged to fall—within a given culture, into an example of an abstract and one-sided idea which is fancied to represent the essence of that culture. In all four respects, it is an unworthy child of the historical studies of the last two hundred years. In each respect it violates elementary dictates of the historical consciousness; in each respect it is far surpassed by the cyclical doctrines of Hegel, a hundred, and Vico, two hundred years ago. [. . .]

[. . .]

Every culture is surrounded not by sheer non-culture, but by other cultures, more or less perfect, perhaps, than itself; higher or lower, perhaps, in the scale of value; but yet cultures. That is the first modification to be made in Spengler's doctrine. Secondly, while recognizing that a given culture has a certain self-consistent character, a fundamental idea which is working itself out into a complete social life, we must assert that this idea or character is not static but dynamic; it is not a single unchanged thing, miraculously born at one time, then persisting unaltered, and finally wiped out of existence, but a process of spiritual development, an idea which grows out of other ideas, in an environment of other ideas, which asserts itself against these other ideas through a process of give-and-take in which it modifies them and is modified by them in turn. In this process, culminating points are reached in which a given idea seems to have achieved an absolute domination. Here the whole culture becomes brilliantly luminous with the light of this idea; luminous to itself, so far as its own human vehicles grasp the idea consciously, luminous to us, so far as we can recreate their idea within our minds and so see what their life meant to them. But the domination is never absolute. It is always a domination over something; there are always other ideas knocking at the gate, kept out by force, whose pressure against the ring-fence of cultural life is equal and opposite to the expansive force of the life within. So the highest summits of culture reveal a contradiction between what they assert and what they deny— Greek liberty resting on Greek slavery, capitalist wealth resting on capitalist poverty—and in the long run the mere attempt to work out the cultural idea consistently, to *live* it (rather than *think* it) to the full, destroys the culture. But the destruction of one culture is the birth of another; for there is no static entity called a culture, there is only a perpetual develop-ment, a development in which what has been won must be lost in order that something further may be won. And everything that is achieved in this process rests on the basis of all that has been achieved in its past phases.

Because this process is always the same, though always new, it is easy to find analogies and homologies between any part of it and any other. But when we cut it up into sections and say "here begins classical culture, and here it ends: here begins Magian culture, and here it ends," we are talking not about history but about the labels we choose to stick upon the corpse of history. Better historical thinking, deeper historical knowledge, would show us within the heart of classical culture, not a single unchanged idea, but a dynamic interplay of ideas, containing elements which, even quite early, prepare it for its conversion into Magian. It is bad history and bad philosophy alike to argue that because the Pantheon is Magian it is not classical. Follow that up, and you will find that nothing is classical. It is truer to say that the classical is not a style but an age, a process, a development, which led to the Magian by its own inner logic. Thus the Pantheon is *both* Magian *and* classical; it is classical in the act of *turning into* Magian. And this conception of "turning into," the conception of becoming, is (as Spengler himself industriously asserts, and industriously forgets) the fundamental idea of all history.

What, then, remains of the conception of historical cycles? Much; for though a "period" of history is an arbitrary fabrication, a mere part torn from its context, given a fictitious unity, and set in a fictitious isolation, yet, by being so treated, it acquires a beginning, and a middle, and an end. And we fabricate periods of history by fastening upon some, to us, peculiarly luminous point and trying to study it as it actually came into being. We find our eye caught, as it were, by some striking phenomenon—Greek life in the fifth century, or the like; and this becomes the nucleus of a group of historical inquiries, asking how it arose and how it passed away; what turned into it, and what it turned into. Thus we form the idea of a period, which we call the Hellenic period; and this period will resemble the Byzantine period or the Baroque period *in being a period*, that is, in having a luminous centre preceded and followed by processes whose only interest to us at the moment is that they lead to and from it. From another point of view, the movement leading away from fifth-century Greece, the "decline of Hellas," will figure as the movement leading up to the Hellenistic world. Was it, then, "really" a decline or an advance? Neither, because both; it was a becoming, a change, a development; and the historian's highest task is to discover *what* developed, through *what* phases, into *what*. If anyone is not interested in that question, he is not interested in history.

Thus the historical cycle is a permanent feature of all historical thought; but wherever it occurs, it is incidental to a point of view. The cycle is the historian's field of vision at a given moment. That is why it has been so often observed that history moves in cycles; that is why, when people have tried, as many have tried, to formulate a system of cycles, that shall be "objectively valid," valid apart from any momentary point of view, they have failed with a failure whose completeness and strikingness has always been proportional to the rigour with which they have pursued the project. In a short essay, slightly written, anyone can expound a plausible system of historical cycles. Perhaps the very length of Spengler's book, and the very learning that he has lavished upon it, are well spent in revealing, as no shorter or less learned work could have done, the impossibility of the task he has attempted.

Note

1   *Untergang des Abendlandes*, 1918. I quote from the admirable English translation, Allen and Unwin, 1926.

Chapter 32

Fernand Braudel

HISTORY AND THE SOCIAL SCIENCES

Fernand Braudel (1902–1985), "History and the Social Sciences", 1958. Trans. Keith Folca, Peter Burke (ed.), *Economy and Society in Early Modern Europe* (London: Routledge, 1972), 11–21.

1 The long-term

THE SOCIAL SCIENCES are experiencing a general crisis: they are all weighed down by their own progress, if only as a result of the accumulation of knowledge and the lack of co-operative work, while no attempt to organize the latter on intelligent lines has yet been made. Whether they like it or not, all social sciences are affected directly or indirectly by the progress of the most vigorous among them; yet they struggle on with a backward-looking, pernicious humanism that can no longer serve as a framework. All, with varying degrees of lucidity, are preoccupied with their own place in the vast body of ancient and modern discovery and this at the very time when it seems that the many paths of the social sciences must converge.

Will the social sciences meet these difficulties with further attempts at self-definition or an outburst of bad temper? Perhaps they have the illusion that these problems can be solved. Today, even more than in the recent past, and even at the risk of going back to unreal problems and arguments already dead, they are too concerned with defining their aims, methods and superiorities. We see them competing with each other, quibbling over the frontiers separating them (or not separating them adequately) from neighbouring sciences. Each one, in fact, longs to stay where it is or go back to where it once was . . . Only a few isolated scholars are bringing these sciences together in a properly organized fashion: for instance, Claude Lévi-Strauss[1] is bringing 'structural' anthropology into the domain of linguistics, the horizons of 'unconscious' history and the youthful empire of 'qualitative' mathematics. His tendency is towards a science which, under the heading of 'science of communication', would connect anthropology, political economy and linguistics. But is anyone else ready to cross frontiers and regroup like this? For the sake of some petty quarrel even history and geography would break their links.

But let us not be unjust; these quarrels and refusals are of some value. The need to maintain a position against others automatically leads to fresh enquiry: to reject something implies at least acquaintance with it. Furthermore, without consciously intending to do so, social sciences cross social life in its entirety, in its 'totality'; each trespasses on its neighbours' territory while convinced that it is still on its own. Economics discovers the sociology that surrounds it; history, perhaps the least structural of all human sciences, absorbs the lessons to be learned from its proximity to so many others, and tries to reflect these lessons. Thus despite silence, opposition and indifferent ignorance, the foundations of a 'common market' are being roughly outlined; in the years to come it will be worth trying to set this common market on a firm footing, even if subsequently each science profits for a time by returning to a narrower individual path.

[. . .]

The other social sciences know little of the crisis that our historical discipline has undergone during the last twenty or thirty years; they tend to misunderstand our work, and in so doing also misunderstand an aspect of social reality that history serves well but does not always make properly known—that is, social time, or those multiple and contradictory forms of time affecting the life of man, which are not only the substance of the past but also the stuff of present-day social life. In the debate that is developing between all the social sciences this is yet another cogent argument for the importance and use of history or rather of the time-dialectic exhibited in the work and sustained observation of historians. Nothing, in our opinion, comes closer to the heart of social reality than this lively, intimate, constantly recurring opposition between the instant and the long-term. Whether we are dealing with the past or present, a clear awareness of the plurality of social time is indispensable to a common methodology of the social sciences.

[. . .]

2 History and time periods

Any historical work analyses past time and chooses between chronological systems according to more or less conscious preferences and rejections. Traditional history, giving its attention to the short-term, the individual and the event, accustomed us long ago to its sudden, dramatic, breathless narrative.

The most recent economic and social history brings cyclical oscillation into the forefront of its research and speculates on its durations: for instance it has pursued the dream, and found the reality, of the cyclical rise and fall of prices, so that there is today, alongside traditional narrative, the description of the 'conjuncture', enquiring into large sections of the past: ten-, twenty- or fifty-year periods.

Beyond this second type of narration again, there is a history of even more sustained breadth, embracing hundreds of years: it is the history of very long time periods. I learned this approach, for good or ill, when attempting to designate the opposite of what François Simiand, one of the first to follow Paul Lacombe, has christened the 'history of the event' ('*l'histoire événementielle*'). The actual terms matter little; in any case our discussion will cover both poles of time, the instant and the long-term.

Not that such terms are absolutely unambiguous. For instance, 'event': personally, I should like to imprison it and restrict it to the short-term. The event is explosive, it is something new ('nouvelle sonnante', as was said in the sixteenth century). It blinds the eyes of contemporaries with clouds of smoke; but it does not endure, and its flame is hardly visible.

Philosophers would no doubt say that this deprives the word of much of its meaning.

Strictly speaking, an event can acquire a whole series of references and associations. It can sometimes point to profound movements and as a result of the artificial (or genuine) game of 'cause' and 'effect', so dear to the historians of the past, it can dominate a time period far beyond its own bounds. It can be extended to infinity and link, however loosely, a whole chain of events and underlying realities, which are thenceforth seemingly inseparable. By playing this adding game, Benedetto Croce would claim that history and man in their entirety are incorporated in every event and can, therefore, be re-discovered at will; no doubt, only if we add to the fragment something it did not contain at first glance, and therefore, only if we also know what can properly be added to it and what cannot. This difficult, dangerous game is proposed by Jean-Paul Sartre[2] in some recent reflections.

Let us try to make ourselves clearer, and speak not of 'events' but of the short-term, the tempo of individuals, of our illusions and rapid judgment—this is, above all, the chronicler's and journalist's time. Alongside great, so-called historical events, chronicles and newspapers present the ordinary accidents of life: a fire, a rail disaster, the price of wheat, a crime, a theatre production, a flood. Anyone can see that there is a short time period for all forms of life, whether economic, social, literary, institutional, religious, geographical (even a gust of wind, a storm), or political.

At first sight, the past consists of this mass of petty details, some striking, others obscure but constantly repeated; and it is they that today form the chief quarry of microsociology and sociometry—(note, too, that there is also microhistory). But this mass of detail does not constitute the whole reality of history in all its density, i.e. the material that scientific reflection can properly use. Social science virtually abhors the event. Not without reason: the short-term is the most capricious and deceptive form of time.

This, for some historians, is at the root of an intense mistrust of traditional history which may also be called the history of the event. With considerable vagueness, some confuse this label with political history, but political history is not necessarily merely the history of the event, nor condemned to be so. However, the fact is that history written in the last hundred years, almost invariably political history centring on the drama of 'great events', has been working in and on the short-term, apart only from the artificial tableaux, totally lacking in time-density ('Europe in 1500', 'the World in 1880', 'Germany on the eve of the Reformation' . . .), which it inserted in its narratives, and the lengthy explanations which were their necessary adjuncts. This was perhaps the price that had to be paid for the progress made in the same period in the acquisition of scientific tools and rigorous methods. The tremendous discovery of the document made historians think that the whole truth lay in documentary authenticity. 'It is sufficient,' Louis Halphen[3] was writing only a few years ago, 'to let oneself be, so to speak, carried along by the documents, read one after another, just as they come, in order to see the chain of events reconstituted almost of itself.' This ideal of 'history as it was born' culminated at the end of the nineteenth century in chronicles written in a new style: in their striving for precision they followed the history of events step by step just as it emerged from ambassadors' letters or parliamentary debates. But the historians of the eighteenth century and the beginning of the nineteenth century had directed their attention elsewhere—to the perspectives of the long-term, which eventually only great thinkers, such as Michelet, Ranke, Jakob Burckhardt and Fustel, were able to rediscover. If we accept the ability to go beyond the short-term as the rarest and most precious asset of the historian of the last hundred years, we shall understand the importance of the history of institutions, religions and civilizations; thanks to archaeology, which has need of vast time-scales, we shall see the pioneering role of studies devoted to classical antiquity. Not long ago they were the saving of our profession.

The recent break with the traditional forms of nineteenth-century history has not meant a total rejection of the short-term. As is well known, this break has benefited economic and social history but harmed political history. It resulted in an upheaval and an undoubted renewal; then, inevitably, came changes in method and the shifting of centres of interest, followed by the arrival of quantitative history, which is still far from exhausted.

But above all there has been a change in traditional historical time. A day or a year might seem like good units of measurement to a political historian in the past. Time was thought of as a sum of days. But a price curve, a demographic progression, the movement of wages, variations in the interest rate, the study of production (dreamed about rather than realized), any close analysis of currency, all require much larger units of measurement.

A new mode of historical narrative is emerging which we may call the 'narrative' of the 'conjuncture', the cycle or even the 'intercycle'; it offers us a choice of periods—decade, quarter-century and, at the outside, the half-century of Kondratieff's classic cycle. For instance, discounting brief, superficial accidents, prices in Europe rise between 1791 and 1817, and sink between 1817 and 1852: this slow rise and fall constitutes a complete intercycle, not simply for Europe, but, generally speaking, for the whole world. True, these chronological periods have no absolute validity. Going by other measures, such as economic growth and national income or production, François Perroux[4] proposes other limits, perhaps more valid ones; but such discussions are not important in themselves. The point is that the historian has at his disposal a new time period, taking the shape of an explanatory scheme in which history may be placed, in accordance with landmarks as yet unknown and the very pulse of the curves we have just mentioned.

[. . .]

Beyond cycles and intercycles there is something the economists call the long-term trend— although they do not always study it. Even now it interests only a few economists, and their reflections on structural crises have not undergone the test of historical analysis, appearing as mere sketches and hypotheses rooted in the very recent past, as far back to 1929, or at the very most the 1870s.[5] However, they offer a useful introduction to long-term history. They are the first key.

The second key, a much more useful one, is the word 'structure'. For good or ill this word dominates questions involving the long-term. The word 'structure', for observers of social life, implies organization, coherence and fairly stable relationships between social realities and masses. For historians, a structure certainly means something that holds together or something that is architectural; but beyond that it means a reality which can distort the effect of time, changing its scope and speed. Certain structures live on for so long that they become stable elements for an indefinite number of generations: they encumber history, they impede and thus control its flow. Others crumble away faster. But all operate simultaneously as a support and an obstacle. As obstacles, they act as limitations ('envelopes' in the mathematical sense) from which man and his experiences can never escape. Just think of the difficulty of breaking down certain geographical frameworks, biological facts or barriers to productivity and even certain constraints of a spiritual order (mental frameworks, too, are long-term prisons).

The most readily accessible example still seems to be that of geographical constraint. For centuries man has remained the prisoner of climate, vegetation, animal population, farming potential and a slowly constructed balance from which he cannot depart without the risk of throwing everything into the melting-pot. Consider the role of the movement of flocks in mountain life, the persistence of certain forms of marine life in privileged spots on the coastline; consider the unchanging situation of towns, the continuity of roads and trade, the surprising rigidity of the geographical framework of civilization.

Similar examples of permanence and survival are to be found in the immense domain of culture. [. . .] Lucien Febvre's study, *Rabelais et le problème de l'incroyance au XVIᵉ siècle*,[6] is devoted to defining the mental equipment ('outillage mental') of French thought at the time of Rabelais—the set of concepts that permeated life and art, thought and belief, long before and after Rabelais, and severely limited from the outset all intellectual adventure for even the freest minds. The work also of Alphonse Dupront[7] is one of the most recent pieces of research undertaken by the French school of history. Here, the idea of the crusade is considered—far beyond the fourteenth century, far beyond the 'actual' crusade—in its continuity as a lasting attitude, constantly renewed, passing through widely different worlds, societies and psychologies, touching even the nineteenth century with a final gleam. [. . .] The history of science, too, involves the construction of universes that constitute so many inadequate explanations, though each is regularly granted centuries of life. They are cast aside only after long service. The Aristotelian universe remained practically uncontested until Galileo, Descartes and Newton; then it faded in the face of a profoundly geometrized universe, which in turn crumbled, much later, in the face of the Einsteinian revolution.[8]

The difficult problem, which is only an apparently paradoxical one, is to show the long-term to be manifest in that field in which historical research has won undisputed success: economic systems—'economic cultures',[9] as some have said, referring to those age-old habits of thought and action, those tough, resilient frameworks of life that often defy all logic.

[. . .]

Among the different sorts of time that make up history, the long-term thus presents itself as a troublesome, complicated, often entirely new character. It will not be an easy matter to admit it into the very centre of our work and this will not only need the usual widening of the field of study and enquiry. Nor will our profession be able simply to make a decision and reap the appropriate benefits. For the historian, acceptance of the long-term means submission to a change of style and attitude; it implies an upheaval of thought and a new conception of the whole of social life; it means becoming familiar with time that is slow-moving, sometimes practically static. Only at this level, and at no other (I shall return to this point below), may one detach oneself from the exacting requirements of historical time to return later with fresh insight, filled with new interests, concerned with new questions. In a word, it is in relation to such vast expanses of slow-moving history and to this infra-structure that the totality of history is to be rethought. Every one of the thousand levels, the thousand explosions of historical time, can be grasped if one starts with this concept of depth and semi-immobility; that is the centre around which everything revolves.

I do not claim to have defined the historian's task in the preceding pages, but rather one conception of his task. It would be naïvely optimistic to think we have found real principles, definite frontiers and the right way at last, after the uncertainties of recent years. In fact every part of social science is constantly being transformed as a result of its own inner activity and the vigorous movement of the whole. History is no exception. So any form of complacency must be avoided; this is no time for disciples. It is a far cry from Charles Victor Langlois and Charles Seignobos to Marc Bloch, but since the time of Marc Bloch the wheel has never stopped turning. For me, history is the sum of all possible histories, a collection of occupational skills and points of view—those of yesterday, today and tomorrow.

The only mistake, in my view, would be to choose one of these histories to the exclusion of the others. This would be the old mistake of 'historizing'. As is well known, it will not be easy to convince all historians, and persuading the social sciences, so desperately eager to lead us back to the history of yesterday, will be even harder. We shall need time and a great deal of hard work to get all these changes and innovations accepted under the old heading of history. And yet a new 'science' of history has been born which will go on questioning and transforming itself. Its advent in France was marked by the appearance of the *Revue de synthèse historique* as early as 1900, then by the *Annales* from 1929 onwards. Historians were beginning to be attentive to *all* the human sciences. That is why our profession has unfamiliar frontiers and subjects of enquiry. What is more, we should not imagine that the barriers and differences still exist which only yesterday separated historians from social scientists.

Every social science, including history, is affected by all the others. They speak, or can speak, the same language.

In the year 1558, or in the year of grace 1958, getting a grasp of what the world is about means defining a hierarchy of forces, currents and individual movements, and refashioning the pattern of their totality. At each moment in the search, distinctions will have to be made between long-term movements and sudden growths, the latter being related to their immediate sources, the former to a long-term span. The world of 1558, so grim for France, was not born at the outset of that dismal year. Nor can this be said of 1958—which for us was another problem year. Each 'current event' brings together movements of different origin and rhythm: today's time dates from yesterday, the day before, and long ago.

Notes

1   *L'Anthropologie structurale*, Paris, 1958, *passim* and esp. p. 329 (English translation: *Structural Anthropology*, New York, 1963, *passim* and esp. pp. 298, 299).
2   Jean-Paul Sartre, 'Questions de méthode', *Les Temps modernes*, 1957, nos. 139, 140.
3   Louis Halphen, *Introduction à l'histoire*, Paris, 1946, p. 50.
4   Cf. his 'Théorie générale du progrès économique', *Cahiers de l'I.S.E.A.*, 1957.
5   Fully developed by René Clemens, *Prolégomènes d'une théorie de la structure économique*, Paris, 1952; see also Johann Ackerman, 'Cycle et structure', *Revue économique*, no. 1, 1952.
6   Paris, 1942.
7   *Le Mythe des Croisades; Essai de sociologie religieuse*, 1959.
8   Further arguments: I should like to bring into the discussion the following powerful articles which all illustrate the same point: Otto Brunner on the social history of Europe, *Historische Zeitschrift*, vol. 177, no. 3; R. Bultmann, ibid., vol. 176, no. 1, on humanism; Georges Lefebvre, *Annales historiques de la révolution française*, 1949, no. 114; F. Hartung, *Historische Zeitschrift*, vol. 180, no. 1, on enlightened despotism.
9   René Courtin, *La civilisation économique du Brésil*, Paris, 1941.

Chapter 33

Thomas Kuhn

The Structure of Scientific Revolutions: A ROLE FOR HISTORY

Thomas Kuhn (1922–1996), "Introduction: A Role for History", *The Structure of Scientific Revolutions* (Chicago: University of Chicago Press, 1963), 1–9.

HISTORY, IF VIEWED as a repository for more than anecdote or chronology, could produce a decisive transformation in the image of science by which we are now possessed. That image has previously been drawn, even by scientists themselves, mainly from the study of finished scientific achievements as these are recorded in the classics and, more recently, in the textbooks from which each new scientific generation learns to practice its trade. Inevitably, however, the aim of such books is persuasive and pedagogic; a concept of science drawn from them is no more likely to fit the enterprise that produced them than an image of a national culture drawn from a tourist brochure or a language text. This essay attempts to show that we have been misled by them in fundamental ways. Its aim is a sketch of the quite different concept of science that can emerge from the historical record of the research activity itself.

Even from history, however, that new concept will not be forthcoming if historical data continue to be sought and scrutinized mainly to answer questions posed by the unhistorical stereotype drawn from science texts. Those texts have, for example, often seemed to imply that the content of science is uniquely exemplified by the observations, laws, and theories described in their pages. Almost as regularly, the same books have been read as saying that scientific methods are simply the ones illustrated by the manipulative techniques used in gathering textbook data, together with the logical operations employed when relating those data to the textbook's theoretical generalizations. The result has been a concept of science with profound implications about its nature and development.

If science is the constellation of facts, theories, and methods collected in current texts, then scientists are the men who, successfully or not, have striven to contribute one or another element to that particular constellation. Scientific development becomes the piecemeal process by which these items have been added, singly and in combination, to the ever growing stockpile that constitutes scientific technique and knowlege. And history of science becomes the discipline that chronicles both these successive increments and the obstacles that have inhibited their accumulation. Concerned with scientific development, the historian then appears to have two main tasks. On the one hand, he must determine by what man and at what point in time each contemporary scientific fact, law, and theory was discovered or invented. On the other, he must describe and explain the congeries of error, myth, and superstition that have inhibited the more rapid accumulation of the constituents of the modern science text. Much research has been directed to these ends, and some still is.

In recent years, however, a few historians of science have been finding it more and more difficult to fulfil the functions that the concept of development-by-accumulation assigns to them. As chroniclers of an incremental process, they discover that additional research makes it harder, not easier, to answer questions like: When was oxygen discovered? Who first conceived of energy conservation? Increasingly, a few of them suspect that these are simply the wrong sorts of questions to ask. Perhaps science does not develop by the accumulation of individual discoveries and inventions. Simultaneously, these same historians confront growing difficulties in distinguishing the "scientific" component of past observation and belief from what their predecessors had readily labeled "error" and "superstition." The more carefully they study, say, Aristotelian dynamics, phlogistic chemistry, or caloric thermodynamics, the more certain they feel that those once current views of nature were, as a whole, neither less scientific nor more the product of human idiosyncrasy than those current today. If these out-of-date beliefs are to be called myths, then myths can be produced by the same sorts of methods and held for the same sorts of reasons that now lead to scientific knowledge. If, on the other hand, they are to be called science, then science has included bodies of belief quite incompatible with the ones we hold today. Given these alternatives, the historian must choose the latter. Out-of-date theories are not in principle unscientific because they have been discarded. That choice, however, makes it difficult to see scientific development as a process of accretion. The same historical research that displays the difficulties in isolating individual inventions and discoveries gives ground for profound doubts about the cumulative process through which these individual contributions to science were thought to have been compounded.

The result of all these doubts and difficulties is a historiographic revolution in the study of science, though one that is still in its early stages. Gradually, and often without entirely realizing they are doing so, historians of science have begun to ask new sorts of questions and to trace different, and often less than cumulative, developmental lines for the sciences. Rather than seeking the permanent contributions of an older science to our present vantage, they attempt to display the historical integrity of that science in its own time. They ask, for example, not about the relation of Galileo's views to those of modern science, but rather about the relationship between his views and those of his group, i.e., his teachers, contemporaries, and immediate successors in the sciences. Furthermore, they insist upon studying the opinions of that group and other similar ones from the viewpoint—usually very different from that of modern science—that gives those opinions the maximum internal coherence and the closest possible fit to nature. Seen through the works that result, works perhaps best exemplified in the writings of Alexandre Koyré, science does not seem altogether the same enterprise as the one discussed by writers in the older historiographic tradition. By implication, at least, these historical studies suggest the possibility of a new image of science. This essay aims to delineate that image by making explicit some of the new historiography's implications.

What aspect of science will emerge to prominence in the course of this effort? First, at least in order of presentation, is the insufficiency of methodological directives, by themselves, to dictate a unique substantive conclusion to many sorts of scientific questions. Instructed to examine electrical or chemical phenomena, the man who is ignorant of these fields but who knows what it is to be scientific may legitimately reach any one of a number of incompatible conclusions. Among those legitimate possibilities, the particular conclusions he does arrive at are probably determined by his prior experience in other fields, by the accidents of his investigation, and by his own individual makeup. What beliefs about the stars, for example, does he bring to the study of chemistry or electricity? Which of the many conceivable experiments relevant to the new field does he elect to perform first? And what aspects of the complex phenomenon that then results strike him as particularly relevant to an elucidation of the nature of chemical change or of electrical affinity? For the individual, at least, and sometimes for the scientific community as well, answers to questions like these are often essential determinants of scientific development. We shall note, for example, in Section II that the early developmental stages of most sciences have been characterized by continual competition between a number of distinct views of nature, each partially derived from, and all roughly compatible with, the dictates of scientific observation and method. What differentiated these various schools was not one or another failure of method—they were all "scientific"—but what we shall come to call their incommensurable ways of seeing the world and of practicing science in it. Observation and experience can and must drastically restrict the range of admissible scientific belief, else there would be no science. But they cannot alone determine a particular body of such belief. An apparently arbitrary element, compounded of personal and historical accident, is always a formative ingredient of the beliefs espoused by a given scientific community at a given time.

That element of arbitrariness does not, however, indicate that any scientific group could practice its trade without some set of received beliefs. Nor does it make less consequential the particular constellation to which the group, at a given time, is in fact committed. Effective research scarcely begins before a scientific community thinks it has acquired firm answers to questions like the following: What are the fundamental entities of which the universe is composed? How do these interact with each other and with the senses? What questions may legitimately be asked about such entities and what techniques employed in seeking solutions? At least in the mature sciences, answers (or full substitutes for answers) to questions like these are firmly embedded in the educational initiation that prepares and licenses the student for professional practice. Because that education is both rigorous and rigid, these answers come to exert a deep hold on the scientific mind. That they can do so does much to account both for the peculiar efficiency of the normal research activity and for the direction in which it proceeds at any given time. When examining normal science in Sections III, IV, and V, we shall want finally to describe that research as a strenuous and devoted attempt to force nature into the conceptual boxes supplied by professional education. Simultaneously, we shall wonder whether research could proceed without such boxes, whatever the element of arbitrariness in their historic origins and, occasionally, in their subsequent development.

Yet that element of arbitrariness is present, and it too has an important effect on scientific development, one which will be examined in detail in Sections VI, VII, and VIII. Normal science, the activity in which most scientists inevitably spend almost all their time, is predicated on the assumption that the scientific community knows what the world is like. Much of the success of the enterprise derives from the community's willingness to defend that assumption, if necessary at considerable cost. Normal science, for example, often suppresses fundamental novelties because they are necessarily subversive of its basic commitments. Nevertheless, so long as those commitments retain an element of the arbitrary, the very nature of normal research ensures that novelty shall not be suppressed for very long. Sometimes a normal problem, one that ought to be solvable by known rules and procedures, resists the reiterated onslaught of the ablest members of the group within whose competence it falls. On other occasions a piece of equipment designed and constructed for the purpose of normal research fails to perform in the anticipated manner, revealing an anomaly that cannot, despite repeated effort, be aligned with professional expectation. In these and other ways besides, normal science repeatedly goes astray. And when it does—when, that is, the profession can no longer evade anomalies that subvert the existing tradition of scientific practice—then being the extraordinary investigations that lead the profession at last to a new set of commitments, a new basis for the practice of science. The extraordinary episodes in which that shift of professional commitments occurs are the ones known in this essay as scientific revolutions. They are the tradition-shattering complements to the tradition-bound activity of normal science.

The most obvious examples of scientific revolutions are those famous episodes in scientific development that have often been labeled revolutions before. Therefore, in Sections IX and X, where the nature of scientific revolutions is first directly scrutinized, we shall deal repeatedly with the major turning points in scientific development associated with the names of Copernicus, Newton, Lavoisier, and Einstein. More clearly than most other episodes in the history of at least the physical sciences, these display what all scientific revolutions are about. Each of them necessitated the community's rejection of one time-honored scientific theory in favor of another incompatible with it. Each produced a consequent shift in the problems available for scientific scrutiny and in the standards by which the profession determined what should count as an admissible problem or as a legitimate problem-solution. And each transformed the scientific imagination in ways that we shall ultimately need to describe as a transformation of the world within which scientific work was done. Such changes, together with the controversies that almost always accompany them, are the defining characteristics of scientific revolutions.

These characteristics emerge with particular clarity from a study of, say, the Newtonian or the chemical revolution. It is, however, a fundamental thesis of this essay that they can also be retrieved from the study of many other episodes that were not so obviously revolutionary. For the far smaller professional group affected by them, Maxwell's equations were as revolutionary as Einstein's, and they were resisted accordingly. The invention of other new theories regularly, and appropriately, evokes the same response from some of the specialists on whose area of special competence they impinge. For these men the new theory implies a change in the rules governing the prior practice of normal science. Inevitably, therefore, it reflects upon much scientific work they have already successfully completed. That is why a new theory, however special its range of application, is seldom or never just an increment to what is already known. Its assimilation requires the reconstruction of prior theory and the re-evaluation of prior fact, an intrinsically revolutionary process that is seldom completed by a single man and never overnight. No wonder historians have had difficulty in dating precisely this extended process that their vocabulary impels them to view as an isolated event.

Nor are new inventions of theory the only scientific events that have revolutionary impact upon the specialists in whose domain they occur. The commitments that govern normal science specify not only what sorts of entities the universe does contain, but also, by implication, those that it does not. It follows, though the point will require extended discussion, that a discovery like that of oxygen or X-rays does not simply add one more item to the population of the scientist's world. Ultimately it has that effect, but not until the professional community has re-evaluated traditional experimental procedures, altered its conception of entities with which it has long been familiar, and, in the process, shifted the network of theory through which it deals with the world. Scientific fact and theory are not categorically separable, except perhaps within a single tradition of normal-scientific practice. That is why the unexpected discovery is not simply factual in its import and why the scientist's world is qualitatively transformed as well as quantitatively enriched by fundamental novelties of either fact or theory.

This extended conception of the nature of scientific revolutions is the one delineated in the pages that follow. Admittedly the extension strains customary usage. Nevertheless, I shall continue to speak even of discoveries as revolutionary, because it is just the possibility of relating their structure to that of, say, the Copernican revolution that makes the extended conception seem to me so important. The preceding discussion indicates how the complementary notions of normal science and of scientific revolutions will be developed in the nine sections immediately to follow. The rest of the essay attempts to dispose of three remaining central questions. Section XI, by discussing the textbook tradition, considers why scientific revolutions have previously been so difficult to see. Section XII describes the revolutionary competition between the proponents of the old normal-scientific tradition and the adherents of the new one. It thus considers the process that should somehow, in a theory of scientific inquiry, replace the confirmation or falsification procedures made familiar by our usual image of science. Competition between segments of the scientific community is the only historical process that ever actually results in the rejection of one previously accepted theory or in the adoption of another. Finally, Section XIII will ask how development through revolutions can be compatible with the apparently unique character of scientific progress. For that question, however, this essay will provide no more than the main outlines of an answer, one which depends upon characteristics of the scientific community that require much additional exploration and study.

Undoubtedly, some readers will already have wondered whether historical study can possibly effect the sort of conceptual transformation aimed at here. An entire arsenal of dichotomies is available to suggest that it cannot properly do so. History, we too often say, is a purely descriptive discipline. The theses suggested above are, however, often interpretive and sometimes normative. Again, many of my generalizations are about the sociology or social psychology of scientists; yet at least a few of my conclusions belong traditionally to logic or epistemology. In the preceding paragraph I may even seem to have violated the very influential contemporary distinction between "the context of discovery" and "the context of justification." Can anything more than profound confusion be indicated by this admixture of diverse fields and concerns?

Having been weaned intellectually on these distinctions and others like them, I could scarcely be more aware of their import and force. For many years I took them to be about the nature of knowledge, and I still suppose that, appropriately recast, they have something important to tell us. Yet my attempts to apply them, even *grosso modo*, to the actual situations in which knowledge is gained, accepted, and assimilated have made them seem extraordinarily problematic. Rather than being elementary logical or methodological distinctions, which would thus be prior to the analysis of scientific knowledge, they now seem integral parts of a traditional set of substantive answers to the very questions upon which they have been deployed. That circularity does not at all invalidate them. But it does make them parts of a theory and, by doing so, subjects them to the same scrutiny regularly applied to theories in other fields. If they are to have more than pure abstraction as their content, then that content must be discovered by observing them in application to the data they are meant to elucidate. How could history of science fail to be a source of phenomena to which theories about knowledge may legitimately be asked to apply?

Further Reading: Chapters 30 to 33

Berlin, Isaiah. *Historical Inevitability: Delivered on 12 May 1953* (Oxford: Oxford University Press, 1954).

Burke, Peter. *The French Historical Revolution: The Annales School, 1929–89* (Cambridge: Polity, 1990).

Costello, Paul. *World Historians and their Goals: Twentieth Century Answers to Modernism* (DeKalb, IL: Northern Illinois University Press, 1993).

Eisenstein, Elizabeth. "Clio and Chronos: An Essay on the Making and Breaking of History-Book Time", *History and Theory* 6 (1966), 36–64.

Kuhn, Thomas Samuel. "Notes on Lakatos", *Boston Studies in the Philosophy of Science* 8 (1971), 137–46.

Lakatos, Imre. "History of Science and its Rational Reconstructions", *Boston Studies in the Philosophy of Science* 8 (1971), 91–136.

Lloyd, Christopher. "The Methodologies of Social History: A Critical Survey and Defense of Structurism", *History and Theory* 30(2) (1991), 180–219.

— . *The Structures of History*. (Oxford UK; Cambridge MA: Blackwell, 1993).

Lovejoy, Arthur. "Reflections on the History of Ideas", *Journal of the History of Ideas* 1 (January 1940), 2–23.

McNeill, William H. "The Changing Shape of World History", *History and Theory* 34(2) (1995), 8–26

Midgeley, Mary. *Evolution as Religion: Strange Hopes and Stranger Fears* (new edn) (London: Routledge, 2002).

Popper, Karl. *The Poverty of Historicism*. 1957. (London: Routledge, 2006).

Toynbee, Arnold J. *A Study of History*. 12 vols (London: Oxford University Press, 1934–61).

Wittgenstein, Ludwig. "Preface", *Philosophical Remarks*. Rush Rhees (ed.). Trans. Raymond Hargreaves and Roger White (Oxford: Blackwell, 1975).

SPENGLER, OSWALD (1880–1936)

Barth, Hans. *Truth and Ideology*. Trans. Frederic Lilge (Berkeley, CA: University of California Press, 1976).

Braun, Martin. "Bury, Spengler and the New Spenglerians", *History Today* 7(8) (1957), 525–9.

Farrenkopf, John. "Hegel, Spengler and the Enigma of World History", *Clio* 19(4) (1990), 331–44.

— . *Prophet of Decline: Spengler on World History and Politics* (Baton Rouge: Louisiana State University Press, 2001).

Fennelly, John F. *Twilight of the Evening Lands: Oswald Spengler a Half Century Later* (New York: Brookdale Press, 1972).

Fischer, Klaus P. *History and Prophecy: Oswald Spengler and the Decline of the West* (New York: Peter Lang, 1989).

Frye, Northrop. "The Decline of the West by Oswald Spengler", *Daedalus* 103(1) (1972), 1–13.

Gibbons, Philip A. and E. H Goddard. *Civilisation or Civilisations: An Essay in the Spenglerian Philosophy of History*, Introduction Ferdinand Canning Scott Schiller (London: Constable, 1926).

Hale, William Harlan. *Challenge to Defeat: Modern Man in Goethe's World and Spengler's Century* (New York: Harcourt, Brace, 1932).

Heller, Erich. *The Disinherited Mind* (New York: Harcourt Brace Jovanovich, 1975), 179–96.

House, Floyd N. "Review: The Decline of the West", *The American Journal of Sociology* 32(1) (1926), 152.

Hughes, H. Stuart. *Oswald Spengler: A Critical Estimate*. 1952 (revd edn). (New York: Scribner, 1962).

McNeill, William. *The Rise of the West: A History of the Human Community* (Chicago: University of Chicago Press, 1992).

Sunic, T. "History and Decadence: Spengler's Cultural Pessimism Today", *Clio* 19(1) (1989), 51–62.

COLLINGWOOD, ROBIN GEORGE (1889–1943)

Bates, David. "Rediscovering Collingwood's Spiritual History (In and Out of Context)", *History and Theory* 35(1) (1996), 29–55.

Boucher, David. *The Social and Political Thought of R. G. Collingwood* (Cambridge: Cambridge University Press, 1989).

Collingwood Studies. Published annually by the University of Wales Press for the R. G. Collingwood Society. Vol 1, 1994–.

Donagan, Alan. *The Later Philosophy of R. G. Collingwood* (Oxford: Clarendon Press, 1962).

Dray, William H. *History as Re-enactment: R.G. Collingwood's Idea of History* (Oxford: Clarendon Press, 1995).

Dussen, W. Jan van der. "Collingwood and the Idea of Progress", *History and Theory* 29(4) (1990), 21–41.

— . "Collingwood's Unpublished Manuscripts", *History and Theory* 18(3) (1979), 287–315.

— . "Collingwood's 'Lost' Manscript of 'The Principles of History' ", *History and Theory* 36(1) (1997), 32–62.

— . *History as a Science: The Philosophy of R. G. Collingwood* (The Hague: Martinus Nijhoff, 1981).

Goldstein, Leon J. "Collingwood's Theory of Historical Knowing", *History and Theory* 9(1) (1970), 3–36.

Hughes-Warrington, Marnie. *"How Good an Historian Shall I Be?": R.G. Collingwood, the Historical Imagination and Education* (Exeter: Imprint Academic, 2003).

Johnson, Peter. *R. G. Collingwood: An Introduction* (Bristol: Thoemmes, 1998).

Johnston, William M. *The Formative Years of R. G. Collingwood* (The Hague: Martinus Nijhoff, 1967).

Krausz, Michael. *Critical Essays on the Philosophy of R. G. Collingwood* (Oxford: Oxford University Press, 1972).

Madood, Tariq. "The Later Collingwood's Alleged Historicism and Relativism", *Journal of the History of Philosophy* 27(1) (1989), 101–25.

Mink, Louis O. *Mind, History, and Dialectic: The Philosophy of R. G. Collingwood* (Bloomington: Indiana University Press, 1969).

Nielson, Margit Hurup. "Re-Enactment and Reconstruction in Collingwood's Philosophy of History", *History and Theory* 20(1) (1981), 1–31.

The Collingwood Society. Cardiff University. October 2007. <http://www.cf.ac.uk/euros/subsites/collingwood/index.html>

Rubinoff, Lionel. *Collingwood and the Reform of Metaphysics: A Study in the Philosophy of the Mind* (Toronto: University of Toronto Press, 1970).

Saari, Heikki. "R. G. Collingwood on the Identity of Thoughts", *Dialogue* 28(1) (1989), 77–89.

Saari, Heikki. *Re-enactment: A Study in R. G. Collingwood's Philosophy of History* (Abo: Abo Akademi, 1984).

Salas, Charles G. "Collingwood's Historical Principles at Work", *History and Theory* 26(1) (1987), 53–71.

BRAUDEL, FERNAND (1902–85)

Bailyn, Bernard. "Braudel's Geohistory: A Reconsideration", *Journal of Economic History* 11(2) (1951), 277–82.

Braudel, Fernand. "History and the Social Sciences: The *Longue Durée*". 1958. *On History*. Trans. Sarah Matthews (Chicago: University of Chicago Press, 1980), 25–54.

— . "Personal Testimony", *The Journal of Modern History* 44(4) (1972), 448–67.

Bulhof, I. N. "The Cosmopolitan Orientation to History and Fernand Braudel", *Clio* 11(1) (1981), 49–63.

Burke, Peter "Fernand Braudel." *The Historian at Work*, John Cannon (ed.) (London: Allen & Unwin, 1980).

— . *The French Historical Revolution: The Annales School, 1929–1989* (Cambridge: Polity Press, 1990).

Hall, J. R. "The Time of History and the History of Times", *History and Theory* 19 (1980), 113–31.

Harris, Olivia. "Braudel: Historical Time and the Horror of Discontinuity", *History Workshop Journal* 57 (2004), 161–74.

Hexter, J. H. "Fernand Braudel and the *Monde Braudelian*", *Journal of Modern History* 44(4) (1972), 480–539.

Hufton, Olwen. "Fernand Braudel", *Past and Present* 112 (1986), 208–13.

Hunt, Lynn. "French History in the Last Twenty Years: The Rise and Fall of the *Annales* Paradigm", *Journal of Contemporary History* 21(2) (1986), 209–24.

Kaplan, Steven Laurence. "Long-Run Lamentations: Braudel on France", *The Journal of Modern History* 63(2) (1991), 341–53.

Kinser, Samuel. "Annaliste Paradigm? The Geohistorical Structuralism of Fernand Braudel", *The American Historical Review* 86(1) (1981), 63–105.

Lai, Cheng-Chung. "Second Thoughts on Fernand Braudel's 'Civilisation and Capitalism' ". *Journal of European Economic History* 24(1) (1995), 177–93.

Morineau, M. "A Fresh Look at Fernand Braudel: Response to Cheng-chung Lai", *Journal of European Economic History* 26(3) (1997), 627–30.

Stoianovich, Traian. "Theoretical Implications of Braudel's 'Civilisation Matérielle' ", *Journal of Modern History* 41(1) (1969), 68–81.

Trevor-Roper, H. R. "Fernand Braudel, the *Annales*, and the Mediterranean", *The Journal of Modern History* 44(4) (1972), 468–79.

Wallerstein, Immanuel. "Braudel on Capitalism, or Everything Upside Down", *The Journal of Modern History* 63(2) (1991), 354–61.

Wesseling, H.L. et al. "Fernand Braudel", *Itinerario* 5 (1981), 15–52.

KUHN, THOMAS SAMUEL (1922–1996)

Agassi, J. "Toward a Historiography of Science", *History and Theory* 2 (1963), 1–79.

Andersson, Gunnar. *Criticism and the History of Science: Kuhn's, Lakatos's, and Feyerabend's Criticisms of Critical Rationalism* (Leiden: E. J. Brill, 1994).

Andreson, Jensine. "Crisis and Kuhn", *Isis* 90 Supplement (1999), S43–S67.

Barnes, Barry. *T. S. Kuhn and Social Science* (London: Macmillan, 1982).

Buchwald, Jed Z. and Smith, George E. "Thomas S. Kuhn, 1922–1996", *Philosophy of Science* 64(2) (1997), 361–76.

Cedarbaum, Daniel G. "Paradigms", *Studies in History and Philosophy of Science* 14 (1983), 173–213.

Cohen, Bernard I. *Revolution in Science* (Cambridge, MA: Harvard University Press, 1985).

Cohen, H. Floris. *The Scientific Revolution: A Historiographical Inquiry* (Chicago: University of Chiacgo Press, 1994).

Fischer, David Hackett. *Historian's Fallacies: Toward a Logic of Historical Thought* (London: Routledge & Kegan Paul, 1971).

Geertz, Clifford. "The Legacy of Thomas Kuhn: The Right Text at the Right Time", *Common Knowledge* 6 (1997), 1–5.

Gutting, Gary (ed.). *Paradigms and Revolutions: Appraisals and Applications of Thomas Kuhn's Philosophy of Science* (Notre Dame: University of Notre Dame Press, 1980).

Hacking, Ian (ed.). *Scientific Revolutions* (Oxford: Oxford University Press, 1981).

History and Theory. "Special Issue: Towards an Historiography of Science" 2(4) (1963).

Hollinger, David A. "T. S. Kuhn's Theory of Science and Its Implications for History", *The American Historical Review* 78(2) (1973), 370–93.

Horwich, Paul (ed.). *World Changes: Thomas Kuhn and the Nature of Science* (Cambridge, MA: MIT Press, 1993).

Hoyningen-Huene, Paul. "The Interrelations between Philosophy, History and Sociology of Science in Thomas Kuhn's Theory of Scientific Development", *The British Journal for the Philosophy of Science* 43(4) (1992), 487–501.

— . *Reconstructing Scientific Revolutions: Thomas S. Kuhn's Philosophy of Science*. Trans. Alexander T. Levine (Chicago, IL: University of Chicago Press, 1993).

Kindi, Vasso. "The Relation of History of Science in *The Structure of Scientific Revolutions* and Kuhn's Later Philosophical Work", *Perspectives on Science* 13(4) (2006), 495–530.

Kragh, Helge. *An Introduction to the Historiography of Science* (Cambridge: Cambridge University Press, 1987).

Masterman, M. "The Nature of a Paradigm", *Criticism and the Growth of Knowledge*, Imre Lakatos and Alan Musgrave (eds) (Cambridge: Cambridge University Press, 1970), 59–89.

Mandelbaum, M. "A Note on Thomas S. Kuhn's *The Structure of Scientific Revolutions*", *Monist* 60(4) (1977), 445–52.

Maudgil, A. "World Pictures and Paradigms: Wittgenstein and Kuhn", *Reports of the Thirteenth International Wittgenstein Symposium 1988*, P. Weingartner and G. Schurz (eds) (Vienna: Höller-Pichler-Tempsky, 1989), 285–90.

Meiland, Jack W. and Michael Krausz (eds). *Relativism, Cognitive and Moral* (Chicago, IL: University of Notre Dame Press, 1982).

Mladenović, Bojana. "Muckraking in History: The Role of the History of Science in Kuhn's Philosophy", *Perspectives on Science* 15(3) (2007), 261–94.

Newton-Smith, W. H. *The Rationality of Science* (London: Routledge, 1981).

Restivo, Sal. "The Myth of the Kuhnian Revolution", *Sociological Theory* 1 (1983), 293–305.

Rorty, Richard. *Philosophy and the Mirror of Nature* (Princeton, NJ: Princeton University Press, 1979).

PART 8

Marxism and "history from below"

INTRODUCTION

THE PREVIOUS TWO SECTIONS introduced social and structural theories that have shaped the concerns of twentieth-century historians. This section opens by focusing more narrowly on the bold ambitions of a small group of predominantly Marxist scholars who founded *Past and Present* in 1952—some years before it emerged as a leading forum for historical scholarship in the English-speaking world.[i] The depth of their influence on the inter-disciplinary vision of younger historians remains unmistakable more than fifty years later. This is especially remarkable since that influence extends to non-Marxists whose research is not concerned with political change but still focuses on the structured nature of social life. This section features three important examples of history from below: historical writing that tries to recover, articulate, and interpret the experience of people who are typically overlooked in studies of political elites and of major historical events.[ii] More socially-oriented than labour history and more attuned to human experience than economic history, descending in part from the people's history written by Michelet (see Part 4), history from below reveals and interprets the cultural expression of ordinary working people. It requires reading documents against the grain and examining materials that previously didn't count as "history." Yet the three examples of such historical writing that are featured in this section first appeared in genres of publication that represented the increasingly professional nature of historical writing. They therefore reveal the range of social and scholarly concerns that defined history from below: the preface to an 850-page study of English working-class culture between 1790 and 1830; a

---

i   The original contributing editors of *Past and Present*, all of whom signed the first editorial, were G. Barraclough, R. R. Betts, V. G. Childe, M. H. Dobb, C. Hill, R. H. Hilton, A. H. M. Jones, D. B. Quinn, J. Morris, and E. J. Hobsbawm. Several appear in Stephen Farthing's portrait, "Historians of *Past and Present*" (NPG 6518), reproduced on the cover of this book; see the Preface, note 1.
ii   The phrase entered into common parlance among historians after E. P. Thompson published "History from Below" in the *Times Literary Supplement,* 7 March 1966.

brief editorial statement written jointly by activists, workers, and scholars; and an academic journal article by a medical historian. Each of these represents research that has been fostered by the aims of this important group of historians. This section also features an influential objection to **ideological** scholarship, whose criticism reveals core values that determine the shape of its project. Once we clarify Marx's own view of society in the context of historical change (building on the Marxist sociology covered in Part 6), this introduction will show how and why the practice of history from below diverged, in productive and revealing ways, from the stylistic, methodological, and political convictions that were voiced so passionately in that resonant first issue of *Past and Present: A Journal of Scientific History*.

In the years leading to the European Revolutions of 1848, Karl Marx had argued that his historical theory reflected the social realities of the working classes with transparent clarity: it did not deduce its ideas from working people's experience nor did it use abstract principles to make sense of what workers do (see Part 6). Rather, Marx asserted, his theory of history simply described what workers already know through the primary importance of work in their lives, which is why Marxism promoted and assumed "the unity of theory and practice". For this reason, we can describe "the early Marx" as an idealist whose theory of history would provide a supportive rhetorical accompaniment to the natural progression of social consciousness, from its origins in feudalism to its enslavement by industrial capitalism to the triumph of communist revolution. However, following the comprehensive failure of the Revolutions of 1848 to raise popular support among property owners, merchants, the military, and even to unite the revolutionaries' own leaders, Marx reconsidered the role he assigned to historical theory in the drama of social revolution: "the later Marx" now believed that his theory, which he called **historical materialism**, should inform, incite, and empower workers towards realizing their communist destiny. One century later, in the wake of the Second World War, the original editors of *Past and Present* were inspired by Marx's notion that historical writing ought to reflect the lives and experiences of working people, and therefore could raise awareness of oppressive economic systems. They were particularly impressed by Marx's focus on the material basis of historical change—each probably would have agreed that it is not possible to understand social history apart from economic structures.

Historical materialism occupies a central place in the conceptual context through which social history was then (and still is) written.[iii] So it may be worthwhile to focus on Marx briefly. Writing in 1857, but looking back to 1848, Marx described historical materialism as a mode of understanding that emerges from a pattern of social evolution:

> In the social production which men carry on they enter into definite relations that are indispensable and independent of their will; these relations of production correspond to a definite stage of development of their material powers of production.

Since it is economic systems that structure society by grouping everyone into classes that reflect their roles in the material production of goods, this theory does not allow for individual identity or for individual will. Workers, whose hands are closer to the production of material goods than those who employ them, therefore constitute the most vital class in the economic structure. However, according to the structure of industrial capitalism, workers have been

---

iii   See, for instance, the emphasis on and then criticism of Marxist approaches to social history in A. J. Reid, *United We Stand: A History of Britain's Trade Unions* (London: Penguin, 2004).

estranged from their labour and have become enslaved by their dependence on wages. Their social consciousness reflects those economic structures that maintain their position in the working class. Economic systems do not only govern our access to the material goods that we need to survive, but they also provide a firm basis for all legal, political, cultural, and even religious institutions—this is why they sustain the class system. In a powerful and famous phrase, Marx declared that

> It is not the consciousness of men that determines their existence, but, on the contrary, their social existence determines their consciousness.[iv]

Through its formation of social classes and stifling of expressive creativity, capitalism blinds us from imagining life beyond the economic structure of its class-based society. Marx argued that, eventually, workers will realize that their special proximity to "the material forces of production" gives them the unique power to revolt effectively against their enslavement. Their turn against "the existing relations of production" therefore constitutes social as well as economic revolution. This theory sounds much like an attempt to impose a narrative structure on history—committing the same kind of "poetic fallacy" that White will find in Spengler's cyclical theory of human civilization (see Parts 7, 10). But for Marxist historians writing in the mid-twentieth century, historical materialism provided an analytic tool rather than an explanatory framework. It elicited a sophisticated, two-part project.

First, Marxist historians would use their scholarly abilities to trace and explain the material basis of social change, using the widest range of research methods available (even from other academic disciplines). Since the material basis of social life touches all aspects of human life in every epoch, this historical work also would entail conducting research that crosses traditional historical boundaries defined by nation and period—in this respect, Marxist history influenced Braudel's notion of **total history** (see Part 7). Second, the task of Marxist historians was to advocate for social change by contributing to class consciousness through scholarship and discussion, recovering the substance of past experience that will inspire readers to envision an alternate social and economic reality. The first editor of *Past and Present* said that he wished for "a vast public of ordinary readers in their tens of thousands, thirsting to understand the past and to learn its lessons for the present".[v]

When the journal was founded and its first editorial was composed, the mix of Marxist and non-Marxist editors meant that this document was drafted and discussed line by line. The result is stylistically terse and conceptually diplomatic, for by asserting that the task of the journal was "to record and explain [the] transformations that society undergoes by its very nature", the editors adopted Marx's emphasis on social change, including the view that change arises from internal forces. But they did this without making any explicit reference to Marxist "modes of production"—leaving the specific causes of such changes open to discussion. Rejecting the abstractions and jargon that had been generated by sociological approaches to history (see Part 6), as well as "romantic" interpretations that refer only to subjective experience (see Part 4), the editors alluded to Bloch and Febvre's commitment to scholarship based

iv K. Marx, "Introduction," *A Contribution to the Critique of Political Economy* [1859]. trans. N. I. Stone (Chicago: Charles H. Kerr, 1904), 11–12. A variant translation appears in *The Marx-Engels Reader*, R. C. Tucker (ed.), 2nd edn (New York: Norton, 1978), 4.

v See Hill, Hilton, and Hobsbawm, "*Past and Present*: Origins and Early Years", *Past and Present* 100 (1983), 4.

on "example and fact" (see Part 5). The editors crowned their statement by speaking to their readers directly: "we believe that it is to history that the great majority of thinking men and women look for strength and understanding. It is to them that we address ourselves". All historians hope to provide a measure of understanding to those who read them. But Marxists took this wish further by making political empowerment and social consciousness a central aim of their historical work.

During the five years that E. P. Thompson spent writing *The Making of the English Working Class* (1963), he taught evening classes on local history to working people. Deeply impressed by their eagerness to learn about their own cultural and social history, this experience confirmed a critical view of historical materialism that Thompson had been formulating, but only in theoretical terms, since the mid-1950s.[vi] Thompson wrote his massive book to show that the gradual formation of class-consciousness is an intrinsic feature of human relationships, one that can only be explained through an appreciation of the actions, ideas, and expressions of working people over the long term. When we recall the impersonal determinism with which Marx linked economic structures to social consciousness, the very first sentences in Thompson's Preface sound refreshingly human: the making of class is "an active process, which owes as much to agency as to functioning. The working class . . . was present at its own making". For Marx, class was a social category created by purely economic forces, a production whose emergence he described in mechanistic terms that suggested individuals are prisoners or victims of their assignment to a particular class.[vii] Thompson picks up this crucial but weak point in Marx's theory of history by exploring the historically and socially dynamic nature of class—as it was expressed, creatively and intellectually, by the individual men who constituted that class.[viii] By showing the degree to which working people had actively and consciously defined their class values, which meant quoting from manuscript and other **primary sources** created by them, Thompson was not merely "rescuing [them] from the enormous condescension of posterity", for there was more to this than correcting his fellow historians. He was also pointing to a crucial tendency among Marxist historians to overlook "the traditions, value-systems, ideas, and institutional forms" that working people used to express themselves. For Thompson, **social history** required the study of creative cultural expression, interpreted through the context of economic relationships—doing so in cogent and accessible language that could appeal to readers beyond academia. Conceptually, methodologically, and stylistically, Thompson's powerful and pioneering example of history from

vi   See E. Thompson, "Socialist Humanism", *The New Reasoner* 1 (Summer 1957), 105–43.

vii In his Preface, Thompson defends Marx against the view "that class is a thing . . . the error vitiates much latter-day 'Marxist' writing". However, in an early essay Thompson indicated that this particular view of class "can be traced to several ambiguities in the thought of Marx". See his "Socialist Humanism", 132–3. Thompson's reluctance to challenge Marx explicitly probably reflects his eagerness to counter the growing popular association of philosophical Marxism with the evident brutality of Stalinism. Similarly, Thompson gestures to Marx's social history of the failed Paris Revolution of 1848, which also opens with the phrase "Men make their own history". This is surprising since later in this text Marx insults the French peasants by describing them as "a sackful of potatoes". See K. Marx, "The Eighteenth Brumaire of Louis Bonaparte", *The Marx-Engels Reader*, 595, 608.

viii For an insightful discussion of the ways through which Thompson's concept of labour and class exclude the history of women's work, and not only in the domestic sphere, see J. W. Scott, "Women in *The Making of the English Working Class*", *Gender and History* (Cambridge, MA: Harvard University Press, 1989), 68–90. For an orthodox Marxist critique of this aspect of Thompson's social analysis, see P. Anderson, *Arguments within English Marxism* (London: Verso, 1980), 26–9.

below signalled both its debts and its departures from Marxist orthodoxy.[ix] Importantly, by focusing on a specific period in English history (from the Gordon Riots in 1780 to the passage of the Reform Bill in 1832), Thompson's detailed study of working-class culture suggested that the grand Marxist vision of producing an integrated history of industrial society is simply not feasible. Still, Thompson's decision to join the editorial board of *Past and Present* in 1969 signalled the degree to which their founding principles invited the innovations that *The Making* brought to social history.

Before returning to the directions that subsequent generations of historians have taken history from below, it might be helpful to shift away from chronology for a moment to focus on Gertrude Himmelfarb's critical discussion of the relation between political ideology and historical scholarship. Writing in 1986, while America and the Soviet Union remained in a state of cold war, Himmelfarb voiced a concern that Marxist history had emerged from the pages of an obscure British journal to dominate the study and teaching of history on both sides of the Atlantic. What, she asked, are the implications and consequences of writing history under an ideological umbrella? Could Marxist historians be trusted to ask the kinds of questions that historical research truly requires? She cited powerful examples of the scholarly and indeed moral failure of Marxist historians to speak out during the years marked by "highly publicized purges and trials, the executions and mass imprisonments, the precipitous changes in the party line". For Himmelfarb, Marxist historians simply could not be serious scholars, because they harboured a primary obligation to incite political change, not to understand the past. Himmelfarb asked us to consider the extent to which social history's emergence from historical materialism binds its practitioners to Marxist ideology, and therefore to Communist policies. This is precisely the sort of question that postcolonial historians of British imperialism ask of cultural anthropologists (see Part 12), even though their philosophical orientation is markedly distinct from Himmelfarb's own belief in the social and political promise of rational self-interest.[x] To what extent, then, is her own historical project ideological?

Himmelfarb recognized that 1956 marked a turning-point in the lives and ideas of Marxist historians in Britain—most of whom abandoned the British Communist Party in disgust over revelations of Stalin's brutality and in protest over the ongoing Soviet invasion of Hungary. For the Marxist editors of *Past and Present*, leaving the Party meant abandoning Soviet loyalties while remaining faithful to elements of historical materialism. For these reasons, the events of 1956 established the crucial difference between a Marxist and a Communist. A founding editor of *Past and Present*, Eric Hobsbawm, described the time as "the political equivalent of a nervous breakdown" for himself and his Marxist colleagues.[xi] So when Himmelfarb argued that one cannot truly understand Thompson's *The Making of the English Working Class* without emphasizing "the Stalinist pieties" that he espoused in an earlier book of 1955, she overlooked Thompson's highly public attack on Soviet and Stalinist communism that he

ix   Dennis Dworkin has remarked that "Tawney once observed that all economic history after Marx was post-Marxist, meaning that historians followed in his footsteps, whether in support of or in opposition to his views. Similarly, socialist history in Britain in the late sixties and seventies may be regarded as post-Thompsonian and post-*The Making of the English Working Class*." See *Cultural Marxism in Postwar Britain: History, the New Left, and the Origins of Cultural Studies* (Durham, NC: Duke University Press, 1997), 182.

x   For discussion of the philosophical concepts expressed by Himmelfarb's approach to history, J. W. Scott, review of *The New History and the Old*, by G. Himmelfarb, *American Historical Review* 94 (June 1989), 699–700.

xi   E. Hobsbawm, "1956: Gareth Stedman Jones Interviews Eric Hobsbawm", *Marxism Today* (November 1986), 19. Quoted in D. Dworkin, *Cultural Marxism*, 46.

published in 1956.[xii] Thompson's criticism of Marx seems especially poignant when we consider the light he had cast on the cultural expressions of working people—it certainly challenges what Himmelfarb called "the Marxist model which relegates consciousness to the superstructure" while contradicting her more general objection, that "the historian committed to [Marxism] has to find it confirmed at every decisive 'moment' of history". Still, Himmelfarb's central objection to Marxist history is important for the questions it raises about history as a political practice. Non-Marxists, she observes, are not resistant to new insights because, unlike Marxists, they interpret historical evidence "on its own merits rather than by reference to some external theory or philosophy". This leads us to return to the concerns that Humboldt and Ranke raised over a century earlier (see Part 5): is it possible to interpret the past using values that do not refer, even implicitly, to an external theory or philosophy? To use Himmelfarb's own phrase, is it possible for historians to abandon "the burden of ideology", separating their political views from their views of history?

As we saw in the writings of Lord Acton, Ranke, and Butterfield, important problems arise when one argues that the historian should discuss the past on its own terms, since evaluating the merits of anything requires a set of values and sense of priorities. Can we empty those of all reference to society and therefore of politics? In another context, Himmelfarb clarifies her own theory of history, seeking to reach beyond ideology:

> Rationality is the precondition of freedom, of the free exercise of individual will. To the extent to which the political realm is more conducive to rational choice, compared with the social realm which is governed by material and economic concerns, it is in politics that the potentiality for freedom lies. This explains why social history tends to be more deterministic than political history, and why political history finds a natural ally in intellectual history.[xiii]

It would seem here that is not the historian's own ideological views that corrupt the writing of history, but rather the historical topic itself. For Himmelfarb, the history of politics is the history of people expressing their views as individuals, free of social, material, and economic pressures. Indeed, in her view politics renders the will of individuals so clearly that its study is

---

xii Thompson published his opposition to Soviet actions and revelations in *The Reasoner*, a journal addressing the British Communist Party. The final two clauses anticipate Thompson's interest in the cultural expression of working people; moreover, reading Thompson's argument, it is difficult to anticipate Himmelfarb's disagreement:

> The subordination of the moral and imaginative faculties to political and administrative authority is wrong: the elimination of moral criteria from political judgement is wrong: the fear of independent thought, the deliberate encouragement of anti-intellectual trends among the people is wrong; the mechanical personification of unconscious class forces, the belittling of the conscious process of intellectual and spiritual conflict, all this is wrong.

See "Through the Smoke of Budapest", *The Reasoner* 3 (November 1956), 3. Thompson frequently restated this view, most recently in a national-radio interview three months before his death: "I think that the orthodox, Stalinist-type Marxism is one of the most discreditable episodes in intellectual life altogether". The interview was aired on *Nightwaves*, BBC Radio 3, 20 May 1993; for an edited transcript, see R. Porter, "Interview with E. P. Thompson", *Socialist History* 6 (1994), 29–33.

xiii See G. Himmelfarb, "History with the Politics Left Out", *The New History and the Old* (revd edn) (Cambridge, MA: Harvard University Press, 1987), 50.

akin to the study of ideas—possibly the most abstract approach to history. In comparison, social history can only be understood as the history of people responding to determinist material forces. Therefore, history from below, with its roots in social realms whose material concerns arise from economic pressures, can never be an appropriate field of historical study. If it were, historians would have to allow for the existence of those forces that shape human will; for Himmelfarb this is undesirable, since the historical writing that would follow cannot feature the practice of freedom through the study of rational choice. Like the Marxists that Himmelfarb examines, she too suggests that when we choose our field of historical research, we express and promote our political ideology.

By 1976, *Past and Present* was one of the most respected historical journals in Europe, whose contributors largely adopted the specialist language and research principles required by academic institutions. To rejuvenate the spirit of animated public discussion on social history that the original editors of *Past and Present* had envisioned, a "history workshop" of students, teachers, local workers, and socialist historians, who had been meeting regularly since 1966, founded *History Workshop Journal*. Recognizing that the private lives of individuals also constitute social history, and indeed could inspire a wider democratization of history through shared resources and dialogue among students, workers, and professional scholars, the *Journal* sought to provide a "workshop" in printed form. Recent attention to the history of women's positions in social organizations, ranging from the nuclear family to the civil-rights movement, from women's roles in domestic life and in professional spheres, had found an eager and sympathetic forum at History Workshop meetings. Consequently, their first editorial agreed that "sex divisions and marriage, family, school, and home" comprise "the fundamental elements of social life". The new *Journal* also was among the first to welcome new developments in critical theories of historical writing. When the first issue of *History Workshop Journal* featured Jeffrey Weeks's article on homosexuality and its social, cultural, and scientific associations with disease, it was a truly groundbreaking effort to provide a historical understanding of homosexuality. This may have been the very first scholarly article on gay history to appear in a peer-reviewed journal.[xiv]

Although the articles featured in the journal's first issue represented historical research of professional quality, the journal widened history from below by writing not only about neglected social groups but also about crucial but neglected social topics, including the history of childhood, the family, education, popular culture, leisure, and crime. It also adopted clear language that was meant to appeal to working readers beyond the academy. Rather than envision their journal as a place for presenting the mere findings of historical research, the *Journal* was designed to engage readers in dialogue on historical topics expressed on its pages, announcing the times and places of meetings at which the material would be discussed. By providing space in each issue for readers to discuss Work in Progress and to point other researchers toward Archives and Sources that they have discovered, the editors sought to demonstrate the old Marxist view that history should become common property. By fostering collaboration among historians in this way, with a thematic emphasis on the material lives of neglected individuals, *History Workshop Journal* both published history from below and sought to inspire readers to pursue such historical work. These innovations took the original aims of *Past and Present* in new directions that were truly engaged with the very readers

xiv See E. D'Emilio, "Not a Simple Matter: Gay History and Gay Historians", *Journal of American History* 76 (1989), 435–42. I am grateful to Jeffrey Weeks for his recollections of this period.

whose histories it tried to recover: sometimes it involved new research methods, including oral, digital, photographic, and televisual sources—methods that probably hadn't been envisioned in 1952.[xv]

The great social historian Roy Porter never published his own research in *Past and Present* or in *History Workshop Journal*, but his amazingly prolific career involved the writing and editing of dozens of books under the obvious influence of history from below. Explaining his turn to medical history, after he had trained as a historian of natural science, Porter described the "three different bodies" that all historians must recognize:

> There's nature—the body natural; society—the body politic; and the inner body as well. All thinking and experience is an attempt to relate nature, society, and self.[xvi]

Porter never associated himself with any ideological theory or group: indeed, his social studies of medical culture developed his suspicions about guiding theories and political ideologies. Interestingly, he voiced this view through an historical argument: he found that "medical truth", which arose during the Enlightenment, was in fact "largely an ideological construct, a myth advanced by a medical profession that was itself not an age-old adamantine institution."[xvii] Explanatory frameworks suggest their own weakness through their dogmatic assumptions. But Porter cited Thompson as having prepared the way for his own attempt to pioneer a study of medicine from below, suggesting that "a people's history of suffering might restore to the history of medicine its human face." In a valuable interview with E. P. Thompson, both historians described "getting hold of documents and reading them upside down", to envision what silent but responsive people thought of what the more vocal and important said and did.[xviii] Examining the history of medical thought and medical treatment from the patient's point of view is not only a more humane approach to a crucial element of scientific and social history, Porter argued, but it also offers a useful entry-point to interpreting the social meaning of suffering and healing. Porter's training in the history of science and the history of ideas, as well as his restless impatience with explanatory frameworks, meant that he was never content with ideological approaches to history. But it was new trends in social history, originating in the "people's history" of the nineteenth century and finding new forums and readers through the twentieth, that led Porter to focus on neglected groups and neglected topics of particular contemporary importance.

In Roy Porter's hands, "history from below" had become a metaphor rather than a method—for the sick patients' experience comprises one half of the two viewpoints that are

xv   For important examples, see: G. Gordon, "Voices from Below: Doing People's History in Cardiff Docklands", *Writing History: Theory and Practice*, Stefan Berger et al. (eds) (London: Hodder Arnold, 2003), 299–320; P. Read, "Presenting Voices in Different Media: Print, Radio, and CD-ROM", *The Oral History Reader*, R. Perks and A. Thomson (eds) (London: Routledge, 1998), 414–20; M. Sturken, "The Image as Memorial: Personal Photographs in Cultural Memory", *The Familial Gaze*, M. Sturken (ed.) (Dartmouth: University Press of New England, 1999), 178–95; J. Keuhl, "History on Film: TV History", *History Workshop Journal* 1 (1976), 127–35.

xvi C. Wood, "Not Past His Sell-By Date: Christopher Wood Interviews Roy Porter", *The Times Higher Education Supplement: Textbook Guide* (30 November 2001), 2.

xvii R. Porter, "Introduction", *The Popularization of Medicine, 1650–1850*, R. Porter (ed.) (London: Routledge, 1992), 8.

xviii See R. Porter, "Interview with E. P. Thompson", 29–33. See note xii.

always required to write a social history of medicine. Since it was the patients who typically financed their more historically vocal counterparts (the physicians), their accounts hardly emerge "from below." But the phrase nicely illustrates a shift that social historians have long aspired to offer, drawing us away from the exclusive history of elite medical men and their honoured institutions towards the historical position of ailing patients and their physical, psychological, and inevitably social lives.

Chapter 34

The Editors

INTRODUCTION TO *PAST AND PRESENT*: INAUGURAL ISSUE

The Editors, "Introduction", *Past and Present*: inaugural issue. *Past and Present* 1 (1952), i–iv.

NEW HISTORICAL PERIODICALS TEND to disclaim controversial views about their subject. PAST AND PRESENT cannot do so. This journal has come into being, not so much because its founders think that there is room for more periodicals in which serious historical work in non-technical language may be published, but because there is room for concern about the state of historical research and discussion at present. The first issue is perhaps a suitable place for the editors to explain what the journal is trying to do. However, in future issues it will do it, in the tradition of the late Marc Bloch and his associate, Lucien Febvre, 'not by means of methodological articles and theoretical dissertations, but by example and fact.'

What kind of historical writing do we wish to encourage? The matter has been well put by the great Arab scholar Ibn Khaldun in the fourteenth century, a period which fortunately acquits him of twentieth-century parti-pris. 'History' he writes (Prolegomena 1, 56)

> is the record of human society, or world civilisation; of the changes that take place in the nature of that society . . .; of revolutions and uprisings by one set of people against another, with the resulting kingdoms and states with their various ranks; of the different activities and occupations of men, whether for gaining their livelihood or in various sciences and crafts; and in general, of all the transformations that society undergoes by its very nature.

Our main task, most of us would agree, is to record and explain these 'transformations that society undergoes by its very nature.' Such a study cannot but prompt some general conclusions, whether or not we call them 'laws of historical development' — though we shall be poor historians if we underrate their complexity. Men are active and conscious makers of history, not merely its passive victims and indices. Each form of human society, and each individual phase therein, has its own special laws of development. Consequently we believe that fashionable attempts to express history in terms of the much simpler changes in the natural sciences (for instance in terms of biological evolution, statistical growth-curves or invariant psychological mechanisms) oversimplify and falsify it. Nor can it be explained merely as a function of outside environment — for instance climate, geography, or, more fashionably, culture-contact. We distrust attempts to explain one phase of history in terms primarily applicable to another — for instance Roman economy in terms of modern capitalism or imperialism, thirteenth-century cathedral-building in terms of Keynesian economic policies, let alone the grosser anachronisms of journalists and political platform-speakers. One need not deny that such theories may throw some light on limited aspects of the subject; but they must be severely kept in their very modest place, and at present they are not.

The main danger of this oversimplification no longer comes, as it did in nineteenth-century, from the misapplication of narrowly mechanical views of the physical sciences, or of biological evolution. It comes rather from the vogue of certain ideas drawn from academic anthropology, sociology, psychology and economics, themselves sciences considerably less advanced than Victorian physics or biology, and much more directly charged with politics. The 'structural-functional approach, as developed in contemporary sociology' has been used, for example, to interpret French history since 1789. The work of economic statisticians and econometricians is recommended to us as the foundation for a new positivism entirely concerned with 'determinismes historiques.' 'Status systems' and 'psychological maladjustments' are used to interpret nations. The economic history of the past century and a half is divided into periods of 'empirical,' 'informed,' and 'cognitive entrepreneurship,' following a fashion to which an entire transatlantic research centre has now been dedicated. Whatever the merits of such ideas and methods — and some are no doubt stimulating, — they are unable to deal with any but the simplest forms of historical change. They are indeed misleading precisely because they hide behind a much greater degree of technical sophistication than Buckle or Comte possessed.

All these methods, however, share the belief that history may be rationally studied, and some of them, though over-simple, have in their time made important contributions to historical understanding. Moreover, it is important to observe, this rationalism is the preserve of no creed or party. The present generation, however, has seen the recrudesence of certain schools of thought, descended directly or indirectly from the anti-rational *Weltanschauung* [ideology] of early nineteenth-century Romanticism, which deny the very possibility of a rational and scientific approach to history. Such views we find difficult to share. That does not mean, of course, that we deny the existence or the influence of irrational forces in the making of the past, nor that we suppose that the past is susceptible of explanation by means of a simple chain of causality. We are as aware as any other historians of the immense force of prejudice and passion in all their manifestations, religious, social and political; we do not deny the impact of the unique, the accidental or the fortuitous, and we are prepared, with the great historian and founder of the modern school of art-history, Max Dvorak, to consider the process of historical change not as the tracing of a single unbroken line of development, but rather as a complex development establishing at every stage new conditions of creative activity and releasing at all stages new shoots from which new developments unfold. But these considerations, we believe, do not invalidate the scientific approach and the application of the scientific technique which nineteenth-century historical scholarship built up to our lasting advantage. We have no sympathy with superficial rationalisations; by the same token we have no sympathy with those for whom the irrational or the providential is the only thing of consequence in their conception of the past. The view of H. A. L. Fisher that history is merely one damned thing after another is, in our belief, unwarrantable. We dissent from it even when presented, by Benedetto Croce and his disciples, in the more sophisticated dress of philosophical idealism. To believe with these writers and others that the pattern we find in the past is merely the subjective one we put into it from the present, is, in effect, to deny that it can be scientific in any real sense. It is no more true, and certainly a great deal more dangerous, than the old view, long since outmoded, that it is possible for the historian — and, indeed, is his sole legitimate function — to establish by a laborious accumulation of 'fact,' a photographically exact reconstruction of an 'objective' past. Neither of these extremes, we believe, reflects accurately the possibilities of history and the functions of the historian. We believe that the methods of reason and science are at least as applicable to history as to geology, palaeontology, ecology or meteorology, though the process of change among humans is immensely more complex. Like these disciplines, history cannot logically separate the study of the past from the present and the future, for it deals with objective phenomena, which do not stop changing when we stop observing them.

Lastly, we agree with Polybius (XII, 25b) that

> the property of history is, first, to ascertain what was actually said (or done) and, second, to discover the causes of success or failure. The facts by themselves may be interesting, but hardly useful. It is the study of causes which makes history fruitful.

> When our minds transfer to present occasions similar conditions from the past, we acquire a basis for estimating the future . . . and are helped to face coming events with confidence.

We should perhaps to-day rely, not on discovering past parallels, but on understanding how change took place in the past; but we share the belief of Polybius in the value of history for the present, and in particular his conception of historical discipline as an instrument enabling us 'to face coming events with confidence.' In a generation which, as Friedrich Meinecke demonstrated, has history in its marrow, and for which an historical mode of thought is second nature, we believe that it is to history that the great majority of thinking men and women look for strength and understanding. It is to them that we address ourselves.

Within these general limits there is plenty of room for difference and disagreement. The Board, and contributors to PAST AND PRESENT study different periods and aspects of history, inherit different preconceptions, and hold differing views. The Editorial Board therefore takes no responsibility for the views of contributors, nor does it seek to impose its own on them, where it is united, nor to exclude contributions which are at odds with some or all its members. We shall, of course, apply certain technical criteria. Articles which merely bring the results of a piece of detailed research whose interest is narrowly restricted will not normally be published; nor, on the other hand, those which deal with wider historical problems without a firm foundation of scholarly research. We shall of course encourage contributions on historical questions which seem to us to be important — but with the object of discovering rather than of confirming the answers. We shall make a consistent attempt to widen the somewhat narrow horizon of traditional historical studies among the English-speaking public. The serious student in the mid-twentieth-century can no longer rest content in ignorance of the history and the historical thought of the greater part of the world. PAST AND PRESENT therefore will make special efforts to bring to non-specialist readers knowledge of Indian, Chinese, Arab, African or Latin-American history, and to make available the work of historians writing in unfamiliar languages, aided by advisers and collaborators from France, China, Italy, India, Czechoslovakia and many other countries.

PAST AND PRESENT will appear, for the time being, twice a year. It will publish articles, review articles and shorter communications on topics of interest to historians — whether specialists or not.

THE EDITORS.

Chapter 35

E. P. Thompson

PREFACE TO *THE MAKING OF THE ENGLISH WORKING CLASS*

E. P. Thompson (1924–1993), "Preface", *The Making of the English Working Class*, 1963 (Harmondsworth: Penguin, 1980), 9–13.

THIS BOOK HAS A CLUMSY TITLE, but it is one which meets its purpose. *Making*, because it is a study in an active process, which owes as much to agency as to conditioning. The working class did not rise like the sun at an appointed time. It was present at its own making.

Class, rather than classes, for reasons which it is one purpose of this book to examine. There is, of course, a difference. 'Working classes' is a descriptive term, which evades as much as it defines. It ties loosely together a bundle of discrete phenomena. There were tailors here and weavers there, and together they make up the working classes.

By class I understand a historical phenomenon, unifying a number of disparate and seemingly unconnected events, both in the raw material of experience and in consciousness. I emphasize that it is a *historical* phenomenon. I do not see class as a 'structure', nor even as a 'category', but as something which in fact happens (and can be shown to have happened) in human relationships.

More than this, the notion of class entails the notion of historical relationship. Like any other relationship, it is a fluency which evades analysis if we attempt to stop it dead at any given moment and anatomize its structure. The finestmeshed sociological net cannot give us a pure specimen of class, any more than it can give us one of deference or of love. The relationship must always be embodied in real people and in a real context. Moreover, we cannot have two distinct classes, each with an independent being, and then bring them *into* relationship with each other. We cannot have love without lovers, nor deference without squires and labourers. And class happens when some men, as a result of common experiences (inherited or shared), feel and articulate the identity of their interests as between themselves, and as against other men whose interests are different from (and usually opposed to) theirs. The class experience is largely determined by the productive relations into which men are born – or enter involuntarily. Class-consciousness is the way in which these experiences are handled in cultural terms: embodied in traditions, value-systems, ideas, and institutional forms. If the experience appears as determined, class-consciousness does not. We can see a *logic* in the responses of similar occupational groups undergoing similar experiences, but we cannot predicate any *law*. Consciousness of class arises in the same way. in different times and places, but never in just the same way.

There is today an ever-present temptation to suppose that class is a thing. This was not Marx's meaning, in his own historical writing, yet the error vitiates much latter-day 'Marxist' writing. 'It', the working class, is assumed to have a real existence, which can be defined almost mathematically — so many men who stand in a certain relation to the means of production. Once this is assumed it becomes possible to deduce the class-consciousness which 'it' ought to have (but seldom does have) if 'it' was properly aware of its own position and real interests. There is a cultural superstructure, through which this recognition dawns in inefficient ways. These cultural 'lags' and distortions are a nuisance, so that it is easy to pass from this to some theory of substitution: the party, sect, or theorist, who disclose class-consciousness, not as it is, but as it ought to be.

But a similar error is committed daily on the other side of the ideological divide. In one form, this is a plain negative. Since the crude notion of class attributed to Marx can be faulted without difficulty, it is assumed that any notion of class is a pejorative theoretical construct, imposed upon the evidence. It is denied that class has happened at all. In another form, and by a curious inversion, it is possible to pass from a dynamic to a static view of class. 'It' – the working class – exists, and can be defined with some accuracy as a component of the social structure. Class-consciousness, however, is a bad thing, invented by displaced intellectuals, since everything which disturbs the harmonious coexistence of groups performing different 'social rôles' (and which thereby retards economic growth) is to be deplored as an 'unjustified disturbance-symptom'.[1] The problem is to determine how best 'it' can be conditioned to accept its social rôle, and how its grievances may best be 'handled and channelled'.

If we remember that class is a relationship, and not a thing, we cannot think in this way. 'It' does not exist, either to have an ideal interest or consciousness, or to lie as a patient on the Adjustor's table. Nor can we turn matters upon their heads, as has been done by one authority who (in a study of class obsessively concerned with methodology, to the exclusion of the examination of a single real class situation in a real historical context) has informed us:

> Classes are based on the differences in legitimate power associated with certain positions, i.e. on the structure of social rôles with respect to their authority expectations. . . . An individual becomes a member of a class by playing a social rôle relevant from the point of view of authority. . . . He belongs to a class because he occupies a position in a social organization; i.e. class membership is derived from the incumbency of a social rôle.[2]

The question, of course, is how the individual got to be in this 'social rôle', and how the particular social organization (with its property-rights and structure of authority) got to be there. And these are historical questions. If we stop history at a given point, then there are no classes but simply a multitude of individuals with a multitude of experiences. But if we watch these men over an adequate period of social change, we observe patterns in their relationships, their ideas, and their institutions. Class is defined by men as they live their own history, and, in the end, this is its only definition.

If I have shown insufficient understanding of the methodological preoccupations of certain sociologists, nevertheless I hope this book will be seen as a contribution to the understanding of class. For I am convinced that we cannot understand class unless we see it as a social and cultural formation, arising from processes which can only be studied as they work themselves out over a considerable historical period. In the years between 1780 and 1832 most English working people came to feel an identity of interests as between themselves, and as against their rulers and employers. This ruling class was itself much divided, and in fact only gained in cohesion over the same years because certain antagonisms were resolved (or faded into relative insignificance) in the face of an insurgent working class. Thus the working-class presence was, in 1832, the most significant factor in British political life.

The book is written in this way. In Part One I consider the continuing popular traditions in the eighteenth century which influenced the crucial Jacobin agitation of the 1790s. In Part Two I move from subjective to objective influences—the experiences of groups of workers during the Industrial Revolution which seem to me to be of especial significance. I also attempt an estimate of the character of the new industrial work-discipline, and the bearing upon this of the Methodist Church. In Part Three I pick up the story of plebeian Radicalism, and carry it through Luddism to the heroic age at the close of the Napoleonic Wars. Finally, I discuss some aspects of political theory and of the consciousness of class in the 1820s and 1830s.

This is a group of studies, on related themes, rather than a consecutive narrative. In selecting these themes I have been conscious, at times, of writing against the weight of prevailing orthodoxies. There is the Fabian orthodoxy, in which the great majority of working people are seen as passive victims of *laissez faire*, with the exception of a handful of far-sighted organizers (notably, Francis Place). There is the orthodoxy of the empirical economic historians, in which working people are seen as a labour force, as migrants, or as the data for statistical series. There is the 'Pilgrim's Progress' orthodoxy, in which the period is ransacked for forerunners-pioneers of the Welfare State, progenitors of a Socialist Commonwealth, or (more recently) early examplars of rational industrial relations. Each of these orthodoxies has a certain validity. All have added to our knowledge. My quarrel with the first and second is that they tend to obscure the agency of working people, the degree to which they contributed by conscious efforts, to the making of history. My quarrel with the third is that it reads history in the light of subsequent preoccupations, and not as in fact it occurred. Only the successful (in the sense of those whose aspirations anticipated subsequent evolution) are remembered. The blind alleys, the lost causes, and the losers themselves are forgotten.

I am seeking to rescue the poor stockinger, the Luddite cropper, the 'obsolete' hand-loom weaver, the 'utopian' artisan, and even the deluded follower of Joanna Southcott, from the enormous condescension of posterity. Their crafts and traditions may have been dying. Their hostility to the new industrialism may have been backward-looking. Their communitarian ideals may have been fantasies. Their insurectionary conspiracies may have been foolhardy. But they lived through these times of acute social disturbance, and we did not. Their aspirations were valid in terms of their own experience; and, if they were casualties of history, they remain, condemned in their own lives, as casualties.

Our only criterion of judgement should not be whether or not a man's actions are justified in the light of subsequent evolution. After all, we are not at the end of social evolution ourselves. In some of the lost causes of the people of the Industrial Revolution we may discover insights into social evils which we have yet to cure. Moreover, the greater part of the world today is still undergoing problems of industrialization, and of the formation of democratic institutions, analogous in many ways to our own experience during the Industrial Revolution. Causes which were lost in England might, in Asia or Africa, yet be won.

Finally, a note of apology to Scottish and Welsh readers. I have neglected these histories, not out of chauvinism, but out of respect. It is because class is a cultural as much as an economic formation that I have been cautious as to generalizing beyond English experience. (I have considered the Irish, not in Ireland, but as immigrants to England.) The Scottish record, in particular, is quite as dramatic, and as tormented, as our own. The Scottish Jacobin agitation was more intense and more heroic. But the Scottish story is significantly different. Calvinism was not the same thing as Methodism, although it is difficult to say which, in the early nineteenth century, was worse. We had no peasantry in England comparable to the Highland migrants. And the popular culture was very different. It is possible, at least until the 1820s, to regard the English and Scottish experiences as distinct, since trade union and political links were impermanent and immature.

This book was written in Yorkshire, and is coloured at times by West Riding sources. My grateful acknowledgements are due to the University of Leeds and to Professor S. G. Raybould for enabling me, some years ago, to commence the research which led to this book; and to the Leverhulme Trustees for the award of a Research Fellowship, which has enabled me to complete the work. I have also learned a great deal from members of my tutorial classes, with whom I have discussed many of the themes treated here. Acknowledgements are due also to the authorities who have allowed me to quote from manuscript and copyright sources: particular acknowledgements will be found at the end of the first edition.

I have also to thank many others. Mr Christopher Hill, Professor Asa Briggs, and Mr John Saville criticized parts of the book in draft, although they are in no sense responsible for my judgements. Mr R. W. Harris showed great editorial patience, when the book burst the bounds of a series for which it was first commissioned. Mr Perry Anderson, Mr Denis Butt, Mr Richard Cobb, Mr Henry Collins, Mr Derrick Crossley, Mr Tim Enright, Dr E. P. Hennock, Mr Rex Russell, Dr John Rex, Dr E. Sigsworth, and Mr H. O. E. Swift, have helped me at different points. I have also to thank Mrs Dorothy Thompson, an historian to whom I am related by the accident of marriage. Each chapter has been discussed with her, and I have been well placed to borrow not only her ideas but material from her notebooks. Her collaboration is to be found, not in this or that particular, but in the way the whole problem is seen.

Halifax, [West Yorkshire] *August 1963*

Notes

1   An example of this approach, covering the period of this book, is to be found in the work of a colleague of Professor Talcott Parsons: N. J. Smelser, *Social Change in the Industrial Revolution* (1959).
2   R. Dahrendorf, *Class and Class Conflict in Industrial Society* (1959), pp. 148–9.

Chapter 36

Gertrude Himmelfarb

THE "GROUP": BRITISH
MARXIST HISTORIANS

Gertrude Himmelfarb, "The 'Group': British Marxist Historians", 1986, *New History and the Old: Critical Essays and Reappraisals* (revd edn) (Cambridge, MA: Harvard University Press, 2004), 70–74, 80–93.

"WHY WAS THERE no Marxism in Great Britain?" A recent issue of the *English Historical Review* poses yet again one of the perennial problems in English history.[1] Why, in the first country to meet all the conditions for a mass Marxist movement, was there no such movement? Why, in the country that gave birth to the industrial revolution, was there no social revolution? Why, in the first country to create a proletariat worthy of the name, was the very word "proletariat" alien and exotic? These questions have been the staple of historical inquiry at least since Elie Halévy early in the century tried to explain the "miracle of modern England": the ability of England, by virtue of its unique institutions and traditions, to accommodate change, conciliate interests, and mitigate conflict.[2]

There is another question, however, that has not often been asked. Why, in a country so resistant to Marxist socialism, have there been so many eminent Marxist historians? And not as mavericks but as members of a respectable and influential (although not, to be sure, dominant) school. And influential precisely in the field of English history, offering Marxist interpretations of a history that has been notably inhospitable to Marxism as a political ideology.

Part of the answer lies in a fascinating and little-known episode in English intellectual history. It is only recently that we have come to learn something of the origins of English Marxist historiography and to appreciate how well organized and consciously ideological it has been. The story of the "Communist Party Historians' Group" (or "collective," as it has also been called)[3] is all the more interesting because it comes from the principals themselves and their disciples—from memoirs, interviews, essays, and, most recently, a full-length book.

In 1983 one of the most influential historical journals in England opened its one-hundredth issue by recalling its founding in 1952: "The history of *Past and Present* begins in the years of the cold war with a group of young Marxist historians, at that time all members of the British Communist Party and enthusiastic participants in the activities of the 'C. P. Historians' Group' which flourished notably in the years 1946 to 1956." Those young historians were, in fact, old "friends and comrades":

> They thus had the quadruple bond of a common past (most had known each other since the late 1930s), a common political commitment, a passion for history, and regular, indeed intensive, contact at the meetings of the Historians' Group at which they debated the Marxist interpretation of historical problems and did their best, in the military jargon then favoured in Bolshevik circles, to 'wage the battle of ideas' on the 'front' most suitable to historians.[4]

This account comes to us with the authority of three distinguished historians who were founders both of the Communist Party Historians' Group and of *Past and Present*—Christopher Hill, R. H. Hilton, and E. J. Hobsbawm—and who are still active in the affairs of the journal. (Today Hill is president of the Past and Present Society, and Hilton and Hobsbawm are chairman and vice-chairman of the editorial board. The fourth founder of the journal and the oldest member of the Historians' Group, Maurice Dobb, died in 1976.)

A memoir by Hobsbawm, "The Historians' Group of the Communist Party," describes the organization that played "a major part in the development of Marxist historiography" and thus in "British historiography in general."[5] The Historians' Group, he reports, was one of many professional and cultural groups operating under the aegis of the National Cultural Committee of the party—"from the Party's point of view, the most flourishing and satisfactory" of them, attracting not only professional historians but also party leaders and union organizers.[6] The founding of *Past and Present* was only one episode in the "battle of ideas" (the "B of I," as it was familiarly known) that was the mission of the Group.[7] It also organized conferences and celebrated anniversaries (1848 was commemorated by a dramatized version of the *Communist Manifesto* in Albert Hall); arranged for translations (of Marx and Engels, Lenin and Stalin, and such latter-day Marxist luminaries as Gramsci); assigned historical projects to be carried out by individual members; and published, among other works, a four-volume collection of historical documents and a volume of essays, *Democracy and the Labour Movement*, that foreshadowed many of the themes now identified with Marxist history.

The Group included some of the best-known historians in Britain today: E. P. Thompson, Eric Hobsbawm, Christopher Hill, Rodney Hilton, George Rudé, Dorothy Thompson, Royden Harrison, John Saville, Victor Kiernan, George Thomson, Raphael Samuel. (Among those no longer alive, and remembered fondly and respectfully by the others, are Maurice Dobb and Dona Torr, whose membership in the party went back almost to its origin.) Hobsbawm comments on the curious fact that so many talented Communist intellectuals chose to become historians.[8] Just as curious is the fact that so many talented historians chose to be Communists—not only in the thirties, when the depression, the Spanish Civil War, and the rise of Nazism made Communism seem, to many intellectuals, the last hope of civilization, but after the war, when they found the Western democracies more menacing than the Soviet Union and Stalinism more congenial and sympathetic than capitalism.

In its early years, Hobsbawm recalls, the members of the Group "segregated themselves strictly from schismatics and heretics," even from Marxists and Marxist sympathizers who had no party credentials.[9] With the advent of the Popular Front in 1951, they became less sectarian. (The founding of *Past and Present* reflected this turn in the party line.) In 1956, after Khrushchev's speech to the Twentieth Congress denouncing Stalin, and the Soviet invasion of Hungary later that year, many historians left the party. They retained their personal associations, however, as well as their commitment to Marxism—unlike their confreres in France, Hobsbawm observes, where the break from the party generally resulted in a disaffection with Marxism. Hobsbawm himself has remained in the party, and the Historians' Group continues to this day.

During the whole of that time (including the period described by Hobsbawm as the "Stalin-Zhdanov-Lysenko years" of "ultra-rigid Stalinism"),[10] the members of the Group saw no conflict between their roles as historians and as Communists.

> Our work as historians was therefore embedded in our work as Marxists, which we believed to imply membership of the Communist Party. It was inseparable from our political commitment and activity . . . We were as loyal, active and committed a group of Communists as any, if only because we felt that Marxism implied membership of the Party. To criticize Marxism was to criticize the Party, and the other way round.[11]

Indeed, their loyalty to both Marxism and the party was such that even Hobsbawm, in retrospect, finds them excessively zealous. "There is no doubt that we ourselves were apt to fall into the stern and wooden style of the disciplined Bolshevik cadres, since we regarded ourselves as such." Thus their arguments on specific historical subjects such as the English Revolution were "sometimes designed *a posteriori* to confirm what we already knew to be necessarily 'correct'." If their work did not suffer more from the "contemporary dogmatism," he explains, it was because the authorized Marxist versions of history dealt with real problems and could be discussed seriously ("except where the political authority of the Bolshevik Party and similar matters were involved"); because there was no party line on most of British history and the work of Soviet historians was largely unknown to them;[12] because "our loyalty and militancy were not in any doubt prior to 1956" so that party officials were well disposed to them; and because a "certain old-fashioned realism" in the party made it possible to criticize and modify some of the orthodox doctrines.[13]

It was in this milieu that some of the distinctive theories of British Marxist history were first formulated: about the nature of feudalism and absolutism, the development of capitalism, the character of the English Civil War, the relation of science and Puritanism to capitalism, the effect of industrialism on the standard of living of the working classes, the nature and role of the "labor aristocracy." The Group also contributed to the new social history—history from below, the history of the common people—which became, as it were, a fellow traveler of Marxist history.

To a young American radical historian looking back on that time, it must seem a heroic age, when radical history had a coherent doctrine, a cohesive community, and a political purposiveness he might well envy. This is certainly the impression one gets from *The British Marxist Historians* by Harvey J. Kaye.[14] The five historians who are the subjects of this study, all members of the original Group, are meant to suggest the range and diversity of Marxist scholarship, their shared concerns and themes, and above all their commitment to a kind of history that is of "scholarly *and* political consequence."[15]

[. . .]

Eric Hobsbawm has been called the "premier" Marxist historian in England[16]—in part because of his continuing relationship with the Communist Party (he is still a member of the Historians' Group and on the editorial board of *Marxism Today*, the official organ of the party), in part because of his far-ranging scholarship and far-flung activities. He himself has attributed his political views and cosmopolitan interests to his personal history, which makes it all the more regrettable that he has given us so tantalizingly few details about that history.[17] We are told that his grandfather, a Russian Jew, emigrated to England in the 1870s, but not when or why his father and Austrian mother moved to Alexandria, where Hobsbawm was born in 1917. Two years later the family settled in Vienna; in 1931 Hobsbawm moved to Berlin and in 1933 to London. Having joined a Communist youth organization in Berlin, he associated himself with the party as a schoolboy in London, selling Communist Party pamphlets and improving his English (and his Marxism) by reading a popular book by Dobb, *On Marxism Today*. At the university he found himself in a congenial political atmosphere. "We were all Marxists as students at Cambridge," he later recalled;[18] and like many of them, he was an active member of the Communist Party. After serving in the education corps during the war, he returned to Cambridge to complete his studies, then took a position at the University of London where he remained until his retirement in 1982.

Hobsbawm's main area of research is nineteenth-century English labor history. Impatient with institutional history, he has devoted himself to such subjects as the effect of the Industrial Revolution on the standard of living of workers, the relationship between the working classes and Methodism, and the nature of the "labor aristocracy." In each case he has brought new empirical evidence to bear on the conventional Marxist view, or has given orthodox Marxism a somewhat different reading. Thus where Marx, and Lenin even more, attributed the "reformism" of the English labor movement to the strength of the labor aristocracy, Hobsbawm emphasized the role of the labor aristocracy in the organization and radicalization of the labor movement.[19] His theses are still the subject of controversy among Marxist as well as non-Marxist historians, but they have reinvigorated some well-worn topics and have given Marxism itself a new lease on life.

Hobsbawm also opened up new frontiers for Marxism with the concept of "primitive rebels," a term that he takes to comprise "social bandits" of the Robin Hood type, "secret societies" like the Mafia, peasant millenarian movements, urban mobs, and religious labor sects.[20] To the orthodox Marxist, the continued existence of these primitive or "archaic" groups is an anomaly. Hobsbawm, by giving them the status of rebels and bringing them together as a "social movement," has legitimized them and made them part of the Marxist schema. Instead of being aberrations, even counter revolutionary deviations, they are represented as the "adaptation of popular agitations to a modern capitalist economy"—"prepolitical" movements, which do not themselves aspire to political power but do promote a "political consciousness" that has made this century "the most revolutionary in history."[21] It is this work that has endeared Hobsbawm to a generation of radical historians committed to "history from below," the history of the "anonymous masses," who are seen as leading lives of quiet (sometimes not so quiet) desperation and who express their alienation and rebellion by means of criminality and other forms of "social deviancy." Many of these historians are attracted by the nonpolitical (at least not overtly political) nature of this rebellion. For a leading American Marxist historian, however, the great achievement of Hobsbawm is that he has kept faith with the political mission of Marxism. "To be 'Hobsbawmian' means to be Marxist," Eugene Genovese has said—that is, to make the "politics of class struggle" central to history, and to make "historical materialism" central to Marxism.[22]

Hobsbawm himself, describing *Primitive Rebels* as "a political as well as a historical" work, has explained the conjunction of circumstances that first brought this subject to his attention in the 1950s: his extensive acquaintance with Italian Communists who were familiar with the Mafia; his reading of Antonio Gramsci, a founder of the Italian Communist Party, who made much of this kind of "nonpolitical protest movement"; an invitation to speak on the European precedents for the Mau Mau uprisings in Kenya; and the Twentieth Congress of the Communist Party in 1956, which inspired a reevaluation of the role of the party and the "bases of revolutionary activity." All of these events, Hobsbawm says, are reflected in the implicit message of the book, that a "strongly organized party" is necessary, although there is no "one railroad" leading to the desired goal.[23]

The reference to 1956 prompts Hobsbawm to observe that the chief effect of that momentous year was to "set us free to do more history, because before '56 we'd spent an enormous amount of our time on political activity."[24] Yet he himself has continued to be politically active, both within the British Communist Party and abroad (in Latin America as well as Europe)—which makes it all the more remarkable that he has been so productive as a historian, a journalist, even (under the pseudonym of Francis Newton) a commentator on jazz.[25]

The best known and, in America at any rate, the most influential of this group is E. P. Thompson. The youngest of them (he was born in 1924), he had joined the party and barely begun his studies at Cambridge when he was called into service. The war itself was more traumatic for him than for the others, his older brother (who had also been a Communist at Cambridge) having been executed by the Nazis while fighting with the Bulgarian partisans. Thompson himself was an officer during the war and afterward spent some months as a railroad construction worker in Yugoslavia and Bulgaria. Returning to Cambridge to complete his degree, he met and married another historian who was also a Communist—indeed, a more active member of the Historians' Group than he. As an extramural lecturer at the University of Leeds, he devoted half his time, by his own estimate, to political activities; his chief responsibility, as a member of the Yorkshire district committee of the Communist Party, was to organize opposition to the Korean War. In 1956 he emerged as one of the leading "dissident Communists," a founder of the *New Reasoner* and of its more influential successor, the *New Left Review*. He was forced off the board of the *Review* in 1962 when it came under the control of the faction led by Perry Anderson and Tom Nairn. At Warwick University in the sixties, he became involved in the radical causes that convulsed that highly politicized university; he later resigned to devote himself to scholarship and politics.

In retrospect it may appear that even in his years as a loyal party member, Thompson displayed "deviationist" tendencies. Yet this may be more a matter of style than substance, the expression of a literary and poetic sensibility (he had originally intended to be a poet) that distinguished him from the more prosaic historians in the Group. It is no accident (as a Marxist might say) that his first book was a biography of William Morris, who had the double virtue of being a poet and a Marxist. Thompson himself claims to see in this book a "muffled 'revisionism'."[26] When it was published, however, in 1955, it was entirely consistent with the party line. As far back as 1934, even before the turn to the Popular Front, the party had tried to appropriate Morris as its spiritual and political ancestor by redeeming him from the "myth" of romantic medievalism and establishing him as an indigenous Marxist Communist.[27] In 1976, shortly before the appearance of the second edition of his biography, Thompson commented on the "Morris/Marx argument" that still looms so large in his thinking. "To defend the tradition of Morris (as I still do) entailed unqualified resistance to Stalinism. But it did *not* entail opposition to Marxism; rather, it entailed rehabilitating lost categories and a lost vocabulary in the Marxist tradition."[28]

In fact there is nothing in the first edition of that book to suggest any "resistance to Stalinism." Indeed, the deletions made in the second edition highlight what Thompson himself calls the "Stalinist pieties" of the earlier edition:[29] the endorsement of the cliché "All roads lead to Communism";[30] the posthumous induction of Morris into the Communist Party ("Were Morris alive today, he would not look far to find the party of his choice");[31] the assurance that Morris' utopian vision of "A Factory as It Might Be" had already been realized in the Soviet Union ("Today visitors return from the Soviet Union with stories of the poet's dream already fulfilled");[32] the long quotation from Stalin that supposedly confirmed Morris' views by providing a "blue-print of the advance to Communism";[33] the suggestion that Morris envisaged "the 'party of a new type' of Lenin—a party of militant *cadres* educated in Socialist theory, the vanguard of the working class, the spearhead 'which is to pierce the armour of Capitalism'."[34] Yet even the Morris of the revised edition, shorn of these "Stalinist pieties," is still a staunch Marxist revolutionary, committed to "scientific Socialism" and repelled by Fabianism, reformism, and "semi-demi-Socialism."[35] (The revised edition was also shorn of some of the philistinism characteristic of Morris in his militant socialist period: "Poetry is tommy-rot," and "Modern tragedy including Shakespeare, is not fit to be put upon the modern stage.")[36]

In his account of Thompson, Kaye inexplicably omits any discussion of the book on Morris. Yet without it one cannot truly understand Thompson's most celebrated work, *The Making of the English Working Class.* Published in 1963, it is still the most influential book produced by any member of the Group. Kaye echoes the opinion of many radical historians when he says that it is probably "the most important work of social history written since the Second World War."[37] If its tone owes much to Morris, its thesis is more boldly Marxist than anything proposed by previous generations of radical and socialist historians. For it maintains that by 1832, even before the rise of Chartism, England had witnessed the emergence of a single "working class" (in contrast to the "working classes" of common usage)—a class that was fully developed, fully conscious of its class identity and class interests, consciously committed to the class struggle, politically organized to carry out that struggle, and ideologically receptive to an alternative economic and social system. There was no actual revolution in England, the argument goes, only because the counterrevolutionary forces succeeded in repressing or suppressing it. But the revolution was a latent historical reality, even if it was only intermittently manifest.

Put so baldly, the thesis is all too easily disputed. But Thompson does not put it so baldly; indeed, it is not the thesis itself that has made the book so influential. What has caught the imagination of a younger generation of radical historians is the passionate tone of the book, the variety of sources, and the latitude given to the crucial concepts. Thus the "working class" is taken to include "the Sunderland sailor, the Irish navvy, the Jewish costermonger, the inmate of an East Anglian village workhouse, the compositor on *The Times*"[38]—and many others who, by social status or occupation, would not normally be consigned to a single "working class." Similarly, expressions of working-class consciousness are found in William Blake's poems as well as in folk ballads; the class struggle is deduced from abortive uprisings, sporadic rickburnings, Irish nationalist conspiracies, and clandestine plots; political organization is attributed to Luddite machine-breakers, secret societies, and trade unions; and a revolutionary alternative to capitalism is seen in any hostility to industrialism, any nostalgia for an old "moral economy" or yearning for a new moral order. In this long, eloquent, richly documented work, these anomalies and contradictions have the perverse effect of appearing to validate a thesis that seems all the more persuasive precisely because it can contain all those anomalies and contradictions. What finally unites these disparate elements is the moral passion of the author, his overt, personal commitment to the working class as he conceives it and to the revolutionary cause with which he identifies it. A sentence from his preface has been so often quoted that it has become the rallying cry of the cause: "I am seeking to rescue the poor stockinger, the Luddite cropper, the 'obsolete' hand-loomer, the 'utopian' artisan, and even the deluded follower of Joanna Southcott, from the enormous condescension of posterity."[39]

More than any other part of his thesis, it is the concept of class consciousness that has attracted a host of disciples and emulators. All of the historians in this group (with the exception of Dobb) have departed, to one degree or another, from the more rigorous classic

Marxist model, which relegates consciousness to the superstructure and which sees the superstructure as derived from and determined by the mode of production and class relations reflecting that mode. But none of the others has made consciousness so integral a part of the concept of class—while at the same time insisting upon the material base of consciousness itself and the materialistic nature of the historical process. And none has been so polemical in defending this version of Marxism against both the conventional historian who finds it excessively materialistic and deterministic, and the Athusserian or Leninist Marxist who finds it excessively empirical and moralistic.

Thompson's great appeal is to the currently fashionable "humanistic" Marxism, the Marxism (or "neo-Marxism," as is sometimes said) supposedly deriving from the young, or early, Marx. Yet Thompson himself, while sometimes referring to the early Marx, does not make much of him, perhaps suspecting that the real young Marx was not quite what he has been made out to be. Instead, Thompson claims to be recovering a "lost vocabulary" in the Marxist tradition, a vocabulary that in Marx himself "was partly a silence—unarticulated assumptions and unrealized mediations."[40] One wonders what Marx would have made of Thompson's vocabulary or of his intention to "rescue" the "deluded follower" of Joanna Southcott, the religious mystic and millenarian who inveighed against the "Whore of Babylon" and prophesied an apocalypse of destruction and salvation. In one of the most memorable sections of the book Thompson describes the "psychic processes of counter-revolution," the "chiliasm of despair" and "psychic blackmail" that characterized this period of "emotional disequilibrium."[41] Yet for all its psychoanalytic overtones, his account is only a more sophisticated version of the "opium of the masses" theme. So too his description of Methodism—the "psychic ordeal" by means of which "the character-structure of the rebellious pre-industrial labourer or artisan was violently recast into that of the submissive industrial worker"[42]—is a modish rendition of the familiar view of Puritanism as an instrument of capitalism.

Since *The Making* (as it is familiarly known to admirers), Thompson's historical research has taken him back into the eighteenth century, where he finds the "plebians" trying to restore an older "moral economy."[43] But more of his energies have gone into political activities, especially the nuclear disarmament movement, and into lengthy and heated polemics. In a hundred-page "Open Letter to Leszek Kolakowski" (complete with seventy-five footnotes), he berated the distinguished Polish philosopher for abandoning Marxism and Communism. And in a series of essays amounting to a good-sized volume, he charged Perry Anderson and the other English "acolytes" of Louis Althusser with a moral obtuseness and "intellectual agoraphobia" reminiscent of Stalinism.[44] To some readers these polemics, in their intensity and turgidity, may recall those of Marx and Engels against the "Holy Family" (the Bauer brothers) and the "Sainted Max" (Stirner). (*The Poverty of Theory*, the title of Thompson's volume, is obviously meant to evoke *The Poverty of Philosophy*, Marx's attack on Proudhon.) Thompson and Anderson have since been partially reconciled, brought together under the umbrella of nuclear disarmament. Anderson praises Thompson as "our finest socialist writer today," while Thompson, who now contributes to the *New Left Review*, calls Anderson a "comrade" and partially absolves him of the sin of Althusserianism.[45]

The controversy between Thompson and Anderson, both claiming to be Marxists, raises once more the old questions about Marxist history. What does it mean to be a Marxist historian? How "revisionist" can Marxist historians be—about the materialist conception of history, for example—and still remain Marxist? To what extent must Marxism be taken into account in understanding and evaluating their work? What, in short, is the relevance of their Marxism?

To address all of these questions adequately would require nothing less than a treatise on Marxism and historiography. But some of them have been implicitly, sometimes explicitly, answered by the Marxist historians themselves, who insist that their Marxism is indeed relevant, that they are not merely historians but Marxist historians. A non-Marxist, believing that every work of history must be evaluated on its own merits rather than by reference to some external theory or philosophy, may choose to disregard such assertions. Indeed, some of the most severe critiques of Marxist histories have been scrupulously empirical, analyzing specific facts and sources, assumptions and generalizations.[46] Some have gone so far as to disallow any consideration of Marxism, as if that would be improper and invidious, rather like an ad hominem argument.

[. . .]

The idea that it is invidious to consider the "substantive philosophy" of a Marxist historian is itself invidious, for it refuses to take seriously what the Marxist historian takes most seriously. Does it really do justice to the historian to ignore the theories and phil-osophy he himself invokes in support of his thesis? (Each of these historians has quoted, sometimes copiously, from Marx, Engels, Lenin, and, in their earlier works, Stalin.) One of the happy by-products of the recently published memoirs is to release us from the conven-tion that holds it improper to allude to these historians as Marxists. If they find Marxism so central to their work, if they think it important to identify themselves as Marxists, surely we can do no less.

There is one other subject that can be explored more candidly, now that the Marxist historians have taken the lead in doing so. That is the intimate (dialectical, a Marxist would say) relationship between history and politics—between writing about the past and acting in the present. Whatever differences Thompson has with Anderson, it is not likely that he would dispute Anderson's comment that each of Thompson's historical works is "a militant intervention in the present, as well as a professional recovery of the past."[47] Nor would he or any of the other Marxist historians take issue with the editors of *Visions of History* (a volume of interviews with Thompson, Hobsbawm, and other radical historians), who commend these historians for the way "their politics inform their practice as historians" and for their commitment to Marx's dictum that the task is "not only to interpret the world but to change it."[48] Marxist history, it would appear, is a continuation of politics by other means.[i]

It is this idea of history more than anything else—more than any specific ideas about class and class struggle, consciousness and culture, mode of production and social relations—that is the common denominator of Marxist history. Marxist historians can be revisionist about almost everything else in the Marxist canon, but they cannot separate politics from history. They cannot abandon, or even hold in abeyance, their political agenda of changing the world while engaged in the historical task of interpreting it.

The Marxist would say, and quite rightly, that all historians reflect in their work a political bias of some sort, that the ideas, interests, and experiences of the historian inevit-ably intrude upon the writing of history, that the very process of selecting sources, present-ing facts, and writing a coherent account necessarily presumes some conception of reality, some order of values, that precludes objectivity. He might also go on to say that the Marxist, in being candid about his bias (unlike the "bourgeois" historian who would conceal it, possibly even be ignorant of it), is giving the reader the opportunity to judge it and make allowance for it. But this is to shift the burden of responsibility from the writer to the reader. The issue is not whether the reader can make the proper discriminations and judgments (he

---

i   Himmelfarb's allusion is to Karl von Clausewitz, "War is nothing but a continuation of politics by other means" (*On War*, 1832–4). [-Ed.]

is generally not in a position to do so), but whether the historian has done so—whether he has made an effort to control and correct his bias, to look for the evidence that might confute his thesis, and, no less important, to construct a thesis capable of confutation. The Marxist, on the other hand, is so assured of the truth of his thesis—its political as well as historical truth—that the temptation, as Hobsbawm says, is to invoke arguments "designed *a posteriori* to confirm what we already knew to be necessarily 'correct'."[49] By the same token (Hobsbawm elsewhere admits) the Marxist is inclined to avoid arguments and facts that he knows to be true lest they undermine the orthodox doctrine or divert him from his polemical task.[50]

The Marxist theory of history, moreover, is so comprehensive—its great appeal is that it makes sense not of this or that part of history but of the whole of history—that the historian committed to it has to find it confirmed at every decisive "moment" of history. Any significant exception would be a denial of the whole, since the theory itself is a whole. Where the "eclectic" or "empirical" historian (pejorative words in the Marxist vocabulary) tries to understand each subject in whatever terms seem appropriate to it, finding evidence of a class struggle in one event but not in another, giving priority to economics in one period and to religion in another, the Marxist historian is bound by a predetermined schema that applies to all periods and events. That schema may be modified, qualified, "revised," but in some basic sense it has to be retained if Marxism itself is to be a meaningful part of his enterprise—and to be meaningful for the present as well as the past, for politics as well as history. It is a formidable burden that the Marxist historian carries.

In addition to the burden of ideology, the Marxist is saddled with the burden—the incubus, some would come to think of it—of party. The editors of the interviews explain that one of their questions could be put only to the older generation of historians: "How did the political repression of the cold war era affect you and your work?"[51] But they did not think to put the corollary question: "How did the intellectual repression of the Communist Party affect you and your work?" Hobsbawm himself has said that for "obvious reasons" they felt "very constrained about twentieth-century history" and shied away from writing about it. One reason he was a nineteenth-century historian, he confessed, was because one could not be an orthodox Communist and write about the period after the founding of the Communist Party. And he also explained that the Group had to abandon one project to which it had given much thought in 1952 and 1953—a history of the British labor movement—because the period since the founding of the British Communist Party "raised some notoriously tricky problems"; the book that was eventually published, in 1956, terminated in 1920, the year the party was founded.[52] (This inhibition seems to have affected *Past and Present* as well. A reviewer of the hundredth anniversary issue pointed out that in the thirty years since its founding there had been no "overt discussion of communism," and that the first article on Stalin appeared only in 1979.)[53]

If admirers of the Group are reluctant to confront the question of what loyalty to the Communist Party entails by way of discipline and conformity, they are even more loath to confront the question of what loyalty to the Soviet Union entails—which is, after all, the sine qua non of membership in the party. Kaye carefully notes the dates when each of the historians joined the party and when most of them left it. But apart from passing references to the events of 1956 [the Soviet invasion of Hungary] that led to the break, there is little or no discussion of what was happening in the world or in the Soviet Union during the period of their membership. Dobb was a party member for more than half a century, from the early twenties until his death in 1976; Hobsbawm's membership covers a different half-century, from the early thirties to the present; Hill and Hilton were members for about twenty years, and Thompson for about fifteen. A good deal of history is contained within those dates.

In his memoir Hobsbawm observes that "it was among the historians that the dissatisfaction with the Party's reactions to the Khrushchev speech at the Twentieth Congress of the CPSU first came into the open."[54] This makes it all the more remarkable that the historians had to wait for Khrushchev to tell them what the informed public had long since known. Both as historians and as party members during the thirties and forties, they had more reason than most to be aware of the highly publicized purges and trials, the executions and mass imprisonments, the precipitous changes in the party line requiring comrades to be Bolsheviks one week and Popular Fronters another, pro-war and anti-Fascist one day and anti-war and pro-German the next. For almost two years while their country was at war with Germany, they had to defend the Hitler-Stalin pact. Asked in a recent interview how he felt about the pact, Hobsbawm replied, "Oh, like most people I was absolutely loyal to the Party line."[55]

That absolute loyalty persisted for a decade after the war. The heyday of the Historians' Group from 1946 to 1956, a period some of them still recall with much satisfaction, was also the era that Thompson calls "High Stalinism." It was a time when intellectuals, scientists, and artists, to say nothing of politicians and political dissidents, were the victims of systematic purges; when Lysenkoism was the official doctrine of state, and when not only Darwinism but other manifestations of "bourgeois science," such as the theory of relativity, were proscribed; when the apotheosis of Stalin took bizarre forms long before Khrushchev exposed the "personality cult"; when the trials in Hungary, Bulgaria, and Czechoslovakia recalled the Moscow trials of the thirties; and when the "Doctor's Plot" of 1952–1953 was accompanied by an anti-Semitic campaign in the course of which a hundred or more Jewish intellectuals were shot. These were, after all, historians, not naive scientists and artists, who lived through these events. As party members they tacitly sanctioned them, and even now, Hobsbawm says, they "look back without regret on their years in the Group."[56]

In describing the meeting of the Group after Khrushchev's speech, Hobsbawm remarks upon the special sense of responsibility felt by the historians qua historians: "The fact is that historians were inevitably forced to confront the situation not only as private persons and communist militants but, as it were, in their professional capacity, since the crucial issue of Stalin was literally one of history: what had happened and why it had been concealed." He quotes one member who protested that they had "stopped being historians" when they accepted the Soviet interpretation of current affairs, and that they "must become historians in respect of present too." In retrospect Hobsbawm endorses that judgment. "Historical analysis," he reflects, "was at the core of Marxist politics."[57]

Yet no member of the Group has undertaken that historical analysis. One can understand why Hobsbawm, who has chosen to remain in the party, has not done so. It is more difficult to understand the reticence of those historians who have left the party. "I commenced to reason," Thompson prefaces a volume of essays, "in my thirty-third year [1956, when he left the party], and despite my best efforts, I have never been able to shake the habit off."[58] But even now he seems reluctant to give his reason free rein lest it give comfort to the enemy. Although he has been more vigorous than the others in denouncing Stalinism, he has done so only in a polemical context. What he has not done is bring his considerable historical talent to bear upon such momentous subjects as the relationship between Stalinism and Leninism, or Leninism and Marxism, or Marxism and the "Libertarian Communism" he now professes. In his "Open Letter" to Kolakowski he prides himself on not following the "well-worn paths of apostasy," on not becoming a "Public Confessor and Renegade"[59]—as if it would be disreputable to write a scholarly work on twentieth-century Communism or even a candid memoir of his experiences in the party.

Kaye concludes his account of the British Marxist historians by reaffirming the intimate relationship between politics and history which is their guiding principle. In this respect, he says, they go beyond Marx—at least beyond the Marx who wrote that "the social revolution of the nineteenth century cannot draw its poetry from the past, but only from the future," that the revolution "must let the dead bury their dead."[60] More than Marx, they believe that the past is a "well of conclusions from which we draw in order to act," and that action itself requires a "historical education." "We must educate those for whom struggle is a determined necessity today with the historical experiences of those for whom struggle was a determined necessity yesterday."[61] The same lesson is drawn by the editors of *Visions of History*, who tell us that the radical historians "have much to teach us about the past and its bearing on the work of liberating the present."[62]

We still await that "historical education." It is thirty years since most of the members of the Group left the party. Yet there is no scholarly study of Marxism or Communism by the historians who were personally, actively committed to those ideologies. Nor has there been any serious reevaluation by them of the histories inspired by those doctrines—or, indeed, of the philosophy of history that posits an intimate relationship between "praxis" and theory, politics and history. This omission is all the more conspicuous in the light of developments in France, where eminent historians have confronted, seriously and candidly, both their experiences in the Communist Party and the implications of Marxist history.[63] For their English confreres, it would seem, Marxism is still a forbidden zone. "Here lie dragons . . ."

Notes

1   Ross McKibbin, "Why Was There No Marxism in Great Britain?" *English Historical Review*, April 1984.

2   Elie Halévy, *A History of the English People in the Nineteenth Century*, trans. E. I. Watkin and D. A. Barker (London, 1960), I, 387.

3   Christopher Hill, R. H. Hilton, and E. J. Hobsbawm, "Past and Present: Origins and Early Years," *Past and Present*, August 1983, p. 3; interview with E. P. Thompson, in *Visions of History*, ed. Henry Abelove et al. (Manchester, 1983), p. 22.

4   "Past and Present," p. 3.

5   It is fitting that this memoir should have been published in a Festschrift [book of essays published in dedication to a senior colleague] for A. L. Morton, one of the founders of the Group and (in 1978 when the volume was published) still the chairman. Morton had a special role in the founding, since one of the initial purposes of the Group was the revision of his *People's History of England*, a popular but embarrassingly unscholarly book. Published by the Left Book Club just before the war, it went through a dozen printings in England and as many translations and editions abroad. The Group was soon diverted into other tasks and never completed the revision.

6   Eric Hobsbawm, "The Historians' Group of the Communist Party," in *Rebels and Their Causes: Essays in Honor of A. L. Morton*, ed. Maurice Cornforth (London, 1978), pp. 21, 27.

7   Bill Schwarz, " 'The People' in History: The Communist Party Historians' Group, 1946–56," in *Making Histories*, ed. Richard Johnson et al. (Minneapolis, 1982), p. 46.

8   In fact, in the 1930s there was an equally prominent group of Communist scientists. Cambridge alone boasted J. D. Bernal, J. B. S. Haldane, Lancelot Hogben, Hyman Levy, and Joseph Needham. When the *Modern Quarterly*, the organ of the Communist Party, was founded in 1938, more than half of the editorial board were scientists.

9   Hobsbawm, "The Historians' Group," p. 23.

10 Ibid., pp. 30–31.

11 Ibid., p. 26.

12 Hobsbawm himself mentions Soviet historians who were translated and were known to the Group. Both Hill and Hilton were familiar with Soviet scholarship on their subjects and were much influenced by it.

13 Ibid., pp. 31–34.

14 Harvey J. Kaye, *The British Marxist Historians* (Cambridge, 1984). This nostalgia is also reflected, though to a lesser extent, in the essay by the young English historian Bill Schwarz, who looks back to

that earlier time when the Group had a "securely founded conception of the politics of intellectual work." Schwarz, " 'The People' in History," p. 44.

15   Kaye, *The British Marxist Historians*, p. x.

16   Eugene Genovese and Warren I. Susman, editorial statement in the first issue of *Marxist Perspectives*, Spring 1978, p. 9; James Cronin, "Creating a Marxist Historiography: The Contribution of Hobsbawm," *Radical History Review*, Winter 1978–79, p. 88

17   The main sources are the interview with Hobsbawm in Abelove et al., *Visions of History*, pp. 30–43; some comments in Hobsbawm, *Revolutionaries: Contemporary Essays* (New York, 1973), pp. 250–251; a profile by Pieter Keuneman written while Hobsbawm was an undergraduate at Cambridge and reprinted in *Culture, Ideology and Politics: Essays for Eric Hobsbawm*, ed. Raphael Samuel and Gareth Stedman Jones (London, 1982), pp. 366–368; and a few remarks in an interview with Miriam Gross in *Time and Tide*, Autumn 1985.

18   Hobsbawm, in Abelove et al., *Visions of History*, p. 30.

19   The key essays appear in Hobsbawm, *Labouring Men: Studies in the History of Labour* (London, 1964), and idem, *Workers: Worlds of Labor* (New York, 1984).

20   Hobsbawm, *Primitive Rebels: Studies in Archaic Forms of Social Movement in the Nineteenth and Twentieth Centuries* (Manchester, 1959), passim.

21   Ibid., pp. 2–3, 9.

22   Eugene D. Genovese, "The Politics of Class Struggle in the History of Society: An Appraisal of the Work of Eric Hobsbawm," in *The Power of the Past: Essays for Hobsbawm*, ed. Pat Thane et al. (Cambridge, 1984), p. 13.

23   Kaye, *The British Marxist Historians*, p. 146 (quoting letter by Hobsbawm); Hobsbawm, in Abelove et al., *Visions of History*, pp. 32–33.

24   Hobsbawm, in Abelove et al., *Visions of History*, p. 33.

25   Hobsbawm's major synthetic works are *The Age of Revolution: Europe, 1789–1848* (London, 1962); *Industry and Empire: An Economic History of Britain since 1750* (London, 1968); and *The Age of Capital, 1848–1875* (London, 1975).

26   E. P. Thompson, *William Morris: Romantic to Revolutionary*, 2nd ed. (New York, 1977), p. 810.

27   After World War II the struggle for Morris' soul was fought on the floor of the House of Commons in a heated exchange between Clement Attlee, leader of the Labour Party, and Willie Gallacher, Communist member of Parliament, each of whom claimed Morris for his party and ideology.

28   Thompson, in Abelove et al., *Visions of History*, p. 21.

29   Thompson, *William Morris*, p. 769.

30   Ibid., 1st ed. (London, 1955), p. 270.

31   Ibid., p. 795.

32   Ibid., p. 760.

33   Ibid.

34   Ibid., p. 485.

35   Ibid., 1st ed., p. 840; 2nd ed., p. 726.

36   Ibid., 1st ed., pp. 731, 881.

37   Kaye, *The British Marxist Historians*, [Cambridge, 1984] p. 173.

38   Thompson, *The Making of the English Working Class* (New York, 1964), p. 194. (The English edition was published in 1963).

39   Ibid., p. 12.

40   Thompson, in Abelove et al., *Visions of History*, p. 21.

41   Thompson, *Making of the English Working Class*, pp. 375, 381, 385.

42   Ibid., pp. 367–368.

43   Thompson, "The Moral Economy of the English Crowd in the Eighteenth Century," *Past and Present*, February 1971; idem, "Patrician Society, Plebeian Culture," *Journal of Social History*, Summer 1974.

44   Thompson, *The Poverty of Theory and Other Essays* (New York, 1978), pp. 4, 111.

45   Perry Anderson, *Arguments within English Marxism* (London, 1980), p. 1; Thompson, in Abelove et al., *Visions of History*, p. 17.

46   See, for example, the review by David Landes of Hobsbawm's *Age of Capital* in the *Times Literary Supplement*, June 4, 1976, pp. 662–664.

47   Anderson, *Arguments*, p. 2.

48   Abelove et al., *Visions of History*, pp. x–xi.

49   Hobsbawm, "The Historians' Group," p. 31.

50   In reconsidering his earlier essays on the labor aristocracy, Hobsbawm explains that he had

deliberately obscured his disagreements with the Leninist thesis "both because he was, for reasons which seemed good at the times of writing, reluctant to stress views which were then heterodox among Marxists, and because he preferred to engage in polemics against those who, on anti-Marxist grounds, denied the existence or analytical value of the concept of a labour aristocracy in nineteenth-century Britain" (*Workers*, p. 249n).

51   Abelove et al., *Visions of History*, p. x.

52   Hobsbawm, in Abelove et al., *Visions of History*, pp. 33–34; idem, "The Historians' Group," pp. 44, 29. Hobsbawm was obviously speaking of the Group's scholarly work. In journalistic articles and popular books some of its members did deal with more recent history. See, for example, Christopher Hill, *Lenin and the Russian Revolution* (London, 1947; rev. ed., 1971). Hobsbawm himself has recently published a scholarly essay, "The 'Moscow Line' and International Communist Policy, 1933–47," in *Warfare, Diplomacy and Politics: Essays in Honour of A. J. P. Taylor*, ed. Chris Wrigley (London, 1986). It is an oddly ambiguous essay, for while he claims to have exposed the "myth" that Communist parties were the "agents of Moscow," much of the evidence he cites seems to substantiate that myth.

53   J. P. Kenyon, "*Past and Present* No. 100," *Times Literary Supplement*, August 5, 1983.

54   Hobsbawm, "The Historians' Group," p. 26.

55   *Time and Tide*, Autumn 1985, p. 53.

56   Hobsbawm, "The Historians' Group," p. 42.

57   Ibid., p. 41.

58   Thompson, *Poverty of Theory*, p. i.

59   Ibid., p. 305.

60   Kaye, *The British Marxist Historians*, p. 248; Marx, *Eighteenth Brumaire*, in *Collected Works*, XI, 106.

61   Kaye, *The British Marxist Historians*, pp. 248–249.

62   Abelove et al., *Visions of History*, p. xi.

63   See, for example, Emmanuel Le Roy Ladurie, *Paris-Montpellier: P.C.-P.S.U. 1945–1963* (Paris, 1982); Natacha Dioujeva and François George, *Staline à Paris* (Paris, 1982); François Furet, "French Intellectuals: From Marxism to Structuralism" (1967), in Furet, *In the Workshop of History* (Chicago, 1984).

Chapter 37

Editorial Collective

INTRODUCTION TO *HISTORY WORKSHOP JOURNAL*: INAUGURAL ISSUE

Editorial Collective, "Introduction", *History Workshop Journal*: inaugural issue, *History Workshop Journal* 1 (1976), 1–3.

THIS JOURNAL COMES OUT of the History Workshops held at Ruskin College, Oxford, over the last ten years. Around these meetings the Workshop developed as a fluid coalition of worker-students (from Ruskin) and other socialist historians. Besides holding meetings it published a number of pamphlets (most of them now out of print); and a series of books based largely on its work have been prepared, of which the first was published in March 1967 and more will appear this year. By setting up this editorial collective to produce the journal we hope to share the work of the Workshop more widely, and to give it more regular and permanent expression. In undertaking it we are setting ourselves a long-term programme of work. Like the Workshops, like the pamphlets, like the books in the Workshop series, the journal will be concerned to bring the boundaries of history closer to people's lives. Like them, it will address itself to the fundamental elements of social life—work and material culture, class relations and politics, sex divisions and marriage, family, school and home. In the journal we shall continue to elaborate these themes, but in a more sustained way, and attempt to coordinate them within an overall view of capitalism as a historical phenomenon, both as a mode of production and as a system of social relations. Like the Workshops, the journal will have a strong grounding in working-class experience, but it will also speak from the start to the internationality of class experience, and will take up theoretical questions in history more explicitly.

We are concerned at the narrowing of the influence of history in our society, and at its progressive withdrawal from the battle of ideas. This shrinking of stature cannot be ascribed to a decline in popular interest. Throughout British society a desire for historical understanding continues to exist; and it is only sometimes fulfilled by the manufacturers of part series, popularizations, television entertainment, and so forth. 'Serious history' has become a subject reserved for the specialist. The restriction is comparatively recent. It can be attributed to the consolidation of the historical profession; to the increasing fragmentation of the subject, especially as it approaches more modern times; and to the narrowness of historians' preoccupations, along with the way that research is organized and shaped. Only academics can be historians, and they have their own territorial rights and pecking orders. The great bulk of historical writing is never intended to be read outside the ranks of the profession, and most is written only for the attention of specialist groups within it. Teaching and research are increasingly divided, and both divorced from wider or explicit social purposes. In the journal we shall try to restore a wider context for the study of history, both as a counter to the scholastic fragmentation of the subject, and with the aim of making it relevant to ordinary people.

The journal is dedicated to making history a more democratic activity and a more urgent concern. We believe that history is a source of inspiration and understanding, furnishing not only the means of interpreting the past but also the best critical vantage point from which to view the present. So we believe that history should become common property, capable of shaping people's understanding of themselves and the society in which they live. We recognize that an open and democratic scholarship requires more work from the historian, not less: a more complex understanding of historical process, more caution in handling the sources, more boldness in extending the boundaries of enquiry, a greater effort to achieve clarity of presentation. Instead of assuming the dutiful interest of the reader, we hope that it can be won by the urgency of what is being said and its relevance to the present. *Women in Nazi Germany*, for example, is a case study of the complex relationships and contradictions between state, ideology, and the sexual division of labour, questions of continuing importance for an understanding of every phase of capitalism, including today's; or again, the account of a peasant museum in Emilia poses a fundamental question about the relationship of dominant and subordinate cultures.

We want the journal to be *Workshop* in character as well as name, to present the workings of historical enquiry not just the results, and to encourage readers in practical criticism, warning them against the automatic acceptance of scholarly findings or text book readings. We hope to bring together working historians of whatever background or experience, and offer them solidarity and practical help, encouraging a collaborative approach to the problems of research. We would like the journal to be used, not just read, to be a place where difficulties are acknowledged, problems defined as well as solved, sources examined for their bias and limitations as well as for the help they may provide, and subjects opened up rather than closed. The content of much of the back part of the journal is workshop in character. In *Work in Progress* readers are invited to discuss their research. We intend contributions to *Archives and Sources* to be as much critical as bibliographical, and perhaps, like David Vaisey's article in this issue, to show how even a single source (in this case seventeenth century court depositions) can open up new subject matter. We hope that the workshop character of the journal will make it useful to those working at all levels of the educational system, by bringing the worlds of teaching and research closer together, by providing teaching materials and aids, and by taking up such themes as the sources of historical imagination (as here in *Children's Historical Novels*), the reconstruction of historical reality (as here in *History on Stage*), and the visual presentation of historical material whether through museum collections or illustrations or the media.

A central feature of the journal will be the publication of original texts and documents. Apart from their intrinsic value, these texts will provide a constant reminder of the kinds of evidence that the historian must answer to as well as build from. The catalogues and borrowings from workers' libraries, in Germany before 1914 and in 1870s inner London, are discussed in the present issue and an account of those of the South Wales miners will appear in the next. They provide fascinating evidence of the variety of influences—often contradictory—which go to make up historical consciousness, and contrast with the conventional geneaology of socialist ideas. Our main document in this issue and the next is the autobiography of Edward Rymer, the nineteenth century pit agitator, which we are reproducing as a facsimile of the pamphlet in which it originally appeared, with an introduction by R. G. Neville, who recently brought it to light. Unlike many working class memoirs, of the familiar 'Pit to Parliament' class, it is no success story: the author was as poor when he wrote it, old and with blindness impending, as he was in childhood. The view of class relations and of workers' lives therefore escapes that retrospective complacency which falsifies so much autobiography of the time.

The socialism of this journal, neither prophetic nor exclusive, and certainly not sectarian, will inform both the content and how it is presented: we want to be read by people outside the quarantine of formal education, as well as by those who chafe at its limitations and work to change it from within. That is why we shall stress clarity and accessibility in what we publish, both in texts and in footnotes. Our socialism determines our concern with the common people in the past, their life and work and thought and individuality, as well as the context and shaping causes of their class experience. Equally it determines the attention we shall pay to capitalism: we are publishing in this issue a contribution from Rodney Hilton on the transition between feudalism and capitalism in Europe, and in our next a major study of capitalism on the South African Rand. Our socialism will also demand the discussion and development of theoretical issues in history. It will make us attack vigorously those types of historical and sociological enquiries which reinforce the structures of power and inequality in our society, and will bring us into critical and constructive debate with bourgeois scholars. We have come together as editors because our various commitments to the cause of socialism lie at the root of our discontent with the present state of history, and at the root of our belief that a different kind of history is possible. We hope to interest and be useful to people who do not share our political commitments but have felt some of the same discontents; we would like the journal to be of service to the reform of history in polytechnics and colleges, and to the cause of history in the schools.

Democratic scholarship means a two-way relationship between writer and reader, and we hope that in the pages of this journal there will be collaboration and understanding between them. We would prefer an active readership not an armchair one, and we want the journal to be a point of contact, a place where experiences are shared, projects encouraged, theoretical issues broached. In particular we hope the journal will reach the many historians who work on their own, often in their spare time, without acknowledgement because they are outside institutions, and we hope that they in turn will write for us. Because this is our first issue there are no letters or contributions from readers. But we want people to write in, not only with critical responses to articles in the journal, but also to reach one another and discuss issues raised by their own work. Our columns (not only in the letter section but also in *Noticeboard* and *Calendar*) can be used to ask for information, to make contacts, to publicize meetings and publications. Far too much research which would be enriched by historical companionship is carried on in conditions of competitive individualism or lonely isolation; too many teachers have to fight an uphill fight unaided. This journal aims to be both critical and supportive, by offering solidarity to the working historian and by exploring the needs of the wider constituency which exists for historical work.

Editorial Collective

Chapter 38

Roy Porter

THE PATIENT'S VIEW: DOING MEDICAL HISTORY FROM BELOW

Roy Porter (1946–2002), "The Patient's View: Doing Medical History From Below", *Theory and Society* 14 (1985), 175–6, 181–7, 192–8.

MEDICINE TODAY is a supremely well-entrenched, prestigious profession, yoked to a body of relatively autonomous, self-directing science, expertise, and practices. It is hardly surprising, then, that it has tended to produce histories of itself essentially cast in the mold of its own current image, stories of successive breakthroughs in medical science, heroic pioneers of surgical techniques, of the supersession of ignorant folkloric remedies and barefaced charlatanry through the rise of medicine as a liberal, ethical, corporate profession. Even historians and historical sociologists who have taken more skeptical views of medicine's past, perhaps stressing its failures or underlining the self-serving features of professionalization, have nevertheless implicitly endorsed the view that the history of healing is par excellence the history of doctors.

But this physician-centered account of the rise of medicine may involve a major historical distortion. For it takes two to make a medical encounter – the sick person as well as the doctor; and for this reason, one might contend that medical history ought centrally to be about the two-way encounters between doctors and patients. Indeed, it often takes many more than two, because medical events have frequently been complex social rituals involving family and community as well as sufferers and physicians. Moreover, a great deal of healing in the past (as, of course, in the present) has involved professional practitioners only marginally, or not at all, and has been primarily a tale of medical self-help, or community care. In medicine's history, the initiatives have often come from, and power has frequently rested with, the sufferer, or with lay people in general, rather than with the individual physician or the medical profession at large.

Yet the sufferers' role in the history of healing – in both its social and cognitive dimensions – has been routinely ignored by scholars. In this article I shall suggest why this has been so, argue that it is undesirable that it should continue so, and suggest some methods and approaches toward developing an alternative history of medicine, largely written from

the patient's point of view. Rather more theoretical models of the historical stages and typical structures of patient-physician relations may in due course emerge and prove penetrating, but we should be cautious about formulating these prematurely. At present, we remain so profoundly ignorant of how ordinary people in the past have actually regarded health and sickness, and managed their encounters with medical men, that our initial priority should be to "defamiliarize" ourselves with the assumptions of modern physician-focused history and sociology of medicine, and hack our way into the empirical forests of the past in all their strangeness and diversity. [. . .]
[. . .]

Bringing sufferers back in: problems and prospects

Obviously, both traditional medical history and its agonistic double will continue. But we also need, as a counterweight, a patient-oriented history, or, to be precise, in the first instance a sick people's or sufferers' history (for the very word "patient" seems dangerously redolent of professional medical relations). In fact, sufferers' history – medical history from below – must be prior to the conventional "in house" accounts. Partly because – banal but incontestible – "no sufferers, no doctors"; but also because, in the past, managing and treating sickness remained very largely in the hands of the sufferers themselves and their circles, the intervention of doctors being only one weapon in the therapeutic arsenal. Your life was in your hands. I accept the point of Foucault and his school that the modern "patient" is in some sense a fabrication of the "medical gaze," a role scripted by the overall scenario of the medical system. But does this claim hold good for any but our heavily professionalized societies? We must beware of retrospectively imposing current sociological models onto the ways of the past.

Obviously, telling the story from the point of view of the sick is fraught with its own pitfalls too. We must avoid the temptation of turning the idylls of the sick into one long bellyache, a primal scream against the atrocities perpetrated by Nature and by social oppression; neither must we sentimentalize victimhood as if suffering were beautiful. No less must we avoid rendering it a Rousseauian version of pastoral, as if the "world we have lost" were some sort of macrobiotic Golden Age, the bloom of health in the paradise garden just before doctors invented pain and disease to make their cut. This is a mistake that some recent feminist history has occasionally made, Suzanne Arms asserting, for example, that before the invasion of male obstetricians, women gave birth "naturally, without pain."[1] Raphael Samuel has recently called for a new kind of "people's history" of the laboring classes that would be neither patronizing nor doctrinaire, neither Romantic nor hectoring.[2] Something like this should be possible for Everyman Sick.

It can't be done, critics might reply. You can only know about the sick through doctors' eyes, their case histories and hospital records; all else is mute prehistory. That is why we have admirable histories of epilepsy and hysteria,[3] but significantly none of epileptics or hysterics. Certainly little has been done, despite Douglas Guthrie's lament back in 1945 that the patient has been neglected.[4] What patient-oriented history there is comprises either collective and statistical profiles of the national health, or the anecdotal reportage of the famous – the "Boswell's Clap" genre,[5] admirably though this is often done. Sometimes what may promise to be sufferers' history proves a mirage, including much work of the French *Annales* historians. Take for example J.-P. Peter's "Disease and the Sick at the End of the Eighteenth Century."[6] Despite the promising title, there's actually little about the sick and certainly nothing from their own point of view; rather it is an account of the surveying ambitions of the Société Royale de Médecine. Vivid proof of how little has been done lies in the published Subject Catalogue of the Wellcome Institute for the History of Medicine in London. Under the heading "Patients," we find just two entries dealing with the whole of the eighteenth and nineteenth centuries.

Yet there is no reason why the history of the sick should prove any more intractable than the history of the laboring classes, of women, criminals, the illiterate, of *Outcast London*, or any other sort of history "from below."[7] In fact, it should be easier. For whereas underdogs such as paupers and criminals in previous centuries were often illiterate, or silenced, or were vocal only in ways leaving few traces in the archives, Pain has been evenhanded enough to visit the rich, educated, and visible scarcely less than the poor; and so the annals of sufferers are neither short nor simple (*vide* Pepys's 1017 entries). At least for the literate, the historian often encounters an embarrassment of riches—diaries, letters, journals, recipes, records of reading, even, occasionally, as in the case of Charles Darwin, a separate Medical Diary – all recording pain, self-examination, self-medication, regimen, and resignation.[8] On rare occasions we even have whole autobiographies of illness, as perhaps with Alice James's *Diary*,[9] or apologiae of the insane such as John Perceval's *Narrative*[10] (the mad, I note in passing, are among the few groups of sufferers to have attracted much interest, and that largely because of the polemics of today's anti-psychiatry movement). So if we cast our nets more widely, a rich haul of materials will tell us about the communal minds and hearts of the sick – proverbs, sayings, folklore, superstitions, remedies, traditional wisdom about diet, the calendar, omens, animals, natural pharmacy, the religious propitiations of *ex-votos*, pilgrimages, shrines, prayers, and so forth.[11]

And then there are fertile sources for history by inference. The visual arts, replete with symbols and myths, and written literature[12] from Medieval ballads up to *Cancer Ward*, provide mirrors and commentaries, often inverted or idealized, sometimes moralistic – catalogues of those stereotypes and methaphors of illness that Susan Sontag has so vociferously deplored.[13] Second, writings for the sick – advice handbooks and self-care manuals such as William Buchan's *Domestic Medicine*,[14] the agony columns of magazines, the breviaries of comfort and consolation, the keep-fit, stay-young-and-beautiful guides – all tell at least about sufferers' hopes and fears, even if we must be cautious before taking them as indices of what was done. And third, the testimony of the doctors themselves. Suitably interrogated, what the doctors recorded[15] can often be decoded to reveal what the sufferers dreaded or demanded, just as Le Roy Ladurie and Carlo Ginzburg have made heresy records eloquent about everyday life in medieval Montaillou or about the mind of a seventeenth-century Friulian miller.[16] In *Mystical Bedlam*, Michael MacDonald has made the consultation case histories of Richard Napier, the early seventeenth-century Buckinghamshire clergyman-physician, the medium for resurrecting the anxieties and tribulations of rural communities.[17]

[. . .]

How disturbance is perceived, and how disease is classified, makes all the difference. Take anthropological studies of East African tribes. These show that tribesmen commonly divide up afflictions into two classes, those "of God" and those "of man."[18] Those of God are natural, tolerable, part of the divine plan, and, for this reason, are to be treated with *natural* remedies, such as herbal wisdom; those of man are the result of witchcraft, and by contrast must be combatted with spiritual and magical medicine. Mutatis mutandis, these insights might illuminate distinctions between physical and spiritual, resignation and action in the European and North American past. But caution is needed, for much medical sociology has been practical and prescriptive. An honorable tradition, led by Michael Balint, awoke to patient dissatisfaction with the medical profession, the gripe that doctors were obtuse or authoritarian.[19] And in the light of present discontents, there is a great temptation in medical sociology either to turn the aloof physician into some timeless, transhistorical law of medical dominance, or to spin a myth of a fall from grace, from some age of the Edenic family doctor.[20] In either case, we must avoid making the past fit into the categories of the present.

As well as "backprojecting" – with caution! – from medical sociology and anthropology, we can learn from social historians in other fields exploring the view "from below." Not directly, for even historians of the family and of childhood have had surprisingly little to say about family and domestic medicine; but by deploying shared perspectives.[21] For long the history of education was the cavalcade of schools and parliamentary acts; the history of crime, a story of law and order, prisons, and police; the history of the poor, the Fabian chronicle of workhouses and reformers. Reacting against these, historians have become more sensitive to the myriad ways people in fact get themselves an education, largely through informal networks, from family and friends, by doing things for themselves; simi- larly historians nowadays argue that "crime" is a shorthand term of analysis, too often masking the clash of deviant and dominant groups, as a work such as E. P. Thompson's *Whigs and Hunters* demonstrates so well; or have shown that the poor have their own "moral economy." Sophisticated recent history from below avoids setting the underdogs apart as mere dumb animals, in Marx's classic evocation, "a sack of potatoes"; far from being passive victims ripe to be invaded and exploited, or cared for paternalistically, those below form communities engaging in complex negotiated exchanges with their betters, flexing their own muscles, much as in the Hegelian master-slave dialectic. Likewise with the sick. Their history mustn't barricade itself in a ghetto, as black studies and women's studies risk doing, perpetuating "separate spheres," mustn't volunteer to be simply a fringe or alternative his- tory of medicine. For it is precisely the dynamic interplay between sufferers and practitioners that requires study, the tug-of-war supply and demand, patient power and doctor power. By starting with the patient we can put medical history back on its feet.

Sufferers' history: a research agenda

Enough of fanfares and trumpets, however. What should the history of the sick actually be like? Although its real challenges lie in reconstructing patterns of consciousness and action, it needs first to root itself in the terra firma of the material conditions of communities in times past, the vital statistics of birth, copulation, and death, standards of living and bills of mortality, in short a biology of humans in history from the cradle to the grave – the sort of profile provided for the nineteenth century by F. B. Smith's *The People's Health*, and which forms the bread-and-butter of *Annales* history in works such as Goubert's *Malades et médecins en Bretagne*.[22] Though assembling such data will involve a degree of history by hindsight – for example, in gauging the distribution of medical personnel throughout a region, or the epidemiology of plagues and fevers – this should not matter, as we can be sure that sufferers themselves had their feet planted on the ground, inhaled the stench of the past, and were aware, however imperfectly, of the implications for health of dearth, vermin, and cold, and knew how many hours' ride away the nearest surgeon was. Due attention to such banausic ballast might help prevent the balloon of sufferers' history floating upwards into space, inflated with the too heady hot air of idealist structuralist anthropology.

Next we need, for our various classes and communities, basic mappings of experience, their belief systems, images and symbols: how did people reflect upon living and dying, the ages and stages of life; the body (was it holy or shameful?), and the functions and meanings of its various organs. How did they explain how and why the frail barque of health capsized into sickness? Were such explanations naturalistic or divine, descriptive or prescriptive? Faced with disease, were people fatalistic or combative? Precisely because they are so universal yet emotionally loaded, such categories as blood, head, guts, or heart could have immensely powerful resonances. For example, Foucault has averred that health and fitness became bourgeois shibboleths during the Englightenment, countering the aristocratic fetishism of blood.[23] Or, Edward Shorter has recently contended that Western distrust of the flesh, and particularly the supposed uncleanness of women, mirrored the physical torments and dangers of childbirth.[24] As childbirth grew safer, the old fear of women as polluting began to fade. Similarly, responses to filth have articulated complicated patterns of beliefs and prejudices. It has been suggested that attitudes toward dirt have undergone a long revolution: back in the late Middle Ages, cleanliness was urged first on essentially aesthetic grounds; then, and in particular in the Calvinist Dutch Republic, it literally became (in John Wesley's phrase) "next to godliness," a prophylactic against sin and sloth, the mark of the elect.[25] Only later did the association of cleanliness with health and hygiene become paramount. Recovering these obsolete thought-patterns may not just be a charming antiquarian exercise, but might make all the difference in explaining behavior. For instance, Lawrence Stone has postulated an inverse relationship between dirt and sexual activity.[26] As Europe cleaned up, fornicating became less of an ordeal, and people coupled more eagerly. The population explosion may owe much to soap.

Next, what happened when people fell ill? I suggest two probes to peer inside the sufferers. One is by monitoring how they experienced and expressed pain, which is very much still a virgin field of research. The language of pain – was it moral, physical, emotional, localized, behavioral? – reveals much about perceptions of selfhood and the hieratic organology of mind, body, heart, soul, nerves; and also about the meaning of maladies. Is pain seen as disease, or divine tribulation? Is it a cry for help, or a cross to be borne? Reference to the Bernsteinian account of elaborated and restricted codes of language can help tell us which complaints were thought natural, chronic or acute, the outriders of death, or earnests of the mysterious healing powers of nature.[27]

The other, obviously, is to fill in sufferers' characterizations and classifications of illnesses. Grasping how people have labelled sickness will illuminate their assumptions about cause, type, prognosis, and remedy. Are the terms used by particular individuals or groups popular or patrician, medical or vernacular, finely differentiated or crude, descriptive or causal, natural, Christian, or pagan, symptomatic or ontological? The paradox is that we almost certainly have a better grasp of the medical world of the Masai than of the Mancunians. Works such as Caplan, Engelhardt, and McCartney's *Concepts of Health and Disease*, and F. Kräupl Taylor's *The Concepts of Illness, Disease and Morbus*, have alerted us to the repertoire of disease characterizations within the *medical* fraternity.[28] It is odd, however, how deaf we have been to lay nosologies. Recent representations of lay perceptions of death, by Ariès, McManners, and others, may point the way ahead.[29]

[. . .]

Conclusion

It is time to draw the threads together. I have been arguing that we should lower the historical gaze onto the sufferers. "Banish money," wrote John Keats, "– banish sofas – Banish wine – Banish Music – But right Jack Health – Honest Jack Health, true Jack Health – banish Health and banish all the world."[30] Health is the backbone of social history, and affliction the *fons et origo* of all history of medicine. For whereas one could plausibly argue, a history of crime should start not with the criminals but with law and police – because these define criminality – the sick cannot possibly be regarded as a class apart, conjured up by the faculty. Moreover, it is especially important to get under the skin of the sufferers, because most maladies have not in fact been treated by the profession but by self- or community help, or in the paramedical marketplace where the sufferers' own initiatives, confidence, and pockets are critical. In addition, lay medical power has also been crucial in a sphere I haven't touched upon here, since I have been concentrating on the sufferer as an individual – in other words, lay-instigated social, civic, and institutional strategies for sickness, above all, in earlier times, for coping with epidemic pestilences such as plague. For what emerges, for example, from recent studies of civic health arrangements in the Italian Renaissance is that physicians regularly had to play second fiddle, in the teeth of various lay interests, to city fathers, philanthropic patrons, and, of course, the Church itself.[31]

Medicine has never enjoyed full monopoly or police powers, and most healing, like charity, begins at home. The upshot is that doctors traditionally had to remember that he who paid the piper called the tune. George Bernard Shaw was well aware of this:

> The doctor learns that if he gets a head of the superstitions of his patients he is a
> ruined man; and the result is that he instinctively takes care not to get ahead of
> them. That is why all the changes come from the laity.[32]

I do not intend to conclude by offering a set of theoretical models for understanding sick person-doctor interaction in times past. That would certainly be premature, and probably also counterproductive, by creating the illusion of patterns of typicality and uniformity. But I should like to tabulate certain strategies and broad interpretive guidelines for future investigations.

1. We need to question medical history's preoccupying concern with *cures* (even cures that don't work). It is modern medicine that is cure-fixated. Pharmaceutical intervention in the past, by contrast, paid great attention to pain control, to fortifying the body, to adjusting the whole constitution. And treatment went far beyond drug interventions, involving complex rituals of comfort and condolence, the consolations of philosophy and grit, acted out by the suffering, with the physician sometimes sharing in the psycho-dynamics of the bedside encounter.

2. We next need to become fully aware that our ancestors were at least as concerned with positive health, and with routine health maintenance, as with sickness, with prevention rather than merely therapeutics. We commit gross historical distortions if we fail to give due weight and attention to traditional medical interest in the weather, in diet, in exercise, in sleep – or, in other words, in the whole field of the "non-naturals."[33] We may tend to regard these strategies as ineffectual, faddish, and even quasi-magical attempts to cope with hostile environments or to placate the deities; yet such self-care regimes may well have had their own physical and psychological wisdom; and as historians we neglect at our peril the key roles played by health-maintenance in forming and sustaining conceptions of the self, of self-respect and autonomy, and (as encapsulated in the goal of "Mens sana in corpore sano") the good man.

3. For us nowadays most sickness experiences are merely troublesome nuisances, and, as Susan Sontag reminds us, only exceptional diseases – mainly fatal ones, like cancers – seem to possess meanings and mythologies that have ramifications for our overall interpretations of the human tragi-comedy.[34] It seems, however, that for people in the past, illness experiences were far more likely to be charged with life meanings, involving and transforming ideas of self, salvation, destiny, providence, reward, and punishment. Sickness and sin, health and holiness were intimately linked, and it is worth remembering that the constant proximity of sickness and death was probably a great sustainer of the religious experience.[35] Sickness cannot be seen in isolation; rather it is important to view responses to health and sickness as constitutive parts of whole cultural sets.

4. Nowadays we tend to think of sickness and the other great bodily events as quintessentially individual, private experiences. That would be a mistake for communities in the past. Until two or three centuries ago, for instance, giving birth was routinely a highly social ritual, involving the close and prolonged attendance on the mother of a supportive group of "gossips,"[36] and we should never underestimate the key role of the family in sickness care and therapeutics in ages before doctors and welfare organizations were common. This is borne out by the vast quantities of family health-care manuals that cascaded off the presses. But the story of family medicine remains curiously neglected.

5. We should stop seeing the doctor as the agent of primary care. People took care before they took physick. What we habitually call primary care is in fact secondary care, once the sufferer has become a patient, has entered the medical arena. And even under medical control, patients have by no means been so passive as the various "medicalization" theories of Foucault and Illich might lead us to believe. From their distinct points of view, Szasz's pleas for the autonomy of the afflicted, and Goffman's studies of the Brechtian survival strategies of the inmates of total institutions, offer a salutory counterbalance, a view of lay initiative, resilience, and capacity to play the system.[37]

Medicalization theory harbors another insidious assumption, the implication that the rise of medical power is in some sense ineluctable and unilinear, the ghost train speeding down the old Whiggish mainline from magic to medicine. But a people's history of health will show something much less monolithic. Here steps toward medical regulation, there the expropriation of lay healing, it is true; but it will also show that sufferers are fertile in their resources, and that feedback processes sometimes mean that medicalization boomerangs back on the faculty, as patients borrow the doctors' lines. Discussing the making of the working class, E. P. Thompson has warned us of over-rigid and mechanistic views of class relations, arguing that class is not a static fact or structure, but a fluid, dynamic process, forming and reforming all the time. The parallel with sufferers' relations with medicine is apt. A people's history of suffering might restore to the history of medicine its human face.[38]

Notes

1   For a critique of such sentimentalization, see E. Shorter, *A History of Women's Bodies* (New York, 1982).

2   R. Samuel, ed., *People's History and Socialist Theory* (London, 1981).

3   O. Temkin, *The Falling Sickness* (Baltimore, 1945); I. Veith, *Hysteria* (Chicago, 1965). This point is implicitly made in S. Gilman, *Seeing the Insane* (London, 1982).

4   D. Guthrie, "The Patient: A Neglected Factor in the History of Medicine," *Proceedings of the Royal Society of Medicine* 37 (1945): 490–94. What Guthrie was chiefly interested in, however, were histories of patients made famous by their doctors – e.g., the first person vaccinated by Jenner – thus perpetuating the concern with priorities set by traditional historiography. See also C. Mullett, "The Lay Outlook on Medicine in England, *circa* 1800–1850," *Bulletin of the History of Medicine* 25 (1951): 168–77.

5   W. B. Ober, *Boswell's Clap and Other Essays* (Carbondale, Ill., 1979).

6   J.-P. Peter, "Disease and the Sick at the End of the Eighteenth Century," in *Biology of Man in History*, ed. R. Forster and O. Ranum (Baltimore, 1975), 81–124.

7   For excellent debates on the nature of "history from below" and the crises of social history, see successive issues of *History Workshop Journal*; also *Theory and Society* 9 (1980): 667–81.

8   For lay people's medical diaries see J. Lane, "The Doctor Scolds Me: The Diaries and Correspondence of Patients in Eighteenth-Century England," in Porter, *Patients and Practitioners*, and J. Barry, "Piety and the Patient: Medicine and Religion in Eighteenth-Century Bristol," ibid.

9   L. Edel, ed., *The Diary of Alice James* (Harmondsworth, 1982).

10   G. Bateson, ed., *Perceval's Narrative* (New York, 1974); cf. D. Peterson, ed., *A Mad People's History of Madness* (Pittsburgh, 1982).

11   For proverbs see F. Loux, *Sagesses du corps* (Paris, 1978); J. Gelis, *Entrer dans la vie* (Paris, 1978).

12   N. Cousins, *The Physician in Literature* (New York, 1982); G. S. Rousseau, "Literature and Medicine: the State of the Field," *Isis* 72 (1981): 406–24.

13   S. Sontag, *Illness as Metaphor* (New York, 1978).

14   C. Lawrence, "William Buchan: Medicine Laid Open," *Medical History* 19 (1975): 20–36; C. Rosenberg, "Medical Text and Medical Context: Explaining William Buchan's *Domestic Medicine*," *Bulletin of the History of Medicine* 57 (1983): 22–42; G. Smith, "Prescribing the Rules of Health: Self Help and Advice in the Late Eighteenth Century," in Porter, *Patients and Practitioners*.

15   A revealing instance is K. Dewhurst, ed., *Willis's Oxford Casebook, 1650–52* (Oxford, 1981).

16   E. Le Roy Ladurie, *Montaillou* (London, 1979); C. Ginzburg, *The Cheese and the Worms* (London, 1980).

17   M. MacDonald, *Mystical Bedlam* (Cambridge, 1981).

[. . .]

18   T. Ranger, "Medical Science and Pentecost: The Dilemma of Anglicanism in Africa," in Sheils, *Church and Healing*, 333–66.

19   E. Balint and J. S. Norell, *Six Minutes for the Patient* (London, 1973); M. Balint, *The Doctor, the Patient and His Illness* (London, 1957).

20   R. Gibson, *The Family Doctor* (London, 1981).

21   Even an admirable work like K. Wrightson, *English Society, 1580–1680* (London, 1982), hardly discusses medicine except in the context of mortality.

22   F. B. Smith, *The People's Health* (London, 1979); L. Clarkson, *Death, Disease and Famine in Pre-Industrial England* (London, 1975); J. P. Goubert, *Malades et médecins en Bretagne, 1770–1790* (Rennes, 1974).

23   M. Foucault, *A History of Sexuality*, vol. 1, *Introduction* (London, 1978).

24   Shorter, *History of Women's Bodies*.

25   See S. Schama, "The Unruly Realm: Appetite and Restraint in Seventeenth-Century Holland," *Daedalus* 108 (1979): 103–23; G. Smith "Prescribing the Rules of Health: Self-Help and Advice in the Late Eighteenth Century," in Porter, *Patients and Practitioners*; N. Elias, *The Civilizing Process* (Oxford, 1983).

26   L. Stone, *The Family, Sex and Marriage in England, 1500–1800* (London, 1977).

27   K. Keele, *Anatomies of Pain* (Oxford, 1957).

28   A. L. Caplan, H. T. Engelhardt Jr., and J. J. MacCartney, eds., *Concepts of Health and Disease* (Reading, Mass., 1981); F. Kräupl Taylor, *The Concepts of Illness, Disease and Morbus* (Cambridge, 1979).

29   J. McManners, *Death and the Enlightenment* (Oxford, 1981); P. Ariès, *The Hour of Our Death* (London, 1981); C. Gittings, *Death, Burial and the Individual in Early Modern England* (London, 1984).

[. . .]

30   R. Gittings, ed., *Keats' Letters* (Oxford, 1979), 3.

31   R. Palmer, "The Church, Leprosy and Plague in Medieval and Early Modern Europe," in Sheils, *Church and Healing*, 79–100; A. W. Russell, ed., *The Town and State Physician in Europe from the Middle Ages to the Enlightenment* (Wolfenbüttel, 1981).

32   G. B. Shaw, *The Doctor's Dilemma* (Harmondsworth, 1979), 67–68.

33   L. J. Rather, "The Six Things Non-Natural: A Note on the Origins and Fate of a Doctrine and a Phrase," *Clio Medica* 3 (1968): 337–47.

34   S. Sontag, *Illness as Metaphor* (New York, 1978).

35   For some general perspectives see Sheils, *Church and Healing*.

36   Wilson, "Participant versus Patient."

37   E. Goffman, *Asylums* (Harmondsworth, 1968).

38   E. P. Thompson, "Eighteenth-Century English Society: Class Struggle without Class?" *Social History* 3 (1978): 133–65; idem, *Whigs and Hunters* (Harmondsworth, 1975); idem, *The Making of the English Working Class* (Harmondsworth, 1968).

Further Reading: Chapters 34 to 38

Adamson, Walter L. *Marx and the Disillusionment of Marxism* (Berkeley: University of California Press, 1985).

Berman, Morris. *Coming to our Senses: Body and Spirit in the Hidden History of the West* (New York: Simon and Schuster, 1989).

Bhattacharya, Sabyasachi. "History from Below", *Social Scientist* 11(4) (1983), 3–20.

Brieger, G. H. "The Historiography of Medicine". *Companion Encyclopedia of the History of Medicine*, W. F. Bynum and R. Porter (eds) (London: Routledge, 1993), 24–44.

Burke, Peter. *Popular Culture in Early Modern Europe* (Aldershot: Ashgate, 1994).

Cohen, G. A. *Karl Marx's Theory of History: A Defence* (Princeton: Princeton University Press, 1978).

Coleman, D. C. *History and the Economic Past. The Rise and Decline of Economic History in Britain* (Oxford: Clarendon, 1987).

Dworkin, Dennis. *Cultural Marxism in Postwar Britain: History, the New Left, and the Origins of Cultural Studies* (Durham, NC: Duke University Press, 1997).

Eley, G. "Marxist Historiography", *Writing History: Theory and Practice*, S. Berger et al. (eds) (London: Hodder Headline, 2003), 71–9.

Evans, Richard J. *In Defence of History*. 1997 (revd edn) (London: Granta, 2000).

Kaye, Harvey J. *The British Marxist Historians: An Introductory Analysis* (Cambridge: Polity Press, 1984).

Krantz, Frederick (ed.). *History from Below: Studies in Popular Protest and Popular Ideology* (Montreal: Concordia University, 1985; Oxford: Basil Blackwell, 1988).

Macfarlane, Alan, Sarah Harrison and Charles Jardine. *Reconstructing Historical Communities* (Cambridge: Cambridge University Press, 1977).

Nield, Keith. "A Symptomatic Dispute? Notes on the Relations Between Marxian Theory and Historical Practice in Britain", *Social Research* 47(3) (1980), 479–506.

Pokrovsky, M. N. "The Task of the Society of Marxist Historians". 1925. *Varieties of History*, F. Stern (ed.) (New York: Macmillan, 1956), 330–35.

Ravetz, Jerome and Richard S. Westfall. "Marxism and the History of Science", *Isis* 72(3) (1981), 393–405.

Samuel, Raphael. "British Marxist Historians: 1880–1980 (Part One)", *New Left Review* 120 (1980), 21–96.

Sharpe, Jim. "History from Below", *New Perspectives on Historical Writing*, Peter Burke (ed.). (2nd edn) (Cambridge: Polity Press, 2001), 25–42.

Thompson, E. P. "History from Below", *The Essential E. P. Thompson*, D. Thompson (ed.) (New York: New Press, 2001), 481–9.

Thompson, Paul. *The Voice of the Past: Oral History*. 1978. (3rd edn) (New York: Oxford University Press, 2000).

Williams, Raymond. "Base and Superstructure in Marxist Cultural Theory", *New Left Review* I(82) (1973), 3–16.

THOMPSON, EDWARD PALMER (1924–1993)

Anderson, Perry. *Arguments Within English Marxism* (London: Verso, 1980).

Best, Geoffrey. "Review: *The Making of the English Working Class*", *Historical Journal* 8(2) (1965), 271–81.

Blackburn, Robin. "Edward Thompson and the New Left", *New Left Review* 201 (1993), 3–9.

Chandavarkar, Rajnarayan. "The Making of the Working Class: E. P. Thompson and Indian History", *History Workshop Journal* 43 (1997), 177–96.

Colloni, Stefan. "Moralist at Work: E. P. Thompson Reappraised", *Times Literary Supplement*, 18 February 2005. <http://tls.timesonline.co.uk>.

Corfield, Penelope. "E. P. Thompson, the Historian: An Appreciation", *New Left Review* 201 (1993), 10–17.

Currie, R. and M. Hartwell. "The Making of the English Working Class?" *The Industrial Revolution and Economic Growth*, Ronald M. Hartwell (ed.) (London: Methuen, 1971), 361–76.

Hill, C. "Worker's Progress", *Times Literary Supplement*, 12 December 1963, 1021–3.

Himmelfarb, Gertrude. "A Tract of Secret History", *New Republic*, 11 April 1964, 24–6.

Hobsbawm, E. "Organised Orphans", *New Statesman* 66 (1963), 787–8.

Johnson, R. "Edward Thompson, Eugene Genovese, and Socialist-Humanist History", *History Workshop Journal* 6 (1978), 79–100.

Kaye, Harvey J. *The British Marxist Historians: An Introductory Analysis* (Cambridge: Polity Press, 1984).

— . and Keith McClelland (eds). *E. P. Thompson: Critical Perspectives* (Oxford: Polity, 1990).

Merill, M. "Interview with E. P. Thomspon", *Visions of History*, H. Abelove et al. (eds) (Manchester: Manchester University Press, 1976), 5–25.

New Left Review. "E. P. Thompson", Special Edition, 201 (1993), 3–25.

Palmer, Bryan D. *The Making of E.P. Thompson: Marxism, Humanism* (Toronto: New Hogtown Press, 1981).

— . *Objections and Oppositions: The Histories and Politics of E.P. Thompson* (London: Verso, 1994).

Rule, John and Robert Malcolmson (eds). *Protest and Survival: Essays for E.P. Thompson* (London: Merlin, 1993).

Scott, Joan W. "Women in the Making of the English Working Class", *Gender and the Politics of History* (New York: Columbia University Press, 1988), 68–92.

Stokes, Peter: "E. P. Thompson", *Twentieth-Century European Cultural Theorists*, Paul Hansom (ed.). (Detroit, MI: Thomson Gale, 2001), 338–44.

HIMMELFARB, GERTRUDE (b. 1922)

Elton, G. R. "Review: The New History and the Old", *The Historical Journal* 31(3) (1988), 761–4.

Himmelfarb, Gertrude. "AHR Forum: Some Reflections on the New History", *The American Historical Review* 94(3) (1989), 661–70.

— . "History." *Times Literary Supplement*, 10 November 2000. <http://tls.timesonline.co.uk>.

Scott, Joan W. "Review: The New History and the Old: Critical Essays and Reappraisals", *The American Historical Review* 94(3) (1989), 699–700.

PORTER, ROY (1946–2002)

Schaffer, Simon. "Obituary: Roy Sydney Porter", *Social Studies of Science* 32(3) (2002), 477–86.

PART 9

History from within: trauma and memory

INTRODUCTION

CONTRIBUTORS TO PREVIOUS SECTIONS have argued that there are specific obligations historians must fulfil to provide meaningful accounts of the past. Among these are Vico's insistence on understanding the past through its own concepts (in Part 2); Braudel's effort to think critically about **historical time**, so that we don't make the mistake of emphasizing the greatness of particular events at the expense of wider and more gradual cultural changes (in Part 7). These also include Bonnie Smith's stimulating questions about the private lives of historians, whose childhoods and intimate relationships shape the questions they ask, the research they conduct, and the reputations they assume (in Part 1). Comteian, Marxist, and later sociological approaches assert that without a sophisticated awareness of the ways individuals recognize themselves through allegiance to social groups, historians cannot understand the organizations that structure society (in Parts 6 and 8). These concerns have reverberated across disciplines and across genres of historical writing — from historical novels to historical films; from historical scholarship to the histories taught to children. Variations on these questions have helped to create a general understanding of divergent approaches to history even among those for whom academic history might seem irrelevant.

Apart from the public circulation of historical narratives, individuals always have harboured personal histories of themselves — even when their memories have not been told to others, let alone published and discussed. Is it private memory, public history, or a combination that shapes our sense of the past? And how does our answer to this question determine the obligations of those who research, interpret, and publish the facts of history? The authors in this section emphasize the urgency of personal memory as well as public history because, in times of peace as well as war, history does not merely inform us of the past: our sense of history justifies our attitudes and treatment of each other. If our moral conscience is created by our sense of who we are and what we have endured, then personal memory — "history from within" — will always touch us more deeply than the history we are taught.[i] This is why a rational emphasis on collecting facts might provide a reliable framework for building chronologies, but it would probably neglect, sometimes with violent consequences, the intimate meaning of history for those who survive it. This might lead us to wonder whether only individuals hold personal memories. Shared memories, even when we adopt them from those we love, create powerful social relationships. For example, if a friend or sibling has no personal experience of slavery, he or she can still share a collective memory of it through concern for someone who continues to suffer its psychological trauma or political legacy.[ii] Nations have always defined themselves in terms of a shared past, frequently when it is a past marked by trauma; this is one reason why nationalism and national **mythology** is defined and defended so aggressively. As these sources suggest, cultural and social memory is not a metaphor: it is a way we make sense of the past through our relationships.

In this section, we will consider the emotional, psychological, and therefore interior significance of history when it is publicized through a narrative of factual events and when it is formed through the intimate memory of personal experience. Historians have tended to view psychological notions of history with suspicion, partly because psychological insight requires a genuine regard for subjective experience, even when it misunderstands the past.[iii] In the approach known as **psychohistory**, which emerged in the late 1950s, historians wrote speculative biographies that presumed the private motives or experiences of historical figures—using sources of variable reliability. Advocates of psychohistory have not helped their case by insisting that resistance to their approach is merely evidence of historians' own fear of facing "the deepest madness of the human mind".[iv] It might be more useful to propose that by valuing memories of past events, historians can better appreciate the human dimensions of history—and that this does not require them to depend only on subjective material as historical evidence. Similarly, historians remain justifiably sceptical about the universal validity of Sigmund Freud's

i   Although sociological approaches to group mentality do not figure explicitly in these sources, for Durkheim's notion of the "collective conscience" (a term that the novelist and critic W. B. Sebald adopts), which unites individuals through their shared beliefs, see Introduction to Part 6, note 10. For Bloch's use of this same term, see Part 1; for its significance in French cultural history, see A. Burguière, "The Fate of the History of *Mentalités* in the *Annales*", *Comparative Studies in Society and History* 24 (1982), 424–37; P. Burke, "Strengths and Weaknesses in the History of Mentalities", *Varieties of Cultural History*, P. Burke (ed.) (Cambridge: Polity Press, 1997), 162–82.
ii   For a useful elaboration, see R. Eyerman, *Cultural Trauma: Slavery and the Formation of African American Identity* (Cambridge: Cambridge University Press, 2002). For a discussion of the ways by which we express and experience collective memory, see Susannah Radstone, "Reconceiving Binaries: The Limits of Memory", *History Workshop Journal* 59 (2005), 134–50.
iii One of the most famous examples of psychohistory is E. H. Erikson, *Young Man Luther: A Study of Psychoanalysis and History* (1958), which examined Luther's ideas in the context of his conflicted identity. For psychohistory as a flawed method for writing history, see F. Weinstein and G. M. Platt, "The Coming Crisis in Psychohistory", *American Historical Review* 47 (1975), 202–28. For a useful discussion of these responses, see P. Gay, *Freud for Historians* (Oxford: Oxford University Press, 1985); D. E. Stannard, *Shrinking History: On Freud and the Failure of Psychohistory* (Oxford: Oxford University Press, 1973). Despite mainstream resistance, psychoanalytic theory has made particularly important contributions to the interpretation of historical catastrophe: see, for example, D. LaCapra, *History and Memory after Auschwitz* (Ithaca: Cornell University Press, 1998); and in conjunction with oral history: see L. Langer, *Holocaust Testimonies: The Ruins of Memory* (New Haven: Yale University Press, 1991).
iv   C. G. Schmidt, "The Perilous Purview of Psychohistory", *Journal of Psychohistory* 14 (1987), 315–25. Quoted in Lynn Hunt, "Psychology, Psychoanalysis, and Historical Thought", *A Companion to Historical Thought* (Oxford: Blackwell, 2002), 340.

influential theory of unconscious conflict. Indeed, by adopting the narrative formula of a classic Greek tale, Freud seems to have invited accusations that the Oedipus complex is as fictional as its namesake. This must be distinguished from the use of personal and subjective memories to construct pictures of the past. Much research in **psychoanalysis** and other fields of psychology has explored the validity and reliability of such data, permitting increasingly confident integration of subjective and objective data. Recent work in psychoanalysis and related fields can be invaluable for developing a sophisticated approach to historical memory, and to traumatic memory in particular. It can help us untangle the interior relationship between historical facts and personal or social mythology, and between intimate memory and public knowledge.

By reflecting on the **historical sensibilities** that emerge from modern warfare, the authors featured in this section discuss the painful rather than theoretical nature of history. Perpetrators of violence typically explain their actions by referring to memories created by their own suffering, which is one reason why these authors suggest that history-writing is an emphatically moral practice (see Part 1). Similarly, what we think about history reflects and determines our feelings about conflict on an individual and political level. Michael Ignatieff was trained in history and philosophy, but his views on ethnic war were shaped by witnessing genocide in Croatia, Bosnia, and Serbia in 1992.[v] He reported on all parties in that conflict, and this brought him so close to the violence that he was once seized by paramilitaries and at another time he heard gunshots around his car.[vi] He made the crucial observation that the memories that fire ethnic hatred cannot be understood simply by analyzing them in objective terms, nor can the bitterness that clouds its past be cleared by reference to facts. Instead, to appreciate the historical sensibility that can encourage old neighbours to kill each other, we need to value the psychological force that myths of victimization hold for those who inflict the very violence they claim to have suffered. This is why he sees a powerful difference between the factual truth of history and the moral truth of memory.

When the British psychoanalyst Adam Phillips discussed the destructive consequences of confusing the past with the present, he alluded to the **screen memories** we create to protect us from real events that are too painful to remember. Although his article appears last in this section, Phillips's reference to an essay that Freud published in 1899 can be valuable at this point. Freud wondered not only why personal memory is more poignant than factual history, but also why those who suffer from psychological trauma cling to subjective memories rather than face the objective past.[vii] In Freud's view, traumatic memory is so forceful that we repress it by unconsciously replacing the painful memory with screen memories that are simpler and easier to understand. But such **repression** always demands a personal and social cost: our mind still struggles with the past and carries its open wounds, so it will express the original trauma in indirect ways, frequently by inflicting similar suffering on others. This is why bringing

---

v   For a cogent history of *genocide* as a term reflecting twentieth-century political, militaristic, and social contexts, see S. Power, "A Crime *With* a Name", *"A Problem from Hell": America and the Age of Genocide* (New York: Basic Books, 2003), 31–45, *passim*.

vi These events took place during production of Ignatieff's documentary film *Blood and Belonging: Journeys into the New Nationalism* (BBC, 1993). For the companion book, see M. Ignatieff, *Blood and Belonging* (Harmondsworth: Penguin, 1993).

vii See S. Freud, "Screen Memories". Trans. J. Strachey, *The Collected Papers of Sigmund Freud*, J. Riviere (ed.) (New York: Basic Books, 1959), 47–69. Freud discusses screen-memories again in "On Childhood Memories and Screen Memories", *The Psychopathology of Everyday Life*, 1901. Trans. A. Bell (Harmondsworth: Penguin, 2002), 45–52.

the true past to light (that is, to consciousness) brings not only pain but also resentment—for by losing the screen, one has lost the safe but familiar motive to justify one's feelings of victimization. This also explains why simply teaching objective history to warring factions cannot solve their conflicts. The German novelist W. G. Sebald has shown in a series of striking essays and novels that objective history can even inhibit the healing that proper attention to screen memories can bring.[viii] Gesturing to Mark Phillips's discussion of historical distance (in Part 3), Adam Phillips observes that we also use distancing as a psychological technique to create and manage our memories, freeing us from the formal and logical coherence required by narrative history.

Freud observed that most of us have forgotten important events from our childhood, but we remember apparently trivial things with astonishing vividness. By exploring the emotional meaning of those memories, Freud argued that these are mental fabrications that we have unconsciously created to distract ourselves from recollections of hurtful events. Freud suggested that these screen memories are not only the mind's defence against the torment of actual memories, but they also show our unconscious wish to remember what did take place so that we can define it as belonging firmly to the past. By relegating present memory to past history, we free our mental resources from the struggle to suppress the past, a process that risks expressing that memory through destructive behaviour towards ourselves or others. Freud concluded by emphasizing the psychological process by which we formulate memories of our individual pasts:

> Our childhood memories show us our earliest years not as they were but as they appeared at the later periods when the memories were revived. In these periods of revival, the childhood memories did not, as people are accustomed to say, *emerge*; they were *formed* at that time. And a number of motives, which had no concern with historical accuracy, had their part in thus forming them as well as in the selection of the memories themselves.[ix]

We create memories not only to protect us from history, but also to validate our actions and to create social identity, as the first three readings in this section show.

In Sebald's compelling reflection on the Allied aerial bombings of Germany during the Second World War, "Air War and Literature", he pointed to the enduring silence and eerie refusal of survivors to commemorate the destruction that took place all around them:

> The death by fire within a few hours of an entire city, with all its buildings and its trees, its inhabitants, its domestic pets, its fixtures and fittings of every kind, must inevitably lead to overload, to paralysis of the capacity to think and feel in those who succeeded in escaping.[x]

But the physical effects of psychological trauma provided only a partial explanation for the lingering inability of German survivors to express their memories. It is more likely that their silence is an expression of their shame and humiliation following factual historical revelations of the Nazi Holocaust. Historical facts have created a social consciousness that would deny

---

viii For his essays, see *On the Natural History of Destruction*. Trans. Anthea Bell (New York: Modern Library, 1999); his novels include: *Austerlitz*. Trans. A. Bell (Harmondsworth: Penguin, 2002); *The Emigrants*. Trans. M. Hulse (London: Vintage, 2002).

ix S. Freud, "Screen Memories", 69.

x See W. G. Sebald, "Air War and Literature", *On the Natural History of Destruction*, 25.

other survivors the chance to depict their tragedy or express their suffering, so that historical discourse imposes a secondary traumatizing silence on personal memory. While memories of personal trauma might not express themselves directly, they form tangible bonds among survivors. More than three years after the bombing of Hamburg, when a train full of passengers was passing through an area still flattened and blackened, a Swedish journalist noticed that "no one looked out of the windows, and he was identified as a foreigner himself *because* he looked out".[xi] Traumatic memory creates social cohesion, by which outsiders are marked by their ability to see or hear things survivors cannot—or will not. As Ignatieff eloquently explained, to those whose memories continue to haunt them, "the past continues to torment because it is *not* past". Similarly, the hostility that greeted Hannah Arendt's 1963 report on the trial and capital punishment of a prominent Nazi war criminal showed, from a different point of view, that memory creates social identity. One critic wrote that Arendt "questioned the myth of the victim [which] guarantees a unified identity"—and it was this questioning of their victimization that led to her condemnation by legions of readers who had survived the Holocaust.[xii] As Ignatieff pointed out when discussing South Africa's Truth and Reconciliation policy, "it is open to question whether justice or truth actually heals", since no supply of objective facts or measure of just retribution can soothe the torment inflicted by traumatic memory.

It remains tempting to equate the execution of justice with the exposure of guilt, especially when it seems to respond to hysterical outbursts of guilty feelings. How should we interpret emotional expression when it refers to the burden of memory? Arendt remarked that Adolf Eichmann, who efficiently arranged the murder of at least three million people, mainly Jews, had wanted "to hang himself in public to lift the burden of guilt from the shoulders of German youngsters".[xiii] She then made the acute observation that Germans who were born after the war "are not staggering under the burden of the past . . . they are trying to escape from the pressure of very present actual problems into a cheap sentimentality". Sebald also referred to what he called the "maudlin sentimentality" of young German writers, whose emotional behaviour upon returning to their ruined cities "hardly seemed to notice the horrors which . . . surrounded them on all sides".[xiv] A literary historian has recently argued, insightfully, that displays of sentiment "*conceal* causal connections and moral form . . . drawing the reader *away* from the dynamic of plot [i.e. the facts of what actually happened] to spectate the scene instead."[xv] Sentimentality is a dramatic performance of a screen memory that shelters

xi   Sebald, 30.

xii See N. Fruchter, "Arendt's Eichmann and Jewish Identity", *For a New America: Essays in History and Politics from "Studies on the Left", 1959–1967*, J. Weinstein and D. W. Eakins (eds) (New York: Vintage, 1970), 424–25. For an effective discussion of the lessons Arendt sought to learn from the Eichmann trial, with reference to the controversies it elicited, see Seyla Benhabib, "Arendt's *Eichmann in Jerusalem*", *The Cambridge Companion to Hannah Arendt*, Dana Villa (ed.) (Cambridge: Cambridge University Press, 2000), 65–87.

xiii On the angry response to the publication of Arendt's report, particularly among Jewish survivors of the Holocaust, with an effective discussion of Arendt's critical understanding of Eichmann's conduct—both as an efficient administrator of the Nazi genocide and as a blandly passive defendant at his trial – see S. Dossa, "Hannah Arendt on Eichmann: The Public, the Private, and Evil", *Review of Politics* 46 (1984), 163–82.

xiv Sebald, 9.

xv   Barbara Benedict proceeds by arguing that "emphasis on visual spectacle elevates the value of watching over that of feeling, or redefines feeling as a kind of watching". See *Framing Feeling: Sentiment and Style in English Prose Fiction* (New York: AMS Press, 1994), 11. My emphasis.

the actors from the reality of history. Similarly, Eichmann's wish for a public punishment would only clarify the merely aesthetic rather than sincerely moral nature of guilt. Emphasizing the fact that those who orchestrated the Holocaust were neither exceptional nor for the most part fanatical, Arendt articulated her famous conclusion: Eichmann embodied the "*banality of evil*". Since Eichmann did not feel any guilt, it simply was not possible for his trial or punishment to validate the depth of suffering he caused by corroborating anyone's traumatic memory. At his trial, he did not challenge historical records of the Holocaust, but he defended his careful logistical organization of the genocide by claiming that he was "only following orders". His position chillingly shows that passive complicity, and not fanatical hatred, is sufficient to kill on an industrial scale.[xvi] Leaving aside whether his punishment brought healing to survivors by referring their memories to the past, Arendt's historical account of his trial elicited a degree of bitterness and resentment that confirmed the unresolved rawness of traumatic memory that remained alive in the present. It also showed that when one generation represses their memories of guilt, it will put emotional pressure on the younger generation, whose consciences are clear.

At the same time, when traumatic memory remains buried and silent its injuries continue to fester. When Sebald surveyed German cultural and intellectual expression after the war, he could not find evidence of moral outrage or even critical discussion about the destruction inflicted by the Allied air assaults: this silence "has its source in the well-kept secret of the corpses built into the foundations of our state"—the horror remained unspeakable for those who were not killed.[xvii] Ironically, by not having to labour under a sense of guilt for crimes committed on their own soil, the British were able to express their shock over the destruction wrought by their own young men. British politicians and policymakers debated the ethical and pragmatic meaning of the Royal Air Force bombing during the war, and the British public expressed revulsion over it after the war. The psychological distance that aerial bombing laid out between those in the planes and those beneath them was captured by the words of a BBC journalist who reported on a night-time raid over Berlin as "the most gigantic display of soundless fireworks in the world".[xviii] But despite the differences in physical proximity between those who planned the raids and those who survived them, even a visiting British official who toured the devastated city of Cologne in 1945 could only say that the area "cried out for a more eloquent piece than I could ever have written".[xix] If historical events require a narrative to communicate their significance, none would emerge from this particular catastrophe. Some other means of representation, including the documentary meditations offered by Sebald himself, will have to be found. Such writing and image-making allows one to explore the nature of screen memories through a narrative that examines and reflects, all the while providing a literary record for others to consider.

It might be useful to conclude by asking ourselves about the role of historians when their work brings them into contact with witnesses to events of unspeakable magnitude. Ignatieff

---

xvi Upon the publication of Eichmann's handwritten memoirs in August 1999, proof emerged that in fact Eichmann was fully aware of the nature and scope of his work—and indeed he had witnessed the murder of thousands at Auschwitz, Treblinka, Misk, and Lemberg. Moreover, when he was told to cease operations in 1946, he continued to organize the detention and deportation of thousands to Auschwitz. See D. Cesarani, *Eichmann: His Life and Crimes* (London: Heinemann, 2004).

xvii Sebald, 13.

xviii Sebald, 21.

xix Sebald, 31.

explained that academic efforts to define history through reliable sources rather than subject-ive experience are hardly relevant for those whose personal feelings define their historical sense:

> The past has none of the fixed and stable identity of a document. The past is an argument, and the function of truth commissions, like the function of honest historians, is simply to purify the argument, to narrow the range of permissive lies.

However, since we seek to defend the record of evident facts, it would be wrong to value the distortions of memory in the same way. It might be more helpful to turn our research skills towards understanding the private and public, personal and social, current and past means by which survivors have sought to make sense of what they have seen—even when they cannot use words to tell it.

Chapter 39

Michael Ignatieff

THE NIGHTMARE FROM WHICH WE ARE TRYING TO AWAKE

Michael Ignatieff, "The Nightmare From Which We Are Trying To Awake", *The Warrior's Honor: Ethnic War and the Modern Conscience* (London: Chatto and Windus, 1998), 166–90.

WHAT IS NIGHTMARISH about nightmare is that it permits no saving distance between dreamer and dream. If history is nightmare, it is because past is not past. As an artist and as an Irishman, [James] Joyce was only too aware that time in Ireland was simultaneous, not linear. In the terrible quarrel at the beginning of *Portrait* over the meaning of the Irish nationalist politician Parnell's disgrace and death, when Dante screams triumphantly, "We crushed him to death!" and Mr. Casey sobs with pain for his dead king and Stephen's father's eyes fill with tears, it is clear that Parnell's death is not in the past at all. In the quarrel, past, present, and future are ablaze together, set alight by time's livid flame.

To awake from history, then, is to recover the saving distance between past and present and to distinguish between myth and truth. Myth is a version of the past that refuses to be just the past. Myth is a narrative shaped by desire, not by truth, formed not by the facts as best we can establish them but by our longing to be reassured and consoled. Coming awake means to renounce such longings, to recover all the sharpness of the distinction between what is true and what we wish were true.

It has become common to believe that we create our identities as much as we inherit them, that belonging is elective rather than tribal, conscious rather than unconscious, chosen rather than determined. Even though we cannot chose the circumstances of our birth, we can chose which of these elements of our fate we make our defining inheritance. Artists like Joyce have helped us think of our identities as artistic creations and have urged us to believe that we too can fly free of the nets of nationality, religion, and language.

The truth is that the nets do bind most of us. Few of us can be artists of our own lives. That does not make us prisoners: we can come awake; we do not need to spend our lives in the twilight of myth and collective illusion; we can become self-conscious. Few of us will ever create as fully as Joyce the imaginative ground on which we stand or the language in which we speak. But though Joyce's hard-won freedom may be beyond most of us, his metaphor of awaking points to a possibility open to us all. In awaking, we return to ourselves. We recover the saving distance between what we are told to be and what we are. This saving distance is the space for irony. We wake: we tell our nightmare to someone; its hold on us begins to break; it begins to seem funny or at least untragic. We may still shudder in the telling, but at least we can share it. We can lighten up. The day can begin.

II

What does it mean for a nation to come to terms with its past? Do nations have psyches the way individuals do? Can a nation's past make a people ill as we know repressed memories sometimes make individuals ill? Conversely, can a nation or contending parts of it be reconciled to its past as individuals can, by replacing myth with fact and lies with truth? Can nations "come awake" from the nightmare of their past, as Joyce believed an individual could?

In his *Introductory Lectures on Psychoanalysis* Freud once baffled his audience by remarking that there was knowing and there was knowing and they were not the same. We think we know a lot of things but we do not really know them at all. We can know something in our heads without knowing it in our guts. We can forgive people in our heads without forgiving them in our hearts. Knowledge can be propositional or dispositional. For the former to become the latter, it must be—in Freud's phrase—"worked through." A two-way process is involved: what we know in our heads must become something we know in our guts; what we know in our guts must become something we know in our heads. Psyche and soma, which have been divided by trauma, must be reunited again. The process is bound to be slow and painful. In working through death or loss, our bodies often resist what our minds know to be true; or our mind resists believing what the body already feels. To master trauma is not just to bring body and mind together in acceptance; it is also to recover, in both body and mind, a sense that the past is past. This means shifting the past out of the present; replacing psychological simultaneity with linear sequence; slowly loosening the hold of a grief or an anger whose power traps us in an unending yesterday.

Can we speak of nations "working through" a civil war or an atrocity as we speak of individuals working through a traumatic memory or event? The question is not made any easier to answer by the ways our metaphors lead us on. We tend to vest our nations with consciences, identities, and memories as if they were individuals. It is problematic enough to vest an individual with a single identity: our inner lives are like battlegrounds over which uneasy truces reign; the identity of a nation is additionally fissured by region, ethnicity, class, and education. It is not merely that each of these elements of a nation will make its own reckoning with trauma but that the real reckoning is molecular—within the conscience of the millions of individuals who compose a nation. Yet nations have a public life and a public discourse, and the molecular reckonings of individuals are decisively affected by the kinds of public discussion of the past that a nation's leaders, writers, and journalists make possible.

Questions about how nations "work through" their past are mysterious, but they are also urgent and of practical significance. In 1993, after seventy-five years of civil war, partition, terrorist insurgency, and intercommunal violence, the people of northern and southern Ireland embarked once again on an attempt to awake from their Joycean nightmare and begin a joint process of healing and reconciliation. In Nelson Mandela's South Africa, a truth commission has been touring the country attempting to provide a forum in which both victims and perpetrators can come to terms with apartheid. If the perpetrators choose truth—that is, if they disclose what they knew and what they did—they can avoid judgment and obtain amnesty and pardon. The War Crimes Tribunal in the Hague is both prosecuting crimes committed in the Balkan war and making them public in order to assist in eventual reconciliation. In the African city of Arusha, a similar tribunal is collecting evidence about the genocide in Rwanda, believing here, too, that truth, justice, and reconciliation are indissolubly linked. In all these instances—Ireland, South Africa, the Balkans, Rwanda—the rhetoric is noble but the rationale is unclear. Justice in itself is not a problematic objective, but whether the attainment of justice always contributes to reconciliation is anything but evident. Truth likewise is a good thing, but as an African proverb reminds us, truth is not always good to say.

In Archbishop Tutu's own words, the aim of his truth commission is "the promotion of national unity and reconciliation" and "the healing of a traumatized, divided, wounded, polarized people." Laudable aims, but are they coherent? Look at the assumptions he makes: that a nation has one psyche, not many; that the truth is certain, not contestable; and that, when the truth is known by all, it has the capacity to heal and reconcile. These are not so much epistemological assumptions as articles of faith about human nature: that the truth is one and, if we know it, it will make us free.

The rest of us look on and applaud, perhaps forgetting to ask how much truth our own societies can stand. All nations depend on forgetting: on forging myths of unity and identity that allow a society to forget its founding crimes, its hidden injuries and divisions, its unhealed wounds. It must be true, for nations as it is for individuals, that we can stand only so much truth. But if too much truth is divisive, the question becomes, How much is enough?

Faith in the healing virtues of truth inspired the commissions in Chile, Argentina, and Brazil that sought to find out what happened to thousands of innocent people "disappeared" by the military juntas during the 1960s and 1970s. All these commissions believed that, if the truth were known, a people made sick by terror and lies would be made well again. The results, though, were ambiguous. As Pilate asked as he washed his hands, What is truth? At the very least, it consists of factual truth and moral truth, of narratives that tell what happened and narratives that attempt to explain why it happened and who is responsible. The truth commissions in South America had more success in establishing the first than in promoting the second. They did succeed in establishing the facts about the disappearance, torture, and death of thousands of persons, and this information allowed relatives and friends the consolation of knowing how the disappeared met their fates. It says much for the human need for truth that the relatives of victims preferred the facts to the false comforts of ignorance. It also says a great deal for the moral appeal of magnanimity that so many of these people should have preferred the truth to vengeance or even justice. It was sufficient for most of them to know what happened; they did not need to punish the transgressors in order to put the past behind them.

But the truth commissions were also charged with the production of public truth and the remaking of public discourse. Their mandate was to generate a moral narrative— explaining the genesis of evil regimes and apportioning moral responsibility for the deeds committed under those governments. And here they were infinitely less successful.

The military, security, and police establishments were prepared to let the truth come out about individual cases of disappearance. Factual truth they could live with; moral truth was out of the question. They fought tenaciously against prosecutions of security personnel and against shouldering responsibility for their crimes. To have conceded ethical responsibility would have weakened their power as institutions. Such was the resistance of the military in Argentina and Chile that the elected governments that created the commissions had to choose between justice and their own survival, between prosecuting the criminals and risking a military coup or letting them go and allowing a democratic tradition to take root.

The record of the truth commissions in Latin America has disillusioned many of those who believe that shared truth is a precondition of social reconciliation. The military and police apparatus survived the inquiries of the truth commissions with their legitimacy undermined but their power intact. The societies in question used the truth commissions to foster the illusion that they had put the past behind them. Indeed, the truth commissions facilitated exactly the kind of false reconciliation with the past that they had been created to forestall. The German writer and thinker Theodor Adorno observed this false reconciliation at work in his native Germany after the war:

> "Coming to terms with the past" does not imply a serious working through of the past, the breaking of its spell through an act of clear consciousness. It suggests, rather, wishing to turn the page and, if possible, wiping it from memory. The attitude that it would be proper for everything to be forgiven and forgotten by those who were wronged is typically expressed by the party that committed the injustice.

The dangers of false reconciliation are real enough but it is possible that disillusion with the truth commissions of Latin America goes too far. It was never the truth commissions' charge to transform the military and security apparatus any more than it is Archbishop Tutu's charge—or within his power—to do the same in South Africa. Truth is truth; it is not social or institutional reform.

Nor, when the truth is proclaimed by an official commission, is it likely to be accepted by those against whom it is directed. The police and military have their own truth—and it exerts its hold precisely because for them it is not a tissue of lies. It is unreasonable to expect those who believed they were putting down a terrorist or insurgent threat to disown this idea simply because a truth commission exposes the threat as having been without foundation. People, especially people in uniform, do not easily or readily surrender the premises upon which their lives are based. Repentance, if it ever occurs, is an individual matter. All that a truth commission can achieve is to reduce the number of lies that circulate unchallenged. In Argentina, it is now impossible to claim, for example, that the military did not throw half-dead victims into the sea from helicopters. In Chile, it is no longer permissible to assert in public that the Pinochet regime did not dispatch thousands of entirely innocent people. Truth commissions can and do change the frame of public discourse and public memory. But they cannot be judged failures because they fail to change behavior and institutions. That is not their function.

A truth commission can winnow out the facts upon which society's arguments with itself should be conducted. But it cannot bring these arguments to a conclusion. Critics of truth commissions sometimes speak as if the past were a sacred text, like the American Constitution or the Bill of Rights, that has been stolen and vandalized and that can be repaired and returned to a well-lit glass case in some grand public rotunda. But the past has none of the fixed and stable identity of a document. The past is an argument, and the function of truth commissions, like the function of honest historians, is simply to purify the argument, to narrow the range of permissible lies.

Truth commissions have the greatest chance of success in societies that already have created a powerful political consensus behind reconciliation, such as in South Africa. This consensus may have less to do with moral agreement about the need to purge the poisons of the past than with a prudential political calculation, shared by most people, that judicial vindictiveness has the potential to tear society apart and even to unleash civil or racial war. In such a context, where truth seems a less divisive objective than justice, Tutu's commission, even as it forces the disclosure of painful truth, may well reinforce the political consensus that created his commission.

In places like the former Yugoslavia, on the other hand, where the parties have murdered and tortured one another for years and where the crimes of the sons and daughters have often built upon the crimes of fathers and grandfathers, the prospects for truth, reconciliation, and justice are much bleaker. These contexts, however bleak, are instructive because they illustrate everything that is problematic in the relation between truth and reconciliation.

The idea that reconciliation depends on shared truth presumes that shared truth about the past is possible. But truth is related to identity. What you believe to be true depends, in some measure, on who you believe yourself to be. And who you believe yourself to be is mostly defined in terms of who you are not. To be a Serb is first and foremost not to be a Croat or a Muslim. If a Serb is someone who believes Croats have a historical tendency toward fascism and a Croat is someone who believes Serbs have a penchant for genocide, then to discard these myths is for both groups to give up a defining element of their own identities. The war [in the Balkans] has created communities of fear, and these communities cannot conceive of sharing a common truth—and a common responsibility—with their enemies until they are less afraid, until fear of the other ceases to be a constitutive part of who they take themselves to be.

Obviously, identity is composed of much more than negative images of the other. Many Croats and Serbs opposed these negative stereotypes and the nationalist madness that over-took their countries. There were many who fought to maintain a moral space between their personal and national identities. Yet even such people—the human-rights activists and anti-war campaigners—are now unable to conceive that one day Zagreb, Belgrade, and Sarajevo might share a common version of the history of the conflict. Agreement on a shared chro-nology of events might be possible, though even this would be contentious; but it is impos-sible to imagine the three sides ever agreeing on how to apportion responsibility. The truth that matters to people is not factual or narrative truth but moral or interpretive truth. And this will always be an object of dispute in the Balkans.

It is an illusion to suppose that "impartial" or "objective" outsiders would ever succeed in getting their moral and interpretive account of the catastrophe accepted by the parties to the conflict. The very fact of being an outsider discredits rather than reinforces one's legitimacy. For there is always a truth that can be known only by those on the inside. Or if not a truth—since facts are facts—then a moral significance to these facts that only an insider can fully appreciate. The truth, if it is to be believed, must be authored by those who have suffered its consequences. But the truth of war is so painful that those who have fought each other rarely if ever sit down to author it together.

The problem of a shared truth is also that it does not lie "in between." It is not a compromise between two competing versions. Either the siege of Sarajevo was a deliberate attempt to terrorize and subvert a legitimately elected, internationally recognized state, or it was a legitimate preemptive defense by the Serbs of their homeland against Muslim attack. It cannot be both. Outside attempts to write a version of the truth that does "justice" to the truth held by both sides are unlikely to be credible to either.

Nor is an acknowledgment of shared suffering equivalent to shared truth. It is relatively easy for both sides to acknowledge each other's pain. Much more difficult—indeed, usually impossible—is shared acknowledgment of who bears the lion's share of responsibility. For if aggressors have their own defense against truth, so do victims. Peoples who believe them-selves to be victims of aggression have an understandable incapacity to believe that they too have committed atrocities. Myths of innocence and victimhood are a powerful obstacle in the way of confronting responsibility, as are atrocity myths about the other side.

Hill-country Serbs in the Foca region of Bosnia told British journalists in the summer of 1992 that their ethnic militias were obliged to cleanse the area of Muslims because it was well known that Muslims crucified Serbian children and floated their bodies down the river past Serbian settlements. Since such myths do not need factual corroboration in order to reproduce themselves, they are not likely to be dispelled by the patient assembly of evidence to the contrary. A version of this particular atrocity myth used to be spread about the Jews in medieval times. The myth was not true about the Jews and it is not true about Muslims, but that is not the point. Myth is so much sustained by the inner world—by paranoia, desire, and longing—that it is dissolved, not when facts from the outer world contradict it, but only when the inner need for it ebbs away.

To speak of myths is not to dispute that one side may be more of a victim than the other or to question that atrocities happen. What is mythic is that the atrocities are held to reveal the essential identity—the intrinsic genocidal propensity—of the peoples in whose name they were committed. All the members of the group are regarded as susceptible to that propensity even though atrocity can be committed only by specific individuals. The idea of collective guilt depends on the idea of a national psyche or racial identity. The fiction at work here is akin to the nationalist delusion that the identities of individuals are or should be subsumed into their national identities.

Ethnic war solders together individual and collective identities. Both aggressors and victims can bear only so much responsibility, as individuals, for what they have done or suffered. They need the absolution provided by collective identity.

Ethnic war isolates aggressors from the truth of their own actions. If ethnic cleansing is successful, it removes victims and leaves the victor in possession of a terrain of undisputed truth. Who, after all, is left to remind the winners that someone else once owned these houses, worshipped here, buried their dead in this ground? Ethnic cleansing eradicates the accusing truth of the past. In its wake, the past may be rewritten so that no record of the victim's presence is allowed to remain. Victory encloses the victor in a forgetting that removes the very possibility of guilt, shame, or remorse, the emotions necessary for any sustained encounter with the truth.

Victims of ethnic war, for their part, have lost the sites that validate their version of the truth. They can no longer point to their homes, their houses of worship, their graves, for those places are gone. In exile, victimhood itself becomes less and less real. The victims keep pleading for a truth to which fewer and fewer people give notice, and outsiders who tell them to face up to the truth are in essence asking them to accept the fact of their defeat. Victims of ethnic war may refuse this truth, preferring to stick together in refugee camps and settlements rather than disperse as individuals to face the world alone. Refusing the truth of defeat is a condition of their dignity but it also traps them in an identity of collective victimhood.

And so both sides in ethnic war end up trapped in collective identities: the victors in their amnesia, the victims in their refusal to accept defeat. These fates shape memory and personality, and, over the long term, make it impossible for either side to be reconciled to the truth.

III

If the prospects for shared truth are grim, and the prospects for reconciliation even grimmer, what is there to be said for the prospects of justice? The vital function of justice in the dialogue between truth and reconciliation is to disaggregate individual and nation, to disassemble the fiction that nations are accountable like individuals for the crimes committed in their name. The most important task of war crimes trials is to "individualize" guilt, to relocate it from the collectivity to the individuals responsible. As Karl Jaspers said of the Nuremberg trials in 1946, "For us Germans this trial has the advantage that it distinguishes between the particular crimes of the leaders and that it does not condemn the Germans collectively."

By analogy with Nuremberg, therefore, the Hague trials are not supposed to put the Serbian, Muslim, or Croatian peoples in the dock but to separate the criminals from the nation and to lay the guilt where it belongs, on the shoulders of individuals. Yet trials inevitably fail to apportion all the guilt to all those responsible. For one thing, small fry tend to pay the price for the crimes committed by big fish, thereby reinforcing the sense that justice is not definitive but arbitrary. For another, such trials do not necessarily break the link between individual and nation. Clearly Nuremberg failed to do so: the world still regards the Germans as being collectively responsible and, indeed, the Germans themselves still accept this responsibility. The German novelist Martin Walser once wrote that when a Frenchman or an American sees pictures of Auschwitz, "he doesn't have to think: We human beings! He can think: Those Germans! Can we think: those Nazis! I for one cannot. . . ." The most that can be said for war crimes trials is that they do something to unburden a people of the fiction of collective guilt, by helping them to transform guilt into shame. This appears to have happened in Germany, to some extent. But Nuremberg alone could not have accomplished it. As Ian Buruma points out in *The Wages of Guilt*, many Germans dismissed the Nuremberg trials as nothing more than "victor's justice." It was not Nuremberg but the strictly German war crimes trials of the 1960s that forced Germans to confront their part in the Holocaust. Verdicts reached in a German courtroom benefited from a legitimacy that the Nuremberg process never enjoyed.

Nor was coming to terms with the past just a matter of digesting the message of the domestic war crimes trials. It took a million visits to concentration camps by German schoolchildren, the publication of a thousand books, the airing of the Hollywood television series *Holocaust*—a vast reckoning between generations, which is still going on.

But such a reckoning is possible only when a publicly sponsored discourse gives it permission to happen. West Germany made a collective attempt to confront its Nazi past; as a vanquished nation occupied by the Western powers, it had no choice. In its classrooms, in its language of public commemoration, and occasionally in its leaders' public gestures of reparation and atonement, West Germany faced up to its past and, in doing so, has gradually allowed the past to become the past.

In East Germany, on the other hand, public discourse passed the burden of the Nazi past westward, to the other side of the "anti-fascist wall"; the official fiction was that the East was the heir of the Communist antifascist resistance and therefore absolved of all responsibility for Hitler's crimes. Even though this fiction must have contradicted ordinary people's memory of their own complicity with Hitler, going along with it was convenient, and for the war criminals among them, organized public amnesia provided a refuge and an exculpation. Over time, however, the public lie became a liability for the regime: official amnesia simply confirmed the suspicion that the regime, as a whole, depended for its survival on historical mendacity. When the public arena is filled with lies, private memory remains in hiding. Indeed, in East Germany, public forgetting engendered private forgetting. But over the very long term, a regime's present-day legitimacy is inevitably undermined if it persists in telling lies about the past. The very rapidity with which East Germany collapsed suggests that the gulf between public lie and private truth had created a long-standing crisis of legitimacy. The breach in the wall brought the whole flimsy structure down. Now that the Stasi is no more, East Germans must awake to the reality that they and their parents colluded not with one dictatorship but with two, Red and Black, from 1933 until 1989.

The enormity of this double inheritance explains why East Germany since 1989 has gone through the most convulsive of all attempts to purge itself of the past: state trials, truth commissions, dismissal of secret police informers, full disclosure of secret police files. The thoroughness of the process was impressive, but its speed was suspect. It was as if the West German elite, which pushed the process through, believed that one single drastic operation could drain away the poison of the past once and for all. Perpetrators and accomplices colluded in this speedy forgiving and forgetting, and many victims did, too, simply to get on with the rest of their lives. Forgetting was made easier by the explosive invasion of the capitalist market into the East. Everyone had waited so long for the consoling bath of capitalist consumption that they could be forgiven for believing that it would cleanse them of the past as well. But the past is tenacious, simply because it holds so many clues to the present. Whenever a people ask themselves, Who are we?—as the East Germans must—they are forced to ask themselves, How did we let ourselves submit? No questions of national identity in the present can ever avoid encountering the painful secrets of the past. In this sense, as long as these questions are alive—and they are perpetually alive in Germany—there can be no forgetting.

IV

Germany's encounter with its Red and Black past was forced upon it by defeat. The Allies insisted on Nuremberg; the West Germans insisted upon de-Stasification in the East. But what happens when societies are *not* forced, by defeat, to face up to the accusing truth of the past? What happens when there are no truth commissions, no war crimes trials? Until the 1980s, Soviet Russia did not—and could not—face up to the crimes of Stalinism. Here official culture actively repressed the collective past because public knowledge of the regime's crimes would undermine whatever legitimacy the regime still retained from its successful defeat of the Nazis. Indeed, the historical mythology of the great patriotic war— of the great victory against fascism—made it extremely difficult for the society to confront the forms of Red fascism that flourished in its midst. Those who fought for the preservation of memory—Solzhenitsyn, Sakharov, Pasternak, and Akhmatova—were persecuted not simply because they demanded rights of free expression but because they spoke a truth about the regime's past that, if publicly known, would have destroyed Soviet legitimacy altogether. This truth—that the regime survived by extermination—was known to millions; hence millions had to be terrorized or killed to maintain the regime's fictions. As early as the mid-1950s, the men of Khrushchev's generation—who had only barely survived the Terror— began admitting that the cost of maintaining a regime based on historical lies was becoming prohibitive. And as a new generation—the men who came to power under Gorbachev— slowly worked their way up the hierarchy, they carried with them the stories of terror and extermination whispered to them by their parents. The increasingly flagrant contradiction between the public lies they were obliged to tell and their own private or family memories of Stalinist repression ended by undermining the Gorbachev elite's determination to hold on to power. The contradiction sowed deep doubt about the moral legitimacy of socialism in the very soul of an elite that was simultaneously confronting economic stagnation and social decomposition. As in East Germany, reconciliation with the past was possible only with the demolition of the system itself, and, as in East Germany, the collapse came very suddenly, as if the edifice had long before developed cracks in its foundation and was awaiting only a final blow from historical events.

But if the will to power of the members of the Gorbachev elite was sapped by the contradiction between their own family memories and mendacious public myth, the same was not true of many millions of ordinary party members. They felt no such contradiction or doubt. Russian society as a whole has never been de-Stalinized. There have been no truth commissions or public trials, and the party's acknowledgment of its guilty past, for example in Khrushchev's speech to the party congress in 1956, occurred only when the facts were too well known to be denied any longer. Indeed, the torturers have been decorated, promoted, and retired with honor. There have been no trials of the executioners of the Lubyanka or the camp commandants of Magadan. Thanks to Solzhenitsyn, there has been some truth about the past, but there has been no justice and hence there cannot be any reconciliation between the two Russias, between the majority who went along with the regime and the minority—whose numbers run into the millions—who were sent to the gulag. The awakening to truth remains confined to a small liberal minority of the old Gorbachev elite and the educated middle and professional classes in the big cities. For countless former party members, there is nothing to repent, nothing to apologize for. In the absence of justice, then, even the truth can be denied.

The case of contemporary Russia indicates that it is not enough to have *some* truth about the past. No matter how magnificent the efforts of Solzhenitsyn and the heroic research of people like Vitaly Shentalinsky, who forced the KGB to give up the secrets of its persecutions of Russian writers, the mere disclosure of truth—of a record of unpunished crime—does not allow the closure, the resolution that judicial trials can force a resisting society to accept.

Justice may be essential, then, but it is best to be modest about what trials can achieve. The great virtue of legal proceedings is that rules of evidence establish otherwise contestable facts. In this sense, war crimes trials make it more difficult for societies to take refuge in denial. But if trials assist the process of uncovering the truth, it is doubtful whether they assist the process of reconciliation. The purgative function of justice tends to operate on the victims' side only. While victims may feel justice has been done, the community from which the perpetrators come may feel that they have been made scapegoats. All one can say is that leaving war crimes unpunished is worse: the cycle of impunity remains unbroken, societies remain free to indulge their fantasies of denial.

V

It is open to question whether justice or truth actually heals. It is an article of faith with us that knowledge, particularly self-knowledge, is a condition of psychic health, yet every society, including ours, manages to function with only the most precarious purchase on the truth of its own past. Every society has a substantial psychological investment in its heroes. To discover that its heroes were guilty of war crimes is to admit that the identities they defended were themselves tarnished. Which is why a society is often so reluctant to surrender its own to war crimes tribunals, why it is so vehemently "in denial" about facts evident to everyone outside the society. War crimes challenge collective moral identities, and when these identities are threatened, denial is actually a defense of everything one holds dear.

There are many forms of denial, ranging from outright refusal to accept facts as facts to complex strategies of relativization. In these, one accepts the facts but argues that the enemy was equally culpable or that the accusing party is also to blame or that such "excesses" are regrettable necessities in time of war. To relativize is to have it both ways: to admit the facts while denying full responsibility for them.

Resistance to historical truth is a function of group identity: nations and peoples weave their sense of themselves into narcissistic narratives that strenuously resist correction.

Similarly, regimes depend for their legitimacy on historical myths that are armored against the truth. The legitimacy of Tito's regime in Yugoslavia depended on the myth that his partisans led a movement of national resistance against the German and Italian occupations. In reality the partisans fought fellow Yugoslavs as much as they fought the occupiers and even made deals with the Germans to strengthen their hand against domestic opponents. Since these facts were common knowledge to any Yugoslav of that generation, the myth of brotherhood and unity required the constant reinforcement of propaganda.

The myth of brotherhood and unity may have been pointing toward a future beyond ethnic hatred, but by lying about the past, the regime perpetuated the hatreds it was trying to get Yugoslavs to overcome. By repressing the real history of the interethnic carnage between 1941 and 1945, the Titoist regime guaranteed that such carnage would return. Competing versions of historical truth—Serb, Croat, and Muslim—that had no peaceful, democratic means of making themselves heard in Tito's Yugoslavia took to the battlefield to make their truths prevail. The result of five years of war is that a shared truth is now inconceivable. In the conditions of ethnic separation that characterize all the major successor republics to Tito's Yugoslavia, a shared truth—and hence a path from truth to reconciliation—is barred, not just by hatreds but by institutions too undemocratic to allow countervailing truth to circulate.

It is not undermining the war crimes tribunal process to maintain that the message of its truth is unlikely to penetrate the authoritarian successor states of the former Yugoslavia. The point is merely that one must keep justice separate from reconciliation. Justice is justice, and within the strict limits of what is possible, it should be done. Justice will also serve the interests of truth. But the truth will not necessarily be believed, and it is putting too much faith in truth to believe that it can heal.

When it comes to healing, one is faced with the most mysterious process of all. For what seems apparent in the former Yugoslavia, in Rwanda, and in South Africa is that the past continues to torment because it is *not* past. These places are not living in a serial order of time but in a simultaneous one, in which the past and the present are a continuous, agglutinated mass of fantasies, distortions, myths, and lies. Reporters in the Balkan war often discovered, when they were told atrocity stories, that they were uncertain whether these stories had occurred yesterday or in 1941 or 1841 or 1441. For the tellers of the tales, yesterday and today were the same. Simultaneity, it would seem, is the dream time of vengeance. Crimes can never be safely fixed in the historical past; they remain locked in the eternal present, crying out for blood. Joyce understood that in Ireland the bodies of the past were never safely dead and buried; they were always roaming through the sleep of the living in search of retribution.

Nations, properly speaking, cannot be reconciled to other nations as individuals can be to individuals. Nonetheless, individuals are helped to heal and to reconcile by public rituals of atonement. When President Alwyn of Chile appeared on television to apologize to the victims of Pinochet's crimes of repression, he created the public climate in which a thousand acts of private repentance and apology became possible. He also symbolically cleansed the Chilean state of its association with these crimes. German Chancellor Willy Brandt's gesture of going down on his knees at a death camp had a similarly cathartic effect by officially associating the German state with the process of atonement.

These acts contrast strikingly with the behavior of the political figures responsible for the war in the Balkans. If, instead of writing books niggling about the numbers exterminated at Jasenovac, President Tudjman of Croatia had gone to the site of the most notorious of the Croatian extermination camps and publicly apologized for the crimes committed by the Croatian Ustashe against Serbs, Gypsies, Jews, and Communist partisans, he would have liberated the Croatian present from the hold of the Ustashe past. He would also have dramatically increased the chances of the Serbian minority's accepting the legitimacy of an independent Croatian state. Had he confronted the past, the war of 1991 might have been prevented. He chose not to, of course: despite having been an anti-Ustashe partisan himself, he depended, in his campaign for independence, on support, both financial and moral, from former Ustashe in exile. Moreover it proved impossible, both for Tudjman and for much of his electorate, to admit Croatia's historical responsibility for war crimes, since it was central to the very rationale behind the drive to independence that Croats were historical victims of the aggrandizing Serbs. Nonetheless, it remains true that a gesture of atonement on Tudjman's part would have purged Croatia of its legacy of genocide; it would have invited Croatians to replace self-pity and hysterical denial of the past with conscientious discourse, and it would have sent an unmistakable message of fraternity to the Serbs, perhaps preventing them from surrendering, with equal self-pity and hysteria, to the Serbian myth that Serbs can be safe only inside a Greater Serbia. Societies and nations are not like individuals, but their leaders can have an enormous impact on the mysterious process by which individuals come to terms with the painfulness of their societies' past. Leaders give their societies permission to say the unsayable, to think the unthinkable, to rise to gestures of reconciliation that people, individually, cannot imagine. In the Balkans, not a single leader had the courage to exorcise his nation's ruling fantasies.

The chief moral obstacle in the path of reconciliation is the desire for revenge. Now, revenge is commonly regarded as a low and unworthy emotion, and because it is regarded as such, its deep moral hold on people is rarely understood. But revenge—morally considered—is a desire to keep faith with the dead, to honor their memory by taking up their cause where they left off. Revenge keeps faith between generations; the violence it engenders is a ritual form of respect for the community's dead—therein lies its legitimacy. Reconciliation is difficult precisely because it must compete with the powerful alternative morality of violence. Political terror is tenacious because it is an ethical practice. It is a cult of the dead, a dire and absolute expression of respect.

When nations or communities fight each other, they are often only continuing a conflict initiated generations earlier. What did or didn't happen at Drogheda, what Cromwell did or didn't do on his conquering passage through Ireland in the civil war—these are the obstacles that continue to stand in the path of reconciliation in the Ireland of the 1990s. Time and again, the slaughter inflicted by one side in Bosnia in 1992 was repaying a slaughter in 1942. This cycle of intergenerational recrimination has no logical end. Sons cannot—in any meaningful sense—pay their fathers' debts or avenge their fathers' wrongs. But it is the very impossibility of intergenerational vengeance that locks communities into the compulsion to repeat. As in nightmare, each side hurls itself at the locked door of the past, seeking in vain to force it open.

Intergenerational conflict can be pacified only when both sides make elementary distinctions between guilt and responsibility. Sons are not guilty for their fathers' crimes and no peace will come until they stop feeling responsible for avenging the wrongs their fathers suffered. They do remain responsible for telling the truth about them. They must admit what was done. But they must also commit themselves to avoiding the repaying of like with like.

Reconciliation means breaking the spiral of intergenerational vengeance. It means substituting the vicious downward spiral of violence with the virtuous upward spiral of mutually reinforcing respect. Reconciliation can stop the cycle of vengeance only if it can equal vengeance as a form of respect for the dead. What each side, in the aftermath of a civil war, essentially demands is that "the other side" face up to the deaths it caused. To deny the reality of these deaths is to treat them as a dream, as a nightmare. Without an apology, without recognition of what happened, the past cannot return to its place as the past. The ghosts will continue to stalk the battlements. Of course, an apology must reflect acceptance of the other side's grief, something deeper than the Englishman Haynes's well-meaning but offhand remark in *Ulysses*: "An Irishman must think like that, I daresay. We feel in England that we have treated you rather unfairly. It seems history is to blame."

Joyce's great rebellion was against the idea of history as fate, compelling each generation to reproduce the hatreds of the previous one because keeping faith with the dead—honoring their memory—seems to require taking up arms to avenge them. Reconciliation built on mutual apology accepts that history is not fate, that history is not to blame. Nor are cultures or traditions—only specific individuals whom history must name. This last dimension of reconciliation—the mourning of the dead—is where the desire for peace must vanquish the longing for revenge. Reconciliation has no chance against vengeance unless it respects the emotions that sustain vengeance, unless it can replace the respect entailed in vengeance with rituals in which communities once at war learn to mourn their dead together. Reconciliation must reach into the shared inheritance of the democracy of death to teach the drastic nullity of all struggles that end in killing, the unending futility of all attempts to avenge those who are no more. For it is an elementary certainty that killing will not bring the dead back to life. This is an inheritance that can be shared, and when it is shared there can be that deep knowing that sometimes comes when one wakes from a dream.

Chapter 40

Hannah Arendt

Eichmann in Jerusalem: JUDGMENT, APPEAL, AND EXECUTION

Hannah Arendt (1906–1975), "Judgment, Appeal, and Execution", 1963, *Eichmann in Jerusalem: A Report on the Banality of Evil* (revd and enlarged edn) (Harmondsworth: Penguin, 1965), 250–52.

THE SPEED WITH WHICH the death sentence was carried out was extraordinary, even if one takes into account that Thursday night was the last possible occasion before the following Monday, since Friday, Saturday, and Sunday are all religious holidays for one or another of the three denominations in the country [Israel]. The execution took place less than two hours after Eichmann was informed of the rejection of his plea for mercy; there had not even been time for a last meal. The explanation may well be found in two last-minute attempts Dr. Servatius made to save his client—an application to a court in West Germany to force the government to demand Eichmann's extradition, even now, and a threat to invoke Article 25 of the Convention for the Protection of Human Rights and Fundamental Freedoms. Neither Dr. Servatius nor his assistant was in Israel when Eichmann's plea was rejected, and the Israeli government probably wanted to close the case, which had been going on for two years, before the defense could even apply for a stay in the date of execution.

The death sentence had been expected, and there was hardly anyone to quarrel with it; but things were altogether different when it was learned that the Israelis had carried it out. The protests were short-lived, but they were widespread and they were voiced by people of influence and prestige. The most common argument was that Eichmann's deeds defied the possibility of human punishment, that it was pointless to impose the death sentence for crimes of such magnitude—which, of course, was true, in a sense, except that it could not conceivably mean that he who had murdered millions should for this very reason escape punishment. On a considerably lower level, the death sentence was called "unimaginative," and very imaginative alternatives were proposed forthwith—Eichmann "should have spent the rest of his life at hard labor in the arid stretches of the Negev, helping with his sweat to reclaim the Jewish homeland," a punishment he would probably not have survived for more than a single day, to say nothing of the fact that in Israel the desert of the south is hardly looked upon as a penal colony; or, in Madison Avenue style, Israel should have reached "divine heights," rising above "the understandable, legal, political, and even human considerations," by calling together "all those who took part in the capture, trial, and sentencing to a public ceremony, with Eichmann there in shackles, and with television cameras and radio to decorate them as the heroes of the century."

Martin Buber called the execution a "mistake of historical dimensions," as it might "serve to expiate the guilt felt by many young persons in Germany"—an argument that oddly echoed Eichmann's own ideas on the matter, though Buber hardly knew that he had wanted to hang himself in public in order to lift the burden of guilt from the shoulders of German youngsters. (It is strange that Buber, a man not only of eminence but of very great intelligence, should not see how spurious these much publicized guilt feelings necessarily are. It is quite gratifying to feel guilty if you haven't done anything wrong: how noble! Whereas it is rather hard and certainly depressing to admit guilt and to repent. The youth of Germany is surrounded, on all sides and in all walks of life, by men in positions of authority and in public office who are very guilty indeed but who *feel* nothing of the sort. The normal reaction to this state of affairs should be indignation, but indignation would be quite risky—not a danger to life and limb but definitely a handicap in a career. Those young German men and women who every once in a while—on the occasion of all the *Diary of Anne Frank* hubbub and of the Eichmann trial—treat us to hysterical outbreaks of guilt feelings are not staggering under the burden of the past, their fathers' guilt; rather, they are trying to escape from the pressure of very present and actual problems into a cheap sentimentality.) Professor Buber went on to say that he felt "no pity at all" for Eichmann, because he could feel pity "only for those whose actions I understand in my heart," and he stressed what he had said many years ago in Germany—that he had "only in a formal sense a common humanity with those who took part" in the acts of the Third Reich. This lofty attitude was, of course, more of a luxury than those who had to try Eichmann could afford, since the law presupposes precisely that we have a common humanity with those whom we accuse and judge and condemn. As far as I know, Buber was the only philosopher to go on public record on the subject of Eichmann's execution (shortly before the trial started, Karl Jaspers had given a radio interview in Basel, later published in *Der Monat*, in which he argued the case for an international tribunal); it was disappointing to find him dodging, on the highest possible level, the very problem Eichmann and his deeds had posed.

Least of all was heard from those who were against the death penalty on principle, unconditionally; their arguments would have remained valid, since they would not have needed to specify them for this particular case. They seem to have felt—rightly, I think—that this was not a very promising case on which to fight.

Adolf Eichmann went to the gallows with great dignity. He had asked for a bottle of red wine and had drunk half of it. He refused the help of the Protestant minister, the Reverend William Hull, who offered to read the Bible with him: he had only two more hours to live, and therefore no "time to waste." He walked the fifty yards from his cell to the execution chamber calm and erect, with his hands bound behind him. When the guards tied his ankles and knees, he asked them to loosen the bonds so that he could stand straight. "I don't need that," he said when the black hood was offered him. He was in complete command of himself, nay, he was more: he was completely himself. Nothing could have demonstrated this more convincingly than the grotesque silliness of his last words. He began by stating emphatically that he was a *Gottgläubiger*, to express in common Nazi fashion that he was no Christian and did not believe in life after death. He then proceeded: "After a short while, gentlemen, *we shall all meet again*. Such is the fate of all men. Long live Germany, long live Argentina, long live Austria. *I shall not forget them.*" In the face of death, he had found the cliché used in funeral oratory. Under the gallows, his memory played him the last trick; he was "elated" and he forgot that this was his own funeral.

It was as though in those last minutes he was summing up the lesson that this long course in human wickedness had taught us—the lesson of the fearsome, word-and-thought-defying *banality of evil.*

Chapter 41

Adam Phillips

CLOSE-UPS

Adam Phillips, "Close-ups", *History Workshop Journal* 57 (2004), 142–9.

> O'HARA: Which reminds me: some of your detractors say that you're merely
> fashionable.
> BARTHELME: Well, the mere has always been a useful category.
> Donald Barthelme: 'The Art of Fiction LXVI', *Paris Review* 80, 1981

IN FREUD'S *Remembering, Repeating, and Working Through*, published in 1914 but written just before the outbreak of war, he wrote that a certain kind of patient, 'does not remember anything of what he has forgotten and repressed, but acts it out. He reproduces it not as a memory but as an action; he repeats it, without, of course, knowing that he is repeating it'.[1] We repeat in action, Freud suggests, what we are unable or unwilling to remember. It is not merely that we fail to construct a historical distance from this past that we repeat; it is that we have not noticed, to all intents and purposes, that such a distance exists. It is as though whatever it is that makes something a memory has not happened. But also, Freud intimates, there is something about remembering that can put a stop to the past as prescriptive. It is precisely the acknowledgement of historical distance – the construction in language of the past as proximate rather than immediate – that is the modern individual's most difficult task. The patients Freud invented, one could say, were living in the past but not living in history. Freud was struck by the fact that modern individuals resisted having a history. They preferred, often at exorbitant personal cost, to go on repeating themselves; as though there was an uncanny sense in the which the personal past – the traumatic personal past – never changed: was itself being actively preserved like an (unconscious) archive.

Where there is repetition, Freud says, there was repression; and where there was repression, there was trauma. Repetition is the sign of trauma; our reiterations, our mannerisms, link us to our losses, to our buried conflicts. When Freud says that the patient repeats as an action what he cannot remember, we should remember that writing is itself an action, and that genre is itself a form of repetition that easily obscures its own history, the conflicts it was born out of, the problems which made it feel like a solution. Freud is inviting us to distinguish between something he calls remembering, which is presumably veracious and potentially transformative, and something called an action, a repeated action in which the so-called patient – like an actor with a script, or a figure in a dream – unwittingly performs something from his past. That he knows he is repeating something, but that he doesn't know he is repeating something from the past means that unwittingly he is living in the present as if it were the past (though it is not an 'as if' to him). The patient who repetitively re-enacts something from the past clearly has no distance from it, because for him there is no it from which he could take his distance. Freud is alerting us to the idea that there is nothing that the individual defends himself against more than the construction of distance from the traumatic past. What Freud refers to as remembering here is a making of links to the past – linking involving a prior separating out; and what Freud is calling psychoanalytic treatment here is a therapeutic technique that makes the past memorable rather than spellbinding. That makes the past into history, into something that one can consider the advantages and disadvantages of knowing about. So Freud's question is: what stops the past becoming available as memory, what is it about the distancing that makes memory possible that the individual cannot bear? What would it mean to have – what kind of sentences would follow on from having – some distance from one's own past? The psychoanalyst, one could say, is trying to help the so-called patient become the historian of himself. There is, Freud can't help but notice, a resistance to history making; and the resistance makes itself known in the ways people tell their histories.

Bill Schwarz, in an essay titled 'Already The Past', reminds us that 'history and memory are not the same', and that 'historiography and memory are not the same'; even though 'historians are not wrong in seeing the enormity of the impact of memory on historiography'.[2] All these nots are in the service of promoting a contemporary historiography, 'troubled by the realm of subjective time', attentive to the preoccupations of the great modernist writers, of whom Freud is one. Indeed, in the example given above, the patient who cannot remember is living entirely in the realm of subjective time, with Freud as his historian (even if the whole notion of subjective time is as perplexing, in its way, as the notion of a private language). Freud is describing the immediacy of something called the past that is mediating (or not) something called the present. Freud has a distance, apparently, that the patient does not have; Freud becomes the historian of how this patient has been unable to have a history. Freud is preoccupied by the immediacy of the past – or rather, its being insufficiently mediated by language – and the resistances to history, by the ways people have, at once, too much and too little distance from their past, and most notably, from their childhoods: the patient is always the failed historian of his own life. But by the same token Freud is tempting us to wonder what it would be to be the successful historians of our own lives. In what would this success consist, and what would be its benefit? And what, if anything, has this got to do with historiography in which, until relatively recently, personal memory has only played a bit part? And in which, in R. G. Collingwood's definition, 'evidence is a collective name for things which singly are called documents, and a document is a thing existing here and now, of such a kind that the historian, by thinking about it, can get answers to the questions he asks about past events';[3] psychoanalysis as a therapy is, of course, merely hearsay; though it is about history, and it produces documents of psychoanalytic theory that may be of historical interest. Freud's writing may be merely a footnote, an afterthought, to Nietzsche's *On the Advantages and Disadvantages of History for Life* (1874), with the figure of the psychoanalyst speaking up for the advantages of history – of personal, remembered history – for life. But in psychoanalysis, as perhaps part of the modern history of historiography, the idea of historical distance, to paraphrase Mark Phillips, has always been a term of art. Indeed, it is inconceivable without the figures of distantiation. Consideration of the word identification alone in historiography and psychoanalytic theory would, I imagine, reveal considerable areas of overlap. Psychoanalysis, like historiography, is about the re-presentation of the significance of events; and about what makes such capacities as we have for representation problematic.

The paradox of Freud's patient is that by re-enacting rather than remembering, by collapsing the present back into the past, he keeps the past at a distance. Freud, in other words, is referring to two forms of distancing. There is the distancing of memory – more akin to Collingwood's documents as evidence – in which there is space for reflection. By thinking about the memories the patient might get answers to the questions he asks about the past. And as memories, again like documents, they can pass into the public realm, and be available for shared consideration. But in the distancing of repeated re-enactment the only evidence is the repeated action, and the disavowal that this is evidence of something that could be called the past; the only evidence of the past is repetition itself, but as evidence this only exists for the psychoanalyst. The repeated actions would be like a set of more or less identical documents with just the word history written on them. The patient who compulsively repeats in this way has very little to reflect upon, other than the fact that he keeps repeating himself. He is living in that infinite distance from the past that is no-memory. Only by describing repeated actions as a defence against memory is the distance between the past and the present constructed. Repetition is the sign of traumatic history that must not or cannot be remembered as such; wherever there is repetition in the Freudian individual's life there is, there has had to be, a breakdown in the making of history. Freud adds repeated action to the stock of available evidence of the past. Distancing – the mapping, in language and/or symptoms, of time on to space – is a prerequisite for psychic survival. And the personal past – re-presenting itself as dream, as screen-memory, as symptom or slip, as desire or repeated action – from a psychoanalytic point of view comes, as Mark Phillips says history writing should come, 'as a family of related genres, rather than (as customarily) a simple unitary one'.[4] Freud finds that for his modern individual personal history can only be inscribed in these hybrid genres. And indeed that the method required for the treatment of personal history problems was itself a hybrid of the methods proposed for historiography by Collingwood and Wilhelm Dilthey; a hybrid of what Phillips calls 'the grand narratives of scientific reason' and the reading of 'every type of human activity as belonging to its own expressive context'. Psychoanalysis, as both theory and practice is, in Phillips's phrase about modern historiography, 'a . . . tension between abstraction and immediacy'.

In the attempt to combine the sciences of nature and the sciences of culture that Freud called psychoanalysis the analyst oscillates – in his quest for a therapeutic oral history – between what Phillips refers to as empathetic imagination, and a more detached sense of the so-called patient as, in Dilthey's words, 'a structure governed by laws'. And what Freud discovers, among other things, are the myriad ways in which the patient keeps himself at a distance. When it comes to memory and desire – the reconstruction of his own history – the modern individual, in Freud's description, is a distancing machine. The patient, as Freud sees him, is always working on his ignorance. So when Phillips says, à propos of Dilthey and the hermeneutic tradition, that 'it is the strangeness or opacity of the historical record that produces the need for a leap of understanding' this would be an accurate description of the psychoanalyst in relation to the patient, and of the patient in relation to himself. The modern individual that Freud describes has an investment, so to speak, in maintaining the strangeness and opacity of his historical record of himself. Freud's therapeutic method of free-association then is itself a disillusionment with, a suspicion of, previous forms of oral historical narrative. Personal history shows through only when narrative coherence is not required. Indeed in the light of Mark Phillips's paper one might see Freud's work as one site in which the constructing of historical distance – at the level of the individual – is being studied. That, at least, personal history is all about, for Freud, the regulation of distance in language; and psychoanalysis, as a body of writing, is a kind of phenomenological account of what Freud's modern individual subject needs to keep his distance from. Psychoanalysis is a close-up on distancing techniques akin, perhaps, to Picasso's close-up on faces, as described by David Hockney. 'On the whole we don't see close up', Hockney writes.

> The only people you ever really see close up are the ones you are in bed with. When your face is close to, moving around, features move to different places, the shapes change, you see double, and so on. The closer things are to you the more difficult it is to locate their exact position – they don't really have an exact position. In genuine close-up, if you look at a face very close to, the subject is far more distorted, similar to the way Picasso would have treated a face. So one of the important things that Picasso was getting at – in cubism as in his later work – was an intimate form of seeing.[5]

'The closer things are to you', Hockney writes, 'the more difficult it is to locate their exact position – they don't really have an exact position.' The closer you get to your internal delirium in free-association, Freud says, or in a dream, things – call them historical events – don't really have an exact position. Indeed the need for things to have an exact position – the determined commitment to a definitive historical narrative – would itself be a sign of internal conflict, of repression at work. It is clearly of interest that we describe the face close up as 'distorted'. As Mark Phillips's paper indicates, our normative assumptions about distance are unusually difficult to discern; and yet, at the same time, distance, and linguistic strategies of distantiation, must be something about which we are most sensitive. Certainly all of psychoanalysis revolves around separation from object of need, and proximity to the forbidden object of desire. Distance from and distance for are the building blocks of the micro-historical enquiry that is psychoanalysis.

If, as Phillips says, 'historicism rests upon a dogmatic relationship to history which it seems unable to examine' Freud's work must be a symptom, a working through, of precisely this problem. The psychoanalytic patient that Freud invented is, in his view, suffering from a dogmatic relationship to his own history that he is unable to examine. The question is whether psychoanalysis has been able to avoid having a dogmatic relationship to both its own history, and the histories of the individuals it has treated. Freud's work certainly makes one wonder – as does Phillips's paper – what it would be to have an undogmatic relationship to history, or whether all we can do is to examine the dogmas.

In psychoanalysis dogma about distance is called phobia; but one could redescribe all of Freud's diagnostic categories – hysteria, obsessionality, paranoia and so on – as the modern individual's repertoire of distancing techniques; with each group having its own kind of dogma about its own history, and its own characteristic inability to examine this history (its own preferred historiography, as it were). And as documents of micro-history it is always interesting to read psychoanalytic case-histories for the ways in which the writer constructs his distance from the patient: the ways in which the clinician as writer keeps his distance from his own history and the history of the so-called patient. The historiography of the case-history – of what Freud refers to in the case of Dora as, 'the patient's inability to give an ordered history of their life',[6] and the doctor's ability or otherwise to construct what he considers to be an ordered history – would clearly be one way to consider how, in Phillips's words, 'historicism protected history itself from deeper enquiry'. Because the questions Philips is asking in his paper are about writing as distantiation. And he is not merely saying that distance is inevitable in the writing of history – in the sense that all writing is by definition after the event and therefore always an after-effect of the event; but rather that this fact serves to obscure the ways in which we are constructing this historical distance, and with animating intentions. It is as though distance is so taken for granted in the writing of history that the writing effects, the rhetorical strategies and the deployed vocabularies that serve to create a sense of proximity and distance, are obscured by their prevalence. The difficulty, as Phillips shows so compellingly in his *Society and Sentiment*, is in describing what these rhetorical strategies of history writing are under pressure from at any given time; what Phillips calls there, 'the impact of new understandings of society on conventional definitions of historical knowledge'.[7] And this becomes both a question of what constitutes historical evidence, and of the contemporary pertinence of historical knowledge and enquiry; of the advantages and disadvantages of history. Phillips describes the historians of the eighteenth and nineteenth centuries as being preoccupied by their negative ideals, by working out what kind of writing history-writing was trying not to be (not like the novel, not like journalism, not like classical models of historiography, and so on). It is a question too of working out the impact of commerce, of a culture of commerce, on inherited forms of historiography. And this is done by making distance a term of art. 'Just because assumptions about distance lie close to the core of history's methods and purposes', Phillips concludes *Society and Sentiment*, 'these assumptions have seldom been brought to the surface, and have more often been the subject of dogmas than questions'.[8] This, of course, is not worlds apart from the psychoanalytic assumption that making something conscious is a way of turning dogma back into its constitutive conflict. But by way of conclusion I want to rephrase Phillips's 'assumptions about distance' as 'assumptions about closeness', and to suggest that there is a peculiar difficulty about historicizing too-closeness; the idea of being too close bringing with it the question of too close for what? For Freud's patients one could say, for example, that they were too close to the traumas of their childhood, or too close to their forbidden desires to have something that we might call a personal history. That too-close is one of the ways we describe both the experience of intimacy and the experience of trauma. There is an interesting moment in *Society and Sentiment* when Phillips comments on Hume's remarks about Clarendon 'hurrying' through the King's death in his *History of the Rebellion*. Hume's 'remarks do stand', Phillips writes,

> as an important recognition that historical distance is itself a product of history. Hume clearly saw that Clarendon did not freely and individually choose his stance in relation to the regicide; rather he shared with his readers a proximity to the event that made a sentimental representation of Charles's death unthinkable. By the same token Hume knew that the passing of the pain of the events had meanwhile opened up for his readers as much as for himself possibilities for finding a new meaning.[9]

Distance from pain makes redescription possible; Hume saw that Clarendon's proximity, and his loyalties, narrowed his narrative options. The regicide could barely be put into words or dwelt upon by Clarendon. Hume's distance – what Phillips calls the 'passing of the pain of events' – makes the killing of the King available for multiple perspectives. 'Proximity to the event', Phillips writes, 'made a sentimental representation of Charles's death unthinkable'; too close means there is an excess, a too-much of something, that hampers representation, what Phillips refers to as 'possibilities for finding new meaning'. Too much closeness means too much of something – call it feeling, though it could be called various things – means too little of something else, call it meaning, or simply words. Language (and therefore) history, Hume and Phillips imply, come into their own at a distance. But the problem might also be how to historicize this very experience of too closeness; and it is noticeable that in his own account Phillips has recourse to the language of psychology. There appears to be little distance between Hume on Clarendon, Phillips on Hume on Clarendon and W. G. Sebald on the bombing of Dresden:

> The death by fire within a few hours of an entire city, with all its buildings and trees, its inhabitants, its domestic pets, its fixtures and fittings of every kind, must inevitably have led to overload, to paralysis of the capacity to think and feel in those who succeeded in escaping. The accounts of individual eye witnesses, therefore, are of only qualified value, and need to be supplemented by what a synoptic and artificial view reveals.[10]

What Sebald refers to as a synoptic and artificial view is the view from a distance that only historians of the event can have. The paradox he presents – not unlike Freud's – is that the survivors of a catastrophe, of what we might call a trauma, do not have a history; there is a history, but not for them; because they are too close, and unlike Picasso studying the faces of the people he is in bed with, they can make nothing of their experience. When it comes to traumatic events – or to certain kinds of event – it is not merely a question of what kind of distance is preferable, but of what kind of distance is possible. To be choosing one's genre is already to be at a sufficient distance.

It would be worth wondering, in Phillips's words, what 'prescriptive views of distance are . . . so embedded in our disciplinary codes' such that a historical account of devastation can sound plausible to us as readers. There is clearly, for example, a preference for coherent, intelligible narrative about events that rendered people vague, incoherent, numbed and hurried. 'The terms in which history congratulates itself on its difference from memory', Phillips writes, 'are remarkably ahistorical and (thankfully) no more than half true.' If history is not as different from memory as it looks; or if we were to model the writing of history on the workings of memory, as the great modernist experiments in writing were prompting us to do, then the coherence and intelligibility of historical narrative, which is itself inevitably and tendentiously distancing, would be radically disfigured. Freud's method of free-association assumed that the coherent account a person can give of their history is, by definition, a defensive account; that a modern person distances themselves from their history through narrative coherence and plausibility. A good story is a bad history. The question is, then, how to historicize too-closeness.

Notes and references

1   Sigmund Freud, *Standard Edition of the Complete Psychological Works*, Vol. XII, p.150.
2   Bill Schwarz, 'Already the Past: Memory and Historical Time', in *Regimes of Memory*, ed. Susannah Radstone and Katharine Hodgkin, Routledge Studies in Memory and Narrative, London, 2003.
3   R. G. Collingwood, *The Idea of History*, Oxford, 1994, p. 10.
4   Mark Salber Phillips, *Society and Sentiment: Genres of Historical Writing in Britain*, Princeton, 2000, p. 343.
5   David Hockney, *Picasso*, New York, 1990, pp. 40–1.
6   Freud, *Standard Edition*, vol. 7, p. 16.
7   Phillips, *Society and Sentiment*, p. 43.
8   Phillips, *Society and Sentiment*, p. 349.
9   Phillips, *Society and Sentiment*, p. 77.
10 W. G. Sebald, *On the Natural History of Destruction*, London, 2003, p. 26.

Further Reading: Chapters 39 to 41

Anderson, Benedict. *Imagined Communities: Reflections on the Origin and Spread of Nationalism* (revd edn) (London: Verso, 2006).

Beevor, Antony. *The Fall of Berlin 1945* (Harmondsworth: Penguin, 2003).

Bodnar, John. *Remaking America: Public Memory, Commemoration, and Patriotism in the Twentieth Century* (Princeton: Princeton University Press, 1992).

Braun, Robert. "The Holocaust and Problems of Historical Representation", *History and Theory* 33(2) (1994), 172–97.

Browning, Christopher. "German Memory, Judicial Interrogation, and Historical Reconstruction: Writing Perpetrator History from Postwar Testimony", *Probing the Limits of Representation: Nazism and the "Final Solution"*, S. Friedlander (ed.) (Cambridge, MA: Harvard University Press, 1992), 22–36.

Brugger, Robert J. (ed.). *Ourselves/Our Past: Psychological Approaches to American History* (Baltimore: Johns Hopkins University Press, 1981).

Cocks, Geoffrey and Travis L. Crosby (eds). *Psycho/History: Readings in the Method of Psychology, Psychoanalysis, and History* (New Haven: Yale University Press, 1987).

Confino, Alon. "Collective Memory and Cultural History: Problems of Method", *The American Historical Review* 102(5) (1997), 1386–403.

Crane, S. *Collecting and Historical Consciousness: New Forms for Collective Memory in Early-Nineteenth Century Germany* (Ithaca: Cornell University Press, 2000).

Denham, Scott and Mark McCulloh (eds). *W.G. Sebald: History, Memory, Trauma* (Berlin: W. de Gruyter, 2006).

Friedrich, Jürg. *The Fire: The Bombing of Germany, 1940–1945*. Trans. Allison Brown (New York: Columbia University Press, 2008).

Freud, Sigmund. "Leonardo da Vinci and A Memory of His Childhood Part IV: Justification of Pathobiography". 1910. Standard edn, James Strachey (ed.) (London: Hogarth Press, 1966), Vol. 11. 130–39.

Gillis, John R. (ed.). *Commemorations: The Politics of National Identity* (Princeton, NJ: Princeton University Press, 1994.

Huyssen, Andreas. "Air War Legacies: From Dresden to Baghdad". *New German Critique* 90 (2003), 163–76.

Ignatieff, Michael. *Blood and Belonging: Journeys into the New Nationalism* (Harmondsworth: Penguin, 1993).

— . *The Lesser Evil: Political Ethics in an Age of Terror* (Edinburgh: Edinburgh University Press, 2005).

Kansteiner, Wulf. "Finding Meaning in Memory: A Methodological Critique of Collective Memory Studies", *History and Theory* 41 (2002), 179–97.

— . *In Pursuit of German Memory: History, Television and Politics After Auschwitz* (Athens, OH: Ohio University Press, 2006), 1.

LaCapra, Dominick. *History and Memory After Auschwitz* (Ithaca: Cornell University Press, 1998).

— . *History in Transit: Experience, Identity, Critical Theory* (Ithaca: Cornell University Press, 2004).

— . "Tropisms of Intellectual History", *Rethinking History* 8 (2004), 499–529.

— . *Writing History, Writing Trauma* (Baltimore: Johns Hopkins University Press, 2001).

Lang, Berel. "Is It Possible to Misrepresent the Holocaust?" *History and Theory* 34 (February 1995), 84–9.

Langer, Lawrence. *Holocaust Testimonies: The Ruins of Memory* (New Haven: Yale University Press, 1991).

Le Goff, Jacques. "Mentalities: A New Field for Historians", *Social Sciences Information* 13(1) (1974), 81–97.

Loewenberg, Peter. *Decoding the Past: The Psychohistorical Approach* (New Brunswick, NJ: Transaction, 1996).

Long, J. J. and Whitehead, Anne. *W. G. Sebald: A Critical Companion* (Edinburgh: Edinburgh University Press, 2004).

Lowenthal, David. *The Past Is a Foreign Country* (Cambridge: Cambridge University Press, 1985).

Marrus, Michael R. *The Holocaust in History* (New York: New American Library, 1987).

Mazlish, Bruce (ed.). *Psychoanalysis and History* (New York: Grosset & Dunlap, 1971).

McGrath, William J. *Freud's Discovery of Psychoanalysis* (Ithaca: Cornell University Press, 1986).

Nora, Pierre. *Realms of Memory: Rethinking the French Past*. Trans. Arthur Goldhammer, 3 vols (New York: Columbia University Press, 1996).

— . and Jacques Le Goff (eds). *Constructing the Past: Essays in Historical Methodology* (Cambridge: Cambridge University Press, 1985).

Power, Samantha. *"A Problem from Hell": America and the Age of Genocide* (London: Flamingo, 2003).

Roper, L. *Oedipus and the Devil: Witchcraft, Sexuality, and Religion in Early Modern Europe, 1500–1700* (London: Routledge, 1994).

Rose, Jacqueline. *The Question of Zion* (Princeton, NJ: Princeton University Press, 2005).

Runyan, W. M. (ed.). *Psychology and Historical Interpretation* (Oxford: Oxford University Press, 1988).

Samuel, Raphael. *Theatres of Memory* (London: Verso, 1994).

Santner, Eric. "History beyond the Pleasure Principle: Some Thoughts on the Representation of Trauma". *Probing the Limits of Representation: Nazism and the "Final Solution"*, Saul Friedlander (ed.) (Cambridge, MA: Harvard University Press, 1992), 143–54.

Scarry, Eliane. *The Body in Pain: The Making and Unmaking of the World* (Oxford: Oxford University Press, 1985).

Schama, Simon. *Landscape and Memory* (London: Vintage, 1996).

Schneider, Peter. "Hitler's Shadow: On Being a Self-Conscious German", *Harper's Magazine* (September 1987), 49–54.

Schwarcz, Vera. *Bridge across Broken Time: Chinese and Jewish Cultural Memory* (New Haven: Yale University Press, 1998).

Sebald, W. G. "Air War and Literature", *On the Natural History of Destruction*. Trans. Anthea Bell (New York: Modern Library, 1999), 3–32.

Solzhenitsyn, Aleksandr I. "Looking Back on It All", *The Gulag Archipelago 1918–1956*. 1973. Trans. Harry Willetts (London: Collins Harvill, 1988), 451–3.

Sontag, Susan, "A Mind in Mourning", *Times Literary Supplement* (25 Feb. 2000). <http://www.tls.timesonline.co.uk>

Taylor, Frederick. *Dresden: Tuesday, February 13, 1945* (New York: HarperCollins, 2005).

ARENDT, HANNAH (1906–1975)

Abraham, David. "Where Hannah Arendt Went Wrong", *Law and History Review* 18(3) (2000), 607–12.

Baade, Hans W. "The Eichmann Trial: Some Legal Aspects", *Duke Law Journal* 1961(3), 400–420.

Barnouw, Dagme. "The Secularity of Evil: Hannah Arendt and the Eichmann Controversy", *Modern Judaism* 3(1) (1983), 75–94.

Bashaw, Rita and Dan Diner. "Hannah Arendt Reconsidered: On the Banal and the Evil in Her Holocaust Narrative", *New German Critique* 71 (1997), 177–90.

Canovan, Margaret. *Hannah Arendt: A Reinterpretation of Her Political Thought* (Cambridge: Cambridge University Press, 1992).

Clarke, Barry. "Beyond 'The Banality of Evil' ", *British Journal of Political Science* 10(4) (1980), 417–39.

Dawidowicz, Lucy S. *The Holocaust and the Historians* (Cambridge, MA: Harvard University Press, 1981).

Dossa, Shiraz. "Hannah Arendt on Eichmann: The Public, the Private and Evil", *The Review of Politics* 46(2) (1984), 163–82.

Sharpe, Barry. *Modesty and Arrogance in Judgment: Hannah Arendt's Eichmann in Jerusalem* (Westport, CT: Praeger, 1999).

Whitfield, Stephen J. *Into the Dark: Hannah Arendt and Totalitarianism* (Philadelphia: Temple University Press, 1980).

PART 10

Postmodernism and "the linguistic turn"

INTRODUCTION

H AYDEN WHITE IS A LEADING FIGURE among numerous critics associated with the linguistic turn, because he has argued that in order to understand the nature of historical writing we should focus on its artistic rather than its scientific basis.[i] The dramatic claims of his article's first paragraph suggest why this argument has been so influential. Indeed, many readers have found that once we consider White's question, certain consequences for the way we think and write about history become unavoidable. He begins with a wise and yet rebellious observation about historical scholarship, and then proceeds to ask the kinds of questions that characterize this "turn":

> In order to write the history of any given scholarly discipline or even of a science, one must be prepared to ask questions *about* it of a sort that do not have to be asked in the practice *of* it . . . What is the structure of a peculiarly *historical* consciousness? What is the epistemological status of historical *explanations*, as compared with other kinds of explanations that might be offered to account for the materials with which historians ordinarily deal? What are the possible *forms* of historical representation and what are their bases?

White wrote this in the early 1970s, in California—at a time and in a place where his students and colleagues were particularly receptive to criticism of authority (including individuals, institutions, and ideas). His eagerness to ask questions from outside the discipline—asking

---

i   According to Richard Rorty, the term was coined by Gustav Bergmann, who has argued that some philosophers ought to focus more rigorously on the purpose and consequences of language—that they require a "linguistic turn" to clarify their use of concrete words to represent abstract things and vice versa. See R. Rorty, "Introduction", *The Linguistic Turn: Essays in Philosophical Method* (Chicago: University of Chicago Press, 1967), 9.

philosophically grand questions about history as a practice — continues to challenge the special status of historical knowledge by asking us to consider its expressive structure.[ii] In turn, this entails questioning the very means by which historians understand and represent that knowledge. By saying that history constitutes a type of consciousness, White is asserting that history requires our awareness rather than our mere existence — history requires a particular kind of structuring through interpretive participation.

White argued in this famous essay that historians, like poets and novelists, communicate their ideas by adopting certain narrative styles — and like poems and novels, historical narratives demand our interpretation, which in turn shapes our historical knowledge. If, as the previous historians in this volume have suggested, historical consciousness is something that is above or beyond "fiction" — above or beyond something created by writers or readers — then we are investing considerable faith in the transparency of linguistic structures that are, in fact, reflections of interpretive viewpoints.[iii] So while White titled his article "The Historical Text as Literary Artifact", in fact he was considering historians as literary authors, with all the implications that imaginative writing and the linguistic shaping of reality such an analogy entails. Just like the novelist, historians use **emplotment** to create the narratives they describe as "historical". At the same time, White organized his article around the view that our awareness of this should not belittle history as a scholarly endeavour: indeed White did not question the ability of rigorous historians to learn about the past, and he does not suggest that historians merely invent fictions rather than uncover facts. Instead, his concern lies with historians as *writers*: he has devoted his distinguished career to arguing that we need to recognize the task of historical writing as truly imaginative and artistic, along with all the associations to literary conventions and rhetorical styles that point requires.[iv]

It is this line of questioning and these kinds of observations that have earned the adjective **postmodern**. Since previous "modern" approaches to history concerned themselves with seeking the best ways to research the past, postmodernism provides the ultimate intellectual consequence: it invites us to challenge our very notion of "the past" by questioning the terms by which we have thought about "history" as a concept and as a practice. Rather than see these questions as examples of historical progress (in terms of History as a field), it is important to point out that many of the leading advocates of the linguistic turn hesitate to call themselves historians: White, for instance, comes close to describing his work as literary criticism, offering vivid examples of why the linguistic turn can and should enrich the study of history.[v] The

ii   Brian Fay describes the year 1973 as "the convenient date to announce the full-bodied linguistic turn" but he provides a bibliography of articles and books that anticipate publications of that date. See his "Introduction", *History and Theory: Contemporary Readings*, Fay et al. (ed.) (Oxford: Blackwell, 1988), 11. This book provides a splendid anthology of the more important evaluations of "the linguistic turn" and its influence on historical writing and scholarship.

iii In Part 12, the anthropologist Clifford Geertz provides a useful definition of *fiction*: "fictions . . . are 'something made', 'something fashioned' — the original meaning of *fictio* [in Latin] — not that they are false, unfactual, or merely 'as if' thought experiments". See his "Thick Description: Toward an Interpretive Theory of Culture" (1975).

iv   Interestingly, there is concern among American professors of English Literature that current training in methods of literary interpretation is suffering because literary scholars have become "amateur historians", abandoning those skills at which they had tended to excel. See J. Gallop, "The Historicization of Literary Studies and the Fate of Close Reading", *Profession*, R. Feal (ed.) (New York: MLA, 2007), 181–6.

v   See the long footnote that opens the Introduction to his frequently-cited book *Metahistory: The Historical Imagination in Nineteenth-Century Europe* (Baltimore: Johns Hopkins University Press, 1973), 2–3. White is currently Professor of Comparative Literature at Stanford University.

French philosopher Paul Ricoeur, who has influenced White, contributed to postmodern debates concerning history by raising and responding to a wider range of theoretical questions related to interpretation (**hermeneutics**). Thankfully, his close critical engagement with Collingwood (see Part 7) and White clarifies his views.

This introduction will survey White's article by exploring his reasons for arguing that historical writing has an "essentially provisional and contingent nature". Next, we will turn to a lecture that Ricoeur gave in 1983, which asked us to think about the real nature of historical writing by engaging closely with the views of Collingwood (see Part 7) and White. Both White and Ricoeur refer to the tendency of historians to make "infinite revisions in the light of new evidence"—which is what Ricoeur means by "the unending rectifications of our configurations"—but they make this observation for different reasons and they develop it in different directions.

For White, descriptions of the past depend on our imaginative interpretations of it as well as on the historian's. It is as if the revisions that historians frequently provide are saying "what I really mean is" or "what I meant to say is"—and we should understand that what they meant, what they said, and what actually happened are three distinct things. Indeed, White goes so far as to describe historical narratives as "verbal fictions, the contents of which are as much *invented* as *found*" since, like poets and novelists, historians create new uses of language and inherit conventional ones, which means that they are tied to certain formal traditions as well as to interpretations of those traditions. This is paradoxical and poses important problems for our sense of their authority, since revision is supposed to indicate that their historical knowledge is about reality and truthfulness and not about imagination and interpretation. After all, if their historical narratives were as reliable as the truth they mean to convey, there would be no need to correct or revise them. No one ever needs to revise the scientific formula "$1+1=2$" since both its terms and its meaning are truthful and therefore beyond interpretation: their truth transcends their expression. But for historians, "the *more* we know about the past, the more difficult it is to generalize about it"—that is, to say anything unambiguous about it. For White, since historians use language to communicate the past, they always must be dependent on their own interpretations as well as ours. The linguistic turn, then, challenges authoritative claims of historians both to understand and to communicate knowledge through language; it also leads us to reconsider the linguistic nature of our own historical understanding.[vi] White then devoted his article—as he has devoted several famous books—to surveying those conventional forms that generate "the fictive component in historical narratives," since it is those conventions that "endow the events of our lives with culturally sanctioned meanings."

Writing as a philosopher interested in hermeneutics, Ricoeur concerned himself with the ways in which historians have thought about interpreting reality. Ricoeur agreed with White that the relationship between words and things is essentially arbitrary (for instance, there is nothing inherently colourful about the word *blue* or deadly about *war*). So this has meant that historians have always struggled to make their language convey reality. (This is what his

vi   Current approaches to linguistic meaning have drawn on cognitive psychology: see D. Herman (ed.) *Narrative Theory and the Cognitive Sciences* (Stanford: Center for the Study of Language and Information, 2003); L. Zunshine, *Why We Read Fiction: Theory of Mind and the Novel* (Columbus: Ohio State University Press, 2006). For a useful critical survey of the role of the reader in the construction of literary and moral meaning, see J. P. Tompkins (ed.) *Reader-Response Criticism: From Formalism to Post-Structuralism* (Baltimore: Johns Hopkins University Press, 1980).

346   INTRODUCTION TO PART 10

complicated formulation, "tropological arbitrariness [requires] endless rectification" means.)
Ricoeur proceeded by examining three ways by which historians have thought about the past
as "real": first, he explained the historians' sense of past reality by considering it as "the
Same" as current reality; as "Other" and foreign to our own sense of reality; and finally, as an
"Analogue" that requires a sense of metaphoric approximation of the past with the familiar. It
is important to show that, from the outset, Ricoeur pointed out that in all three types of
interpretation, historians and their readers experience "*incitements* to redescription that come
from the past itself". If we look at that incitement to describe the past and what he calls our
"debt of gratitude with respect to the dead", and if we take it seriously, we can begin to look
beyond the slipperiness or arbitrariness of language to value instead the non-linguistic nature
of the obligation historians feel to stay true to what they know of the past. In his conclusion,
Ricoeur pointed to the "*such as*" or "*as if*" that major historians such as Ranke used
when describing their ambitions. They claimed only to recount "the facts such as they really
occurred" (see Part 5). This important and fundamental "*such as*" illustrates Ranke's awareness that he can only give us an approximate sense of history, one that is both familiar and
unfamiliar. For Ricoeur, that openness to approximation should temper our enthusiasm for
claiming that Ranke felt he knew what "really" took place, or that Ranke thought that he
really could communicate history through writing.[vii]

The important issue for White is our conventional tendency to think of history as if it were
itself a logical and linear narrative. That conventional or **modern** view assumed (and continues
to assume) that narratives deliver understanding self-evidently, as if historical events were
structured according to specific episodes that contained their own preface, introduction, plot,
and conclusion—and as if historical events argued their own importance in the same way that
a narrator or storyteller provides direction to readers overtly (through direct claims) or implicitly (adjusting tone or style). White is eloquent on this point: "We do not *live* stories, even if
we give our lives meaning by retrospectively casting them in the form of stories. And so too
with nations or whole cultures."

In literary history, critics refer to "the canon"—a class of classic and indisputably
important books or authors—as the means by which influential readers have structured the
literary past. Most of us probably agree that Shakespeare, for instance, is the quintessential
English poet, even though we know that this is an opinion that needs to be explained rather
than a real fact that is beyond dispute. Similarly in political, national, cultural, and other forms
of history, it is those books that have become classics that structure our sense of the past—
and the classical value of those narratives (be they by Leopold von Ranke, Winston Churchill,
or anyone else) needs to be considered critically and sceptically if we are truly devoted to a
sophisticated awareness of what constitutes human history. White's project did not merely
require that we challenge the canonical status of particular texts, but rather that we engage
critically with the historical meanings that inform our very use of language—and which have
become intrinsic to language itself.

It is helpful to consider White in the context of postmodernism for several reasons, but
perhaps the most useful one is his own debt and yet movement beyond **structuralist** approaches
to narrative. At a crucial point in his argument, White echoed the influential structural linguist
Ferdinand de Saussure: "As a symbolic structure, the historical narrative does not *reproduce*

vii For lexical evidence of Ranke's concern about abilities of language in historical writing, see Part
     5, introduction, note vi.

the events it describes . . ." This observation concerning the arbitrary relation of language to things, or its essentially representative rather than constitutive means of presenting reality, had already been made by Saussure at least as early as 1907.[viii] For various reasons, including its enormous influence in subsequent linguistic, literary, and philosophical theory—as well as their practice—we can accept it as a modern view. But White took this observation further by quickly adding that

> it [the historical narrative] tells us in what direction to think about the events and charges our thought about the events with different emotional valences [forces]. The historical narrative does not *image* the things it indicates; it *calls to mind* images of the things it indicates, in the same way that a metaphor does.

This is White's central point concerning the value of the linguistic turn for History: historians use emplotment to structure the human past in the form of those linguistic documents that they write. Moreover, as readers of historical narratives, we are already familiar with conventional images of, say, heroic battles, tragic suffering, romantic escapes, and hilarious twists of fate, and therefore we already participate in literary interpretations of historical narratives. It is through our unavoidable fluency in that literary system of imagery and its figurative use of language, that we actively emplot, interpret, and therefore distort the non-literary and non-linguistic facts of history. As White reminded us, historical reality is not a story, nor is it truly structured like a narrative. This also clarifies White's view that historical understanding actually refers to increased familiarity with other narratives, rather than to specific moments in historical reality.

White warned us of the tempting "poetic fallacy", and devoted his important book *Metahistory* (1973) to identifying and clarifying those **metanarratives** or powerful literary models that inform our interpretation of historical classics.[ix] This enabled him to make far-reaching observations from his close analysis of canonical historical narratives: for example, he observed that Michelet's immersion in Romantic writings of the post-Revolutionary period led him to deliver, in his depiction of those times, "words that were never spoken" in his attempt to "make the silences of history speak" (see Part 4).[x] White's attunement with the location and meaning of linguistic structures allowed him to make sense of Michelet's impossible scholarly

viii See F. de Saussure, "Nature of the Linguistic Sign", *General Course in Linguistics*. Trans. Roy Harris (London: Duckworth, 1983), 65–9. This chapter is a reconstruction of lectures Saussure delivered in Geneva between 1907 and 1911.

ix In Part 7, I suggested that Spengler's theory of historical cycles is an example of White's "poetic fallacy". Remembering Spengler's avowed debts to Nietzsche, it is ironic that White's own concern with the relationships between language and knowledge is also an apparent response to Nietzsche. In "Language as an Alleged Science" (1872), Nietzsche observes:

> The importance of language for the development of culture lies in the fact that, in language, man juxtaposed to the world another world of his own, a place which he thought so sturdy that from it he could move the rest of the world from its foundations and make himself lord over it. To the extent he believed over long periods of time in the concepts and names of things as if they were *aeternae veritates* [eternal truths], man has acquired that pride by which he has raised himself above the animals: he really did believe that in language he had knowledge of the world.

See F. Nietzsche, *Human All Too Human: A Book for Free Spirits*. Trans. M. Faber with S. Lehmann (Lincoln: University of Nebraska Press, 1996), 18–19.

x White, *Metahistory*, 158–9.

ambition, which in one sense aimed beyond the abilities of written narrative, but in another attempted to do what all historians do by seeking to represent reality through writing.

Paul Ricoeur acknowledged White's view that literary elements structure our historical consciousness. However he devoted his lecture to providing a logical map of what he saw as the three "great classes" of critical approaches that can explain the view that history represents reality. In contrast to White, Ricoeur did not go so far as to conclude that a particular historical or literary method can provide a satisfactory or comprehensive answer. However, his own approach occupies an important place in recent postmodern discourse because Ricoeur agreed that meaning is generated through symbolic representation, and that his critical task is undertaken from within the linguistic system that he attempted to critique. Ricoeur eagerly pointed out, at least twice in this lecture, that it is our idea of debt to the past that motivates historical reading and writing. Essentially, this idea emerges from an emotional valence or feeling (to use White's term) that exists independently from language and narrative. In other words, Ricoeur also believed that historical consciousness and even our sense of historical time are structured by language and narrative. But we are not *trapped* within those structures, because we retain a persistent desire to know more and to fill out the gaps left open by attempts to record past reality.

Ricoeur began with a complex formulation of what historians do with the evidence that their narratives are meant to represent. Acting out their sense of indebtedness to the past, historians adopt the notion of *trace*.[xi] Ricoeur elaborates:

> Inasmuch as it is *left* by the *past*, it *stands for* the past, it "represents" the past, not in the sense that the past would appear itself in the mind (*Vorstellung*) but in the sense that the trace takes place of (*Vertretung*) the past, absent from historical discourse.

Since traces are left behind by the past, we can think of the trace as an actual memento or physical piece of the past, something that language clearly is not but something that language can inspire to provide. For White, language is by its very nature poetical and allusive—it always evokes other words which in turn we associate with other images (hence the German term *Vorstellung*: "imaginative association"). Ricoeur was saying that some historians want to escape, deny, or avoid that allusiveness and instead to use narrative to stand in place of (*Vertretung*: "replacement") those traces of past reality. The first kind of historical writing is representational: it presents history again (re-presents) using non-historical terms, hoping to capture the past poetically even though past reality is neither of a literary nature nor should it be open to endless imaginative recreation. The second kind of historical writing makes a much grander claim on reality by using language to replace the past—that is, by using language as if it is providing us with a trace of the real past. Examining the ways in which historians have adopted either or both of these uses of narrative was interesting for Ricoeur because it allowed

---

xi   This is not the "trace" used by Jacques Derrida to denote an unsubstantial but meaningful part of a representative object; see J. Derrida, *Of Grammatology*. Trans. G. Chakravorty Spivak (Baltimore: Johns Hopkins University Press, 1976), 70–2. For an accessible introduction to this and to related concepts in Derrida, see J. Culler, *On Deconstruction: Theory and Criticism after Structuralism* (Ithaca: Cornell University Press 1982), 156–79. Nor is Ricoeur referring to Walter Benjamin's notion of "the trace", which is the material residue and thus symbolic evidence of everyday life. See W. Benjamin, "Louis Philippe, or The Interior", [1935] *Walter Benjamin: Selected Writings, Volume 3: 1935–1938* ed. and trans. E. Jephcott et al. (Cambridge, MA: Harvard University Press, 2002), 38–47.

him to explore the theories of interpretation (or hermeneutics) that have dominated recent historiography.

Collingwood provided a familiar example of what Ricoeur called a rendering of the past as "the Same" as the present. We recall from Part 7 that Collingwood was concerned with **historical sensibility**, the emotional and intellectual ability of historians to experience elements of the past and to communicate effectively the insights that sensibility provides. While this would provide historians and their readers with a meaningful sense of the past—it would make history feel real—for Ricoeur there is an essential problem with this approach: "The idea of re-enactment is precisely intended to . . . [abolish] the temporal distance between the past and the present by the very act of *rethinking* the past." Imagining the past in the present denies those traces of the past that are emphatically not of the present: our interpretive experience, assisted by presenting the past in the present tense, abolishes our sense of time. This, by the way, is one reason why traumatized survivors of the past might be incapable of representing the past—as Adam Phillips pointed out in Part 9: bringing the past into the present through narrative shrinks **historical distance**, and this loss of time as a protective shield against memories of the past causes intolerable pain. As Mark Phillips showed in Part 3, historians orchestrate different kinds of historical distance as ways of demonstrating their vision of the past. Similarly, for Ricoeur, Collingwood's representation through imaginative re-enactment only uses those parts of the trace that are available for interpretation: this distorts the past by ignoring those parts of it that cannot be interpreted. For example, if a wartime diary is the trace found by a historian, and a transcription of it comprises his or her historical narrative (or basis of interpretation), this would represent only those textual aspects of it that are familiar to us, leaving aside and therefore "abolishing" other aspects of it—aspects which, possibly, cannot be communicated through language. Our interpretation distorted its historical object. This is why Ricoeur classifies Collingwood's approach to the past as "Same". It can only re-enact what is already familiar.

The class of "Other" can be explained by brief reference to Dilthey. As we recall from Part 6, Dilthey wanted to underline the essential fact that we are not those past figures we study: they are strangers, utterly foreign to us. We must make an imaginative effort to use empathy (*Verstehen*) in order to understand those others, and so accept that the past exists at a distance from ourselves. Ricoeur suggested that this is a promising approach, since it recognizes the importance of temporal difference (difference in time). However, by focusing only on the relationship between individuals (the historian and her or his dead subjects), in fact this approach "eludes the specific difficulty of the survival of the past in the present". Traces of the past are not actual people (unless they are, unusually, bones) and so Dilthey's notion of *Verstehen* stops us from interpreting the meaning of what that trace meant in the past and what it still might mean in the present.

Finally, Ricoeur considered White's approach to the past as an "Analogue" of the present, by which language represents history through allusion. As we know from White's article, the best that historical narrative can do is pretend to represent the past, since narrative represents things only by using the shifting meanings of language. Yet this can be immensely useful, for White and for Ricoeur, because critical study of historical narratives, themselves written and interpreted over time, can offer us insight into "the deep structure of the historical imagination" by evoking what specific terms meant at specific times. For Ricoeur, however, when White proposes that historical past can only be seen as an analogy for the present (since its traces are limited and contained by language), "we are in danger of concealing the intentionality that *crosses through* [what White calls] the tropics of discourse." For Ricoeur, our very wish to recover and make sense of the past is central to our wish to interpret the past as reality; White's theory of linguistic representation "must not lead us to give more value to the verbal power invested in our redescriptions than to the *incitements* to redescription that come from the past itself". In conclusion, as mentioned earlier, Ricoeur cites Ranke, the apparent inventor of historical science, who was eager to point out that his task was to depict the past *such as it happened*—this "such as" reveals the openness with which dedicated historians declare their understanding that their representations of history can never be truly successful. At best, they will communicate, evocatively, their wish to do justice to an aim that exceeds their grasp.

Chapter 42

Hayden White

THE HISTORICAL TEXT AS
LITERARY ARTIFACT

Hayden White, "The Historical Text as Literary Artifact", *Tropics of Discourse* (Baltimore: Johns Hopkins University Press, 1978), 81–100.

O NE OF THE WAYS that a scholarly field takes stock of itself is by considering its history. Yet it is difficult to get an objective history of a scholarly discipline, because if the historian is himself a practitioner of it, he is likely to be a devotee of one or another of its sects and hence biased; and if he is not a practitioner, he is unlikely to have the expertise necessary to distinguish between the significant and the insignificant events of the field's development. One might think that these difficulties would not arise in the field of history itself, but they do and not only for the reasons mentioned above. In order to write the history of any given scholarly discipline or even of a science, one must be prepared to ask questions *about* it of a sort that do not have to be asked in the practice *of* it. One must try to get behind or beneath the presuppositions which sustain a given type of inquiry and ask the questions that can be begged in its practice in the interest of determining why this type of inquiry has been designed to solve the problems it characteristically tries to solve. This is what metahistory seeks to do. It addresses itself to such questions as, What is the structure of a peculiarly *historical* consciousness? What is the epistemological status of historical *explanations*, as compared with other kinds of explanations that might be offered to account for the materials with which historians ordinarily deal? What are the possible *forms* of historical representation and what are their bases? What authority can historical accounts claim as contributions to a secured knowledge of reality in general and to the human sciences in particular?

Now, many of these questions have been dealt with quite competently over the last quarter-century by philosophers concerned to define history's relationships to other disciplines, especially the physical and social sciences, and by historians interested in assessing the success of their discipline in mapping the past and determining the relationship of that past to the present. But there is one problem that neither philosophers nor historians have looked at very seriously and to which literary theorists have given only passing attention. This question has to do with the status of the historical narrative, considered purely as a verbal artifact purporting to be a model of structures and processes long past and therefore not subject to either experimental or observational controls. This is not to say that historians and philosophers of history have failed to take notice of the essentially provisional and contingent nature of historical representations and of their susceptibility to infinite revision in the light of new evidence or more sophisticated conceptualization of problems. One of the marks of a good professional historian is the consistency with which he reminds his readers of the purely provisional nature of his characterizations of events, agents, and agencies found in the always incomplete historical record. Nor is it to say that literary theorists have *never* studied the structure of historical narratives. But in general there has been a reluctance to consider historical narratives as what they most manifestly are: verbal fictions, the contents of which are as much *invented as found* and the forms of which have more in common with their counterparts in literature than they have with those in the sciences.

Now, it is obvious that this conflation of mythic and historical consciousness will offend some historians and disturb those literary theorists whose conception of literature presupposes a radical opposition of history to fiction or of fact to fancy. As Northrop Frye has remarked, "In a sense the historical is the opposite of the mythical, and to tell the historian that what gives shape to his book is a myth would sound to him vaguely insulting." Yet Frye himself grants that "when a historian's scheme gets to a certain point of comprehensiveness it becomes mythical in shape, and so approaches the poetic in its structure." He even speaks of different kinds of historical myths: Romantic myths "based on a quest or pilgrimage to a City of God or classless society"; Comic "myths of progress through evolution or revolution"; Tragic myths of "decline and fall, like the works of Gibbon and Spengler"; and Ironic "myths of recurrence or casual catastrophe." But Frye appears to believe that these myths are operative only in such victims of what might be called the "poetic fallacy" as Hegel, Marx, Nietzsche, Spengler, Toynbee, and Sartre—historians whose fascination with the "constructive" capacity of human thought has deadened their responsibility to the "found" data. "The historian works inductively," he says, "collecting his facts and trying to avoid any informing patterns except those he sees, or is honestly convinced he sees, in the facts themselves." He does not work "from" a "unifying form," as the poet does, but "toward" it; and it therefore follows that the historian, like any writer of discursive prose, is to be judged "by the truth of what he says, or by the adequacy of his verbal reproduction of his external model," whether that external model be the actions of past men or the historian's own thought about such actions.

What Frye says is true enough as a statement of the *ideal* that has inspired historical writing since the time of the Greeks, but that ideal presupposes an opposition between myth and history that is as problematical as it is venerable. It serves Frye's purposes very well, since it permits him to locate the specifically "fictive" in the space between the two concepts of the "mythic" and the "historical." As readers of Frye's *Anatomy of Criticism* will remember, Frye conceives fictions to consist in part of sublimates of archetypal myth-structures. These structures have been displaced to the interior of verbal artifacts in such a way as to serve as their latent meanings. The fundamental meanings of all fictions, their thematic content, consist, in Frye's view, of the "pre-generic plot-structures" or *mythoi* derived from the corpora of Classical and Judaeo-Christian religious literature. According to this theory, we understand *why* a particular story has "turned out" as it has when we have identified the archetypal myth, or pregeneric plot structure, of which the story is an exemplification. And we see the "point" of a story when we have identified its theme (Frye's translation of *dianoia*), which makes of it a "parable or illustrative fable." "Every work of literature," Frye insists, "has both a fictional and a thematic aspect," but as we move from "fictional projection" toward the overt articulation of theme, the writing tends to take on the aspect of "direct address, or straight discursive writing and cease[s] to be literature." And in Frye's view, as we have seen, history (or at least "proper history") belongs to the category of "discursive writing," so that when the fictional element—or mythic plot structure—is *obviously* present in it, it ceases to be history altogether and becomes a bastard genre, product of an unholy, though not unnatural, union between history and poetry.

Yet, I would argue, histories gain part of their explanatory effect by their success in making stories out of *mere* chronicles; and stories in turn are made out of chronicles by an operation which I have elsewhere called "emplotment." And by emplotment I mean simply the encodation of the facts contained in the chronicle as components of specific *kinds* of plot structures, in precisely the way that Frye has suggested is the case with "fictions" in general.

The late R. G. Collingwood insisted that the historian was above all a story teller and suggested that historical sensibility was manifested in the capacity to make a plausible story out of a congeries of "facts" which, in their unprocessed form, made no sense at all. In their efforts to make sense of the historical record, which is fragmentary and always incomplete, historians have to make use of what Collingwood called "the constructive imagination," which told the historian—as it tells the competent detective—what "must have been the case" given the available evidence and the formal properties it displayed to the consciousness capable of putting the right question to it. This constructive imagination functions in much the same way that Kant supposed the *a priori* imagination functions when it tells us that even though we cannot preceive both sides of a tabletop simultaneously, we can be certain it has *two* sides if it has one, because the very concept of *one side* entails at least *one other*. Collingwood suggested that historians come to their evidence endowed with a sense of the *possible* forms that different kinds of recognizably human situations *can* take. He called this sense the nose for the "story" contained in the evidence or for the "true" story that was buried in or hidden behind the "apparent" story. And he concluded that historians provide plausible explanations for bodies of historical evidence when they succeed in discovering the story or complex of stories inplicitly contained within them.

What Collingwood failed to see was that no given set of casually recorded historical events can in itself constitute a story; the most it might offer to the historian are story *elements*. The events are *made* into a story by the suppression or subordination of certain of them and the highlighting of others, by characterization, motific repetition, variation of tone and point of view, alternative descriptive strategies, and the like—in short, all of the techniques that we would normally expect to find in the emplotment of a novel or a play. For example, no historical event is *intrinsically* tragic; it can only be conceived as such from a particular point of view or from within the context of a structured set of events of which it is an element enjoying a privileged place. For in history what is tragic from one perspective is comic from another, just as in society what appears to be tragic from the standpoint of one class may be, as Marx purported to show of the 18th Brumaire of Louis Buonaparte, only a farce from that of another class. Considered as potential elements of a story, historical events are value-neutral. Whether they find their place finally in a story that is tragic, comic, romantic, or ironic—to use Frye's categories—depends upon the historian's decision to configure them according to the imperatives of one plot structure or mythos rather than another. The same set of events can serve as components of a story that is tragic *or* comic, as the case may be, depending on the historian's choice of the plot structure that he considers most appropriate for ordering events of that kind so as to make them into a comprehensible story.

This suggests that what the historian brings to his consideration of the historical record is a notion of the *types* of configurations of events that can be recognized as stories by the audience for which he is writing. True, he can misfire. I do not suppose that anyone would accept the emplotment of the life of President Kennedy as comedy, but whether it ought to be emplotted romantically, tragically, or satirically is an open question. The important point is that most historical sequences can be emplotted in a number of different ways, so as to provide different interpretations of those events and to endow them with different meanings. Thus, for example, what Michelet in his great history of the French Revolution construed as a drama of Romantic transcendence, his contemporary Tocqueville emplotted as an ironic Tragedy. Neither can be said to have had more knowledge of the "facts" contained in the record; they simply had different notions of the kind of story that best fitted the facts they knew. Nor should it be thought that they told different stories of the Revolution because they had discovered different *kinds* of facts, political on the one hand, social on the other. They sought out different kinds of facts because they had different kinds of stories to tell. But why did these alternative, not to say mutually exclusive, representations of what was substantially the same set of events appear equally plausible to their respective audiences? Simply because the historians shared with their audiences certain preconceptions about how the Revolution might be emplotted, in response to imperatives that were generally extra historical, ideological, aesthetic, or mythical.

Collingwood once remarked that you could never explicate a tragedy to anyone who was not already acquainted with the kinds of situations that are regarded as "tragic" in our culture. Anyone who has taught or taken one of those omnibus courses usually entitled Western Civilization or Introduction to the Classics of Western Literature will know what Collingwood had in mind. Unless you have some idea of the generic attributes of tragic, comic, romantic, or ironic situations, you will be unable to recognize them as such when you come upon them in a literary text. But historical situations do not have built into them intrinsic meanings in the way that literary texts do. Historical situations are not *inherently* tragic, comic, or romantic. They may all be inherently ironic, but they need not be emplotted that way. All the historian needs to do to transform a tragic into a comic situation is to shift his point of view or change the scope of his perceptions. Anyway, we only think of situations as tragic or comic because these concepts are part of our generally cultural and specifically literary heritage. *How* a given historical situation is to be configured depends on the historian's subtlety in matching up a specific plot structure with the set of historical events that he wishes to endow with a meaning of a particular kind. This is essentially a literary, that is to say fiction-making, operation. And to call it that in no way detracts from the status of historical narratives as providing a kind of knowledge. For not only are the pregeneric plot structures by which sets of events can be constituted as stories of a particular kind limited in number, as Frye and other archetypal critics suggest; but the encodation of events in terms of such plot structures is one of the ways that a culture has of making sense of both personal and public pasts.

We can make sense of sets of events in a number of different ways. One of the ways is to subsume the events under the causal laws which may have governed their concatenation in order to produce the particular configuration that the events appear to assume when considered as "effects" of mechanical forces. This is the way of scientific explanation. Another way we make sense of a set of events which appears strange, enigmatic, or mysterious in its immediate manifestations is to encode the set in terms of culturally provided categories, such as metaphysical concepts, religious beliefs, or story forms. The effect of such encodations is to familiarize the unfamiliar; and in general this is the way of historiography, whose "data" are always immediately strange, not to say exotic, simply by virtue of their distance from us in time and their origin in a way of life different from our own.

The historian shares with his audience *general notions* of the *forms* that significant human situations *must* take by virtue of his participation in the specific processes of sense-making which identify him as a member of one cultural endowment rather than another. In the process of studying a given complex of events, he begins to perceive the *possible* story form that such events *may* figure. In his narrative account of how this set of events took on the shape which he perceives to inhere within it, he emplots his account as a story of a particular kind. The reader, in the process of following the historian's account of those events, gradually comes to realize that the story he is reading is of one kind rather than another: romance, tragedy, comedy, satire, epic, or what have you. And when he has perceived the class or type to which the story that he is reading belongs, he experiences the effect of having the events in the story explained to him. He has at this point not only successfully *followed* the story; he has grasped the point of it, *understood* it, as well. The original strangeness, mystery, or exoticism of the events is dispelled, and they take on a familiar aspect, not in their details, but in their functions as elements of a familiar kind of configuration. They are rendered comprehensible by being subsumed under the categories of the plot structure in which they are encoded as a story of a particular kind. They are familiarized, not only because the reader now has more *information* about the events, but also because he has been shown how the data conform to an *icon* of a comprehensible finished process, a plot structure with which he is familiar as a part of his cultural endowment.

This is not unlike what happens, or is supposed to happen, in psychotherapy. The sets of events in the patient's past which are the presumed cause of his distress, manifested in the neurotic syndrome, have been defamiliarized, rendered strange, mysterious, and threatening and have assumed a meaning that he can neither accept not effectively reject. It is not that the patient does not *know* what those events were, does not know the facts; for if he did not in some sense know the facts, he would be unable to recognize them and repress them whenever they arise in his consciousness. On the contrary, he knows them all too well. He knows them so well, in fact, that he lives with them constantly and in such a way as to make it impossible for him to see any other facts except through the coloration that the set of events in question gives to his perception of the world. We might say that, according to the theory of psychoanalysis, the patient has overemplotted these events, has charged them with a meaning so intense that, whether real or merely imagined, they continue to shape both his perceptions and his responses to the world long after they should have become "past history." The therapist's problem, then, is not to hold up before the patient the "real facts" of the matter, the "truth" as against the "fantasy" that obsesses him. Nor is it to give him a short course in psychoanalytical theory by which to enlighten him as to the true nature of his distress by cataloguing it as a manifestation of some "complex." This is what the analyst might do in relating the patient's case to a third party, and especially to another analyst. But psychoanalytic theory recognizes that the patient will resist both of these tactics in the same way that he resists the intrusion into consciousness of the traumatized memory traces in the *form* that he obsessively remembers them. The problem is to get the patient to "reemplot" his whole life history in such a way as to change the *meaning* of those events for him and their *significance* for the economy of the whole set of events that make up his life. As thus envisaged, the therapeutic process is an exercise in the refamiliarization of events that have been defamiliarized, rendered alienated from the patient's life-history, by virtue of their overdetermination as causal forces. And we might say that the events are detraumatized by being removed from the plot structure in which they have a dominant place and inserted in another in which they have a subordinate or simply ordinary function as elements of a life shared with all other men.

Now, I am not interested in forcing the analogy between psychotherapy and historiography; I use the example merely to illustrate a point about the fictive component in historical narratives. Historians seek to refamiliarize us with events which have been forgotten through either accident, neglect, or repression. Moreover, the greatest historians have always dealt with those events in the histories of their cultures which are "traumatic" in nature and the meaning of which is either problematical or overdetermined in the significance that they still have for current life, events such as revolutions, civil wars, large-scale processes such as industrialization and urbanization, or institutions which have lost their original function in a society but continue to play an important role on the current social scene. In looking at the ways in which such structures took shape or evolved, historians *refamiliarize* them, not only by providing more information about them, but also by showing how their developments conformed to one or another of the story types that we conventionally invoke to make sense of our own life-histories.

Now, if any of this is plausible as a characterization of the explanatory effect of historical narrative, it tells us something important about the *mimetic* aspect of historical narratives. It is generally maintained—as Frye said—that a history is a verbal model of a set of events external to the mind of the historian. But it is wrong to think of a history as a model similar to a scale model of an airplane or ship, a map, or a photograph. For we can check the adequacy of this latter kind of model by going and looking at the original and, by applying the necessary rules of translation, seeing in what respect the model has actually succeeded in reproducing aspects of the original. But historical structures and processes are not like these originals; we cannot go and look at them in order to see if the historian has adequately reproduced them in his narrative. Nor should we want to, even if we could; for after all it was the very strangeness of the original as it appeared in the documents that inspired the historian's efforts to make a model of it in the first place. If the historian only did that for us, we should be in the same situation as the patient whose analyst merely told him, on the basis of interviews with his parents, siblings, and childhood friends, what the "true facts" of the patient's early life were. We would have no reason to think that anything at all had been *explained* to us.

This is what leads me to think that historical narratives are not only models of past events and processes, but also metaphorical statements which suggest a relation of similitude between such events and processes and the story types that we conventionally use to endow the events of our lives with culturally sanctioned meanings. Viewed in a purely formal way, a historical narrative is not only a *reproduction* of the events reported in it, but also a *complex of symbols* which gives us directions for finding an *icon* of the structure of those events in our literary tradition.

I am here, of course, invoking the distinctions between sign, symbol, and icon which C. S. Peirce developed in his philosophy of language. I think that these distinctions will help us to understand what is fictive in all putatively realistic representations of the world and what is realistic in all manifestly fictive ones. They help us, in short, to answer the question, What are historical representations *representations of?* It seems to me that we must say of histories what Frye seems to think is true only of poetry or philosophies of history, namely that, considered as a system of signs, the historical narrative points in two directions simultaneously: *toward* the events described in the narrative and *toward* the story type or mythos which the historian has chosen to serve as the icon of the structure of the events. The narrative itself is not the icon; what it does is *describe* events in the historical record in such a way as to inform the reader *what to take as an icon* of the events so as to render them "familiar" to him. The historical narrative thus mediates between the events reported in it on the one side and pregeneric plot structures conventionally used in our culture to endow unfamiliar events and situations with meanings, on the other.

The evasion of the implications of the fictive nature of historical narrative is in part a consequence of the utility of the concept "history" for the definition of other types of discourse. "History" can be set over against "science" by virture of its want of conceptual rigor and failure to produce the kinds of universal laws that the sciences characteristically seek to produce. Similarly, "history" can be set over against "literature" by virtue of its interest in the "actual" rather than the "possible," which is supposedly the object of representation of "literary" works. Thus, within a long and distinguished critical tradition that has sought to determine what is "real" and what is "imagined" in the novel, history has served as a kind of archetype of the "realistic" pole of representation. I am thinking of Frye, Auerbach, Booth, Scholes and Kellogg, and others. Nor is it unusual for literary theorists, when they are speaking about the "context" of a literary work, to suppose that this context—the "historical milieu"—has a concreteness and an accessibility that the work itself can never have, as if it were easier to perceive the reality of a past world put together from a thousand historical documents than it is to probe the depths of a single literary work that is present to the critic studying it. But the presumed concreteness and accessibility of historical milieux, these contexts of the texts that literary scholars study, are themselves products of the fictive capability of the historians who have studied those contexts. The historical documents are not less opaque than the texts studied by the literary critic. Nor is the world those documents figure more accessible. The one is no more "given" than the other. In fact, the opaqueness of the world figured in historical documents is, if anything, increased by the production of historical narratives. Each new historical work only adds to the number of possible texts that have to be interpreted if a full and accurate picture of a given historical milieu is to be faithfully drawn. The relationship between the past to be analyzed and historical works produced by analysis of the documents is paradoxical; the *more* we know about the past, the more difficult it is to generalize about it.

But if the increase in our knowledge of the past makes it more difficult to generalize about it, it should make it easier for us to generalize about the forms in which that knowledge is transmitted to us. Our knowledge of the past may increase incrementally, but our understanding of it does not. Nor does our understanding of the past progress by the kind of revolutionary breakthroughs that we associate with the development of the physical sciences. Like literature, history progresses by the production of classics, the nature of which is such that they cannot be disconfirmed or negated, in the way that the principal conceptual schemata of the sciences are. And it is their nondisconfirmability that testifies to the essentially *literary* nature of historical classics. There is something in a historical masterpiece that cannot be negated, and this nonnegatable element is its form, the form which is its fiction.

It is frequently forgotten or, when remembered, denied that no given set of events attested by the historical record comprises a *story* manifestly finished and complete. This is as true as the events that comprise the life of an individual as it is of an institution, a nation, or a whole people. We do not *live* stories, even if we give our lives meaning by retrospectively casting them in the form of stories. And so too with nations or whole cultures. In an essay on the "mythical" nature of historiography, Lévi-Strauss remarks on the astonishment that a visitor from another planet would feel if confronted by the thousands of histories written about the French Revolution. For in those works, the "authors do not always make use of the same incidents; when they do, the incidents are revealed in different lights. And yet these are variations which have to do with the same country, the same period, and the same events—events whose reality is scattered across every level of a multilayered structure." He goes on to suggest that the criterion of validity by which historical accounts might be assessed cannot depend on their elements"—that is to say—their putative factual content. On the contrary, he notes, "pursued in isolation, each element shows itself to be beyond grasp. But certain of them derive consistency from the fact that they can be integrated into a system whose terms are more or less credible when set against the overall coherence of the series." But his "coherence of the series" cannot be the coherence of the *chronological* series, that sequence of "facts" organized into the temporal order of their original occurrence. For the "chronicle" of events, out of which the historian fashions his story of "what really happened," already comes preencoded. There are "hot" and "cold" chronologies, chronologies in which more or fewer dates appear to demand inclusion in a full chronicle of what happened. Moreover, the dates themselves come to us already grouped into classes of dates, classes which are constitutive of putative domains of the historical field, domains which appear as problems for the historian to solve if he is to give a full and culturally responsible account of the past.

All this suggests to Lévi-Strauss that, when it is a matter of working up a comprehensive account of the various domains of the historical record in the form of a story, the "alleged historical continuities" that the historian purports to find in the record are "secured only by dint of fraudulent outlines" imposed by the historian on the record. These "fraudulent outlines" are, in his view, a product of "abstraction" and a means of escape from the "threat of an infinite regress" that always lurks at the interior of every complex set of historical "facts." We can construct a comprehensible story of the past, Lévi-Strauss insists, only by a decision to "give up" one or more of the domains of facts offering themselves for inclusion in our accounts. Our *explanations* of historical structures and processes are thus determined more by what we leave out of our representations than by what we put in. For it is in this brutal capacity to exclude certain facts in the interest of constituting others as components of comprehensible stories that the historian displays his tact as well as his understanding. The "overall coherence" of any given "series" of historical facts is the coherence of story, but this coherence is achieved only by a tailoring of the "facts" to the requirements of the story form. And thus Lévi-Strauss concludes: "In spite of worthy and indispensable efforts to bring another moment in history alive and to possess it, a clairvoyant history should admit that it never completely escapes from the nature of myth."

It is this mediative function that permits us to speak of a historical narrative as an extended metaphor. As a symbolic structure, the historical narrative does not *reproduce* the events it describes; it tells us in what direction to think about the events and charges our thought about the events with different emotional valences. The historical narrative does not *image* the things it indicates; it *calls to mind* images of the things it indicates, in the same way that a metaphor does. When a given concourse of events is emplotted as a "tragedy," this simply means that the historian has so described the events as to *remind us* of that form of fiction which we associate with the concept "tragic." Properly understood, histories ought never to be read as unambiguous signs of the events they report, but rather as symbolic structures, extended metaphors, that "liken" the events reported in them to some form with which we have already become familiar in our literary culture.

Perhaps I should indicate briefly what is meant by the *symbolic* and *iconic* aspects of a metaphor. The hackneyed phrase "My love, a rose" is not, obviously, intended to be understood as suggesting that the loved one is *actually* a rose. It is not even meant to suggest that the loved one has the specific attributes of a rose—that is to say, that the loved one is red, yellow, orange, or black, is a plant, has thorns, needs sunlight, should be sprayed regularly with insecticides, and so on. It is meant to be understood as indicating that the beloved shares the *qualities* which the rose has come to *symbolize* in the customary linguistic usages of Western culture. That is to say, considered as a message, the metaphor gives directions for finding an entity that will evoke the images associated *with loved ones and roses alike* in our culture. The metaphor does not *image* the thing it seeks to characterize, *it gives directions* for finding the set of images that are intended to be associated with that thing. It functions as a symbol, rather than as a sign: which is to say that it does not give us either a *description* or an *icon* of the thing it represents, but *tells us* what images to look for in our culturally encoded experience in order to determine how we *should feel* about the thing represented.

So too for historical narratives. They succeed in endowing sets of past events with meanings, over and above whatever comprehension they provide by appeal to putative causal laws, by exploiting the metaphorical similarities between sets of real events and the conventional structures of our fictions. By the very constitution of a set of events in such a way as to make a comprehensible story out of them, the historian charges those events with the symbolic significance of a comprehensible plot structure. Historians may not like to think of their works as translations of fact into fictions; but this is one of the effects of their works. By suggesting alternative emplotments of a given sequence of historical events, historians provide historical events with all of the possible meanings with which the literary art of their culture is capable of endowing them. The real dispute between the proper historian and the philosopher of history has to do with the latter's insistence that events can be emplotted in one and only one story form. History-writing thrives on the discovery of all the possible plot structures that might be invoked to endow sets of events with different meanings. And our understanding of the past increases precisely in the degree to which we succeed in determining how far that past conforms to the strategies of sense-making that are contained in their purest forms in literary art.

Conceiving historical narratives in this way may give us some insight into the crisis in historical thinking which has been under way since the beginning of our century. Let us imagine that the problem of the historian is to make sense of a hypothetical *set* of events by arranging them in a *series* that is at once chronologically *and* syntactically structured, in the way that any discourse from a sentence all the way up to a novel is structured. We can see immediately that the imperatives of chronological arrangement of the events constituting the set must exist in tension with the imperatives of the syntactical strategies alluded to, whether the latter are conceived as those of logic (the syllogism) or those of narrative (the plot structure).

Thus, we have a set of events

(1) $a, b, c, d, e, \ldots \ldots \ldots, n,$

ordered chronologically but requiring description and characterization as elements of plot or argument by which to give them meaning. Now, the series can be emplotted in a number of different ways and thereby endowed with different meanings without violating the imperatives of the chronological arrangement at all. We may briefly characterize some of these emplotments in the following ways:

(2) $A, b, c, d, e, \ldots \ldots \ldots, n,$
(3) $a, B, c, d, e, \ldots \ldots \ldots, n$
(4) $a, b, C, d, e, \ldots \ldots \ldots, n$
(5) $a, b, c, D, e, \ldots \ldots \ldots, n$

And so on.

The capitalized letters indicate the privileged status given to certain events or sets of events in the series by which they are endowed with explanatory force, either as causes explaining the structure of the whole series or as symbols of the plot structure of the series considered as a story of a specific kind. We might say that any history which endows any putatively original event (a) with the status of a decisive factor (A) in the structuration of the whole series of events following after it is "deterministic." The emplotments of the history of "society" by Rousseau in his *Second Discourse*, Marx in the *Manifesto*, and Freud in *Totem and Taboo* would fall into this category. So too, any history which endows the last event in the series (e), whether real or only speculatively projected, with the force of full explanatory power (E) is of the type of all eschatological or apocalyptical histories. St. Augustine's *City of God* and the various versions of the Joachite notion of the advent of a millenium, Hegel's *Philosophy of History*, and, in general, all Idealist histories are of this sort. In between we would have the various forms of historiography which appeal to plot structures of a distinctively "fictional" sort (Romance, Comedy, Tragedy, and Satire) by which to endow the series with a perceivable form and a conceivable "meaning."

If the series were simply recorded in the order in which the events originally occurred, under the assumption that the ordering of the events in their temporal sequence itself provided a kind of explanation of why they occurred when and where they did, we would have the pure form of the *chronicle*. This would be a "naive" form of chronicle, however, inasmuch as the categories of time and space alone served as the informing interpretative principles. Over against the naive form of chronicle we could postulate as a logical possibility its "sentimental" counterpart, the ironic denial that historical series have any kind of larger significance or describe any imaginable plot structure or indeed can even be construed as a story with a discernible beginning, middle, and end. We could conceive such accounts of history as intending to serve as antidotes to their false or overemplotted counterparts (nos. 2, 3, 4, and 5 above) and could represent them as an ironic return to mere chronicle as constituting the only sense which any cognitively responsible history could take. We could characterize such histories thus:

(6) "*a, b, c, d, e . . . ., n*"

with the quotation marks indicating the conscious interpretation of the events as having nothing other than seriality as their meaning.

This schema is of course highly abstract and does not do justice to the possible mixtures of and variations within the types that it is meant to distinguish. But it helps us, I think, to conceive how events might be emplotted in different ways without violating the imperatives of the chronological order of the events (however they are construed) so as to yield alternative, mutually exclusive, and yet, equally plausible interpretations of the set. I have tried to show in *Metahistory* how such mixtures and variations occur in the writings of the master historians of the nineteenth century; and I have suggested in that book that classic historical accounts always represent attempts both to emplot the historical series adequately and implicitly to come to terms with other plausible emplotments. It is this dialectical tension between two or more possible emplotments that signals the element of critical self-consciousness present in any historian of recognizably classical stature.

Histories, then, are not only about events but also about the possible sets of relationships that those events can be demonstrated to figure. These sets of relationships are not, however, immanent in the events themselves; they exist only in the mind of the historian reflecting on them. Here they are present as the modes of relationships conceptualized in the myth, fable, and folklore, scientific knowledge, religion, and literary art, of the historian's own culture. But more importantly, they are, I suggest, immanent in the very language which the historian must use to *describe* events prior to a scientific analysis of them or a fictional emplotment of them. For if the historian's aim is to familarize us with the unfamiliar, he must use figurative, rather than technical, language. Technical languages are familiarizing only *to* those who have been indoctrinated in their uses and only *of* those sets of events which the practitioners of a discipline have agreed to describe in a uniform terminology. History possesses no such generally accepted technical terminology and in fact no agreement on what kind of events make up its specific subject matter. The historian's characteristic instrument of encodation, comunication, and exchange is ordinary educated speech. This implies that the only instruments that he has for endowing his data with meaning, of rendering the strange familiar, and of rendering the mysterious past comprehensible, are the techniques of *figurative* language. All historical narratives presuppose figurative characterizations of the events they purport to represent and explain. And this means that historical narratives, considered purely as verbal artifacts, can be characterized by the mode of figurative discourse in which they are cast.

If this is the case, then it may well be that the kind of emplotment that the historian decides to use to give meaning to a set of historical events is dictated by the dominant figurative mode of the language he has used to *describe* the elements of his account *prior* to his composition of a narrative. Geoffrey Hartman once remarked in my hearing, at a conference on literary history, that he was not sure that he knew what historians of literature might want to do, but he did know that to write a history meant to place an event within a context, by relating it as a part of some conceivable whole. He went on to suggest that as far as he knew, there were only two ways of relating parts to wholes, by metonymy and by synecdoche. Having been engaged for some time in the study of the thought of Giambattista Vico, I was much taken with this thought, because it conformed to Vico's notion that the "logic" of all "poetic wisdom" was contained in the relationships which language itself provided in the four principal modes of figurative representation: metaphor, metonymy, synecdoche, and irony. My own hunch—and it is a hunch which I find confirmed in Hegel's reflections on the nature of nonscientific discourse—is that in any field of study which, like history, has not yet become disciplinized to the point of constructing a formal terminological system for describing its objects, in the way that physics and chemistry have, it is the types of figurative discourse that dictate the fundamental forms of the data to be studied. This means that the *shape* of the *relationships* which will appear to be inherent in the objects inhabiting the field will in reality have been imposed on the field by the investigator in the very *act of identifying and describing* the objects that he finds there. The implication is that historians *constitute* their subjects as possible objects of narrative representation by the very language they use to *describe* them. And if this is the case, it means that the different kinds of historical interpretations that we have of the same set of events, such as the French Revolution as interpreted by Michelet, Tocqueville, Taine, and others, are little more than projections of the linguistic protocols that these historians used to *pre*-figure that set of events prior to writing their narratives of it. It is only a hypothesis, but it seems possible that the conviction of the historian that he has "found" the form of his narrative in the events themselves, rather than imposed it upon them, in the way the poet does, is a result of a certain lack of linguistic self-consciousness which obscures the extent to which descriptions of events *already* constitute interpretations of their nature. As thus envisaged, the difference between Michelet's and Tocqueville's accounts of the Revolution does not reside only in the fact that the former emplotted his story in the modality of a Romance and the latter his in the modality of Tragedy; it resides as well in the tropological mode—metaphorical and metonymic, respectively—with each brought to his apprehension of the facts as they appeared in the documents.

I do not have the space to try to demonstrate the plausibility of this hypothesis, which is the informing principle of my book *Metahistory*. But I hope that this essay may serve to suggest an approach to the study of such discursive prose forms as historiography, an approach that is as old as the study of rhetoric and as new as modern linguistics. Such a study would proceed along the lines laid out by Roman Jakobson in a paper entitled "Linguistics and Poetics," in which he characterized the difference between Romantic poetry and the various forms of nineteenth-century Realistic prose as residing in the essentially metaphorical nature of the former and the essentially metonymical nature of the latter. I think that this characterization of the difference between poetry and prose is too narrow, because it presupposes that complex macrostructural narratives such as the novel are little more than projections of the "selective" (i.e., phonemic) axis of all speech acts. Poetry, and especially Romantic poetry, is then characterized by Jakobson as a projection of the "combinatory" (i.e., morphemic) axis of language. Such a binary theory pushes the analyst toward a dualistic opposition between poetry and prose which appears to rule out the possibility of a metonymical poetry and a metaphorical prose. But the fruitfulness of Jakobson's theory lies in its suggestion that the various forms of both poetry and prose, all of which have their counterparts in narrative in general and therefore in historiography too, can be characterized in terms of the dominant trope which serves as the paradigm, provided by language itself, of all significant relationships conceived to exist in the world by anyone wishing to represent those relationships in language.

Narrative, or the syntagmatic dispersion of events across a temporal series presented as a prose discourse, in such a way as to display their progressive elaboration as a comprehensible form, would represent the "inward turn" that discourse takes when it tries to *show* the reader the true form of things existing behind a merely apparent formlessness. Narrative *style*, in history as well as in the novel, would then be construed as the modality of the movement from a representation of some original state of affairs to some subsequent state. The primary *meaning* of a narrative would then consist of the destructuration of a set of events (real or imagined) originally encoded in one tropological mode and the progressive restructuration of the set in another tropological mode. As thus envisaged, narrative would be a process of decodation and recodation in which an original perception is clarified by being cast in a figurative mode different from that in which it has come encoded by convention, authority, or custom. And the explanatory force of the narrative would then depend on the contrast between the original encodation and the later one.

For example, let us suppose that a set of experiences comes to us as a grotesque, i.e., as unclassified and unclassifiable. Our problem is to identify the modality of the relationships that bind the discernible elements of the formless totality together in such a way as to make of it a whole of some sort. If we stress the similarities among the elements, we are working in the mode of metaphor; if we stress the differences among them, we are working in the mode of metonymy. Of course, in order to make sense of any set of experiences, we must obviously identify both the parts of a thing that appear to make it up and the nature of the shared aspects of the parts that make them identifiable as a totality. This implies that all original characterizations of anything must utilize *both* metaphor and metonymy in order to "fix" it as something about which we can meaningfully discourse.

In the case of historiography, the attempts of commentators to make sense of the French Revolution are instructive. Burke decodes the events of the Revolution which his contemporaries experience as a grotesque by recoding it in the mode of irony; Michelet recodes these events in the mode of synecdoche; Tocqueville recodes them in the mode of metonymy. In each case, however, the movement from code to recode is narratively described, i.e., laid out on a time-line in such a way as to make the interpretation of the events that made up the "Revolution" a kind of drama that we can recognize as Satirical, Romantic, and Tragic, respectively. This drama can be followed by the reader of the narrative in such a way as to be experienced as a progressive revelation of what the *true* nature of the events consists of. The revelation is not experienced, however, as a restructuring of perception so much as an illumination of a field of occurrence. But actually what has happened is that a set of events originally encoded in one way is simply being decoded by being recoded in another. The events themselves are not substantially changed from one account to another. That is to say, the data that are to be analyzed are not significantly different in the different accounts. What is different are the modalities of their relationships. These modalities, in turn, although they *may* appear to the reader to be based on different theories of the nature of society, politics, and history, ultimately have their origin in the figurative characterizations of the whole set of events as representing wholes of fundamentally different sorts. It is for this reason that, when it is a matter of setting different interpretations of the same set of historical phenomena over against one another in an attempt to decide which is the best or most convincing, we are often driven to confusion or ambiguity. This is not to say that we cannot distinguish between good and bad historiography, since we can always fall back on such criteria as responsibility to the rules of evidence, the relative fullness of narrative detail, logical consistency, and the like to determine this issue. But it is to say that the effort to distinguish between good and bad interpretations of a historical event such as the Revolution is not as easy as it might at first appear when it is a matter of dealing with alternative interpretations produced by historians of relatively equal learning and conceptual sophistication. After all, a great historical classic cannot be disconfirmed or nullified either by the discovery of some new datum that might call a specific explanation of some element of the whole account into question or by the generation of new methods of analysis which permit us to deal with questions that earlier historians might not have taken under consideration. And it is precisely because great historical classics, such as works by Gibbon, Michelet, Thucydides, Mommsen, Ranke, Burckhardt, Bancroft, and so on, cannot be definitely disconfirmed that we must look to the specifically literary aspects of their work as crucial, and not merely subsidiary, elements in their historiographical technique.

What all this points to is the necessity of revising the distinction conventionally drawn between poetic and prose discourse in discussion of such narrative forms as historiography and recognizing that the distinction, as old as Aristotle, between history and poetry obscures as much as it illuminates about both. If there is an element of the historical in all poetry, there is an element of poetry in every historical account of the world. And this because in our account of the historical world we are dependent, in ways perhaps that we are not in the natural sciences, on the techniques of *figurative language* both for our *characterization* of the objects of our narrative representations and for the *strategies* by which to constitute narrative accounts of the transformations of those objects in time. And this because history has no stipulatable subject matter uniquely its own; it is always written as part of a contest between contending poetic figurations of what the past *might* consist of.

The older distinction between fiction and history, in which fiction is conceived as the representation of the imaginable and history as the representation of the actual, must give place to the recognition that we can only know the *actual* by contrasting it with or likening it to the *imaginable*. As thus conceived, historical narratives are complex structures in which a world of experience is imagined to exist under at least two modes, one of which is encoded as "real," the other of which is "revealed" to have been illusory in the course of the narrative. Of course, it is a fiction of the historian that the various states of affairs which he constitutes as the beginning, the middle, and the end of a course of development are all "actual" or "real" and that he merely recorded "what happened" in the transition from the inaugural to the terminal phase. But both the beginning state of affairs and the ending one are inevitably poetic constructions, and as such, dependent upon the modality of the figurative language used to give them the aspect of coherence. This implies that all narrative is not simply a recording of "what happened" in the transition from one state of affairs to another, but a progressive *redescription* of sets of events in such a way as to dismantle a structure encoded in one verbal mode in the beginning so as to justify a recoding of it in another mode at the end. This is what the "middle" of all narratives consist of.

All of this is highly schematic, and I know that this insistence on the fictive element in all historical narratives is certain to arouse the ire of historians who believe that they are doing something fundamentally different from the novelist, by virtue of the fact that they deal with "real," while the novelist deals with "imagined," events. But neither the form nor the explanatory power of narrative derives from the different contents it is presumed to be able to accommodate. In point of fact, history—the real world as it evolves in time—is made sense of in the same way that the poet or novelist tries to make sense of it, i.e., by endowing what originally appears to be problematical and mysterious with the aspect of a recognizable, because it is a familiar, form. It does not matter whether the world is conceived to be real or only imagined; the manner of making sense of it is the same.

So too, to say that we make sense of the real world by imposing upon it the formal coherency that we customarily associate with the products of writers of fiction in no way detracts from the status as knowledge which we ascribe to historiography. It would only detract from it if we were to believe that literature did not teach us anything about reality, but was a product of an imagination which was not of this world but of some other, inhuman one. In may view, we experience the "fictionalization" of history as an "explanation" for the same reason that we experience great fiction as an illumination of a world that we inhabit along with the author. In both we recognize the forms by which consciousness both constitutes and colonizes the world it seeks to inhabit comfortably.

Finally, it may be observed that if historians were to recognize the fictive element in their narratives, this would not mean the degradation of historiography to the status of ideology or propaganda. In fact, this recognition would serve as a potent antidote to the tendency of historians to become captive of ideological preconceptions which they do not recognize as such but honor as the "correct" perception of "the way things *really* are." By drawing historiography nearer to its origins in literary sensibility, we should be able to identify the ideological, because it is the fictive, element in our own discourse. We are always able to see the fictive element in those historians with whose interpretations of a given set of events we disagree; we seldom perceive that element in our own prose. So, too, if we recognized the literary or fictive element in every historical account, we would be able to move the teaching of historiography onto a higher level of self-consciousness than it currently occupies.

What teacher has not lamented his inability to give instruction to apprentices in the *writing* of history? What graduate student of history has not despaired at trying to comprehend and imitate the model which his instructors *appear* to honor but the principles of which remain uncharted? If we recognize that there is a fictive element in all historical narrative, we would find in the theory of language and narrative itself the basis for a more subtle presentation of what historiography consists of than that which simply tells the student to go and "find out the facts" and write them up in such a way as to tell "what really happened."

In my view, history as a discipline is in bad shape today because it has lost sight of its origins in the literary imagination. In the interest of *appearing* scientific and objective, it has repressed and denied to itself its own greatest source of strength and renewal. By drawing historiography back once more to an intimate connection with its literary basis, we should not only be putting ourselves on guard against *merely* ideological distortions; we should be by way of arriving at that "theory" of history without which it cannot pass for a "discipline" at all.

Chapter 43

Paul Ricoeur

THE REALITY OF THE
HISTORICAL PAST

Paul Ricoeur (1913–2005), *The Reality of the Historical Past* (Milwaukee: Marquette University Press, 1984), 1–11, 14–17, 20–21, 25–51.

WHAT DOES THE TERM "real" signify when it is applied to the historical past? What do we mean when we say that something really happened?

This is the most troublesome question that historiography puts to historical thinking. And yet, if it is difficult to find a reply, the question itself is inevitable: it makes the difference between history and fiction [. . .]

A solid conviction animates the historian here; regardless of the selective nature of collecting, preserving, and consulting documents, and of their relation to the questions put to them by the historian, even including the ideological implications of all these manoeuvres —the recourse to documents marks a dividing line between history and fiction. Unlike the novel, the constructions of the historian are intended to be reconstructions of the past. Through documents and by means of documentary proof, the historian is constrained by *what once was*. He owes a *debt* to the past, a debt of *gratitude* with respect to the dead, which makes him an *insolvent debtor*. This is the conviction that is expressed by the notion of trace. Inasmuch as it is *left* by the *past*, it *stands for* the past, it "represents" the past, not in the sense that the past would appear itself in the mind *(Vorstellung)* but in the sense that the trace takes place of *(Vertretung)* the past, absent from historical discourse. I shall thus venture to speak of *taking-the-place-of* in order to distinguish the relation of *Vertretung* from that of *Vorstellung*. It characterizes the *indirect* reference specific to knowledge through traces and distinguishes from any other the referential mode of the history of the past. This referential mode is inseparable from the work of configuration itself: for it is only by means of the unending rectification of our configurations that we form an idea of the inexhaustible resources of the past.

[. . .] For the historian, the notion of trace constitutes a sort of *terminus* in the series of referrals that, from archives, lead to the document, and from the document to the trace. However, the historian does not usually linger over the enigma of historical reference, over its essentially indirect character. For the historian, the ontological question implicitly contained in the notion of trace ["does this object exist as the historical evidence?"] is immediately covered over by the epistemological question of the document, namely, its value as warrant, support, proof in the explanation of the past.[1]

In the pages that follow, an attempt will be made, if not to resolve, at least to articulate the enigma of *representing* or *of taking-the-place-of*: we shall attempt to say what is original in the historical past's position of *vis-à-vis* in relation to the *limiting-concepts* of critical thinking. [. . .] With the idea of the past, the undeniably positive features of the limiting-idea come to the forefront: something once took place. What is no longer, one day was. This pre-dominance of the positive side of the limiting-idea is evident in that it is the past *such as* it was that moves historians to provide historical configurations and that is behind their endless rectifications, as they touch up the painting. This is what I wanted to suggest when I spoke of the historian's *inexhaustible debt* with respect to the past. The past is thus a guiding-concept as much as a limiting-concept.

The question is then to know if the gap that is opened in this way between the historian's *vis-à-vis* and [. . .] limiting-concepts does not express the very originality of the idea [of] the past in relation to the *thing-in-itself*, [. . .]
[. . .]

I propose, more for didactic than for dialectical reasons, to place the idea of historical past under the incomparable categories that Plato in the *Sophist* called the "great classes." For reasons that will become more apparent as our work of thinking progresses, I have chosen the three great classes of the Same, the Other, and the Analogue. I do not claim that the idea of the past is constructed dialectically by the very interconnection of these three great classes, I merely hold that we are talking sense about the past by thinking of it, in turn, under the sign of the Same, then of the sign of the Other, and finally under that of the Analogue.

1. Under the sign of the Same: "Re-enacting" the past in the present.

Under the sign of the Same I place the conception of history as "re-enactment" of the past, following Collingwood.[2] The discussion will show in what way this conception calls for, as its counterpart, that of the past as history's *absent* partner.

In order to avoid any confusion, it is important to indicate at the outset Collingwood's true place in the philosophy of history. *Re-enactment* is not a method of understanding – even less of explanation – which would take its place somewhere between William Dray and Henrik von Wright. The fact that it has served as a warrant for intuitionist variations of understanding and that, as such, it is generally dismissed by most epistemologists has done it a great disservice. From this stems the major misunderstanding concerning Collingwood's work, which is that of a philosopher more than that of an epistemologist. From the outlying regions of epistemology, Collingwood moves into the realm of philosophy, which he defines in the Introduction to *The Idea of History* as thought about thought.[3] Three themes are connected to this second-order reflection. They concern: a) the *documentary* character of historical thought; b) the work of *imagination* in the interpretation of documentary data; c) finally, the desire that the constructions of the imagination *re-enact* the past. The theme of re-enactment must be maintained in third place, in order clearly to indicate that it does not designate an alternative method but the result aimed at by documentary interpretation and by the constructions of the imagination.[4]

The interpretation of documents is so closely tied to the definition of history that it suffices to distinguish the history of human affairs from the study of natural changes, including that of evolution in biology.[5] More precisely, the notion of documentary proof, placed at the forefront of the investigation refers directly to the problem that concerns us, that of knowledge through traces. Of what, exactly, are documents the trace? Essentially, of the "inside" of events, which has to be called *thought*. Not that the "outside" of the event, that is to say the physical changes affecting bodies, is itself inessential. On the contrary, *action* is the union of the inside and the outside of an event. This is why the historian is the one who is obliged "to think himself into the action, to discern the thought of its agent" (213).[6] On the other hand, the term "thought" has to be taken in a broader sense than that of rational thought; it covers the whole field of intentions and motivations, to the extent that a desire can figure in the major premise of a practical syllogism by its character of desirability, which is hypothesized to be expressible. This vast sense given to thought allows us to say that knowing *what* happened is already knowing *why* it happened (214).

This twofold delimitation of the concept of "historical evidence" by means of the notion of the "inside" of the event and that of the "thought" of the historical agent leads directly to that of re-enactment. To introduce oneself through thought into an action in order to discern in it the thought of its agent is precisely to *re-think* in one's own mind what was once thought. This sudden access to re-enactment has, nevertheless, the drawback of giving support to the idea that re-enactment is a type of method: "All history," it is affirmed, "is the re-enactment of past thought in the historian's own mind" (215). On the other hand, a warning is contained in the very definition of re-enactment: re-enacting does not consist in reliving but in rethinking, and rethinking already contains the critical moment that forces us to take the detour by way of the historical imagination.[7]

The document, in fact, raises the question of the relation of historical thought to the past as past. But it can only raise it: the reply lies in the role of *historical imagination* that marks the specificity of history in relation to the observation of a given present, as in perception. The section on "historical imagination" is surprisingly audacious. Confronting the authority of written sources, the historian is his own source, "his own authority" (236). His *autonomy* combines the selective character of the work of thought, the audacity of "historical construction," and the tenacity of the suspicions of the one who, following Bacon's adage, "puts Nature to the question." Nor does Collingwood hesitate to speak of "*a priori* imagination," to signify that the historian is the judge of his sources and not the opposite. The criterion for his judgement is the coherence of his construction.
[. . .]

Unlike the novelist, the historian has a double task: to construct a coherent picture, one that makes sense, and "to construct a picture of things as they really were and of events as they really happened" (246). The second task is only partially accomplished, if one considers the "rules of method" that distinguish the work of the historian from that of the novelist: localizing all historical narratives in the same space and the same time, being able to relate all historical narratives to a single historical world, making the picture of the past agree with the documents in their known state or as historians discover them. If one were to stop at this, the problem of the past as such would not arise; for to localize events in the same space and in the same time not implying the notion of the present is also to leave aside the notion of the past. This is why, in the paragraph on the historical imagination, Collingwood frankly states that "as Descartes might have said . . . the idea of the past is an 'innate' idea" (247).[8]

The idea of re-enactment is precisely intended to [. . .] [abolish] the temporal distance between the past and the present by the very act of *rethinking* what was once thought. [. . .]

[. . .] Thoughts, it is stated, are in a sense events happening in time, but in another sense, for the person who is concerned with the act of re-thinking, thoughts are not in time at all (217).[9] The fact that this thesis is put forward in the context of a comparison between the ideas of human *nature* and of human *history* is easy to understand. It is in nature that the past is separated from the present: "The past, in a natural process, is a past superseded and dead" (225). In nature, instants die and are replaced by others. On the other hand, the same event, known historically, "survives in the present" (225).

[. . .] All that is finally meaningful is the current possession of the activity of the past. Might it be objected that it was necessary that the past *survive* by leaving a trace, and that we become *inheritors* of the past in order to be able to re-enact past thoughts? Survival and inheritance are natural processes. Historical knowledge begins with the way in which we enter into possession of them. [. . .]

[. . .]

Collingwood's entire enterprise collapses when confronted with the possibility of passing from the thought of the past as *mine* to the thought of the past as *other*. [. . .]

At the same time, Collingwood's failure indicates the direction to be pursued: his theory of re-enactment decomposes the notion of historical time into two notions, both of which deny it. On one side we find change, where one occurrence replaces another; on the other, the intemporality of the act of thinking: the survival of the past which makes us its trace possible, tradition which makes us its heirs, and preservation which allows new possession. These mediations cannot be placed under the "great class" of the Same.

2. Under the sign of the "Other": A negative ontology of the past?

Dialectical reversal: if the past cannot be thought under the great category of the Same, could it be grasped better under that of the Other?

In those historians who remain open to philosophical questioning, we find a number of suggestions which, despite their diversity, point in the direction of what could be called a negative ontology of the past.

Taking the opposite tack from Collingwood, many contemporary historians see in history an admission of otherness, a restitution of temporal distance, even an apology for difference, pushed to the point of temporal exoticism. But very few have ventured to cast in theoretical terms this pre-eminence of the Other in historical *thought*.

The concern with recovering the sense of temporal *distance* stands in opposition to the ideal of re-enactment when the main emphasis is placed, in the idea of historical inquiry, on *taking a distance* with respect to the temptation of or the attempt at "empathy." Problematization then predominates over received traditions, and conceptualization over the simple transcription of lived experience in its own language; history then tends as a whole to *make the past remote* from the present. It can even expressly attempt to produce an effect of strangeness in contrast to the desire to make the unfamiliar familiar again, to use Hayden White's vocabulary. And why would the effect of strangeness not go so far as to make us feel we are in a foreign, unknown land? The historian has only to become the ethnologist of days gone by. This strategy of putting-at-a-distance is placed in the service of the attempt at spiritual *decentering* practiced by those historians most concerned with repudiating the Western ethnocentrism of traditional history.[10]

Under what category can we think of taking-a-distance in this way?

It is not without importance that we begin with what is most familiar to the authors influenced by the German tradition of *Verstehen*: the understanding of *others* is for this tradition the best analogue of historical understanding. Dilthey was the first to found all the human sciences – including history – on the capacity the mind possesses to transport itself into an alien psychic life, on the basis of signs that "express" – that is, carry to the outside – another's personal experience. Correlatively, the transcendence of the past has as its first model the alien psychic life carried outside by "signitive" conduct. A bridge is thus built from two sides; on the one hand, expression crosses the gap separating the outside and the inside; on the other hand, the transfer in imagination into an alien life spans the gap separating the self and its other. From these two converging externalizations results the first objectification by which a private life and an alien life open up one to the other. Onto this first objectification are grafted the second-order objectifications resulting from the inscription of the expression in lasting signs – first and foremost among these, writing.

[This] model of other people is certainly a very solid one inasmuch as it not only involves otherness but joins the Same to the Other. But the paradox is that by abolishing the difference between others today and others of yesteryear, it obliterates the problematic of temporal distance and eludes the specific difficulty related to the survival of the past in the present – a difficulty that constitutes the difference between knowledge of other people and knowledge of the past.

[. . .]

I want to conclude this review of the various figures of otherness with Michel de Certeau's contribution, which seems to me to go farthest in the direction of a negative ontology of the past.[11] This, too, is an apology for difference but in a context of thought that pulls it in almost the opposite direction from the preceding one. This context is that of a "sociology of historiography," in which it is no longer the *object* or the *method* of history that is rendered problematical but the historian himself with regard to his operation. To do history is to produce something. The question then arises concerning the social place of the historical operation.[12]

Now this place, according to de Certeau, is the unsaid *par excellence* of historiography; in its scientific claim, history indeed believes it is – or claims to be – produced from no particular position, from nowhere. This argument, we note, holds just as much for the critical school as for the positivist school. Where, in fact, does the tribunal of historical judgement reside?

This is the context of questions in which a new interpretation of the event as difference comes to light. How? Once the false claim of the historian to produce history in what approximates a state of socio-cultural weightlessness is unmasked, the suspicion dawns that any history that claims to be scientific is vitiated [corrupted] by a desire for mastery, which sets the historian up as the arbiter of meaning. This desire for mastery constitutes the ideology implicit in history.[13]

[. . .]

3. Under the sign of the "Analogue": a tropological approach?

The two groups of approaches examined above are not useless to us, despite their unilateral character.

One way of "saving" their respective contributions to the question of history's ultimate referent is to join their efforts together under the sign of the "great class" which itself associates the Same and the Other. The Similar is this great category. Or better, the Analogue which is a resemblance between relations rather than between simple terms.

It is not just the dialectical, nor the merely didactical quality of the series: Same, Other, Analogue that has goaded me on to search a solution to our problem in the direction we are now going to explore. What first caught my attention were the veiled anticipations of this way of categorizing the relation of taking-the-place-of or of representing in the preceding analyses, where we repeatedly encountered expressions of the form: *such as* (such as it was). When one wants to indicate the difference between fiction and history, one unavoidably invokes the idea of a certain correspondence between the narrative and what really happened. At the same time, we are well aware that this re-construction is a different construction than the course of events reported. This is why many authors reject the term "representation" which seems to them to be tainted by the myth of a term-by-term reduplication of reality in the image we have of it. But the problem of correspondence to the past is not thereby eliminated by the change of vocabulary. If history is a construction, the historian instinct-ively would like this construction to be a reconstruction. It would even appear that this intention to reconstruct by constructing is part of the workload of the good historian. Whether this undertaking is placed under the sign of friendship or under that of curiosity, the historian is moved by the vow to do justice to the past. The relation of historians to the past is first of all that of an unpaid debt in which they represent us all, we the readers of their works. This idea of debt, which may seem strange at first, appears to me to emerge out of an expression common to the painter and to the historian: both seek to "render" a landscape, a course of events. Under the term "render" can be recognized the intention of "rendering its due to what is and to what was."

[. . .]

It is at this stage in my reflection that I encounter Hayden White's effort in *Metahistory* and in *Tropics of Discourse*,[14] to complete a theory of emplotment by means of a theory of "tropes" (metaphor, metonymy, synecdoche, irony). This recourse to tropology is imposed by the singular structure of historical discourse, in contrast to simple fiction. This discourse, in fact, appears to call for a double allegiance: on the one hand, to the constraints related to the privileged *type* of plot, and on the other, to the past itself through the documentary information accessible at a given moment. The historian's work then consists in making the narrative structure a "model," an "icon" of the past, capable of "representing" it.[15]

How does the theory of tropes reply to the second challenge? Reply: ". . . before a given domain can be interpreted, it must first be construed as a ground inhabited by discernible figures" (30). "In order to figure 'what really happened' in the past . . . the historian must first *prefigure* as a possible object of knowledge the whole set of events reported in the documents" *(ibid.)*[16] The function of this poetic operation is to trace out possible itineraries in the "historical field" and in this way to give an initial contour to the possible objects of knowledge. The intention is certainly oriented toward what really happened in the past, but the paradox is that one can designate what it is that precedes all narrative only by *prefiguring* it.

The advantage of the four basic tropes of classical rhetoric is that they offer a variety of figures of discourse for this work of prefiguration and thus preserve the wealth of sense belonging to the historical object, both by the equivocity peculiar to each trope and by the multiplicity of the available figures.[17]

Actually, of the four tropes considered – metaphor, metonymy, synecdoche, and irony – it is the first that has an expressly *representative* function. But White seems to mean that the other tropes, though distinct, are but variants of metaphor,[18] and serve as correctives to the naiveté of metaphor, which tends to hold as adequate the asserted resemblance (my love, a rose). It is not the first time in the rhetorical tradition that metaphor is taken by turns as the generic term and as a species on the level of the tropes. In this way, metonymy, by equating the part and the whole, would tend to make the historical factor the mere mani-festation of another factor. Synecdoche, by connecting the extrinsic relation of two orders of phenomena to an intrinsic relation among shared qualities, is held to figure an integration rather than a reduction. Irony is taken to be responsible for introducing a negative note in this work of prefiguration – something like a "second thought." In contrast to metaphor, which inaugurates and in another sense holds the tropological domain together, White calls irony "metatropological," inasmuch as it provokes the awareness of the possible misuse of figurative language and continually recalls the problematical nature of language as a whole. None of these attempts at structuring constitutes a logical constraint and the figurative operation can stop at the first stage, that of metaphorical characterization. But only the complete route from the most naive apprehension (metaphor) to the most reflective (irony) authorizes us to speak of a tropological structure of consciousness.[19] As a whole, the theory of tropes, by its deliberately linguistical character, can be integrated into the table listing the modalities of historical imagination, without thereby being integrated into its properly explanatory modes. As such, it constitutes the deep structure of the historical imagination.[20]

The benefit expected from this tropological chart of consciousness, concerning the *representative* ambition of history, is immense: rhetoric governs the description of the historical field, as logic governs an explanatory argument: "For it is by figuration that the historian virtually *constitutes* the subject of the discourse."[21] In this sense, identifying the type of plot is the domain of logic, but the intention of the series of events that history, as the system of signs, attempts to describe is the province of tropology. Tropological prefiguration proves to be more specific, to the extent that explanation by emplotment is held to be more generic.[22]

[. . .]

I should now like to say a few words about where I situate myself with respect to the subtle and often obscure analyses of Hayden White. I do not hesitate to say that, to me, they constitute a decisive contribution to the exploration of the third dialectical moment of the idea of taking-the-place-of or representing by which I am attempting to express the relation of the historical narrative to the real past. By giving the support of *tropological* resources to the matching up of a given plot with a given course of events, these analyses provide precious credibility to our suggestion that the relation to the reality of the past must move in succession by way of the framework of the Same, the Other, and the Analogue. Tropological analysis is the sought after explicitation of the category of the Analogue. It says only one thing: things must have happened *as* it is stated in the narrative considered. Thanks to the tropological frame of reference, the *being-as* of the past event is brought to language.

Having said this, I readily grant that [. . .] the recourse to the theory of tropes runs the risk of erasing the dividing line between *fiction* and *history*.[23]

By placing the accent almost exclusively on the rhetorical *process*, we are in danger of concealing the intentionality that *crosses through* the "tropics of discourse in the direction of past events." [. . ..] I like the formula: "We can only know the actual by contrasting it with or likening it to the imaginable" (*The Writing of History*, p. 60). If this formula is to maintain its full force, the concern with "drawing historiography nearer to its origins in literary sensibility" (*ibid.*, p. 61) must not lead us to give more value to the verbal power invested in our redescriptions than to the *incitements* to redescription that come from the past itself. In other words, a certain tropological arbitrariness[24] must not make us forget the kind of constraint that the past exerted on historical discourse through known documents, by demanding an endless *rectification* on its part. The relation between history and fiction is certainly more complex than we can ever say. Of course, we must combat the prejudice that the historian's language could be made entirely transparent, so that the facts would speak for themselves, as if it were enough to get rid of the *ornaments of prose* in order to do away with the *figures of poetry*. But we would be unable to combat this first prejudice if we did not at the same time combat the second, according to which the literature of imagination, because it constantly makes use of fiction, can have no hold on reality. These two prejudices must be fought together.[25]

This is the role that can be assigned to the "great class" of the Analogue in the pursuit of what once was. The aporia of the trace as "standing for" the past finds in *seeing-as* a partial resolution. This *as* was already utilized in Ranke's expression, which has unceasingly goaded us on: the facts *such as* they *really* occurred. In the analogical interpretation of the relation of taking-the-place-of or representing, the accent has shifted from "really" to "such as." Better: *really* has meaning only in terms of *such as*. It is the equivalent of *being as* to which *seeing as* responds and corresponds.

[. . .]

It remains that this exploration of the relation of *taking-the-place-of* or of *representing* cannot help but be incomplete – incomplete because it is abstract. As we have learned from phenomenology, and in particular from that of Heidegger, the past, cut off from the dialectic between future, past, and present remains an abstraction. This is why the present study constitutes no more than an attempt to think more clearly what remains *enigmatic* in the pastness of the past as such. By placing it successively under each of the "great classes" of the Same, the Other, and the Analogue, we have at least preserved the mysterious character of the debt which makes the master of plots into a servant of the memory of men of the past.

Notes

1   Marc Bloch's example in *Apologie pour l'histoire; Le métier d'historien* is revealing in this regard. He is well familiar with the problematic of the trace, which presents itself to him through that of the document ("what do we mean by documents, if not a 'trace', that is to say the perceptible mark left by a phenomenon itself impossible to grasp" [56]). But the enigmatic relation of the trace is immediately connected up to the notion of *indirect observation* familiar to the empirical sciences, to the extent that the physicist, the geographer, for example, rely upon observations made by others (*ibid.*). What differs with respect to the other sciences of observation is indeed to be sought elsewhere than in the *indirect* nature of the observation: the historian, unlike the physicist, cannot bring about the appearance of the trace. But this drawback belonging to historical observation is compensated for in two ways: the historian can multiply the reports of witnesses, and confront them with one another; Marc Bloch speaks here of the "handling of testimonies of opposite types" (65). In particular, the historian can give precedence to "witnesses in spite of themselves," that is, to documents that were not intended to inform or to instruct contemporaries and even less, future historians (62). For a philosophical investigation concerned with the ontological import of the notion of trace, the desire to show that knowledge through traces belongs to the field of observation, tends to conceal the enigmatic character of the notion of the trace of the *past*. Authenticated testimony functions like a delegated *eye witness* account: I see through the eyes of someone else. An illusion of contemporaneousness is thus created which allows us to place knowledge through traces along the line of indirect observation. And yet no one has more magnificently stressed than has Marc Bloch the bond of history to time, when he defines it as the "science of men in time" (36).

2   *The Idea of History* is a posthumous work published by T.M. Knox in 1946 (Clarendon Press; Oxford University Press, 1956), on the basis of lectures given at Oxford in 1936, after Collingwood's appointment to the chair of metaphysical philosophy, and partially revised by the author up to 1940. The most complete parts of the manuscript have been grouped together by the editor in the fifth part, entitled *Epilegomena*, pp. 205–324.

3   "Philosophy is reflective . . . thought about thought" (p. 1). It has opposite it "the past, consisting of particular events in space and time which are no longer happening" (5). Again: "actions of human beings that have been done in the past" (9). The question is: what about them makes it possible for historians to know them? The accent placed on the past character of events means that the question can be answered only by people that are qualified in two ways, as historians having experience of their profession, and as philosophers capable of reflecting on this experience.

4   In the table of contents adopted by the editor of *The Idea of History*, the paragraph on "History as Reenactment of Past Experience" (282–302) follows that on "The Historical Imagination" (231–249) – this was the first in the series of Oxford lectures, and that on "Historical Evidence," where the concept of human history is opposed to that of human nature, and where re-enactment is examined directly, without passing by way of the reflection on imagination. This order of presentation is understandable if re-enactment, without constituting the methodological process characteristic of history, defines its *telos*, and with this its place in knowledge. I shall follow the order: historical

evidence, historical imagination, history as re-enactment of past experience in order to indicate that the concept of re-enactment is more philosophical than epistemological.

5   For Collingwood the question is less knowing how history differs from the sciences of nature than knowing if there can be knowledge of man other than historical. To this question he gives a clearly negative answer, for the simple reason that the concept of human history takes the place assigned by Locke and Hume to that of human nature: "the right way of investigating mind is by the methods of history" (209). "History is what the science of human nature professed to be" (*ibid.*). "All knowledge of mind is historical" (219). "The science of human mind resolves itself into history" (220). It will be noted that Collingwood calls "interpretation of evidence" (9–10) what we translate here by "*preuve documentaire*" (documentary proof). Here, he says, "evidence is a collective name for things which singly are called documents, and a document is a thing existing here and now, of such a kind that the historian, by thinking about it, can get answers to the questions he asks about past events" (10).

6   The semiological character of the problem is evident, although Collingwood does not use these terms: external changes are not those the historian looks *at* but *those through which* he looks, in order to discern the thought within them (214). This relation between the inside and the outside corresponds to what Dilthey called *Ausdruck* (expression).

7   "All thinking is critical thinking: the thought which re-enacts past thoughts, therefore, criticizes them in re-enacting them" (216). If, indeed, the cause is the inside of the event itself, then only a long work of interpretation permits us to picture ourselves in the situation, to think for ourselves what an agent in the past judged appropriate to do. Rethinking what was once thought cannot help but be an extremely complex operation, if the original thought already was complex in itself.

8   "Every present has a past of its own, and any imaginative reconstruction of the past aims at reconstructing the past of this present, the present in which the act of imagination is going on, as here and now perceived" (247). Note the sui-referential definition of the present, implied in the referral to the act of imagination as it is perceived here and now.

9   The Roman constitution, or its modification by Augustus, once it is re-thought, is not less an eternal object than Whitehead's triangle: "The peculiarity which makes it historical is not the fact of its happening in time, but the fact of its becoming known to us by our re-thinking the same thought which created the situation we are investigating, and thus coming to understand that situation" (218).

10 This concern with taking a distance is very strong in French historians; François Furet demands, in the beginning of *Penser la Révolution française*, that intellectual curiosity break with the spirit of commemoration or of denouncing. *Un autre Moyen Age*, to use J. Le Goff's title, is the Middle Ages seen as different from our age. For Paul Veyne, in *L'Inventaire des différences*, "the Romans existed in a manner just as exotic and just as ordinary as the Tibetans or the Nambikwara, for example, neither more nor less; so that it becomes impossible to continue to consider them as a sort of value-standard" (8).

11 "L'opération historique," in *Faire de l'Histoire*, edited by Le Goff and Nora (Paris: Gallimard), 1976, I.

12 "Conceiving of history as an operation would be trying . . . to understand it as the relation between a *place* (a recruitment, a milieu, a profession, etc.) and procedures of analysis (a discipline)" (4).

13 This argument will not surprise readers of Horkheimer and Adorno – the great leaders of the Frankfurt School – who revealed the will for domination at work in the rationalism of the Enlightenment. One finds something similar to this in Habermas's first works, where he denounces the claim of intrumental reason to annex the historico-hermeneutical sciences.

14 *Metahistory. The Historical Imagination in XIXth Century Europe* (Baltimore and London: The Johns Hopkins University Press, 1973), pp. 31–38. *Tropics of Discourse* is the title of a collection of articles published between 1966 and 1978 (Baltimore: The John Hopkins University Press, 1978). I shall be considering mainly the articles written after *Metahistory*: "The Historical Text as Literary Artifact," *Clio* 3, no. 3 (1974); "Historicism, History and the Figurative Imagination," *History and Theory* 14, no. 4 (1975); "The Fictions of Factual Representation," in *The Literature of Fact*, edited by Angus Fletcher (New York: Columbia University Press, 1976). The article published in *Clio* is also included in *The Writing of History*, edited by Canary and Kozecki (University of Wisconsin Press, 1978).

15 "I will consider the historical work as what it most manifestly is – that is to say, a verbal structure in the form of a narrative prose discourse that purports to be a model, or icon, of past structures and processes in the interest of *explaining what they were by representing* them" (*Metahistory*, 2). Further on it is stated: "Historical accounts purport to be verbal models, or icons, of specific segments of the historical process" (30). Similar expressions can be read in articles written after *Metahistory*: the

desire to construct "the kind of story that best fitted" the known facts (*The Writing of History*, 48). The historian's subtlety consists "in matching up a specific plot-structure with a set of historical events that he wishes to endow with a meaning of a particular kind" (*ibid.*). With these two image-laden expressions the entire problem of the representation of the past is posed in conjunction with the operation of emplotment.

16   "This preconceptual linguistic protocol will in turn be – by virtue of its essentially *prefigurative* nature – characterizable in terms of the dominant tropological mode in which it is cast" (*Metahistory*, 30). It is termed *prefigurative*, not in our sense (*Mimèsis* I), namely as a structure of human praxis preceding the work of configuration by the historical narrative or by the fictional narrative, but in the sense of a *linguistical* operation unfolding on the level of the still indiscriminate mass of documentary data: "By identifying the dominant mode (or modes) of discourse, one penetrates to that level of conscious-ness on which a world of experience is *constituted* prior to being analyzed" (*Metahistory*, 33).

17   This is why, in opposition to the binarism fashionable in linguistics and in structural anthropology, Hayden White goes back to the four tropes of Ramus and Vico. The 1974 article "Historicism, History and the Figurative Imagination," offers a well-argued criticism of Jakobson's binary analysis. It is not surprising that *Tropics of Discourse* contains several essays that deal directly or indirectly with Vico's logical poetics, Vico who is shown to be Hayden White's true master, along with Kenneth Burke and his *Grammar of Motives* (the expression "master-tropes" comes from the latter).

18   I understand in this sense the following statement, which at first sight is disconcerting: "Irony, Metonymy, and Synecdoche are kinds of Metaphor, but they differ from one another in the kinds of *reductions or integrations* they effect on the literal level of their meanings and by the kinds of illuminations they aim at on the figurative level. Metaphor is essentially *re-presentational*, Metonymy is *reductionist*, Synecdoche is *integrative*, and Irony is *negational*" (*Metahistory*, 34).

19   The problem is taken up again in "Fictions of Factual Representation" (*Tropics of Discourse*, 122–144): metaphor gives preference to resemblance, metonymy to continuity, hence *dispersion* in mechanical series of relations (it is Burke who is responsible for characterizing dispersion as "reduction"); synecdoche gives preference to the part-whole relation, hence to integration, from which result holistic or organicist interpretations. Irony, suspension, gives preference to contradiction, aporia, by stressing the *inadequacy* of any *characterization*. It is also recalled, as it was in *Metahistory*, that there is a certain affinity between a given trope and a given mode of emplotment: between metaphor and the romanesque, between metonymy and the tragic, etc.

20   The introduction to *Tropics of Discourse*: "Tropology, Discourse and Modes of Human Consciousness" (1–26) ascribes to this "tropical element in all discourse, whether of the realistic or the more imaginative kind," a more ambitious function than that accorded it by *Metahistory*: tropology now covers all the deviations leading from one meaning *toward* another meaning "with full credit to the possibility that things might be expressed otherwise" (2). This field is no longer limited to the prefiguration of the historical field; it extends to any sort or preinterpretation. Tropology bears the colors of rhetoric as it confronts logic, wherever understanding strives to render familiar the unfamiliar or the alien, by paths irreducible to logical proof. Its role is so vast and so fundamental that it can, little by little, become the equivalent of a *cultural critique* of a rhetorical type of all the areas where consciousness, in its cultural *praxis*, enters into a debate with its milieu. Any new system of encoding is, at this deep level, figurative.

21   "Historicism, History and the Imagination," *Tropics of Discourse*, 106.

22   "This conception of the historical discourse permits us to consider the specific *story* as an *image* of the events *about which* the story is told, while the generic story-type serves as a *conceptual model* to which the events are to be likened in order to permit their encodation as elements of a recognizable structure" (*Tropics of Discourse*, 110). The division between the rhetoric of tropes and the logic of modes of explanation is substituted for the overly basic distinction between fact (information) and interpretation (explication). Conversely, their imbrication in the past allows us to reply to the paradox posed by Lévi-Strauss in *The Savage Mind*, based on the fact that history was held to be torn between a *micro-level* where events are disolved in aggregates of physicochemical reactions and a *macro-level* where history is lost in the vast cosmologies that rhythm the rise and decline of civiliza-tions of the past. There is thus held to be a *rhetorical* solution to the paradox according to which an excess of information ruins understanding and an excess of understanding impoverishes informa-tion (*Tropics of Discourse*, 102). Insofar as the work of figuration adjusts *facts* and *explanations* to one another, it allows the historian to stay half-way between the two extremes underscored by Lévi-Strauss.

23   Hayden White is not unaware of this danger. This is why he invites us "to understand what is fictive

in all putatively realistic representations of the world and what is realistic in all manifestly ficti
ones" (*The Writing of History*, 52). In the same sense: . . . we experience the fictionalization of history
as an explanation for the same reason that we experience great fiction as an illumination of a world
that we inhabit along with the author. In both we re-cognize the forms by which consciousness both
constitutes and colonizes the world it seeks to inhabit comfortably" (*ibid.*, 61). Having said this,
White is not too far away from what we mean by the *interweaving reference* of fiction and of history.
But, as he does not really show us what is realistic in all fiction, only the fictive side of the
purportedly realistic representation of the world is stressed.

24 "The implication is that historians *constitute* their subjects as possible objects of narrative representation by the very language they use to *describe* them" (*ibid.*, 57).

25 Hayden White readily grants this: novel and history are not simply indistinguishable as verbal
artifacts, both of them purport to offer a verbal image of reality. One is not concerned with
consistency and the other with correspondence; both, by different paths, aim at consistency *and*
at correspondence: "It is in these twin senses that all written discourse is cognitive in its aims
and mimetic in its means" (*Tropics of Discourse*, 122). He also states: ". . . history is no less a form of
fiction than the novel is a form of historical representation" *(ibid.).*

g: Chapters 42 and 43

The Origins of Postmodernity (London: Verso, 1998).

istory and Postmodernism", History and Theory 28 (1989), 137–53.

Tropology: The Rise and Fall of Metaphor (Berkeley: University of
    Press, 1994).

— . *Narrative Logic: A Semantic Analysis of the Historian's Language* (London: Martinus
    Nijhoff, 1983).

Appleby, Joyce. "One Good Turn Deserves Another: Moving Beyond the Linguistic; A Response
    to David Harlan", *The American Historical Review* 94(5) (1989), 1326–32.

Barthes, Roland. "The Discourse of History". Trans. Stephen Bann. *Comparative Criticism: A
    Yearbook* 3 (1981), 3–28.

— . "Writing and the Novel", *Writing Degree Zero*. 1953. Trans. A. Lavers and C. Smith
    (London: Jonathan Cape, 1967), 35–46.

Burke, Peter. "History of Events and the Revival of Narrative", *New Perspectives on
    Historical Writing*. 2nd edn, Peter Burke (ed.) (Cambridge: Polity Press, 2001),
    283–301.

Cameron, Averil (ed.). *The History as Text: The Writing of Ancient History* (Chapel Hill:
    University of North Carolina Press, 1989).

Canary, Robert H. and Henry Kozicki. *The Writing of History: Literary Form and Historical
    Understanding* (Madison: University of Wisconsin Press, 1978).

Carr, David. "Narrative and the Real World: An Argument for Continuity", *History and Theory*
    25(2) (1986), 117–31.

— . *Time, Narrative and History* (Bloomington: Indiana University Press, 1986).

Danto, Arthur C. *Narration and Knowledge* (New York: Columbia University Press, 1985).

Davis, Natalie Zemon. *Fiction in the Archives: Pardon Tales and their Tellers in Sixteenth-
    Century France* (Stanford: Stanford University Press, 1987).

— . *The Return of Martin Guerre* (Cambridge, MA: Harvard University Press, 1983).

Gallagher, Catherine and Stephen Greenblatt. *Practicing New Historicism* (Chicago: Uni-
    versity of Chicago Press, 2001).

Gorman, J. L. "Objectivity and Truth in History", *Inquiry* 17 (1974), 373–94.

Harlan, David. "Intellectual History and the Return of Literature", *The American Historical
    Review* 94(3) (1989), 581–609.

Jameson, Fredric. *The Political Unconscious: Narrative as a Socially Symbolic Act.* (new edn)
    (London: Routledge, 2002).

Jenkins, Keith. *The Postmodern History Reader* (London: Routledge, 1997).

— . "Why Bother with the Past?" *Rethinking History* 1(1) (1997), 56–66.

Kellner, Hans. "The Politics of Interpretation", *The Politics of Interpretation*, W. J. T. Mitchell
    (ed.) (Chicago: University of Chicago Press, 1982), 301.

LaCapra, Dominick. "History, Language, and Reading: Waiting for Crillon", *American Historical
    Review* 100 (1995), 799–828.

— . "Rhetoric and History", *History and Criticism* (Ithaca: Cornell University Press,
    1985), 15–44.

Lorenz, Chris. "Historical Knoweldge and Historical Reality", *History and Theory* 33(3)
    (1994), 297–327.

Megill, Allan. " 'Grand Narratives' and the Discipline of History", *A New Philosophy of
    History*, Frank Ankersmit and Hans Kellner (eds) (Chicago: University of Chicago
    Press, 1995), 151–73.

Mink, Louis. "History and Fiction as Modes of Comprehension", *New Literary History* 1 (1970), 514–58.

Partner, Nancy F. "Making Up Lost Time: Writing on the Writing of History", *Speculum* 61 (1986), 90–117.

Pocock, J. G. A. "The Concept of a Language and the Métier d'Historien: Some Considerations on Practice", *The Languages of Political Theory in Early-Modern Europe*, Anthony Pagden (ed.) (Cambridge: Cambridge University Press, 1987), 19–40.

Rorty, Richard. (ed.). *The Linguistic Turn: Essays in Philosophical Method* (Chicago: University of Chicago Press, 1967).

Stone, Lawrence. "Notes: History and Postmodernism", *Past and Present* 131 (1991), 217–18.

— . "The Revival of Narrative: Reflections on a New Old History", *Past and Present* 85 (1979), 3–24.

Toews, John E. "Intellectual History after the Linguistic Turn: The Autonomy of Meaning and the Irreducibility of Experience", *American Historical Review* 92 (1987), 879–907.

Tompkins, Jane P. (ed.). *Reader-Response Criticism: From Formalism to Post-Structuralism* (Baltimore: Johns Hopkins University Press, 1980).

Waugh, Patricia. *Practising Postmodernism/Reading Modernism* (London: Edward Arnold, 1992).

Zagorin, Perez. "History, the Referent, and Narrative: Reflections on Postmodernsim Now", *History and Theory* 38(1) (1999), 1–24.

Zunshine, Lisa. *Why We Read Fiction: Theory of Mind and the Novel* (Columbus: Ohio State University Press, 2006).

WHITE, HAYDEN (b. 1928)

Carroll, N. "Interpretation, History and Narrative", *Monist* 73(2) (1990), 134–66.

Cohen, Sande. *Historical Culture: On the Recoding of an Academic Discipline* (Berkeley, CA: University of California Press, 1987).

Constan, D. "The Function of Narrative in Hayden White's *Metahistory*", *Clio* 11(1) (1981), 65–78.

Jenkins, Keith. *On "What is History?": From Carr and Elton to Rorty and White* (London: Routledge, 1995).

Kansteiner, Wulf. "Hayden White's Critique of the Writing of History", *History and Theory* 32(3) (1993), 273–95.

Kellner, Hans. "Narrativity in History: Post-Structuralism and Since", *History and Theory* 26(4) (1987), 1–29.

— . *Language and Historical Representation: Getting the Story Crooked* (Madison, WI: University of Wisconsin Press, 1989).

La Capra, Dominick. *Rethinking Intellectual History: Texts, Contexts, Language* (Ithaca: Cornell University Press, 1983).

Marwick, Arthur. "Two Approaches to Historical Study: The Metaphysical (Including 'Postmodernism') and the Historical", *Journal of Contemporary History* 30(1) (1995), 5–35.

McCullagh, B. "Metaphor and Truth in History", *Clio* 23(1) (1993), 23–49.

"*Metahistory*: Six Critiques", *History and Theory* 19(4) (1980), 1–101.

Momgliano, A. "The Rhetoric of History and the History of Rhetoric: On Hayden White's Tropes", *Comparative Criticism* 3 (1981), 259–68.

Roth, Michael S. "Cultural Criticism and Political Theory: Hayden White's Rhetorics of History", *Political Theory* 16(4) (1988), 636–46.

Vann, Richard T. "The Reception of Hayden White", *History and Theory* 37(2) (1998), 143–62.

RICOEUR, PAUL (1913–2005)
Carr, David, Paul Ricoeur, C. Taylor and Hayden White. "Round Table on *Temps et récit,* vol. 1", *University of Ottawa Quarterly* 55(4) (1985), 287–322.
Clark, S. H. *Paul Ricoeur* (London: Routledge, 1990).
Gehart, Mary. "Imagination and History in Ricoeur's Interpretation Theory". *Philosophy Today* 23(1) (1979), 51–68.
Ihde, Don. *Hermeneutic Phenomenology: The Philosophy of Paul Ricoeur.* Foreword Paul Ricoeur (Evanston, IL: Northwestern University Press, 1971).
Joy, Morny (ed.). *Paul Ricoeur and Narrative: Context and Contestation* (Calgary: University of Calgary Press, 1997).
Kellner, H. "Narrativity in History: Post-structuralism and Since", *History and Theory* 26(4) (1987), 1–29.
Kemp, T. Peter and David Ramussen. *The Narrative Path: the Later Works of Paul Ricoeur* (Cambridge, MA: MIT Press, 1989).
Klemm, David E. *The Hermeneutical Theory of Paul Ricoeur: A Constructive Analysis* (Lewisburg, WV: Associated University Press, 1983).
Lowe, Walter James. "The Coherence of Paul Ricoeur", *The Journal of Religion* 61(4) (1981), 384–402.
Nordquist, Joan. *Paul Ricoeur: A Bibliography* (Santa Cruz, CA: Reference and Research Services, 1999).
Pucci, E. "History and the Question of Identity: Kant, Arendt, Ricoeur", *Philosophy and Social Criticism* 21(5/6) (1995), 125–36.
Reagan, Charles E. *Paul Ricoeur: His Life and Work* (Chicago: University of Chicago Press, 1996).
— . (ed.). *Studies in the Philosophy of Paul Ricoeur* (Athens, OH: Ohio University Press, 1979).
Robinson, G. D. "Paul Ricoeur and the Hermeneutics of Suspicion: A Brief Overview and Critique", *Premise* 2(8) (1995).
Schwartz, Sanford. "Hermeneutics and the Productive Imagination: Paul Ricoeur in the 1970s", *The Journal of Religion* 63(3) (1983), 290–300.
Thompson, Martyn P. "Reception Theory and the Interpretation of Historical Meaning", *History and Theory* 32(3) (1993), 248–72.
White, Hayden. *The Content of the Form: Narrative Discourse and Historical Representation* (Baltimore: Johns Hopkins University Press, 1987).
— . "The Question of Narrative in Contemporary Historical Theory", *History and Theory* 23(1) (1984), 1–33.
Wood, David. *On Paul Ricoeur: Narrative and Interpretation* (London: Routledge, 1991).
Zagorin, Perez. "Historiography and Postmodernism: Reconsiderations", *History and Theory* 29(3) (1990), 263–274.

PART 11

History and sexual identity

INTRODUCTION

A T THE MIDPOINT OF JOAN WALLACH SCOTT'S article, she observed that various political regimes created laws "that put women in their place". Such laws included denying women the right to vote, controlling their choice to bear children, forbidding mothers from taking paid employment, and imposing certain standards of dress. Although it might appear that Scott's interpretation of those policies offered a conventional feminist viewpoint on legal or social history, in fact it presented a new and innovative argument:

> These actions and their timing make little sense in themselves; in most instances,
> the state had nothing immediate or material to gain from the control of women.
> The actions can only be made sense of as part of an analysis of the construction
> and consolidation of power. An assertion of control or strength was given form as
> a policy about women.

When this article was first published in 1986, these remarks defined a new departure from current feminist approaches to history (often described as second wave), that recovered and then described women's history by focusing on their experiences. By emphasizing both the real existence and importance of women's experience, the second wave sought to correct a sexist bias that previously ignored the history of women. For example, the feminist historian Rosalind Miles explained that "it is essential to acknowledge that the interests of women have been opposed to, and by, those of men . . . historical periods of great progress for men have often involved losses and setbacks for women".[i] Now, Scott suggested, discriminatory treatment of

---

i   R. Miles, *The Women's History of the World* (London: Paladin, 1989), 13. For a suggestive
    discussion of feminist scholarship from the 1970s that argues "the history of women demands
    different periodization than does political history", see G. Lerner, "Placing Women in History",
    The Majority Finds Its Past: Placing Women in History (New York: Oxford University Press,
    1979), 122–4.

women makes little sense apart from its social meaning; discrimination cannot be explained simply by acknowledging certain beliefs or by pointing to certain facts. Therefore she questioned what had long been accepted by feminist historians and their sympathetic readers: that women have been mistreated simply because it was in powerful men's interests to do so. Scott addressed this point by asking a bold question: "Why (and since when) have women been invisible as historical subjects, when we know they participated in the great and small events of history?" By focusing on the construction and consolidation of power, Scott advocates a new way for historians to think, research, and write about the historical meaning of **sexual identity** through experience and representation. Her argument is that our social and cultural ideas about gender (those things that we consider "feminine" and "masculine") determine what we mean when we refer to sex ("female" and "male" or "woman" and "man"). By emphasizing the social processes by which powerful ideas create biological categories, Scott has complicated conventional ways of thinking about history—especially, perhaps, for those who remained committed to the basic claims of "second wave" feminism.

In the passage just quoted, Scott showed that governments have legitimated themselves by identifying one group of citizens and then representing them as weak by legally forcing them to act weakly. The result was a powerful representation of the "fact" that women are naturally dependent on the male protection of the ruling regime—in other words, the regime created and enforced a particular meaning for sexual identity. The implication for historians is that we must shift our attention away from recovering women's experience to examining the meaning of "woman" as a social or legal or psychological category. This approach does not invalidate conventionally feminist approaches: certainly, social and political forces have defined sexual identity in a binary way, and the recovery of neglected material will remain valuable. Still, by asking us to focus on the process by which sexual identity has been created and experienced (some would say "performed," emphasizing its range of possible meanings),[ii] Scott has asked us to think critically about conceptual approaches and basic values that have informed feminist history. Writing in 1973, when feminist history was starting to achieve a measure of academic respect, Adrienne Rich (then a professor) clarified a basic belief of the second wave:

> In terms of the *content* of her education, there is no discipline that does not obscure or devalue the history and experience of women as a group. . . . That the true business of civilization has been in the hands of men is the lesson absorbed by every student of the traditional sources.[iii]

ii   Interestingly, one of the most innovative theorists of gender, Judith Butler, also tends to view its expression in narrative terms. It is important to emphasize that definitions of gender that focus on identity rather than materiality do not minimize fundamentally activist concerns—using scholarship to identify and rectify injustice. Butler points to the "performative" nature of gender identity in social and ideological terms: "the tacit collective agreement to perform, produce, and sustain discrete and polar genders as cultural fictions is obscured by the credibility of those productions—and the punishments that attend not agreeing to believe in them." See *Gender Trouble: Feminism and the Subversion of Identity* (London: Routledge, 1989), 140.

iii   A. Rich, "Toward a Woman-Centered University," in *On Lies, Secrets, and Silence: Selected Prose 1966–1978* (New York: Norton, 1979), 135. When this article was first published, Rich was Professor of English at the City University of New York.

Scott reconsiders the relations of sex to gender in using a modified **historicism** rather than **ideological** approach. This allows our engagement with actual historical evidence to guide our research, taking into account the **mythologies** that inform such engagement. Indeed, in this article Scott argued that we need to generate a critical approach to history that can "disrupt the notion of fixity, to discover the nature of the debate or repression that lends to the appearance of timeless permanence in binary gender representation". Only by researching the many meanings that gender identity has constituted in the past, and by tracing their origins, representation, and consequences, can we develop a sophisticated understanding of human history—which, in turn, can illuminate legacies of injustice.[iv]

Like Hayden White (in Part 10), Scott understands that her approach to history requires new methods. Recent feminist scholars have asked whether language can contain the richness and diversity of social and psychological experience,[v] and yet Miles's "second wave" view that history should give a narrative voice to women's silence does suggest a certain eagerness to fit women's history into a textual structure: "Any women's history . . . has to be alert to the blanks, the omissions and the half-truths. It must listen to the silences and make them cry out."[vi] Paradoxically, Miles's call echoed Michelet's rather literary ambition, which required more imagination and conjecture than actual historical research (see Parts 1, 4, and 10). Just as White argued that historical narratives distort our ability to make sense of the past by implying that history is structured like a story, for Scott sexual identity is created by variable social contexts that extend into the present. This is why "we need to subject our categories to criticism, our analyses to self-criticism".[vii] For Scott, the history of sexual identity (**gender history**) should adopt a constantly nuanced view, identifying what femininity and masculinity has meant, both in specific instances and across the *longue durée* (see Part 7), "deal[ing] with the individual subject as well as social organization," resisting the pull of traditional terms or current social ambitions to define our historical scope.

In each section preceding this one, written documents formed the primary basis of historical research (including White, despite his suspicion of textual authority). Indeed in every section **primary sources** has referred to a printed or manuscript narrative. Scott asserts that, historically, "attention to gender is often not explicit, but it is nonetheless a crucial part of the organization of equality and inequality". If developing a new approach to social history is one

---

iv   This remains a controversial view, not only for its focus on gender construction rather than sexual discrimination but also for its suggestion that a complete narrative history of sexual identity or "women's lives" is even possible: June Purvis and Amanda Weatherill argue that, regarding gender history,

> we find it a problematic term since it implies an equivalence of consideration to women and men, femininity and masculinity, within the field of study. This is a naïve position to take. At present, we simply do not know enough about women's lives in the past nor about cultural constructions/representations of femininity and masculinity to write a fully fledged gender history. There is the danger, therefore, that gender history is yet another variation of men's history, peppered with frequent references to "gender" but with little reference to women's lives.

See "Playing the Gender History Game: A Reply to Penelope J. Corfield," *Rethinking History* 3 (1999): 334.

v   See, for example, A. R. Jones, " 'Writing the Body: Toward An Understanding of *L'Écriture Féminine*," *Feminist Studies* 7 (Summer 1972): 247–63.

vi   Miles proceeds by indicating that "women's history, then, must hope to explain as well as narrate." See Miles, 13; consider, too, the view of narrative implicit in the title of her book.

vii See J. Scott, *Gender and the Politics of History* (New York: Columbia University Press, 1999), 41.

of the challenges posed by the authors in this section, then it also concerns our **methodology**: how can we research the history of gender when its meaning is not always articulated literally or linguistically? Scott lists instances in which gender might be encoded: they include political upheavals, demographic crises, shifting patterns of employment, and "the emergence of new kinds of cultural symbols". These codes develop through social and political processes, and "the nature of that process, of the actors and their actions, can only be determined specifically, in the context of time and place". Keeping White in mind, how might our interpretation of historical materials, in search of a constantly-redefined category such as gender, avoid the kind of creative interpretation and false historical consciousness that previous historical "classics" have promoted? One approach is through biography: Scott lists several biographical studies that have examined the lives of individuals—and of groups of individuals—incorporating sophisticated approaches to sexual identity. Nevertheless, by closing her chapter with a series of questions concerning the nature of historical inquiries into the social construction of gender, Scott indicates that such studies remain a source of scholarly challenges that our commitment to history cannot avoid.

David Halperin, an American scholar of classical Greece, provides a convincing example of how historians can rise to Scott's challenge. He does this in an impressive way: Halperin's chapter, provocatively titled "Forgetting Foucault", examines several cultural symbols (including an ancient Greek or Roman scare-image, and frequently-told tale from classical Rome and medieval Italy) to clarify the historically-specific meaning of sexual acts and sexual identity. Halperin reflects on the social meaning of sexual identity by focusing on historical interpretations of activities that we would now consider sexual, illustrating a view about contemporary Western sensibility that has been expressed elsewhere:

> It is not the Greeks who were weird about sex but rather it is we today, particularly men and women of the professional classes, who have a culturally and historically unique organization of sexual and social life and, therefore, have difficulty understanding the sex/gender systems of other cultures.[viii]

Just as the historicist ambitions of Vico, Humboldt, Ranke, and Collingwood require imaginative effort as well as careful attention to historical details, Halperin finds that the historical meaning of sexual identities and sexual practices forces us to notice the "weirdness" of our own views. This, Halperin hopes, constitutes an important step toward recognizing the socially constructed nature of those values that we are most likely to consider normal or natural or correct. Although Halperin's article is not concerned with feminist theory, nor is Scott's article concerned with sexual practices, both historians share a critical approach to history that emphasizes the changing and social nature of sexual identity.

Before returning to Halperin, it might be useful to consider Michel Foucault's influential and controversial *History of Sexuality: An Introduction*—to which Scott and Halperin refer. It is important to point out, particularly in a Reader designed for historians, that although Foucault wrote books with "history" in their titles and he is reputed to have uncovered ground-shifting historical evidence, Foucault was not a social historian—indeed he called

---

viii D. Halperin, "Introduction: In Defense of Historicism," *How to Do the History of Homosexuality* (Chicago: University of Chicago Press, 2002), 3.

himself a "historian of systems of thought."[ix] His defiant and spirited rhetorical style can inspire but also confuse readers, particularly when he used sensational terms to describe historical events,[x] which is only one reason why many historians have been reluctant to engage with the challenging questions Foucault asks.[xi] Nevertheless, nearly twenty-five years after his death, most historians agree that on the topic of historical methodology, few philosophers have been more influential or deservedly important than Foucault. This is particularly true when historians address the conceptual frames that shape our perceptions and experiences of sexual identity.

Approaching Foucault's chapter for the first time, it might be helpful to be forewarned that his initial point is actually one side of a philosophical paradox. Foucault asserted at the start that "in Western societies since the Middle Ages, the exercise of power has always been formulated in terms of law." This means that as historical researchers who are concerned with the nature of meaning, we must accept that "sex is to be deciphered on the basis of its relation to the law." This is a strange observation, for if it's the law that provides the basis for sexual conduct, then why shouldn't we just study those laws? Why refer to society? To make matters even more confusing, Foucault closed his chapter by demanding that "we must construct an analytics of power that no longer takes law as a model and a code". Now why would it be useful to consider the ideas and behaviours that constitute sexuality in terms of "law" when, at the same time, we need to consider power as something apart from legal language and legal structures? Foucault required this paradox, because his approach to history tries not only to decipher what people thought about sexual identity but also to make sense of the means by which related ideas and knowledge were shaped, circulated, and enforced. In other words, he opened the way to examine relationships between different types and sources of power. Scott is helpful here:

> Changes in the organization of social relationships always correspond to changes in representations of power, but the direction of change is not necessarily one way.

This formulation is probably indebted to Foucault, who wanted us to think about the dynamic relationship between the power of social institutions (such as law, medicine, and religion) and its representation of that power. He also wanted us to use our own notions of what legal,

---

ix   In 1969, Foucault was elected to the prestigious Collège de France as the newly-created Chaire de l'Histoire des systèmes de pensée.

x   Perhaps the most notorious example is found in Foucault's widely-cited book *Madness and Civilization: A History of Insanity in an Age of Reason* (1965), whose central thesis is that the social and intellectual project known as the Enlightenment entailed a "great confinement" of "unreasonables." Foucault's terms seem to argue that the insane and outspoken were systematically silenced through forced confinement in mental hospitals and other similar institutions across Europe from the late seventeenth and throughout the eighteenth centuries. But as Roy Porter has shown, such confinement did not take place even on a modest scale. See R. Porter, "Foucault's Great Confinement," *History of the Human Sciences* 3 (1990): 47–54; *Mind-Forg'd Manacles: A History of Madness in England from the Restoration to the Regency* (Cambridge, MA: Harvard University Press, 1987). On the fundamental problems in Foucault's research in medical history, see A. Scull, "Scholarship of Fools," Review of Michel Foucault, *History of Madness, TLS* (17 March 2007). <http://www.tls.timesonline.co.uk>.

xi   See Allan Megill, "Foucault, Structuralism, and the Ends of History," *Journal of the History of Ideas* 51 (1979): 451–503.

medical or religious knowledge is to explain how they discipline our beliefs and police our behaviour. Like Foucault's contemporary Paul Ricoeur, who asserted that narrative shapes our sense of time in history and yet allowed us to retain our wish to understand the past on its own terms (see Part 10), Foucault offered us a way out. Foucault argued that subtle forms of power define our very notions of what constitutes sexual desire and sexual identity (he says that "there is no escaping from power"). Although this means that we cannot easily understand those meanings from a different point in history, it also allows that we might gain some perspective by defining the so-called laws that influenced past values and actions.

Foucault's rhetorical flourishes (Halperin calls them "extravagances") sometimes suggest that he would be better appreciated in French than in English translation. For instance, Foucault claimed that "in political thought and analysis, we still have not cut off the head of the king"—surely this allusion would make more sense to French rather than British readers (whose monarch retains her head). However, because Foucault was interested in representation as well as the meanings it implies, such flourishes are useful, for instance in light of his subsequent remarks:

> [Consider] the importance that the theory of power gives to the problem of right and violence, law and illegality, freedom and will, and especially the state and its sovereignty. . . . [Consider] new methods of power whose operation is not ensured by right but by technique, not by law but by normalization, not by punishment but by control, methods that are employed on all levels and in forms that go beyond the state and its apparatus.

Since nearly every noun in that quotation is an abstraction, it would seem that Foucault required either our creative imagination or leap of faith to make sense of the difference between the state's ability to enforce ideas and the normalization of beliefs about sexuality that circulate apart from state control. Another possibility is to consider the degree to which we can use our own experience to supply examples that would support (or deny) Foucault's theory of power. To what extent does "rejection, exclusion, refusal" characterize the relation between "sex and pleasure" in historical and in contemporary terms? Does the objective language of sex enforce a subjective sense of containment and denial?[xii] At its worst, these rhetorical flourishes are distracting; at their best, they are suggestive of further conceptual possibilities.

Foucault mentioned **psychoanalysis** as an alternative to considering the meaning of sexuality over time, but Freud's theory of repression is incompatible with Foucault's theory of power. This is because psychoanalysis holds out the promise that one can be liberated from the

xii For a pioneering study of middle-class Victorian attitudes to sex, whose conclusions rely on the strongly binary language then used to describe pornography, see Steven Marcus, *The Other Victorians: A Study of Pornography and Sexuality in Mid-Nineteenth Century England* (New York: Basic Books, 1966). Foucault made an ironic reference to Marcus by providing the title "We 'Other Victorians' " for the first part of his *History of Sexuality: An Introduction*. Peter Gay observes that Marcus's own terms of reference are themselves evidence of a reactionary response to Victorian morality (hence Foucault's title), which helpfully suggests the extent to which sex history is itself evidence of particular moral codes. See P. Gay, *The Bourgeois Experience, Victoria to Freud*, vol. 1 (Oxford: Oxford University Press, 1984), 468. Foucault's awareness of this is, arguably, one of his strengths.

emotional and physical effects of **repression** through analysis. For Foucault, the methods of power that define our notions of sexual identity are beyond our control—they cannot be surmounted through psychoanalytic treatment nor are they instilled through trauma or violence, because they are impersonal and pervasive. Sexual identity, then, is not a matter that can be defined independently or freely: for Foucault, power has already disciplined our notions of what sexual identity is and can be, and so as historians we need to consider the institutions and discourses (these can include hospitals and medical terminology; prisons and penal codes; religion and its commandments). It is tempting to argue, as Carolyn Dean has noted of sex historians of the 1960s, that "sexual attitudes measure human progress"[xiii] and therefore to consider Foucault's sweeping analysis as evidence of our superior morality—for by asking ourselves these questions, are we not envisioning better realities? Actually Foucault is hardly an optimist, since he found that "normalization" continues to "discipline" our concepts of sex. At the same time, Foucault suggested that research into the sources of control and the means of defining sexual concepts and behaviour might provide us with a measure of useful insight.

This excerpt from Halperin's book opens with his attempt to clarify a point he shares with Foucault: "sexuality is indeed . . . a distinctly modern production." For some readers, Foucault had seemed to say as much by showing that early-modern law and medicine distinguished a physical act (sodomy) from a sexual identity (male homosexual). Those readers of Foucault (and of Halperin) have mistakenly concluded that there were only sexual acts, and no sexual identities, before the nineteenth century. But, as Halperin is keen to emphasize, Foucault did not say that deviant behaviour or deviant sexual taste are new inventions, only that these are phenomena that social institutions tried to deny:

> As almost always in *The History of Sexuality*, Foucault is speaking about discursive and institutional practices, not about what people really did in bed or what they thought about it.

Since Halperin and many other historians want to look beyond discourse to uncover what sexual identity means, why should Foucault's focus on institutional practices matter?

The answer, Halperin shows, is that Foucault's larger project examined the "new persecution of the peripheral sexualities" that coincided with the historical formation of our current ideas. It is those social institutions, and their discourses, which have defined sexual identities that are normal and healthy, and those that are perverse and sick. There are three important points to notice that are central to the social processes that define sexual identity, and which are inseparable from historical discourse about them:

- the associations we make between physical acts and sexual identity are produced by concepts that have changed over time;
- our actual practices and even our thoughts about them can still allow us to draw conclusions about sexuality that would seem self-contradictory to others;
- those aspects of "power" that negate or forbid certain sexual identities allow and encourage other sexual identities.

xiii See C. Dean, "Sexuality, Gender, and the Self," *A Companion to Western Historical Thought*, ed. L. Kramer and S. Maza (Oxford: Blackwell, 2002), 360.

Perhaps the most familiar example to current historians in the West is the condemnation of conduct equated with male homosexuality.[xiv] Illustrating those three elements: Those who share that view do so for reasons that extend beyond their beliefs about the morality of certain physical acts, and the moral values that we now attach to certain acts are in no way natural — they have changed over time and according to social context; anyone, regardless of their personal conduct or ideas about it, can share that condemnation; by condemning homosexuality, one is encouraging acceptance of heterosexuality. Ironically, however, the processes that condemn a sexual identity can achieve precisely the opposite — negative ideas about sexual identity actually create its social manifestation. For Foucault, social forces will attach those ideas to specific groups of real people, "for only by that means could the subject's body itself become so deeply, so minutely invaded and colonized by the agencies of normalization." Since our concerns are with those approaches to history that can reveal the processes by which sexual identity is created, it might be useful to note that, for Foucault, those three elements are studied through examination of the codes and practices of "formal discursive systems" (law, medicine, and religion). But as we will see, Halperin suggests in addition that the forces that motivate such processes should also be examined through wider reading in historical material pertaining to "popular moral attitudes and behaviours." Only then will our historical analysis reflect a truly meaningful range of social, cultural, and structural forces that govern sexual identity.

Halperin offers two examples from Western culture that nicely illustrate the ultimately social and therefore flexible meaning of sexual identity. Both examples illustrate the crucial point that, historically, sexual identity has not always been associated with particular physical acts. Correct or deviant sexual acts can be used to define correct or deviant people in a variety of ways, and in the ancient and medieval past some of those ways of linking acts with identity were different from the way we link them today. Halperin's analysis itself provides us with a useful example of the kind of historical approach that rises, fruitfully, to Scott's challenge.

First, Halperin describes the *kinaidos*, a male scare-image that appears in the scientific and literary records of classical antiquity, and was designed to terrify men into making strenuous efforts to avoid being mistaken for it. Representing a social view of the period, that masculinity requires a constant struggle to control sexual desires, the *kinaidos* existed to warn men of what happens when they surrender to the sensual appetites that all men harbour. Appearing as "a repugnant and perplexing freak," whose behaviour sometimes involved acting in a sexually deviant way, the *kinaidos* did not represent a real or even fictional individual, nor did it represent a certain attitude or point of view — in Halperin's terms, it is a **morphology** (a physical being) without subjectivity (its own perspective): it was not a person or representation of a person in the modern sense. The *kinaidos* was meaningful (it was terrifying for men and laughable for women) because in its social context, it represented the consequences that all men would face if they failed to behave in a particular way. It was like a human signpost with a shiny coating: we would recognize what it means because we can see ourselves reflected in it. But apart from its classical social context, it means nothing.

xiv For a survey of the laws contemporary with the translation of Foucault's book into English, see "The Constitutionality of Laws Forbidding Private Homosexual Conduct," *Michigan Law Review* 72 (August 1974): 1613–1637. Demonstrating the current link between conduct and identity, the authors explain that, "although not every society has condemned homosexuality, [religious] abhorrence of homosexual conduct [has] resulted in its prohibition in many Western states" (1627).

The second example shows the prevalence of an ancient tale that has circulated in Western literature from the time of Apuleius (c. AD 125) to Giovanni Boccaccio (mid-fourteenth century). The tale was once funny or at least made sense because its characters and their thoughts were familiar—like all texts, its degree of popularity reflected its degree of popular relevance. In the classical version, a dinner guest has to return home early because his host has discovered, during dinner, that his wife is hiding her young lover in their house. The guest returns to his own house only to find that his own wife is hiding a young man. The outraged husband (a mere guest no longer) rapes the young man. The first point to notice here is that, in Apuleius's version of the story, the husband who rapes the boy has no particular preference for boys: his sexual act—if it could even be called "sexual" in the context of ancient Greece—demonstrates his anger and not his desire. In the medieval version, the husband clearly has a sexual preference for young males and the rape expresses his desire. However, and this is the second point that Halperin emphasizes, the husband's deviant sexual taste is not visible in any aspect of his appearance: unlike the *kinaidos*, "*You wouldn't know* [the husband] *was a paederast or a sodomite by looking at him.*" The husband's actions were not, for either the classical or medieval reader, anything remarkable at all. Indeed, the story was funny because its characters were so familiar. The story displays the husband's **subjectivity** clearly: he has a viewpoint, emotions, and desires. But his expression of these does not create or amount to what we might now consider a sexual identity: his gender, in other words, does not depend on what he did with the boy. Indeed, Halperin concludes, if "sensibility, a set of personal mannerisms, a style of gender presentation, or a psychology" constitutes sexual identity, then in the social context of his representation in Apuleius and in Boccaccio, the sodomite husband is unremarkable. Is it even possible for Western readers in the early twenty-first century to describe (let alone envision) a man who desires homosexual sex in terms that are not synonymous with homosexual identity?

Halperin's analysis of these historical representations illustrate that an approach to the social construction of sexual identity requires a historicist commitment—defining historical meaning only in terms of the codes of its time. In antiquity, referring to a physical being (the *kinaidos*) was one way to identify sex acts with a person; in the medieval period, this could be done by attribution of subjectivity (the medieval husband who desires boys)—neither of these would probably constitute a sexual identity in the modern sense, since each lacks a true matrix of psychological depth, erotic desires, and sexual practices. This analysis should enable us to understand our present historical moment with fresh insight. If we accept Foucault's position, that social codes discipline sexual expression and sexual contexts, then the historical study of sexual identity is a tool that works to release us from repressive power. Scott's concern for making sense of the past must examine both the representation and organization of sexual identity; it must draw on a wide range of historical sources—including political, literary, legal, medical, and religious materials—and interpret them comparatively. Only such an ambitious historical project will bring us closer to appreciating the social construction of sexual identity.

Chapter 44

Joan Wallach Scott

GENDER: A USEFUL CATEGORY OF HISTORICAL ANALYSIS

Joan Wallach Scott, "Gender: A Useful Category of Historical Analysis", 1985, *Gender and the Politics of History* (New York: Columbia University Press, 1988), 41–50.

CONCERN WITH GENDER as an analytic category has emerged only in the late twentieth century. It is absent from the major bodies of social theory articulated from the eighteenth to the early twentieth century. To be sure, some of those theories built their logic on analogies to the opposition of male and female, others acknowledged a "woman question," still others addressed the formation of subjective sexual identity, but gender as a way of talking about systems of social or sexual relations did not appear. This neglect may in part explain the difficulty that contemporary feminists have had incorporating the term "gender" into existing bodies of theory and convincing adherents of one or another theoretical school that gender belongs in their vocabulary. The term "gender" is part of the attempt by contemporary feminists to stake claim to a certain definitional ground, to insist on the inadequacy of existing bodies of theory for explaining persistent inequalities between women and men. It seems to me significant that the use of the word "gender" has emerged at a moment of great epistemological turmoil that takes the form, in some cases, of a shift from scientific to literary paradigms among social scientists (from an emphasis on cause to one on meaning, blurring genres of inquiry, in anthropologist Clifford Geertz's phrase)[1] and, in other cases, the form of debates about theory between those who assert the transparency of facts and those who insist that all reality is construed or constructed, between those who defend and those who question the idea that "man" is the rational master of his own destiny. In the space opened by this debate and on the side of the critique of science developed by the humanities, and of empiricism and humanism by post-structuralists, feminists have begun to find not only a theoretical voice of their own but scholarly and political allies as well. It is within this space that we must articulate gender as an analytic category.

What should be done by historians who, after all, have seen their discipline dismissed by some recent theorists as a relic of humanist thought? I do not think we should quit the archives or abandon the study of the past, but we do have to change some of the ways we've gone about working, some of the questions we have asked. We need to scrutinize our methods of analysis, clarify our operative assumptions, and explain how we think change occurs. Instead of a search for single origins, we have to conceive of processes so intercon-nected that they cannot be disentangled. Of course, we identify problems to study, and these constitute beginnings or points of entry into complex processes. But it is the processes we must continually keep in mind. We must ask more often how things happened in order to find out why they happened; in anthropologist Michelle Rosaldo's formulation, we must pursue not universal, general causality but meaningful explanation: "It now appears to me that women's place in human social life is not in any direct sense a product of the things she does, but of the meaning her activities acquire through concrete social interaction."[2] To pursue meaning, we need to deal with the individual subject as well as social organization and to articulate the nature of their interrelationships, for both are crucial to understanding how gender works, how change occurs. Finally, we need to replace the notion that social power is unified, coherent, and centralized with something like Michel Foucault's concept of power as dispersed constellations of unequal relationships, discursively constituted in social "fields of force."[3] Within these processes and structures, there is room for a concept of human agency as the attempt (at least partially rational) to construct an identity, a life, a set of relationships, a society within certain limits and with language—conceptual language that at once sets boundaries and contains the possibility for negation, resistance, reinterpre-tation, the play of metaphoric invention and imagination.

My definition of gender has two parts and several subsets. They are interrelated but must be analytically distinct. The core of the definition rests on an integral connection between two propositions: gender is a constitutive element of social relationships based on perceived differences between the sexes, and gender is a primary way of signifying relation-ships of power. Changes in the organization of social relationships always correspond to changes in representations of power, but the direction of change is not necessarily one way. As a constitutive element of social relationships based on perceived differences between the sexes, gender involves four interrelated elements: first, culturally available symbols that evoke multiple (and often contradictory) representations—Eve and Mary as symbols of woman, for example, in the Western Christian tradition—but also, myths of light and dark, purification and pollution, innocence and corruption. For historians, the interesting ques-tions are, Which symbolic representations are invoked, how, and in what contexts? Second, normative concepts that set forth interpretations of the meanings of the symbols, that attempt to limit and contain their metaphoric possibilities. These concepts are expressed in religious, educational, scientific, legal, and political doctrines and typically take the form of a fixed binary opposition, categorically and unequivocally asserting the meaning of male and female, masculine and feminine. In fact, these normative statements depend on the refusal or repression of alternative possibilities, and sometimes overt contests about them take place (at what moments and under what circumstances ought to be a concern of historians). The position that emerges as dominant, however, is stated as the only possible one. Subsequent history is written as if these normative positions were the product of social consensus rather than of conflict. An example of this kind of history is the treatment of the Victorian ideology of domesticity as if it were created whole and only afterwards reacted to instead of being the constant subject of great differences of opinion. Another kind of example comes from contemporary fundamentalist religious groups that have forcibly linked their practice to a restoration of women's supposedly more authentic "traditional" role, when, in fact, there is little historical precedent for the unquestioned performance of such a role. The point of new historical investigation is to disrupt the notion of fixity, to discover the nature of the debate or repression that leads to the appearance of timeless permanence in binary gender representation. This kind of analysis must include a notion of politics and reference to social institutions and organizations—the third aspect of gender relationships.

Some scholars, notably anthropologists, have restricted the use of gender to the kinship system (focusing on household and family as the basis for social organization). We need a broader view that includes not only kinship but also (especially for complex modern societies) the labor market (a sex-segregated labor market is a part of the process of gender construction), education (all-male, single-sex, or coeducational institutions are part of the same process), and the polity (universal male suffrage is part of the process of gender construction). It makes little sense to force these institutions back to functional utility in the kinship system, or to argue that contemporary relationships between men and women are artifacts of older kinship systems based on the exchange of women.[4] Gender is constructed through kinship, but not exclusively; it is constructed as well in the economy and the polity, which, in our society at least, now operate largely independently of kinship.

The fourth aspect of gender is subjective identity. I agree with anthropologist Gayle Rubin's formulation that psychoanalysis offers an important theory about the reproduction of gender, a description of the "transformation of the biological sexuality of individuals as they are enculturated."[5] But the universal claim of psychoanalysis gives me pause. Even though Lacanian theory may be helpful for thinking about the construction of gendered identity, historians need to work in a more historical way. If gender identity is based only and universally on fear of castration, the point of historical inquiry is denied. Moreover, real men and women do not always or literally fulfill the terms either of their society's prescriptions or of our analytic categories. Historians need instead to examine the ways in which gendered identities are substantively constructed and relate their findings to a range of activities, social organizations, and historically specific cultural representations. The best efforts in this area so far have been, not surprisingly, biographies: Biddy Martin's interpretation of Lou Andreas Salomé, Kathryn Sklar's depiction of Catharine Beecher, Jacqueline Hall's life of Jessie Daniel Ames, and Mary Hill's discussion of Charlotte Perkins Gilman.[6] But collective treatments are also possible, as Mrinalina Sinha and Lou Ratté have shown in their respective studies of the terms of construction of gender identity for British colonial administrators in India and for British-educated Indians who emerged as anti-imperialist, nationalist leaders.[7]

The first part of my definition of gender consists, then, of all four of these elements, and no one of them operates without the others. Yet they do not operate simultaneously, with one simply reflecting the others. A question for historical research is, in fact, what the relationships among the four aspects are. The sketch I have offered of the process of constructing gender relationships could be used to discuss class, race, ethnicity, or, for that matter, any social process. My point was to clarify and specify how one needs to think about the effect of gender in social and institutional relationships, because this thinking is often not done precisely or systematically. The theorizing of gender, however, is developed in my second proposition: gender is a primary way of signifying relationships of power. It might be better to say, gender is a primary field within which or by means of which power is articulated. Gender is not the only field, but it seems to have been a persistent and recurrent way of enabling the signification of power in the West, in the Judeo-Christian as well as the Islamic tradition. As such, this part of the definition might seem to belong in the normative section of the argument, yet it does not, for concepts of power, though they may build on gender, are not always literally about gender itself. French sociologist Pierre Bourdieu has written about how the "di-vision du monde," based on references to "biological differences and notably those that refer to the division of the labor of procreation and reproduction," operates as "the best founded of collective illusions." Established as an objective set of references, concepts of gender structure perception and the concrete and symbolic organization of all social life.[8] To the extent that these references establish distributions of power (differential control over or access to material and symbolic resources), gender becomes implicated in the conception and construction of power itself. The French anthropologist Maurice Godelier has put it this way: "It is not sexuality which haunts society, but society which haunts the body's sexuality. Sex-related differences between bodies are continually summoned as testimony to social relations and phenomena that have nothing to do with sexuality. Not only as testimony to, but also testimony for—in other words, as legitimation."[9]

The legitimizing function of gender works in many ways. Bourdieu, for example, showed how, in certain cultures, agricultural exploitation was organized according to concepts of time and season that rested on specific definitions of the opposition between masculine and feminine. Gayatri Spivak has done a pointed analysis of the uses of gender and colonialism in certain texts of British and American women writers.[10] Natalie Davis has shown how concepts of masculine and feminine related to understandings and criticisms of the rules of social order in early modern France.[11] Historian Caroline Bynum has thrown new light on medieval spirituality through her attention to the relationships between concepts of masculine and feminine and religious behavior. Her work gives us important insight into the ways in which these concepts informed the politics of monastic institutions as well as of individual believers.[12] Art historians have opened a new territory by reading social implications from literal depictions of women and men.[13] These interpretations are based on the idea that conceptual languages employ differentiation of establish meaning and that sexual difference is a primary way of signifying differentiation.[14] Gender, then, provides a way to decode meaning and to understand the complex connections among various forms of human interaction. When historians look for the ways in which the concept of gender legitimizes and constructs social relationships, they develop insight into the reciprocal nature of gender and society and into the particular and contextually specific ways in which politics constructs gender and gender constructs politics.

Politics is only one of the areas in which gender can be used for historical analysis. I have chosen the following examples relating to politics and power in their most traditionally construed sense, that is, as they pertain to government and the nation-state, for two reasons. First, the territory is virtually uncharted, since gender has been seen as antithetical to the real business of politics. Second, political history—still the dominant mode of historical inquiry—has been the stronghold of resistance to the inclusion of material or even questions about women and gender.

Gender has been employed literally or analogically in political theory to justify or criticize the reign of monarchs and to express the relationship between ruler and ruled. One might have expected that the debates of contemporaries over the reigns of Elizabeth I in England and Catherine de Medici in France would dwell on the issue of women's suitability for political rule, but, in the period when kinship and kingship were integrally related, discussions about male kings were equally preoccupied with masculinity and femininity.[15] Analogies to the marital relationship provide structure for the arguments of Jean Bodin, Robert Filmer, and John Locke. Edmund Burke's attack on the French Revolution is built around a contrast between ugly, murderous *sansculotte* hags ("the furies of hell, in the abused shape of the vilest of women") and the soft femininity of Marie Antoinette, who escaped the crowd to "seek refuge at the feet of a king and husband" and whose beauty once inspired national pride. (It was in reference to the appropriate role for the feminine in the political order that Burke wrote, "To make us love our country, our country ought to be lovely.")[16] But the analogy is not always to marriage or even to heterosexuality. In medieval Islamic political theory, the symbols of political power alluded most often to sex between man and boy, suggesting not only forms of acceptable sexuality akin to those that Foucault's last work described in classical Greece but also the irrelevance of women to any notion of politics and public life.[17]

Lest this last comment suggest that political theory simply reflects social organization, it seems important to note that changes in gender relationships can be set off by views of the needs of state. A striking example is Louis de Bonald's argument in 1816 about why the divorce legislation of the French Revolution had to be repealed:

> Just as political democracy, "allows the people, the weak part of political society, to rise against the established power," so divorce, "veritable domestic democracy," allows the wife, "the weak part, to rebel against marital author-ity. . . . in order to keep the state out of the hands of the people, it is necessary to keep the family out of the hands of wives and children."[18]

Bonald begins with an analogy and then establishes a direct correspondence between divorce and democracy. Harking back to much earlier arguments about the well-ordered family as the foundation of the well-ordered state, the legislation that implemented this view redefined the limits of the marital relationship. Similarly, in our own time, conservative political ideologues would like to pass a series of laws about the organization and behavior of the family that would alter current practices. The connection between authoritarian regimes and the control of women has been noted but not thoroughly studied. Whether at a crucial moment for Jacobin hegemony in the French Revolution, at the point of Stalin's bid for controlling authority, the implementation of Nazi policy in Germany, or with the triumph in Iran of the Ayatollah Khomeini, emergent rulers have legitimized domination, strength, central authority, and ruling power as masculine (enemies, outsiders, subversives, weakness as feminine) and made that code literal in laws (forbidding women's political participation, outlawing abortion, prohibiting wage-earning by mothers, imposing female dress codes) that put women in their place.[19] These actions and their timing make little sense in themselves; in most instances, the state had nothing immediate or material to gain from the control of women. The actions can only be made sense of as part of an analysis of the construction and consolidation of power. An assertion of control or strength was given form as a policy about women. In these examples, sexual difference was conceived in terms of the domination or control of women. These examples provide some insight into the kinds of power relation-ships being constructed in modern history, but this particular type of relationship is not a universal political theme. In different ways, for example, the democratic regimes of the twentieth century have also constructed their political ideologies with gendered concepts and translated them into policy; the welfare state, for example, demonstrated its protective paternalism in laws directed at women and children.[20] Historically, some socialist and anarchist movements have refused metaphors of domination entirely, imaginatively present-ing their critiques of particular regimes or social organizations in terms of transformations of gender identities. Utopian socialists in France and England in the 1830s and 1840s conceived their dreams for a harmonious future in terms of the complementary natures of individuals as exemplified in the union of man and woman, "the social individual."[21] Euro-pean anarchists were long known not only for refusing the conventions of bourgeois mar-riage but for their visions of a world in which sexual difference did not imply hierarchy.

These examples are of explicit connections between gender and power, but they are only a part of my definition of gender as a primary way of signifying relationships of power. Attention to gender is often not explicit, but it is nonetheless a crucial part of the organiza-tion of equality or inequality. Hierarchical structures rely on generalized understandings of the so-called natural relationships between male and female. The concept of class in the nineteenth century relied on gender for its articulation. While middle-class reformers in

France, for example, depicted workers in terms coded as feminine (subordinated, weak, sexually exploited like prostitutes), labor and socialist leaders replied by insisting on the masculine position of the working class (producers, strong, protectors of their women and children). The terms of this discourse were not explicitly about gender, but they were strengthened by references to it. The gendered "coding" of certain terms established and "naturalized" their meanings. In the process, historically specific, normative definitions of gender (which were taken as givens) were reproduced and embedded in the culture of the French working class.[22]

The subject of war, diplomacy, and high politics frequently comes up when traditional political historians question the utility of gender in their work. But here, too, we need to look beyond the actors and the literal import of their words. Power relations among nations and the status of colonial subjects have been made comprehensible (and thus legitimate) in terms of relations between male and female. The legitimizing of war—of expending young lives to protect the state—has variously taken the forms of explicit appeals to manhood (to the need to defend otherwise vulnerable women and children), of implicit reliance on belief in the duty of sons to serve their leaders or their (father the) king, and of associations between masculinity and national strength.[23] High politics itself is a gendered concept, for it establishes its crucial importance and public power, the reasons for and the fact of its highest authority, precisely in its exclusion of women from its work. Gender is one of the recurrent references by which political power has been conceived, legitimated, and criticized. It refers to but also establishes the meaning of the male/female opposition. To vindicate political power, the reference must seem sure and fixed, outside human construction, part of the natural or divine order. In that way, the binary opposition and the social process of gender relationships both become part of the meaning of power itself; to question or alter any aspect threatens the entire system.

If significations of gender and power construct one another, how do things change? The answer in a general sense is that change may be initiated in many places. Massive political upheavals that throw old orders into chaos and bring new ones into being may revise the terms (and so the organization) of gender in the search for new forms of legitimation. But they may not; old notions of gender have also served to validate new regimes.[24] Demographic crises, occasioned by food shortages, plagues, or wars, may have called into question normative visions of heterosexual marriage (as happened in some circles, in some countries in the 1920s), but they have also spawned pronatalist policies that insist on the exclusive importance of women's maternal and reproductive functions.[25] Shifting patterns of employment may lead to altered marital strategies and to different possibilities for the construction of subjectivity, but they can also be experienced as new arenas of activity for dutiful daughters and wives.[26] The emergence of new kinds of cultural symbols may make possible the reinterpreting or, indeed, rewriting of the oedipal story, but it can also serve to reinscribe that terrible drama in even more telling terms. Political processes will determine which outcome prevails—political in the sense that different actors and different meanings are contending with one another for control. The nature of that process, of the actors and their actions, can only be determined specifically, in the context of time and place. We can write the history of that process only if we recognize that "man" and "woman" are at once empty and overflowing categories. Empty because they have no ultimate, transcendent meaning. Overflowing because even when they appear to be fixed, they still contain within them alternative, denied, or suppressed definitions.

Political history has, in a sense, been enacted on the field of gender. It is a field that seems fixed yet whose meaning is contested and in flux. If we treat the opposition between male and female as problematic rather than known, as something contextually defined, repeatedly constructed, then we must constantly ask not only what is at stake in proclamations or debates that invoke gender to explain or justify their positions but also how implicit understandings of gender are being invoked and reinscribed. What is the relationship between laws about women and the power of the state? Why (and since when) have women been invisible as historical subjects, when we know they participated in the great and small events of human history? Has gender legitimized the emergence of professional careers?[27] Is (to quote the title of a recent article by French feminist Luce Irigaray) the subject of science sexed?[28] What is the relationship between state politics and the discovery of the crime of homosexuality?[29] How have social institutions incorporated gender into their assumptions and organizations? Have there ever been genuinely egalitarian concepts of gender in terms of which political systems were projected, if not built?

Investigation of these issues will yield a history that will provide new perspectives on old questions (about how, for example, political rule is imposed, or what the impact of war on society is), redefine the old questions in new terms (introducing considerations of family and sexuality, for example, in the study of economics or war), make women visible as active participants, and create analytic distance between the seemingly fixed language of the past and our own terminology. In addition, this new history will leave open possibilities for thinking about current feminist political strategies and the (utopian) future, for it suggests that gender must be redefined and restructured in conjunction with a vision of political and social equality that includes not only sex but class and race.

Notes

1   Clifford Geertz, "Blurred Genres," *American Scholar* (1980) 49:165–79.
2   Michelle Zimbalist Rosaldo, "The Uses and Abuses of Anthropology: Reflections on Feminism and Cross-Cultural Understanding," *Signs* (1980) 5:400.
3   Michel Foucault, *The History of Sexuality*, Vol. I, *An Introduction* (New York: Vintage, 1980); Michel Foucault, *Power/Knowledge: Selected Interviews and Other Writings, 1972–1977* (New York: Pantheon, 1980).
4   For this argument, see Rubin, "The Traffic in Women," p. 199.
5   *Ibid.*, p. 189.
6   Biddy Martin, "Feminism, Criticism and Foucault," *New German Critique* (1982) 27:3–30; Kathryn Kish Sklar, *Catharine Beecher: A Study in American Domesticity* (New Haven: Yale University Press, 1973); Mary A. Hill, *Charlotte Perkins Gilman: The Making of a Radical Feminist, 1860–1896* (Philadelphia: Temple University Press, 1980); Jacqueline Dowd Hall, *Revolt Against Chivalry: Jesse Daniel Ames and the Women's Campaign Against Lynching* (New York: Columbia University Press, 1974).
7   Lou Ratté, "Gender Ambivalence in the Indian Nationalist Movement," unpublished paper, Pembroke Center Seminar, Spring 1983; and Mrinalina Sinha, "Manliness: A Victorian Ideal and the British Imperial Elite in India," unpublished paper, Department of History, State University of New York, Stony Brook, 1984, and Sinha, "The Age of Consent Act: The Ideal of Masculinity and Colonial Ideology in Late 19th Century Bengal," *Proceedings*, Eighth International Symposium on Asian Studies, 1986, pp. 1199–1214.
8   Pierre Bourdieu, *Le Sens Pratique* (Paris: Les Editions de Minuit, 1980), pp. 246–47, 333–461, especially p. 366.
9   Maurice Godelier, "The Origins of Male Domination," *New Left Review* (1981) 127:17.
10   Gayatri Chakravorty Spivak, "Three Women's Texts and a Critique of Imperialism," *Critical Inquiry* (1985) 12:243–46. See also Kate Millett, *Sexual Politics* (New York: Avon, 1969). An examination of how feminine references work in major texts of Western philosophy is carried out by Luce Irigaray in *Speculum of the Other Woman*, translated by Gillian C. Gill (Ithaca, N.Y.: Cornell University Press, 1985).
11   Natalie Zemon Davis, "Women on Top," in her *Society and Culture in Early Modern France* (Stanford: Stanford University Press, 1975), pp. 124–51.
12   Caroline Walker Bynum, *Jesus as Mother: Studies in the Spirituality of the High Middle Ages* (Berkeley: University of California Press, 1982); Caroline Walker Bynum, "Fast, Feast, and Flesh: The

Religious Significance of Food to Medieval Women," *Representations* (1985) 11:1–25; Caroline Walker Bynum, "Introduction," *Religion and Gender: Essays on the Complexity of Symbols* (Boston: Beacon Press, 1987).

13   See, for example, T. J. Clark, *The Painting of Modern Life* (New York: Knopf, 1985).

14   The difference between structuralist and post-structuralist theorists on this question rests on how open or closed they view the categories of difference. To the extent that post-structuralists do not fix a universal meaning for the categories or the relationship between them, their approach seems conducive to the kind of historical analysis I am advocating.

15   Rachel Weil, "The Crown Has Fallen to the Distaff: Gender and Politics in the Age of Catherine de Medici," *Critical Matrix* (Princeton Working Papers in Women's Studies) (1985), I. See also Louis Montrose, "Shaping Fantasies: Figurations of Gender and Power in Elizabethan Culture," *Representations* (1983) 1:61–94; and Lynn Hunt, "Hercules and the Radical Image in the French Revolution," *Representations* (1983) 1:95–117.

16   Edmund Burke, *Reflections on the French Revolution* (1892; reprint ed., New York, 1909), pp. 208–9, 214. See Jean Bodin, *Six Books of the Commonwealth* (1606; reprint ed., New York: Barnes and Noble, 1967); Robert Filmer, *Patriarchia and Other Political Works* (Oxford: B. Blackwell, 1949); and John Locke, *Two Treatises of Government* (1690; reprint ed., Cambridge: Cambridge University Press, 1970). See also Elizabeth Fox-Genovese, "Property and Patriarchy in Classical Bourgeois Political Theory," *Radical History Review* (1977) 4:36–59; and Mary Lyndon Shanley, "Marriage Contract and Social Contract in Seventeenth Century English Political Thought," *Western Political Quarterly* (1979) 3:79–91.

17   I am grateful to Bernard Lewis for the reference to Islam. Michel Foucault, *Historie de la Sexualité*, Vol. 2, *L'Usage des plaisirs* (Paris: Gallimard, 1984). On women in classical Athens, see Marilyn Arthur, " 'Liberated Woman': The Classical Era," in Renate Bridenthal and Claudia Koonz, eds., *Becoming Visible: Women in European History* (Boston: Houghton Mifflin, 1977), pp. 75–78.

18   Cited in Roderick Phillips, "Women and Family Breakdown in Eighteenth Century France: Rouen 1780–1800," *Social History* (1976) 2:217.

19   On the French Revolution, see Darlene Gay Levy, Harriet Applewhite, and Mary Durham Johnson, eds., *Women in Revolutionary Paris, 1789–1795* (Urbana: University of Illinois Press, 1979), pp. 209–20; on Soviet legislation, see the documents in Rudolph Schlesinger, *Changing Attitudes in Soviet Russia: Documents and Readings*, Vol. I, *The Family in the USSR* (London: Routledge and Kegan Paul, 1949), pp. 62–71, 251–54; on Nazi policy, see Tim Mason, "Women in Nazi Germany, *History Workshop* (1976) 1:74–113, and Tim Mason, "Women in Germany, 1925–40: Family, Welfare and Work," *History Workshop* (1976) 2:5–32.

20   Elizabeth Wilson, *Women and the Welfare State* (London: Tavistock, 1977); Jane Jenson, "Gender and Reproduction"; Jane Lewis, *The Politics of Motherhood: Child and Maternal Welfare in England, 1900–1939* (London: Croom Helm, 1980); Mary Lynn McDougall, "Protecting Infants: The French Campaign for Maternity Leaves, 1890s–1913," *French Historical Studies* (1983) 13:79–105.

21   On English utopians, see Barbara Taylor, *Eve and the New Jerusalem* (New York: Pantheon, 1983).

22   Louis Devance, "Femme, famille, travail et morale sexuelle dans l'idéologie de 1848," in *Mythes et représentations de la femme au XIXe siècle* (Paris: Champion, 1977); Jacques Rancière and Pierre Vauday, "En allant à l'éxpo: L'ouvrier, sa femme et les machines," *Les Révoltes Logiques* (1975) 1:5–22.

23   Gayatri Chakravorty Spivak, " 'Draupadi' by Mahasveta Devi," *Critical Inquiry* (1981) 8:381–401; Homi Bhabha, "Of Mimicry and Man: The Ambivalence of Colonial Discourse," *October* (1984) 28:125–33; Karin Hausen, "The German Nation's Obligations to the Heroes' Widows of World War I," in Margaret R. Higonnet et al., *Behind the Lines: Gender and the Two World Wars* (New Haven: Yale University Press, 1987), pp. 126–40. See also Ken Inglis, "The Representation of Gender on Australian War Memorials," *Daedalus* (1987) 116:35–59.

24   On the French Revolution, see Levy et al., *Women in Revolutionary Paris*. On the American Revolution, see Mary Beth Norton, *Liberty's Daughters: The Revolutionary Experience of American Women* (Boston: Little, Brown, 1980); Linda Kerber, *Women of the Republic* (Chapel Hill: University of North Carolina Press, 1980); Joan Hoff-Wilson, "The Illusion of Change: Women and the American Revolution," in Alfred Young, ed., *The American Revolution: Explorations in the History of American Radicalism* (DeKalb: Northern Illinois University Press, 1976), pp. 383–446. On the French Third Republic, see Steven Hause, *Women's Suffrage and Social Politics in the French Third Republic* (Princeton: Princeton University Press, 1984). An extremely interesting treatment of a recent case is Maxine Molyneux, "Mobilization without Emancipation? Women's Interests, the State and Revolution in Nicaragua," *Feminist Studies* (1985) 11:227–54.

25   On pronatalism, see Riley, *War in the Nursery*, and Jenson, "Gender and Reproduction." On the
     1920s, see the essays in *Stratégies des Femmes* (Paris: Editions Tierce, 1984).
26   For various interpretations of the impact of new work on women, see Louise A. Tilly and Joan
     W. Scott, *Women, Work and Family* (New York: Holt, Rinehart and Winston, 1978; Methuen, 1987);
     Thomas Dublin, *Women at Work: The Transformation of Work and Community in Lowell, Massachusetts,
     1826–1860* (New York: Columbia University Press, 1979); and Edward Shorter, *The Making of the
     Modern Family* (New York: Basic Books, 1975).
27   See, for example, Margaret Rossiter, *Women Scientists in America: Struggles and Strategies to 1914*
     (Baltimore: Johns Hopkins University Press, 1982).
28   Luce Irigaray, "Is the Subject of Science Sexed?" *Cultural Critique* (1985) 1:73–88.
29   Louis Crompton, *Byron and Greek Love: Homophobia in Nineteenth-Century England* (Berkeley: Uni-
     versity of California Press, 1985). This question is touched on also in Jeffrey Weeks, *Sex, Politics and
     Society: The Regulation of Sexuality Since 1800* (London: Leyman, 1981).

Chapter 45

Michel Foucault

OBJECTIVE

Michel Foucault (1926–1984), "Objective", 1976. Trans. Robert Hurley. *The History of Sexuality: An Introduction* (London: Allen Lane, 1978), 81–91.

WHY THESE INVESTIGATIONS? I am well aware that an uncertainty runs through the sketches I have drawn thus far, one that threatens to invalidate the more detailed inquiries that I have projected. I have repeatedly stressed that the history of the last centuries in Western societies did not manifest the movement of a power that was essentially repressive. I based my argument on the disqualification of that notion while feigning ignorance of the fact that a critique has been mounted from another quarter and doubtless in a more radical fashion: a critique conducted at the level of the theory of desire. In point of fact, the assertion that sex is not "repressed" is not altogether new. Psychoanalysts have been saying the same thing for some time. They have challenged the simple little machinery that comes to mind when one speaks of repression; the idea of a rebellious energy that must be throttled has appeared to them inadequate for deciphering the manner in which power and desire are joined to one another; they consider them to be linked in a more complex and primary way than through the interplay of a primitive, natural, and living energy welling up from below, and a higher order seeking to stand in its way; thus one should not think that desire is repressed, for the simple reason that the law is what constitutes both desire and the lack on which it is predicated. Where there is desire, the power relation is already present: [it is] an illusion, then, to denounce this relation for a repression exerted after the event; but [it is] vanity as well, to go questing after a desire that is beyond the reach of ["legal"] power.

But, in an obstinately confused way, I sometimes spoke, as though I were dealing with equivalent notions, of *repression*, and sometimes of *law*, of prohibition or censorship. Through stubbornness or neglect, I failed to consider everything that can distinguish their theoretical implications. And I grant that one might justifiably say to me: By constantly referring to positive technologies of power, you are playing a double game where you hope to win on all counts; you confuse your adversaries by appearing to take the weaker position, and, discussing repression alone, you would have us believe, wrongly, that you have rid yourself of the problem of law; and yet you keep the essential practical consequence of the principle of power-as-law, namely the fact that there is no escaping from power, that it is always-already present, constituting that very thing which one attempts to counter it with. As to the idea of a power-repression, you have retained its most fragile theoretical element, and this in order to criticize it; you have retained the most sterilizing political consequence of the idea of power-law, but only in order to preserve it for your own use.

The aim of the inquiries that will follow is to move less toward a "theory" of power than toward an "analytics" of power: that is, toward a definition of the specific domain formed by relations of power, and toward a determination of the instruments that will make possible its analysis. However, it seems to me that this analytics can be constituted only if it frees itself completely from a certain representation of power that I would term—it will be seen later why—"juridico-discursive." It is this conception that governs both the thematics of repression and the theory of the law as constitutive of desire. In other words, what distinguishes the analysis made in terms of the repression of instincts from that made in terms of the law of desire is clearly the way in which they each conceive of the nature and dynamics of the drives, not the way in which they conceive of power. They both rely on a common representation of power which, depending on the use made of it and the position it is accorded with respect to desire, leads to two contrary results: either to the promise of a "liberation," if power is seen as having only an external hold on desire, or, if it is constitutive of desire itself, to the affirmation: you are always-already trapped. Moreover, one must not imagine that this representation is peculiar to those who are concerned with the problem of the relations of power with sex. In fact it is much more general; one frequently encounters it in political analyses of power, and it is deeply rooted in the history of the West.

These are some of its principal features:

—*The negative relation.* It never establishes any connection between power and sex that is not negative: rejection, exclusion, refusal, blockage, concealment, or mask. Where sex and pleasure are concerned, power can "do" nothing but say no to them; what it produces, if anything, is absences and gaps; it overlooks elements, introduces discontinuities, separates what is joined, and marks off boundaries. Its effects take the general form of limit and lack.

—*The insistence of the rule.* Power is essentially what dictates its law to sex. Which means first of all that sex is placed by power in a binary system: licit and illicit, permitted and forbidden. Secondly, power prescribes an "order" for sex that operates at the same time as a form of intelligibility: sex is to be deciphered on the basis of its relation to the law. And finally, power acts by laying down the rule: power's hold on sex is maintained through language, or rather through the act of discourse that creates, from the very fact that it is articulated, a rule of law. It speaks, and that is the rule. The pure form of power resides in the function of the legislator; and its mode of action with regard to sex is of a juridico-discursive character.

—*The cycle of prohibition:* thou shalt not go near, thou shalt not touch, thou shalt not consume, thou shalt not experience pleasure, thou shalt not speak, thou shalt not show thyself; ultimately thou shalt not exist, except in darkness and secrecy. To deal with sex, power employs nothing more than a law of prohibition. Its objective: that sex renounce itself. Its instrument: the threat of a punishment that is nothing other than the suppression of sex. Renounce yourself or suffer the penalty of being suppressed; do not appear if you do not want to disappear. Your existence will be maintained only at the cost of your nullification. Power constrains sex only through a taboo that plays on the alternative between two nonexistences.

—*The logic of censorship.* This interdiction is thought to take three forms: affirming that such a thing is not permitted, preventing it from being said, denying that it exists. Forms that are difficult to reconcile. But it is here that one imagines a sort of logical sequence that characterizes censorship mechanisms: it links the inexistent, the illicit, and the inexpressible in such a way that each is at the same time the principle and the effect of the others: one must not talk about what is forbidden until it is annulled in reality; what is inexistent has no right to show itself, even in the order of speech where its inexistence is declared; and that which one must keep silent about is banished from reality as the thing that is tabooed above all else. The logic of power exerted on sex is the paradoxical logic of a law that might be expressed as an injunction of nonexistence, nonmanifestation, and silence.

—*The uniformity of the apparatus.* Power over sex is exercised in the same way at all levels. From top to bottom, in its over-all decisions and its capillary interventions alike, whatever the devices or institutions on which it relies, it acts in a uniform and comprehensive manner; it operates according to the simple and endlessly reproduced mechanisms of law, taboo, and censorship: from state to family, from prince to father, from the tribunal to the small change of everyday punishments, from the agencies of social domination to the structures that constitute the subject himself, one finds a general form of power, varying in scale alone. This form is the law of transgression and punishment, with its interplay of licit and illicit. Whether one attributes to it the form of the prince who formulates rights, of the father who forbids, of the censor who enforces silence, or of the master who states the law, in any case one schematizes power in a juridical form, and one defines its effects as obedience. Confronted by a power that is law, the subject who is constituted as subject—who is "subjected"—is he who obeys. To the formal homogeneity of power in these various instances corresponds the general form of submission in the one who is constrained by it—whether the individual in question is the subject opposite the monarch, the citizen opposite the state, the child opposite the parent, or the disciple opposite the master. A legislative power on one side, and an obedient subject on the other.

Underlying both the general theme that power represses sex and the idea that the law constitutes desire, one encounters the same [reputed] mechanics of power. It is defined in a strangely restrictive way, in that, to begin with, this power is poor in resources, sparing of its methods, monotonous in the tactics it utilizes, incapable of invention, and seemingly doomed always to repeat itself. Further, it is a power that only has the force of the negative on its side, a power to say no; in no condition to produce, capable only of posting limits, it is basically anti-energy. This is the paradox of its effectiveness: it is incapable of doing anything, except to render what it dominates incapable of doing anything either, except for what this power allows it to do. And finally, it is a power whose model is essentially juridical, centered on nothing more than the statement of the law and the operation of taboos. All the modes of domination, submission, and subjugation are ultimately reduced to an effect of obedience.

Why is this juridical notion of power, involving as it does the neglect of everything that makes for its productive effectiveness, its strategic resourcefulness, its positivity, so readily accepted? In a society such as ours, where the devices of power are so numerous, its rituals so visible, and its instruments ultimately so reliable, in this society that has been more imaginative, probably, than any other in creating devious and supple mechanisms of power, what explains this tendency not to recognize the latter except in the negative and emaciated form of prohibition? Why are the deployments of power reduced simply to the procedure of the law of interdiction?

Let me offer a general and tactical reason that seems self-evident: power is tolerable only on condition that it mask a substantial part of itself. Its success is proportional to its ability to hide its own mechanisms. Would power be accepted if it were entirely cynical? For it, secrecy is not in the nature of an abuse; it is indispensable to its operation. Not only because power imposes secrecy on those whom it dominates, but because it is perhaps just as indispensable to the latter: would they accept it if they did not see it as a mere limit placed on their desire, leaving a measure of freedom—however slight—intact? Power as a pure limit set on freedom is, at least in our society, the general form of its acceptability.

There is, perhaps, a historical reason for this. The great institutions of power that developed in the Middle Ages—monarchy, the state with its apparatus—rose up on the basis of a multiplicity of prior powers, and to a certain extent in opposition to them: dense, entangled, conflicting powers, powers tied to the direct or indirect dominion over the land, to the possession of arms, to serfdom, to bonds of suzerainty and vassalage. If these institutions were able to implant themselves, if, by profiting from a whole series of tactical alliances, they were able to gain acceptance, this was because they presented themselves as agencies of regulation, arbitration, and demarcation, as a way of introducing order in the midst of these powers, of establishing a principle that would temper them and distribute them according to boundaries and a fixed hierarchy. Faced with a myriad of clashing forces, these great forms of power functioned as a principle of right that transcended all the heterogeneous claims, manifesting the triple distinction of forming a unitary regime, of identifying its will with the law, and of acting through mechanisms of interdiction and sanction. The slogan of this regime, *pax et justitia*, in keeping with the function it laid claim to, established peace as the prohibition of feudal or private wars, and justice as a way of suspending the private settling of lawsuits. Doubtless there was more to this development of great monarchic institutions than a pure and simple juridical edifice. But such was the language of power, the representation it gave of itself, and the entire theory of public law that was constructed in the Middle Ages, or reconstructed from Roman law, bears witness to the fact. Law was not simply a weapon skillfully wielded by monarchs; it was the monarchic system's mode of manifestation and the form of its acceptability. In Western societies since the Middle Ages, the exercise of power has always been formulated in terms of law.

A tradition dating back to the eighteenth or nineteenth century has accustomed us to place absolute monarchic power on the side of the unlawful: arbitrariness, abuse, caprice, willfulness, privileges and exceptions, the traditional continuance of accomplished facts. But this is to overlook a fundamental historical trait of Western monarchies: they were constructed as systems of law, they expressed themselves through theories of law, and they made their mechanisms of power work in the form of law. The old reproach that Boulainvilliers directed at the French monarchy—that it used the law and jurists to do away with rights and to bring down the aristocracy—was basically warranted by the facts. Through the development of the monarchy and its institutions this juridico-political dimension was established. It is by no means adequate to describe the manner in which power was and is exercised, but it is the code according to which power presents itself and prescribes that we conceive of it. The history of the monarchy went hand in hand with the covering up of the facts and procedures of power by juridico-political discourse.

Yet, despite the efforts that were made to disengage the juridical sphere from the monarchic institution and to free the political from the juridical, the representation of power remained caught within this system. Consider the two following examples. Criticism of the eighteenth-century monarchic institution in France was not directed against the juridico-monarchic sphere as such, but was made on behalf of a pure and rigorous juridical system to which all the mechanisms of power could conform, with no excesses or irregularities, as opposed to a monarchy which, notwithstanding its own assertions, continuously overstepped the legal framework and set itself above the laws. Political criticism availed itself, therefore, of all the juridical thinking that had accompanied the development of the monarchy, in order to condemn the latter; but it did not challenge the principle which held that law had to be the very form of power, and that power always had to be exercised in the form of law. Another type of criticism of political institutions appeared in the nineteenth century, a much more radical criticism in that it was concerned to show not only that real power escaped the rules of jurisprudence, but that the legal system itself was merely a way of exerting violence, of appropriating that violence for the benefit of the few, and of exploiting the dissymmetries and injustices of domination under cover of general law. But this critique of law is still carried out on the assumption that, ideally and by nature, power must be exercised in accordance with a fundamental lawfulness.

At bottom, despite the differences in epochs and objectives, the representation of power has remained under the spell of monarchy. In political thought and analysis, we still have not cut off the head of the king. Hence the importance that the theory of power gives to the problem of right and violence, law and illegality, freedom and will, and especially the state and sovereignty (even if the latter is questioned insofar as it is personified in a collective being and no longer a sovereign individual). To conceive of power on the basis of these problems is to conceive of it in terms of a historical form that is characteristic of our societies: the juridical monarchy. Characteristic yet transitory. For while many of its forms have persisted to the present, it has gradually been penetrated by quite new mechanisms of power that are probably irreducible to the representation of law. As we shall see, these power mechanisms are, at least in part, those that, beginning in the eighteenth century, took charge of men's existence, men as living bodies. And if it is true that the juridical system was useful for representing, albeit in a nonexhaustive way, a power that was centered primarily around deduction (*prélèvement*) and death, it is utterly incongruous with the new methods of power whose operation is not ensured by right but by technique, not by law but by normalization, not by punishment but by control, methods that are employed on all levels and in forms that go beyond the state and its apparatus. We have been engaged for centuries in a type of society in which the juridical is increasingly incapable of coding power, of serving as its system of representation. Our historical gradient carries us further and further away from a reign of law that had already begun to recede into the past at a time when the French Revolution and the accompanying age of constitutions and codes seemed to destine it for a future that was at hand.

It is this juridical representation that is still at work in recent analyses concerning the relationships of power to sex. But the problem is not to know whether desire is alien to power, whether it is prior to the law as is often thought to be the case, when it is not rather the law that is perceived as constituting it. This question is beside the point. Whether desire is this or that, in any case one continues to conceive of it in relation to a power that is always juridical and discursive, a power that has its central point in the enunciation of the law. One remains attached to a certain image of power-law, of power-sovereignty, which was traced out by the theoreticians of right and the monarchic institution. It is this image that we must break free of, that is, of the theoretical privilege of law and sovereignty, if we wish to analyze power within the concrete and historical framework of its operation. We must construct an analytics of power that no longer takes law as a model and a code.

This history of sexuality, or rather this series of studies concerning the historical relationships of power and the discourse on sex, is, I realize, a circular project in the sense that it involves two endeavors that refer back to one another. We shall try to rid ourselves of a juridical and negative representation of power, and cease to conceive of it in terms of law, prohibition, liberty, and sovereignty. But how then do we analyze what has occurred in recent history with regard to this thing—seemingly one of the most forbidden areas of our lives and bodies—that is sex? How, if not by way of prohibition and blockage, does power gain access to it? Through which mechanisms, or tactics, or devices? But let us assume in turn that a somewhat careful scrutiny will show that power in modern societies has not in fact governed sexuality through law and sovereignty; let us suppose that historical analysis has revealed the presence of a veritable "technology" of sex, one that is much more complex and above all much more positive than the mere effect of a "defense" could be; this being the case, does this example—which can only be considered a privileged one, since power seemed in this instance, more than anywhere else, to function as prohibition—not compel one to discover principles for analyzing power which do not derive from the system of right and the form of law? Hence it is a question of forming a different grid of historical decipherment by starting from a different theory of power; and, at the same time, of advancing little by little toward a different conception of power through a closer examination of an entire historical material. We must at the same time conceive of sex without the law, and power without the king.

Chapter 46

David Halperin

FORGETTING FOUCAULT: ACTS, IDENTITIES, AND THE HISTORY OF SEXUALITY

David Halperin, "Forgetting Foucault: Acts, Identities, and the History of Sexuality", *How to do the History of Homosexuality* (Chicago: Chicago University Press, 2002), 26–44 (excerpt).

IN WHAT FOLLOWS I propose to explore [an] aspect of the oblivion that has engulfed Foucault's approach to sexuality since his death, one particular "forgetting" that has had important consequences for the practice of both the history of sexuality and lesbian/gay studies. I refer to the reception and deployment of Foucault's distinction between the sodomite and the homosexual—a distinction often taken to be synonymous with the distinction between sexual acts and sexual identities. The passage in *The History of Sexuality*, volume I, in which Foucault makes this fateful distinction is so well known that it might seem unnecessary to quote it, but what that really means, I am contending, is that the passage is in fact so well forgotten that nothing but direct quotation from it will do. Foucault writes,

> As defined by the ancient civil or canonical codes, sodomy was a category of forbidden acts; their author was nothing more than the juridical subject of them. The nineteenth-century homosexual became a personage—a past, a case history and a childhood, a character, a form of life; also a morphology, with an indiscreet anatomy and possibly a mysterious physiology. Nothing in his total being escapes his sexuality. Everywhere in him it is present: underlying all his actions, because it is their insidious and indefinitely active principle; shamelessly inscribed on his face and on his body, because it is a secret that always gives itself away. It is consubstantial with him, less as a habitual sin than as a singular nature. . . . Homosexuality appeared as one of the forms of sexuality when it was transposed from the practice of sodomy onto a kind of interior androgyny, a hermaphroditism of the soul. The sodomite was a renegade [or "backslider"]; the homosexual is now a species.

[La sodomie—celle des anciens droits civil ou canonique—était un type d'actes interdits; leur auteur n'en était que le sujet juridique. L'homosexuel du xixe siècle est devenu un personnage: un passé, une histoire et une enfance, un caractère, une forme de vie; une morphologie aussi, avec une anatomie indiscrète et peut-être une physiologie mystérieuse. Rien de ce qu'il est au total n'échappe à sa sexualité. Partout en lui, elle est présente: sous-jacente à toutes ses conduites parce qu'elle en est le principe insidieux et indéfiniment actif; inscrite sans pudeur sur son visage et sur son corps parce qu'elle est un secret qui se trahit toujours. Elle lui est consubstantielle, moins comme un péché d'habitude que comme une nature singulière. . . . L'homosexualité est apparue comme une des figures de la sexualité lorsqu'elle a été rabattue de la pratique de la sodomie sur une sorte d'androgynie intérieure, un hermaphrodisme de l'âme. Le sodomite était un relaps, l'homosexuel est maintenant une espèce.][1]

Foucault's formulation is routinely taken to authorize the doctrine that before the nineteenth century the categories or classifications typically employed by European cultures to articulate sexual difference did not distinguish among different kinds of sexual actors but only among different kinds of sexual acts. In the pre-modern and early modern periods, so the claim goes, sexual behavior did not represent a sign or marker of a person's sexual identity; it did not indicate or express some more generalized or holistic feature of the person, such as that person's subjectivity, disposition, or character. The pattern is clearest, we are told, in the case of deviant sexual acts. Sodomy, for example, was a sinful act that anyone of sufficient depravity might commit; it was not a symptom of a type of personality. To perform the act of sodomy was not to manifest a deviant sexual identity but merely to be the author of a morally objectionable act. Whence the conclusion that before the modern era sexual deviance could be predicated only of acts, not of persons or identities.

There is a good deal of truth in this received view, and Foucault himself may even have subscribed to a version of it at the time he wrote *The History of Sexuality*, volume I. Although I am about to argue strenuously against it, I want to be very clear that my aim is to revise it, not to reverse it. I do not want to return us to some unreconstructed or reactionary belief in the universal validity and applicability of modern sexual concepts or to promote an uncritical acceptance of the categories and classifications of sexuality as true descriptors of the basic realities of human erotic life—and, therefore, as unproblematic instruments for the historical analysis of human culture in all times and places. It is certainly not my intention to undermine the principles and practices of the new social history, let alone to recant my previous arguments for the historical and cultural constitution of sexual identity (which have sometimes been misinterpreted as providing support for the view I shall be criticizing here). Least of all do I wish to revive an essentialist faith in the unqualified existence of homosexual and heterosexual persons in Western societies before the modern era. I take it as established that a large-scale transformation of social and personal life took place in Europe as part of the massive cultural reorganization that accompanied the transition from a traditional, hierarchical, status-based society to a modern, individualistic, mass society during the period of industrialization and the rise of a capitalist economy. One symptom of that transformation, as a number of researchers (both before and after Foucault) have pointed out, is that something new happens to the various relations among sexual roles, sexual object-choices, sexual categories, sexual behaviors, and sexual identities in bourgeois Europe between the end of the seventeenth century and the beginning of the twentieth. Sex takes on new social and individual functions, and it assumes a new importance in defining and normalizing the modern self. The conception of the sexual instinct as an autonomous human function without an organ appears for the first time in the nineteenth century, and without it the currently prevailing, heavily psychologized model of sexual subjectivity—which knits up desire, its objects, sexual behavior, gender identity, reproductive function, mental health, erotic sensibility, personal style, and degrees of normality or deviance into an individuating, normativizing feature of the personality called "sexuality" or "sexual orientation"—is inconceivable.[2] Sexuality is indeed, as Foucault claimed, a distinctively modern production. Nonetheless, the canonical reading of the famous passage in *The History of Sexuality*, volume I, and the conclusion conventionally based on it—namely, that before the modern era sexual deviance could be predicated only of acts, not of persons or identities—is, I shall contend, as inattentive to Foucault's text as it is heedless of European history.

Such a misreading of Foucault can be constructed only by setting aside, and then forgetting, the decisive qualifying phrase with which his famous pronouncement opens: "*As defined by the ancient civil or canonical codes*," Foucault begins, "sodomy was a category of forbidden acts." Foucault, in other words, is making a carefully limited point about the differing styles of disqualification applied to male love by pre-modern legal definitions of sodomy and by nineteenth-century psychiatric conceptualizations of homosexuality, respectively. The intended effect of his rhetorical extravagance in this passage is to highlight what in particular was new and distinctive about the modern discursive practices that produced the category of "the homosexual." As almost always in *The History of Sexuality*, Foucault is speaking about discursive and institutional practices, not about what people really did in bed or what they thought about it. He is not attempting to describe popular attitudes or private emotions, much less is he presuming to convey what actually went on in the minds of different historical subjects when they had sex. He is making a contrast between the way something called "sodomy" was typically defined by the laws of various European states and municipalities as well as by Christian penitentials and canon law, on the one hand, and the way something called "homosexuality" was typically defined by the writings of nineteenth-century and early-twentieth-century sexologists, on the other.

A glance at the larger context of the much-excerpted passage in *The History of Sexuality*, volume I, is sufficient to make Foucault's meaning clear. Foucault introduces his account of "the nineteenth-century homosexual" in order to illustrate a more general claim, which he advances in the sentence immediately preceding: the "new persecution of the peripheral sexualities" that occurred in the modern era was accomplished in part through "an *incorporation of perversions* and a new *specification of individuals*."[3] (Earlier efforts to regulate sexual behavior did not feature such tactics, according to Foucault.) The whole discussion of this distinctively modern method of sexual control is embedded, in turn, within a larger argument about a crucial shift in the nature of sexual prohibitions as those prohibitions were constructed in formal discursive practices, a shift that occurred in Europe between the pre-modern period and the nineteenth century. Comparing medieval moral and legal codifications of sexual relations with nineteenth-century medical and forensic ones, Foucault contrasts various pre-modern styles of sexual prohibition, which took the form of specifying rules of conduct, making prescriptions and recommendations, and discriminating between the licit and the illicit, with modern styles of sexual prohibition. These latter-day strategies took the form of establishing norms of self-regulation—not by legislating standards of behavior and punishing deviations from them but rather by constructing new species of individuals, discovering and "implanting" perversions, and, in this way, elaborating more subtle and insidious means of social control. The ultimate purpose of the comparison is to support Foucault's "historico-theoretical" demonstration that power is not only negative but also positive, not only repressive but also productive.

Foucault is analyzing the different modalities of power at work in pre-modern and modern codifications of sexual prohibition, which is to say in two historical instances of sexual discourse attached to institutional practices. He carefully isolates the formal discursive systems that he will proceed to discuss from popular moral attitudes and behaviors about which he will have nothing to say and that he dismisses from consideration with barely a parenthetical glance: "Up to the end of the eighteenth century, three major explicit codes [*codes*]—*apart from regularities of custom and constraints of opinion*—governed sexual practices: canon law [*droit canonique*], Christian pastoral, and civil law."[4] Foucault goes on to expand this observation in a passage that directly anticipates and lays the groundwork for the famous portrait he will later sketch of the differences between "the sodomy of the old civil and canonical codes" and that novel invention of modern psychiatry, "the nineteenth-century homosexual." Describing the terms in which pre-modern sexual prohibitions defined the scope of their operation and the nature of their target, he writes, "What was taken into account in the civil and religious jurisdictions alike was a general unlawfulness. Doubtless acts 'contrary to nature' were stamped as especially abominable, but they were perceived simply as an extreme form of acts 'against the law'; they, too, were infringements of decrees—decrees which were just as sacred as those of marriage and which had been established in order to rule the order of things and the plan of beings. Prohibitions bearing on sex were basically of a juridical nature [*de nature juridique*]."[5] This passage prepares the reader to gauge the differences between these "juridical" prohibitions against "acts" " 'contrary to nature' " and the nineteenth-century prohibitions against homosexuality, which did not simply criminalize sexual relations between men as illegal but medically disqualified them as pathological and—not content with pathologizing the act—constructed the perpetrator as a deviant form of life, a perverse personality, an anomalous species, thereby producing a new specification of individuals whose true nature would be defined from now on by reference to their abnormal "sexuality." The nineteenth-century disciplining of the subject, though it purported to aim at the eradication of "peripheral sexualities," paradoxically required their consolidation and "implantation" or "incorporation" in individuals, for only by that means could the subject's body itself become so deeply, so minutely invaded and colonized by the agencies of normalization. The discursive construction of the new sexual perversions was therefore a ruse of power, no longer simply prohibiting behavior but now also controlling, regulating, and normalizing embodied subjects. As Foucault sums up his argument, "The implantation of perversions is an instrument-effect: it is through the isolation, intensification, and consolidation of peripheral sexualities that the relations of power to sex and pleasure branched out and multiplied, measured the body and penetrated modes of conduct."[6] Want an example? Take the case of homosexuality. "The sodomy of the old civil and canonical codes was a category of forbidden acts; their author was nothing more than the juridical subject of them. The nineteenth-century homosexual became a personage. . . ." So that's how the overall argument works.

Foucault narrowly frames his comparison between sodomy and homosexuality with the purpose of this larger argument in mind. The point-by-point contrast—between legal discourse (*codes* and *droits*) and psychiatric discourse, between juridical subjects and sexual subjects, between laws and norms, between acts contrary to nature and embodied subjects or species of individuals—is ruthlessly schematic. That schematic reduction is in keeping with the general design of the first volume of Foucault's *History*, which merely outlines, in an admittedly preliminary and tentative fashion, the principles intended to guide the remaining five unfinished studies that Foucault projected for his *History* at the time. His schematic opposition between sodomy and homosexuality is first and foremost a discursive analysis, not a social history, let alone an exhaustive one. *It is not an empirical claim about the historical existence or non-existence of sexually deviant individuals*. It is a claim about the internal logic and systematic functioning of two different discursive styles of sexual disqualification—and, ultimately, it is a heuristic device for foregrounding what is distinctive about modern techniques of social and sexual regulation. As such, it points to a historical development that will need to be properly explored in its own right (as Foucault intended to do in a separate volume), and it dramatizes the larger themes of Foucault's *History*: the historical triumph of normalization over law, the decentralization and dispersion of the mechanisms of regulation, the disciplining of the modern subject, the traversal of sexuality by relations of power, the productivity of power, and the displacement of state coercion by the technical and bureau-cratic administration of life ("biopower"). By documenting the existence of both a discursive and a temporal gap between two dissimilar styles of defining, and disqualifying, male same-sex sexual expression, Foucault highlights the historical and political specificity of "sexual-ity," both as a cultural concept and as a tactical device, and so he contributes to the task of "introducing" the history of sexuality as a possible field of study—and as a radical scholarly and political project. Nothing Foucault says about the differences between those two histor-ically distant, and operationally distinct, discursive strategies for regulating and delegitimat-ing forms of male same-sex sexual contacts prohibits us from inquiring into the connections that pre-modern people may have made between specific sexual acts and the particular ethos, or sexual style, or sexual subjectivity, of those who performed them.

A more explicit argument to this effect was advanced in the late 1980s by John J. Winkler, in opposition less to Foucault than to what even then were already well-established, conventional, and highly dogmatic misreadings of Foucault. Winkler, a classical scholar, was discussing the ancient Greek and Roman figure of the *kinaidos* or *cinaedus*, a "scare-image" (or phobic construction) of a sexually deviant and gender-deviant male, whose most salient distinguishing feature was a supposedly "feminine" love of being sexually penetrated by other men.[7] "Scholars of recent sex-gender history," Winkler wrote in his 1990 book, *The Constraints of Desire*, "have asserted that pre-modern systems classified not persons but acts and that 'the' homosexual as a person-category is a recent invention." He went on to qualify that assertion as follows: "The *kinaidos*, to be sure, is not a 'homosexual' but neither is he just an ordinary guy who now and then decided to commit a kinaidic act. The conception of a *kinaidos* was of a man socially deviant in his entire being, principally observable in behavior that flagrantly violated or contravened the dominant social defin-ition of masculinity. To this extent, *kinaidos* was a category of person, not just of acts."[8] Ancient Mediterranean societies, of course, did not exactly have "categories of person," types of blank individuals, in the modern sense, as Winkler himself pointed out. The ancient conception of the *kinaidos*, Winkler explained, depended on indigenous notions of gender. It arose in the context of a belief system in which, first of all, the two genders are conceived as opposite ends of a much-traveled continuum and, second, masculinity is thought to be a difficult accomplishment—one that is achieved only by a constant struggle akin to warfare against enemies both internal and external—and thus requires great forti-tude in order to maintain. In a situation where it is so hard, both personally and culturally, to be a man, Winkler observed, "the temptation to desert one's side is very great." The *kinaidos* succumbed to that temptation.

The *kinaidos* could be conceived by the ancients in both universalizing and minoritizing terms—as a potential threat to the masculine identity of every male, that is, and as the disfiguring peculiarity of a small class of deviant individuals.[9] Because ancient Mediterranean discourses of sex and gender featured the notion that "the two sexes are not simply opposite but stand at poles of a continuum which can be traversed," as Winkler pointed out, " 'woman' is not only the opposite of a man; she is also a potentially threatening 'internal emigré' of masculine identity."[10] The prospect of losing one's masculine gender status and being reduced to the social ranks of women therefore represented a universal possibility for all men. In such a context, the figure of the *kinaidos* stood as a warning to men of what could happen to them if they gave up the internal struggle to master their desires and surrendered, in womanly fashion, to the lure of pleasure. The clear implication of this warning is that the only thing that prevents men from allowing other men to use them as objects of sexual degradation, the only thing that enables men to resist the temptation to let other men fuck them like whores, is not the nature of their own desires, or their own capacities for sexual enjoyment, but their hard-won masculine ability to withstand the seductive appeal of pleasure-at-any-price. The *kinaidos*, on this view, is not someone who has a different sexual orientation from other men or who belongs to some autonomous sexual species. Rather, he is someone who represents what *every* man would be like if he were so shameless as to sacrifice his dignity and masculine gender status for the sake of gratifying the most odious and disgraceful, though no doubt voluptuous, bodily appetites. Such a worthless character is so radical and so complete a failure as a man that he could be understood, at least by the ancients, as wholly reversing the internal gender hierarchy that structured and defined normative masculinity for men and that maintained it against manifold temptations to effeminacy. The catastrophic failure of male self-fashioning that the *kinaidos* represented was so complete, in other words, that it could not be imagined as merely confined within the sphere of erotic life or restricted to the occasional performance of disreputable sexual acts: it defined and determined a man's social identity in its totality, and it generated a recognizable social type—namely, the "scare-image" and phobic stereotype of the *kinaidos*, which Winkler so eloquently described.

As the mere existence of the stereotype implies, the ancients were quite capable of conceptualizing the figure of the *kinaidos*, when they so desired, not only in anxiously universalizing terms but also in comfortably minoritizing ones. Although some normal men might acknowledge that the scandalous pleasures to which the *kinaidos* succumbed, and which normal men properly avoided, were universally pleasurable in and of themselves, still the very fact that the *kinaidos* did succumb to such pleasure, whereas normal men did not, contributed to defining his difference and marked out the vast distance that separated the *kinaidos* from normal men. Just as some moderns may think that, whereas anyone *can* get addicted to drugs, only people who have something fundamentally wrong with them actually *do*, so some ancients evidently thought that, although the pleasures of sexual penetration in themselves might be universally pleasurable, any male who actually pursued them suffered from a specific constitutional defect—namely, a constitutional lack of the masculine capacity to withstand the appeal of pleasure (especially pleasure deemed exceptionally disgraceful or degrading) as well as a constitutional tendency to adopt a specifically feminine attitude of surrender in relations with other men. Hence, the desire to be sexually penetrated by other men, which was the most dramatic and flagrant sign of the *kinaidos*'s constitutional femininity, could be interpreted by the ancients in sharply minoritizing terms as an indication of a physiological anomaly in the *kinaidos* or as the symptom of a moral or mental "disease." Conceived in these terms, the *kinaidos* did not represent the frightening possibility of a failure of nerve on the part of every man, a collapse in the face of the ongoing struggle that all men necessarily waged to maintain and defend their masculinity, he was simply a peculiar, repugnant, and perplexing freak, driven to abandon his sexual and gender identity in pursuit of a pleasure that no one but a woman could possibly enjoy. (And there were even some abominable practices, like fellatio, which a *kinaidos* might relish but no decent woman would so much as contemplate.)

The details in this minoritizing conception of the *kinaidos* have been filled in with great skill and documented at fascinating length by Maud Gleason, most recently in her 1995 book, *Making Men*. "The essential idea here," writes Gleason, corroborating Winkler's emphasis on the gender deviance of the *kinaidos* and calling attention to what she fittingly terms the ancient "semiotics of gender" that produced the *kinaidos* as a visibly deviant kind of being, "is that there exist [according to the axioms of Greek and Roman social life] masculine and feminine 'types' that do not necessarily correspond to the anatomical sex of the person in question."[11] Gleason approaches the figure of the *kinaidos* from an unexpected and original scholarly angle—namely, from a close study of the neglected scientific writings of the ancient physiognomists, experts in the learned technique of deciphering a person's character from his or her appearance. Gleason's analysis of the ancient corpus of physiognomic texts makes clear that the portrait they construct of the figure of the *kinaidos* agrees with the stereotypical features commonly ascribed by the ancients to the general appearance of gender-deviant or "effeminate" men. Like such men, the *kinaidos* could be identified, or so the Greeks thought, by a variety of physical features: weak eyes, knees that knock together, head tilted to the right, hands limply upturned, and hips that either swing from side to side or are held tightly rigid. Latin physiognomy agrees largely with the Greek tradition in its enumeration of the characteristics of the *cinaedus:* "A tilted head, a mincing gait, an enervated voice, a lack of stability in the shoulders, and a feminine way of moving the body." Gleason adds that a *kinaidos* could also be known by certain specific mannerisms: "He shifts his eyes around in sheep-like fashion when he speaks; he touches his fingers to his nose; he compulsively obliterates all traces of spittle he may find—his own or anyone else's—by rubbing it into the dust with his heel; he frequently stops to admire what he considers his own best feature; he smiles furtively while talking; he holds his arms turned outward; he laughs out loud; and he has an annoying habit of clasping other people by the hand."[12] The *kinaidos*, in short, is considerably more than the juridical subject of deviant sexual acts. To recur to Foucault's terminology, the *kinaidos* represents at the very least a full-blown morphology. As Gleason observes, "Foucault's description of the nineteenth-century homosexual fits the *cinaedus* remarkably well. . . . The *cinaedus* was a 'life-form' all to himself, and his condition was written all over him in signs that could be decoded by those practiced in the art." Gleason hastens to add, however, that "what made [the *cinaedus*] different from normal folk . . . was not simply the fact that his sexual partners included people of the same sex as himself (that, after all, was nothing out of the ordinary), nor was it some kind of psychosexual orientation—a 'sexuality' in the nineteenth-century sense—but rather an inversion or reversal of his gender identity: his abandonment of a 'masculine' role in favor of a 'feminine' one."[13]

Gleason's conclusion has now been massively confirmed by Craig Williams, a specialist in ancient Roman literature, who has undertaken an exhaustive survey of the extant Latin sources. William's careful discussion makes it clear that the *cinaedus* does not correspond closely to any type of individual defined by more recent, canonical categories of "sexuality": "When a Roman called a man a *cinaedus*," Williams explains, "he was not ruling out the possibility that the man might play sexual roles other than that of the receptive partner in anal intercourse." Hence,

> the *cinaedus* was not the same thing as a "passive homosexual," since it was neither his expression of sexual desire for other males nor his proclivity for playing the receptive role in anal intercourse that gave him his identity or uniquely defined him as a *cinaedus:* he might engage in sexual practices with women and still be a *cinaedus*, and a man did not automatically become a *cinaedus* simply by being penetrated (victims of rape, for example, would not normally be described as such). A *cinaedus* was, rather, a man who failed to be fully masculine, whose effeminacy showed itself in such symptoms as feminine clothing and mannerisms and a lascivious and oversexed demeanor that was likely to be embodied in a proclivity for playing the receptive role in anal intercourse. *Cinaedi* were, in other words, a prominent subset of the class of effeminate men (*molles*) . . . but hardly identical to that whole class.[14]

Williams goes on to align his own analysis of the *cinaedus* with the tradition of interpretation that extends from Winkler and Gleason to the argument proposed here:

> Likewise I am suggesting that the Roman *cinaedus* was in fact a category of person who was considered "socially deviant," but that his social identity was crucially different from that of the "homosexual," since his desire for persons of his own sex was not a defining or even problematic feature of his makeup as a deviant: his desire to be penetrated was indeed one of his characteristics, but, as we have seen, men called *cinaedi* were also thought capable of being interested in penetrative sexual relations with women. Thus the deviance of the *cinaedus* is ultimately a matter of gender identity rather than sexual identity, in the sense that his predilection for playing the receptive role in penetrative acts was not the single defining feature of his identity but rather a sign of a more funda-mental transgression of gender categories.[15]

There may well be modern categories of deviance—and there may well be contemporary forms of sexual rebellion, transgression, or affirmation—that correspond in some ways to the ancient figure of the *cinaedus* or *kinaidos*. But such categories would only partly overlap with the category of "the homosexual." And if "homosexuality" today is sometimes under-stood to *apply* to figures such as the *cinaedus*, that tells us less about the particular character-istics of those figures than it does about the elasticity of the category of homosexuality itself. To capture the defining features of the *kinaidos*, it is necessary to begin, at least, by situating him in his own conceptual and social universe, as I have tried to do here.

One significant difference between the *kinaidos* and "the homosexual" is that the *kinaidos* was defined more in terms of gender than in terms of desire. For whether he was imagined in universalizing or minoritizing terms, the *kinaidos* in any case offended principally against the order of masculinity, not against the order of heterosexuality. As such, the *kinaidos* does not represent a salient example of deviant sexual subjectivity. Although he was distinguished from normal men in part by the pleasure he took in being sexually penetrated, his peculiar taste was not sufficient, in and of itself, to individuate him as a sexual subject. Rather, it was a generic sign of femininity. Even the *kinaidos*'s desire to play a receptive role in sexual intercourse with other men—which was about as close to manifesting a distinctive sexual orientation as the *kinaidos* ever got—represented to the ancients "merely a symptom of the deeper disorder, his gender deviance," as Williams emphasizes, and so it did not imply a different kind of specifically sexual subjectivity. Inasmuch as the ancients did not distinguish systematically between gender and sexuality, the *kinaidos*'s desire to be sexually penetrated could be seen as part and parcel of his singular, transgendered condition: it represented at once a symptom and a consequence of the categorical reversal of his masculine gender identity, and it identified the *kinaidos* as womanly in both his gender identity and his sexual desire. To be "womanly," in such a context, is of course a sexual as well as a gendered trait, and "gender deviance" should not be conceptualized as hermetically sealed off from matters of desire. Nonetheless, the *kinaidos*'s desire did not distinguish him as the bearer of a unique or distinct sexuality as such. Neither did his lust for bodily pleasure, since—far from being considered a deviant desire, as we have seen—such lust was thought common to all men. Nor was there anything peculiar about the *kinaidos*'s sexual object-choice: as Gleason men-tions, it was quite possible in the ancient Mediterranean world for a male to desire and to pursue sexual contact with other males without impugning in the slightest his own masculin-ity or normative identity as a man—just so long as he played an insertive sexual role, observed all the proper phallocentric protocols in his relations with the objects of his desire, and maintained a normatively masculine style of personal deportment. Unlike the modern homosexual, then, the *kinaidos* was not defined principally by his "sexuality." Even without a sexuality of his own, however, the *kinaidos*'s betrayal of his masculine gender identity was so spectacular as to brand him a deviant type of person and to inscribe his deviant identity all over his face and body. To put it very schematically, the *kinaidos* represents an instance of deviant sexual morphology without deviant sexual subjectivity.

Let's move on, then, from matters of sexual morphology and gender presentation and take up matters of sexual subjectivity itself. My chief exhibit in this latter department will be an ancient erotic fable told by Apuleius in the second century and retold by Giovanni Boccaccio in the fourteenth. The two texts have been the subject of a trenchant comparative study by Jonathan Walters in a 1993 issue of *Gender and History*. I have taken Walters's analysis as the basis of my own, and my interpretation closely follows his, although I have a somewhat different set of questions to put to the two texts.[16]

Here, first of all, in bare outline, is the plot of the erotic fable under scrutiny. A man dining out at the home of a friend finds his dinner interrupted when his host detects an adulterous lover concealed in the house by the host's wife, who had not expected her husband to arrive home for dinner, much less with a guest in tow. His meal abruptly terminated, the disappointed guest returns to his own house for dinner ahead of schedule and tells the story to his righteously indignant wife, only to discover that she herself has hidden in his house a young lover of her own. Instead of threatening to kill the youth, however, the husband fucks him and lets him go. The end. This bare summary does little justice to the artistry and wit with which the two stories are told by their respective authors, but the point I wish to make is a historical one, not a literary one. I trust it will emerge from the following comparison.

Apuleius's tale of the baker's wife in book 9 of *The Golden Ass* begins with a description of her lover. He is a boy (*puer*), Apuleius's narrator tells us, still notable for the shiny smoothness of his beardless cheeks, and still delighting and attracting the sexual attention of wayward husbands (*adulteros*) (9.22). According to the erotic postulates of ancient Mediterranean societies, then, there will be nothing out of the ordinary about a normal man finding him sexually desirable. So the first thing to notice is that Apuleius explains the sexual motivation of the wronged husband by reference to erotic qualities inherent in the sexual object, not by reference to any distinguishing characteristics of the sexual subject—not, in other words, by reference to the husband's own sexual tastes, to his erotic subjectivity. This emphasis on the attractiveness of the boy thereby prepares the way for the ending of the story; it is not necessary for the narrator to invoke any specific sort of erotic inclination, much less a deviant one, on the part of the husband in order to anticipate the denouement of the plot. In fact, as Walters observes, the husband "is not described in any way that marks him out as unusual, let alone reprehensible: he is portrayed as blameless, 'a good man in general and extremely temperate' "; that is in keeping with a story designed, within the larger context of Apuleius's narrative, to illustrate the mischief caused to their husbands by devious, depraved, and adulterous wives.[17] When the baker discovers the boy, he locks up his wife and takes the boy to bed himself, thereby (as Apuleius's narrator puts it) enjoying "the most gratifying revenge for his ruined marriage." At daybreak he summons two of his slaves and has them hold the boy up while he flogs his buttocks with a rod, leaving the boy "with his white buttocks the worse for their treatment" both by night and by day. The baker then kicks his wife out of the house and prepares to divorce her (9.28).

Boccaccio's tale of Pietro di Vinciolo of Perugia, the Tenth Story of the Fifth Day of the *Decameron*, is based directly on Apuleius; its departures from its model are therefore especially telling.[18] Boccaccio's narrator begins further back in time, at the point when Pietro takes a wife "more to beguile others and to abate the general suspect [*la generale oppinion*] in which he was held by all the Perugians, than for any desire [*vaghezza*] of his own" (trans. Payne-Singleton). As Walters remarks, "Boccaccio . . . is at pains to tell us from the beginning that something is wrong with the husband."[19] What Boccaccio marks specifically as deviant about Pietro, or so the foregoing quotation from the *Decameron* implies, is his desire.[20] This turns out to refer to his sexual object-choice and to comprehend, in particular, two different aspects of it: first, the customary objects of his sexual desire are young men, not the usual objects of desire for a man, and, second, Pietro (unlike the baker in Apuleius) has no desire for the usual objects of male desire—namely, women. So he has a non-standard erotic subjectivity, insofar as he both desires the wrong objects and fails to desire the right objects.

Both of these erotic errors are dramatized by the narrative. We are told that his wife's lover is "a youth [*garzone*], who was one of the goodliest and most agreeable of all Perugia," and that when Pietro discovers him he instantly recognizes him as "one whom he had long pursued for his own lewd ends." Understandably, Pietro "no less rejoiced to have found him than his wife was woeful"; when he confronts her with the lad, "she saw that he was all agog with joy because he held so goodly a stripling [*giovinetto*] by the hand." No wonder that, far from punishing his wife, Pietro hastens to strike an obscene bargain with her to share the young man between them. As for Pietro's sexual indifference to women, we are told that his lusty, red-haired, highly sexed young wife, "who would liefer have had two husbands than one," is frustrated by her husband's inattention and realizes that she will exhaust herself arguing with him before she will change his disposition. Indeed, he has "a mind far more disposed otherwhat than to her [*molto piú ad altro che a lei l'animo avea disposto*]." At the culmination of the story, Pietro's wife reproaches him for being as desirous of women as "a dog of cudgels [*cosí vago di noi come il can delle mazze*]."

Note that Boccaccio's narrator says nothing to indicate that Pietro is effeminate or in any way deviant in terms of his personal style or sexual morphology.[21] *You wouldn't know he was a paederast or a sodomite by looking at him.* Nothing about his looks or his behavior gives him away—or gives his wife any advance warning about the nature of his sexual peculiarities. As she says, she had supposed he desired what men typically do desire and should desire when she married him; otherwise, she would never have done so. "He knew I was a woman," she exclaims to herself; "why, then, did he take me to wife, if women were not to his mind [*contro all'animo*]?" Nothing in his morphology made her suspect he harbored deviant desires. And why in any case should we presume that the husband would exhibit signs of effeminacy? He no more resembles the ancient figure of the *kinaidos* than does his literary forebear in Apuleius. Far from displaying a supposedly "feminine" inclination to submit himself to other men to be sexually penetrated by them, the husband in Boccaccio plays a sexually insertive role in intercourse with his wife's lover. That, after all, is the point of the story's punchline: "On the following morning the youth was escorted back to the public square not altogether certain which he had the more been that night, wife or husband"—meaning, obviously, *wife* to *Pietro* or *husband to Pietro's wife*.[22] What is at issue in Boccaccio's portrait of Pietro di Vinciolo, then, is not gender deviance but sexual deviance.

Finally, in Apuleius's tale the husband's enjoyment of his wife's lover is an incidental component of his revenge and does not express any special or distinctive sexual taste on his part, much less a habitual preference, whereas in Boccaccio's tale the husband is identified as the subject of deviant sexual desires and is only too happy to exploit his wife's infidelity for the purposes of his own pleasure.

A comparison of these two pre-modern texts indicates that it is possible for sexual acts to be represented in such texts as either *more* or *less* related to sexual dispositions, desires, and subjectivities. Whereas Apuleius's text makes no incriminating association between the baker's sexual enjoyment of the adulterous youth and the baker's character, masculinity, or sexual disposition, Boccaccio's text connects the performance of sodomitical acts with a deviant sexual taste and a deviant sexual subjectivity. In order to update Apuleius's plot it seems to have been necessary for Boccaccio to posit a sodomitical disposition or inclination on the husband's part: he seems to have had no other way of motivating the scandalously witty conclusion of the tale as he had inherited it from Apuleius. Pietro's inclination is not the same thing as a sexual orientation, much less a sexual identity or form of life, to be sure. For one thing, his sexual preference seems contained, compartmentalized, and does not appear to connect to any other feature of his character, such as a sensibility, a set of personal mannerisms, a style of gender presentation, or a psychology. Nonetheless, Pietro's sexual taste for young men represents a notable and perhaps even a defining feature of his life as a sexual subject, as well as a distinctive feature of his life as a social and ethical subject. Pietro may not be a deviant life-form, like the ancient Greek or Roman *kinaidos*—a traitor to his gender whose deviance is visibly inscribed in his personal demeanor—but neither is he nothing more than the juridical subject of a sodomitical act. Rather, his sexual preference for youths is a settled feature of his character and a significant fact about his social identity as a moral and sexual agent.

To sum up, I have tried to suggest that the current doctrine that holds that sexual acts were unconnected to sexual identities in European discourses before the nineteenth century is mistaken in at least two different respects. First, sexual acts could be interpreted as representative components of an individual's sexual morphology. Second, sexual acts could be interpreted as representative expressions of an individual's sexual subjectivity. A sexual morphology is not the same thing as a sexual subjectivity: the figure of the *kinaidos*, for example, represents an instance of deviant morphology without subjectivity, whereas Boccaccio's Pietro represents an instance of deviant subjectivity without morphology. Thus, morphology and subjectivity, as I have been using those terms, describe two *different* logics according to which sexual acts can be connected to some more generalized feature of an individual's identity. In particular, I've argued that the ancient figure of the *kinaidos* qualifies as an instance of a sexual life-form or morphology and, therefore, that the property of *kinaidia* (or being a *kinaidos*) is a property of social beings, not merely of sexual acts. Nonetheless, what defines the *kinaidos* is not a unique or peculiar subjectivity but a shameless appetite for pleasure, which is common to all human beings, along with a deviant gender-style, which assimilates him to the cultural definition of woman. By contrast, the sodomitical character of Boccaccio's Pietro di Vinciolo does not express itself through a deviant morphology but through his sexual tastes, preferences, inclinations, or desires—that is, through a deviant subjectivity. Sodomy, in Boccaccio's world, like *kinaidia* in classical antiquity, is a property of social beings, not merely of sexual acts. The relation between the sodomitical act and the subject who performs it is constructed differently in the case of the sodomite from the way that acts and social identities are connected in the case of the *kinaidos*.

Neither the sexual morphology of the *kinaidos* nor the sexual subjectivity of the fourteenth-century Italian sodomite should be understood as a sexual identity, or a sexual orientation in the modern sense—much less as equivalent to the modern formation known as homosexuality. At the very least, popular notions of homosexual identity and homosexual orientation today tend to insist on the *conjunction* of sexual morphology and sexual subjectivity: they presume a convergence in the sexual actor of a deviant personal style with a deviant erotic desire. In addition, what historically distinguishes "homosexuality" as a sexual classification is its unprecedented combination of at least three distinct and previously uncorrelated conceptual entities: (1) a psychiatric notion of a perverted or pathological *orientation*, derived from nineteenth-century medicine, which is an essentially psychological concept that applies to the inner life of the individual and does not necessarily entail same-sex sexual behavior or desire; (2) a psychoanalytic notion of same-sex *sexual object-choice* or desire, derived from Sigmund Freud and his coworkers, which is a category of erotic intentionality and does not necessarily imply a permanent psychosexual orientation, let alone a patho- logical or deviant one (since, according to Freud, most normal individuals make an unconscious homosexual object-choice at least at some point in their fantasy lives); and (3) a sociological notion of *sexually deviant behavior*, derived from nineteenth- and twentieth- century forensic inquiries into "social problems," which focuses on non-standard sexual practice and does not necessarily refer to erotic psychology or psychosexual orientation (since same-sex sexual behavior is widely distributed in the population, as Kinsey showed, and is not the exclusive property of those with a unique psychology or a homosexual sexual orientation). Despite their several failures to meet the requirements of the modern defin- ition of the homosexual, however, both the *kinaidos* and Boccaccio's Pietro, in their quite different and distinctive ways, challenge the orthodox pseudo-Foucauldian doctrine about the supposedly strict separation between sexual acts and sexual identities in European culture before the nineteenth century.

My argument, then, does not refute Foucault's claim about the different ways male same-sex eroticism was constructed by the discourse of "the ancient civil or canonical codes" and by the discourse of nineteenth-century sexology. Nor does it demolish the absolutely indispensable distinction between sexual acts and sexual identities that historians of homo- sexuality have extracted from Foucault's text (where the term "identity" nowhere occurs) and that, in any case, antedated it by many years. Least of all does my argument undermine a rigorously historicizing approach to the study of the social and cultural constitution of sexual subjectivity and sexual identity. (Whatever I may be up to in this essay, a posthumous rapprochement with John Boswell is not it.) What my argument does do, I hope, is to encourage us to inquire into the construction of sexual identities before the emergence of sexual orientations and to do this *without* recurring necessarily to modern notions of "sexual- ity" or sexual orientation. To temper the overly schematic fashion whereby historicist histories of homosexuality have distinguished and sealed off from each other sexual acts and sexual identities is not, I hope, to contribute to an anti-historicist backlash or to imply some permanent, historically invariable relation between particular sexual acts and individual sexual identities. Perhaps we need to supplement our notion of sexual identity with a more refined concept of, say, partial identity, emergent identity, transient identity, semi-identity, incomplete identity, proto-identity, or sub-identity. In any case, my intent is not to reinstall a notion of sexual identity as a historical category so much as to indicate *the multiplicity of possible historical connections between sex and identity*, a multiplicity whose existence has been obscured by the necessary but narrowly focused, totalizing critique of sexual identity as a unitary concept. We need to find ways of asking how different historical cultures fashioned different sorts of links between sexual acts, on the one hand, and sexual tastes, styles, dispositions, characters, gender presentations, and forms of subjectivity, on the other.

It is a matter of considerable irony that Foucault's influential distinction between the discursive construction of the sodomite and the discursive construction of the homosexual, which had originally been intended to open up a domain of historical inquiry, has now become a major obstacle blocking further research into the rudiments of sexual identity- formation in pre-modern and early modern European societies. Foucault himself would surely have been astonished. Not only was he much too good a historian ever to have authorized the incautious and implausible claim that no one had ever had a sexual subjectiv- ity, a sexual morphology, or a sexual identity of any kind before the nineteenth century (even if he painstakingly demonstrated that the conditions necessary for having a *sexuality*, a psychosexual orientation in the modern sense, did not in fact obtain until then). His approach to what he called "the history of the present" was also too searching, too experimental, and too open-ended to tolerate converting a heuristic analytic distinction into an ill-founded historical dogma, as his more forgetful epigones have not hesitated to do.

Notes

1   Foucault, *The History of Sexuality*, 1:43 (translation considerably modified); *La volonté de savoir*, 59.
2   See the very careful demonstration of this point by Arnold I. Davidson, "Closing up the Corpses: Diseases of Sexuality and the Emergence of the Psychiatric Style of Reasoning," in *Meaning and Method: Essays in Honor of Hilary Putnam*, ed. George Boolos (Cambridge: Cambridge University Press, 1990), 295–325.
3   Foucault, *The History of Sexuality*, 1:42–43; *La volonté de savoir*, 58–59. Emphasis in original.
4   Foucault, *The History of Sexuality*, 1:37 (translation modified); *La volonté de savoir*, 51. Emphasis added.
5   Foucault, *The History of Sexuality*, 1:38 (translation modified); *La volonté de savoir*, 52–53. Foucault explains, in a sentence that follows the conclusion of the passage quoted here, that "the 'nature' on which [sexual prohibitions] were based was still a kind of law."
6   Foucault, *The History of Sexuality*, 1:48; *La volonté de savoir*, 66.
7   A complete and systematic definition of the Latin form of this ancient term has now been provided by Craig. A. Williams, *Roman Homosexuality: Ideologies of Masculinity in Classical Antiquity* (New York: Oxford University Press, 1999), 175–78, esp. 175–76.
8   John J. Winkler, *The Constraints of Desire: The Anthropology of Sex and Gender in Ancient Greece* (New York: Routledge, 1990). 45–46. The formulation is repeated, somewhat less emphatically, by Winkler in "Laying Down the Law: The Oversight of Men's Sexual Behavior in Classical Athens," in *Before Sexuality: The Construction of Erotic Experience in the Ancient Greek World*, ed. David M. Halperin, John J. Winkler, and Froma I. Zeitlin (Princeton, N.J.: Princeton University Press, 1990), 171–209, esp. 176–77.
9   I borrow the distinction between universalizing and minoritizing concepts of (homo)sexual identity from Eve Kosofsky Sedgwick, *Epistemology of the Closet* (Berkeley: University of California Press, 1990), 1, 9, 85–86.
10 Winkler, *The Constraints of Desire*, 50, and "Laying Down the Law," 182.
11 Maud W. Gleason, "The Semiotics of Gender: Physiognomy and Self-Fashioning in the Second Century C.E.," in *Before Sexuality*, ed. Halperin, Winkler, and Zeitlin, 389–415 (quotation on 390), *Making Men: Sophists and Self-Presentation in Ancient Rome* (Princeton, N.J.: Princeton University Press, 1995), 58.
12 Gleason, *Making Men*, 64; Gleason, "The Semiotics of Gender," 396.
13 Gleason, "The Semiotics of Gender," 411–12. Cf. Halperin, *One Hundred Years of Homosexuality* (New York: Routledge, 1990), 22–24.
14 Williams, *Roman Homosexuality*, 178.
15 Ibid., 210–11.
16 Jonathan Walters, " 'No More Than a Boy': The Shifting Construction of Masculinity from Ancient Greece to the Middle Ages," *Gender and History* 5, no. 1 (spring 1993): 20–33.
17 Ibid., 22–23, quoting Apullius, *The Golden Ass* 9.14.
18 See Walters, " 'No More Than a Boy,' " 22. On April 13, 2001, Professor Carla Freccero of the University of California, Santa Cruz, presented a critique of my argument in a paper delivered at the University of Michigan, entitled "Were Fourteenth Century Perugini Homophobic? Foucault, Halperin, and Early Modern Sexual Subjectivities." I did not hear the paper myself, and Freccero has not shared it with me, so I have been unable to take advantage of her remarks in reformulating my argument here.
19 Walters, " 'No More Than a Boy,' " 24.
20 Ibid., 26: "In Boccaccio's version . . . we find the husband defined wholly in terms of his sexual desire, which marks him as abnormal from the start and indeed sets the plot in motion."
21 Walters, " 'No More Than a Boy,' " 27, also emphasizes this point.
22 See, further, ibid., 27–28. Whereas the ancient conception of the *kinaidos* foregrounded his effeminacy and passivity, the fourteenth- and fifteenth-century Florentine definitions of "sodomy" and "sodomite" referred only to the "active" or insertive partner in anal intercourse: see Rocke, *Forbidden Friendships and Male Culture in Renaissance Florence* (Oxford: Oxford University Press, 1998), 14, 110.

Further Reading: Chapters 44 to 46

Anderson, Bonnie S. and Judith P Zinsser. *A History of Their Own: Women in Europe from Prehistory to the Present* (New York: Harper and Row, 1988).

Badran, Margot and Miriam Cooke (eds). *Opening the Gates: A Century of Arab Feminist Writing* (Bloomington: Indiana University Press, 1990).

Bailey, Joanne and Arnold, John. "Is the Rise of Gender History 'Hiding' Women from History Once Again?". *History in Focus: Gender History*. London: Institute of Historical Research 8 (2005).

Basu, Aparna. "Women's History in India", *Writing Women's History: International Perspectives*, Karen Offen, Ruth Roach Pierson and Jane Rendall (eds) (London: Macmillan, 1991), 181–209.

"Bibliography". *History in Focus: Gender History*. London: Institute of Historical Research 8 (2005).

Bock, Gisela. "Women's History and Gender History: Aspects of an International Debate", *Gender and History* 1(1) (1989), 7–30.

Bridenthal, Renate, Claudia Koonz and Susan Stuard (eds). *Becoming Visible: Women in European History*. 1977 (3rd edn) (Boston: Houghton Mifflin, 1998).

Bullough, Vern L. *Science in the Bedroom: A History of Sex Research* (New York: Basic Books, 1994).

Burret, Jean (ed.). *Looking into My Sister's Eyes: An Exploration in Women's History* (Toronto: Multicultural History Society of Ontario, 1986).

Butler, Judith. *Gender Trouble: Feminism and the Subversion of Identity*. 1990. (London: Routledge, 2006).

Connell, R. W. *Masculinities* (London: Polity Press, 1995).

D'Emilio, John and Estelle B. Freedman. *Intimate Matters: A History of Sexuality in America* (New York: Harper and Row, 1988).

Davis, Natalie Zemon. " 'Women's History' in Transition: The European Case", *Feminist Studies* 3 (1976), 83–103.

Downs, Laura Lee. *Writing Gender History* (London: Hodder Arnold, 2004).

Duberman, Martin et al. *Hidden from History: Reclaiming the Gay and Lesbian Past* (New York: New American Library, 1989).

DuBois, Ellen, et al. "Politics and Culture in Women's History: A Symposium", *Feminist Studies* 6(1) (1980), 26–64.

Editorial Collective, (The). "Why Gender and History?" *Gender and History* 1(1) (1989), 1–6.

Greenberg, David F. *The Construction of Homosexuality* (Chicago: University of Chicago Press, 1988).

Hall, Catherine. *White, Male and Middle-Class: Explorations in Feminism and History* (New York: Routledge, 1992).

Halperin, David M. (ed.). *Before Sexuality: The Construction of Erotic Experience in the Ancient Greek World* (Princeton, NJ: Princeton University Press, 2001).

——. "Is There a History of Sexuality?" *History and Theory* 28 (1989), 257–74.

——. *One Hundred Years of Homosexuality and other essays on Greek Love* (New York: Routledge, 1990).

——. *Saint Foucault: Towards A Gay Hagiography* (Oxford: Oxford University Press, 1997).

Harvey, Karen. "The History of Masculinity, circa 1650–1800", *Journal of British Studies* 44(2) (2005), 296–312.

Herdt, G. (ed.). *Third Sex, Third Gender: Beyond Sexual Dimorphism in Culture and History* (Zone Books, 1994).

Hoff, Joan. "Gender as a Postmodern Category of Paralysis", *Women's History Review* 3 (1994), 149–68.

Hunt, Nancy Rose. "Placing African Women's History and Locating Gender", *Social History* 14 (1989), 359–79.

Johnson-Odim, Cheryl and Margaret Strobel (eds). *Expanding the Boundaries of Women's History: Essays on Women in the Third World* (Bloomington: Indiana University Press, 1992).

Karttunen, Frances. *Between Worlds: Interpreters, Guides and Survivors* (New Brunswick, NJ: Rutgers University Press, 1994).

Keddie, Nikki R. and Beth Baron (eds). *Women in Middle Eastern History* (New Haven, CT: Yale University Press, 1991).

Kerber, Linda K. "Separate Spheres, Female Worlds, Woman's Place: The Rhetoric of Women's History", *Journal of American History* 75(1) (1988), 9–39.

Kumar, Nita (ed.). *Women as Subjects: South Asian Histories* (Charlottesville, VA: University of Virginia Press, 1994).

Lerner, Gerda. *The Majority Finds its Past: Placing Women in History* (Oxford: Oxford University Press, 1979).

Manicom, Linzi. "Ruling Relations: Rethinking State and Gender in South African History", *Journal of African History* 33(3) (1992), 441–65.

Morgan, David H. J. "Man Made Manifest: Histories and Masculinities", *Gender and History* 1(1) (1989), 87–89.

Nicholson, Linda. "Interpreting Gender", *SIGNS* 20(1) (1994), 79–105.

Offen, Karen, Ruth Roach Pierson and Jane Rendall (eds). *Writing Women's History: International Perspectives* (London: Macmillan, 1991).

Oram, Alison and Annmarie Turnbull (eds). *The Lesbian History Sourcebook: Love and Sex Between Women in Britain from 1780 to 1970* (London: Routledge, 2001).

Partner, Nancy, "No Sex, No Gender", *Speculum* 68 (1993), 419–43.

Rajan, Rajeswari Sunder. *Real and Imagined Women, Gender, Culture, Postcolonialism* (London: Routledge, 1993).

Rose, Sonya O. "Gender History/Women's History: Is Feminist Scholarship Losing its Critical Edge?", *Journal of Women's History* 5(1) (1993), 89–101.

Rowbotham, Sheila. *Hidden From History* (London: Pluto Press, 1973).

Sanday, Peggy and Ruth Goodenough. *Beyond the Second Sex: New Directions in the Anthropology of Gender* (Philadelphia: University of Pennsylvania Press, 1990).

Sangari, Kumkum and Sudesh Vaid (eds). *Recasting Women: Essays in Indian Colonial History* (New Brunswick, NJ: Rutgers University Press, 1990).

Schmidt, Elizabeth. *Peasants, Traders and Wives. Shona Women in the History of Zimbabwe, 1870–1939* (Portsmouth, NH: Heinemann, 1992).

Scott, Joan Wallach. "The Evidence of Experience", *Critical Enquiry* 17 (1991), 773–97.

——. "Women's History", *New Perspectives on Historical Writing*. Peter Burke (ed.) (Cambridge: Polity Press, 2001).

Sedgwick, Eve Kosofsky. *Epistemology of the Closet* (Berkeley: University of California Press, 1990).

Shapiro, Anne-Louise (ed.). *Feminists Revision History* (New Brunswick, NJ: Rutgers University Press, 1994).

Smith, Bonnie G. "Women's Contribution to Modern Historiography in Great Britain, France, and the United States, 1750–1940", *The American Historical Review* 89(3) (1984): 709–32.

Spivak, Gayatri Chakravorty. *A Critique of Postcolonial Reason: Toward a History of the Vanishing Present* (London: Harvard University Press, 1999).

—— . *In Other Worlds.* 1987. (London: Routledge, 2006).

Vogel, Lise. "Telling Tales: Historians of Our Own Lives", *Journal of Women's History* 2(3) (1991), 89–102.

Whittig, Monique. "The Straight Mind", *Modern Language Association Conference* (New York, 1978).

SCOTT, JOAN WALLACH

Anderson, Margo. "Review: Gender and the Politics of History", *Gender and Society* 5(3) (1991), 408–9.

Gordon, Linda. "Review: Gender and the Politics of History", *The American Historical Review* 95(4) (1990), 1156–7.

Scott, Joan Wallach. "History in Crisis: The Others' Side of the Story", AHR Forum: The Old History and the New, *The American Historical Review* 94(3) (1989), 680–92.

Whitney, Susan B. "History through the Lens of Gender", *Journal of Women's History* 11(1) (1999), 193–202.

FOUCAULT, MICHEL (1926–1984)

Bernauer, James and David Rasmussen (eds). *The Final Foucault* (Cambridge, MA: MIT Press, 1988).

Best, Steven. *The Politics of Historical Vision: Marx, Foucault, Habermas* (New York: Guileford, 1995).

Burke, Peter (ed.). *Critical Essays on Michel Foucault* (Cambridge: Scholar Press, 1992).

—— . *History and Social Theory* (Cambridge: Polity Press, 1992).

Clark, Michael. *Michel Foucualt, An Annotated Bibliography Toolkit for a New Age* (New York: Garland, 1983).

Dean, Mitchell. *Critical and Effective Histories: Foucault's Methods and Historical Sociology* (Oxford: Blackwell, 1994).

Derrida, Jacques. "Cogito and the History of Madness", *Writing and Difference* (London: Routledge & Kegan Paul, 1978), 31–63.

Diamond, Irene and Lee Quinby (ed). *Feminism and Foucault: Reflections on Resistance* (Boston, MA: Northwestern University Press, 1988).

Dreyfus, Hubert L. and Paul Rabinow. *Michel Foucault: Beyond Structuralism and Hermeneutics* (Chicago, IL: University of Chicago Press, 1982).

Goldstein, Jan (ed.). *Foucault and the Writing of History* (Oxford: Basil Blackwell, 1994).

Gutting, Gary. *The Cambridge Companion to Foucault* (2nd edn) (Cambridge: Cambridge University Press, 2005).

—— . *Michel Foucault's Archaeology of Scientific Reason* (Cambridge: Cambridge University Press, 1989).

Hoy, David C. (ed.). *Foucault: A Critical Reader* (Oxford: Blackwell, 1986).

Huppert, G. "Divinatio et Eruditio: Thoughts on Foucault", *History and Theory* 13(3) (1974), 191–207.

Kelly, Michael (ed.). *Critique and Power: Recasting the Foucault/Habermas Debate* (Cambridge, MA: MIT Press, 1994).

Leland, D. "On Reading and Writing the World: Foucault's History of Thought", *Clio* 4(2) (1975), 225–43.

Macey, David. *The Lives of Michel Foucault* (London: Hutchinson, 1993).

McNay, Lois. *Foucault: A Critical Introduction* (Cambridge: Polity Press, 1994).

Midelfort, H. C. E. "Madness and Civilization in Early Modern Europe: A Reappraisal of Michel Foucault", *After the Reformation: Essays in Honor of J. H. Hexter*, Barbara C. Malament (ed.) (Philadelphia, PA: University of Philadelphia Press, 1980), 247–65.

O'Brien, Patricia. "Crime and Punishment as Historical Problem", *Journal of Social History* 11(4) (1978), 508–20.

O'Farrell, Clare. *Foucault: Historian or Philosopher?* (London: Macmillan, 1989).

Poster, Mark. *Foucault, Marxism and History: Mode of Production versus Mode of Information* (Cambridge: Polity Press, 1994).

Roth, Michael S. "Foucault's 'History of the Present' ", *History and Theory* 20(1) (1981), 32–46.

Rousseau, G. S. "Whose Enlightenment? Not Man's: The Case of Michel Foucault", *Eighteenth Century Studies* 6(2) (1972), 238–56.

Sheridan, Alan. *Michel Foucault: The Will to Truth* (London: Tavistock, 1980).

Still, Arthur and Velody, Irving. *Rewriting the History of Madness: Studies in Foucault's 'Histoire de la folie' "* (London: Routledge, 1992).

White, Hayden. *The Tropics of Discourse: Essays in Cultural Criticism* (Baltimore, MD: Johns Hopkins University Press, 1973).

Wilson, Timothy H. "Foucault, Genealogy, History", *Philosophy Today* 39(2) (1995), 157–70.

HALPERIN, DAVID M.

Haggerty, George E. "The Gay Canon", *American Literary History* 12(1) (2000), 284–97.

Halperin, David. "How to do the History of Male Homosexuality", *GLQ: A Journal of Lesbian and Gay Studies* 6(1) (2000), 87–124.

—— . *One Hundred Years of Homosexuality* (New York: Routledge, 1990).

—— . *Saint Foucault: Towards a Gay Hagiography* (Oxford: Oxford University Press, 1995).

Howard, John. "Review: How to do the History of Homosexuality", *The American Historical Review* 109(2) (2004): <http://www.historycooperative.org>

Thorp, John. "The Social Construction of Homosexuality", *Phoenix* 46(1) (1992), 54–65

PART 12

Anthropological description and objects of history

INTRODUCTION

THE AMERICAN ANTHROPOLOGIST Clifford Geertz published this essay in 1973 to clarify his innovative approach to "culture". Despite his relaxed and at times conversational tone, Geertz made the provocative point that "anthropological writings are themselves interpretations ... they are, thus, fictions in the sense that they are 'something made' ". This was a powerful remark by an eminent member of a profession that considered itself at the vanguard of social science, and which had maintained that view of itself since emerging "out of the intersection of European discovery, colonialism, and natural science" a century earlier.[i] Geertz's emphasis on the interpretive and imaginative elements of anthropology's analysis of foreign cultures did not call for an overhaul of its fieldwork. But it did clarify the kinds of analytic work that cultural anthropologists had been doing. Geertz's emphasis on the interpretive nature of cultural analysis—indeed, he "read" cultures as "texts"—brought anthropology closer to the concerns of historians writing at the same time. Yet Geertz's approach invited criticism that questioned whether anthropology really could "converse" on an equal footing and in a truly mutual way with the "other" cultures that constituted its objects of study. Anthropologists like Geertz have tended to be very much at home with historical approaches to research since, unlike the influential sociologists discussed earlier in this book (see Part 6), anthropologists are empiricists who tend not to conduct their work with a hypothesis that they seek to prove. Like historians, anthropologists try to use the materials available to them to shape their knowledge as well as their questions. At the same time, like anthropologists, historians retain their own history of using cultural, geographical, and racial categories in their research and in their writing. To what extent have these terms described, or

i   See J. Morgan and P. Just, *Social and Cultural Anthropology: A Very Short Introduction* (Oxford: Oxford University Press, 2000), 1. It is useful to keep in mind that "Thick Description: Toward an Interpretive Theory of Culture" introduces a series of essays by Geertz that elaborate these concepts and which were originally published between 1957 and the mid-1960s.

in fact fictionalized (that is, created) human objects of historical study? And how does our thinking about the "fictionalization" of the human past make such studies more or less meaningful to a study of historiography?

The classic anthropological definition of culture has been taught and quoted often since Edward B. Tylor articulated it in 1871:

> Culture, or civilization . . . is that complex whole which includes knowledge, belief, art, morals, law, custom, and any other capabilities and habits acquired by man as a member of society.[ii]

Culture, according to Tylor, is a set of things whose meaning can be determined through fact-gathering and classification. To offer insight into a foreign culture, then, anthropological research requires a collection of data that represents a set of learned behaviours and ideas; these will be internally consistent and shared by all members of a given group, and are accessible to outsiders. But Geertz argued that in order to identify, describe, and make sense of culture, we must engage in an interpretive process that involves meaningful *interaction* with that culture. This is because the subjects within that culture communicate meaning—meaning that goes beyond their "capabilities and beliefs"—in a way that needs to be listened to (actively) and not merely heard (passively). Now even for the most orthodox historicist, whose scientific methods of textual research recognize the crucial relationship between intuitive imagination and scholarly insight, Geertz's definition of culture will sound familiar:

> Believing, with Max Weber, that man is an animal suspended in webs of significance he himself has spun, I take culture to be those webs, and the analysis of it to be therefore not an experimental science in search of law, but an interpretive one in search of meaning.

In the mid-1970s, it appeared that Geertz was unmasking his scientific field as a truly humanistic one, locating it closer to textual than statistical studies.[iii] Geertz believed that it is not possible to engage meaningfully with the *individuals* we encounter while doing fieldwork, so we need to understand his or her *culture*—or at the very least, culture needs to be interpreted before individuals can be studied. As we will see, Geertz assumes that the relationship between the researcher and his or her human objects of study is egalitarian, mutual, and therefore free of political or ideological interference. It was this unquestioned aspect of the anthropologist's relationship with his objects of study that invited responses from commentators such as Edward Said, responses that themselves referred directly to urgent social concerns.

ii   E. B. Tylor, *Primitive Culture* (London: John Murray, 1871), vol. 1, 1.
iii   The essays that "Thick Description" introduces "stand as a permanent record, not only of Geertz's thinking but of an important trend in social science. They reflect the optimism of the 1950s, when social scientists sought to chart and abet the great leap forward of the Third World, the disillusionment of the 1960s when the prophesies failed, and the current redirection of so many of that generation into stylistic and symbolic studies, which associates them with literary critics and theologians rather than with administrators, politicians, and economists". See E. Colson, Review of *The Interpretation of Cultures* by C. Geertz, *Contemporary Sociology* 4 (1975), 638.

Geertz's interpretive theory of culture considers its subject **semiotically**, which means that the anthropologist's task is "to sort out the structures of signification" to "determine their social ground and import". For Geertz, culture is an "acted document" whose meaning must be understood in the social context of its action and not through the anthropologist's own preconceptions. Since culture must be read as a documentary text (it requires reflection and interpretation), its analysis requires a form of deliberately detailed "reading" whose expression calls for a unique narrative style.[iv] As a method of analysis, Geertz distinguished this from the means by which anthropologists have distorted their understanding and description of foreign cultures—they have adopted an analytic method that he calls "thin description". For Geertz, culture is a thick lens or heavy web through which we view the world as well as ourselves, but thin description treats culture as a series of transparent, objectively-quantifiable, and socially-functional beliefs—"whatever it is one has to know or believe in order to operate in a manner acceptable to its members". Once those beliefs have been identified thinly, the anthropologist (or "ethnoscientist") analyzes them by formulating those beliefs in the form of systematic rules, "an ethnographic algorithm which, if followed, would make it possible to operate, to pass . . . for a native". If the real aim of anthropology is to understand what culture means for the individuals within it, then this approach fails because it includes only those "mental phenomena which can be analyzed by formal methods similar to those of mathematics and logic". So, like the Whig interpretation of history (see Part 5) that adopts a circular approach to its sources, the anthropologist's thin description defines and defends its conclusions even before the analysis—or, indeed, the data collection—has commenced. In other words, for Geertz conventional anthropology has cut cultures down to their cognitive parts, because it is those parts that have suited the anthropologist's analytic and descriptive methods—to which they have a prior professional commitment. Meaning, from the cultural subject's point of view, therefore has been lost or distorted both by the researcher's scientific method and by his or her formal means of analysis.

Rather than provide information that would allow one to pass as someone else—or to believe that anthropology holds the key to knowing the other as well as one knows oneself—Geertz wanted "to converse" with that other culture through an interpretive process that was mutually meaningful. For Geertz, cultural symbols require interpretation, and this realizes the morally-desirable vision of two subjects in open and fruitful dialogue with each other: "the aim of anthropology is the enlargement of human discourse". This means that "culture is not a power to which social events, behaviours, institutions, or processes can be causally attributed; it is a context, something within which they can be intelligibly—that is, thickly—described". Through the process of detailed and reflective description, an interpretive approach to the symbolic structure of culture would "aid us in gaining access to the conceptual world in which our subjects live". Thick description "renders [other cultures] accessible: setting them in the frame of their own banalities, it dissolves their opacity". Geertz was clear about this: "our formulations of other peoples' symbol systems must be actor-oriented"—the object of study must be interpreted by focusing on its own viewpoint, its **subjective** rather than **objective** meaning.

iv Hayden White's essay (in Part 10), on the "poetic fallacy" committed by historians who mistakenly believe that the past is structured like "classic" texts, shares some critical vocabulary with Geertz's essay—for he is inviting anthropologists to read human cultures as texts. Although Geertz's essay was published when White was circulating early versions of "The Literary Text as Historical Artifact", the two authors were not aware of each other's work. I am grateful to Hayden White for this information.

Particularly since the publication of Geertz's essay, historians have been eager to engage with these methods and insights.[v] Some have remarked that, although as formal academic fields history and anthropology "may appear bounded and mutually exclusive . . . that is an image of disciplinarity, no more".[vi] We have already noted fundamental concepts that are shared by Geertz's semiotic approach to culture and the historicist's valuation of interpretation and careful scrutiny of archival texts. Read in a context that values the analytic strengths and insights of both fields, surely this call for cross-disciplinary discussion can lead to new understandings of the ways through which anthropology can inform historical studies—and vice versa. For many years, the distinguished historian Robert Darnton taught an undergraduate course at Princeton with Geertz, and he formulated a variation on the following for their students:

> Where the historian of ideas traces the filtration of formal thought from philosopher to philosopher, the ethnographic historian studies the way ordinary people made sense of the world. He attempts to uncover their cosmology, to show how they organized reality in their minds and expressed it in their behaviour. He does not try to make a philosopher out of the man in the street but to see how street life called for a strategy.[vii]

Darnton and others have described this as "cultural history", and quickly addressed the problem inherent in studying the "native" thoughts and habits of the past, realizing that "other people are other. They do not think the way we do".[viii] Darnton proceeded by trying "to set out with the idea of capturing otherness" by "wandering through the archives" and "picking at the document where it is most opaque".[ix] Surely this historical adoption of Geertz's approach to French popular culture during the eighteenth century produces few moral or ideological concerns. But when we turn to the living communities in which Geertz practised and formulated his ideas, crucial ethical problems might arise—problems that have since been highlighted by studies in the history of cultural anthropology.

This excerpt from Said's famous and influential study of "Western" fascination with the "East", *Orientalism,* does not address the field of anthropology explicitly. But Said's argument opens up "thick description" to scrutiny by scrutinizing the "configurations of power" that exist between the fascinated Western researcher and his or her Oriental object—when that

v   Probably the most influential example of "thick description" for historians is C. Geertz, "Deep Play: Notes on the Balinese Cockfight". *Daedalus* 101 (1972), 1–37. It has been reprinted in *The Interpretation of Cultures,* 412–53.

vi   J. Goodman, "History and Anthropology", *Companion to Historiography,* M. Bentley (ed.) (London: Routledge, 1997), 784. Historical studies that feature Geertz are included in P. Burke (ed.) *New Perspectives on Historical Writing* (Cambridge: Polity Press, 1991). Ann Swindler lists Geertz's direct influence on historians such as Robert Darnton, Natalie Zemon Davis, and Lynn Hunt in "Geertz's Ambiguous Legacy", *Contemporary Sociology* 25 (May 1996), 299–302. See also L. Jordanova's critical discussion of Geertz's prominence among historians in "Resisting Reflexivity", *History of the Social Sciences* 5 (1992), 59–67. For a useful survey of his legacy among historians, see *Special Issue: The Fate of "Culture": Geertz and Beyond, Representations* 59 (Summer 1997).

vii R. Darnton, *The Great Cat Massacre and Other Episodes in French Cultural History* (New York: Basic Books, 1984), 3–4.

viii For a fine introduction to the problems, methods, and concerns of cultural history in the West, see P. Burke, *What is Cultural History?* (Cambridge: Polity, 2004).

ix   R. Darnton, 5.

object is a human "text" and not an archival one.[x] Said's view was that the West's colonial domination in Asia and Africa did not only entail subjugation of its indigenous peoples and plunder of its resources. Western rule also created powerful and yet subtle ideas about the concept of culture, by which "the East" or "the Orient" continues to exist as an enchanting but also demeaning reflection of the West's desire to define itself as inherently powerful, superior, and sophisticated—in the unquestionable position of "cultural leadership". For Said, this view of the Orient operates on the basis of

> the collective notion identifying "us" Europeans as against all "those" non-Europeans, and indeed it can be argued that the major component in European culture is . . . the idea of European identity as a superior one in comparison with all the non-European peoples and cultures.

This widespread belief, which Said described as "a cultural and political fact", does not express itself solely through explicit legal or institutional policies—for example as racist or segregationalist policies in America, the apartheid system in South Africa, or in European colonial policies in the Middle East that have favoured the rights of certain people over others. In ways that are subtle, coded, and therefore in some respects more powerful, Orientalism is

> A *distribution* of geopolitical awareness into aesthetic, scholarly, economic, socio-logical, historical, and philological [literary] texts; it is an *elaboration* not only of a basic geographical distinction (the world is made up of two unequal halves, Orient and Occident) but also . . . it *is*, rather than expresses, a certain *will* or *intention* to understand, in some cases to control, manipulate, even to incorporate, what is a manifestly different (or alternative and novel) world.

As historians sympathetic to Said's argument, we may wonder whether Geertz's enthusiasm for cross-cultural "conversation" with a desirable moral purpose, "the enlargement of the universe of human discourse", suggests the inescapable legacy of less desirable episodes in the history of his own profession. Could Geertz have been motivated by remorse for the kinds of knowledge about "ethnicity" that his predecessor anthropologists generated and promoted? To what extent does the prestige of his profession rest on a history of cultural misunderstanding, and to what extent has that history challenged his ability to promote more ethically desirable goals?

It is ironic that Geertz embraced the same view of scholarly interpretation—that it creates ("fictionalizes") its objects of study—on which Said's entire argument depends. Indeed Geertz's open admission to fictionalization as a primary element of thick description also invites criticism

---

x   Although Said does not mention anthropology specifically in *Orientalism*, Said has addressed Geertz directly to the book's central thesis, remarking that, "as a discipline, anthropology has not yet dealt with this inherently political limitation upon its supposedly disinterested universality"; on the history of anthropology and anthropological concepts of culture, Said directs readers to T. Asad, *Anthropology and the Colonial Encounter* (New York: Humanities Press, 1973). See "*Orientalism* Reconsidered", *Cultural Critique* 1 (1985), 94. See also L. Baker, *From Savage to Negro: Anthropology and the Construction of Race, 1896–1954* (Berkeley: University of California Press, 1998); and the essays collected in P. Pels and O. Salemink (eds), *Colonial Subjects: Essays on the Practical History of Anthropology* (Ann Arbor: University of Michigan Press, 2000). On the imperialist legacy of anthropological ethnology, and its symbolic means of interpretation, see J. Fabian, *Time and the Other: How Anthropology Makes Its Object* (New York: Columbia University Press, 1983).

that has been directed, more recently, at historians who use cultural symbols to define collect-ive memory: "we end up constructing [a meaningful] history ... from visible signs whose significance is taken for granted".[xi] Could Geertz's eagerness to appreciate the differences between his and his cultural subjects' view of the world still be bound by the imperial project that created anthropology in the first place? What are the kinds of empirical evidence that would ground Geertz's fictionalization in the actual experience of his subjects? Said suggested that no cultural analysis, even at its most self-critical, can shake off its imperialist past:

> Orientalism brings one up directly against [the] question—that is to realizing that political imperialism governs an entire field of study, imagination, and schol-arly institutions—in such a way as to make its avoidance an intellectual and historical impossibility.

Said is quick to point out that the Orientalist roots of these scholarly endeavours did not simply limit the work that anthropologists could do. On the contrary, and with an important reference to Foucault (see Part 11), Said asserted that "internal constraints upon writers and thinkers [are] *productive*, not unilaterally inhibiting"—in other words, Orientalism uses its ideological power to create certain kinds of knowledge. This means that, for Said, Geertz's assumption of, rather than concern for, his own position as an interpreter of other cultures provided rich terrain for a study of imperialist and colonialist concepts.[xii] The question we might consider is: is there any element of thick description that retains anthropology's traditional refusal to examine its relational nature (or "*positional* authority") to its objects of study? Is Geertz's anthropological paradigm inherently colonialist?

David Cannadine offers an implicit but compelling answer, one which challenges Said's vision of a binary separation between imperial power and colonial experience—indeed it is reminiscent of recent approaches to gender that critique earlier views of sexual difference (see Part 11).[xiii] In his study of the ways imperial Britain viewed its colonies between 1850 and 1950, Cannadine challenged the basic notions that underwrite Orientalism as an approach to history. First, he doubted that an imperial project, on the Foucauldian or hegemonic terms used by Said, ever existed.[xiv] Second, Cannadine showed that Britain's relationship to its

---

xi   Alon Confino, "Collective Memory and Cultural History: Problems of Method", *American His-torical Review* 102 (Dec. 1997), 1397.

xii See Said's recommendation of Asad in note x.

xiii Numerous scholars have explored the notion that colonial encounters entail a "hybridization" of imperial and colonial identities: no one is the same (psychologically, culturally, ideologically) once contact has been made—this provides a productive challenge to implications of a binary character distinguishing imperialists and colonials. For concrete examples and discussion of hybridity in colonial and postcolonial contexts, see R. Young, *Colonial Desire: Hybridity in Theory, Race, and Culture* (London: Routledge, 1995).

xiv "I am not sure that there ever was such a thing as 'the imperial project': even at its apogee, the British Empire was too ramshackle a thing ever to display such unanimity of action and consist-ency of purpose": see D. Cannadine, *Ornamentalism: How the British Saw their Empire* (Harmondsworth: Penguin, 2001), 197–8. Said provided a brief definition of hegemony in the excerpt: "certain cultural forms predominate over others, just as certain ideas are more influen-tial than others; the form of this cultural leadership Gramsci has identified as *hegemony*." Therefore one could argue that Cannadine—who focused on those elements of imperial power that were "displayed" rather than felt—considered Said's position but engaged instead with different aspects of empire. Focusing only on methodology, since Said addressed French imperial-ism as well as British, Cannadine's exclusively British focus cannot refute Said's claim.

colonial empire was one that saw the colonies as social extensions of itself: they were remade in Britain's own image and not in exotic, foreign, or even different terms. Once we survey the insights and problems of these two arguments, both of which recognize that Europe's own history cannot be studied without considering its colonial past, we may wonder whether the very terms we use to describe culture fictionalizes its meaning—and in doing so, it can provide us with material through which to explore its ideological values. This will suggest that a critical approach to Geertz's relationship to culture would need to examine the degree to which he seeks his own values reflected or replicated in his objects of study.

In Cannadine's view, the imperial project was devoted to recreating a society that was familiar to what the British had at home, "a great chain of being" with a named monarch at the top and with nameless subjects below—it did not perceive the colonies as "other" to itself, and therefore did not try to create an oriental fantasy from the lands and people that it controlled. Unlike Said's interest in the meanings generated by concepts and ideology, Cannadine dwelled on concrete examples of social perception during a specific period of time. It is useful to contrast the historical method that Cannadine used to explain his argument:

> To be sure, the Enlightenment brought about a new, collective way of looking at people, races and colours, based on distance and separation and otherness. But it did not subvert the earlier, individualistic, analogical way of thinking, based on the observation of status similarities and the cultivation of affinities, that projected domestically originated perceptions of the social order overseas.

Now it is true that Said did not focus on race or ethnicity in *Orientalism*, but on more subtle and perhaps even more insidious concepts by which Western values "created" an inferior East. However, as Cannadine suggested, since Said treated Western discourse about the Orient as if its perceptions and preferences remained stable across two millennia (from the composition of Aeschylus's *The Persians* to the present), Orientalism cannot account for conceptual and social changes that took place over long periods. Also, as other critics of *Orientalism* have pointed out, the theory cannot account for the wide range of Eastern experiences of contact with the West—so, ironically, Said could be interpreted as having viewed the Orient as a simple and passive rather than as a sophisticated and responsive player in European imperial history. Similarly, although Said's historical material consists of Western literary, historical, geographical, linguistic, and political writings, his analysis may be weakened by the exclusion of imaginative writings that could reveal perspectives at odds with Orientalism.[xv]

Both Cannadine and Said argued, quite innovatively, that it is not possible to write the political history of empire apart from its social history. However, readers have pointed out that their respective studies pay little attention to colonial viewpoints—their respective discussions of social perception represent only one side (even a sophisticated one side) of what must have been a richly-layered and multivocal dialogue between imperial Europe and its colonials.[xvi] Their agreement, that social consciousness is a defining element of the historical past, led them to select and interpret sources that brought them to different definitions of empire, and to argue very different conclusions. Cannadine observed that empire must be understood "as a functioning social structure and as an imagined social entity", but this is a view of empire that

---

xv For a useful collection of the more frequently-cited responses to *Orientalism*, which both support and challenge various aspects of Said's position, see P. Williams and L. Chrisman (eds). *Colonial Discourse and Post-Colonial Theory: A Reader* (New York: Columbia University Press, 1994).

xvi See note xiii.

leaves its existence firmly in the past. Cannadine's history of social perceptions drew on the writings, speeches, and policies of British politicians and their colonial administrators, so naturally the empire belongs to the past—indeed he considered the British handover of Hong Kong to China in 1997 as the empire's final sunset. Evoking a narrative metaphor familiar to readers of Hayden White (see Part 10), he claimed this historic moment as "the *end* of that story".[xvii] Indeed, if the empire does still exist, then for Cannadine it shows its demise through the dismantling of hierarchical social institutions at home: Cannadine pointed out that most hereditary peers lost their seats in the British Parliament's House of Lords only months after Prince Charles sailed out of Hong Kong's Victoria Harbour. Perhaps Said would interpret rather than depict such events with the same critical approach that Fernand Braudel brought to *l'histoire evènementielle* (see Part 7). This is because, for Said, empire is a hegemonic force that creates certain kinds of knowledge (about race, rights, and nationality) that cannot be understood merely through reference to judicial facts and political events. Even the most triumphant declarations of political independence take place within the centripetal force of social **discourses** that sustain powerful notions of imperial privilege and status. For Said, this is precisely why the British and American empires are still with us, and why his reading of imaginative travel memoirs by European colonialists that constructed the Orient continued to provide effective sources for understanding imperial projects on their own imaginative terms. For those who have inherited what Said considers the empire's hegemonic legacy—for those who still work in its specialist professions (such as anthropology) and for those who find themselves either in its shadow on under its scrutiny—Said provided an analysis that, like Cannadine, emphasized the empire's perceptions of itself.

To what extent can any account of the historical past, and of its continuing presence, be meaningful when historians understand it as a one-way street rather than as a complicated series of exchanges? George Fredrickson's compelling survey of racism since it emerged as a concept among early twentieth-century historians suggests that, even without explicit quotation from "other" sources, the very terms we use to define social groups reveal the degree to which we envision a dynamic relationship with them. Our conceptual vocabulary itself should be examined, both by readers and by the authors who invent its terms and those who use them—and this constitutes an important step towards clarifying the degree to which historical discourse creates its human objects of study. Thus far in this section we have gestured to three means by which the past can be created or "fictionalized" by historians: these include interpretation of cultural symbols using familiar terms of reference; through a concept of cultural hegemony whereby one group defines itself against differences that it imagines to exist only in another group; and through social self-perceptions, by which one group tries to extend its own values to a subjugated group.

In his book on the history of racism, Fredrickson showed that race has been used as a powerful tool to define a group of people according to an invented notion of ethnicity:

> There are ... cases—and African American ethnicity would be a prime example—in which ethnic identity is created by the racialization of people who would not otherwise have shared an identity. [For example] Blacks did not think of themselves as black, Negroes, or even Africans when they lived in the various kingdoms and tribal communities of West Africa before the advent of the slave trade.

xvii See D. Cannadine, 181.

In this important respect, "black" is a linguistic construction through which one shared feature, found among millions of people, has been used to provide them with a common identity. Not only has that assertion of racial identity ignored and therefore implicitly denied means of self-identification that were used before the slave trade, but it also suggested that the biological notion of "race" is itself an invention—for this category would also ignore the cultural, genetic, and physiological differences to be found within these populations. As an American historian who has written six books on racial politics, Fredrickson was aware of the distortions that his descriptive vocabulary creates. As he has shown, he is only one of many historians who have tried to find new terms to describe social groups without reference to the past stigmas, misunderstandings, and dismissals that racial categories continue to evoke. Even here, by settling on a definition of racism "as the ideas, practices, and institutions associated with a rigid form of ethnic hierarchy", he has remarked that it is inadequate because it excludes anti-Semitic racism—which is not based strictly on a notion of national or linguistic origins, but rather on clusters of cultural and historical beliefs. Still, despite these problems, Fredrickson asked us to consider the history of the terms we use to better understand the context through which they were invented and applied.

In "Thick Description", Geertz observed that interpretive analysis which is truly "actor-centred" (that is, focused on what the "other" is doing and feeling) will provide some insurance against us speaking of culture when we are truly speaking of ourselves. While Said and Cannadine both showed that historical approaches to culture should always include a measure of critical reflection on our methods of study and our interpretive values, Fredrickson concluded his chapter by providing a useful connection between historical concepts and social ideology: "If racism is defined as an ideology rather than as a theory, links can be established between belief and practice that the history of ideas may obscure". Ideologies are beliefs that pretend to be truths; theories are intellectual positions that are open to discussion. Since descriptive categories play an important part in the creation of social and political structures that we assume are natural and therefore reflect the universal order of things, Fredrickson was urging us to consider the social *practices* that those categories encourage. Any historical study that defines its terms without also considering the intellectual and ideological needs that continue to lend them validity, runs the truly practical risk of creating its human subjects as historical objects.

Chapter 47

Clifford Geertz

THICK DESCRIPTION: TOWARD AN INTERPRETIVE THEORY OF CULTURE

Clifford Geertz (1926–2006), "Thick Description: Toward an Interpretive Theory of Culture", *The Interpretation of Cultures: Selected Essays* (London: Hutchinson, 1973), 3–16, 24–27, 30.

I

IN HER BOOK, *Philosophy in a New Key*, Susanne Langer remarks that certain ideas burst upon the intellectual landscape with a tremendous force. They resolve so many fundamental problems at once that they seem also to promise that they will resolve all fundamental problems, clarify all obscure issues. Everyone snaps them up as the open sesame of some new positive science, the conceptual center-point around which a comprehensive system of analysis can be built. The sudden vogue of such a *grande idée*, crowding out almost everything else for a while, is due, she says, "to the fact that all sensitive and active minds turn at once to exploiting it. We try it in every connection, for every purpose, experiment with possible stretches of its strict meaning, with generalizations and derivatives."

After we have become familiar with the new idea, however, after it has become part of our general stock of theoretical concepts, our expectations are brought more into balance with its actual uses, and its excessive popularity is ended. A few zealots persist in the old key-to-the-universe view of it; but less driven thinkers settle down after a while to the problems the idea has really generated. They try to apply it and extend it where it applies and where it is capable of extension; and they desist where it does not apply or cannot be extended. It becomes, if it was, in truth, a seminal idea in the first place, a permanent and enduring part of our intellectual armory. But it no longer has the grandiose, all-promising scope, the infinite versatility of apparent application, it once had. The second law of thermodynamics, or the principle of natural selection, or the notion of unconscious motivation, or the organization of the means of production does not explain everything, not even everything human, but it still explains something; and our attention shifts to isolating just what that something is, to disentangling ourselves from a lot of pseudoscience to which, in the first flush of its celebrity, it has also given rise.

Whether or not this is, in fact, the way all centrally important scientific concepts develop, I don't know. But certainly this pattern fits the concept of culture, around which the whole discipline of anthropology arose, and whose domination that discipline has been increasingly concerned to limit, specify, focus, and contain. It is to this cutting of the culture concept down to size, therefore actually insuring its continued importance rather than undermining it, that the essays below are all, in their several ways and from their several directions, dedicated. They all argue, sometimes explicitly, more often merely through the particular analysis they develop, for a narrowed, specialized, and, so I imagine, theoretically more powerful concept of culture to replace E. B. Tylor's famous "most complex whole," which, its originative power not denied, seems to me to have reached the point where it obscures a good deal more than it reveals.

The conceptual morass into which the Tylorean kind of *pot-au-feu* theorizing about culture can lead, is evident in what is still one of the better general introductions to anthropology, Clyde Kluckhohn's *Mirror for Man*. In some twenty-seven pages of his chapter on the concept, Kluckhohn managed to define culture in turn as: (1) "the total way of life of a people"; (2) "the social legacy the individual acquires from his group"; (3) "a way of thinking, feeling, and believing"; (4) "an abstraction from behavior"; (5) a theory on the part of the anthropologist about the way in which a group of people in fact behave; (6) a "storehouse of pooled learning"; (7) "a set of standardized orientations to recurrent problems"; (8) "learned behavior"; (9) a mechanism for the normative regulation of behavior; (10) "a set of techniques for adjusting both to the external environment and to other men"; (11) "a precipitate of history"; and turning, perhaps in desperation, to similies, as a map, as a sieve, and as a matrix. In the face of this sort of theoretical diffusion, even a somewhat constricted and not entirely standard concept of culture, which is at least internally coherent and, more important, which has a definable argument to make is (as, to be fair, Kluckhohn himself keenly realized) an improvement. Eclecticism is self-defeating not because there is only one direction in which it is useful to move, but because there are so many: it is necessary to choose.

The concept of culture I espouse, and whose utility the essays below attempt to demonstrate, is essentially a semiotic one. Believing, with Max Weber, that man is an animal suspended in webs of significance he himself has spun, I take culture to be those webs, and the analysis of it to be therefore not an experimental science in search of law but an interpretive one in search of meaning. It is explication I am after, construing social expressions on their surface enigmatical. But this pronouncement, a doctrine in a clause, demands itself some explication.

II

[. . .]

In anthropology, or anyway social anthropology, what the practitioners do is ethnography. And it is in understanding what ethnography is, or more exactly *what doing ethnography is*, that a start can be made toward grasping what anthropological analysis amounts to as a form of knowledge. This, it must immediately be said, is not a matter of methods. From one point of view, that of the textbook, doing ethnography is establishing rapport, selecting informants, transcribing texts, taking genealogies, mapping fields, keeping a diary, and so on. But it is not these things, techniques and received procedures, that define the enterprise. What defines it is the kind of intellectual effort it is: an elaborate venture in, to borrow a notion from Gilbert Ryle, "thick description."

Ryle's discussion of "thick description" appears in two recent essays of his (now reprinted in the second volume of his *Collected Papers*) addressed to the general question of what, as he puts it, "*Le Penseur*" is doing: "Thinking and Reflecting" and "The Thinking of Thoughts." Consider, he says, two boys rapidly contracting the eyelids of their right eyes. In one, this is an involuntary twitch; in the other, a conspiratorial signal to a friend. The two movements are, as movements, identical; from an I-am-a-camera, "phenomenalistic" observation of them alone, one could not tell which was twitch and which was wink, or indeed whether both or either was twitch or wink. Yet the difference, however unphotographable, between a twitch and a wink is vast; as anyone unfortunate enough to have had the first taken for the second knows. The winker is communicating, and indeed communicating in a quite precise and special way: (1) deliberately, (2) to someone in particular, (3) to impart a particular message, (4) according to a socially established code, and (5) without cognizance of the rest of the company. As Ryle points out, the winker has not done two things, contracted his eyelids and winked, while the twitcher has done only one, contracted his eyelids. Contracting your eyelids on purpose when there exists a public code in which so doing counts as a conspiratorial signal *is* winking. That's all there is to it: a speck of behavior, a fleck of culture, and—*voilà!*—a gesture.

That, however, is just the beginning. Suppose, he continues, there is a third boy, who, "to give malicious amusement to his cronies," parodies the first boy's wink, as amateurish, clumsy, obvious, and so on. He, of course, does this in the same way the second boy winked and the first twitched: by contracting his right eyelids. Only this boy is neither winking nor twitching, he is parodying someone else's, as he takes it, laughable, attempt at winking. Here, too, a socially established code exists (he will "wink" laboriously, overobviously, perhaps adding a grimace—the usual artifices of the clown); and so also does a message. Only now it is not conspiracy but ridicule that is in the air. If the others think he is actually winking, his whole project misfires as completely, though with somewhat different results, as if they think he is twitching. One can go further: uncertain of his mimicking abilities, the would-be satirist may practice at home before the mirror, in which case he is not twitching, winking, or parodying, but rehearsing; though so far as what a camera, a radical behaviorist, or a believer in protocol sentences would record he is just rapidly contracting his right eyelids like all the others. Complexities are possible, if not practically without end, at least logically so. The original winker might, for example, actually have been fake-winking, say, to mislead outsiders into imagining there was a conspiracy afoot when there in fact was not, in which case our descriptions of what the parodist is parodying and the rehearser rehearsing of course shift accordingly. But the point is that between what Ryle calls the "thin description" of what the rehearser (parodist, winker, twitcher . . .) is doing ("rapidly contracting his right eyelids") and the "thick description" of what he is doing ("practicing a burlesque of a friend faking a wink to deceive an innocent into thinking a conspiracy is in motion") lies the object of ethnography: a stratified hierarchy of meaningful structures in terms of which twitches, winks, fake-winks, parodies, rehearsals of parodies are produced, perceived, and interpreted, and without which they would not (not even the zero-form twitches, which, *as a cultural category*, are as much nonwinks as winks are nontwitches) in fact exist, no matter what anyone did or didn't do with his eyelids.

Like so many of the little stories Oxford philosophers like to make up for themselves, all this winking, fake-winking, burlesque-fake-winking, rehearsed-burlesque-fake-winking, may seem a bit artificial. In way of adding a more empirical note, let me give, deliberately unpreceded by any prior explanatory comment at all, a not untypical excerpt from my own field journal to demonstrate that, however evened off for didactic purposes, Ryle's example presents an image only too exact of the sort of piled-up structures of inference and implication through which an ethnographer is continually trying to pick his way:

The French [the informant said] had only just arrived. They set up twenty or
so small forts between here, the town, and the Marmusha area up in the middle
of the mountains, placing them on promontories so they could survey the
countryside. But for all this they couldn't guarantee safety, especially at night,
so although the *mezraq*, trade-pact, system was supposed to be legally abolished
it in fact continued as before.

One night, when Cohen (who speaks fluent Berber), was up there, at Marmusha, two
other Jews who were traders to a neighboring tribe came by to purchase some goods from
him. Some Berbers, from yet another neighboring tribe, tried to break into Cohen's place,
but he fired his rifle in the air. (Traditionally, Jews were not allowed to carry weapons; but at
this period things were so unsettled many did so anyway.) This attracted the attention of the
French and the marauders fled.

The next night, however, they came back, one of them disguised as a woman who
knocked on the door with some sort of a story. Cohen was suspicious and didn't want to let
"her" in, but the other Jews said, "oh, it's all right, it's only a woman." So they opened the
door and the whole lot came pouring in. They killed the two visiting Jews, but Cohen
managed to barricade himself in an adjoining room. He heard the robbers planning to burn
him alive in the shop after they removed his goods, and so he opened the door and, laying
about him wildly with a club, managed to escape through a window.

He went up to the fort, then, to have his wounds dressed, and complained to the local
commandant, one Captain Dumari, saying he wanted his '*ar*—i.e., four or five times the
value of the merchandise stolen from him. The robbers were from a tribe which had not
yet submitted to French authority and were in open rebellion against it, and he wanted
authorization to go with his *mezraq*-holder, the Marmusha tribal *sheikh*, to collect the
indemnity that, under traditional rules, he had coming to him. Captain Dumari couldn't
officially give him permission to do this, because of the French prohibition of the *mezraq*
relationship, but he gave him verbal authorization, saying, "If you get killed, it's your
problem."

So the *sheikh*, the Jew, and a small company of armed Marmushans went off ten or
fifteen kilometers up into the rebellious area, where there were of course no French,
and, sneaking up, captured the thief-tribe's shepherd and stole its herds. The other tribe
soon came riding out on horses after them, armed with rifles and ready to attack. But
when they saw who the "sheep thieves" were, they thought better of it and said, "all right,
we'll talk." They couldn't really deny what had happened—that some of their men had
robbed Cohen and killed the two visitors—and they weren't prepared to start the serious
feud with the Marmusha a scuffle with the invading party would bring on. So the two
groups talked, and talked, and talked, there on the plain amid the thousands of sheep, and
decided finally on five-hundred-sheep damages. The two armed Berber groups then lined
up on their horses at opposite ends of the plain, with the sheep herded between them,
and Cohen, in his black gown, pillbox hat, and flapping slippers, went out alone among
the sheep, picking out, one by one and at his own good speed, the best ones for his
payment.

So Cohen got his sheep and drove them back to Marmusha. The French, up in their
fort, heard them coming from some distance ("Ba, ba, ba" said Cohen, happily, recalling the
image) and said, "What the hell is that?" And Cohen said, "That is my '*ar*." The French couldn't
believe he had actually done what he said he had done, and accused him of being a spy for the
rebellious Berbers, put him in prison, and took his sheep. In the town, his family, not having
heard from him in so long a time, thought he was dead. But after a while the French released
him and he came back home, but without his sheep. He then went to the Colonel in the

town, the Frenchman in charge of the whole region, to complain. But the Colonel said, "I can't do anything about the matter. It's not my problem."

Quoted raw, a note in a bottle, this passage conveys, as any similar one similarly presented would do, a fair sense of how much goes into ethnographic description of even the most elemental sort—how extraordinarily "thick" it is. In finished anthropological writings, including those collected here, this fact—that what we call our data are really our own constructions of other people's constructions of what they and their compatriots are up to—is obscured because most of what we need to comprehend a particular event, ritual, custom, idea, or whatever is insinuated as background information before the thing itself is directly examined. (Even to reveal that this little drama took place in the highlands of central Morocco in 1912—and was recounted there in 1968—is to determine much of our understanding of it.) There is nothing particularly wrong with this, and it is in any case inevitable. But it does lead to a view of anthropological research as rather more of an observational and rather less of an interpretive activity than it really is. Right down at the factual base, the hard rock, insofar as there is any, of the whole enterprise, we are already explicating: and worse, explicating explications. Winks upon winks upon winks.

Analysis, then, is sorting out the structures of signification—what Ryle called established codes, a somewhat misleading expression, for it makes the enterprise sound too much like that of the cipher clerk when it is much more like that of the literary critic—and determining their social ground and import. Here, in our text, such sorting would begin with distinguishing the three unlike frames of interpretation ingredient in the situation, Jewish, Berber, and French, and would then move on to show how (and why) at that time, in that place, their copresence produced a situation in which systematic misunderstanding reduced traditional form to social farce. What tripped Cohen up, and with him the whole, ancient pattern of social and economic relationships within which he functioned, was a confusion of tongues.

I shall come back to this too-compacted aphorism later, as well as to the details of the text itself. The point for now is only that ethnography is thick description. What the ethnographer is in fact faced with—except when (as, of course, he must do) he is pursuing the more automatized routines of data collection—is a multiplicity of complex conceptual structures, many of them superimposed upon or knotted into one another, which are at once strange, irregular, and inexplicit, and which he must contrive somehow first to grasp and then to render. And this is true at the most down-to-earth, jungle field work levels of his activity: interviewing informants, observing rituals, eliciting kin terms, tracing property lines, censusing households . . . writing his journal. Doing ethnography is like trying to read (in the sense of "construct a reading of") a manuscript—foreign, faded, full of ellipses, incoherencies, suspicious emendations, and tendentious commentaries, but written not in conventionalized graphs of sound but in transient examples of shaped behavior.

III

Culture, this acted document, thus is public, like a burlesqued wink or a mock sheep raid. Though ideational, it does not exist in someone's head; though unphysical, it is not an occult entity. The interminable, because unterminable, debate within anthropology as to whether culture is "subjective" or "objective," together with the mutual exchange of intellectual insults ("idealist!"—"materialist!"; "mentalist!"—"behaviorist!"; "impressionist!"—"positivist!") which accompanies it, is wholly misconceived. Once human behavior is seen as (most of the time; there *are* true twitches) symbolic action—action which, like phonation in speech, pigment in painting, line in writing, or sonance in music, signifies—the question as to whether culture is patterned conduct or a frame of mind, or even the two somehow mixed together, loses sense. The thing to ask about a burlesqued wink or a mock sheep raid is not what their ontological status is. It is the same as that of rocks on the one hand and dreams on the other—they are things of this world. The thing to ask is what their import is: what it is, ridicule or challenge, irony or anger, snobbery or pride, that, in their occurrence and through their agency, is getting said.

This may seem like an obvious truth, but there are a number of ways to obscure it. One is to imagine that culture is a self-contained "superorganic" reality with forces and purposes of its own; that is, to reify it. Another is to claim that it consists in the brute pattern of behavioral events we observe in fact to occur in some identifiable community or other; that is, to reduce it. But though both these confusions still exist, and doubtless will be always with us, the main source of theoretical muddlement in contemporary anthropology is a view which developed in reaction to them and is right now very widely held—namely, that, to quote Ward Goodenough, perhaps its leading proponent, "culture [is located] in the minds and hearts of men."

Variously called ethnoscience, componential analysis, or cognitive anthropology (a terminological wavering which reflects a deeper uncertainty), this school of thought holds that culture is composed of psychological structures by means of which individuals or groups of individuals guide their behavior. "A society's culture," to quote Goodenough again, this time in a passage which has become the *locus classicus* of the whole movement, "consists of whatever it is one has to know or believe in order to operate in a manner acceptable to its members." And from this view of what culture is follows a view, equally assured, of what describing it is—the writing out of systematic rules, an ethnographic algorithm, which, if followed, would make it possible so to operate, to pass (physical appearance aside) for a native. In such a way, extreme subjectivism is married to extreme formalism, with the expected result: an explosion of debate as to whether particular analyses (which come in the form of taxonomies, paradigms, tables, trees, and other ingenuities) reflect what the natives "really" think or are merely clever simulations, logically equivalent but substantively different, of what they think.

As, on first glance, this approach may look close enough to the one being developed here to be mistaken for it, it is useful to be explicit as to what divides them. If, leaving our winks and sheep behind for the moment, we take, say, a Beethoven quartet as an, admittedly rather special but, for these purposes, nicely illustrative, sample of culture, no one would, I think, identify it with its score, with the skills and knowledge needed to play it, with the understanding of it possessed by its performers or auditors, nor, to take care, *en passant*, of the reductionists and reifiers, with a particular performance of it or with some mysterious entity transcending material existence. The "no one" is perhaps too strong here, for there are always incorrigibles. But that a Beethoven quartet is a temporally developed tonal structure, a coherent sequence of modeled sound—in a word, music—and not anybody's knowledge of or belief about anything, including how to play it, is a proposition to which most people are, upon reflection, likely to assent.

To play the violin it is necessary to possess certain habits, skills, knowledge, and talents, to be in the mood to play, and (as the old joke goes) to have a violin. But violin playing is neither the habits, skills, knowledge, and so on, nor the mood, nor (the notion believers in "material culture" apparently embrace) the violin. To make a trade pact in Morocco, you have to do certain things in certain ways (among others, cut, while chanting Quranic Arabic, the throat of a lamb before the assembled, undeformed, adult male members of your tribe) and to be possessed of certain psychological characteristics (among others, a desire for distant things). But a trade pact is neither the throat cutting nor the desire, though it is real enough, as seven kinsmen of our Marmusha sheikh discovered when, on an earlier occasion, they were executed by him following the theft of one mangy, essentially valueless sheepskin from Cohen.

Culture is public because meaning is. You can't wink (or burlesque one) without knowing what counts as winking or how, physically, to contract your eyelids, and you can't conduct a sheep raid (or mimic one) without knowing what it is to steal a sheep and how practically to go about it. But to draw from such truths the conclusion that knowing how to wink is winking and knowing how to steal a sheep is sheep raiding is to betray as deep a confusion as, taking thin descriptions for thick, to identify winking with eyelid contractions or sheep raiding with chasing woolly animals out of pastures. The cognitivist fallacy—that culture consists (to quote another spokesman for the movement, Stephen Tyler) of "mental phenomena which can [he means "should"] be analyzed by formal methods similar to those of mathematics and logic"—is as destructive of an effective use of the concept as are the behaviorist and idealist fallacies to which it is a misdrawn correction. Perhaps, as its errors are more sophisticated and its distortions subtler, it is even more so.

The generalized attack on privacy theories of meaning is, since early Husserl and late Wittgenstein, so much a part of modern thought that it need not be developed once more here. What is necessary is to see to it that the news of it reaches anthropology; and in particular that it is made clear that to say that culture consists of socially established structures of meaning in terms of which people do such things as signal conspiracies and join them or perceive insults and answer them, is no more to say that it is a psychological phenomenon, a characteristic of someone's mind, personality, cognitive structure, or whatever, than to say that Tantrism, genetics, the progressive form of the verb, the classification of wines, the Common Law, or the notion of "a conditional curse" (as Westermarck defined the concept of 'ar in terms of which Cohen pressed his claim to damages) is. What, in a place like Morocco, most prevents those of us who grew up winking other winks or attending other sheep from grasping what people are up to is not ignorance as to how cognition works (though, especially as, one assumes, it works the same among them as it does among us, it would greatly help to have less of that too) as a lack of familiarity with the imaginative universe within which their acts are signs. As Wittgenstein has been invoked, he may as well be quoted:

> We . . . say of some people that they are transparent to us. It is, however, important as regards this observation that one human being can be a complete enigma to another. We learn this when we come into a strange country with entirely strange traditions; and, what is more, even given a mastery of the country's language. We do not *understand* the people. (And not because of not knowing what they are saying to themselves.) We cannot find our feet with them.

IV

Finding our feet, an unnerving business which never more than distantly succeeds, is what ethnographic research consists of as a personal experience; trying to formulate the basis on which one imagines, always excessively, one has found them is what anthropological writing consists of as a scientific endeavor. We are not, or at least I am not, seeking either to become natives (a compromised word in any case) or to mimic them. Only romantics or spies would seem to find point in that. We are seeking, in the widened sense of the term in which it encompasses very much more than talk, to converse with them, a matter a great deal more difficult, and not only with strangers, than is commonly recognized. "If speaking *for* someone else seems to be a mysterious process," Stanley Cavell has remarked, "that may be because speaking *to* someone does not seem mysterious enough."

Looked at in this way, the aim of anthropology is the enlargement of the universe of human discourse. That is not, of course, its only aim—instruction, amusement, practical counsel, moral advance, and the discovery of natural order in human behavior are others; nor is anthropology the only discipline which pursues it. But it is an aim to which a semiotic concept of culture is peculiarly well adapted. As interworked systems of construable signs (what, ignoring provincial usages, I would call symbols), culture is not a power, something to which social events, behaviors, institutions, or processes can be causally attributed; it is a context, something within which they can be intelligibly—that is, thickly—described.

The famous anthropological absorption with the (to us) exotic—Berber horsemen, Jewish peddlers, French Legionnaires—is, thus, essentially a device for displacing the dulling sense of familiarity with which the mysteriousness of our own ability to relate perceptively to one another is concealed from us. Looking at the ordinary in places where it takes unaccustomed forms brings out not, as has so often been claimed, the arbitrariness of human behavior (there is nothing especially arbitrary about taking sheep theft for insolence in Morocco), but the degree to which its meaning varies according to the pattern of life by which it is informed. Understanding a people's culture exposes their normalness without reducing their particularity. (The more I manage to follow what the Moroccans are up to, the more logical, and the more singular, they seem.) It renders them accessible: setting them in the frame of their own banalities, it dissolves their opacity.

It is this maneuver, usually too casually referred to as "seeing things from the actor's point of view," too bookishly as "the *verstehen* approach," or too technically as "emic analysis," that so often leads to the notion that anthropology is a variety of either long-distance mind reading or cannibal-isle fantasizing, and which, for someone anxious to navigate past the wrecks of a dozen sunken philosophies, must therefore be executed with a great deal of care. Nothing is more necessary to comprehending what anthropological interpretation is, and the degree to which it *is* interpretation, than an exact understanding of what it means—and what it does not mean—to say that our formulations of other peoples' symbol systems must be actor-oriented.[1]

[What it means is that descriptions of Berber, Jewish, or French culture must be cast in terms of the constructions we imagine Berbers, Jews, or Frenchmen to place upon what they live through, the formulae they use to define what happens to them. What it does not mean is that such descriptions are themselves Berber, Jewish, or French—that is, part of the reality they are ostensibly describing; they are anthropological—that is, part of a developing system of scientific analysis.] They must be cast in terms of the interpretations to which persons of a particular denomination subject their experience, because that is what they profess to be descriptions of; they are anthropological because it is, in fact, anthropologists who profess them. Normally, it is not necessary to point out quite so laboriously that the object of study is one thing and the study of it another. It is clear enough that the physical world is not physics and *A Skeleton Key to Finnegan's Wake* not *Finnegan's Wake* [James Joyce's difficult novel]. But, as, in the study of culture, analysis penetrates into the very body of the object—that is, *we begin with our own interpretations of what our informants are up to, or think they are up to, and then systematize those*—the line between (Moroccan) culture as a natural fact and (Moroccan) culture as a theoretical entity tends to get blurred. All the more so, as the latter is presented in the form of an actor's-eye description of (Moroccan) conceptions of everything from violence, honor, divinity, and justice, to tribe, property, patronage, and chiefship.

[In short, anthropological writings are themselves interpretations, and second and third order ones to boot. (By definition, only a "native" makes first order ones: it's *his* culture.)[2] They are, thus, fictions; fictions, in the sense that they are "something made," "something fashioned"⌉—the original meaning of *fictiō*—not that they are false, unfactual, or merely "as if" thought experiments. To construct actor-oriented descriptions of the involvements of a Berber chieftain, a Jewish merchant, and a French soldier with one another in 1912 Morocco is clearly an imaginative act, not all that different from constructing similar descriptions of, say, the involvements with one another of a provincial French doctor, his silly, adulterous wife, and her feckless lover in nineteenth century France. In the latter case, the actors are represented as not having existed and the events as not having happened, while in the former they are represented as actual, or as having been so. This is a difference of no mean importance; indeed, precisely the one Madame Bovary had difficulty grasping. But the importance does not lie in the fact that her story was created while Cohen's was only noted. The conditions of their creation, and the point of it (to say nothing of the manner and the quality) differ. But the one is as much a *fictiō*—"a making"—as the other.

Anthropologists have not always been as aware as they might be of this fact: that although culture exists in the trading post, the hill fort, or the sheep run, anthropology exists in the book, the article, the lecture, the museum display, or, sometimes nowadays, the film. To become aware of it is to realize that the line between mode of representation and substantive content is as undrawable in cultural analysis as it is in painting; and that fact in turn seems to threaten the objective status of anthropological knowledge by suggesting that its source is not social reality but scholarly artifice.

It does threaten it, but the threat is hollow. The claim to attention of an ethnographic account does not rest on its author's ability to capture primitive facts in faraway places and carry them home like a mask or a carving, but on the degree to which he is able to clarify what goes on in such places, to reduce the puzzlement—what manner of men are these?—to which unfamiliar acts emerging out of unknown backgrounds naturally give rise. This raises some serious problems of verification, all right—or, if "verification" is too strong a word for so soft a science (I, myself, would prefer "appraisal"), of how you can tell a better account from a worse one. But that is precisely the virtue of it. If ethnography is thick description and ethnographers those who are doing the describing, then the determining question for any given example of it, whether a field journal squib or a Malinowski-sized monograph, is whether it sorts winks from twitches and real winks from mimicked ones. It is not against a body of uninterpreted data, radically thinned descriptions, that we must measure the cogency of our explications, but against the power of the scientific imagination to bring us into touch with the lives of strangers. It is not worth it, as Thoreau said, to go round the world to count the cats in Zanzibar.

[. . .]

VII

Which brings us, finally, to theory. The besetting sin of interpretive approaches to any-thing—literature, dreams, symptoms, culture—is that they tend to resist, or to be permit-ted to resist, conceptual articulation and thus to escape systematic modes of assessment. You either grasp an interpretation or you do not, see the point of it or you do not, accept it or you do not. Imprisoned in the immediacy of its own detail, it is presented as self-validating, or, worse, as validated by the supposedly developed sensitivities of the person who presents it; any attempt to cast what it says in terms other than its own is regarded as a travesty—as, the anthropologist's severest term of moral abuse, ethnocentric.

For a field of study which, however timidly (though I, myself, am not timid about the matter at all), asserts itself to be a science, this just will not do. There is no reason why the conceptual structure of a cultural interpretation should be any less formulable, and thus less susceptible to explicit canons of appraisal, than that of, say, a biological observation or a physical experiment—no reason except that the terms in which such formulations can be cast are, if not wholly nonexistent, very nearly so. We are reduced to insinuating theories because we lack the power to state them.

At the same time, it must be admitted that there are a number of characteristics of cultural interpretation which make the theoretical development of it more than usually difficult. The first is the need for theory to stay rather closer to the ground than tends to be the case in sciences more able to give themselves over to imaginative abstraction. Only short flights of ratiocination [rational reasoning] tend to be effective in anthropology; longer ones tend to drift off into logical dreams, academic bemusements with formal symmetry. The whole point of a semiotic approach to culture is, as I have said, to aid us in gaining access to the conceptual world in which our subjects live so that we can, in some extended sense of the term, converse with them. The tension between the pull of this need to penetrate an unfamiliar universe of symbolic action and the requirements of technical advance in the theory of culture, between the need to grasp and the need to analyze, is, as a result, both necessarily great and essentially irremovable. Indeed, the further theoretical development goes, the deeper the tension gets. This is the first condition for cultural theory: it is not its own master. As it is unseverable from the immediacies thick description presents, its freedom to shape itself in terms of its internal logic is rather limited. What generality it contrives to achieve grows out of the delicacy of its distinctions, not the sweep of its abstractions.

And from this follows a peculiarity in the way, as a simple matter of empirical fact, our knowledge of culture . . . cultures . . . a culture . . . grows: in spurts. Rather than following a rising curve of cumulative findings, cultural analysis breaks up into a disconnected yet coherent sequence of bolder and bolder sorties. Studies do build on other studies, not in the sense that they take up where the others leave off, but in the sense that, better informed and better conceptualized, they plunge more deeply into the same things. Every serious cultural analysis starts from a sheer beginning and ends where it manages to get before exhausting its intellectual impulse. Previously discovered facts are mobilized, previously developed concepts used, previously formulated hypotheses tried out; but the movement is not from already proven theorems to newly proven ones, it is from an awkward fumbling for the most elementary understanding to a supported claim that one has achieved that and surpassed it. A study is an advance if it is more incisive—whatever that may mean—than those that preceded it; but it less stands on their shoulders than, challenged and challenging, runs by their side.

It is for this reason, among others, that the essay, whether of thirty pages or three hundred, has seemed the natural genre in which to present cultural interpretations and the theories sustaining them, and why, if one looks for systematic treatises in the field, one is so soon disappointed, the more so if one finds any. Even inventory articles are rare here, and anyway of hardly more than bibliographical interest. The major theoretical contributions not only lie in specific studies—that is true in almost any field—but they are very difficult to abstract from such studies and integrate into anything one might call "culture theory" as such. Theoretical formulations hover so low over the interpretations they govern that they don't make much sense or hold much interest apart from them. This is so, not because they are not general (if they are not general, they are not theoretical), but because, stated independently of their applications, they seem either commonplace or vacant. One can, and this in fact is how the field progresses conceptually, take a line of theoretical attack developed in connection with one exercise in ethnographic interpretation and employ it in another, pushing it forward to greater precision and broader relevance; but one cannot write a "General Theory of Cultural Interpretation." Or, rather, one can, but there appears to be little profit in it, because the essential task of theory building here is not to codify abstract regularities but to make thick description possible, not to generalize across cases but to generalize within them.

To generalize within cases is usually called, at least in medicine and depth psychology, clinical inference. Rather than beginning with a set of observations and attempting to subsume them under a governing law, such inference begins with a set of (presumptive) signifiers and attempts to place them within an intelligible frame. Measures are matched to theoretical predictions, but symptoms (even when they are measured) are scanned for theoretical peculiarities—that is, they are diagnosed. In the study of culture the signifiers are not symptoms or clusters of symptoms, but symbolic acts or clusters of symbolic acts, and the aim is not therapy but the analysis of social discourse. But the way in which theory is used—to ferret out the unapparent import of things—is the same.

Thus we are led to the second condition of cultural theory: it is not, at least in the strict meaning of the term, predictive. The diagnostician doesn't predict measles; he decides that someone has them, or at the very most *anticipates* that someone is rather likely shortly to get them. But this limitation, which is real enough, has commonly been both misunderstood and exaggerated, because it has been taken to mean that cultural interpretation is merely post facto: that, like the peasant in the old story, we first shoot the holes in the fence and then paint the bull's-eyes around them. It is hardly to be denied that there is a good deal of that sort of thing around, some of it in prominent places. It is to be denied, however, that it is the inevitable outcome of a clinical approach to the use of theory.

It is true that in the clinical style of theoretical formulation, conceptualization is directed toward the task of generating interpretations of matters already in hand, not toward projecting outcomes of experimental manipulations or deducing future states of a determined system. But that does not mean that theory has only to fit (or, more carefully, to generate cogent interpretations of) realities past; it has also to survive—intellectually survive—realities to come. Although we formulate our interpretation of an outburst of winking or an instance of sheep-raiding after its occurrence, sometimes long after, the theoretical framework in terms of which such an interpretation is made must be capable of continuing to yield defensible interpretations as new social phenomena swim into view. Although one starts any effort at thick description, beyond the obvious and superficial, from a state of general bewilderment as to what the devil is going on—trying to find one's feet—one does not start (or ought not) intellectually empty-handed. Theoretical ideas are not created wholly anew in each study; as I have said, they are adopted from other, related studies, and, refined in the process, applied to new interpretive problems. If they cease being useful with respect to such problems, they tend to stop being used and are more or less abandoned. If they continue being useful, throwing up new understandings, they are further elaborated and go on being used.[3]

Such a view of how theory functions in an interpretive science suggests that the distinction, relative in any case, that appears in the experimental or observational sciences between "description" and "explanation" appears here as one, even more relative, between "inscription" ("thick description") and "specification" ("diagnosis")—between setting down the meaning particular social actions have for the actors whose actions they are, and stating, as explicitly as we can manage, what the knowledge thus attained demonstrates about the society in which it is found and, beyond that, about social life as such. Our double task is to uncover the conceptual structures that inform our subjects' acts, the "said" of social discourse, and to construct a system of analysis in whose terms what is generic to those structures, what belongs to them because they are what they are, will stand out against the other determinants of human behavior. In ethnography, the office of theory is to provide a vocabulary in which what symbolic action has to say about itself—that is, about the role of culture in human life—can be expressed.

[. . .]

The danger that cultural analysis, in search of all-too-deep-lying turtles, will lose touch with the hard surfaces of life—with the political, economic, stratificatory realities within which men are everywhere contained—and with the biological and physical necessities on which those surfaces rest, is an ever-present one. The only defense against it, and against, thus, turning cultural analysis into a kind of sociological aestheticism, is to train such analysis on such realities and such necessities in the first place. It is thus that I have written about nationalism, about violence, about identity, about human nature, about legitimacy, about revolution, about ethnicity, about urbanization, about status, about death, about time, and most of all about particular attempts by particular peoples to place these things in some sort of comprehensible, meaningful frame.

To look at the symbolic dimensions of social action—art, religion, ideology, science, law, morality, common sense—is not to turn away from the existential dilemmas of life for some empyrean realm of demotionalized forms; it is to plunge into the midst of them. The essential vocation of interpretive anthropology is not to answer our deepest questions, but to make available to us answers that others, guarding other sheep in other valleys, have given, and thus to include them in the consultable record of what man has said.

Notes

1   Not only other peoples': anthropology *can* be trained on the culture of which it is itself a part, and it increasingly is; a fact of profound importance, but which, as it raises a few tricky and rather special second order problems, I shall put to the side for the moment.

2   The order problem is, again, complex. Anthropological works based on other anthropological works (Lévi-Strauss', for example) may, of course, be fourth order or higher, and informants frequently, even habitually, make second order interpretations—what have come to be known as "native models." In literate cultures, where "native" interpretation can proceed to higher levels—in connection with the Maghreb, one has only to think of Ibn Khaldun; with the United States, Margaret Mead—these matters become intricate indeed.

3   Admittedly, this is something of an idealization. Because theories are seldom if ever decisively disproved in clinical use but merely grow increasingly awkward, unproductive, strained, or vacuous, they often persist long after all but a handful of people (though *they* are often most passionate) have lost much interest in them. Indeed, so far as anthropology is concerned, it is almost more of a problem to get exhausted ideas out of the literature than it is to get productive ones in, and so a great deal more of theoretical discussion than one would prefer is critical rather than constructive, and whole careers have been devoted to hastening the demise of moribund notions. As the field advances one would hope that this sort of intellectual weed control would become a less prominent part of our activities. But, for the moment, it remains true that old theories tend less to die than to go into second editions.

Chapter 48

Edward Said

INTRODUCTION TO *ORIENTALISM*

Edward Said (1935–2003), "Introduction", *Orientalism* (New York: Random House, 1978), 4–9, 12–15.

II

I HAVE BEGUN with the assumption that the Orient is not an inert fact of nature. It is not merely *there*, just as the Occident itself is not just *there* either. We must take seriously Vico's great observation that men make their own history, that what they can know is what they have made, and extend it to geography: as both geographical and cultural entities—to say nothing of historical entities—such locales, regions, geographical sectors as "Orient" and "Occident" are man-made. Therefore as much as the West itself, the Orient is an idea that has a history and a tradition of thought, imagery, and vocabulary that have given it reality and presence in and for the West. The two geographical entities thus support and to an extent reflect each other.

Having said that, one must go on to state a number of reasonable qualifications. In the first place, it would be wrong to conclude that the Orient was *essentially* an idea, or a creation with no corresponding reality. When Disraeli said in his novel *Tancred* [1847] that the East was a career, he meant that to be interested in the East was something bright young Westerners would find to be an all-consuming passion; he should not be interpreted as saying that the East was *only* a career for Westerners. There were—and are—cultures and nations whose location is in the East, and their lives, histories, and customs have a brute reality obviously greater than anything that could be said about them in the West. About that fact this study of Orientalism has very little to contribute, except to acknowledge it tacitly. But the phenomenon of Orientalism as I study it here deals principally, not with a correspondence between Orientalism and Orient, but with the internal consistency of Orientalism and its ideas about the Orient (the East as career) despite or beyond any correspondence, or lack thereof, with a "real" Orient. My point is that Disraeli's statement about the East refers mainly to that created consistency, that regular constellation of ideas as the pre-eminent thing about the Orient, and not to its mere being, as Wallace Stevens's phrase has it.

A second qualification is that ideas, cultures, and histories cannot seriously be understood or studied without their force, or more precisely their configurations of power, also being studied. To believe that the Orient was created—or, as I call it, "Orientalized"—and to believe that such things happen simply as a necessity of the imagination, is to be disingenuous. The relationship between Occident and Orient is a relationship of power, of domination, of varying degrees of a complex hegemony, and is quite accurately indicated in the title of K. M. Panikkar's classic *Asia and Western Dominance*.[1] The Orient was Orientalized not only because it was discovered to be "Oriental" in all those ways considered commonplace by an average nineteenth-century European, but also because it *could be*—that is, submitted to being—*made* Oriental. There is very little consent to be found, for example, in the fact that Flaubert's encounter with an Egyptian courtesan produced a widely influential model of the Oriental woman; she never spoke of herself, she never represented her emotions, presence, or history. *He* spoke for and represented her. He was foreign, comparatively wealthy, male, and these were historical facts of domination that allowed him not only to possess Kuchuk Hanem physically but to speak for her and tell his readers in what way she was "typically Oriental." My argument is that Flaubert's situation of strength in relation to Kuchuk Hanem was not an isolated instance.[i] It fairly stands for the pattern of relative strength between East and West, and the discourse about the Orient that it enabled.

This brings us to a third qualification. One ought never to assume that the structure of Orientalism is nothing more than a structure of lies or of myths which, were the truth about them to be told, would simply blow away. I myself believe that Orientalism is more particularly valuable as a sign of European-Atlantic power over the Orient than it is as a veridic [truthful] discourse about the Orient (which is what, in its academic or scholarly form, it claims to be). Nevertheless, what we must respect and try to grasp is the sheer knitted-together strength of Orientalist discourse, its very close ties to the enabling socioeconomic and political institutions, and its redoubtable durability. After all, any system of ideas that can remain unchanged as teachable wisdom (in academies, books, congresses, universities, foreign-service institutes) from the period of Ernest Renan in the late 1840s until the present in the United States must be something more formidable than a mere collection of lies. Orientalism, therefore, is not an airy European fantasy about the Orient, but a created body of theory and practice in which, for many generations, there has been a considerable material investment. Continued investment made Orientalism, as a system of knowledge about the Orient, an accepted grid for filtering through the Orient into Western consciousness, just as that same investment multiplied—indeed, made truly productive—the statements proliferating out from Orientalism into the general culture.

Gramsci has made the useful analytic distinction between civil and political society in which the former is made up of voluntary (or at least rational and noncoercive) affiliations like schools, families, and unions, the latter of state institutions (the army, the police, the central bureaucracy) whose role in the polity is direct domination. Culture, of course, is to be found operating within civil society, where the influence of ideas, of institutions, and of other persons works not through domination but by what Gramsci calls consent. In any society not totalitarian, then, certain cultural forms predominate over others, just as certain ideas are more influential than others; the form of this cultural leadership is what Gramsci has identified as *hegemony*, an indispensable concept for any understanding of cultural life in the industrial West. It is hegemony, or rather the result of cultural hegemony at work, that gives Orientalism the durability and the strength I have been speaking about so far.

i   See G. Flaubert, "Up the Nile to Wadi Haifa," [1849] *Flaubert in Egypt*, ed. and trans. F. Steegmuller (Hardmondsworth: Penguin, 1972) 97–137. [-Ed.]

Orientalism is never far from what Denys Hay has called the idea of Europe,[2] a collective notion identifying "us" Europeans as against all "those" non-Europeans, and indeed it can be argued that the major component in European culture is precisely what made that culture hegemonic both in and outside Europe: the idea of European identity as a superior one in comparison with all the non-European peoples and cultures. There is in addition the hegemony of European ideas about the Orient, themselves reiterating European superiority over Oriental backwardness, usually overriding the possibility that a more independent, or more skeptical, thinker might have had different views on the matter.

In a quite constant way, Orientalism depends for its strategy on this flexible *positional* superiority, which puts the Westerner in a whole series of possible relationships with the Orient without ever losing him the relative upper hand. And why should it have been otherwise, especially during the period of extraordinary European ascendancy from the late Renaissance to the present? The scientist, the scholar, the missionary, the trader, or the soldier was in, or thought about, the Orient because he *could be there*, or could think about it, with very little resistance on the Orient's part. Under the general heading of knowledge of the Orient, and within the umbrella of Western hegemony over the Orient during the period from the end of the eighteenth century, there emerged a complex Orient suitable for study in the academy, for display in the museum, for reconstruction in the colonial office, for theoretical illustration in anthropological, biological, linguistic, racial, and historical theses about mankind and the universe, for instances of economic and sociological theories of development, revolution, cultural personality, national or religious character. Additionally, the imaginative examination of things Oriental was based more or less exclusively upon a sovereign Western consciousness out of whose unchallenged centrality an Oriental world emerged, first according to general ideas about who or what was an Oriental, then according to a detailed logic governed not simply by empirical reality but by a battery of desires, repressions, investments, and projections. If we can point to great Orientalist works of genuine scholarship like Silvestre de Sacy's *Chrestomathie arabe* [1806], or Edward William Lane's *Account of the Manners and Customs of the Modern Egyptians* [1836], we need also to note that Renan's and Gobineau's racial ideas came out of the same impulse, as did a great many Victorian pornographic novels (see the analysis by Steven Marcus of "The Lustful Turk"[3]).

And yet, one must repeatedly ask oneself whether what matters in Orientalism is the general group of ideas overriding the mass of material—about which who could deny that they were shot through with doctrines of European superiority, various kinds of racism, imperialism, and the like, dogmatic views of "the Oriental" as a kind of ideal and unchanging abstraction?—or the much more varied work produced by almost uncountable individual writers, whom one would take up as individual instances of authors dealing with the Orient. In a sense the two alternatives, general and particular, are really two perspectives on the same material: in both instances one would have to deal with pioneers in the field like William Jones [1746–94], with great artists like Nerval or Flaubert. And why would it not be possible to employ both perspectives together, or one after the other? Isn't there an obvious danger of distortion (of precisely the kind that academic Orientalism has always been prone to) if either too general or too specific a level of description is maintained systematically?

My two fears are distortion and inaccuracy, or rather the kind of inaccuracy produced by too dogmatic a generality and too positivistic a localized focus. In trying to deal with these problems I have tried to deal with three main aspects of my own contemporary reality that seem to me to point the way out of the methodological or perspectival difficulties I have been discussing, difficulties that might force one, in the first instance, into writing a coarse polemic on so unacceptably general a level of description as not to be worth the effort, or in the second instance, into writing so detailed and atomistic a series of analyses as to lose all track of the general lines of force informing the field, giving it its special cogency. How then to recognize individuality and to reconcile it with its intelligent, and by no means passive or merely dictatorial, general and hegemonic context?

III

[. . .]

My idea is that European and then American interest in the Orient was political according to some of the obvious historical accounts of it that I have given here, but that it was the culture that created that interest, that acted dynamically along with brute political, economic, and military rationales to make the Orient the varied and complicated place that it obviously was in the field I call Orientalism.

Therefore, Orientalism is not a mere political subject matter or field that is reflected passively by culture, scholarship, or institutions; nor is it a large and diffuse collection of texts about the Orient; nor is it representative and expressive of some nefarious "Western" imperialist plot to hold down the "Oriental" world. It is rather a *distribution* of geopolitical awareness into aesthetic, scholarly, economic, and sociological, historical, and philological texts; it is an *elaboration* not only of a basic geographical distinction (the world is made up of two unequal halves, Orient and Occident) but also of a whole series of "interests" which, by such means as scholarly discovery, philological reconstruction, psychological analysis, land-scape and sociological description, it not only creates but also maintains; it *is*, rather than expresses, a certain *will* or *intention* to understand, in some cases to control, manipulate, even to incorporate, what is a manifestly different (or alternative and novel) world; it is, above all, a discourse that is by no means in direct, corresponding relationship with political power in the raw, but rather is produced and exists in an uneven exchange with various kinds of power, shaped to a degree by the exchange with power political (as with a colonial or imperial establishment), power intellectual (as with reigning sciences like comparative linguistics or anatomy, or any of the modern policy sciences), power cultural (as with orthodoxies and canons of taste, texts, values), power moral (as with ideas about what "we" do and what "they" cannot do or understand as "we" do). Indeed, my real argument is that Orientalism is—and does not simply represent—a considerable dimension of modern political-intellectual culture, and as such has less to do with the Orient than it does with "our" world.

Because Orientalism is a cultural and a political fact, then, it does not exist in some archival vacuum; quite the contrary, I think it can be shown that what is thought, said, or even done about the Orient follows (perhaps occurs within) certain distinct and intel-lectually knowable lines. Here too a considerable degree of nuance and elaboration can be seen working as between the broad superstructural pressures and the details of composition, the facts of textuality. Most humanistic scholars are, I think, perfectly happy with the notion that texts exist in contexts, that there is such a thing as intertextuality, that the pressures of conventions, predecessors, and rhetorical styles limit what Walter Benjamin once called the "overtaxing of the productive person in the name of . . . the principle of 'creativity,' " in which the poet is believed on his own, and out of his pure mind, to have brought forth his work.[4] Yet there is a reluctance to allow that political, institutional, and ideological con-straints act in the same manner on the individual author. A humanist will believe it to be an interesting fact to any interpreter of Balzac that he was influenced in the *Comédie humaine* by the conflict between Geoffroy Saint-Hilaire and Cuvier, but the same sort of pressure on Balzac of deeply reactionary monarchism is felt in some vague way to demean his literary "genius" and therefore to be less worth serious study. Similarly—as Harry Bracken has been tirelessly showing—philosophers will conduct their discussions of Locke, Hume, and empiricism without ever taking into account that there is an explicit connection in these classic writers between their "philosophic" doctrines and racial theory, justifications of slavery, or arguments for colonial exploitation.[5] These are common enough ways by which contemporary scholarship keeps itself pure.

Perhaps it is true that most attempts to rub culture's nose in the mud of politics have been crudely iconoclastic; perhaps also the social interpretation of literature in my own field has simply not kept up with the enormous technical advances in detailed textual analysis. But there is no getting away from the fact that literary studies in general, and American Marxist theorists in particular, have avoided the effort of seriously bridging the gap between the superstructural and the base levels in textual, historical scholarship; on another occasion I have gone so far as to say that the literary-cultural establishment as a whole has declared the serious study of imperialism and culture off limits.[6] For Orientalism brings one up directly against that question—that is, to realizing that political imperialism governs an entire field of study, imagination, and scholarly institutions—in such a way as to make its avoidance an intellectual and historical impossibility. Yet there will always remain the perennial escape mechanism of saying that a literary scholar and a philosopher, for example, are trained in literature and philosophy respectively, not in politics or ideological analysis. In other words, the specialist argument can work quite effectively to block the larger and, in my opinion, the more intellectually serious perspective.

Here it seems to me there is a simple two-part answer to be given, at least so far as the study of imperialism and culture (or Orientalism) is concerned. In the first place, nearly every nineteenth-century writer (and the same is true enough of writers in earlier periods) was extraordinarily well aware of the fact of empire: this is a subject not very well studied, but it will not take a modern Victorian specialist long to admit that liberal cultural heroes like John Stuart Mill, Arnold, Carlyle, Newman, Macaulay, Ruskin, George Eliot, and even Dickens had definite views on race and imperialism, which are quite easily to be found at work in their writing. So even a specialist must deal with the knowledge that Mill, for example, made it clear in *On Liberty* and *Representative Government* that his views there could not be applied to India (he was an India Office functionary for a good deal of his life, after all) because the Indians were civilizationally, if not racially, inferior. The same kind of paradox is to be found in Marx, as I try to show in this book. In the second place, to believe that politics in the form of imperialism bears upon the production of literature, scholarship, social theory, and history writing is by no means equivalent to saying that culture is therefore a demeaned or denigrated thing. Quite the contrary: my whole point is to say that we can better understand the persistence and the durability of saturating hegemonic systems like culture when we realize that their internal constraints upon writers and thinkers were *productive, not unilaterally inhibiting.* It is this idea that Gramsci, certainly, and Foucault and Raymond Williams in their very different ways have been trying to illustrate. Even one or two pages by Williams on "the uses of the Empire" in *The Long Revolution* tell us more about nineteenth-century cultural richness than many volumes of hermetic textual analyses.[7]

Therefore I study Orientalism as a dynamic exchange between individual authors and the large political concerns shaped by the three great empires—British, French, American —in whose intellectual and imaginative territory the writing was produced. What interests me most as a scholar is not the gross political verity but the detail, as indeed what interests us in someone like Lane or Flaubert or Renan is not the (to him) indisputable truth that Occidentals are superior to Orientals, but the profoundly worked over and modulated evidence of his detailed work within the very wide space opened up by that truth. One need only remember that Lane's *Manners and Customs of the Modern Egyptians* is a classic of historical and anthropological observation because of its style, its enormously intelligent and brilliant details, not because of its simple reflection of racial superiority, to understand what I am saying here.

The kind of political questions raised by Orientalism, then, are as follows: What other sorts of intellectual, aesthetic, scholarly, and cultural energies went into the making of an imperialist tradition like the Orientalist one? How did philology, lexicography, history, biology, political and economic theory, novel-writing, and lyric poetry come to the service of Orientalism's broadly imperialist view of the world? What changes, modulations, refinements, even revolutions take place within Orientalism? What is the meaning of originality, of continuity, of individuality, in this context? How does Orientalism transmit or reproduce itself from one epoch to another? In fine, how can we treat the cultural, historical phenomenon of Orientalism as a kind of *willed human work*—not of mere unconditioned ratiocination—in all its historical complexity, detail, and worth without at the same time losing sight of the alliance between cultural work, political tendencies, the state, and the specific realities of domination? Governed by such concerns a humanistic study can responsibly address itself to politics *and* culture. But this is not to say that such a study establishes a hard-and-fast rule about the relationship between knowledge and politics. My argument is that each humanistic investigation must formulate the nature of that connection in the specific context of the study, the subject matter, and its historical circumstances.

Notes

1   K. M. Panikkar, *Asia and Western Dominance* (London: George Allen & Unwin, 1959).
2   Denys Hay, *Europe: The Emergence of an Idea*, 2nd ed. (Edinburgh: Edinburgh University Press, 1968).
3   Steven Marcus, *The Other Victorians: A Study of Sexuality and Pornography in Mid-Nineteenth Century England* (1966; reprint ed., New York: Bantam Books, 1967), pp. 200–19.
4   Walter Benjamin, *Charles Baudelaire: A Lyric Poet in the Era of High Capitalism*, trans. Harry Zohn (London: New Left Books, 1973), p. 71.
5   Harry Bracken, "Essence, Accident and Race," *Hermathena* 116 (Winter 1973): 81–96.
6   In an interview published in *Diacritics* 6, no. 3 (Fall 1976): 38.
7   Raymond Williams, *The Long Revolution* (London: Chatto & Windus, 1961), pp. 66–7.

Chapter 49

David Cannadine

BEGINNINGS

David Cannadine, "Beginnings", *Ornamentalism: How the British Saw Their Empire* (Oxford: Oxford University Press, 2001), 3–10.

Prologue

NATIONS, it has recently become commonplace to observe, are in part imagined communities, depending for their credibility and identity both on the legitimacy of government and the apparatus of the state, and on invented traditions, manufactured myths, and shared perceptions of the social order that are never more than crude categories and oversimplified stereotypes.[1] If this has been true (as indeed it has) of a relatively compact and contained country like Britain, then how much more true must this have been of the empire that the British conquered and peopled, administered and ruled? At its territorial zenith, shortly after the end of the First World War, it consisted of naval stations and military bases extending from Gibraltar to Hong Kong, the four great dominions of settlement, the Indian Empire that occupied an entire subcontinent, the crown colonies in Asia, Africa and the Caribbean, and the League of Nations Mandates, especially in the Middle East.[2] But, as with all such transoceanic realms, the British Empire was not only a geopolitical entity: it was also a culturally created and imaginatively constructed artifact. How, then, in the heyday of its existence, did Britons imagine and envisage their unprecedentedly vast and varied imperium, not so much geographically as sociologically? How did they try to organize and to arrange their heterogeneous imperial society, as they settled and conquered, governed and ruled it, and what did they think the resulting social order looked like?[3]

To the extent that they tried to conceive of these diverse colonies and varied populations beyond the seas as 'an entire interactive system, one vast interconnected world', most Britons followed the standard pattern of human behaviour when contemplating and comprehending the unfamiliar. Their 'inner predisposition' was to begin with what they knew – or what they thought they knew – namely, the social structure of their own home country.[4]

But what sort of a starting point was this, and what were the implications and consequences of British perceptions of their domestic social order for British perceptions of their imperial social order? From Hegel to Marx, and from Engels to Said, it has been commonplace to suggest that Britons saw their own society (and, by extension, that of what became their settler dominions) as dynamic, individualistic, egalitarian, modernizing – and thus superior. By comparison with such a positive and progressive metropolitan perception, this argument continues, Britons saw society in their 'tropical' and 'oriental' colonies as enervated, hierarchical, corporatist, backward – and thus inferior.[5] But among its many flaws, this appealingly simplistic (and highly influential) contrast is based on a mistaken premise, in that it fundamentally misunderstands most Britons' perceptions of their domestic social world when their nation was at its zenith as an imperial power.

Far from seeing themselves as atomized individuals with no rooted sense of identity, or as collective classes coming into being and struggling with each other, or as equal citizens whose modernity engendered an unrivalled sense of progressive superiority, Britons generally conceived of themselves as belonging to an unequal society characterized by a seamless web of layered gradations, which were hallowed by time and precedent, which were sanctioned by tradition and religion, and which extended in a great chain of being from the monarch at the top to the humblest subject at the bottom.[6] That was how they saw themselves, and it was from that starting point that they contemplated and tried to comprehend the distant realms and diverse society of their empire. This in turn meant that for the British, their overseas realms were at least as much about sameness as they were about difference. For insofar as they regarded their empire as 'one vast interconnected world', they did not necessarily do so in disadvantaged or critical contrast to the way they perceived their own metropolitan society. Rather, they were at least as likely to envisage the social structure of their empire – as their predecessors had done before them – by analogy to what they knew of 'home', or in replication of it, or in parallel to it, or in extension of it, or (sometimes) in idealization of it, or (even, and increasingly) in nostalgia for it.[7]

This means that we need to be much more attentive to the varied – sometimes, even, contradictory – ways in which the British understood, visualized and imagined their empire hierarchically. To be sure, *one* of the ways in which they did so was in racial terms of superiority and inferiority. Like all post-Enlightenment imperial powers, only more so, Britons saw themselves as the lords of all the world and thus of humankind. They placed themselves at the top of the scale of civilization and achievement, they ranked all other races in descending order beneath them, according to their relative merits (and de-merits), and during the period 1780 to 1830 they increasingly embodied these views in imperial institutions and codes.[8] And when it came to the systematic settlement of Canada, Australia, New Zealand and South Africa, they did not hesitate to banish the indigenous peoples to the margins of the new, imperial society. By the end of the nineteenth century these notions of racial hierarchy, supremacy and stereotyping had become more fully developed, and stridently hardened, as exemplified in Cecil Rhodes's remark that 'the British are the finest race in the world, and the more of the world they inhabit, the better it will be for mankind' [1877], or in Lord Cromer's belief that the world was divided between those who were British and those who were merely 'subject races' [1908].[9]

In short, and as Peter Marshall has observed, 'Empire reinforced a hierarchical view of the world, in which the British occupied a preeminent place among the colonial powers, while those subjected to colonial rule were ranged below them, in varying degrees of supposed inferiority.'[10] These facts are familiar and incontrovertible. But this mode of imperial ranking and imaging was not just based on the Enlightenment view of the intrinsic inferiority of dark-skinned peoples: it was also based on notions of metropolitan–peripheral analogy and sameness. For as the British contemplated the unprecedented numbers massed together in their new industrial cities, they tended to compare these great towns at home with the 'dark continents' overseas, and thus equate the workers in factories with coloured peoples abroad. The 'shock cities' of the 1830s and 1840s were seen as resembling 'darkest Africa' in their distant, unknown and unfathomable menaces; and during the third quarter of the nineteenth century London's newly discovered 'residuum' and 'dangerous classes' were likened – in their character and their conduct – to the 'negroes' of empire. And these domestic–imperial analogies were worked and extended in the opposite direction as well: one additional reason why 'natives' in the empire were regarded as collectively inferior was that they were seen as the overseas equivalent of the 'undeserving poor' in Britain.[11]

To some degree, then, these analogies and comparisons that Britons drew and made between domestic and overseas societies, from the eighteenth to the twentieth centuries, served to reinforce the prevailing Enlightenment notions of racial superiority and inferiority. And it is from this premise that the British Empire has been viewed by contemporaries and by historians as an enterprise that was built and maintained on the basis of the collective, institutionalized and politicized ranking of races. But, as these analogies and comparisons also suggest, this was not the only way in which Britons envisioned their empire, and its imperial society, as an essentially hierarchical organism. For there was another vantage-point from which they regarded the inhabitants of their far-flung realms, which was also built around notions of superiority and inferiority, but which frequently cut across, and sometimes overturned and undermined, the notion that the British Empire was based solely and completely on a hierarchy of race. This alternative approach was, indeed, the conventional way in which the English (and latterly the British) had regarded the inhabitants of other, alien worlds, for it was a perspective that long antedated the Enlightenment.

It has certainly been traced back to the sixteenth and seventeenth centuries, for when the English first encountered the native peoples of North America, they did not see them collectively as a race of inferior savages; on the contrary, they viewed them individually as fellow human beings. It was from this pre-Enlightenment perspective that the English concluded that North American society closely resembled their own: a carefully graded hierarchy of status, extending in a seamless web from chiefs and princes at the top to less worthy figures at the bottom. Moreover, these two essentially hierarchical societies were seen as coexisting, not in a relationship of (English) superiority and (North American) inferiority, but in a relationship of equivalence and similarity: princes in one society were the analogues to princes in another, and so on and so on, all the way down these two parallel social ladders. In short, when the English initially contemplated native Americans, they saw them as social equals rather than as social inferiors, and when they came to apply their conventionally hierarchical tools of observation, their prime grid of analysis was individual status rather than collective race.[12]

It is the argument of this book that these attitudes, whereby social ranking was as important as (perhaps more important than?) colour of skin in contemplating the extra-metropolitan world, remained important for the English and, latterly, for the British long after it has been generally supposed they ceased to matter. To be sure, the Enlightenment brought about a new, collective way of looking at peoples, races and colours, based on distance and separation and otherness. But it did not subvert the earlier, individualistic, analogical way of thinking, based on the observation of status similarities and the cultivation of affinities, that projected domestically originated perceptions of the social order overseas.[13] On the contrary, this essentially pre-racial way of seeing things lasted for as long as the British Empire lasted. Here is one example. In the summer of 1881 King Kalakaua of Hawaii was visiting England and, in the course of an extensive round of social engagements, he found himself the guest at a party given by Lady Spencer. Also attending were the prince of

Wales, who would eventually become King Edward VII, and the German crown prince, who was his brother-in-law and the future kaiser. The prince of Wales insisted that the king should take precedence over the crown prince, and when his brother-in-law objected, he offered the following pithy and trenchant justification: 'Either the brute is a king, or he's a common or garden nigger; and if the latter, what's he doing here?'[14]

Read one way, this is, to our modern sensibilities, a deeply insensitive and offensively racist observation; read from another viewpoint, this was, by the conventions of its own time, a very *un*racist remark. The traditional, pre-Enlightenment freemasonry [instinctive sense of brotherhood] based on the shared recognition of high social rank – a freemasonry to which Martin Malia has suggestively given the name 'aristocratic internationalism' – both trumped and transcended the alternative and more recent freemasonry based on the unifying characteristic of shared skin colour. From *this* perspective, the hierarchical principle that underlay Britons' perceptions of their empire was not exclusively based on the collective, colour-coded ranking of social groups, but depended as much on the more venerable colour-blind ranking of individual social prestige.[15] This means there were at least two visions of empire that were essentially (and elaborately) hierarchical: one centred on colour, the other on class. So, in the *Raj Quartet*, Major Ronald Merrick, whose social background was relatively lowly, believed that 'the English were superior to all other races, especially black'. But the Cambridge-educated Guy Perron feels a greater affinity with the Indian Hari Kumar, who went to the same public school as he did, than he does with Merrick, who is very much his social inferior.[16]

The British Empire has been extensively studied as a complex *racial* hierarchy (and also as a less complex *gender* hierarchy); but it has received far less attention as an equally complex *social* hierarchy or, indeed, as a social organism, or construct, of any kind. This constant (and largely unquestioned) privileging of colour over class, of race over rank, of collectivities over individualities, in the scholarly literature has opened up many important new lines of inquiry. But it has also meant that scarcely any attention has been paid to empire as a functioning social structure and as an imagined social entity, in which, as Karen Ordahl Kupperman puts it, 'status is fundamental to all other categories'.[17] Yet throughout its history, the views expressed by the prince of Wales reflected generally held opinions about the social arrangements existing in the empire. These attitudes and perceptions were certainly still in existence in the late eighteenth and early nineteenth centuries.[18] But they were no less important between the 1850s and the 1950s, when the ideal of social hierarchy was seen as the model towards which the great dominions should approximate, when it formed the basis of the fully elaborated Raj in India, when it provided the key to the doctrine of 'indirect rule' in Africa, when it formed the template for the new nations created in the British Middle East, when it was codified and rationalized by the imperial honours system, and when it was legitimated and unified by the imperial monarchy. In all these ways, the theory and the practice of social hierarchy served to eradicate the differences, and to homogenize the heterogeneities, of empire.

Of course, even in the heyday of empire these hierarchical structures and constructs, impulses and images, imaginings and ideologies, based on status rather than race, were never wholly pervasive or persuasive. And they were often founded on serious misunderstandings (sometimes deliberate, sometimes inadvertent) of imperial society, whether in the metropolis or on the periphery. But they *were* the conventional wisdom of the official mind in the metropolis, and of their collaborators on the peripheries, and of many people in Britain and the empire who also envisaged this 'vast interconnected world' in traditional, Burkeian terms. The rest of this book will sketch out, in a necessarily abridged and schematic form, an account of the British Empire in which the concept of hierarchy as social prestige is brought more closely to the centre of things than historians have generally allowed. As such, it urges the importance of seeing and understanding the British Empire as a mechanism for the export, projection and analogization of domestic social structures and social perceptions. For most of its history, the British visualized and understood their empire *on their own terms*, and we need to know more about what they were, and about how they did so. We should never forget that the British Empire was first and foremost a class act, where individual social ordering often took precedence over collective racial othering.

Notes

1   B. Anderson, *Imagined Communities: Reflections on the Origin and Spread of Nationalism* (London, 1983); E. J. Hobsbawm and T. O. Ranger (eds.), *The Invention of Tradition* (Cambridge, 1983).

2   J. Morris, *Pax Britannica: The Climax of an Empire* (London, 1968), p. 9; R. Hyam, *Britain's Imperial Century, 1815–1914* (London, 1976), p. 15; A. J. Stockwell, 'Power, Authority and Freedom', in P. J. Marshall (ed.), *The Cambridge Illustrated History of the British Empire* (Cambridge, 1996), pp. 154–6.

3   E. Hinderaker, 'The "Four Indian Kings" and the Imaginative Construction of the First British Empire', *W & MQ*, 3rd ser., liii (1996), p. 487.

4   M. Malia, *Russia Under Western Eyes: From the Bronze Horseman to the Lenin Mausoleum* (Cambridge, Mass., 1990), p. 9.

5   D. A. Washbrook, 'Economic Depression and the Making of "Traditional" Society in Colonial India, 1820–1855', *TRHS*, 6th ser., iii (1993), p. 239; E. W. Said, *Orientalism: Western Conceptions of the Orient* (Harmondsworth, 1995 edn.). For the most well-grounded historical critiques of the Said thesis, see J. M. MacKenzie, *Orientalism: History, Theory and the Arts* (Manchester, 1995); D. A. Washbrook, 'Orients and Occidents: Colonial Discourse Theory and the Historiography of the British Empire', in *OHBE* v, pp. 596–611. This contrast between an 'egalitarian' west and a 'hierarchical' orient has also been made by L. Dumont, *Homo Hierarchicus: The Caste System and Its Implications* (Chicago, 1991). See S. Barnett, L. Fruzzetti and A. Stor, 'Hierarchy Purified: Notes on Dumont and His Critics', *Journal of Asian Studies*, xxxv (1976), pp. 627–46.

6   D. Cannadine, *Class in Britain* (London, 1998); idem, 'Beyond Class? Social Structures and Social Perceptions in Modern England', *Proceedings of the British Academy*, xcvii (1997), pp. 95–118.

7   G. W. Stocking, *Race, Culture and Evolution: Essays in the History of Anthropology* (Chicago, 1982), p. 45; K. Malik, *The Meaning of Race: Race, History and Culture in Western Society* (London, 1996), pp. 5–6.

8   V. Kiernan, *The Lords of Human Kind: European Attitudes towards the Outside World in the Imperial Age* (London, 1969); A. Pagden, *Lords of All the World: Ideologies of Empire in Spain, Britain and France, c. 1500–c. 1800* (London, 1995); P. J. Marshall and G. Williams, *The Great Map of Mankind: British Perceptions of the World in the Age of Enlightenment* (London, 1982); C. A. Bayly, *Imperial Meridian: The British Empire and the World, 1780–1830* (London, 1989), pp. 147–55, 222; T. R. Metcalf, *Ideologies of the Raj* (Cambridge, 1995), pp. 30–34.

9   Hyam, *Britain's Imperial Century*, pp. 37–40, 78–85, 156–62; Lord Cromer, *Political and Literary Essays, 1908–1913* (Freeport, NY, 1969 edn.), pp. 12–14, 40–43.

10   P. J. Marshall, 'Imperial Britain', *JICH*, xxiii (1995), p. 385; idem, 'Britain without America – A Second Empire?', in *OHBE* ii, pp. 591–2; A. N. Porter, 'Introduction', in *OHBE* iii, pp. 21–5. For similar views, see J. Harris, *Private Lives, Public Spirit: A Social History of Britain, 1870–1914* (Oxford, 1993), pp. 6, 234–5; A. Marwick, *Class: Image and Reality in Britain, France and the USA since 1930* (London, 1980), p. 30.

11   A. Briggs, *Victorian Cities* (Harmondsworth, 1968), pp. 62–4, 313–16; G. Stedman Jones, *Outcast London: A Study in the Relationship between the Classes in Victorian Society* (Oxford, 1971); G. Himmelfarb, *The Idea of Poverty: England in the Early Industrial Age* (London, 1984), pp. 307–70; Malik, *The Meaning of Race*, pp. 92–100; M. J. Daunton and R. Halpern, 'Introduction: British Identities, Indigenous Peoples, and the Empire', and C. A. Bayly, The British and Indigenous Peoples, 1760–1860: Power, Perception and Identity', both in M. J. Daunton and R. Halpern (eds.), *Empire and Others: British Encounters with Indigenous Peoples, 1600–1850* (London, 1999), pp. 12, 33.

12   K. O. Kupperman, *Settling with the Indians: The Meeting of English and Indian Cultures in America, 1580–1640* (Totowa, NJ, 1980), pp. vii, 2–5, 35–8, 47–54, 120–27, 143–8.

13   This argument has been well made for the first half of the nineteenth century by D. Lorimer, *Colour, Class and the Victorians: Attitudes to the Negro in the Mid-Nineteenth Century* (Leicester, 1978), esp. pp. 67–8. But it underestimates the extent to which later Victorians persisted in seeing coloured people in this way. See B. Brereton, *Race Relations in Colonial Trinidad, 1870–1900* (Cambridge, 1979), p. 211; J. Fingard, 'Race and Respectability in Victorian Halifax', *JICH*, xx (1992), pp. 169–95.

14   P. Magnus, *King Edward the Seventh* (Harmondsworth, 1967), pp. 217–18. For an earlier instance of the prince of Wales's encounter with ruling monarchs, see F. Harcourt, 'The Queen, the Sultan and the Viceroy: A Victorian State Occasion', *The London Journal*, v (1979), pp. 35–56.

15   Malia, *Russia Under Western Eyes*, pp. 36–9. P. Mason, *Prospero's Magic: Some Thoughts on Class and Race* (London, 1962), p. 4, also noted the 'tacit alliance across a race barrier between top people'. See below, pp. 123–6.

16   H. Spurling, 'Paul Scott: Novelist and Historian', in W. R. Louis (ed.), *Adventures with Britannia: Personalities, Politics and Culture in Britain* (London, 1995), pp. 35–6; M. Gorra, *After Empire: Scott, Naipaul, Rushdie* (Chicago, 1997), pp. 35–6. In this regard, it is also worth noting this Colonial Office confidential memorandum on appointments: 'He must above all not be infected with racial snobbery. Colour prejudice in the colonial civil servant is the one unforgivable sin.': A. H. M. Kirk-Greene, *On Crown Service: A History of HM Colonial and Overseas Civil Services, 1837–1997* (London, 1999), p. 99. There was also, of course, a third imperial hierarchy, built around gender. For a suggestive discussion of the interrelatedness on these class, race and gender hierarchies, see A. McClintock, *Imperial Leather: Race, Gender and Sexuality in the Colonial Contest* (London, 1995), pp. 4–9.

17   Kupperman, *Settling with the Indians*, p. 4.

18   P. J. Marshall, 'Empire and Authority in the Later Eighteenth Century', *JICH*, xv (1987), pp. 105–22.

Chapter 50

George Fredrickson

THE CONCEPT OF RACISM IN HISTORICAL DISCOURSE

George Fredrickson, "The Concept of Racism in Historical Discourse", *Racism: A Short History*. (Princeton, NJ: Princeton University Press, 2003), 151–63, 167–70.

ALTHOUGH COMMONLY USED, "RACISM" has become a loaded and ambiguous term. Both sides in the current debate over affirmative action in the United States, for example, have used it to describe their opponents. It can mean either a lamentable absence of "color blindness" in an allegedly postracist age *or* insensitivity to past and present discrimination against groups that to be helped must be racially categorized. Once considered primarily a matter of belief or ideology, "racism" may now express itself in institutional patterns or social practices that have adverse effects on members of groups thought of as "races," even if a conscious belief that they are inferior or unworthy is absent. The term is clearly in danger of losing the precision needed to make it an analytical tool for historians and social scientists examining the relations among human groups or collectivities. But few would deny that we need, as a bare minimum, a strong expression to describe some horrendous acts of brutality and injustice that were clearly inspired by beliefs associated with the concept of race—the vilification, lynching, and segregation of African Americans in the South during the Jim Crow era; the Nazis' demonization and extermination of European Jewry; and the noncitizenship and economic servitude of South African blacks under apartheid.

These three clear-cut examples of racism in both theory and practice draw our attention to the fact that two kinds of people have been conspicuously victimized by this proclivity to denigrate and abuse others because of their physical characteristics, ancestry, and alleged spiritual deficiencies: people of color (especially blacks) and Jews. In the main body of this study I compare these two principal manifestations of racism and probe the connections between them. Insight into the genesis and context of this undertaking can perhaps be enhanced by a review of how previous scholarship, including my own, has dealt with racism as a historical subject—what meanings have been given to it and what lessons may be learned from this historiography about where we might go from here. In light of the multiple current meanings of the term, some historians and social scientists, including myself, have been tempted at times to exclude the word from our vocabularies. In the introduction to an early book on "white supremacy" in the United States and South Africa, "I concluded that racism is too ambiguous and loaded a term to describe my subject effectively."[1] In a recent essay, Loïc Wacquant, a prominent sociologist of race, advocates "forsaking once and for all the inflammatory and exceedingly ductile category of 'racism' save as a descriptive term referring to empirically analyzable doctrines and beliefs about 'race.' "[2]

Most historians of race and racism have in fact limited themselves to the study of racial doctrines and beliefs and would therefore be permitted by Wacquant to continue using the term. But it was in part the limitations of considering racism simply as a doctrine or set of ideas that encouraged me to substitute the term "white supremacy" to designate the white-over-black manifestation of it. I wanted to examine the relationship between the cultural aspects—racist attitudes, beliefs, and ideas—and structures and politics of racial domination. To put it another way, my interest was not merely in the history of ideas and attitudes but in the history of ideology in the broadest sense of that term. What also concerned me, therefore, was the relationship between attitudes and beliefs on the one hand and practices and institutions on the other. But I would insist that certain kinds of ideas and beliefs must be present, at some level of consciousness, in the minds of the practitioners of racism. If not, we would have no way to distinguish racism from classism, ethnocentrism, sexism, religious intolerance, ageism, or any other mode of allotting differential advantages or prestige to categories of people that vary, or seem to vary, in some important respect.

A further conceptual refinement can be derived from Kwame Anthony Appiah's distinction between racism and "racialism." He defines racialism as the belief "that there are heritable characteristics, possessed by members of our species, that allow us to divide them into a small set of races, in such a way that all the members of these races share certain traits and tendencies with each other that they do not share with members of any other race."[3] Such a belief essentializes differences but does not necessarily imply inequality or hierarchy. As a moral philosopher, Appiah finds such a viewpoint mistaken but not immoral. Racialists do not become racists until they make such convictions the basis for claiming special privileges for members of what they consider to be their own race, and for disparaging and doing harm to those deemed racially Other. In an early work on color-coded racism in the United States, I implicitly made a similar distinction when I coined the phrase "romantic racialism" to describe the belief commonly held by antebellum abolitionists of both races that blacks were intrinsically different from whites in temperament and psychology (more "spiritual" and less aggressive). I did not wish to use the pejorative "racism," because, for at least some of these antislavery men and women, the alleged peculiarities of blacks did not sanction a belief in their inferiority or justify enslaving them or discriminating against them.[4] But when groups whose differing ancestry is culturally and/or physically marked come into adversarial contact, there is a powerful temptation, especially on the part of the more powerful group, to justify aggression, domination, or extermination by invoking differences defined as "racial"—meaning that they are intrinsic and unchangeable.

Unlike some sociologists, I do not believe that one can regard race and ethnicity as clearly distinct and unrelated phenomena. To my way of thinking, groups designated as races could also be regarded as "ethnic" in the Weberian sense of being historical collectivities claiming descent from a common set of ancestors. Race can therefore be described as what happens when ethnicity is deemed essential or indelible and made hierarchical.[5] There are, however, cases—and African American ethnicity would be a prime example—in which ethnic identity is created by the racialization of people who would not otherwise have shared an identity. (Blacks did not think of themselves as blacks, Negroes, or even Africans when they lived in the various kingdoms and tribal communities of West Africa before the advent of the slave trade.) From this perspective, racism is the evil twin of ethnocentrism. The latter may involve racialism in Appiah's sense but can also be based on individual cultural identities that are not viewed as unchangeable. (Many pre-modern communities—American Indian tribes, for example—have regarded themselves as superior beings and their enemies as utterly unworthy of respect but have nevertheless readily assimilated captives and other strangers regardless of phenotype or cultural background.) The erroneous but relatively harmless doctrine of simple racialism is rarely found among members of the advantaged or dominant groups in a plural society, but *racism* is all too common. One is more likely to find tolerant or egalitarian racialism among stigmatized groups: they may embrace and reevaluate some of the differences traditionally attributed to them, attempting to change them from defects into virtues, thus affirming a positive cultural identity and making the case that difference does not mean inferiority.

The reason that my efforts to dispense with the problematic term "racism" in some of my earlier work came to naught was simply because I could not find a satisfactory alternative to describe the phenomena that I wished to study. "White supremacy" is limited in its application to only one type of racism—what I would now call the "colorcoded" or somatic variety. A review of the historical discourse on racism that began in the 1920s reveals that the term was first applied to ideologies making invidious distinctions among divisions of the "white" or Caucasian race, and especially to show that Aryans or Nordics were superior to other people normally considered "white" or "Caucasian." The term "race" has a long history, but "racism" goes back only to the early twentieth century, and the "ism" reflected the understanding of historians and others who wrote about it that they were dealing with a questionable set of beliefs and not undeniable facts of nature. It might be said that the concept of racism emerges only when the concept of race, or at least some of its applications, begin to be questioned. Our understanding of the core function of racism—its assigning of fixed or permanent differences among human descent groups and using this attribution of difference to justify their differential treatment—has changed less during the past century than have the specific categories of people who are viewed as its victims.

The historiographies of the two most conspicuous manifestations of racism—white supremacism and antisemitism—have proceeded along different tracks. Historians and sociologists concerned with one kind of racism have generally shown little interest in the work done on the other. When racism has been a central concept in this work, it has often been defined in such a group-specific way that a wider application is made difficult, if not foreclosed entirely. For example, one can readily agree with the British sociologist Zygmunt Bauman's short definition of racism, which precedes his discussion of how it applies to the Holocaust: "Man is before he acts; nothing he does may change what he is. This is roughly the philosophical essence of racism." But he then proceeds to limit the concept to cases where the aim is the extermination or expatriation of the racialized other.[6] Hence white supremacy, which normally involves the domination rather than elimination of the Other, ceases to be racism. When I myself defined the essence of racism as the ideas, practices, and institutions associated with a rigid form of ethnic hierarchy, I was unwittingly privileging the white supremacist variant over the antisemitic form, which presses toward the dissolution of the hierarchy through the expulsion or destruction of the lower-status group.[7]

Although the historiographies of white supremacy and antisemitism have not, for the most part, engaged each other, a small number of scholars, going back to the 1920s, have examined racism historically in a way that was not group-specific—as a mode of thought or set of attitudes with varying or multiple targets. Understanding which groups were considered the primary victims and how the racists whose ideas were being analyzed identified themselves and the group to which they belonged may provide a kind of lineage for my short history. But there is one aspect of these studies that may trouble some advocates of scholarly objectivity. Scholars who were hostile to what they were writing about have produced virtually all such examinations of racism. In many cases (especially at times when racism was respectable) a central purpose of their work was to discredit the ideas they were describing. While this did not mean that they were producing propaganda rather than scholarship, it did mean that they either argued for, or clearly assumed, the falsity and perniciousness of the beliefs or attitudes they were examining. But is an objective or nonjudgmental history of racism really possible? The history of racism or (as some would have it) "racisms" began as a branch of intellectual history, or the history of ideas, at a time when concepts of racial hierarchy were widely accepted. If the historian had simply described the ideas in the terms that their proponents would have found acceptable and given no direct or implicit indication that they were false and harmful, he or she would in fact have been encouraging their promulgation and contributing to their legitimization. The most fruitful orientation at a time like our own, when racism is generally condemned in principle, is a clinical one. It is legitimate to assume, at the beginning of the twenty-first century—as it might not have been at the beginning of the twentieth—that racism is an evil analogous to a deadly disease. But the responsibility of the historian or sociologist who studies racism is not to moralize and condemn but to understand this malignancy so that it can be more effectively treated, just as a medical researcher studying cancer does not moralize about it but searches for knowledge that might point the way to a cure.

[. . .]

[. . .] Frank H. Hankins's *The Racial Basis of Civilization*, published in 1926, [was] the first work by an American that dealt in part with the history of what the author called "racialism." It was an attack on the theory of Nordic superiority that was popularized in the United States by the writings of Madison Grant and the successful campaign for the restriction of immigration from southern and eastern Europe.[8] A sociologist who taught at Smith College, Hankins was himself a racialist in Appiah's sense (if not his own) and would today be considered a racist in his attitude toward blacks, although for him a belief in black genetic inferiority did not constitute racism or "racialism" but was simply established scientific fact. "While we are denying the extravagant claims of the Nordicists," he wrote, "we also deny the equally perverse and doctrinaire claim of the race egalitarians. There is no respect apparently in which the races are equal; but their differences must be thought of in terms of relative frequencies and not as absolute differences in kind."[9] Hankins described and sharply criticized the views of the classic European exponents of Nordicism, Teutonism, or Aryanism. "The most obvious error of the *racialists*," he concluded, "has been the claim of a purity of blood and of a specific civilizing potency which the facts do not bear out." During the recent world war, "the doctrines of race purity and superiority had a perceptibly larger significance in Germany than elsewhere."[10] Like Simar, therefore, Hankins was striking back at claims of Nordic or Teutonic supremacy that he associated with the German aggressiveness that had allegedly caused World War I. But as an American, Hankins could scarcely avoid thinking of race as also being color-coded, and here he accepted the judgments of most of his white fellow citizens. "Although the negro [*sic*] has on many occasions lived in contact with centers of advanced culture or even in the midst of them," he wrote, "he has generally lagged behind the level of such cultures." Negro backwardness is the product of biological factors, especially brain size, and therefore cannot be "explained by lack of opportunity."[11]

Hankins, the professed critic of European "racialism," thus stood on the enduring bedrock of American racism—the belief that Americans of European or white ancestry are collectively superior in intelligence and creativity to people of African descent. His single heresy, from this white supremacist perspective, was his general approval of race mixture, including intermarriage between blacks and whites. Mulattoes, he thought, had a good chance to adapt to "advanced culture," and if they were light enough to pass for white, so much the better. His biological racism was therefore more logical (some would say more Brazilian) in its application than the conventional American "one-drop rule."[12] In his references to Jews, Hankins showed little or no awareness of the dangers of a politicized antisemitism, although he did heap ridicule on some myths about Jews, such as Houston Chamberlain's fantasy that Jesus was really an Aryan. Denying that Jews were "a race in any strict sense," he described them as "a social group which in many times and places has been more vigorously hated than the negro [sic] in many parts of the United States during the last half century. The Jew has not only fought his own battle but he has 'come back' with almost obnoxious persistency and 'nerve' after every rebuff."[13] Hankins thus managed to put down blacks for their failure to rebound as Jews did, while at the same time, in his use of the adjective "obnoxious," revealing a touch of the genteel Anglo-American antisemitism that was rife in the 1920s.

With the rise of Hitler to power in Germany in 1933, the centrality of antisemitism to "the doctrine of races" or "racialism" in the modern world became fully apparent for the first time. It was Magnus Hirschfeld, prominent German sexologist of the Weimar era and early champion of homosexual rights, who first gave real currency to the term "racism" by making it the title of a book. Hirschfeld, an assimilated Jew, had the good sense to flee when the Nazis took power, and he finished his critique of Nazi ethnological theories as an exile in Nice, where he died in 1935, leaving the work unpublished. The manuscript entitled "Rassismus" was subsequently translated into English and published as Racism in 1938.[14] As might be expected, the book is primarily a history, analysis, and refutation of the racial doctrines that the Nazis brought with them and put into practice when they gained control of Germany. As a scientist who was ahead of his time, Hirschfeld had found little of value or substance in the concept of race: "If it were practicable, we should certainly do well to eradicate the term 'race' as far as subdivisions of the human species are concerned."[15] Hirschfeld, who thought of himself as an objective scholar and a cosmopolitan rather than an ethnic loyalist, could make analogies between Germans and Jews, which, in light of the Holocaust, would now seem offensive. "Both peoples regard themselves as elect or chosen, and both are very strongly disliked by everyone else."[16] But he perceptively described the psychosocial sources of racism when he explained the ascendancy of German antisemitism as a reaction to the loss of the First World War and the difficulties that followed. Racism, he wrote, serves as a safety valve against a sense of catastrophe. It seems "to provide for a restoration of self-esteem, for satisfaction for the assertive impulse of a will to power by tyrannizing over an enemy within the gates who was certainly more accessible and less dangerous to tackle than a reputed enemy across the national frontiers."[17]

[. . .]

Since the bifurcation of studies of white supremacy and antisemitism that took place after World War II, there have been few serious efforts to write histories of racism that encompass both the antisemitic and the color-coded varieties. The first comprehensive history of American racism, Thomas Gossett's Race: The History of an Idea in America (1963) traced consciousness of race to the ancient world.[18] Its treatment of specifically American manifestations cast its net quite wide to include representation and treatment of American Indians and immigrants from southern and eastern Europe, including Jews, as well as blacks. But most subsequent work on the history of American racism has been group-specific and has concentrated most heavily on attitudes toward African Americans. On the other hand, George Mosse's general history of European racism, published in 1978, focused mainly on the growth of racist antisemitism and paid relatively little attention to the colorcoded racism associated with imperial expansion.[19] There appear to be only two significant attempts to cover Western attitudes toward race comprehensively: Ivan Hannaford's *Race: The History of an Idea in the West* (1996)[20] and Imanuel Geiss, *Geschichte der Rassismus* (History of racism) published in Germany in 1988 and never translated into English.[21] Hannaford's study, as its title indicates, is strictly an intellectual history and considers race as a concept more than racism as an ideology. It argues strenuously that no clear concept of race existed before the seventeenth century, thus raising the issue of whether anything that existed before the invention of race in the modern sense can legitimately be labeled racism. Geiss, to the contrary, sees racism as anticipated in most respects by the ethnocentrism or xenophobia that developed in the ancient world, as reflected, for example, in the Old Testament.

My own conception, as set forth in the introduction and applied throughout the *Short History*, falls between Hannaford's view that race and racism are peculiarly modern ideas and Geiss's notion that they are simply manifestations of the perennial phenomena of ethnocentrism and xenophobia. I have attempted to develop an understanding that is neither too broad for historical specificity nor too narrow to cover more than the limited span of Western history during which a racism based on scientific theories of human variation was widely accepted. If racism is defined as an ideology rather than as a theory, links can be established between belief and practice that the history of ideas may obscure. But ideologies have content, and it is necessary to distinguish racist ideologies from other belief systems that emphasize human differences and can be used as rationalizations of inequality. The classic sociological distinction between racism and ethnocentrism is helpful, but not perhaps in the usual sense, in which the key variable is whether differences are described in cultural or physical terms. It is actually quite difficult in specific historical cases to say whether appearance or "culture" is the source of the salient differences, because culture can be reified and essentialized to the point where it has the same deterministic effect as skin color. But we would be stretching the concept of racism much too far if we attempted to make it cover the pride and loyalty that may result from a strong sense of ethnic identity. Such group-centeredness may engender prejudice and discrimination against those outside the group, but two additional elements would seem to be required before the categorization of racism is justified. One is a belief that the differences between the ethnic groups involved are permanent and ineradicable. If conversion or assimilation is a real possibility, we have religious or cultural intolerance but not racism. The second is the social and political side of the ideology—its linkage to the exercise of power in the name of race and the resulting patterns of domination or exclusion. To attempt a short formulation, we might say that racism exists when one ethnic group or historical collectivity dominates, excludes, or seeks to eliminate another on the basis of differences that it believes are hereditary and unalterable.

Notes

1   George M. Fredrickson, *White Supremacy: A Comparative Study in American and South African History* (New York, 1981), xii.

2   Loïc J. D. Wacquant, "For an Analytic of Racial Domination," in *Political Power and Social Theory*, vol. 11, ed. Diane E. Davis (Greenwich, Conn., 1997), 222.

3   Kwame Anthony Appiah, "Racisms," in *Anatomy of Racism*, ed. David Theo Goldberg (Minneapolis, 1990), 4–5.

4   See George M. Fredrickson, *The Black Image in the White Mind: The Debate on Afro-American Character and Destiny, 1817–1914* (Middletown, Conn., 1987; orig. pub. 1971), 97–129.

5   I develop this argument in my essay "Understanding Racism," in *The Comparative Imagination: On the History of Racism, Nationalism, and Social Movements* (Berkeley, 1997), 77–97.

6   Zygmunt Bauman, *Modernity and the Holocaust* (Ithaca, 1989), 60–82 (quotation on 60).

7   "Understanding Racism."

8   See chap. 2 [the original source].

9   Frank H. Hankins, *The Racial Basis of Civilization: A Critique of the Nordic Doctrine* (New York, 1926), ix.

10   Ibid., 89, 93.

11   Ibid., 306–307.

12   Ibid., 343–348.

13   Ibid., 307.

14   Magnus Hirschfeld, *Racism* (Port Washington, N.Y., 1973; orig. pub. 1938).

15   Ibid., 57.

16   Ibid., 228.

17   Ibid., 360.

18   Thomas F. Gossett, *Race: The History of an Idea in America* (Dallas, 1963).

19   George L. Mosse, *Toward the Final Solution: A History of European Racism* (Madison, 1978).

20   Ivan Hannaford, *Race: The History of an Idea in the West* (Baltimore, 1996).

21   Imanuel Geiss, *Geschichte der Rassismus* (Frankfurt am Main, 1988).

Further Reading: Chapters 47 to 50

Abdel-Malek, A. "Orientalism In Crisis", *Diogenes* 44 (1963), 103–401.

Ahmed, Aijaz. *In Theory: Classes, Nations, Literatures* (London: Verso, 1992).

Anderson, Benedict R. O'G. *Imagined Communities: Reflections on the Origin and Spread of Nationalism* (2nd edn) (London: Verso, 1991).

Axel, Brian Keith. *From the Margins: Historical Anthropology and Its Futures* (Durham, NC: Duke University Press, 2002).

Balibar, Etienne. "The Nation Form: History and Ideology". Trans. Immanuel Wallerstein and Chris Turner, *Review* 13(3) (1990), 329–61.

Ballantyne, Tony (ed.). "Special Issue: From Orientalism to Ornamentalism", *Journal of Colonialism and Colonial History* 3(1) (2002).

Bennett, Tony. *The Birth of the Museum: History, Theory, Politics* (London: Routledge, 1994).

Bernstein, Barton J. (ed.). *Towards A New Past: Dissenting Essays in American History* (New York: Pantheon Books, 1968).

Bhaba, Homi. "Of Mimicry and Man: The Ambivalence of Colonial Discourse", *The Location of Culture* (London: Routledge, 1994), 125–33.

Boas, F. *Primitive Art* (New York: Dover Publications, 1955).

— . "Some Principles of Museum Administration", *Science* 25 (1907), 921–33.

Boehmer, Elleke. *Colonial and Postcolonial Literature* (Oxford: Oxford University Press, 1995).

Brightman, Robert. "Forget Culture: Replacement, Transcendence, Relexification", *Cultural Anthropology* 10(4) (1995), 509–46.

Burckhardt, Jacob. "The Three Powers", *Reflections on History* Trans. Marie D. Hottinger (London: George Allen & Unwin, 1943), 33–65.

Carrier, J. L. "Occidentalism: the World Turned Upside Down", *American Ethnologist* 19(2) (1992), 195–212.

Chakrabarty, Dipesh. "Postcoloniality and the Artifice of History: Who Speaks for the 'Indian' Pasts?" *Representations* 37 (1992), 1–26.

— . *Provincializing Europe: Postcolonial Tics of Ethnography* (Berkeley: University of California Press, 1986).

Chaudhuri, Nupur and Ruth R. Pierson (eds). *Nation, Empire, Colony: Historicizing Race and Gender* (Bloomington: Indiana University Press, 1998).

Clifford, James. *The Predicament of Culture* (Cambridge, MA: Harvard University Press, 1988).

— . *Writing Culture: The Poetics and Polical Thought and Historical Difference* (Princeton, NJ: Princeton University Press, 2000).

Cohen, Bernard. *An Anthropologist Amongst Historians* (Oxford: Oxford University Press, 1987).

Comaroff, John and Jean Comaroff. *Modernity and Its Malcontents: Ritual Power in Post-Colonial Africa* (Chicago: University of Chicago Press, 1993).

Confino, Alon. "Collective Memory and Cultural History: Problems of Method", *The American Historical Review* 102(5) (1997), 1386–403.

Cooper, Frederick and Ann Laura Stoler. "Between Metropole and Colony: Rethinking a Research Agenda", *Tensions of Empire: Colonial Cultures in a Bourgeois World*, Cooper and Stoler (eds) (Berkeley: University of California Press, 1997).

Darnton, Robert. *The Great Cat Massacre and Other Episodes in French Cultural History* (New York: Basic Books, 1984).

Droysen, J. G. "Cultural History", *Texte zur Geschichtstheorie*. Trans. Robert M. Burns (Göttingen: Vandenhoeck & Ruprecht, 1972), 27–30.

Fabian, Johannes. *Time and the Other* (New York: Columbia University Press, 1983).

Fieldhouse, D. K. " 'Imperialism': An Historiographical Revision", *Economic History Review* 14(2) (1961), 187–209.

Gandhi, Leela. *Postcolonial Theory: A Critical Introduction* (Edinburgh: Edinburgh University Press, 1998).

Ginsburg, Carlo. *The Cheese and the Worms: The Cosmos of a Sixteenth-Century Miller*. Trans. J. and A. Tedeschi (Baltimore: Johns Hopkins University Press, 1980).

Green, Anna. *Cultural History* (Basingstoke: Palgrave Macmillan, 2008).

Greenblatt, Stephen. "Culture", *Critical Terms for Literary Study*, Frank Lentricchia and Thomas McLaughlin (eds) (Chicago: University of Chicago Press, 1995), 225–31.

Guha, Ranajit (ed). *A Subaltern Studies Reader, 1986–1995* (Minneapolis: University of Minnesota Press, 1997).

Holt, Thomas C. "Marking: Race, Race-making, and the Writing of History", *The American Historical Review* 100(1) (1995), 1–20.

Hourani, A. *Islam in European Thought* (Cambridge: Cambridge University Press, 1992).

Huizinga, Johan. "The Task of Cultural History", *Men and Ideas: History, the Middle Ages, the Renaissance*. Trans. James S. Holmes and Hans van Marle (New York: Meridian).

Hunt, Lynn (ed.). *The New Cultural History* (Berkeley: University of California Press, 1989).

Jörn, Rüsen. "Some Theoretical Approaches to Intercultural Comparative Historiography", *History and Theory* 35(4) (1996), 5–22.

Kelley, Donald R. "The Old Cultural History", *History of the Human Sciences* 9(3) (1996), 101–26.

Kolchin, Peter. "Re-evaulating the Antebellum Slave Community: A Comparative Perspective", *Journal of American History* 70(3) (1983), 579–601.

Kramer, Lloyd. "Historical Narratives and the Meaning of Nationalism", *Journal of the History of Ideas* 58(3) (1997), 524–45.

Leela, Gandhi. *Postcolonial Theory* (Edinburgh: Edinburgh University Press, 1998).

Lévi-Strauss, Claude. *Tristes Tropiques*. Trans. J. Russell (London: Atheneum, 1963).

Lorenz, Chris. "Comparative Historiography: Problems and Persepctives", *History and Theory* 38(1) (1999), 25–39.

Marcus, George. *Writing Culture* (Berkeley: University of California Press, 1986).

— . and Michael Fischer. *Anthropology as Cultural Critique* (Chicago: University of Chicago Press, 1986).

Medick, Hans. "Missionaries in the Row Boa", *Comparative Studies in Society and History* 29 (1987), 76–98.

Moore-Gilbert, Bart. *Postcolonial Theory: Contexts, Practices, Politics* (London: Verso, 1997).

Nugent, Paul. *Postcolonial History and the Longue Durée: Africa Since Independence, A Comparative History* (Basingstoke: Palgrave Macmillan, 2004).

O'Hanlon, Rosalind and David Washbrook. "After Orientalism: Culture, Criticism, and Politics in the Third World", *Comparative Studies in Society and History* 34(1) (1992), 141–67.

Parish, Peter J. *Slavery: History and Historians* (New York: Harper & Row, 1989).

Prakash, Gyan. "Writing Post-Orientalist Histories of the Third World: Perspectives from Indian Historiography", *Comparative Studies in Society and History* 32(2) (1990), 383–408.

Renan, Ernest. "What Is a Nation?" *Becoming National: A Reader*, Geoff Eley and Ronald Grigor Suny (eds) (Oxford: Oxford University Press, 1996), 41–55.

Rodinson, Maxime. "The Western Image and Western Studies of Islam", *The Legacy of Islam*, Joseph Schacht and C. E. Boswarth (eds) (2nd edn). (Oxford: Clarendon Press, 1974).

Schapera, I. "Should Anthropologists Be Historians?", *Journal of the Royal Anthropological Institute* 92 (1962), 143–56.

— . "Language and Practice in Cultural History", *French Historical Studies* 21(2) (1998), 241–54.

Scott, James C. *Weapons of the Weak: Everyday Forms of Peasant Resistance* (New Haven: Yale University Press, 1985).

Simpson, Moira G. *Making Representations: Museums in the Post-Colonial Era* (London: Routledge, 1996).

Spivak, Gayatri Chakravorty. *The Post-Colonial Critic: Essays, Strategies, Dialogues*, Sarah Harasym (ed.) (New York: Routledge, 1990).

Steedman, C. "Culture, Cultural Studies, and the Historians", *Cultural Studies*, Grossberg et al. (eds) (London: Routledge, 1992).

Stone, L. "History and the Social Sciences in the Twentieth Century", *The Future of History*, C. Delzell (ed.) (Nashville, TN: Vanderbilt University Press, 1977).

Stovall, Tyler. "The Color Line behind the Lines: Racial Violence in France during the Great War", *The American Historical Review* 103(3) (1998), 737–69.

Taussig, Michael. *The Devil and Commodity Fetishism in South America* (Chapel Hill: University of North Carolina Press, 1980).

Thomas, Keith. "History and Anthropology", *Past and Present* 24 (1963), 3–24.

Thomas, Nicholas. *Colonialism's Culture* (Princeton: Princeton University Press, 1994).

Washbrook, D. A. "Orients and Occidents: Colonial Discourse Theory and the Historiography of the British Empire", *Oxford History of the British Empire: Historiography*, R. W. Winks (ed.) (Oxford: Oxford University Press, 1999), 596–611.

Wolfe, Patrick. "History and Imperialism: A Century of Theory from Marx to Postcolonialism", *The American Historical Review* 102(2) (1997): 388–420.

Young, Robert. *Colonial Desire: Hybridity in Theory, Culture and Race* (London: Routledge, 1995).

—— . *Postcolonialism: An Historical Introduction* (Oxford: Blackwell, 2001).

GEERTZ, CLIFFORD (1926–2006)

Abu-Lughod, Lila. "The Interpretation of Culture(s) After Television", *Representations* 59 (1997), 109–34.

Colson, Elizabeth. "Review: The Interpretation of Cultures", *Contemporary Sociology* 4(6) (1975), 637–8.

Geertz, Clifford. *After the Fact: Two Countries, Four Decades, One Anthropologist* (Cambridge, MA: Harvard University Press, 1995).

Ortner, Sherry B. (ed.). *The Fate of "Culture": Geertz and Beyond* (Berkeley: University of California Press, 1999).

— . "Introduction: Special Issue: The Fate of 'Culture': Geertz and Beyond", *Representations* 59 (1997), 1–13.

Rice, Kenneth A. *Geertz and Culture* (Ann Arbor: University of Michigan Press, 1980).

Sewell Jr., William H. "Geertz, Cultural Systems, and History: From Synchrony to Transformation", *Representations* 59 (1997), 35–55.

Shankman, Paul et al. "The Thick and the Thin: On the Interpretive Theoretical Program of Clifford Geertz [and Comments and Reply]", *Current Anthropology* 25(3) (1984), 261–80.

Shweder, Richard A. and Byron Good (eds). *Clifford Geertz By His Colleagues* (Chicago: University of Chicago Press, 2005).

Swidler, Ann. "Review: Geertz's Ambiguous Legacy", *Contemporary Sociology* 25(3) (1996), 299–302.

Windschuttle, Keith: "The Ethnocentrism of Clifford Geertz", *New Criterion* 21(2) (2002), 5–12.

SAID, EDWARD (1935–2003)

Chambers, Ross and Amal Rassam. "Comments on Orientalism. Two Reviews", *Comparative Studies in Society and History* 22(4) (1980), 505–12.

Dawn, C. Ernest. "Review: Orientalism", *The American Historical Review* 84(5) (1979), 1334.

Inden, Ronald. "Orientalist Constructions of India", *Modern Asian Studies* 20(3) (1986), 401–46.

Mudimbe, V. Y. *The Idea of Africa* (Bloomington: Indiana University Press, 1994).

Prakash, Gyan. "Writing Post-Orientalist Histories of the Third World", *Colonialism and Culture*, N. B. Dirks (ed.) (Ann Arbor: University of Michigan Press, 1992), 353–88.

—— . "Orientalism Now", *History and Theory* 34(3) (1995), 199–212.

Rich, Paul John. *The Invasions of the Gulf: Radicalism, Ritualism and the Shaikhs* (Cambridge: Allborough Press, 1991).

Said, Edward. "Orientalism Reconsidered", *Cultural Critique* 1 (1985), 89–107.

Spivak, Gayatri Chakravorty. "Subaltern Studies: Deconstructing Historiography", *Selected Subaltern Studies*, Ranajit Guha and Gayatri Chakravorty Spivak (eds) (Oxford: Oxford University Press, 1988).

Sprinker, Michael (ed.). *Edward Said: A Critical Reader* (Oxford: Blackwell, 1992).

PART 13

The social history of material objects

INTRODUCTION

FOR MOST OF THE CONTRIBUTORS to this volume, and especially those who approach history under Ranke's influence (see Part 5), historical research limits itself to printed or manuscript documents. This legacy runs deep, because even those who point to the restrictions that language enforces on our historical perspective (see Part 10) have chosen to use writing as their means of historical expression. For centuries before the advent of German historicism, non-literary objects such as old paintings, royal medals and stamps, antique statues, inscribed monuments, and even woven tapestries provided the primary sources and vehicles for historical research.[i] Thinking beyond the linguistic frame through which modern historiography has been shaped, this section considers the material objects that document the history of human relationships. These include the objects that reveal our historical relationship

---

i The best indication of the range of methods and objects used by antiquarians during this period is Montfaucon, *L'Antiquité expliquée et representé en figures* (1719, trans. 1721–2), whose ten illustrated volumes catalogued every conceivable object that could cast light on the ancient past. It was organized by topic, with sections devoted to religious objects, objects of warfare, transport, dress, and so on. For a comprehensive study of the artists, craftsmen, and antiquaries who chose non-literary methods to depict and interpret history, see F. Haskell, *History and Its Images: Art and the Interpretation of the Past* (New Haven: Yale University Press, 1993), esp. 131–58. As late as 1777, Voltaire's article on "History" in *L'Encyclopédie* called attention to marble friezes as "our only incontestable knowledge that we have of the *history* of antiquity." On contemporary history-writing in the form of public etchings, see note xi. For a much more recent survey of current trends in visual history, see Ivan Gaskell, "Visual History", *New Perspectives on Historical Writing*, P. Burke (ed.) (2nd edn) (Cambridge: Polity Press, 2001), 187–217. More recently, documentary cinema is a popular means by which historians have sought to engage with the past, particularly when depicting personal memories: see P. Rabinowitz, "Wreckage upon Wreckage: History, Documentary, and the Ruins of Memory", *History and Theory* 32 (1993), 119–37. For an animated discussion of television as a medium for communicating "public history", see S. Schama, "Fine-Cutting Clio", *The Public Historian* 25 (Summer 2003), 15–25.

to physical things (like clothing or dishes), representational things (such as money or credit), and to the idea of things (like personal cleanliness or parenthood). The social history of objects also provides a suggestive contrast to the enduring Rankeian interest in the history of great men and great events, for its equally focused concerns and analytic methods recover and examine the objects that fill the history of everyday life. The authors who prepared the sources in this section address readers from across fields and contexts, from a British historian of eighteenth-century shopping habits to a German archaeologist digging in Sicily to a French anthropologist writing about gift-giving rituals in the South Pacific. Yet each is preoccupied with the same questions all of us raise when considering the methods we use to examine the past: what defined the meaning of a historical object? What is our justification for such a definition? And how do associated concepts reflect past opinions of that same object? By considering the social history of things, this section suggests the broad range of directions that approaches to history have sought to develop, even when they have united around one topic.

Researchers who are interested in material history need to be particularly aware of the methods they adopt when defining their objects of study, and not only because their questions emerge from numerous disciplines. They discover, immediately, that the technical functions, emotional resonance, and social meaning of objects change readily. As these sources show, this critical self-awareness means occupying a paradoxical position with regard to any claim to historicism. How can we envision or enact a historical sensibility that assumed something was familiar when that thing is now considered exotic—or disgusting? This point might best be illustrated by showing its inverse: look around at the objects that surround you right now. These things might include interior lighting, a table, a chair, a writing instrument, perhaps a porcelain cup filled with a warm drink. We might assume that these objects are so typical of domestic life that they have always been here, performing the same roles. Historians of material culture research not only the history of books, furniture, dishes, and food, but also the ways we have thought about those things, and why. Some even go further, to study the history of material habits: one of the following readings shows that it is only during the past 220 years or so that Europeans have used water when washing ourselves, and that in turn we have come to believe that washing with water is required for cleanliness, healthiness, attractiveness, and even moral purity.[ii] So it might be difficult to imagine that cleanliness had been signified (for much longer than 220 years) by the display of white linen, not clean skin. Indeed, for many centuries, the very idea of bathing in water was considered sickening—because water was considered a primary source of disease. Writing a social history of cleanliness, then, poses challenges that relate to methods (how do we locate sources for something whose presence or absence was just assumed?) and to sensibility: how should we interpret such assumptions? Recalling the challenging historicist questions raised by Vico, Collingwood, Butterfield, and others, it takes significant imaginative and scholarly effort to interpret the meaning of something when that thing is at once so familiar to us, was quite foreign to the past, and yet understanding it remains crucial for our project as historians.

The first source in this section describes the editorial goals of the *Journal of Material Culture*.

---

ii   Apart from Vigarello, for an insightful discussion on historical associations between immersion and purity (which ranges from the Romans to the present), see V. Smith, *Clean: A History of Personal Hygiene and Purity* (Oxford: Oxford University Press, 2007).

Like two other journals discussed in this book (in Part 8), the *JMC* has sought to provide a forum for collaboration among scholars working in different areas of research. Since "no single discipline can claim a monopoly on knowledge", studies in the materiality of human existence require particular contributions from fields that concern the making, meaning, consumption, and interpretation of material objects across time and across social contexts. Taking the example of domestic architecture and landscape design, as well as the organization of museums, the editors pointed out that a deeper understanding of the ways people manage physical space requires specialist expertise—in cultural anthropology, urban and interior design, economics, aesthetics, and psychology. Thinking critically about the psychological (individual) or symbolic (cultural) meaning of "physical space", the editors have addressed the atmosphere created by "the materiality of music", pointing out that even a non-physical thing like rock music shapes our experience of our surroundings, whether that music is transmitted discreetly through headphones or through speakers that shake furniture. But should we assume that a current perception of an auditory experience is universal? What factors contribute to a variation in perceptions of an identical physical event? We know that the production of music involves objects: which criteria should we use to define their design?

Taking these questions further, the editors gesture to anthropological studies of Melanesia (the vast area extends from parts of Indonesia to New Caledonia to Fiji), remarking that "the dichotomy of persons and things is itself a particular historical and regional phenomenon". Addressing the historicity of that presumed "dichotomy" means questioning our very ideas of what constitutes a specific object, its ownership, and its exchange-value. The editors are referring indirectly to the widely-influential French anthropologist Marcel Mauss, nephew and student of Émile Durkheim (see Part 6).[iii] Mauss contributed to numerous fields, from sociology to political science, by examining the social values represented by the gifts we give to one another. By focusing on the sense of obligation that governs the practice of gift-giving in numerous societies, Mauss showed that the exchanged object should be considered as important as the people who give or receive it. Indeed, in some cases the gift should be understood as a social "subject" rather than "object," and not only for the personified language locals used to describe it. One example that Mauss offers is the practice whereby Samoan families present a child for adoption and then expect to receive gifts from the adoptive family. The child is the initial gift whose continuing presence in the new family requires eternal repayment, continuing for the child's entire life. Strong social taboos prevent either family from breaking this system of "legal and economic exchange"; the trading of objects by both families provides material proof of the child's identity and confirms the fact of his or her own origin. These so-called gifts, in this social context, cannot be considered simply as objects since they carry such powerful meanings to everyone involved. Unfortunately, Mauss says nothing about what this exchange means for the children involved—marking the limitations of his research and of the concerns of his time.

Nevertheless, Mauss' insight here is crucial for historians, and not only because it requires us to consider our own notions of what constitutes a material object. For by describing the exchange of gifts as a "total social fact," Mauss opened up legal and economic contracts to moral and social analysis, directing us to their broad associations among everyone who participates in their exchange. For these reasons, Mauss advanced an integrated view of social

iii   With Durkheim, Mauss was co-founder of *L'Année Sociologique*, and the original version of the text from which this reading is taken appeared in that journal, between 1923–4. See M. Fournier, *Marcel Mauss: A Biography*, trans. J. M. Todd (Princeton: Princeton University Press, 2005).

behaviour, avoiding the kind of sociological reductionism of actions to formal institutions that distinguished the work of his mentor.[iv] For Mauss, the rules that govern these "total" events are particularly powerful because they are not set down in writing or talked about explicitly. This attention to the powerful yet unspoken structures that govern social relationships anticipates Michel Foucault's focus on discourse, the "legally coded" power that concentrates on the construction of knowledge rather than the imposition of formal laws (see Part 11). Similarly, Foucault adopted Mauss' focus on the productive significance of such social structures: Mauss discussed the ways that structured rituals such as gift-giving build relationships by binding people together through mutual obligation. Also, like Marx (see Part 8), Mauss suggested that there are no true individuals at all in the system of commerce governing the exchange of gifts, but rather there are only social groups whose roles are defined quite apart from individual choices, preferences, and concerns. This is why Mauss specified, importantly, that the obligations involved in the commerce of gift-giving are "disinterested"—they are determined by social custom and not by the wishes, interests, or true consent of individuals. Paradoxically, this remains the case even when "to make a gift of something to someone is to make a present of some part of oneself".[v] By moving beyond the social institutions that continue to symbolize themselves through material objects (such as marriage and wedding-rings, or funerals and black clothing), to examine the complex meaning of what has often been termed by sociologists as simple "consumption", Mauss' study of gifts has been cited regularly for nearly a century.[vi]

Writing his essay for publication in a French sociology journal eighty-five years ago, Mauss revealed methodological weaknesses obvious to twenty-first-century readers. He realized that, by restricting his cultural research to the writings of visiting anthropologists, his commitment to examining "the consciousness of the societies themselves" depended on Western observations that found their way into print.[vii] His study examined local words to describe customs unique to their context, but his little reflection on the relationships between the visiting anthropologists and their indigenous subjects meant that he could not offer readers any interpretive context relating to the original fieldwork. By focusing on the social circulation of goods in eighteenth-century Britain, and by focusing particularly on the changing notions of ownership during that period, Neil McKendrick's history of eighteenth-century consumer culture in England showed Mauss's influence while anticipating the cross-disciplinary ambitions of the *Journal of Material Culture*.

iv For a discussion of the "productionist bias" in most sociological studies of material culture, which probably originates in Durkheim's emphasis on the prescriptive social roles of formal institutions, see C. Campbell, *The Romantic Ethic and the Spirit of Modern Consumerism* (Oxford: Basil Blackwell, 1987).

v M. Mauss, *The Gift: The Form and Reason for Exchange in Archaic Societies*. Trans. W. D. Halls (London: Routledge, 1990), 16.

vi *The Gift* has been widely misinterpreted, particularly by readers who suggested that Mauss intended to showcase "primitive" customs in order to celebrate Western cultural superiority: for a fine survey of such misinterpretations, see J. Parry, " *The Gift*, The Indian Gift, and the 'Indian Gift' ", *Man* 21 (1986), 453–73. There has been sufficient interest in Mauss to justify a new translation of his book into English: Ian Cunnison's translation appeared in 1954; W. D. Halls' was published in 1990 and has since been reprinted three times.

vii For a further example of Mauss' willingness to develop his theory on the basis of printed texts, note that the Old Norse poem that he cites at length in his Introduction was one he could read only in translation. See M. Mauss, *The Gift*, 108; on ancient Eddic poetry, see R. J. Glendinning and H. Bessason, *Edda: A Collection of Essays* (Winnipeg: University of Manitoba Press, 1983).

McKendrick has been concerned not only with the availability of new consumer objects, such as fashionable clothing, leather-covered books, fine china tea-sets, and shaving utensils. More importantly, and in response to Mauss, in his influential essay he examined the social and economic reasons why these new luxury items quickly became necessities, attempting to identify the nature of consumer taste and the ways by which these tastes shaped people's sense of themselves. His historical scholarship made innovative use of sources that had been neglected prior to the early 1980s, including clothing advertisements from eighteenth-century newspapers; household financial records; allusions to material goods by poets, novelists, and moral philosophers; and by tracing the changing perceptions of fashion mannequins, from their invention in the early years of the century to their apparent ubiquity only a few decades later. Taking these concerns in numerous directions, he argued that we should recognize not only the Industrial Revolution in British economic history, but also a Consumer Revolution in British social history—for both arose simultaneously, and their relationships are so closely related that they ought to be studied together. Focusing on the eighteenth-century consumer as an individual who didn't merely consume material goods through ownership, but who associated his or her personal identity with the desire and ability to consume things, McKendrick encouraged us to examine the political, intellectual, and social adjustments that consumers created to serve those desires and to test those abilities. These adjustments extended to personal relationships, leisure activities, commercial techniques, and changes in lifestyle. These changes touched everyone involved in every aspect of consumption: from manufacture to advertising, selling, financing, and disposing. This is why McKendrick referred to the "social circulation of goods" whose conceptual meanings and material significance affected a wide range of people, enabling a study of material consumption whose social consequences could extend as widely as the methods of those who research it. Twenty-five years after the publication of McKendick's groundbreaking essay, material historians tend to emerge from curatorial and decorative-arts backgrounds. This means that in many cases their primary scholarly task is to describe historic objects, usually in the economic context of the object's technical fabrication and social function.[viii]

Bringing the history of material culture in another fruitful direction, Georges Vigarello has pointed to the challenges of addressing, in historical terms, notions of personal cleanliness before the widespread use of water for washing. Before the mid-eighteenth century, "attention to cleanliness was a matter of sight and smell"; since bodies were kept warm by covering them with clothing and scented by dousing them in perfume, it was the sensory qualities of those things that were most important—not the idea of bodily cleanliness that is so crucial to us now. Since such careful attention was paid to the whiteness of linen and the sweetness of perfume, "it is foolish to deny the existence of practices of cleanliness in a pre-scientific culture". Despite the unscientific nature of this culture (in Vigarello's terms), his research drew on medical treatises and practices to show that water was then thought to enter the body through the skin, thus causing diseases as fatal as plague. Therefore, the very effort to avoid water indicates a rational concern for cleanliness that preserved health, based on then-current knowledge. Vigarello referred to Norbert Elias, whose pioneering study on the history of personal etiquette shows that "civilized behaviour" begins with the imposition of rules that restrain our behaviour before developing into what we think are just normal instances of

viii See, for example, Aileen Ribiero, *The Art of Dress: Fashion in England and France, 1750–1820* (New Haven: Yale University Press, 1995).

self-control.[ix] Perhaps more influentially for sociological and material history, Elias argues that it is a sense of self-esteem or shame that regulates our bodies and our appetites (for food, sex, sleep, and sneezing). Over time, these very personal feelings become shared values that, in turn, create cohesive social groups. So when Vigarello examined the literary and "scientific" sources that document the ways material objects were used to demonstrate personal cleanliness, he emphasized the fact that these previous generations were engaged in a "civilizing process" of their own. Refusing a **positivist** view that would simply condemn past behaviour as uncivilized (see Part 6), Vigarello asked us to consider the meaningfulness of past practices in their own terms: they compel us to examine fashions for particular clothing, interpretations of current medical concepts, and the choreography of social events that featured typical displays of outward appearance.

The final source in this section was written by an archaeologist who reflects on the process by which historians "create the material remains of the past". Cornelius Holtorf narrated the events that determine whether a ceramic potshard, found by a student at an excavation site, will become a museum piece or a simple number in a darkened inventory of "archaeology rubbish". Leaving aside the important point that yesterday's rubbish provides splendid evidence of past lives, Holtorf highlighted our "momentary, fluid, and flexible" methods of classifying and interpreting historical artifacts. The actual object itself never changes (unless it is dropped), but the ideas projected onto it reflect professional values that in turn define its meaning. Although professional historians and archaeologists are trained to identify evidence of the past, their classifications attach meaning to an object in ways that reflect "the result of relationships of people and things". If we do not re-evaluate the terms that define our interpretation of which materials are of historical interest and which are not, we simply create a material history unconsciously, according to our personal taste, and not deliberately, using professional principles that are subjects of discussion. Given the informality, speed, and frequency with which such processes take place, should historians think of themselves as creators or as interpreters of historic objects? Why would we consider one role preferable to another? How does the answer to that question reflect on our notions of historical authority? Turning to the collaborative and cross-disciplinary forums made possible by publications such as the *Journal of Material Culture*, such reports from the field elicit the kind of cross-disciplinary responses we require to prevent us from creating rather than interpreting the past. Those insights will cast new light on the nature of our historical methods and assumptions about the purpose of historical writing.

Like the closing verse of a poem or last word in a speech, the final section in an anthology tends to carry the presumption of special emphasis. That is unfortunate in this *Reader* because the history of historical writing continues to expand in many directions—so no single section can represent the state of historiography. Also, when we look at the sections that precede this one, we can see shared concerns about history that surfaced at different times and in various places during the past three hundred years. Although some trends preceded others, it might not be useful to suggest that one is more important than another. To sum them up or to predict their futures would presume that this book should shape rather than introduce them.

ix See N. Elias, *The Civilizing Process*, 1939. Trans. E. Jephcott. E. Dunning et al. (eds). (Oxford: Blackwell, 2000). For a thoughtful article that proposes methodological and conceptual similarities between Elias and Foucault (see Part 11), see D. Smith, "*The Civilizing Process* and *The History of Sexuality*: Comparing Norbert Elias and Michel Foucault", *Theory and Society* (1999), 79–100.

The cross-disciplinary approach to history called for by many of the contributors to this volume is not new, but several historians have called for innovative methods of achieving it. History as an authorial pursuit and history as an interest of readers predates, by many centuries, the creation of history as a profession and History as an academic discipline (see Part 5).[x] When French historians decided to rename their scholarly organization in 1718, they did so by emphasizing its general literary qualities: they renamed themselves L'Académie des Inscriptions et Belles Lettres.[xi] Vico argued that the ideal theory of history would rely not on the chronicles of past events, but on the literature of well-read poets—to which his own brilliant if chaotic writing would contribute (see Part 2).[xii] The conjectural historians of the mid-eighteenth century sought to contribute to "literature" or "polite learning": their sources balanced ancient poetry with political biography; their authorial task meant displaying a refined prose style; and their most committed readers considered themselves "men of letters" and not "historians" (see Part 3).[xiii] Despite the increased specialization of historians over the final decades of the twentieth century, we may have returned to a similar outlook, since it is now difficult to find anyone working in any area of the humanities and social sciences (from Philosophy to Film Studies, or from English to Economics) who doesn't consider her or himself a historian of some aspect of their field—even though "historian" is not how most would describe themselves, probably because their viewpoint incorporates the perspectives of numerous disciplines. One of the first criteria by which any piece of academic writing is judged refers to the author's grasp of the topic's "background", by which we mean "perspectives on its history"—regardless of the topic itself.

Across disciplines, the wish for deeper historical understanding has become a defining mark of intellectual eagerness and academic seriousness, especially when it seeks to include the critical vocabulary of numerous fields. At the same time, as each of these contributors has suggested, by articulating the ambitions and assumptions of historical writing, we bring it closer to reflecting effectively on the widest range of concerns about our past.

x   For an excellent survey, from ancient Greece to German Romanticism, see D. R. Kelley, *Faces of History: Historical Inquiry from Herodotus to Herder* (New Haven: Yale University Press, 1998).

xi   It had been called L'Académie Royale des Médailles et des Inscriptions, since one of its official tasks was to advise on suitable inscriptions for royal medals and monuments. *Belles-lettres* (or "literature" in English) was used well into the nineteenth century by English-language authors; when Samuel Johnson defined *literature* in his *Dictionary of the English Language* (1755), he provided a near-exact translation of *belles-lettres*: "skill in letters". For a history of the Académie, see *L'Académie des Inscriptions et Belles-Lettres. Histoire, Prix et Fondations, Publications* (Paris: A. Picard, 1938).

xii See G. Vico, *New Science* (1744). Trans. David Marsh (Harmondsworth: Penguin, 2001), 5.

xiii For one of clearest explanations of the goals of historical writing (and reading) during the mid-eighteenth century, see David Hume's whimsical and yet detailed essay, "Of the Study of History", in *Essays Moral, Political, and Literary*, E. Miller (ed.) (Indianapolis: Liberty Fund, 1985), 563–8.

Chapter 51

Daniel Miller and Christopher Tilley

INTRODUCTION TO *JOURNAL OF MATERIAL CULTURE:* INAUGURAL ISSUE

Daniel Miller and Christopher Tilley, "Introduction", *Journal of Material Culture:* inaugural issue, *Journal of Material Culture*, 1 (1996), 5–14.

THE LAUNCH of this new journal emerges from an extraordinary range of innovative research on material culture that has taken place across the humanities and social sciences during the last two decades. The aim, quite simply, is to provide a forum for interdisciplinary discussion and debate to bring together and encourage communication between scholars working within different fields. The common focus of this interdisciplinary research is on the ways in which artefacts are implicated in the construction, maintenance and transformation of social identities.

The study of material culture may be most broadly defined as the investigation of the relationship between people and things irrespective of time and space. The perspective adopted may be global or local, concerned with the past or the present, or the mediation between the two. Defined in this manner, the potential range of contemporary disciplines involved in some way or other in studying material culture is effectively as wide as the human and cultural sciences themselves.

Definitions of the origins of being human abound, and have altered historically, but two in particular have always taken centre stage: to be human is to speak, and to make and use tools. Consideration of the linguistic basis of humanity has given rise to linguistics. The use and meanings of artefacts have, by contrast, no obvious disciplinary home. Yet it could have been otherwise; the systematic study of language might be scattered through as large a number of different disciplines as the study of material culture is today.

The fact that no discipline called 'material culture studies' exists may be regarded as a positive advantage. Disciplines, with their boundary-maintaining devices, institutional structures, accepted texts, methodologies, internal debates and circumscribed areas of study tend, by virtue of their very constitution, to be rather conservative in nature. Changes within them most frequently come about through borrowing ideas from outside. Our aim, therefore, in developing this journal is *not* to draw together studies of contemporary consumer goods, landscapes, archaeological finds, studies of architecture, artworks or ethnographic collections into a new, 'disciplined' subject area, or even a subdiscipline, but to encourage the cross-fertilization of ideas and approaches between people concerned with the material constitution of social relations. As such we have no obvious genealogy of ancestors to whom we should pay homage, and are not concerned to invent any. In developing this journal we remain firmly committed to a politics of inclusion. There are already enough constraints imposed on our ability to think and to write fresh and creative work without inventing any new ones.

An adequate understanding of any social actions and relations, we would maintain, demands an understanding of material culture and vice versa. The world is constituted through a continuous dynamism, a dialectic of object-subject relations that can only be more fully explored through developing theoretical perspectives, methodologies and empirical studies drawing on different types of evidence from alternative contexts. We hope, through the contributions to this journal, to further stimulate a general comparative approach to the study of the embeddedness of humanity in society.

Let us take two obvious aspects of the materiality of human existence. All human groups dwell in space, most commonly in houses in settlements that form part of wider landscapes. Houses and landscapes form an evident concern for sociologists, historians, archaeologists, anthropologists, geographers, architects, psychologists, museologists, and people involved in design and consumer studies (to name but a few). Whether or not it is placed in the foreground, the physical presence of houses and landscapes is there as a material environment that creates people (has an impact, or effects, facilitates or constrains activities) as much as it comprises structures that people create. Scholars from different disciplines make extremely valuable contributions to an understanding of houses and land-scapes, but usually only of a limited number of aspects. For example, a psychologist might be interested in the emotional impact of houses or landscapes on people using or entering them: the effects of high or low ceilings, dark or light rooms, rocky or wooded valleys. An anthropologist might be interested in gender symbolism in landscapes and houses in high-land Papua New Guinea, an archaeologist in temporal changes in houses and landscapes over the long term. No single discipline can claim a monopoly of knowledge. An archaeologist, through his or her particular expertise and knowledge of the evidence, has a great deal to teach an anthropologist or a geographer about landscapes and houses, and vice versa. Breaking down the kind of disciplinary chauvinism in which anthropologists and sociologists may read only the work of other anthropologists and sociologists, our aim is to make the *Journal of Material Culture* a forum in which people from disparate intellectual backgrounds can learn from and inform each other and engage in debate. Most productively, we would like to see the journal developing into an arena where, say, archaeologists and geographers, anthropologists and psychologists, might write together and interpret houses and land-scapes, whether the empirical database be Bronze Age hut circles in south-west Britain, house compounds in Cameroon or the streets of Harlem.

As another example, the last decade has seen museums come of age, in the sense that questions about their role and about what had seemed almost an intrinsic conservatism have led to a new self-consciousness about their function, and, more important, the consequences of that function with regard to the people who come to them. As museums give rise to museology, it becomes clear that the point of articulation with the rest of the academic world is through material culture studies. Without material culture studies, museums have substantive problems and issues but no foundation for the study of objects in context. If we were to attempt to create a material culture discipline we would probably find some resistance from both archaeologists and museum workers, who may not wish to cross boundaries and have to ascribe to yet another set of constraints and definitions. By not being a discipline, however, we become a point of articulation instead of division and we are able to unite such people with many others who share common interests.

Attempts to establish interdisciplinary links and collaboration are not new, and one can readily identify a number of conferences and their published proceedings together with collaborative books. But what has been entirely lacking within material culture studies has been the kind of continuous focus drawing together a community of interested scholars that only a periodical published at regular intervals can provide. It is our hope that the *Journal of Material Culture* will fill that gap. There are many academics in a whole variety of disciplines who do not relate their work to the term 'material culture studies', or who are not even particularly aware that such a category exists. A general 'raising of consciousness' about the possibilities latent in this category may well help to facilitate a greater freedom of communication and collaboration.

The lack of a disciplinary foundation could lead to a lack of confidence in the independent contribution we might make. At worst we would merely become followers of disciplines hitching on to the bandwagons of academic fashion. We hope we do not represent merely an addition to a sequence of 'structuralism and material culture', 'Marxism and material culture', 'postmodernism and material culture', etc. Of course some application of new ideas to our particular concerns may well prove valuable and of common interest. Furthermore, such appropriation can still be creative. Structuralism may have developed through linguistics, but in studying the relationship between symbol and object advances occurred in the elaboration of semiotic theory precisely because objects are not like language.

In addition, however, we hope this journal will represent the independent contribution that material culture studies can make to wider concerns in the humanities and social sciences. For example, theories of objectification have helped to transcend subject-object dualities. Focusing upon both the transience and longevity of objects has helped develop new approaches to the nature of social memory. Studies of the consumption of commodities helped stimulate the study of consumption in media and cultural studies. The fact that objects tend to be meaningful rather than merely communicate meaning has helped move our concerns from narrow questions of semantics to larger issues of identity. In this journal we would wish to promote such approaches, which take from the specific qualities of materiality and lead us to rethink general theory.

What links all these studies together is a common focus on the material aspects of human existence, theories and methodologies. The last few decades have seen a burgeoning of theoretical approaches in the humanities and the social sciences. It is now strikingly obvious that no one single theoretical or conceptual approach can provide a grand solution to the study of material culture. Different perspectives, from structuralism to phenomenology, poststructuralism to hermeneutics, exploit alternative aspects of the evidence in the interpretations they provide. Critical theory and discourse perspectives have led us all to be increasingly self-reflexive: what exactly are we doing and why? The aim of this journal will be to foster a non-partisan approach to the study of material culture in which scholars coming from different theoretical backgrounds can hopefully talk to, rather than past, each other. We would hope to avoid some of the empty rhetorical gestures and open (and unpleasant) competitiveness that individual disciplines more often than not encourage and relish. Through the systematic exploration of different theories in relation to material culture we would hope to foster an increased understanding of both their strengths and weaknesses. What we do hope to foster in all the papers published in the journal is a critical perspective on the world. Our project is, of necessity, a political one, in relation to both academia and the society in which we live and work. A greater appreciation of the material basis of our social conditions of life will hopefully lead to their transformation.

Materiality and the material legacy of the past

In considering material culture, the comparison is often most easily made with linguistics. Material culture certainly gained a great deal from the highly energized study of language that culminated this century in the development of structuralism. But this had its drawbacks as well as advantages. It has become increasingly apparent that taking artefacts, images and performances as quasi-texts is to overlook their most fundamental properties so far as users and witnesses might be concerned. Current theories of material culture do not advocate any simple physicalist attention to the material quality of things, but they do acknowledge that materiality often plays an important role in creating their particular significance and meaningfulness *as well* as their symbolic efficacy.

The domain of linguistics should be comparatively easy to define, but even here too pedantic an attempt to define what constitutes language would be tiresome, and much of the most interesting work occurs at the fringes of linguistics. We assume a similar situation with regard to material culture. Thus we would hope, for example, that debates within this journal will interest academics interested in music and sound. The materiality of sound is already recognized as a major issue in the study of music. The atmosphere created by heavy metal rock music, the private domain constituted by a lonely listener at home with the radio and the uses of 'piped' music in the public domain all immediately reflect upon sound's material presence. While there are many issues of ethno-musicology that are not particularly relevant for us, a debate on the material presence of sound in comparison with other cultural forms might prove invaluable.

As in the case of rock music, materiality is something that is often hard to ignore and often present as a sign of other people's agency and not one's own. Most often, as in the landscape and buildings that surround us, the agents so signified are historical, representing the accrued labour of generations. As Bourdieu amongst others has pointed out, it is not just the material environment of agricultural field systems, buildings and boundaries that we inherit, it is also our specific taxonomies and ways of interacting with that environment, ranging from whether we sit or squat to the way religious traditions in our area have conceptualized over millennia the gross world of material form.[i]

It is interesting to note, in this context, that one of the key debates that has emerged in sociology during the past 5 years has been over modernism and its relation to postmodernism and the supposed development of a postmodern cultural condition. Whether the latter is viewed, as by Jameson, as the 'cultural logic of late capitalism' or by others as a liberalizing force in society, considerations of the material form of architecture, seen as the physical manifestation of powerful cultural codes and ideologies, have played a key role in the debates.[ii] This further serves to emphasize both the embeddedness of material culture in schemes of perception and cultural categories and the intended and unintended consequences that can, as often as not, be best highlighted and understood through study of their physical manifestations and effects. The materiality of history, as our inherited legacy,

---

i   See Pierre Bourdieu, *Distinction: A Social Critique of the Judgement of Taste,* trans. R. Nice (Cambridge, MA: Harvard University Press, 1984). [-Ed.]
ii   See Fredric Jameson, *Postmodernism, or The Cultural Logic of Late Capitalism* (Durham, NC: Duke University Press, 1991). [-Ed.]

brings out two of the main branches of material culture studies. The first is the study of historical artefacts, the second resides in the wider connotations of the term materialism.

The potential of material culture studies is perhaps nowhere more evident than when we consider the integration of studies of the present and studies of the past. Precisely because of the devotion of archaeology, to excavation, of prehistory to research in archives and of anthropology to ethnography, for a considerable time a gap has existed which periodically has led to the emergence of particular schools of material culture studies. For example, in the 1950s in France a group of scholars associated with Leroi-Gourhan developed an approach to technology that included both prehistoric and contemporary sources.[iii] In the 1960s scholars such as Deetz and Glassie working in the United States saw the potential of historical archaeology for again transcending the dichotomy between synchronic and diachronic studies.[iv] In the 1980s in Britain two groups emerged. One, based at University College, developed the study of longterm social structure as a contribution to the emergence of neo-Marxist studies, while others working with David Clarke and Ian Hodder at Cambridge created a similar contribution to structuralist studies.

In the 1990s new regional foci seem to be emerging which exploit this same niche. Examples might include work by Australian scholars interested in material culture as a means of studying the colonial encounter in the Pacific, or work in the United States on trying to theorize diaspora communities of the past in relation to a new sense of transcending national identity felt by many groups today. It is perhaps time that students of material culture capitalized upon what has been an immensely positive contribution to interdisciplinary studies sustained over many decades and build still further on these foundations. Few groups have so consistently refused to be characterized as either diachronically or synchronically based.

Materialism and de-fetishism

A consideration of the material legacy of the past leads us equally to the recognition of the importance of materialism per se. One of the many contributions made by Karl Marx was his commitment to understanding how the materiality within which we live constrains who we can become. In the particular circumstance of the industrial revolution this became largely a concern with the grounding of history in labour and the economy. Today this notion of materialism may be enlarged. For example, we might feel constrained by the presence of the consumer world of commodities within which most of us live. We might recognize this as overwhelming in the same sense that the industrial revolution was an overwhelming presence a century and a half ago. We may have many different responses to this condition but still recognize that in a profound sense we are constituted by it.

Materialism stresses our limited control over the forces that create us. In the case of Marx this led to an empathy with those who were most oppressed by history and least able to see themselves in the world created around them and often by them. We may wish to retain a perspective that prevents us from too easily blaming the victim for their circumstance. This is but one example of the way in which attempts to understand the significance of buildings, commodities, agricultural systems and soundscapes are important. So, far from detracting from the understanding of people, they are the foundation for a more genuine empathy for and sympathetic comprehension of the lives of others.

---

iii André Leroi-Gourhan (1911–1986). [-Ed]
iv James Deetz (1930–2000); Henry Glassie (1941–). [-Ed]

This is important because many academics outside our concerns tend to assume that by using the label 'material culture studies' we enhance an already present fetishism of the object. By contrast, many of us believe it is a simple-minded humanism, which views persons outside the context and constraints of their material culture and thereby establishes a dichotomy between persons and objects, that is the true source of such fetishism. Indeed, it may be only material culture studies that has the will and knowledge to undertake the key task of de-fetishising objects that is today as important a form of emancipating humanity as it was a century ago.

The dichotomy of persons and things is itself a particular historical and regional phenomenon. The literature on Melanesia is famous for illustrating just how thing-like people can be and people-like things can be. Most historians recognize the discovery of (a clearly gendered) 'man' as a particular product of the European Enlightenment, although it no doubt had its equivalents in other times and places. The Enlightenment enthroned man as the measure of all things, such that the material world become defined as an object of knowledge and separated out as dehumanized science and technology. Only the arts retained the project of transcending this dichotomy, and they become an increasingly specialized subfield of human practice.

In the last 20 years a considerable literature has developed that suggests that after several centuries this period of explicit humanism is in decline, and that the relationship between persons and things is becoming once again a less dichotomous and more fluid one. This has been one of the core contentions of the debates over postmodernism. The cause of this shift is generally felt to be the rise of commodities, where, as Simmel[v] first pointed out, the sheer quantitative increase is such as to constitute a qualitative change in many of our lives. So far the debate over what this change portends is relatively crude. There is now one well-established line, most clearly associated with Baudrillard, that views this transformation as the loss of humanity.[vi] We are all reduced to being the sign-servants of the object world. On the other hand, there are many other possibilities that have been less fully explored. We might, for example, simply be returning to the kind of precommodified relationship encountered in anthropology and history. It is clear that material objects appear pervasively in adjudications about modern life, but grand generalizations about whether they overwhelm us or whether they (or we) have become mere simulacra tend to involve the projection of philosophical logics upon self-evident objects, whereas this journal will be concerned to demonstrate that such things are by no means self-evident and require constant dedicated analysis.

In the rapidly growing study of commodities and consumption other contradictions have emerged. For example, consumption might be viewed as the labour of housewives who gain little by way of credit or respect for their skills as consumers. At the same time there is the sense that such consumption, when translated into the increasing power of retail on the one hand and economic institutions such as GATT on the other, has become the major source of power in the contemporary world.[vii] Precisely because this is not recognized, it would follow that the labour of consumers is now as important an area of fetishism as the labour of producers once was. Material culture studies that aim to uncover such contradictions thereby become an important instrument of de-fetishism with significant potential

v   See D. Frisby and Mike Featherstone, eds., *Simmel on Culture: Selected Writings* (London: Sage, 1997). [-Ed.]

vi See Jean Baudrillard, *The Consumer Society: Myths and Structures.* 1970. Trans. C. Turner (London: Sage, 2000). [-Ed.]

vii GATT: The General Agreement on Tariffs and Trade (1947–1994), superseded by The World Trade Organization. [-Ed.]

political consequences. This is only one example of arguments that would place material culture studies at the heart of any rethinking of contemporary critical theory.

The advantages of being un–disciplined

As already noted, the term 'discipline' is highly appropriate for the established categories of academic teaching. We fight for resources with grant-giving agencies on the basis of boundaries drawn that include our academic 'territory' and also set boundaries on who may use this label of being a 'proper' historian or student of design. Now it would be disingenuous for us to argue that such disciplines or boundaries should not exist. We would not survive in a libertarian academic anarchy. We do have to take responsibility for jobs, students, allocating resources and other tasks that depend upon the maintenance of categories and taxonomies. Parochialism must unfortunately be maintained. But in a sense material culture studies has been blessed with an unusual and potentially fruitful legacy. Dismissed for many decades as the antiquated end point of evolutionary studies, it was able to lie dormant while other structures came into being and were sedimented into more concrete forms. As a result people working in material culture studies have been able to maintain a dynamic presence in the interstices between other activities. An example already noted is the combination of archaeology, history and ethnography into a general study of the evolution of social structures in the 1970s. Another example has been the virtual reinvention of consumer studies apart from some highly parochial economics and psychology in the later 1980s. The new concern with consumption, with its redirection of attention to the social life of commodities, has in turn become an idiom through which many other facets of modern life such as nationalism or morality can be studied, since these are often highly pertinent to the labour of consumption.

The phenomenal growth of cultural studies in the 1980s provides the best example of the advantages of remaining undisciplined and pursuing a field of study without respect to prior claims of disciplinary antecedents. Many disciplines had – or increasingly claim to have – a concept of cultural studies as central to their respective fields, such that analysis of meaning and interpretation has become one of the most powerful synthesizing modes of thought in the social sciences. As a field, cultural studies has been immensely productive precisely because it lacked constraints on what should be investigated and how phenomena should be conceptualized. Some of the aims of cultural studies are similar to those advanced in this journal. The major differences are our emphasis on the material constitution of sociality and a greater commitment to comparative studies.

We argue then that being undisciplined can be highly productive if it leads us to focus upon areas that established disciplines have ignored because of boundary constraints. This is lack of discipline with a purpose, not merely the eclectic play of a libertarian's individualism for its own sake. At every level the construction of our categories means making decisions. For example, there are already journals that relate to particular cultural forms, journals for textiles, for buildings, for glass, for other bodies of artefacts. Clearly there are particular issues that are specific to buildings that are of limited interest to those working on dress. The term 'material culture' looks to areas such as issues of identity or a critique of the concept of function that would equally address both. We recognize that if we unite some studies that appear parochial from the point of view of our domain, so we in turn appear parochial to those who do not want to consider materiality as an issue and are looking for still more general philosophical, political or aesthetic concerns. For them also this journal would be the wrong outlet. We hope that the criteria are general enough that the concern is genuinely interdisciplinary and of interest to people involved in other classes of subject matter. We want to see this concern illustrated as much through specific domains of objects as through specific regions and periods.

It would also be disingenuous to pretend that a journal does not itself have to adopt certain disciplines such as criteria of acceptance and scholarship. This journal has editors, there are criteria by which articles will be selected and there is an educational agenda that affirms knowledge and, above all, understanding as goals in the Enlightenment tradition. We would wish therefore to be clear that our 'indiscipline' is seen as potentially creative. We are looking for papers that are more than the anecdotes and opinions of individuals looking for self-expression. There are a number of other journals that seem to have taken that turn, and we do not propose to follow them. If we have not seen 'the death of the author' that was proclaimed in the 1970s then at least we might expect the humility of authors who have taken the trouble to immerse themselves in the labour of others – be they informants, the objects produced by labour, or a community of academics – and who have had the patience to work out and present clearly the relationship between what they have to say and the academic context in which they are saying it.

We hope that we can escape some of the least-necessary disciplinary features. We hope we will have the integrity to publish the most interesting and significant papers from whatever quarter, irrespective of the official qualification or position of the authors. We hope that the initial format will be open to criticism and change so that the journal continues to fill a genuine niche. In future issues we intend to include review articles of major texts. We are also considering a section reviewing relevant debates on the internet. If this serves a genuine purpose in archiving for longer-term usage conversations whose ephemeral quality results in genuine loss, then we feel that is the kind of task our journal should take on. But if it turns out that it is better to regard the two media as complementary, with the internet employed for working out ideas and this journal for establishing a reference collection of studies, then it is best we remain apart. We hope that the readers of this journal will feel free to write and comment directly on what we are doing and feel part of the production, rather than just the consumption, of the journal.

Finally, we do not want to be limited by any regional base. We would particularly welcome papers from areas that have their own traditions of material culture analysis or contemporary concerns they may wish to share. Equally, we would welcome papers from areas that are not often involved in particular considerations of material culture because their base in artefacts is less obviously material. These might range from the study of the social consumption of electronic communications, through the cultural significance of sensory media such as smell, taste and sound, to discursive analyses of text and film.

These then are the aims; we do not know yet how long it will take us to refine and develop them, but it will only happen with support and participation from a large inter-disciplinary group. We already know there is considerable enthusiasm behind the develop-ment of this journal from many regions and quarters, but our ability to realize these goals depends upon contributions coming from as wide a sphere as possible and being maintained in the longer term. Above all, in developing this journal, we are interested in the *creativity* of different disciplines and bringing about dialogues that will stimulate the development of new ideas, providing a wider context for more 'parochial' concerns. Together, then, we hope that being 'undisciplined' can be constructive and contribute to a critical understanding of the present and the past.

Chapter 52

Marcel Mauss

INTRODUCTION TO *THE GIFT: FORMS AND FUNCTIONS OF EXCHANGE IN ARCHAIC SOCIETIES*

Marcel Mauss (1872–1950), "Introduction", *The Gift: Forms and Functions of Exchange in Archaic Societies,* 1923–4. Trans. W. D. Halls (London: Routledge, 1990), 1–9. Footnotes have been excised.

The gift, and especially the obligation to return it

Epigraph

BELOW WE GIVE a few stanzas from the Havamal, one of the old poems of the Scandinavian Edda [early medieval poet]. They may serve as an epigraph for this study, so powerfully do they plunge the reader into the immediate atmosphere of ideas and facts in which our exposition will unfold.

> (39) I have never found a man so generous
> And so liberal in feeding his guests
> That 'to receive would not be received',
> Nor a man so . . . [the adjective is missing]
> Of his goods
> That to receive in return was disagreeable to
> Him

> (41) With weapons and clothes
> Friends must give pleasure to one another;
> Everyone knows that for himself [through his Own experience].
> Those who exchange presents with one another

Remain friends the longest
If things turn out successfully.

(42) One must be a friend
To one's friend,
And give present for present;
One must have
Laughter for laughter
And sorrow for lies

(44) You know, if you have a friend
In whom you have confidence
And if you wish to get good results
Your soul must blend in with his
And you must exchange presents
And frequently pay him visits.

(44) But if you have another person
(sic) Whom you mistrust
And if you wish to get good results,
You must speak fine words to him
But your thoughts must be false
And you must lament in lies.

(46) This is the way with him
In whom you have no trust
And whose sentiments you suspect,
You must smile at him
And speak in spite of yourself:
Presents given in return must be similar to
Those received.

(47) Noble and valiant men
Have the best life;
They have no fear at all
But a coward fears everything:
The miser always fears presents.

Cahen also points out to us stanza 145:

(145) It is better not to beg [ask for something]
Than to sacrifice too much [to the gods]:
A present given always expects one in return.
It is better not to bring any offering
Than to spend too much on it.

Programme

The subject is clear. In Scandinavian civilization, and in a good number of others, exchanges and contracts take place in the form of presents; in theory these are voluntary, in reality they are given and reciprocated obligatorily.

The present monograph is a fragment of more extensive studies. For years our attention has been concentrated on both the organization of contractual law and the system of total economic services operating between the various sections or subgroups that make up so-called primitive societies, as well as those we might characterize as archaic. This embraces an enormous complex of facts. These in themselves are very complicated. Everything inter-mingles in them, everything constituting the strictly social life of societies that have pre-ceded our own, even those going back to protohistory. In these 'total' social phenomena, as we propose calling them, all kinds of institutions are given expression at one and the same time – religious, juridical, and moral, which relate to both politics and the family; likewise economic ones, which suppose special forms of production and consumption, or rather, of performing total services and of distribution. This is not to take into account the aesthetic phenomena to which these facts lead, and the contours of the phenomena that these institutions manifest.

Among all these very complex themes and this multiplicity of social 'things' that are in a state of flux, we seek here to study only one characteristic – one that goes deep but is isolated: the so to speak voluntary character of these total services, apparently free and disinterested but nevertheless constrained and self-interested. Almost always such services have taken the form of the gift, the present generously given even when, in the gesture accompanying the transaction, there is only a polite fiction, formalism, and social deceit, and when really there is obligation and economic self-interest. Although we shall indicate in detail all the various principles that have imposed this appearance on a necessary form of exchange, namely, the division of labour in society itself – among all these principles we shall nevertheless study only one in depth. *What rule of legality and self-interest, in societies of a backward or archaic type, compels the gift that has been received to be obligatorily reciprocated? What power resides in the object given that causes its recipient to pay it back?* This is the problem on which we shall fasten more particularly, whilst indicating others. By examining a fairly large body of facts we hope to respond to this very precise question and to point the way to how one may embark upon a study of related questions. We shall also see to what fresh problems we are led. Some concern a permanent form of contractual morality, namely, how the law relating to things even today remains linked to the law relating to persons. Others deal with the forms and ideas that, at least in part, have always presided over the act of exchange, and that even now partially complement the notion of individual self-interest.

We shall thus achieve a dual purpose. On the one hand, we shall arrive at conclusions of a somewhat archeological kind concerning the nature of human transaction in societies around us, or that have immediately preceded our own. We shall describe the phenomena of exchange and contract in those societies that are not, as has been claimed, devoid of economic markets – since the market is a human phenomenon that, in our view, is not foreign to any known society – but whose system of exchange is different from ours. In these societies we shall see the market as it existed before the institution of traders and before their main invention – money proper. We shall see how it functioned both before the discovery of forms of contract and sale that may be said to be modern (Semitic, Hellenic, Hellenistic, and Roman), and also before money, minted and inscribed. We shall see the morality and the organization that operate in such transactions.

As we shall note that this morality and organization still function in our own societies, in unchanging fashion and, so to speak, hidden, below the surface, and as we believe that in this we have found one of the human foundations on which our societies are built, we shall be able to deduce a few moral conclusions concerning certain problems posed by the crisis in our own law and economic organization. There we shall call a halt. This page of social history, of theoretical sociology, of conclusions in the field of morality, and of political and economic practice only leads us after all to pose once more, in different forms, questions that are old but ever-new.

Method

We have followed the method of exact comparison. First, as always, we have studied our subject only in relation to specific selected areas: Polynesia, Melanesia, the American Northwest, and a few great legal systems. Next, we have naturally only chosen those systems of law in which we could gain access, through documents and philogical studies, to the consciousness of the societies themselves, for here we are dealing in words and ideas. This again has restricted the scope of our comparisons. Finally, each study focused on systems that we have striven to describe each in turn and in its entirety. Thus we have renounced that continuous comparison in which everything is mixed up together, and in which institutions lose all local colour and documents their savour.

The rendering of total services. The gift and potlatch

The present study forms part of a series of researches that Davy[i] and myself have been pursuing for a long time, concerning the archaic forms of contract. A summary of these is necessary.

Apparently there has never existed, either in an era fairly close in time to our own, or in societies that we lump together somewhat awkwardly as primitive or inferior, anything that might resemble what is called a 'natural' economy. Through a strange but classic aberration, in order to characterize this type of economy, a choice was even made of the writings by Cook relating to exchange and barter among the Polynesians. Now, it is these same Polynesians that we intend to study here. We shall see how far removed they are from a state of nature as regards law and economics.

In the economic and legal systems that have preceded our own, one hardly ever finds a simple exchange of goods, wealth, and products in transactions concluded by individuals. First, it is not individuals but collectivities that impose obligations of exchange and contract upon each other. The contracting parties are legal entities: clans, tribes, and families who confront and oppose one another either in groups who meet face to face in one spot, or through their chiefs, or in both these ways at once. Moreover, what they exchange is not solely property and wealth, movable and immovable goods, and things economically useful. In particular, such exchanges are acts of politeness: banquets, rituals, military services, women, children, dances, festivals, and fairs, in which economic transaction is only one element, and in which the passing on of wealth is only one feature of a much more general and enduring contract. Finally, these total services and counter-services are committed to in a somewhat voluntary form by presents and gifts, although in the final analysis they are strictly compulsory, on pain of private or public warfare. We propose to call all this the *system of total services*. The purest type of such institutions seems to us to be characterized by

i   Georges Davy (1868–1938). [-Ed.]

the alliance of two phratries in Pacific or North American tribes in general, where rituals, marriages, inheritance of goods, legal ties and those of self-interest, the ranks of the military and priests – in short everything, is complementary and presumes co-operation between the two halves of the tribe. For example, their games, in particular, are regulated by both halves. The Tlingit and the Haïda, two tribes of the American Northwest, express the nature of such practices forcefully by declaring that 'the two tribal phratries show respect to each other'.

But within these two tribes of the American Northwest and throughout this region there appears what is certainly a type of these 'total services', rare but highly developed. We propose to call this form the 'potlatch', as moreover, do American authors using the Chinook term, which has become part of the everyday language of Whites and Indians from Vancouver to Alaska. The word potlatch essentially means 'to feed', 'to consume'. These tribes, which are very rich, and live on the islands, or on the coast, or in the area between the Rocky Mountains and the coast, spend the winter in a continual festival of feasts, fairs, and markets, which also constitute the solemn assembly of the tribe. The tribe is organized by hierarchical confraternities and secret societies, the latter often being confused with the former, as with the clans. Everything – clans, marriages, initiations, Shamanist seances and meetings for the worship of the great gods, the totems or the collective or individual ancestors of the clan – is woven into an inextricable network of rites, of total legal and economic services, of assignment to political ranks in the society of men, in the tribe, and in the confederations of tribes, and even internationally. Yet what is noteworthy about these tribes is the principle of rivalry and hostility that prevails in all these practices. They go as far as to fight and kill chiefs and nobles. Moreover, they even go as far as the purely sumptuary destruction of wealth that has been accumulated in order to outdo the rival chief as well as his associate (normally a grandfather, father-in-law, or son-in-law). There is total service in the sense that it is indeed the whole clan that contracts on behalf of all, for all that it possesses and for all that it does, through the person of its chief. But this act of 'service' on the part of the chief takes on an extremely marked agonistic character. It is essentially usurious and sumptuary. It is a struggle between nobles to establish a hierarchy amongst themselves from which their clan will benefit at a later date.

We propose to reserve the term potlatch for this kind of institution that, with less risk and more accuracy, but also at greater length, we might call: *total services of an agonistic type.*

Up to now we had scarcely found any examples of this institution except among the tribes of the American Northwest, Melanesia, and Papua. Everywhere else, in Africa, Polynesia, Malaysia, South America, and the rest of North America, the basis of exchanges between clans and families appeared to us to be the more elementary type of total services. However, more detailed research has now uncovered a quite considerable number of inter-mediate forms between those exchanges comprising very acute rivalry and the destruction of wealth, such as those of the American Northwest and Melanesia, and others, where emulation is more moderate but where those entering into contracts seek to outdo one another in their gifts. In the same way we vie with one another in our presents of thanks, banquets and weddings, and in simple invitations. We still feel the need to *revanchieren*[ii], as the Germans say. We have discovered intermediate forms in the ancient Indo-European world, and especially among the Thracians.

Various themes – rules and ideas – are contained in this type of law and economy. The

ii   To return a favour or get one's revenge. [-Ed.]

most important feature among these spiritual mechanisms is clearly one that obliges a person to reciprocate the present that has been received. Now, the moral and religious reason for this constraint is nowhere more apparent than in Polynesia. Let us study it in greater detail, and we will plainly see what force impels one to reciprocate the thing received, and generally to enter into real contracts.

Chapter 53

Neil McKendrick

INTRODUCTION TO *THE BIRTH OF A CONSUMER SOCIETY*

Neil McKendrick, "Introduction", *The Birth of a Consumer Society: The Commercialization of Eighteenth-Century England* (London: Europa, 1982), 1–6.

'The English of those several denominations [Peasants and Mechanics, Farmers, Free-holders, Tradesmen and Manufacturers in Middling Life, Wholesale Dealers, Merchants and all persons of Landed Estates] have better Conveniences in their Houses and affect to have more in Quantity of clean, neat Furniture, and a greater variety, such as Carpets, Screens, Window Curtains, Chamber Bells, polished Brass Locks, Fenders etc., (Things Hardly known abroad among persons of such Rank) than are to be found in any other Country of Europe . . . were an inventory to be taken of Household Goods and Furniture of a Peasant, or Mechanic, in France, and of a Peasant, or Mechanic in England, the latter would be found on average to Exceed the former in Value by at least three to one.'

JOSIAH TUCKER [(1713–1799)]

THERE WAS A CONSUMER REVOLUTION in eighteenth-century England. More men and women than ever before in human history enjoyed the experience of acquiring material possessions. Objects which for centuries had been the privileged possessions of the rich came, within the space of a few generations, to be within the reach of a larger part of society than ever before, and, for the first time, to be within the legitimate aspirations of almost all of it. Objects which were once acquired as the result of inheritance at best, came to be the legitimate pursuit of a whole new class of consumers.

What men and women had once hoped to inherit from their parents, they now expected to buy for themselves. What were once bought at the dictate of need, were now bought at the dictate of fashion. What were once bought for life, might now be bought several times over. What were once available only on high days and holidays through the agency of markets, fairs and itinerant pedlars were increasingly made available every day but Sunday through the additional agency of an ever-advancing network of shops and shop-keepers. As a result 'luxuries' came to be seen as mere 'decencies', and 'decencies' came to be seen as 'necessities'. Even 'necessities' underwent a dramatic metamorphosis in style, variety and availability.

Where once material possessions were prized for their durability, they were now increasingly prized for their fashionability. Where once a fashion might last a lifetime, now it might barely last a year. Where once women had merely dreamed of following the prevailing London fashions, they could now follow them daily in the advertisements in the provincial press, and actually buy them from the ever-increasing number of commercial outlets dedicated to satisfying their wants and their needs. Where once consumers eager for new fashions were dependent on the chance of rumour and the impressions of gossip, they could now rely on the accurate details of the illustrated fashion print or ring the changes for themselves on the endless combinations made possible by the English fashion doll; instead of what a quick eye and a retentive memory could glean from the dress of the rich or a visit of the fashionable, there were now precise details minutely recorded in the pages of the fashion magazines for a new and larger market to pore over. Where once the ability to wear such fashions was limited to the very few, now rising real family incomes brought them increasingly within the reach of the many.

All these changes took place within the confines of the eighteenth century. The result of these changes for those engaged in making and selling objects for the person and for the home were revolutionary. And those making and selling such consumer goods had not only responded to those changes; they had, as a result of their earnest commercial endeavours, played a substantial and a positive role in bringing them about. They had helped to release and to satisfy a consumer boom of major proportions.

This is not to suggest, of course, that the *desire* to consume was an eighteenth-century novelty. It was the *ability* to do so which was new. The ferocious pursuit of getting and spending has a long history. The feverish pursuit of fashion is just as ancient. Extravagant patterns of consumer behaviour can be easily traced back to antiquity; and one does not need to trouble post-seventeenth century Europe for the most grotesque examples of conspicuous consumption. But in the past the acquisitive part of society was a tiny one. Its indomitable pursuit of possessions satisfied more than personal greed and personal whim. It signalled more than simple, or even ornate, extravagances. It served important social and political functions too. Rich clothes, fine furs and precious gems, for instance, could mark the divinity of a king, and radiate the splendour and standing of his court. They could underline the exclusive status of the nobility, or the professional status of lawyers, doctors, and the educated élite. To preserve those distinctions sumptuary laws might be required to reinforce the effects of poverty, to buttress the conservative effects of custom, to insist on the unavailability of a desired cloth, to prevent commercial cunning from bringing it within the reach of those who aspired to wear it.

The barriers to a consumer society were therefore numerous and effective. To overcome them required changes in attitude and thought, changes in prosperity and standards of living, changes in commercial technique and promotional skills, sometimes changes even in the law itself. Above all it required the commercialization of society—the process with which this book is mainly concerned. That process was so pervasive that to do justice to it requires that it be followed beyond the world of advertising and selling, beyond the world of fashion and credit. It needs to be pursued into the political world of eighteenth-century England, into the commercialization of leisure, and of childhood, and into the world of invention and creation, where unabashed by any sense of the plenitude of Nature men deliberately sought to create new and improved species and exciting novelties with which to delight the eye, to exhibit one's taste and to assert one's wealth. The avowed intention was to proclaim one's ability constantly to improve on the old and the inherited, and of course, to swell the demand for what was new and exciting and modern.

The changes in attitude encompassed major political, intellectual and social adjustments as well as the more obvious economic realignments. To demonstrate the revolutionary nature of these changes, it will be necessary to marshal a wide array of diverse evidence, to explain in detail some of the reasons for, and the methods by which, the changes were effected, and to dissect some case studies of the changes themselves and the individual techniques of those who brought them about.

In claiming for the cumulative outcome a qualitative and distinctively important change of lifestyles, in speaking of a commerical revolution, in announcing the birth of a consumer society, it is not intended to dismiss the evidence for commercial change before the eighteenth century. Indeed an appreciation of the developments and embryonic growth of consumer behaviour in earlier periods is a necessary prerequisite for the dramatic turning point which is claimed for Georgian England.

But if there is no intention to condemn the value of what German historians call the *Frühgeschichte* of commercial activity, it is intended to put it firmly into perspective.

One could easily be forgiven for thinking that historians have been too prodigal in their inventive labelling of the past. Their zeal in finding revolutions, renaissances and rebirths— each one predating the last—has often been altogether excessive. One has to admit that there have been many false pregnancies, and some births so premature that the infant so fondly announced by one historian has been allowed to die without regret by the consensus of his historical colleagues.

Some of these unjustified announcements in the birth columns of the academic journals have performed a useful role. They have provoked a reevaluation of the evidence and, in doing so, often established the recognition of significant economic developments in periods previously dismissed under labels so unpromising for commerical development as the Dark Ages or the Bronze Age.[1] But their importance is often absurdly exaggerated by titles proclaiming the 'commercial revolutions' of Bronze Age and even Stone Age Britain, where first the wide distribution of bronze cauldrons has been held by respected scholars to herald industrial and commercial revolutions of the eighth century B.C.; and the distribution of axe heads from the flint mines of Grimes Graves has been held to point to an even earlier retailing revolution. Compared with these extreme examples the commercial revolutions found lurking unexpectedly in medieval and early modern Europe seem highly respectable and certainly more understandable.[2] Gibbon's sardonic dismissal of Charlemagne's economic activities as being little more than a preoccupation 'with the care of his poultry and the sale of his eggs' perhaps explains the medievalists' attempts to redress the balance,[3] but the titles under which they announce their revisionary exercise are often comically exaggerated. 'Le grand commerce' of the Merovingian Age, 'The Resurgence of Commerce' in the tenth century, the commercial Revolutions revolving remorselessly and repetitively in virtually every century, 'big business' booming in 'The Birth of Western Economy in the Dark Ages', are, as the more cautious scholars have readily admitted, 'too grandiose to describe the modest activities' in which most of these early traders were engaged.[4]

The evidence too is often exiguous in the extreme, as modest in amount as the activities it has been used to misdescribe, as unimportant as the developments it has been used to exaggerate. The evidence in favour of Merovingian 'shops' consists of little more than a mere mention in Gregory of Tours of *domus negociatorum*;[5] and even the negative evidence is often disturbingly meagre—the fact that *vague* is a word of Scandinavian origin is used as 'decisive proof of Frankish indifference to things of the sea' and therefore of seaborne trade.[6]

It is very proper for historians to identify these first stirrings of commercial activity— 'merchants settling down in one place, goods warehouses being built in towns, stalls appearing, then small shops and workshops, and populations no longer consisting solely of clerics, nobles and peasants . . . capitalism making its timid appearance under the name *commenda*, the oldest form of production loan'—but it is equally necessary to remember that 'these origins are not easy to discern, since they are few and far between and often obscure'.[7] The evidence must not be overstated. Their importance must not be exaggerated. The labels offered to the work of such great scholars as Henri Pirenne, Ferdinand Lot, Alfons Dopsch and Robert Latouche are often heavily qualified in the text. The very proper doubts, the anxious evaluation, the tentative conclusions and, reassuringly often, the final negative verdicts of the historical profession are far more appropriate to the identification of a false pregnancy than to anything as dramatic and certain as birth.

It requires evidence as unambiguous and changes as obvious as those which can be found in the eighteenth century to justify the vital metaphor of birth. One can see the embryonic signs of a consumer society appearing clearly enough in seventeenth-century England,[8] but to speak merely of the continued *development* of a consumer society in the eighteenth century would not acknowledge sufficiently the sharp break in trend between Stuart England and Georgian England. To speak of the further *growth* of a consumer society would be even more banal—far too flat a description of an event which excited such a positive reaction, such an excited response from contemporary observers, and which introduced such marked changes into so many people's lives.

To speak of a birth indicates the organic nature of the whole development, the need for a long preceding period of growth, and the necessity for many further stages[9] before the maturity of 'a society of high mass consumption' would be reached;[10] and yet also indicates the importance, the excitement, the novel sense of a dramatic event which is what I want to convey.

To claim that there is ample evidence to justify regarding these pervasive changes in commercial technique and consumer behaviour as an event of dramatic importance in English life is, by implication, to chide earlier historians for doing insufficient justice to it.

Some explanation is necessary, therefore, of why historians so willing to discuss the nature and causes and impact of the Industrial Revolution have been so chary in proclaiming a Consumer Revolution.[11] Some explanation is needed to explain why the widespread commercial changes which accompanied the decisive changes in production have received, relatively speaking, so much less attention. Some discussion is required of why attention has centred on the great industrialists and the supply side of the supply-demand equation, and why so little attention has been given to those hordes of little men who helped to boost the demand side and who succeeded in exciting new wants, in making available new goods, and in satisfying a new consumer market of unprecedented size and buying power. When Napoleon dismissed England as a nation of shopkeepers, he little knew how eager English historians would be to try to live down the jibe, and to efface from the record of historical significance the efforts of those busy, inventive, profit-seeking men of business whose eager advertising, active marketing and inspired salesmanship did so much in eighteenth-century England to usher in a new economy and a new demand structure in English society.[12]

Notes

1   V. Gordon Childe, *Prehistoric Communities of the British Isles* (1940), pp. 168–74, where he described 'a drastic reorganisation of the distributive side of the industry'.

2   For example R. de Roover, 'The Commercial Revolution of the Thirteenth Century', *Bulletin of the Business Historical Society*, vol. xvi (1942). Mrs. J. R. Green found another 'commercial revolution' skulking in the fifteenth century (*Town Life in the Fifteenth Century*. (1894). Vol. II, ch. 3. pp. 75–123), and many others have labelled the quickening of trade with such unfortunate labels. This is not the place to discuss these claims, but for a discussion of some of the evidence and arguments of

historians of the calibre of Henri Pirenne, Ferdinand Lot, Alfons Dopsch and others, see Robert Latouche, *Les Origins de l'Economie Occidentale*, (Paris 1956) part iv, ch. II, pp. 235–68, and Philip Grierson's foreword to the English translation, *The Birth of the Western Economy: Economic Aspects of the Dark Ages* (London 1961).

3   Philip Grierson, op. cit., p. xi.

4   Latouche, op. cit., p. 123.

5   Quoted by Grierson, op. cit., p. xi.

6   Latouche, op. cit., p. 121. As Latouche trenchantly commented 'Shops were rare, and the few allusions which might consciously refer to them are not very convincing'.

7   Latouche, op. cit., p. 235.

8   Joan Thirsk, *Economic Policy and Projects: The Development of a Consumer Society in Early Modern Europe* (1978); R. Davis, *A Commercial Revolution* (Historical Association Pamphlet, no. 64, 1967); and for a general review R. M. Hartwell, 'Economic Growth in England before the Industrial Revolution', *The Industrial Revolution and Economic Growth* (1971), pp. 21–41.

9   For a later stage of the process of commercialization, see Peter Mathias, *Retailing Revolution: A History of Multiple Retailing in the Food Trades* (1967).

10 W. W. Rostow, *The Stages of Economic Growth* (Cambridge 1960).

11 Some of the constituent parts of such a revolution have been identified (as can be seen in the work of E. W. Gilboy, E. B. Schumpeter, A. H. John, D. E. C. Eversley, E. A. Wrigley, E. L. Jones, A. W. Coats, H. J. Perkin and Joyce Appleby in particular, and as will be seen below), and some historians have been willing to recognize 'a rise of internal demand which permanently affected the level of expectations of most classes in English society. . . . One might say that the appetite for mass consumption had been roused': A. H. John, 'Aspects of English Economic Growth in the First Half of the Eighteenth Century', *Economica*, vol. XXVIII, no. 110 (May 1961), pp. 176–90. But many other aspects have been very much neglected—shamefully so in comparison with the supply side of the Industrial Revolution. As a result the Consumer Revolution of the Eighteenth Century still lacks its historian.

12 Those unhappily familiar with the near illegibility of my handwriting will realize that my thanks to Mrs. Patricia McCullagh for typing my manuscript greatly exceed those implied in the customary formal note of acknowledgement. I am grateful, too, to the British Academy and to the Wolfson Foundation for research grants which made possible some of the research involved in chapters 2 and 4. Finally my indebtedness to my wife, Dr. Melveena McKendrick of Girton College, Cambridge, is as usual more comprehensive than can easily be imagined and my thanks are, in consequence, beyond measure.

Chapter 54

Georges Vigarello

INTRODUCTION TO *CONCEPTS OF CLEANLINESS: CHANGING ATTITUDES IN FRANCE SINCE THE MIDDLE AGES*

Georges Vigarello, "Introduction", *Concepts of Cleanliness: Changing Attitudes in France since the Middle Ages* (Cambridge: Cambridge University Press, 1988), 1–3.

IN THE COURSE OF recounting the familiar exploits of Don Carlos, mysteriously abducted by masked ruffians, *Le Roman comique* (1651) describes its hero [washing and dressing]. The prisoner is noble and the surroundings are sumptuous. Scarron describes both actions and objects: the attentiveness of the servants, naturally, and the magnificence of certain objects, such as the chandelier of chased silver-gilt, but also the indicators of cleanliness. These, however, defy our understanding; they are at the same time close to, and totally remote from, our own. They may bear some resemblance to certain practices of today, but they are, in fact, far removed from them. Scarron's interest focusses on indications which have today become subsidiary, whilst he pays little attention to others which have become, in contrast, essential. There are things missing and things left vague; it is as if our own most routine actions have yet to be invented, though some, nevertheless, have their equivalents here. In particular, the single act of washing which he mentions is very brief: 'I forgot to tell you that I think he washed his mouth, as I know he took great care of his teeth.'[1] Attention to cleanliness is more explicitly concentrated on linen and clothes. 'The masked dwarf stepped forward to serve him, and had him take the most beautiful linen in the world, the whitest and the most sweet-smelling.'[2]

There is no mention of water at any point in these scenes, except for the water which washed his mouth. Attention to cleanliness was a matter of sight and smell. It existed, with its own requirements, routines and frame of reference, but it served appearance above all. A norm was expressed and visible. The difference from today is that it applied primarily not to the skin but to linen, to what was most immediately visible. This example alone shows that it is foolish to deny the existence of practices of cleanliness in a pre-scientific culture. The norms, in this regard, do not start from nothing. They have their basis and their purpose.

What we need to examine is how they change and are elaborated, how they are manifested and transformed.

A history of cleanliness should first, therefore, show how new requirements and constraints gradually emerge. It has to retrace a journey in which the scene from *Le Roman comique* constitutes only a stage. Other, less refined, scenes have preceded it, where, for example, changing the shirt did not have the same importance. Linen, in particular, received little attention, and did not serve as a criterion of distinction, in the scenes of royal receptions described two centuries earlier in *Le Roman de Jehan de Paris*.

Cleanliness here reflects the civilising process, in its gradual moulding of bodily sensations, its heightening of their refinement, and its release of their subtlety. It is a history of the refining of behaviour, and of the growth of private space and of self-discipline: the care of oneself for one's own sake, a labour ever more squeezed between the intimate and the social. On a wider plane, it is the history of the progressive pressure of civilisation on the world of direct sensations.[3] It reveals the extension of their range. A cleanliness defined by regular washing of the body supposes, quite simply, a greater sharpness of perception and a stronger self-discipline than a cleanliness which is essentially defined by the changing of linen and its degree of whiteness.

It is essential, before embarking on such a history, to put aside our own frame of reference; cleanliness has to be recognised in behaviour long forgotten. The 'dry' wash of the courtier, for example, who wiped his face with a white cloth rather than wash it, responded to a standard of cleanliness which was altogether rational in the seventeenth century. It was considered and justified, even though it makes little sense today, when feelings and meanings have changed. We have to rediscover this lost sensibility.

It is also necessary to overturn the hierarchy of categories of authority; it was not, for example, hygienists who laid down the criteria of cleanliness in the seventeenth century, but the authors of manuals of etiquette, experts in manners, not scholars. The slow accumulation of constraints was accompanied by the displacement of the knowledge on which they were based.

Representing this process as a succession of accretions, or as an accumulation of pressures brought to bear on the body, however, risks giving a false picture. It was not simply a question of the accumulation of constraints. Such a history needs to connect with other histories. Cleanliness is inevitably affected by images of the body, by images, more or less obscure, of the corporeal shell, by even obscurer images of the body's physical composition. It was, for example, because water was seen as capable of penetrating the body, that bathing had a very special significance in the sixteenth and seventeenth centuries; hot water, in particular, was believed to weaken the organs and leave the pores open to unwholesome air. Thus there existed a set of ideas about the body which had their own history and causes. They, too, affected sensibility, and influenced norms, which could not change in isolation from them. They operated on ground already occupied, and never controlled a passive body. Images of the body had to change before constraints could change. So, too, did latent conceptions of the body, such as those which dictated its functioning and its capabilities.

So a history of bodily cleanliness brings into play a wider and more complex history. All the ideas which gave the body its contours, shaped its appearance and suggested its internal mechanisms had primarily a social terrain. The cleanliness of the seventeenth century, attached essentially to linen and external appearance, and expressed in, for example, the display of objects or the fine points of vestimentary symbols, was obviously very different from the cleanliness which, at a later date, was expressed in the protection of the body's organism, or of whole populations. In the same way, a court society which conformed to the aristocratic criteria of appearance and display, differed from a bourgeois society more concerned with the physical and demographic strength of peoples. A concentration on purely external appearance changed to a more complex attention to physical resources, to strength, and to hidden forces. Thus the history of bodily cleanliness is also social history.

Finally, the word 'cleanliness' is employed here in a wide sense, as applying to the whole body or to the whole collection of objects capable of standing for it.

Notes

1   P. Scarron, *Le Roman comique* (1651) in *Romanciers du XVIIe siècle* (Paris, 1973), p. 560.
2   *Ibid.*
3   The work of Norbert Elias, *La Civilisation des moeurs* (Paris, 1973, 1st ed. in German, 1939, trans. English as *The Civilising Process*, Oxford, 1978) is crucial here.

Chapter 55

Cornelius Holtorf

NOTES ON THE LIFE HISTORY OF
A POTSHARD

Cornelius Holtorf, "Notes on the Life History of a Potshard". Unpublished MS, 2007.

THE PRESENT CHAPTER will investigate how archaeologists transform a contemporary object into an *ancient* artefact of a particular age. [. . .] It has become a truism that every generation has the past it desires or deserves. But the material basis of these changing understandings of the past is usually taken for granted: ideas change, while the artefacts stay the same. Current presentations of the archaeological heritage have been criticised for their commodification of the past as well as for the ideological messages they convey, but the very materiality of the artefacts themselves remained largely unchallenged and was never subjected to the same critical analysis (but see Shanks 1998). We may be able to interpret and 'construct' the meaning of an object in any way we like, but we are seemingly unable to construct the object 'itself'. The task of the archaeologist is usually described as finding, documenting, and interpreting, but not as *creating* the material remains of the past. By the same token, the archaeologists and other experts are expected to establish, and not negotiate, the age of genuine archaeological artefacts. Yet ultimately it is a particular kind of contemporary practice which brings ancient artefacts about.

One of the reasons why this may seem counter-intuitive at first is the power of the life-history metaphor. [. . .] Like human bodies, things that have once been 'born' appear to live as what they 'are' until they die. They may have been used and interpreted in different ways along the way, but their material identity seems to remain unchangeable and continuous all along: a megalith has always been a megalith, a stone-axe has always been a stoneaxe. Arguably, however, the radically different meanings such things can have in different contexts put even the assumption of a continuing material 'core' in doubt. [. . .]
[. . .]

An ethnographic approach

In order to understand how archaeologists add age-value to the properties of an artefact, it is therefore essential to focus on its present context alone. No life of the artefact before the moment of discovery can be assumed: any assertions about its origins and earlier uses and interpretations are the outcome of processes that take place today. However, I do not mean to imply that the artefact did not *exist* previously. The point is rather that this is of no great concern, since *all* its properties and characteristics, including its material identity and age, are ascribed to it some time after the moment of discovery. They are not gradually revealed but slowly assembled (Shanks 1998). [. . .] [A]rchaeological objects may [. . .] be different things to different people today – they can have parallel identities in parallel present contexts. Crucially, this does not imply that a thing's properties and characteristics are completely arbitrary, but that they are determined by various factors effective in their present lives. An archaeologist [. . .] is constrained in his or her assessment not only by the limits of his own knowledge and experience, but also by available techniques and by the dominant norms and values of academic discourse.

To study the actual processes that shape an artefact's identity today requires an ethnographic approach, employing direct observation and interviews as its main methodologies. One of the most important characteristics of the 'ethnographic' approach is that the observer maintains an independence from both normative prescriptions of how things ought to be and from the insiders' own perceptions of what they are doing (see also Edgeworth 1990, 1991). A similar ethnographic approach relating to the natural sciences has long been applied by sociologists of science. One of the most influential, so-called 'laboratory studies' was Karin Knorr-Cetina's study of *The Manufacture of Knowledge* (1981). In this chapter, I will be applying a similar approach to archaeological practice, studying what happens to an artefact from the moment of discovery on the site to its display in a museum. I will be taking laboratory studies into the field. What is to be gained from such research? The greatest benefit is to find out more about what it actually is that archaeologists are doing when they 'study the past'. How do they transform certain things into archaeological evidence? How do they learn what kind of artefacts they are dealing with? And how do they actually get to know their ancient-ness, i.e. the fact that they are associated with a particular age of the past?

Ethnography of a potshard

I will be focussing on a thing that was quickly to become a 'potshard'. It began its life on 4 July 2000, at 11:01 to be precise. It was 'born' right on top of Monte Polizzo, where Erica Grijalva helped it along emerging out of the ground. Monte Polizzo is a large hilltop settlement in Western Sicily. Most of the occupation deposits on the mountain date to the 6th and 5th centuries BC. That settlement was possibly associated with a people known to the Greeks as Elymians who lived in an inland area that was disputed between the Elymians, the Greeks and the Carthaginians. Among the participants of the large international excavation project that now occupies Monte Polizzo every summer, its highest part is known as 'The Acropolis'. This is where, during the summer of 2000, a team led by Ian Morris of Stanford University began their excavations. He and his team revealed a semi-circular stone structure on the very top of the mountain, as well as the remains of a rectangular building nearby (Morris et al [2001]). In 2001, this building turned out to be one of a complex of at least three rectilinear rooms with a courtyard and multiple terrace walls." [. . .]
[. . .]

On an excavation, not everything is kept. (One day at Monte Polizzo I kept a bag for things we did not usually keep.) So what made Erica discover and keep this thing? – just for a minute ignoring the fact that I was hovering over Erica and taking pictures of the 'thing' in front of her, then squatting nearby and observing the proceedings. Julian Thomas said (1996: 62) that "in order to 'do archaeology' we have to recognise certain things as representing evidence. Archaeological analysis is consequently a specific form of 'clearing' which enables entities to be recognised in a very specific kind of way". As Matthew Edgeworth argued (1990; 1991: 104, 149–52), emerging objects are generally at least half-expected and therefore to a certain extent already known and understood even before they are 'found'. What is anticipated jumps quickly into the eye when the soil's manipulation by the towel and the associated movement of the excavator's body, head, and eyes brings a host of possible objects of significance into view. In the Monte Polizzo project diggers routinely find, and keep artefacts, bones, and a variety of scientific samples, for example for pollen, charcoal and macrofossil analysis. Such object categories are highly contingent. They are adopted because of particular research interests, old habits, established conventions or historical accidents, not because they are necessarily the best possible way to categorise things archaeologists come across (Conolly 2000, Lucas 2001: chapter 3). The categories used are subject to change at any time, and they could be very different. Ian Hodder figured (1997: 695) that

> If the object categories on which archaeological research is founded can be seen to be the product of the conventional lenses used in analysis, the door is opened for constructing 'new' objects of study which partition the object-world in different and multi-scalar ways. 'Objects' such as 'burning', or 'decoration', or 'rubbish' cut across the lower-level domains based on conventional artefact categories.

The project Erica was working for did not have any such far-reaching ambitions, although it did (and does) introduce a range of innovative methodologies to Sicilian archaeology. At the moment the thing was found, Erica had to make the crucial decision as to whether or not that thing was valuable evidence, i.e. an artefact, a bone, a useful sample, or something else worth keeping. This is a routine decision which diggers like Erica make hundreds of times every day. But what is worth keeping anyway? In 1958, Lewis Binford provoked James Griffin when he decided to keep and catalogue large amounts of fire-cracked rock as well as coke bottle tops and nails (Binford 1972: 128). But value is not only linked to classification. Very small things are often not deemed worth classifying and worth keeping in the same way that others are – which is why on many excavations not all earth is routinely being sieved and why size does matter (Hodder 1999: 15–17, Orton et al 1993: 47).

Based on a superficial resemblance with other 'potshards', Erica recognised the thing as as a potshard and deemed it worth keeping. Erica then carefully cleaned away the dirt around it and gradually revealed more and more of what she still believed was a shard. My watch showed 11:25. As in this case, it is usually the trowelling excavator who transforms 'natural' material into 'cultural' material by making sense of it in a particular way (Edgeworth 1991: 135, 174; Yarrow 2000: 17–20). The initial identification may later be revised when more of the object is revealed, or when it is first touched, or when it snaps, or when it is carefully cleaned between the fingers, or when the trench supervisor is consulted. In the space of a split-second, a 'shard' may thus become 'dirt', or a 'stone' a 'bone', or a 'root' a 'single find'. Clearly this, if anything, is interpretation at the trowel's edge (Hodder 1997, 1999: chapter 5). Later, people may change their minds. Some classifications can later be undone, for example when a shard is recovered from among the bones, but others are irreversible, for example when a 'shard' is later discovered on the dirt heap (with the original location unknown).

At 11:43 Erica placed the shard into the pottery bowl on the side of the trench she was working in. It carried a label stating

MP 2000
Acropolis
July 4, 2000
Trench 17651
East Bulk
8

This written information is the first step in a series of inscriptions, including drawn plans, photographs, context-sheets, and eventually site reports, through which discovered artefacts are transformed into textual objects and 'objective' data (Edgeworth 1991: 146 [. . .]).

Later the content of the bowl was transferred into a plastic bag, which was labelled and then carried down the mountain to the parked cars, from where it got a ride directly to the dig house in the nearby town of Salemi. At 15:43 on that same afternoon, Erica began washing 'her' shards. This gave her a chance to review whether all items in the pottery bag were indeed potshards. Any things that she no longer felt were appropriately classified would now have been removed from the bag. A 'bone' would have been removed and put into the bones bag, while a 'pebble' in the bag would in practice probably have been thrown into the bushes behind the table where much of the washing took place. Again, people may later change their views or admit mistakes or others may disagree with their classifications, but probably more often than we would like, facts are created that cannot be undone. Moreover, there are types of pottery that dissolve in water, and there are types of decoration that suffer from scrubbing, and there are countless little bits and pieces that break off and are thrown out with the water, while other pieces are mixed up during the subsequent drying process in the sun. I remember from my very first excavation in 1986 how a tiny strange thing which my trench supervisor had just identified as the fragment of a bronze fibula a short time later simply disappeared out of my hand, and was never found again. What this means is that a pot is a bone is a piece of dirt is nothing left. At the end of the process of cleaning, inspecting and drying the shard under investigation was still in the bag, which was good news for my project.

What I have established so far is that the thing, which Erica discovered in the morning on Monte Polizzo, had by the same evening become a clean and dry shard of pottery in a plastic bag which also contained a number of other shards found on the same day in the same context. All this was mostly due to Erica Grijalva, an undergraduate student in Mechanical Engineering from Stanford University, California. Knowing something as a potshard is to know a lot already:

> This is a material which is familiar to us, and from the moment when it is turned up by the trowel the way in which we understand it is already con-strained by a range of prejudices and understandings. We know certain things about how pottery is made, what it can be used for, and the conditions under which people can routinely make use of pots. Before we begin, these will inevitably colour the way in which we will interpret the artefact. When the artefact is recovered, it is already a part of a world. (Thomas 1996: 63)

But the really crucial moment in the life of the shard lay still ahead: the attribution of age.

Artefacts found on an excavation can be of very different ages – from a few months (or even contemporaneous with the archaeologists) to many millennia. Diggers are usually encouraged to keep and record all artefacts, although most of them would in practice not look twice at rusty nails or beer bottles that are 'obviously' of no great antiquity and therefore not 'worth' keeping. [. . .]

Things that derive from the archaeological excavation itself, such as bent nails, small ends of string, or food remains are quickly discarded, too. All such things are often not considered to be finds but 'rubbish'. As a result, the most recent phases of occupation of archaeological sites tend to be systematically undervalued. This raises the question on what grounds diggers are able to identify relatively quickly that one artefact is 'ancient' (which I take to mean from before a possible local person's own memory, i.e. older than 50–80 years), and another one is mere recent rubbish. This is not a trivial question, considering that the digger is not able to apply any kind of sophisticated dating method on site. Instead he or she will glance at the object, maybe remove some dirt that is stuck to it, look again, and make a decision after these few moments.

Based on my observations at various excavations I have taken part in (and not applying specifically to Monte Polizzo), diggers come to their decisions about the age of an artefact in a negative way: if it isn't clearly recent, it must be old. Recent artefacts are identified and subsequently discarded if they

(1)   are positively identified by the digger as belonging to the project (from personal memory),
(2)   resemble artefacts known to be recent AND come from layers that are likely to be recent (e.g. surface, infills from top layers etc),
(3)   are considered as recent by consulted authorities on site (e.g. trench supervisor).

In case of doubt, the object is likely to be kept and treated 'as if ancient', until it can be re-evaluated after washing, possibly consulting further authorities.

The point of this brief discussion is not to complain about any possible misidentifications. It is more interesting to note that by the time a find reaches the finds laboratory and its team, the antiquity of that find has not yet been positively established. The same was true for the 'shard' I was following. [. . .] Erica of course had never had any doubts about the fact that this was an 'ancient shard' just like all the others that she and the other diggers had been recovering for the past few weeks. My own decision to follow this particular thing also relied on my judgement that it was an ancient artefact that would go through the normal process of finds analysis, or I would not have selected it. We could of course both have been proven wrong. For example by a thermoluminescence date for the shard. But in practice such direct dating methods are not often employed in archaeological projects, and usually restricted to a few carefully selected individual pieces. Instead, finds from Monte Polizzo were usually dated by Emma Blake and her team in the project's finds laboratory.

The moment of truth came one day after the discovery of the shard, on 5 July 2000 at 13:43, to be precise. Emma Blake had at that point opened the plastic bag with 'my' shard in it, and the contents spread out on a table. With a small team of helpers, one of her main tasks was to go through all the bags of pottery and enter the information they contained into the project's database. This database would become the primary and most important source of information for later post-excavation analysis. Whatever Emma listed here, would to a large extent determine the information that the project could ever get out of that thing. To paraphrase Douglas Adams, it would be the answer to the question of the meaning of the thing in the universe. Emma came to the conclusion that that answer was "F 24" – confirming a hunch she had had at 10:55 when she first saw the shard while putting all the dry shards in the cassette into the plastic bag. When I asked her, Emma defined F 24 to me as a "generic, coarse ware, pithos/storage-vessel, grey-red-brown-orange colours, grey core, handmade, undecorated, grog as primary inclusion, a couple of centimetres thick".

This identification was made in the space of about one or two seconds after picking up the shard and looking at it. Emma clearly had a lot of experience, and a lot of intuition. My shard was neither the first nor the only fabric F24 she had come across; this was one of the most common fabrics on site and not usually one that was difficult to identify. Hence Emma did not consider it a potentially controversial decision. She did not see a need to consult others in the room for their opinion but I really do not think that her classification as F24 could seriously be questioned by anyone. Having said that, it is well known among pottery specialists that the association of potshards with a particular fabric type depends partly on the psychology of the person who is associating (Orton et al. 1993: 73).

To complete the process of analysis, the F24 shards were weighed, returned to their bag, and the bag was marked "undiagnostic". Undiagnostic shards are such shards that are effect-ively not deemed worth being looked at again in any detail; they are not drawn and not photographed. By now it was 13:58 and after quarter of an hour of fame the shard was basically over and done with. What followed was entry of the data on the recording sheet into the computer, and then the bag being stored in a cassette and moved around . . . and moved around again . . . for over a week . . . until it was moved again and finally being transported on 13 July, at 9:58 to be precise, to the local Museum where it was carried through the gate at 10:15, and up the stairs, and finally found its final resting place in a large store room.

All this may sound pretty mundane and unsurprising. But what had effectively happened is that a thing found in the ground on 4 July 2000 had been authenticated, identified and dated by an archaeological project. When it entered the museum's store room, at 10:16 on 13 July 2000, the thing had become a fragment of a large storage vessel of the Iron Age settlement on top of Monte Polizzo. This transformation was due to specific archaeological formation processes, featuring Erica Grijalva who placed the thing repeatedly into the right bowls and bags so that it became established as a potshard, and Emma Blake who saw quickly that this shard was of the fabric F24. Also important was, of course, that the shard was meaningfully constituted inasmuch as Erica was working in a particular excavation trench on a particular site, that Emma knew about the origin of the shard when she made her judgement, and that the cassettes in the Museum were clearly labelled as coming from the Monte Polizzo archaeological project.

This is where I left the shard. But it is not hard to imagine the next events, whenever they might actually happen. There may be archaeologists of the Monte Polizzo Project who will study the material in detail, although it is perhaps less likely that anybody will ever look through the masses of undiagnostic material. Eventually all the finds will formally be handed over to the museum for permanent storage and display. Susan Pearce argued (1999: 17–8):

> Once material has been received into the museum, it has achieved the official *imprimatur* of value and significance conveyed by the institution and its cura-torial complement [. . .] and henceworth it will be treated in ways which make its meaning manifest, meaning which is thought of as 'inherent' and 'natural' but which is, in fact, a matter for deliberation and contrivance on the part of the curators.

As a new addition to a museum's collection the shard is likely to be moved around a few more times, and eventually re-classified and labelled in a general way, determining its place in the overall collection. This particular shard is unlikely to be exhibited to the public, but no doubt others from the same site will be placed in cases together with their museum labels. Whether displayed or not, the museum will provide the permanent new context of the finds from Monte Polizzo, and the archaeological project which in some sense created not only the artefacts as such but also the entire site will have become invisible and written out of the objects' life-stories. Whereas the archaeologists labelled what they associated with the history of Monte Polizzo, future visitors will associate with the history of Monte Polizzo (and beyond) what they see labelled in the museum. In this sense, the label is indeed more important than the object itself, which only comes to illustrate the statements made by the label (Pearce 1999: 18, 20).

The bottom line of this chapter is that the lives of artefacts in the present are not half as exciting as those they had in the past. And yet, those past lives are the direct outcome of their present lives. Only with a secure identity as an artefact and its ancient-ness being established can archaeologists ever hope to involve a thing in any kind of academically plausible relationships with people of a past period. These crucial properties of things are not in every case verified through detailed analysis and careful evaluation of the results by an expert in the field who is able to recognise things for *what they are* and therefore *what they were*. Instead, most decisions appear to be made in an *ad hoc* kind of way in a matter of seconds. When Emma was determining the fabric of the shard, she effectively also verified its ancient-ness. Important evaluations emerge as the by-product of unquestioned routine processes and are partly owed to non-specialists such as Erica Grijalva. Such classifications and verifications are contextually specific constructions which bear the mark of the situational contingency by which they are generated. In effect, archaeological projects are not the consequence of ancient artefacts but ancient artefacts are the consequence of archaeological projects.

The argument I am making here is not about the flaws of objectivity and the inevitability of being subjective. Thomas Yarrow has shown in an ethnographic analysis of an archaeological excavation project (2000) how objectivity and subjectivity are firmly intertwined. The objectivity of an archaeological artefact is established by diggers who are each trying to act and conceptualise things objectively, i.e. by applying collectively known archaeological expertise and rules of discourse. Similarly, the academic credibility and thus objectivity of the entire site depends on the ability of the site director to act conventionally and attract the association of eminent archaeologists and institutions. People can thus embody objectivity. Artefacts, on the other hand, do not only owe their status and existence entirely to individual subjects' discoveries (Edgeworth 1991) but can also literally embody people's subjectivities. Finding and recovering artefacts in a conventional way partly make a person an archaeologist. Private collectors may even regard the ordered artefacts they possess as extensions of themselves (Pearce 1999: 15). On an excavation project, the identity of diggers is firmly linked to the trenches they work in and the artefacts they discover. Moreover, Yarrow also showed how finds made through re-excavating previously dug trenches come to stand for the subjectivities of the archaeologists who missed them and thus call the objectivity of the original work into question. In these instances, artefacts objectify subjectivities, although these will often be hidden in their subsequent public presentations. Both objectivity and subjectivity are thus not essential characteristics of things and people respectively but the result of particular social relations between people and things. Their subjectivities and objectivities are partly embodied by each other.

It was the aim of scientific laboratory studies to study scientific processes in action (Knorr-Cetina 1981). "The result, to summarize it in one sentence, was that nothing extraordinary and nothing 'scientific' was happening inside the sacred walls of these temples" (Latour 1983: 141). It has become clear in this chapter that this statement is no less valid in the case of an archaeological excavation.

This result has more general implications for our understanding of the way we classify and interpret material culture, because scientific practice is not categorically different from anything which is engaged in other (non-scientific) practices (Thomas 1996: 63). They illustrate in some detail how 'momentary, fluid and flexible' our classifications and interpretations often are (Hodder 1997). The material identities ascribed to things are not their essential properties but the result of relationships of people and things: their very materiality is potentially multiple and has not only a history but more than likely also a future (Shanks 1998, Thomas 1996: 70–82). I do not think that this insight has any grand consequences for the way we should or should not do archaeology in the future. It is more the other way around: the way we will do archaeology in the future may have consequences for our insights about the characteristics of material culture and the practices surrounding its interpretation. The past then is of the present; it is not a property that resides, and can be recovered in the materiality of the archaeological discoveries themselves. We cannot re-present the past in the present, and we cannot predict which past the future will have.

References

Binford, Lewis (1972) *An Archaeological Perspective*. New York and London: Seminar Press.

Conolly, James (2000) 'Çatalhöyük and the Archaeological "Object" ', in Ian Hodder (ed.) *Towards Reflexive Method in Archaeology: The Example of Çatalhöyük*, pp. 51–56. Cambridge: McDonald Institute of Archaeological Research.

Edgeworth, Matthew (1990) 'Analogy as practical reason: the perception of objects in excavation practice', *Archaeological Review from Cambridge* 9: 243–252.

Edgeworth, Matthew (1991) The Act of Discovery. An Ethnography of the Subject-Object Relation in Archaeological Practice. Unpublished Doctoral Dissertation. University of Durham.

Hodder, Ian (1997) ' "Always momentary, fluid and flexible": towards a reflexive excavation methodology', *Antiquity* 71: 691–700.

Hodder, Ian (1999) *The Archaeological Process. An Introduction*. Oxford: Blackwell.

Knorr-Cetina, Karin (1981) *The Manufacture of Knowledge*. Oxford: Pergamon Press.

Latour, Bruno (1983) 'Give Me a Laboratory and I Will Raise the World', in Karin Knorr-Cetina and Michael Mulkay (eds) *Science Observed*, pp. 141–170. London: Sage.

Lowenthal, David (1992) Authenticity? The dogma of self-delusion. In: M. Jones (ed.) *Why Fakes Matter. Essays on Problems of Authenticity*, pp. 184–192. London: British Museum Press.

Lucas, Gavin (2001) *Critical Approaches to Fieldwork. Contemporary and Historical Archaeological Practice*. London and New York: Routledge.

Morris, Ian, Trinity Jackman and Emma Blake (2001) 'Stanford University excavations on the acropolis of Monte Polizzo, Sicily, I: preliminary report on the 2000 season', *Memoirs of the American Academy in Rome* 46, 2001, 253–71.

Orton, Clive, Paul Tyers and Alan Vince (1993) *Pottery in Archaeology*. Cambridge: Cambridge University Press.

Pearce, Susan (1999) Presenting Archaeology. In: M. Merriman (ed.) *Making Early History in Museums*, pp. 12–27. London and New York: University of Leicester Press.

Shanks, Michael (1998) 'The Life of an Artefact in an Interpretive Archaeology', *Fennoscandia Archaeologica* 15: 15–42.

Thomas, Julian (1996) *Time, Culture & Identity. An interpretive archaeology*. London and New York: Routledge.

Yarrow, Thomas (2000) Excavating Knowledge: the relational capacities of persons and things on an archaeological dig. Unpublished undergraduate dissertation. University of Cambridge, Department of Social Anthropology.

Further Reading: Chapters 51 to 55

Appadurai, A. *The Social Life of Things: Commodities in Cultural Perspective* (Cambridge: Cambridge University Press, 1986).

Attfield, J. *Wild Things: The Material Culture of Everyday Life* (Oxford: Berg, 2000).

Bahn, Paul. *The Bluffer's Guide to Archaeology*. (revd edn) (London: Oval Books, 1999).

Belk, R. W. *Collecting in a Consumer Society* (London: Routledge, 2001).

Binford, Lewis R. *An Archaeological Perspective* (New York: Academic Press, 1972).

Bourdier, Jean-Paul and Nevar AlSayyad (eds). *Dwellings, Settlements and Tradition: Cross-Cultural Perspectives* (Lanham MD: University Press of America, for the International Association for the Study of Traditional Environment, 1989).

Braudel, Fernand. *Capitalism and Material Life, 1400–1800*. Trans. Miriam Kochan (New York: Harper and Row, 1975).

Brieger, G. H. "The Historiography of Medicine", *Companion Encyclopedia of the History of Medicine*, W. F. Bynum and Roy Porter (eds) (London: Routledge, 1993), 24–44.

Burrison, John A. *Brothers in Clay: The Story of Georgia Folk Pottery* (Athens: University of Georgia Press, 1983).

Bushman, Richard L. and Claudia L. Bushman. "The Early History of Cleanliness in America", *The Journal of American History* 74(4) (1988): 1213–38.

Classen, Constance. *Worlds of Sense: Exploring the Senses in History and across Cultures* (London: Routledge, 1993).

Corbin, Alain. *The Foul and the Fragrant: Odor and the French Social Imagination* (Cambridge, MA: Harvard University Press, 1986).

Eggener, Keith L. *American Architectural History: A Contemporary Reader* (London: Routledge, 2004).

Elias, Norbert. *The Civilizing Process: Sociogenetic and Psychogenetic Investigations*. Trans. Edmund Jephcott. (revd edn), Eric Dunning, Johan Goudsbloum and Stephen Mennell (eds) (Oxford: Blackwell, 2000).

Feathersone, M. "The Body in Consumer Culture", *Theory, Culture & Society* 1 (1982), 18–33.

Forman, Benno M. "Furniture for Dressing in Early America, 1650–1730: Forms, Nomenclature, and Use", *Winterthur Portfolio* 22(2/3) (1987), 149–64.

Gosden, Chris and Yvonne Marshall. "The Cultural Biography of Objects", *World Archaeology* 31(2) (1999): 169–178.

Hicks, Dan and Marcy C. Beaudry (eds). *The Cambridge Companion to Historical Archaeology* (Cambridge: Cambridge University Press, 2006).

Hodder, Ian. *The Archaeological Process: An Introduction* (Oxford: Blackwell, 1999).

— . *Theory and Practice in Archaeology* (London: Routledge, 1992).

Holtorf, Cornelius. "The Life-Histories of Megaliths in Mecklenburg-Vorpommern (Germany)", *World Archaeology* 30(1) (1998), 23–38.

— and Hakan Karlsson. *Philosophy and Archaeological Practice: Perspectives for the 21st Century* (Gotenburg: Bricoleur Press, 2000).

Hoy, Suellen. *Chasing Dirt: The American Pursuit of Cleanliness* (New York: Oxford University Press, 1995).

Kingery, W. David (ed.). *Learning From Things: Method and Theory of Material Culture Studies* (Washington, DC; London: Smithsonian Institution Press, 1996).

Lubar, Steven and W. David Kingery (eds). *History From Things: Essays on Material Culture* (London: Smithsonian Institution Press, 1993).

Ladurie, Emmanuel Le Roy. *Times of Feast, Times of Famine: A History of the Climate Since the Year 1000*. Trans. Barbara Bray (London: Allen & Unwin, 1971).

MacKenzie, M. *Androgynous Objects* (Melbourne: Harwood Academic Press, 1991).

Mintz, Sidney. *Sweetness and Power: Sugar in Modern History* (London: Sifton, 1985).

Numbers, Ronald L. (ed.). *Medicine in the New World: New Spain, New France and New England* (Knoxville: University of Tennessee Press, 1987).

Perry, Curtis (ed.). *Material Culture and Cultural Materialisms in the Middle Ages and Renaissance* (Turnhout, Belgium: Brepols, 2001).

Porter, Roy. "History of the Body Reconsidered", *New Perspectives on Historical Writing*, Peter Burke (ed.). (2nd edn) (Cambridge: Polity Press, 2001), 233–61.

Pounds, Norman J. G. *Hearth and Home: A History of Material Culture* (Bloomington: Indiana University Press, 1989).

Ramsey, Matthew. *Professional and Popular Medicine in France, 1770–1830: The Social World of Medical Practice* (Cambridge: Cambridge University Press, 1988).

Ribiero, Aileen. *Dress in Eighteenth-Century Europe, 1715–1789*. (revd edn) (New Haven: Yale University Press, 2002).

Riley, James C. *The Eighteenth-Century Campaign to Avoid Disease* (New York: St Martin's Press, 1987).

Roberts, K. B. and J. D. W. Tomlinson. *The Fabric of the Body* (Oxford: Clarendon Press, 1992).

Robertson, Cheryl. "Male and Female Agendas for Domestic Reform: The Middle-Class Bungalow in Gendered Perspective", *Winterthur Portfolio* 26(2/3) (1991), 123–41.

Roche, Daniel. *The Culture of Clothing: Dress and Fashion in the Ancien Regime*. (new edn) (Cambridge: Cambridge University Press, 1996).

— . *A History of Everyday Things: The Birth of Consumption in France, 1600–1800*. Trans. Brian Pearce (Cambridge: Cambridge University Press, 2000).

Schlereth, Thomas J. "Material Culture Research and Historical Explanation", *The Public Historian* 7(4) (1985), 21–36.

Smith, Virginia. *Clean: A History of Personal Hygiene and Purity* (Oxford: Oxford University Press, 2007).

Stafford, Barbara Maria. *Body Criticism: Imaging the Unseen in Enlightenment Art and Medicine* (Cambridge, MA: Massachusetts Institute of Technology Press, 1991).

Stocking, G. (ed.). *Objects and Others: Essays on Museums and Material Culture* (Madison: University of Wisconsin Press, 1985).

Styles, John. *The Dress of the People: Everyday Fashion in Eighteenth-Century England* (New Haven, CT: Yale University Press, 2008).

— and Amanda Vickery (eds). *Gender, Taste, and Material Culture in Britain and North America, 1700–1830*. New Haven, CT: Yale University Press, 2007.

Thomas, N. *Entangled Objects: Exchange, Material Culture, and Colonialism in the Pacific* (Cambridge, MA: Harvard University Press, 1991).

Tilden, Freeman. *Interpreting Our Heritage*. (3rd edn) (Chapel Hill: University of North Carolina Press, 1977).

Tilley, C. "Ethnography and material culture", *Handbook of Ethnography*, P. Atkinson, A. Coffey, S. Delamont, J. and L. Lofland (eds) (London: Sage, 2000), 258–72.

— . *Metaphor and Material Culture* (Oxford: Blackwell, 1999).

Trigger, Bruce G. *A History of Archaeological Thought* (Cambridge: Cambridge University Press, 1989).

Turner, Bryan S. "Recent Developments in the Theory of the Body", *The Body: Social Process and Cultural Theory*, Mike Featherstone, Mike Hepworth and Bryan S. Turner (eds) (London: Sage, 1991), 1–35.

Vlach, John Michael. "Studying African American Artifacts: Some Background for the Winterthur Conference, "Race and Ethnicity in American Material Life", *Winterthur Portfolio* 33(4) (1998), 211–14.

Wright, Lawrence. *Clean and Decent. The Fascinating History of the Bathroom and the Water Closet* (London: Routledge & Kegan Paul, 1960).

MAUSS, MARCEL (1872–1950)

Allen, Nicholas J. *Categories and Classifications: Maussian Reflections on the Social* (New York; Oxford: Berghahn Books, 2000).

Douglas, Mary. "Foreword: Introduction to Mauss's essay on the Gift", *Risk and Blame: Essays in Cultural Theory* (London: Routledge, 1992).

Fournier, Marcel. *Marcel Mauss: A Biography*. Trans. Jane Marie Todd (Princeton, NJ: Princeton University Press, 2006).

Fuller, C. J. "Review: The Gift", *Man* New Series 27(2) (1992), 431–3.

Hart, Keith. "Marcel Mauss: In Pursuit of the Whole. A Review Essay", *Comparative Studies in Society and History* 49(2) (2007), 473–85.

James, Wendy and Nicholas J. Allen (eds). *Marcel Mauss. A Centenary Tribute* (Oxford: Berghahn Books, 1998).

Lévy-Strauss, Claude. *Introduction to the Work of Marcel Mauss.* Trans. Felicity Baker (London: Routledge & Kegan Paul, 1987).

Parry, Jonathan. "The Gift, the Indian Gift and the 'Indian Gift' ", *Man* New Series 21(3) (1986), 453–73.

Richman, Michèle H. "Marcel Mauss (1872–1950)", *The Columbia History of Twentieth-Century French Thought*, Lawrence D. Kritzman and Brian J. Reilly (eds). Trans. Malcolm DeBevoise (New York: Columbia University Press, 2006), 615–17.

Schrift, Alan D. (ed.). *The Logic of the Gift: Toward an Ethic of Generosity* (New York: Routledge, 1997).

Glossary of critical terms

These terms and their associated theorists are listed in the Index.

For biographies of the authors mentioned here, see the Further Reading section at the close of each respective Part.

- For updated biographies of deceased British figures (those whose dates appear at the top of their text), with valuable bibliographies, see the *Oxford Dictionary of National Biography*, in print and online at http://www.oxforddnb.com
- For Americans, see *American National Biography*, in print and online at http://anb.org
- For Europeans, see Daniel Woolf (ed.). *A Global Encyclopedia of Historical Writing* (New York: Garland, 2003) 2 vols; M. Hughes-Warrington, *Fifty Key Historians* (London: Routledge, 2000).

A list of more extensive glossaries follows.

Archive and **archives** (from Greek, *public office* or *government*)
Until the arrival of digital conservation technology, **archive** (the singular form) referred to any depository for cataloguing, preserving, and consulting **primary materials**, normally accessible only to qualified scholars (for the sake of conserving the documents over time). It could also refer simply to a collection of **primary materials**, in printed or electronic formats. When used in the plural, **archives** usually refers to a public or institutional department that houses historical records and official documents. A digital archive can provide access to documents that have been scanned or transcribed, and therefore are not physically examined. **Methodological** and **hermeneutic** debates addressing the merits and limitations of consulting digital rather than original documents for the purposes of historical research are ongoing.

Landis, William E. and Robin L Chandler (eds). *Archives and the Digital Library* (London: Routledge, 2007).

McGann, Jerome. *Radiant Textuality: Literature after the World Wide Web* (Basingstoke: Palgrave, 2004).

Walch, T. and M. Daniels (eds). *A Modern Archives Reader: Basic Readings on Archival Theory and Practice* (Washington, DC: National Archives, 1984).

Empiricism (noun, from Greek, *experience; skill; experiment*)

To be called an **empiric** during the early eighteenth century was to be labelled with an insult—for the word's strict association with information derived only from the physical senses was seen to be atheistic, anti-philosophical, and therefore unsophisticated. Even John Locke, the great **empirical** philosopher of the late seventeenth century, was religious for reasons that he could not explain by reference to his sensory experience. During the eighteenth century, however, **empiricism** came into favour as moralists and scientists associated sensory experience with rationality, clarity of thought, depth of feeling, and honesty. Throughout, however, empiricism has been tied to the scientific method, by which one develops a theory or hypothesis only after one has gathered sufficient **object-ive** evidence—something that can only be discovered through careful experimentation and strict observation. Since empirical analysis begins with questions rather than theories, it can be contrasted usefully with the **deductive method**, by which one confirms or disconfirms a basic hypothesis either through abstract reasoning or experimentation.

G. Elton, *Return to Essentials: Some Reflections on the Present State of Historical Study* (Cambridge: Cambridge University Press, 1991).

Comparative method

Although historians have always compared their descriptions of social groups, sets of ideas, or other elements of their research with contrasting or similar examples, the **comparative method** remains most characteristic of the *Annaliste* historians who were well-versed in French sociology: they included Marc Bloch, Lucien Febvre, and Fernand Braudel. Famously embraced by late-nineteenth-century sociologists as a fundamental aspect of their practice, **comparativists** generate their analysis by studying the similarities and differences between things. Ideally, the comparative method will generate a richer sense of context, and prevent narrow-minded conclusions developed through the use of isolated examples. Of course an important challenge lies in the determination of appropriate comparisons, and whether to emphasize differences or similarities.

C. C. Ragin, *The Comparative Method: Moving beyond Qualitative and Quantitative Strategies* (Berkeley: University of California Press, 1987).

Conjectural history

Also known as philosophical history, **conjectural history** is a method of historical explanation that emerged out of the Scottish Enlightenment. An important component of the Science of Man, by which moral philosophers sought to chart the natural progress of Western civilization through a theoretical understanding of the human mind, conjectural history allowed historians to speculate on the nature of historical events for which no documentation existed. Its **progressive** logic and **deduct-ive** method helps to explain the prevalence of **stadial history** as a key feature of conjectural histories. At its simplest, **conjecturists** used their understanding of human nature to predict the origins and causes of historical phenomena (e.g. D. Hume, "The Origin of Government", 1741); in more sophis-ticated examples, conjectural history emboldened historians to explore the human motivations that led to important political or technological outcomes (e.g. W. Robertson, *History of America*, 1777). In the famous instance of Smith's *Wealth of Nations* (1776), **conjecturalism** comprised the notion of "the economic man" and "the invisible hand" as the guiding forces in modern history—Smith's entire historical project rested on these abstract and speculative constructs. Conjectural history was but one method of historical explanation that flourished in the second half of the eighteenth and early nineteenth centuries, and it can be a useful way to consider new trends in social, psychological, and political thought in the decades before and after the French Revolution.

Berry, Christopher J. *Social Theory of the Scottish Enlightenment* (Edinburgh: Edinburgh University Press, 1997).

Kidd, Colin. *Subverting Scotland's Past: Scottish Whig Historians and the Creation of an Anglo-British Identity 1689–c.1830* (Cambridge: Cambridge University Press, 1993).

les conjonctures (French, *economic or political trends*)
See historical time.

Cultural history
An ancient historical method that has risen to prominence only in the past thirty years, largely through the research and writings of Robert Darnton and Natalie Zemon Davis. Cultural historians use the widest range of archival, material, and visual materials to study the historical meaning of cultural expression. Therefore, like material historians, they are interested not only in the expression of ideas but also in the ways such expression was interpreted and circulated in the past. This has entailed borrowing insights from fields as diverse as literary criticism, cultural anthropology, art history, sociology, and even sexology. Instinctively populist, with an apparent commitment to engaging with theories and materials that explain past experiences of everyday life, cultural history has been accused of making dramatic interpretations based on arcane and possibly insignificant evidence; it has also, unquestionably, widened the range of historical inquiry by developing intellectual connections between fields and encouraging serious study of neglected materials.

Darnton, Robert. *The Great Cat Massacre and Other Episodes in French Cultural History* (New York: Vintage, 1985).

Davis, Nathalie Zemon. *Fiction in the Archives* (Stanford: Stanford University Press, 1987).

Hunt, Lynn (ed.). *The New Cultural History* (Berkeley: University of California Press, 1989).

Deductive approach (from medieval Latin, *to infer logically*)
Deductive approaches to history begin with a theory or hypothesis and then engage in research to explain, test, or prove its validity. One logical limitation of the deductive method is that a theory never disproved can still be incorrect—since, by placing the burden of proof on historical research rather than on the theory itself, one could make extensive use of the theory without encountering a reason to doubt it. For example, if one uses the deductive method to study the history of handwriting with the guiding theory that writers have always been left-handed, one could potentially conduct research for many years without ever encountering evidence to disprove that theory (which, of course, is false). On the other hand, the deductive method is crucial for widening one's range of historical concerns and depth of analysis, for two main reasons. First, if we approach historical scholarship without a guiding theory, we would have no clear set of ideas or questions through which to analyze the facts we find. Second, as twentieth-century advocates of historiography have shown, even the most orthodox empiricist or historicist will approach historical sources with unconscious or ideological priorities—and so the deductive method allows for a certain explicit clarity of our concerns as historians.

R. Keat and J. Urry, *Social Theory as Science* (London: Routledge, 1975).

Discourse (from Latin and French, *running to and fro; to traverse*)

For French philosopher Michel Foucault, **discourse** refers to the kinds of knowledge that are determined and imposed by social institutions such as law, religion, and medicine. Sometimes expressed through narrative means (such as printed rules, sacred texts, and spoken commandments) and non-narrative means (through anxiety of shame, normalization of behaviour, and fear of punishment), discourse has provided a tool for historical inquiry that continues to divide historians. Some historians have suggested that the term implies a **deductive** method that determines rather than examines historical phenomena (much like **ideological** approaches); others have found that an appreciation of discourse is essential to appreciate the subtle social and psychological meaning of everything they study.

Berkhofer, Robert. *Beyond the Great Story: History as Text and Discourse* (Princeton, NJ: Princeton University Press, 1995).
Foucault, Michel. *The Archaeology of Knowledge*. 1969. Trans. A. M. Sheridan Smith (London: Routledge, 2002).

Emplotment

Drawing on Kant's late-eighteenth-century belief that understanding requires organization of sensations into logical components; and on the Canadian literary critic Northrop Frye, who showed that Western literature comprises archetypal **metanarratives** (which include heroic tales of victory, tragic songs of loss, and comedies featuring hilarious twists of fate), the American historical theorist Hayden White argues that Western historians use **emplotment** both to convey and to understand the past. For White, emplotment is above all a narrative device that properly belongs to novelists, poets, and other writers of fiction. But historians use this device to express their ideas through narratives that have recognizable structures (or plots) or which use metaphors (analogues or figurative language), that always refer to other narratives whose meanings usually have nothing to do with the historical past that they mean to represent. For example, when a historian describes or analyzes the 1997 funeral of Princess Diana, she or he will use language that will allude to depictions of other grand state funerals, tragedies involving dead princesses, abandoned children, guilty ex-husbands, wicked mother-in-laws, and vengeful crowds—but none of these things is intrinsic to the history we want to discuss, nor are those allusions intended by the historian. In White's view, dependence on emplotment to represent the past does not suggest that rigorous historians are "making it all up" or turning to narrative as a way to escape the challenge of **historicism** or **historical sensibility**. Rather, White is concerned with the literary task in which all historians must engage, and who should do so fully aware of the classical meanings their **emplotment** will express. The **linguistic turn** of the 1970s and 1980s refers to the concerns and questions that have arisen as a consequence of White's argument regarding the relationships among language, writing, and historical understanding.

McCullagh, C. Behan. *Justifying Historical Descriptions* (Cambridge: Cambridge University Press, 1984).
White, Hayden. "Historical Emplotment and the Problem of Truth", *Probing the Limits of Representation*, S. Friedlander (ed.) (Cambridge: Cambridge University Press, 1982), 37–53.

Gender history

Historians of gender research the historical meaning of **sexual identity**. This means that they usually have three concerns: first, to identify the behaviours and beliefs that historically have distinguished men and boys from women and girls. Second, they analyze how and why those particular activities and ideas have been associated with masculinity and femininity. Third, since the meaning of gender has shaped social structures such as government, religion, work, and families, **gender historians** examine the ways people both have generated and responded to associations that define sexual identity. In the same way that feminist historians use their insights into women's history for political purposes, some gender historians advocate for greater understanding of the ways gender has limited human rights by enabling those with certain traits to enjoy privileges denied to others. However, unlike **second-wave feminist historians**, gender historians have questioned conventional approaches that firmly connect sex to gender by linking women with oppression and men with privilege: since masculinity and femininity have always embodied a variable range of meanings, which men and women have understood, enjoyed, and resisted in many ways, blanket notions of "women's experience" or "men's experience" distort that historical complexity. Moreover, like **cultural historians**, gender historians argue that meaning has been socially encoded in subtle as well as explicit ways—and this means that they adopt innovative and cross-disciplinary research methods.

Scott. Joan W. "Gender: A Useful Category of Historical Analysis", *American Historical Review* 91 (Dec. 1986), 1053–1075.

Hermeneutics

The philosophical study of interpretation, referring to written texts, human actions, and social institutions. Prior to the late nineteenth century, **hermeneutics** was a primarily theological enterprise that focused on the kinds of interpretive possibilities offered by Biblical scripture. Once the German philosopher Dilthey brought the term into philosophical and historical studies, historians were compelled to examine the values, concepts, and practical strategies that informed their interpretation of their research materials. This entailed critical discussion of the ways by which understanding (see **Verstehen**) can be possible, given the changing nature of the contexts in which documents are produced, **archived**, and interpreted by historians—not to mention the problems posed by cultural, linguistic, and behavioural differences between individual and groups of individuals.

Mueller-Vollmer, K. *The Hermeneutics Reader* (Oxford: Blackwell, 1986).
Owensby, Jacob. *Dilthey and the Narrative of History* (Ithaca: Cornell University Press, 1994).

l'histoire evènementielle (French, *history of events*)
See **historical time.**

Historical distance
When historians study the past and compose their narratives, they do so from a perspective that implies imagining themselves in proximity to their historical subject—intellectually, emotionally, physically. This spatial sense of distance can mean that historians will depict the past with an urgency and immediacy characteristic of romantic history, or they may adopt a more abstract or distant view of the past, typical of **conjectural historians**. In more sophisticated ways, historians can imagine themselves close to the past, but then represent that proximity using language that puts readers at a distance from it. Mark Salber Phillips has suggested that the fashioning of **historical distance** in historical narratives of the late eighteenth and early nineteenth centuries enabled authors to define their reputations; to develop new directions in history-writing that referred to related literary genres (such as biography, memoir, and the novel); and to position themselves and their subjects in ways that commented on political, social, and religious institutions, as well as **ideology**. Moreover, by charting the ways readers have responded to historical distance—historians

have stood accused of being unsympathetic, insensitive, or too enthusiastic—we can use notions of distance to interpret the critical values that inform historical reading and writing.

Mark Salber Phillips, *Society and Sentiment: Genres of Historical Writing in Britain, 1740–1820* (Princeton, NJ: Princeton University Press, 2000).

Historical materialism (adjective form: **materialist history**, not to be confused with the non-ideological field of **material history**)
Asserting that all consciousness relates to one's place in a specific socio-economic class, Marx's classic theory of history is rooted in the belief that the past, present, and future can only be understood through the economic relationships among people, their labour, and their access to material things they need to survive. These relationships become increasingly obvious to those whose labour is closest to the physical production of material goods, but whose ability to work has been exploited by those who prefer not to do such work. Once social consciousness of **materialist history** emerges among the working class, social revolution against capitalism towards communism becomes inevitable. The following is Marx's argument for **historical materialism**:

> In the social production which men [i.e., people] carry on they enter into definite relations that are indispensable and independent of their will; these relations of production correspond to a definite stage of development of their material powers of production. At a certain stage of their development, the material forces of production in society come into conflict with the existing relations of production, or—what is but a legal expression for the same thing—with the property relations within which they had been at work before. It is not the consciousness of men that determines their existence, but, on the contrary, their social existence determines their consciousness. From forms of development of the forces of production these relations turn into their fetters. Then comes the period of social revolution.
> (See K. Marx, "Introduction", *A Contribution to the Critique of Political Economy*, 1859. Trans. N. I. Stone (Chicago: Charles H. Kerr, 1904) 11–12.)

Like other **deductive** approaches characteristic of nineteenth-century social science, **materialist history** is **progressive** because it envisions a positive outcome to historical events; it is also explicitly **ideological** because it both determines and assumes a system of beliefs that attempts to explain all aspects of individual, social, and political life.

S. H. Rigby, *Marxism and History. A Critical Introduction* (2nd edn) (Manchester: Manchester University Press, 1998).

Historical sensibility or **historical imagination**
The early twentieth-century archaeologist, historian, and philosopher R. G. Collingwood argued, in a series of eloquent lectures and essays, that in order to understand the historical past we must have the intellectual and emotional ability to imaginatively re-enact it. Since history can never be witnessed first-hand, first we need to trust the authority of our sources. Next, we need to consider them critically by comparing their accounts with things we know to be true from our own experience. In this important respect, **historical sensibility** requires the empathetic capability to understand others that Dilthey, Collingwood's near-contemporary, called *Verstehen*. This requires that we construct a coherent imaginative sense of what has taken place in the past even though such coherence cannot

be supplied by the sources alone. To do this carefully and truthfully, we require a sensitive and reflective historical sensibility, one which will allow us to imagine the neglected details and to piece together facts only implied by historical sources. Collingwood offers a familiar example: when we look at the horizon and see a ship in one place, then look again and see it in another, we use our imagination and our experience to construct the ship's unseen movement. Without such an imaginative ability, meaningful understanding would not be possible. Unlike the imaginative capacity described by Macaulay (in Part 4), which merely energizes narrative style, historical imagination allows us to make sense of historical authorities that have not provided a coherent depiction of reality. Since historical analysis and historical narrative always imply the historian's own understanding of the past, she or he needs to be able to use their own knowledge of facts, feelings, and ideas to re-enact that past. For Collingwood, this is a necessary part of the historian's task, one which supplies the basis for criticism of sources and for describing past realities.

Collingwood, R. G. "The Historical Imagination". 1935. *The Idea of History* (revd edn) (Oxford: Oxford University Press, 1993), 231–49.

Dray, William H. *History as Re-enactment: R. G. Collingwood's Idea of History* (Oxford: Oxford University Press, 1995).

Historical time

Even if they do not address this topic explicitly, all historians are concerned with the nature of time in history, assuming the most appropriate ways to represent it and to express it in their analyses of the past. In a famous essay (1958), the French cultural and social historian Fernand Braudel presented a new vocabulary for defining and examining the nature of historical time. Observing that periodization had limited the scope and methods of historians, he argued for a new approach to the past: total history (*l'histoire globale*) would research gradual changes, not necessarily progressive changes, over the very long term (*longue durée*). This method departed from the short-term history of political events (*l'histoire evènementielle*) and of cyclical economic patterns over the medium term (*les conjonctures*) that Braudel saw as arbitrary periodizations that merely invited historians to define causes and effects easily, even though doing so entailed limiting their perspective to just those facts that seemed relevant and to inserting their own previous knowledge of outcomes. Essential to his notion of total history, Braudel advocated for using physical geography to define field of research—for example, his massive study of the Mediterranean world crossed linguistic, national, religious, and cultural borders. This approach to historical time remains influential, but also idealistic; as the linguistic turn has shown, there are inalienable aspects of historical scholarship that make truly total history impossible to achieve.

Braudel, Fernand. "History and the Social Sciences: The *Longue Durée*". 1958. *On History*. Trans. Sarah Matthews (Chicago: University of Chicago Press, 1980). 25–54.

Burke, Peter. *The French Historical Revolution: The Annales School, 1929–89* (Stanford: Stanford University Press, 1990).

Stone, Lawrence. *The Crisis of the Aristocracy: 1558–1661* (Oxford: Clarendon Press, 1965).

Historicism also historism

This is a key term in the historiography of the modern period; indeed, as Auerbach (in Part 2) has observed, it is historicism that defines modern approaches to the past. There are two definitions to historicism: the first (and the one used throughout this book), is the English translation of *historismus*, a late-nineteenth-century German term for Ranke's strictly empirical approach to historical scholarship, which demanded that we do our utmost to understand the past through its own values rather than our own—a view first espoused by Vico one century earlier. This means that all research must focus on those historical events that were motivated by human agency, so that our study of the sources will provide documentary evidence of the ideas, plans, actions, and intended developmental consequences of that past in its own terms. This theory presupposes an attitude to the past requiring a certain **historical sensibility**, through which historians will cultivate their intuition in order to make sense of the past rather than to impose their current views on it. The second definition, used by the Austro-British philosopher Karl Popper in the mid-twentieth century, understood **historicism** in a completely different way: for Popper, the **deductive sociological** theories that guided much history-writing in the early twentieth century (see Parts 6 and 7) started with an **ideological** theory of human nature to explain how history had developed and to determine its destiny. Such a **progressive** series of predictions were used, particularly in Stalin's Russia and Hitler's Germany, to legitimate a fascist vision of national characteristics, with horrific human consequences. Popper used the term **historicism** in this way because **deductive** theorists have used the same rhetoric as Ranke to justify their views on history.

Iggers, Georg. "Historicism: The History and Meaning of the Term", *Journal of the History of Ideas* 56 (1995), 129–52.
Popper, Karl. *The Poverty of Historicism*. 1957 (London: Routledge, 2002).

Historiography (from Greek, *history-writing*)
This word has retained several meanings over the past three centuries: Samuel Johnson's great *Dictionary* (1755) defined a historiographer simply as anyone who writes history. Over the years, as historians and their readers have become increasingly interested in the methods, values, and perspectives that history-writing entails, this meaning has shifted. Since the mid-twentieth century **Historiography** refers to historical commentary on the writing of history, which is how the word is used in this book. Similarly, when one mentions the historiography of a particular historian, we are referring to the critical values and **methodology** that informs that historian's writing.

Woolf, Daniel. "Historiography", *New Dictionary of the History of Ideas*, M. C. Horowitz (ed.) (New York: Scribners, 2004), 6 vols. Vol. 1, xxxv–lxxxviii.
History and Theory. Wesleyan University Press, 1960–. <http://www.historyandtheory.org>.
See also the Further Reading list following the Preface.

History from below
This term entered historians' parlance following the publication of E. P. Thompson's social history *The Making of the English Working Class* (1963), entering more common parlance upon the publication of Thompson's article of that title in the *Times Literary Supplement* (7 April 1966). Thompson, under the influence of other Marxist historians and the Italian political theorist Antonio Gramsci, observed that most history has been written from the perspective (and to serve the interests) of ruling-class elites: this not only includes familiar genres such as political biography, but also labour and economic history, which had neglected to uncover and consider the lives of working people. Particularly in Britain, where Thompson pointed to extensive **archival** holdings that document the lives, labour, and expression of working people, the statistical basis of labour and economic history seemed to ignore these available materials. **History from below** has since developed to encompass the methods and concerns of **cultural history** and **material history** by examining neglected topics as well as social groups, including the history of leisure, daily life, the family, loneliness, and old age.

Eric Hobsbawm, "On History from Below", *On History* (London: New Press, 1997), 201–16.

Ideal presence
This is a state of mind described by the prominent Scottish intellectual Lord Kames, in his widely popular treatise on aesthetics, *Elements of Criticism* (1762). Drawing on the moral theory of his cousin and friend David Hume, who famously argued that we determine right and wrong on the basis of our feelings rather than our ideas, Kames sought to describe and explain our emotional response to works of art—particularly to events on a stage and to depictions that we read. For Kames, our powerful natural capacities for sympathy lead us to become so emotionally and intellectually involved in depictions of suffering that we momentarily forget that we are merely spectators: this is why we might weep or become fearful while reading or watching a tragedy. Such experiences are like "a waking dream" because, on the one hand, we know that what we are seeing is not actual suffering and that it does not really pertain to us personally. And yet, like a memory of something that has once happened to us, we are strongly affected by the fiction—it plays on our capacity for sympathy with others, and this is why Kames remarks that the degree and frequency by which we experience ideal presence indicates the depth of our moral capacities. Paradoxically, sympathetic feelings of pity produce pleasurable sensations (again relating to Hume's theory of the mind, which is naturally inclined to activity and abhors boredom), and this is another reason why we are susceptible to the liveliness of "ideal" experiences of "presence." Kames concludes by suggesting that the best historians are able to affect their readers through those literary devices that elicit ideal presence, which in turn improves society by promoting sympathetic feelings for others. This theory is particularly useful for interpretations of romantic historians; Kames's book was widely read and taught well into the mid-nineteenth century, particularly in America.

Rothstein, Eric. " 'Ideal Presence' and the 'Non Finito' in Eighteenth-Century Aesthetics", *Eighteenth-Century Studies* 9 (1976), 307–32.

Ideology (from Greek, *idea* and *field of study*)
From the time this word entered the English language (probably in a 1796 translation from French) until one century later, **ideology** referred simply to the science or study of ideas—without reference to any particular ideas or way of studying them. According to the critic Raymond Williams, the current use of this word follows from Napoleon Bonaparte's use of **ideology** to define those doctrines that sought to impose particular ideas on political structures (such as government and the law). This pejorative sense, that ideology is something that misleads us by providing false ideas, still remains: if we remark on the ideological basis of an argument we are saying that it is biased by previous ideas and therefore is not sufficiently **empirical**. Similarly, outside historiography, ideology retains an association with the ideas that inform government policies. Yet a more technical use of the word by historians, which intends to be free of those particular associations, refers to any coherent system of beliefs—of which we may or may not be aware. While some theorists (namely Marxists) would argue that no experiences or ideas can ever be free of **ideology**, others would respond by accusing such theorists of using ideology as a form of determinism or as an excuse for their own **deductive** project. See also **mythology**.

Raymond Williams. "Ideology", *Keywords: A Dictionary of Culture and Society* (revd edn) (Oxford: Oxford University Press, 1983), 153–7.

Linguistic turn
For the history of this term, see Part 10, Introduction, note i. For its definition, see **emplotment**.

la longue durée (French, *the long term*)
See historical time.

Material history or history of material culture (not to be confused with historical
materialism or materialist history)
Closely related to archaeology, which locates and examines physical remains, material historians
refer to tangible things to study the past. Also related to social history, material historians focus not
only on neglected objects and their human value, but also on the hermeneutics of physical things:
for without an interpretation of the cultural and economic contexts that contributes to their value, it
is not possible to analyze an object's social or individual meanings. This means that material history
is a flexibly interdisciplinary field concerned with the ways objects represent and express relationships between people and things; people and habits; people in the past and researchers of their lives
in the present. While it has been inspired by history from below, material historians devote themselves to objects that document the everyday life of elites as well as unknowns—for example in
histories of dress, table-manners, cleanliness, and reading.

Buchli, Victor. *The Material Culture Reader* (Oxford: Berg, 2002).
Woodward, Ian. *Understanding Material Culture* (London: Sage, 2007).

Metanarrative
See emplotment

Methodology
This word refers to the general study of the concepts and methods that inform research, and to the
critical examination of academic investigation in ways that reveal ideology.

Peter Novick. *That Noble Dream: The "Objectivity Question" and the American Historical Profession*
    (Cambridge: Cambridge University Press, 1988).

Modernity (from Latin, *right now*)
A familiar instance of periodization, the modern period is normally considered to range from the
Enlightenment in the early eighteenth century to the present. In the mid-eighteenth century, when
the word entered common parlance, to modernize meant to change things for the sake of convenience
and comfort—a progressive notion synonymous with improvement. By the late nineteenth century,
with the influence of sociological theories developed by Marx, Durkheim, and Weber, modernity was
associated in the West with industrialization, the valuation of rationality, and increased political
awareness of the relationships between individuals and social groups. With the spread of Freudian
psychoanalytic concepts into popular culture in the twentieth century, modernity has been defined by
self-consciousness of emotions, desires, and associated states of mind. Related to all of these developments, the German-American literary critic Erich Auerbach has described historicism, the comprehensive effort to think about the past through its own concepts—implying awareness of our own
values and abilities (see historical sensibility)—as a defining element of the modern period. Debates
continue on the question of whether we have entered a postmodern period, reflecting critically on
the progressive elements of modernity.

Anthony Giddens. *The Consequences of Modernity* (Stanford: Stanford University Press, 1991).

Morphology (from Ancient Greek: *the science of forms*)

This biological term was brought into literary and historical vocabulary by the German romantic poet and novelist Johann Wolfgang von Goethe in 1790. Spengler adopted the term just over a century later to describe his "scientific" attempt to analyze humanity's origins and destiny by seeking out the essential "natural" meanings that distinguish different cultures (or "civilizations"). The word's origins in biological science are important, because they lent Spengler a language signifying **progressive ideology**—even though its organic rhetoric suggests a mystical and ultimately poetic project.

John Farrenkopf. "The Transformation of Spengler's Philosophy of World History", *Journal of the History of Ideas 52* (1991), 463–85.

Mythology

Until the mid-nineteenth century, **mythology** referred to interpretive commentaries on fictional tales, but it was later used to describe stories that reveal meanings more subtle and significant than those that can be provided by factual history or scientific explanation. For this reason, by the twentieth century the word carried negative and positive connotations, depending on one's view of the relative truth-value of metaphoric *vis-à-vis* literal explanations. Since mythology still retains the sense that it exists to explain mysterious origins, it can be understood either as a cynical justification or as a genuine attempt to understand specific phenomena, such as historical events or formal institutions. Using mythic terms and adopting a mythic tone, historians use the cultural resonance of mythology to generate powerful rhetoric. This famous example is from W. E. B. Du Bois's climactic conclusion to his history of American racism, written in 1935:

> The most significant drama in the last thousand years of human history is the transportation of ten million human beings out of the dark beauty of their mother continent into the new-found Eldorado of the West. They descended into Hell; and in the third century they arose from the dead, in the finest effort to achieve democracy for the working millions the world had ever seen. It was a tragedy that beggared the Greek; it was an upheaval of humanity like the Reformation and French Revolution. Yet we are blind and led by the blind. We discern in it no part of our labour movement; no part of our industrial triumph; no part of our religious experience.
> ("The Propaganda of History", *Black Reconstruction in America*
> (Philadelphia: Albert Saifer, 1935) 727.)

Like **ideology**, mythology refers to a set of beliefs, but those that are consciously recognized and refer directly to a specific concern. Mythology can also be understood as both the consequence and originator of historical **emplotment**, where certain texts, events, figures, and event literary styles, reference a system of consciously-shared ideas.

Donald Brown. *Hierarchy, History, and Human Nature: The Social Origins of Historical Consciousness* (Tucson: University of Arizona Press, 1988).

New History, The

An articulate revolt against the dominance of **empirical methodology** and preoccupations with documented political history, based in America in the first decades subsequent to the founding of History departments in the US by German-trained academics—from 1898 to the mid-1920s. Described by Roosevelt and Robinson, **The New History** sought to make history relevant for readers within and beyond universities by adopting the intellectual, social, and economic concerns that mattered at the time. Usefully understood through comparison with the founding principles of the *Annales* journal in France and with Butterfield's critique of the "Whig Interpretation of History" (for both see Part 5), New Historians sought to adopt methods from the social sciences and other fields to make history practically useful by explaining the causes and nature of current events. Impatient with narrative styles that intrigued rather than informed readers, as well as with narrow studies dictated by the holdings of **archives**, the New Historians faced an ultimately unresolved dilemma: to study history objectively while serving current social and political needs.

John Hingham, *History: The Development of Historical Studies in the United States* (2nd edn) (Baltimore: Johns Hopkins University Press, 1989).

Objectivity (for etymology, see **subjectivity**)

In **modern historiography**, this term now refers to self-evident knowledge unaffected by perspective; this was not always the case (see **subjective**). Normally considered the guiding vision of **empirical** research, **objectivity** has been associated with impartiality and freedom from external influence. While most historians would agree that objectivity refers to an ideal goal rather than a realistic accomplishment, some (such as the philosopher Richard Rorty) would argue that objectivity is a pragmatic issue—we identify certain things as objectively valid because they have "paid their way and made themselves useful" through particular kinds of cultural and intellectual exposure or tradition. See **subjective**.

In its adverbial form, to analyze something **objectively** is to consider it as an inanimate or inarticulate object, with self-evident components, rather than **subjectively**, which requires meaningful engagement with an internal viewpoint. See **subjective** and *Verstehen*.

Novick, Peter. *That Noble Dream: The "Objectivity Question" and the American Historical Profession* (Cambridge: Cambridge University Press, 1988).
Rorty, Richard. *Consequences of Pragmatism* (Princeton, NJ: Princeton University Press, 1982).

Paradigm shift (from Greek, *pattern, example,* or *precedent*)

This term was coined in 1962 by the American physicist and historian, Thomas Kuhn, to describe the only apparently **progressive** historical event that takes place when a major scientific discovery replaces the theories and concepts that existed before. Paradigm shifts define the nature of scientific **progress** at a certain cost to historians: since these shifts entail the creation of new questions that relegate old ideas as obsolete, we tend to view the history of science as a series of successes when in fact it is those now-neglected questions and viewpoints that defined the intellectual and cultural environments of the past. This theory provides a critique of **periodization** and **emplotment** since it asks us to question the ways by which discoveries have structured our view of history, obscuring a more subtle investigation of past ideas and inquiries.

Hollinger, David A. "T. S. Kuhn's Theory of Science and its Implications for History", *In the American Province: Studies in the History and Historiography of Ideas* (Bloomington: Indiana University Press, 1985), 105–29.
Kuhn, Thomas S. *The Structure of Scientific Revolutions* (Chicago: University of Chicago Press, 1962).

Periodization

The tendency to impose a structure on the past dates back to ancient times, and awareness that such structuring should be viewed more as a problem than a convenience dates back at least as far as

Petrarch (who lamented, back in the fourteenth century, that a Dark Age separates the present from classical antiquity). As Hayden White's notion of **emplotment** suggests, the notion that the past can be structured using a **metanarrative** says more about the values of that narrative than about the history it is meant to contain. Over the past three centuries, historians have used various criteria to **periodize** the past: they have used numerical chronology (by referring to the nineteenth century), political events (Revolutionary France or Victorian Britain), aesthetic concepts (the Enlightenment), and critical values (the modern period).

Dietrich Gerhard. "Periodization in European History", *American Historical Review* 61 (July 1956), 900–913.

Poetic fallacy

For Hayden White, historians commit the **poetic fallacy** when they distort the non-linguistic nature of human history by structuring it according to a familiar literary formula. All **stadial historians** commit the poetic fallacy by envisioning the past as a kind of literary plot, complete with increasingly mature stages, moving in a **progressive** direction toward a utopic conclusion or tragic decline. See **emplotment**.

Positive as an adjective for **positivism** and **progressivism** and not for logical positivism (which is not addressed in this book; see V. Kraft, *The Vienna Circle* (New York: Greenwood Press, 1953)).
This term originates in Auguste Comte's *Positive Philosophy*, in which he argued: (1) that all knowledge is scientific, and therefore the past, present, and future can be described accurately through a **deductive** and systematic philosophy called **positivism**; (2) using a **stadial** theory of human history, positivism and progressivism define the past as a series of stages by which humanity is destined to move away from simple barbarism toward intelligent civilization. A classic instance of **emplotment**, it was this view of history that elicited Butterfield's *Whig Interpretation of History* (see Part 5).

Burke, Peter. *History and Social Theory* (2nd edn) (Cambridge: Polity Press, 2005).
Comte, Auguste. *Introduction to Positive Philosophy*. 1830. Ed. and trans. Frederick Ferré (Indianapolis: Hackett, 1988).

Postmodernity (from Latin, *after* and *right now*)

Postmodernism remains a controversial term that simultaneously suggests connection to and departure from **modernity** to characterize the present moment (from the 1950s). Challenging the **ideology** of **progressivism** that once defined **modernity**, **postmodernity** refers to ideas and expressions that challenge fundamental concepts that underlie modernity: the relationship between language and meaning; artistic greatness and **metanarrative**; personal and political identity; the presumptive aims and effective **discourse** of institutions. In **historiography**, postmodernist concerns have informed the **linguistic turn** of the 1970s and 1980s. While advocates of postmodernism have denied social and political motivations, their challenge to the modern notion that experience can be known and expressed linguistically or **semiotically** has led to accusations that postmodern theorists are sophisticated agents of social and intellectual conservatism.

Keith Jenkins. *The Postmodern History Reader* (London: Routledge, 1997).

Primary sources

Historians refer to **primary sources** as evidence that provides an immediate and first-hand account of a historical event. Normally associated with **archival** documents, but also including **material** objects or the evidence of witnesses, primary sources provide the closest possible documentation of the past. They can be usefully contrasted with secondary sources, which comment on other sources (including primary sources) rather than on the past itself. Since modern historiography is concerned with the interpretation and representation of history rather than the events it recounts, historiography treats secondary sources as primary sources—since they document the history of historical scholarship.

Progressivism
See positive.

Psychoanalysis
A psychological theory developed by the Austrian psychiatrist Sigmund Freud, but extended and revised considerably since Freud's death in 1939; thus "classical psychoanalysis" normally refers to Freud's clinical techniques and prolific writings, and "contemporary psychoanalysis" refers to the widening body of research, writing, and techniques developed afterward. Classical psychoanalysis, as a theory of the mind rather than a clinical technique (which is not discussed in this book), posits that all thought and action are the expression of psychological conflicts that originate in early childhood. Those conflicts are unconscious, because we are not aware of them and therefore their expression takes place indirectly and involuntarily, through dreams, screen memories, "neurotic" behaviour, and personal or collective investment in particular mythologies. For Freud, the instincts that drive human thought and action are not limited to securing food and shelter; we also have fundamental sexual drives that operate right from birth—and since those drives are normally frustrated during childhood due to social taboo, consequent life experiences can be usefully understood as a playing-out of the struggle to manage interior conflicts between the wish to express those desires and the social requirement that we deny them. We respond to the taboo on sexual desire through repression, by denying ourselves even the recognition of sexual drives. Healthy forms of repression result in creative "sublimation" through socially normative expression in public and private life; unhealthy repression, which is the normal result of painful traumatic experiences that should be treated rather than denied, results in behaviour that is damaging to ourselves and others, of whose nature and effects we may remain unconscious. Freud insisted that he was a medical empiricist whose theory emerged through many years of caring for psychiatric patients, and indeed his writings normally take the form of case-studies designed for his medical colleagues. Nevertheless, psychoanalysis has been accused of residing in the deductive tradition of contemporary sociological theorists, which means it has been understood to provide a mere metanarrative of personal history. Such debate will continue, but in the meantime it is unlikely that any historian writing after 1950 would doubt the valuable methodological influence and insights that psychoanalysis continues to offer.

Peter Gay. *The Freud Reader* (New York: Vintage, 1995).

Psychohistory
A deductive method of biography that adopts classical Freudian concepts to speculate on the unconscious thoughts and motivations of historical figures and historical events. It developed in the late 1950s with the publication of Erik Erikson's *Young Man Luther* (1958) but had its roots in Norbert Elias's interpretation of social manners and beliefs in *The Civilizing Process* (1939).

D. Stannard. *Shrinking History: On Freud and the Failure of Psychohistory* (Oxford: Oxford University Press, 1980).

Repression

A **psychoanalytic** concept describing the psychological process by which the mind manipulates unacceptable desires and painful memories so that they seem to have disappeared. Freud argues that **repression** merely banishes these desires and memories to unconsciousness, through which their meaning will either resurface through unhealthy ("neurotic") behaviour or, through a healthy process of "sublimation," it will be expressed in creative and useful ways. See **psychoanalysis**.

Screen memory

Freud developed this classical **psychoanalytic** concept in a clinical paper of 1901 (see Part 9, Introduction, note vii). In that essay, Freud speculated on the reasons why adults usually remember the painful events of childhood, but easily recall seemingly meaningless memories from that time. His explanation focused on the **repression** of childhood wishes, which entailed that the **unconscious** creates false and simple memories to provide a screen from the true memories that would be too painful to recollect in later life. Freud emphasized the psychological process by which we formulate memories of our individual pasts:

> Our childhood memories show us our earliest years not as they were but as they appeared at the later periods when the memories were revived. In these periods of revival, the child-hood memories did not, as people are accustomed to say, *emerge*; they were *formed* at that time. And a number of motives, which had no concern with historical accuracy, had their part in thus forming them as well as in the selection of the memories themselves.
> ("Screen Memories". Trans. J. Strachey, *The Collected Papers of Sigmund Freud,*
> J. Riviere (ed.) (New York: Basic Books, 1959), 69.)

This is a valuable concept for any **historiography** that addresses differences between memory and history, and which examines the personal significance of memory, particularly in the context of a traumatic past.

Adam Phillips. "Close-Ups", *History Workshop Journal* 57 (2004), 142–9.

Second-wave feminism

In American **social history**, first-wave feminism refers to the late-nineteenth and early-twentieth-century movement for women's political rights, primarily the right to vote in democratic elections. **Second-wave feminism** refers to broader activist goals that emerged in tandem with the civil rights struggles of the 1960s, focusing on women's equality in the workplace and in educational institutions, reproductive rights, and social valuation of motherhood. The key phrase that defined its **methodology** was "the personal is political": the experiences of girls and women in private life can only be understood as expressions of their places in public spheres—and *vice-versa*. So when **post-modern** and **gender** historians question both the logic of representation as well as the notion of unified experience as a criterion of **sexual identity**, they place the **methodology** and political project of second-wave feminism under scrutiny.

I. Whelehan. *Modern Feminist Thought: From the Second Wave to "Post-Feminism"* (New York: New York University Press, 1995).

Semiotics or semiology

The study of the relationship between representations and their intended meanings—classically defined as the science of signs. To address the **semiotics** of any form of representation (such as visual, linguistic, behavioural, or auditory) is to examine the kinds of interpretations that are permitted by the social and linguistic codes that govern communication. Historians who focus on the transmission of ideas and their methods of explanation engage in semiotic analysis because it provides a useful way to consider why particular words or symbols have been chosen, and why those particular symbols would anticipate certain interpretations.

Daniel Chandler. *Semiotics: The Basics* (London: Routledge, 2007).

Sexual identity
See **Gender History**

Stadial history
An explanation of historical **progress** that divides the past, present, and future into distinct stages or epochs. This **deductive** form of **periodization** has been prevalent throughout the modern period. Vico, Durkheim, and Spengler (for example) envisioned a three-stage structure in their **stadial** histories; Marx and Freud use variations on stadial history in their conceptions of social and psychological development.

Karen O'Brien. *Narratives of Enlightenment: Cosmopolitan History from Voltaire to Gibbon* (Cambridge: Cambridge University Press, 1997).

Social history
Historical studies which focus on any aspect of social life—ranging from statistical analyses of demographic research to examining the **material** elements of everyday experience. Unlike political history, which traditionally had focused biographically on specific individuals or groups that held powerful state offices, **social history** concerns itself with relatively neglected individuals or groups. Although social history existed before the advent of **history from below**, notably as an area of **conjectural**, romantic, and **New History**, its range of topics, methods, and analysis has widened and deepened considerably under the influence of Marxist, feminist, and **cultural history**. Gender historians and historians interested in the meaning and consequences of social **discourse** expand and interpret **social history**, which is why it has attracted controversy, with advocates such as Scott and Halperin extolling its **progressive** political significance and its critics such as Himmelfarb accusing it of **ideological deductivism**.

Peter N. Stearns (ed.) *Expanding the Past: A Reader in Social History* (New York: New York University Press, 1988).

Sociology (from Latin *companions* and Greek *study of*)
This term was coined in 1824 by the French **positivist** Auguste Comte, who argued that the only valuable study is one which focuses on the structure of social relationships. Without understanding the ways individuals organize themselves into groups (or, for other social scientists of the period, how individuals are forced into groups), historical phenomena make little sense. By the end of the century, Émile Durkheim held France's first academic position in social science (1896), founded its journal *L'Année Sociologique* (1898), and was elected (1906) to the first professorial chair in Sociology (1913). For Durkheim, Sociology was not only independent from History but was also more deeply analytical, scientific, and morally meaningful than its stale and narrowly fact-gathering ancestor. A further century later, sociology comprises a diversity of **methodologies** and theories; even as its founding methods depend on a **deductive approach**, few would doubt its permanent value for nearly all aspects of historical inquiry.

Burke, Peter. *History and Social Theory* (2nd edn) (Cambridge: Polity Press, 2005).

Nisbet, R. A. *The Sociological Tradition* (London: Heinemann, 1967).

Structuralism

This term has been adopted by various academic fields since it was first used by anthropologists in the 1950s and 1960s; its definitions shift according to one's scholarly interests. In modern historiography, structuralism usually refers to a preoccupation with the social, linguistic, semiotic, and ideological structures that can be empirically observed and analyzed; it refers also to the deeper meanings that underlie those structures. Historians employ structuralist methodology to locate and analyze statistical information, mythology, discourse, repression, or any other belief structures that help us understand the function and formation of behaviours, ideas, and institutions. Ultimately, most twentieth-century structuralists refer to a psychological or social theory. With the emergence of postmodernism, concern has shifted away from examining underlying structures to question the very assumptions that have led us to distinguish visible structures from the meanings they are meant to represent. This preoccupation with strategies of representation has found its expression in the linguistic turn.

Allan Megill. "Foucault, Structuralism, and the Ends of History", *Journal of Modern History* 51 (1979), 451–503.

Subjectivity (from Latin, *to throw* or *cast* and *under*)

The original Latin sense was sustained until the nineteenth century; until that time, subjective referred to things-in-themselves (*cast under our view*) and objective to things as they were presented (*thrown before us*). Since the mid-nineteenth century, these meanings have undergone a near-reversal: subjectivity now refers to a perspective defined by its interiority—in other words, a viewpoint worthy of consideration on its own variable terms. Its opposite, objectivity, is associated with empiricism and self-evident meaning; subjectivity is associated with interpretive nuance, mutable states of mind, and relativism. See objectivity.

R. Williams. *Keywords: A Vocabulary of Culture and Society*, 308–12.

Total history (*l'histoire globale*)

See historical time.

Verstehen (from German, *understanding*)

This term found its way from theology to sociology in the late nineteenth century, in the writings of Dilthey and Weber that respond critically to deductive methods that sought to analyse society objectively. Rather than reduce historical events to the political history of actions, *Verstehen* requires a nuanced methodology and study of the social history of ideas, intentions, and experiences, paving the way for psychoanalysis. A concept crucial for hermeneutics, historical sensibility, and therefore modern historiography, *Verstehen* refers to the interpersonal understanding that historians require if they are to make meaningful sense of other people's experiences. It has been accepted in principle by historicists who also criticize it for lacking any empirical means of demonstrating its accuracy or effectiveness.

William Outhwaite. *Understanding Social Life: The Method Called Verstehen* (2nd edn) (Lewes, UK: Stroud and Pateman, 1986).

Further glossaries in modern historiography

Bennett, Tony et al. (eds). *New Keywords: A Revised Vocabulary of Culture and Society* (Oxford: Blackwell, 2005).

Bullock, Alan and Stephen Trombley (eds). *The New Fontana Dictionary of Modern Thought* (3rd edn) (London: Fontana, 1999).

Munslow, Alun. *The Routledge Companion to Historical Studies* (London: Routledge, 2000).

Williams, Raymond. *Keywords: A Vocabulary of Culture and Society* (2nd edn) (Oxford: Oxford University Press, 1983).

Woolf, Daniel (ed.). *A Global Encyclopedia of Historical Writing* (New York: Garland, 2003), 2 vols.

Index

This index refers to topics and scholars discussed in the individual chapters and editorial introductions. Page numbers of terms that are defined in the Glossary appear in **bold**.

Michelangelo 66
Michelet, Athénaïs 43–7
Michelet, Jules 43–5, 108, 122–6, 253, 267,
  347–8, 354, 361–2, 381; *author of Chapter 15*
Middle Ages 7, 11, 14, 26, 67–8, 174, 176, 191,
  239–44, 305, 373, 383, 401
Miles, Rosalind 379, 381
Mill, John Stuart 12, 49, 106–7, 113–14,
  199–201, 204, 447; *author of Chapter 25*
Millar, John 80
Miller, Daniel *co-author of Chapter 51*
Mitzman, Arthur 45, 50
modern history 5–12, 15, 17–8, 35, 101,
  173–4, 186, 210, 345, 393, 510
modernity, modernism 107, 121, 201, 240,
  242–3, 450, 478, **517**, 520
Momigliano, Arnaldo 43
Mommsen, Theodor 9, 363
Monod, Gabriel 43–5, 49
Montesquieu, Baron 6, 67, 79, 137
moral value of historical writing 87–8
morphology 246–8, 386, 404, 410, 412–5, **518**
Morris, Ian 498
Morris, William 289–90
Mosse, George 459
Motley, John Lothrop 36–9, 47–8
Mozley, James 15
Müller, Max 42
museum practice 108–9
myth, mythic and mythology 24–5, 28, 30, 55,
  61, 64–5, 68–71, 113, 121, 127, 239, 244,
  245, 258, 274, 289, 297, 303, 306, 312–5,
  319–21, 323–9, 352–4, 356–8, 360, 370,
  381, 390, 444, 449, **518**, 521, 524

Nairn, Tom 289
names, use of 184
Napier, Richard 303
Napoleon 7, 11, 13, 68, 234, 240, 246, 492,
  516
Napoleon III 45
natural law 62, 64, 67–8, 150
Neville, R.G. 300
New England 125–6, 150
New History 163–5, 184–94, 395, **518–19**, 523
New Left Review 289, 291
Newman, John Henry 9, 12, 447
Newton, Sir Isaac 32, 62, 165, 236, 242, 255,
  260
Nicholas V 176
Niebuhr, Barthold 38–41, 48, 180–1
Niebuhr, Carsten 37
Niebuhr, Helmut Richard 12
Nietzsche, Friedrich 26, 107, 122, 234, 243,
  247, 335, 347, 352
novels 42, 75, 80, 85, 87, 102–3, 112, 121–5,
  130–1, 135, 361, 367, 205, 223, 248,
  259–60, 311, 314, 338, 344, 353, 357, 359,
  362
Nuremberg trials 325

Oates, Titus 13
objectivity 3, 22, 35, 38, 41, 46, 86, 108, 160,
  204, 292, 314, 458, 503, **519**, 524; *see also*
  truth in history
Ong, Walter 39
Orientalism 424–8, 443–8; definition of,
  425

painting 87, 89, 94, 96, 108, 130, 246, 436,
  439, 467
Panikkar, K.M. 444
papacy, the 175, 177
paradigm shift 234–7, **519**
Parkman, Francis 122, 125–7, 178; *author of
  Chapter 17*
Parnell, Charles Stewart 319
Pascal, Blaise 22
Past and Present 14, 108, 267–74, 277–80,
  285–6, 293
Pearce, Susan 502
Peel, Sir Robert 8
Péguy, Charles 34
Peirce, C.S. 356
Perceval, John 303
periodization 121, 234, 252–6, 379, 514, 517,
  519–20, 523
Perroux, François 254
Peter, J.-P. 302
Petrie, Flinders 247
Phillips, Adam 200, 313–4, 349; *author of
  Chapter 41*
Phillips, Mark 86, 88, 314, 335–9, 349, 513;
  author of Chapter 12
philology 37, 48, 68, 448
philosophical history 161, 170, 509; *see also*
  conjectural history
Philosophism 139
Picasso, Pablo 66, 337, 339
Pinochet, Augusto 322, 328
Pirenne, Henri 492–3
Pitt, William (the Elder) 13, 16
Place, Francis 283
Plato 37, 55, 63, 71, 242, 245, 247, 366
Plutarch 10, 63, 76, 90, 101, 112
poetic fallacy 235, 269, 347, 352, 423, **520**
poetry 61–5, 66–71, 89, 103, 122, 125, 168,
  244, 290, 295, 353, 356, 361–3, 371, 448,
  470, 473
politics and political history 5–8, 35, 185,
  253–4, 394, 399, 427
Pollock, Frederick 37
Polybius 74, 77, 247, 250, 279
Pope, Alexander 66
Porter, Roy 274, 383; *author of Chapter 38*
positive philosophy 200–1
positivism 278, 472, **520**; see also progressivism
postmodernity and post-modernism 205,
  344–6, 477–8, 480, **520**, 524
potlatch 486–7
Prévost, Abbé 48, 102–3